Implementing SOA

Implementing SOA

Total Architecture in Practice

Paul C. Brown

✦✦Addison-Wesley

Upper Saddle River, NJ • Boston • Indianapolis • San Francisco
New York • Toronto • Montreal • London • Munich • Paris • Madrid
Capetown • Sydney • Tokyo • Singapore • Mexico City

Many of the designations used by manufacturers and sellers to distinguish their products are claimed as trademarks. Where those designations appear in this book, and the publisher was aware of a trademark claim, the designations have been printed with initial capital letters or in all capitals.

The author and publisher have taken care in the preparation of this book, but make no expressed or implied warranty of any kind and assume no responsibility for errors or omissions. No liability is assumed for incidental or consequential damages in connection with or arising out of the use of the information or programs contained herein.

The publisher offers excellent discounts on this book when ordered in quantity for bulk purchases or special sales, which may include electronic versions and/or custom covers and content particular to your business, training goals, marketing focus, and branding interests. For more information, please contact:

U.S. Corporate and Government Sales
(800) 382-3419
corpsales@pearsontechgroup.com

For sales outside the United States please contact:

International Sales
international@pearson.com

This Book Is Safari Enabled

The Safari® Enabled icon on the cover of your favorite technology book means the book is available through Safari Bookshelf. When you buy this book, you get free access to the online edition for 45 days.

Safari Bookshelf is an electronic reference library that lets you easily search thousands of technical books, find code samples, download chapters, and access technical information whenever and wherever you need it.

To gain 45-day Safari Enabled access to this book:

- Go to www.informit.com/onlineedition
- Complete the brief registration form
- Enter the coupon code INL6-UPXM-Z2CQ-WWMN-IEMD

If you have difficulty registering on Safari Bookshelf or accessing the online edition, please e-mail customer-service@safaribooksonline.com.

Visit us on the Web: informit.com/aw

Library of Congress Cataloging-in-Publication Data

Brown, Paul C.
  Implementing SOA : total architecture in practice / Paul C. Brown.
      p.   cm.
  Includes index.
  ISBN 0-321-50472-0 (pbk. : alk. paper)
 1. Computer architecture. 2. Computer network architectures. 3. Business enterprises—Computer networks—Management. 4. Web services. I. Title.
QA76.9.A73B82 2008
  004.2'2—dc22   2008005257

ISBN-13: 978-0-321-50472-2
ISBN-10:   0-321-50472-0

Text printed in the United States on recycled paper at Courier in Stoughton, Massachusetts.
First printing, April 2008

For Maria

Contents

Preface

If you are an architect responsible for a service-oriented architecture (SOA) in an enterprise, you face many challenges. Whether intended or not, the architecture you create defines the structure of your enterprise at many different levels, from business processes down to data storage. It defines the boundaries between organizational units as well as between business systems. Your architecture must go beyond defining services and provide practical solutions for a host of complex distributed system design problems, from orchestrating business processes to ensuring business continuity. Implementing your architecture will involve many projects over an extended period, and your guidance will be required.

In *Succeeding with SOA*, I discussed the need for an enterprise to pay close attention to its architecture, the role of its architects, and the importance of setting the right organizational context for their success. In this book, *Implementing SOA*, I turn to the work of the architects themselves—your work—guiding you through the process of defining a service-oriented architecture at both the project and enterprise levels. Whether you are an architect putting SOA into practice or you are an engineer aspiring to be an architect and wanting to learn more, I wrote this book for you.

Doing SOA well can be very rewarding. Done properly, your enterprise will comprise a robust and flexible collection of reusable business and infrastructure services. The enterprise will be able to efficiently recombine these services to address changing business needs. On the other hand, if you do SOA poorly, your enterprise will be encumbered with a fragile and rigid set of functionality (which I hesitate to call services) that will retard rather than promote enterprise evolution. You don't want to end up there. *Implementing SOA* will show you the pitfalls as well as the best practices. In short, it will guide you to doing SOA well.

The SOA Architectural Challenges

Doing SOA well presents you with four interrelated architectural challenges.

1. Services define the structure of both business processes and systems. Business processes and systems have become so hopelessly intertwined that it is no longer possible to design one without altering the other. They have to be designed together, a concept I call *total architecture*. Thus, building your service-oriented architecture is not just a technical exercise, it is also a business exercise that requires the active participation of the business side of the house.

2. You are not building your SOA from scratch. Your enterprise today operates using a working set of business processes and systems. You can't afford to disrupt business operations just because you want to build an SOA. Practically speaking, you need to evolve your existing business processes and systems into an SOA. During this transition, individual projects must continue to deliver tangible business value, independent of your SOA initiative.

3. Your SOA is a vision that requires a consistent interpretation as it is put into practice. The actual implementation of your SOA will happen piecemeal, project by project. Services that are developed in today's project must satisfy future needs, and today's projects must leverage the services developed in yesterday's projects. Ensuring that existing services are appropriately used, and that new services will meet future needs, requires coordination and planning across multiple projects, both present and future.

4. A service-oriented architecture is actually a distributed system. As such, your SOA must incorporate self-consistent solutions to all of the classic distributed system design problems: trading off service granularity against communications delays, coping with communications breakdowns, managing information that is distributed across services and sites, coordinating service execution and load distribution, ensuring service and business process availability and fault tolerance, securing your information, and monitoring and managing both business processes and services. The requirements driving your solution choices stem from the needs of the business processes involved and are thus tied in with business process design as well as systems design. As before, solutions to these problems require consistent approaches across all of your projects.

At the end of the day, your challenge as an architect is to organize your enterprise's collaboration between business processes, people, information, and systems, and to focus it on achieving your enterprise's goals.

About the Book

Implementing SOA is a comprehensive guide to addressing your architectural challenges. It shows you how to smoothly integrate the design of both business processes and business systems. It will tell you how to evolve your existing architecture to achieve your SOA objectives, maintaining operational support for the enterprise during the transition. It demonstrates how to use a proactive enterprise architecture group to bring a consistent and forward-looking architectural perspective to multiple projects. Finally, it shows you how to address the full spectrum of distributed system design issues that you will face.

This book is organized into nine parts. Part I presents the fundamental concepts of architecture, services, and the total architecture synthesis methodology. Parts II through VIII discuss a series of architectural design issues, ranging from understanding business processes to monitoring and testing your architecture. Part IX then builds on these discussions to address the large-scale issues associated with complex business processes and workflow, concluding with a summary discussion of the workings of the enterprise architecture group.

In Parts II through VIII, each of the architecture topics is discussed from two perspectives: the project perspective and the enterprise architecture perspective. Each part first discusses the design issues as though the project architect were creating the entire architecture from scratch. The last chapter in each part then addresses the realities of a multi-project environment and the role that the enterprise architecture group must play to ensure that the design issues are appropriately addressed throughout the total architecture. This separation highlights the relative roles of the project and enterprise architects as well as the manner in which they need to collaborate. The enterprise architecture group chapter in Part IX then summarizes the activities of this group.

The book as a whole, and each individual chapter, can be approached in two ways. One way is prescriptive. The book presents a structured approach to tackling individual projects and managing the overall enterprise architecture. The other way is to use the book as a review guideline. Each chapter discusses a topic and concludes with a list of key questions related to that topic. Use the questions as a self-evaluation guide for your current projects and enterprise architecture efforts. Then use the content of the individual chapters to review the specific issues and the various ways in which they can be addressed. Either way, you will strengthen your enterprise architecture.

Implementing SOA is a comprehensive guide to building your enterprise architecture. While the emphasis is clearly on SOA, SOA is just a style of distributed system architecture. Real-world enterprise architectures contain a mixture of SOA and non-SOA elements. To reflect this reality, the discussions in this book extend beyond SOA to cover the full scope of distributed business systems architecture.

The pragmatic approach of *Implementing SOA* will guide your understanding of each issue you will face, your possible solution choices, and the tradeoffs to consider in building your solutions. The key questions at the end of each chapter not only provide a convenient summary, but also serve as convenient architecture review questions. These questions, and the supporting discussions in each chapter, will guide you to SOA success.

Acknowledgments

This book is dedicated to my wife, Maria. Without her love and support, neither this book nor the previous one would ever have come into existence. She picked up the slack for many things I should have been doing and gave me encouragement when I grew weary of the task. Mere words are inadequate to express my love and appreciation.

There are many who have helped along the way as well. I thank my mentors who helped me learn how to explore uncharted territory: John Reschovsky, Joel Sturman, David Oliver, David Musser, and Mukkai Krishnamoorthy. I thank my colleagues who have provided an intellectual foil for these ideas: Jonathan Levant, John Hutchison, James Rumbaugh, Michael Blaha, and William Premerlani. For their support of my enterprise methodology work, I thank Brian Pierce, Bruce Johnson, Paul Beduhn, and Paul Asmar. For their help in sharpening the real-world architectural concepts, I thank Paul Asmar, David Leigh, Saul Caganoff, and Janet Strong. For helping me turn a concept into a book, I thank Michael Blaha and William Premerlani. For helping me make this book a reality, I thank Paul Asmar, Ram Menon, Roger Strukhoff, Scott Fingerhut, Peter Gordon, Michael Blaha, and Charly Paelinck.

PCB
Schenectady, NY
February 19, 2008

Part I

Fundamentals

Chapter 1

SOA and the Enterprise

Service-oriented architecture (SOA) is an architectural style that modularizes information systems into services. You then orchestrate collections of these services to bring business processes to life. In a successful SOA, you can readily recombine these services in various ways to implement new or improved business processes.

SOA is a logical evolutionary descendant of the software modularization techniques that began more than 50 years ago with the introduction of structured programming. SOA's novelty is that it gives you increased flexibility in the choice of implementation technologies and locations for the service providers and consumers. The abstracted service interfaces also enable providers and consumers to evolve independently—as long as the interfaces remain stable.

The benefits of an SOA derive primarily from a single characteristic: the stability of the service interface. This stability, relative to the overall rate of systems changes, isolates service consumers from changes in service implementations. This isolation limits the scope of changes and thus reduces the cost of subsequent changes. You derive a much larger benefit when you are able to reuse services—exactly as they are. Reuse avoids the cost of re-implementing or modifying the functionality encapsulated in the service.

The Challenge

The stability of service interfaces is the key to SOA success. A stable interface isolates the service user from the ongoing changes in the service provider and thus reduces the scope of work that is required each time the service provider is modified. This reduction in scope carries with it a corresponding reduction in cost in the form of cost avoidance. Interface stability is also the key enabler for service reuse. If the existing interface cannot support the needs of a future service user or service provider, then changes to the interface will be required. The cost of making these changes diminishes or eliminates the anticipated savings that justified the development of the service in the first place.

Actually achieving this interface stability is the dominant SOA challenge. Why? Because a business service interface does more than establish a boundary between systems. A business service encapsulates a piece of a business process. It establishes an interface between the encapsulated portion of the business process and the rest of the business process. A `sales order management service` encapsulates the portions of business processes that create and maintain sales orders. Thus when you define business services, you are architecting your business processes as well as your systems.

Business processes run on information. All but the most trivial of services manage some set of information. The definition of the service determines what information it manages, distinguishing this information from information managed by other system components and services. For example, a `sales order management service` is the system of record for sales order information, but it does not manage warehouse inventory. Thus, business services modularize information.

Business processes (and systems, for that matter) rely on people. Even in a highly automated business process, people are the final recourse for finding and fixing problems. In many other business processes, people are an integral part of the process, making decisions and otherwise contributing their knowledge and skills to the process. These people belong to organizations—and so do the business services. When you define business services, you are establishing the responsibilities of organizations as well as systems. You are establishing the roles of people in the organization along with the responsibility for managing the service itself.

The architecture of the modern enterprise defines the structure of more than its systems. It defines the structure of the people, processes, and information as well. It is the *total architecture* of the enterprise.

The Concept of Total Architecture

Business processes, people, information, and systems have become so intertwined in the modern enterprise that you can no longer design them independently. You have to address them in toto—as a whole. Furthermore, the scale and complexity of enterprise business processes requires that you do this design hierarchically. A high-level architecture—the *total architecture*—determines the participants, their roles and responsibilities, and the dynamics of their interaction required to achieve the business goals (Figure 1–1). Subsequent steps then detail and execute this architecture.

Total architecture is not a choice. It is a concession to reality. Attempts to organize business processes, people, information, and systems independently result in structures that do not fit together particularly well. The development process becomes inefficient, the focus on the ultimate business objective gets lost, and it becomes increasingly difficult to respond to changing opportunities and pressures. The only real choice you have lies in how to address the total architecture.

The word *total* is appropriate for another reason as well. Traditionally in the business world, architecture has almost exclusively been the concern of the IT community. The business really didn't care as long as IT got

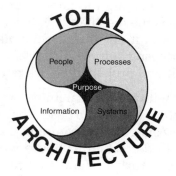

Figure 1–1: *Total Architecture*

the job done. But what are we saying here? The structuring of the business processes has to be done in concert with the structuring of the systems. Architecture is no longer an IT issue—it is an enterprise issue. We are talking about nothing less than total enterprise architecture. IT can't do it alone!

Architecture Is Structure for a Purpose

Every architecture is created for a specific purpose. Imagine that there has been a magnificent mansion under construction near where you live. You have been watching it evolve for months with growing curiosity. One day you are given an opportunity to tour the property, and you are delighted. You drive in and are impressed with the broad sweep of the expansive circular driveway—it will provide more than enough parking for even the largest party! You walk up the steps of the exquisite portico and through the huge brass-trimmed oak double doors into a spacious marble foyer. You wander through wide corridors leading to dozens of magnificently furnished rooms until you finally reach the mansion's crown jewel, the ballroom. What a palace! A work of art—well conceived and well executed, although more than a little extravagant.

Then one of your fellow wanderers approaches you and asks you what you think of this new concept in retail sales. Sales, you ask? Yes—the mansion is a new concept for retailing home furnishings. The merchandise is laid out exactly as it would be in your home—or at least the home you *wished* you had! Suddenly you begin to wonder. As big as that driveway is, will it hold hordes of holiday shoppers? Are the doors and hallways wide enough to handle crowds of shoppers with their packages? Where is the merchandise that you actually purchase? The more you think about it, the less sense it all makes. The architecture is just wrong—it doesn't suit the purpose. It may look like a magnificent mansion, but it will probably make a poor store.

What has all this to do with software architecture? An architecture, any architecture, is a structure with a purpose. That purpose is to support some form of activity. A good architecture will advance this purpose. A poor architecture will detract. Your house would not make a good factory, nor would New York's Grand Central Station make a good house. This is as true for the architecture of information systems as it is for the architecture of buildings. And just as it is with buildings, the creation of a good architecture requires a clear understanding of its intended purpose.

Because this is a book about the architecture of the enterprise information systems, we must begin by asking this: What is the purpose of the architecture? Simply put, it is to enable the business processes of the enterprise. That enablement can take a variety of forms, ranging from simple record keeping to completely automating business processes.

Increasingly, automation is becoming the focus. As you automate, systems become active participants in the business processes, making decisions and taking action. The systems and the business processes become so intertwined that you cannot even define the business process without discussing the role of the system. You now have a chicken-and-egg situation in which the business process cannot be designed without making assumptions about how and when the system should participate, and you cannot evaluate the reasonableness of that participation without beginning to design the system itself.

The traditional waterfall requirements-followed-by-system-design paradigm does not accomplish this. You need a new paradigm in which business process design and system design are addressed concurrently. It is this concurrent design paradigm, this Total Architecture Synthesis (TAS), that is the subject of this book.

The TAS paradigm is not a radical departure from the past. It is a simple restructuring of the traditional design activities to produce a more efficient iterative design technique. It is similar in concept to agile software development, but at the architectural level. Sketch a business process and its requirements, sketch an architecture to support it, then evaluate. Like it? Add more detail to the process, refine the architecture, evaluate again. Don't like it? Try something else—you haven't made a big investment, so there's nothing holding you back.

Constant Changes

The environment in which your enterprise lives is constantly changing. Customers and partners expect increasing levels of service and responsiveness. Your current competitors are constantly maneuvering to get the upper hand, and new companies threaten with disruptive technologies. And, of course, you have your own initiatives to improve your competitive position. Simply having a good implementation of today's business processes is not sufficient. Your enterprise needs to be able to adapt to these changes and initiate its own in order to remain viable.

The winner in such situations will be the enterprise that is most agile. The total architecture perspective is the critical enabler. With a solid understanding of the interactions between business processes, information, people, and systems, you will be able to quickly adapt and, at the same time, preserve future agility. This is particularly important when defining services. Because service interfaces are points of stability in the design, you need a good understanding of the flexibility that your enterprise requires to ensure that these stable interfaces will support future needs.

As I discussed at length in *Succeeding with SOA*, attempting adaptive changes without this understanding is risky at best and catastrophic at worst. You won't have a good understanding of the consequences of your changes, even in the near term. In the long term, you are likely to end up with a fragile chewing-gum and bailing-wire hodge-podge of systems that nobody understands. Such situations inhibit change and place your enterprise at a competitive disadvantage.

Total Architecture Synthesis

The good news is that considering your total architecture does not have to take longer or cost more than doing it on the cheap. It simply requires focusing on what's important. What are the business goals of the project? What business process changes are required to achieve those goals? Which business processes (and changes) are most likely to present challenges to the systems? What systems architecture (or changes) will it take to address those challenges?

Realize that you must eventually answer all of these questions. The trick is to answer them before you have committed to implementation, or even to detailed design. At this point, making mistakes and changing direction is quick and cheap. It's only a paper design, and easy to adjust. Then, once you are satisfied that you are headed in the right direction, you can detail the design and begin implementation with confidence. This is the philosophy of TAS.

Will your architecture be perfect? Of course not. Nor does it need to be. But the overall structure and organization—your total architecture—

will be both solid and flexible. Structure is what is expensive and time consuming to alter. You will find that, in practice, the types of subsequent alterations you will need to make are minor and easily accommodated.

You will find TAS to be efficient. While it does involve analysis, it avoids the analysis-paralysis problem by focusing on those things that really make a difference to the overall structure, and leaving the details for later. How efficient? There is no faster way to success—because you prioritize the work and only address questions that absolutely have to be answered. You can get to failure faster—and many do—but not success. The failure may not show up until you try to make subsequent changes, but without the total architecture perspective you are flying blind. Eventually you will crash.

So how do you do this? How do you organize business processes, people, information, and systems and focus them on achieving enterprise goals? And how do you do this efficiently and quickly? *Implementing SOA* will show you how.

Making Total Architecture Work in Your Enterprise

The issues and concerns addressed by Total Architecture are ubiquitous. You will find them in every enterprise and every project, and you must address them. However, you don't want to become fixated on finding the best possible solution to each issue or concern. The most common failing is not one of addressing an issue improperly; rather, it is failing to address the issue at all. Total Architecture will guide you in understanding what those issues are.

If Total Architecture teaches nothing else, it shows you that these issues and their resolution are interdependent. The "best possible" solution to one issue, viewed in isolation, may turn out to be less than optimal when its impact on other issues is taken into account. Use Total Architecture as a guide to understanding these dependencies and arriving at solutions that are optimal for the enterprise.

Finally, you should note that while the issues and concerns addressed by Total Architecture are ubiquitous, the prescriptive techniques presented here are but one approach among many. The detailed techniques you ultimately use and the manner in which you organize to apply them will vary depending upon the degree of centralization in the enterprise, the level of formality the organization is accustomed to, and the culture of the organization. Use the techniques in this book as a benchmark against which to compare your present processes and methods. Identify the gaps, and determine the best way of filling those gaps in your enterprise. Then act.

Total Architecture is a mindset—one that keeps you focused on the purpose of the enterprise. It reminds you that the interactions of business processes, people, information, and systems are but a means to help the enterprise achieve its ends. To achieve those ends, you must consciously architect those interactions. Architects must be charged with this responsibility and given the executive support to make it happen. Total Architecture is the lens that focuses the enterprise on its purposes.

Key Overview Questions

1. Does your present architecture facilitate business change or get in its way?

2. Do your projects have clearly defined business goals? How do you maintain the focus on achieving these goals during design?

3. Do you consciously design your business processes?

4. Does your approach to designing business services take into consideration the structure that the services impose upon the business processes?

5. What steps do you take to ensure that your services (a) can be reused, and (b) are, in fact, being reused?

Chapter 2

Architecture Fundamentals

Architecture is the characterization of the organization of a system in terms of its constituent parts. It characterizes the physical structure, functional organization, and collaborative behavior of those constituent parts and relates them to the system's intended purpose. A completed architectural description serves as a reference for the stakeholders—those who charter, fund, design, implement, and utilize the systems—as they strive to ensure that the systems that are realized satisfy the purpose that motivated their construction.

Upon reflection, you will see that this definition is as applicable to the architecture of physical buildings as it is to that of business systems. A hotel, for example, is a temporary place of residence, and its structure and organization must support that purpose. Similarly, the architecture of an enterprise exists to support the business processes of the enterprise. The ensuing discussion draws upon examples from both domains to clarify this definition of architecture and its implications for your work.

Structural Organization

When you think of architecture, your intuition probably leads you first to the notion of structure (Figure 2–1). At the highest physical level, an

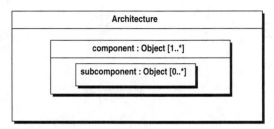

Figure 2–1: *Structure*

architecture consists of one or more components. In a city, there are many buildings. In an enterprise there are many applications. Each of these components, in turn, can comprise subcomponents. Remember that a service (since this is a book about SOA) is just a specialized form of component, so everything said here about components applies to services as well.

Components

Some architectural components are obvious when you consider the purpose of the overall system. In the city you find houses, stores, hotels, restaurants, offices, and movie theaters, all playing obvious roles in supporting daily life. In the enterprise you find order management systems, customer management systems, account management systems, claims systems, and financial accounting systems, again playing obvious roles in the operation of the enterprise. I will refer to these obvious components as the major components of the architecture.

There are other components that play supporting roles. Their roles do not become obvious until you consider the details of how the major components actually execute their roles. In the city there are components involved in the distribution of power, water, gas, sewage, and information. Their role does not become obvious until, for example, you consider how a restaurant prepares its food. Only then do you discover the restaurant's need for water, power, gas, sewage, and even for information as it places orders for supplies and manages accounts. In enterprise systems the supporting components are the power distribution, networks, file systems, databases, and the machines on which the applications run. It is not until you consider how the order management system actually manages orders that you discover the need for file systems, databases, network communications, machines to run the applications, and power to support the networks, machines, and file systems.

In understanding an architecture, you begin with knowledge of the major components and the manner in which they collaborate to satisfy the business purpose. Then, as you begin to consider the mechanics of how the components collaborate, you refine this high-level understanding by determining how the major components accomplish their tasks. In so doing, you identify the need for the supporting components and show how they participate in the overall collaboration.

Subcomponents

Components have an internal substructure of their own. The structure of a building, for example, is an organization of spaces. Larger spaces comprise smaller spaces, both interior and exterior. Consider a large hotel and the plot of land upon which it rests. One wing contains ballrooms and meeting rooms. Another wing contains the pool, fitness center, and spa. The tower contains the guest rooms. These large spaces all connect to a lobby area, which contains the registration desk, shops, and restaurants. Other spaces house the kitchens, laundry, storage rooms, heating and air conditioning equipment, and maintenance shops. The hotel has exterior space as well, comprising driveways, parking lots, patios, and recreational spaces. The organization of these spaces is the subcomponent structure of the hotel.

Business systems have internal structure as well. An application might be implemented in a two-tier or 3-tier architectural style (Figure 2–2). Each of the components will, in turn, have substructure.

When it comes to subcomponents, the architect must make a judgment call as to how much substructure he or she must consider. An architect

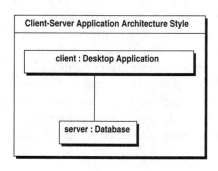
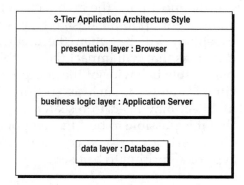

Figure 2–2: *Application Architecture Styles*

designing a house, for example, shows the placement of rooms and closets and specifies the type of wall construction but does not show the detailed internal structure of the walls. The exact placement of 2×4s and sheetrock is left up to the framing contractor.

In distributed systems, for the most part, you want to at least identify all of the individual software executables that are involved in the business processes. Generally, the internal structure of each process is left up to the designer of that process, although the architect may choose to specify the technology to be used and the style of the design. In the end, what you need to identify are the "moving parts" of the system— the components that take action.

While ideally you want to understand all of the moving parts of the design, you have to be somewhat pragmatic about the level of detail you seek. This is particularly true when there are large and complex applications involved in the overall business process—applications that comprise two or more software executables. To what extent do you need to understand the internal structure of these applications?

The pragmatic answer is that if you are modifying the application, then you need to understand its internal structure. If you are not modifying the application, and the application owner can accurately determine the performance characteristics and shared resource demands (network and disk in particular), then you can treat that application as a black box. But I warn you now, you are trusting the veracity of that system owner's claims. If they turn out to be inaccurate, your architecture may not work. You need to convince yourself that the system owner knows what he or she is talking about. Otherwise, you have no choice but to model the application's internal structure.

For the most part, the architect will leave the internal design of each component up to the design team responsible for the component. The exception will be when the architect can anticipate specific design decisions that will impact the feasibility of the design or the externally observable behavior of the component. When there are complex algorithms involved, such as sorting and searching large data sets, the architect may need to research the available algorithms to determine that it is possible to build a component with the required performance characteristics. In such cases, the architect should specify the specific type of algorithm to be used.

Functional Organization

You don't build systems for fun—you build them for a purpose. That purpose is to provide support for one or more kinds of activities. As an architect, one of the things you need to consider and specify is which component is involved in which activities and what that component's responsibilities are with respect to those activities (Figure 2–3).

The purpose of a hotel, for example, is to provide short-term support for the activities you associate with living in a residence: sleeping, personal hygiene, and perhaps eating, physical fitness, and recreation as well. For an enterprise, the purpose is to support the business processes of the enterprise that enable it to provide goods and services. These business processes comprise sequences of activities. By identifying which system components support which activities, and indicating exactly what each component does with respect to an activity, you define the role that the component is expected to play *with respect to the intended purpose of the overall architecture*. More precisely, the role identifies the set of behaviors that the component is expected to exhibit.

In your role as architect, it is your responsibility to clearly define the role of each component. You record your intent by labeling each component with the name of the role it will play. In the blueprints for your house, for example, you will find the cooking space labeled *kitchen*, the sleeping spaces labeled *bedrooms*, and the personal hygiene spaces labeled *bathrooms*. Subsequently, you will define the behaviors that are expected of each role.

The roles to be played by business system components are derived from the business processes they are intended to support. A retail business has an order-to-cash business process that transforms goods into

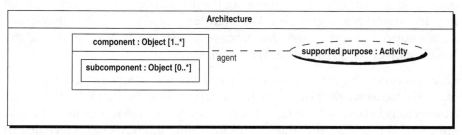

Figure 2–3: *Functional Organization*

revenue, a stock-replenishment business process that ensures goods are on the shelf when needed, and financial business processes to close the books at the end of each day, week, quarter, and year. In modularizing an architecture, the architect decomposes these business processes into activities and assigns the functional responsibility for executing those activities to the components of the architecture. In so doing, the architect is functionally organizing the architecture and defining the intended business role of each component. But sometimes labeling the components with clearly recognizable role names is not easy.

Shared Resources

In the architecture of buildings, the relationship between the physical spaces and their functional purpose is, for the most part, straightforward. In the architecture of business systems this relationship is often more complicated. Computers, databases, networks, application servers, and web browsers are all general-purpose components. Any given computer might house the order management function, the warehouse management function, or the accounting function—or all three. Because these components are general purpose, many of them end up being shared resources—resources that support more than one business purpose. A single database, for example, might house data associated with several functions. Such sharing can make it difficult for the architect to relate the component back to its functional business purposes in a clear and unambiguous manner.

This relationship between components and the business processes they support must be clear. The functional requirements for the components derive from their business roles. The nonfunctional requirements such as response time, throughput, and availability are, in turn, derived from these functional requirements and the needs of the overall business process. Unless you clearly understand the roles of the component, you can only guess at the functional and nonfunctional requirements. Such guesswork generates risk—risk that the component's support for the business process will be inadequate and that the business itself will consequently suffer.

One reason such guesswork is risky is that each component has a finite capacity to do work. This capacity is determined by factors such as the number and speed of the CPUs, the amount of RAM, the capacity and speed of the disks, and the bandwidth and latency characteristics of the networks. Sizing these components—determining their required capacity—requires an understanding of both their intended functional purpose and the volume of business activity they must support.

When components are shared, these finite capacity limitations can also cause unintended adverse interactions between business processes. If one business process is consuming more than its fair share of a component's resources, it may starve another business process of the resources that it needs. If a single database is supporting order management, warehouse management, and accounting applications, then the end-of-quarter financial accounting activity may place such a burden on the database that the enterprise's ability to take orders and ship goods is degraded. Such interactions are the unintended consequences resulting from an architectural decision to share the resource.

Another reason that guesswork is risky is the show-stopping impact that system component failures can have on the business process. If the component is the sole provider of a needed function in a business process, the loss of the component will keep that business process from executing. Without understanding which components are supporting which business processes, you cannot determine the business consequences of a component failure. Absent this understanding, you can only guess at the level of high availability, fault tolerance, and business continuity investment that is appropriate for each component.

Guessing at requirements and guessing at investment levels generates risk for the enterprise—risk that is unnecessary and avoidable. As an architect, you must define the functional role that each component is expected to play in each business process that it participates in. These role definitions are as much a part of the architecture definition as are the physical structures of the business systems. Not only must you understand these roles, you must also document and pass this understanding on to others to guide them in their evaluation and implementation of the architecture.

Coping with Evolving Requirements

Most enterprises are in a continual state of flux, responding to changing business goals and environmental pressures. This state of flux results in continually evolving business processes which, in turn, result in continually evolving system requirements. This continuing evolution presents an ongoing challenge for the enterprise architect to maintain clearly defined roles for each component. Without clearly defined roles, the requirements for the individual components become unclear. This, in turn, exposes the enterprise to the risks discussed previously.

One powerful tool the architect has for managing this risk is to clearly label each component with its intended business role. A role identifies expected behaviors (which will be subsequently defined), and the ability to clearly label the component is an indication that the expected behavior has been clearly identified. Furthermore, labeling provides an evolutionary guide for future architects and designers as the architecture evolves. Role names help the architects and designers determine the appropriate home for new functionality—unless that functionality actually belongs to a newly emerging role!

The Temptation of Expediency

When new functionality is required, particularly functionality that is part of a newly emerging role, there is a temptation to be expedient and simply place that functionality in whichever component seems to be the most convenient. This temptation is to be avoided, as it leads to a loss of clarity with respect to the role each component is expected to play in the enterprise. A loss of clarity makes it increasingly difficult to understand the component's requirements. This introduces guesswork into the requirement's definition—guesswork that brings risk.

Consider an operational data store containing sales order information. The purpose of this data store is to maintain sales order information in support of the order-to-cash business process. Now consider the fate of orders that have been shipped and paid. There is information in these old orders that is of value to the business. Should these orders be allowed to accumulate in the operational data store? The expedient answer is yes. Historically, however, this has not been the right answer.

This situation, of course, was the genesis of the role commonly referred to as the *data warehouse*. If you allow old orders to accumulate in the operational data store, its performance deteriorates as the number of completed orders piles up. Slice-and-dice data mining queries further tax the data store and degrade its operational performance. In response, the historical data was moved into a separate component— the data warehouse.

For those who allow the data to accumulate in the operational data store, the transition to a data warehouse is, in many cases, traumatic. The accumulating data in the operational data store leads to a gradual degradation in order-to-cash business process performance and a growing realization that some type of change was required. By the time the data warehouse is introduced, the operational data store performance problems make completing the split a time-critical exercise, further increasing the complexity of an already difficult project.

Recognizing that a new business process—in this case, historical data analysis—is emerging gives the enterprise time to make a graceful transition. With such recognition, the short-term accumulation of transactions while an appropriate data analysis process and supporting architecture is being developed will probably be acceptable. This allows the business to begin reaping value from the data while the data warehouse is put into place without excessive deterioration of the operational data store performance.

It is important to recognize that new functionality often indicates the emergence of new roles. You, as an architect, must continually be on the lookout for such indications. When you recognize the emergence of a new role, it is your responsibility to determine the appropriate home for this new role. The key here is to ensure that you remain involved in the evolution of the business processes and systems so that you can observe the emergence of new roles and evolve the architecture accordingly. You must watch databases, in particular. They are particularly vulnerable to expedient-driven growth that muddies their business purpose.

The consequences of expedient-driven database growth often do not become apparent until site disaster recovery is considered. Then it becomes apparent that there is some data in the database (current order information) that cannot be lost and therefore must be kept synchronized at the recovery site in real time or near real time. At the same time, there is other data (data warehouse information) that is less critical. The enterprise can actually tolerate a small level of data loss in this information during the unlikely event of a site disaster recovery.

The dilemma this mixed utilization presents is that real-time data synchronization is expensive, and that expense is proportional to the amount of data being synchronized. Real-time data synchronization impacts application performance and requires costly inter-site network bandwidth, not to mention the cost of the software and hardware required. Periodic synchronization, on the other hand, is transparent to applications and relatively inexpensive. The presence of both types of data in the same database creates a massive design problem for which there is no happy solution. Either all data is replicated in real time (imposing the performance and cost penalties on all applications updating data), or a hand-crafted mixed-mode synchronization strategy must be devised. Such strategies are complex to design, expensive to implement, and nearly impossible to test. And an untested failover is unlikely to actually work.

These two examples illustrate the need to have well-defined component roles. One of your chief challenges as an architect is to ensure that component roles remain clearly defined in the face of business processes and systems evolution. Ignore this challenge, or do it poorly, and your architecture will become a chewing gum and bailing wire concoction that is fragile, inflexible, and costly to maintain. Keep roles clearly defined and your architecture will be able to evolve gracefully, efficiently, and cost-effectively.

Collaborative Behavior

The components of an architecture are not isolated from one another, and their mere ability to perform certain functions does not, by itself, satisfy their business purpose. The components must collaborate together to make this happen. Furthermore, it is not until you examine this collaboration that you can understand whether your architecture effectively supports the business process—or inhibits it.

Activities

Understanding collaboration begins with understanding activities. *An activity is a function performed by one or more agents that uses one or more inputs and produces one or more results* (Figure 2–4). The activity's inputs include the event that triggers the performance of the activity, and for some activities this event may be the only input. The results of an activity include its completion status, and for some activities this may be the only result.

How does this apply to building architecture? You probably think it strange to talk about the spaces of a building being participants in activities. After all, people are the primary agents in most of the activities that take place in buildings. However, buildings actually do contribute to the activities that take place within them. Your kitchen, for example, provides heat, light, running water, drains, refrigeration,

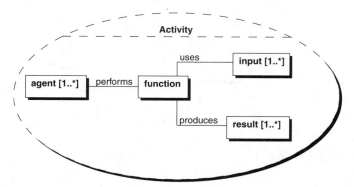

Figure 2–4: *Activity Structure*

heating elements, and storage spaces. These are secondary agents for performing activities. But buildings can provide primary agents as well. Your dishwasher completely automates the function of washing the dishes, although it does not load the dishwasher or put the dishes away. If you stop and think about it, as buildings become more sophisticated, they play increasingly important agent roles in the activities they support.

The role of business systems as agents in business processes is a bit more obvious, but people play prominent agent roles as well. The mix, of course, varies depending upon the degree of automation in the business process. If you purchase a piece of software and take delivery online, the entire transaction is being handled by the business systems. You are the only human participant in the process. Hiring an employee, on the other hand, tends to involve many people who work in conjunction with a number of business systems to bring the new person on board and provision them to play their role as an employee.

Objects

The inputs, results, and agents associated with an activity are all objects (things) of one sort or another (Figure 2–5).[1] Lumping agents with inputs and outputs may seem a bit odd until you consider that some activities have inputs or results that are agents for other activities.

---

1. Don't confuse the term *object* here with the programming language concept—objects in this context are simply things.

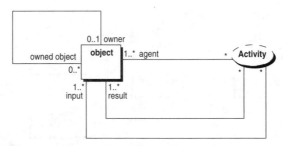

Figure 2–5: *Objects and Activities*

For example, the activities of hiring employees, making tools, and implementing information systems all produce results that then become agents for other activities.

Another important relationship involving objects is ownership. Ownership is not a structural relationship between objects, but rather a responsibility relationship. The sales order management system owns (is responsible for) sales orders. The warehouse management system owns (is responsible for) the inventory in the warehouse.

Ownership implies management responsibility. The owning object is responsible for (and therefore needs to control) the objects that it owns. This has implications for systems design. The sales order management system owns the data in its underlying database. To carry out this responsibility, access to the underlying data needs to be under the control of the order management system. Changes to the underlying data must be managed by the order management system so that it can enforce the business rules associated with altering the data. The implication is that if other participants are going to change the data, the order management system must provide interfaces so that other participants can ask it to make the required changes. The order management system becomes a service provider.

Ownership tends to be one of those relationships that is not very clearly defined in business systems. Pieces of information (the most commonly owned objects in business systems) tend to be replicated haphazardly in various systems. Many organizations struggle to simply identify the system of record for pieces of information—the one truly accurate copy. The problem this presents is that you can't manage something you don't control, and the value added for most business services is all about management. A sales order management service that cannot guarantee the accuracy of the sales order information isn't worth anything. For this reason, the identification of ownership rela-tionships is an important aspect of architecture.

Communications

Activities are related to one another through the objects involved in their execution. The most common relationship is that one activity produces a result that is an input to another activity. This is called a producer-consumer relationship. Generally, when the same agent is responsible for carrying out both activities, you tend to ignore (from an architec-tural perspective) the details of how that result gets to the next activity. You leave that up to the designer of the agent that will carry out the activities. However, when the two activities are being carried out by different agents, communication between those agents is required to convey the results of one agent's activity to the next agent.

Communication itself is a specialized form of activity (Figure 2–6). A communication has at least two agents, the Sender and Recipient, and one or more items that are delivered by the activity. There may be a number of intermediary agents involved in delivering the items, and some address information as well. When you send a letter, the postal service serves as the intermediary and the address on the envelope tells the service where to deliver the letter. The envelope itself contains the items to be delivered. When you send an e-mail, you have a similar scenario, with the e-mail servers and networks being the intermediaries.

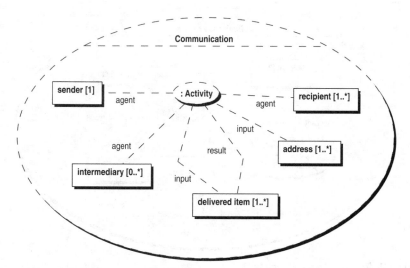

Figure 2–6: *Structure of a Communication*

Business Processes

Armed with the notions of activity, object, and communication, you can now model the structure of a business process as a collaboration between participants (Figure 2–7). This model makes a somewhat artificial distinction between the objects that play the role of agent, which from now on I will refer to as participants, and the objects that are the inputs and outputs of activities, which I will continue to refer to as objects. This distinction is valid for most business processes because with respect to a specific business process, each object tends to be either an active participant (a performer of activities) or a passive object involved in the activity. Even the hiring of a new employee fits this model, with the new employee truly being a participant and the inputs and outputs of the activities being the paperwork, records, and system configuration changes that result from the process.

Another somewhat artificial distinction in this model is the differentiation between communications and other kinds of activities. This separation distinguishes the functional responsibilities of an individual participant (the activities for which it is the sole agent) from the communications between the participants.

Figure 2–8 shows an example of an order-to-cash business process for an online merchant. Here you can see the participants along with their activities and communications. This UML activity diagram notation

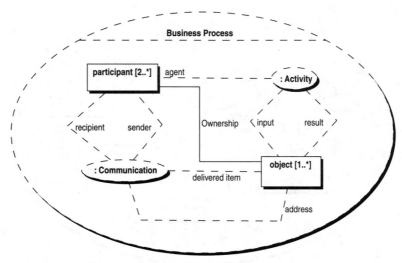

Figure 2–7: *Business Process*

enables you to clearly show the structure of a business process. It shows the participants in the process, the individual activities they perform, the communications between them, and the objects being conveyed in the communications.

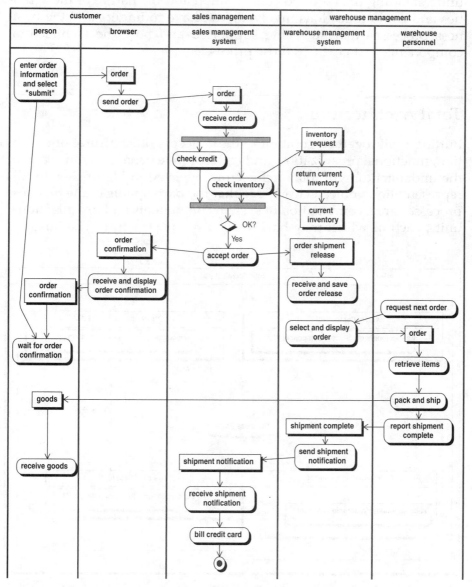

Figure 2–8: *Order-to-Cash Business Process Normal Execution*

At this point it should be very clear that the components of an architecture do not live in isolation. On the contrary, their suitability for their intended purpose depends entirely upon their ability to collaborate with one another to bring business processes to life. You can't evaluate this ability—and therefore cannot evaluate your architecture—without understanding the required collaboration and the nature of the activities and communications involved. You have to understand the business processes that are being supported and how the architectural components participate in those processes.

Total Architecture

Putting it all together, combining the concepts of structural organization, functional organization, and collaborative behavior, you arrive at the understanding of total architecture depicted in Figure 2–9. In this representation you can clearly see that the participants in the business processes are a combination of system components and organizational units, each of which may have their own substructure. The business

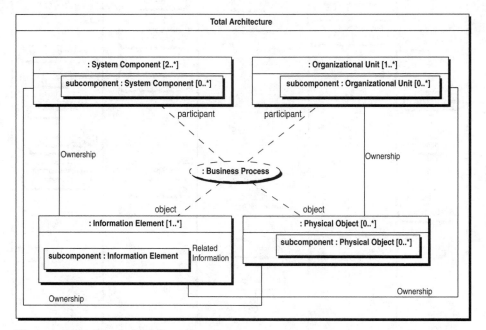

Figure 2–9: *Total Architecture*

process produces, consumes, and communicates objects that may be either informational elements or physical objects, both of which may have substructure as well. A complete description of an architecture must address the total architecture in its entirety.

However, while a complete architectural description must characterize all of this structure, you as an architect may not be responsible for defining it all. For example, business processes are commonly defined by the business stakeholders from the perspective of the human participants. These business process definitions indicate which activities are being performed by the systems, but not necessarily by which systems components. Your responsibility as a systems architect is to identify which systems components are performing those activities and further detail the activities and objects involved. Your job, then, is to ensure that the total architecture picture is clear, the collaborations will actually work, and the implementation can be accomplished within the cost and schedule guidelines.

Nonfunctional Requirements

To completely characterize a business process, you need to go beyond the activities and consider what are commonly referred to as the non-functional requirements, which are also referred to as quality attributes. This catch-all category includes all of the constraints that the business process must satisfy to ensure that it meets the business requirements, constraints such as the rate at which the business process must execute and the time frame in which the results are expected. Any constraint that the business process must satisfy constitutes a nonfunctional requirement.

From the nonfunctional requirements for the overall business process you can determine the nonfunctional requirements for the individual participants in the process—but only after you have defined the collaborative behavior that brings the business process to life. Given a requirement that orders are being received at a particular rate and must be shipped within a day of order receipt, you can use your understanding of the collaborative behavior shown in Figure 2–8 to determine what each participant must be able to do to satisfy those requirements.

Translating nonfunctional business process requirements to nonfunctional participant requirements often requires some analysis and some design decisions. If you expect 10,000 orders a day and the warehouse is a single-shift operation, then the warehouse must be able to pack and ship 10,000 orders in an eight-hour period. If the business process requires that the confirmation of the order takes no longer than 30 seconds, then the credit check and inventory check operations need to be completed within this time frame. As an architect, part of your responsibility is to budget this time and establish response-time service-level agreement (SLA) requirements for the warehouse management system and credit-checking services.

Refinement

At this point you may be saying to yourself that defining a collaboration sounds more like design than architecture—and you may be wondering what the difference is after all. This understandable confusion arises because architecture and design are the same kind of activity. They differ only in their level of detail. You can think about architecture and design as two points along a continuous spectrum of refinement that ranges from concept to operation (Figure 2–10). Movement along this spectrum represents the process of refinement.

The *New Oxford American Dictionary* defines refinement as "the improvement or clarification of something by the making of small changes."[2] To make this definition work for architecture, I need to add a clarification: After an architecture has been defined, refinement cannot alter the architecture; it can only add detail. The reason for this restriction is that you want to ensure that any reasoning that you have done about the architecture prior to refinement remains valid after the

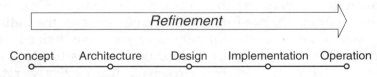

Figure 2–10: *Refinement*

---

2. Elizabeth J. Jewell, Frank Abate, and Erin McKean. 2005. *The New Oxford American Dictionary.* New York, NY: Oxford University Press, p. 1423.

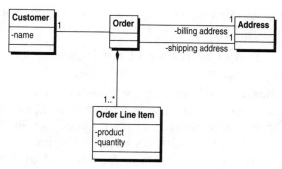

Figure 2–11: *Class Model of an Order*

refinement. If a change to the architecture becomes necessary, you—the architect—must be involved.

For example, consider the model of an order shown in Figure 2–11. This model is typical of the architectural specification you would expect for the order being communicated between the `browser` and the `sales management system` in Figure 2–8. Any specific representation of the order that contains all of the information in the model constitutes a proper refinement of the order. The refinement could, for example, indicate that the name consists of three fields containing the person's first, middle, and last name respectively. Similarly, an address representation consisting of street address, city, state, country, and postal code would also be a refinement. In contrast, a representation that omitted any of the information in the model or added additional information (such as the customer's e-mail address) would not be considered a refinement.

The Role of the Architect

The notion of refinement is an important one in architecture. The architect's job is to identify the components of the system and specify the components in sufficient detail that any proper refinement of the architecture will lead to a successful implementation. The architect adds only enough detail to be confident that if different design teams implement (refine) different components, the components will still collaborate properly to bring the business processes to life. Implementations that are not strict refinements are alterations to the architecture and require the architect's review and approval.

An architectural specification must, at a minimum, provide the following information:

1. An identification of each type of participant required (whether a system component or organizational unit).

2. A specification for each system component, including the information and physical objects owned by the component, a detailed specification of each interface, and a specification of the component's externally observable behavior. Optionally, the architect may choose to further constrain the internal architecture of the component.

3. A specification for each organizational participant detailing the information and physical objects owned by the organizational unit, the movement of information and physical objects to and from that participant, and the characterization of the observable behavior of the participant.

4. A detailed specification of each communication and communication mechanism.

5. A specification of the geographic deployment of the participants including the number and type of each participant at each location and the connectivity between the participants and between the locations.

6. A description of the collaboration of the participants that indicates how the collaboration satisfies the business need.

Enterprise Architecture

Characterizing an architecture by describing how it supports business processes seems to present a dilemma when you look at architecture from the enterprise perspective. There are many business processes in your enterprise, and the future will bring business processes you haven't even thought of yet. How do you define an architecture for the enterprise under such circumstances?

Architecture Styles

A commonly used but ultimately unsatisfactory approach is to completely ignore collaborative behavior and focus entirely on specifying the structural organization and a few principles of functional organization. You've already seen a couple of examples back in Figure 2–2 that sketched client-server and 3-tier application architectures.

Architecture styles generally describe the structure of an architecture and provide a set of principles for determining which type of functionality belongs in each portion of the structure. The Client-Server Application Architecture style of Figure 2–2 partitions an application into server components that are responsible for data management and client components that are responsible for business logic and user interface. The 3-Tier Application Architecture style in the same figure partitions the application into three components, essentially separating the Client of the Client-Server style into a user interface presentation layer and a business logic layer.

Of course enterprise architectures involve more than one application, and immediately you begin to see one of the limitations of this approach. When there is more than one application, application architecture styles do not provide any guidance regarding what functionality belongs in one application versus another, nor do they provide any guidance as to how, when, and why those applications ought to communicate with one other.

The enterprise version of an architecture style generally looks something like Figure 2–12. Here you see the enterprise characterized as a collection of applications that share a common communications service. There has been some evolution in this picture as the communications service has evolved from a raw network to what is now loosely called an enterprise service bus, but the principles remain the same—as do the weaknesses. There is no guidance in this style about which functionality belongs in which applications, nor is there any guidance surrounding

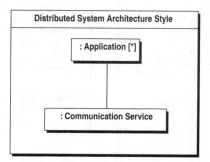

Figure 2–12: *Distributed System Architecture Style*

when applications should communicate. In other words, there is no guidance around collaboration.

Guidance on collaboration is essential. Poorly conceived collaborations will not satisfy business needs. To illustrate this, consider the two functional assignment alternatives shown in Figure 2–13. Now ask yourself which of the two functional responsibility assignments for `activity 2` is preferable.

This type of question arises whenever you consider making an activity a part of a service. You might, for example, be considering making `activity 2` into a service performed by `participant B`—the service provider. Is this a good idea or not?

Well, what if `activity 2` were a trivial operation—say subtraction. Does it make sense for `participant A` to package two numbers as a message, send them to `participant B`, and then wait for `participant B` to compute the answer, package up the answer, and send it back? Probably not. The overhead of the communication and the delays involved far exceed the cost of performing the subtraction operation in `participant A`. Making it into a service would not be efficient.

Now consider the opposite extreme. `activity 2` is an operation that generates a huge data set as a result, and `activity 3` analyzes that

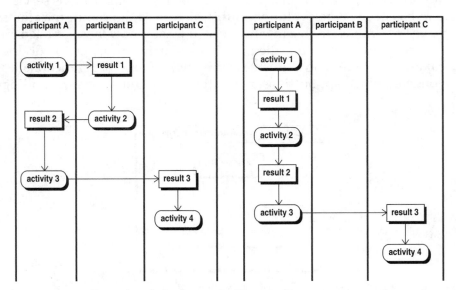

Figure 2–13: *Functional Assignment Alternatives*

data set and reduces it to a simple yes/no answer. Does it make sense to have `activity 2` performed by another participant and incur the cost of having to move that huge data set from `participant B` back to `participant A`? Or would it make more sense to have `participant A` perform both activities and save the communications costs?

To answer these questions, you need to have some understanding of the nature of the activities and the size of the results. In other words, you need to understand something about the business process and the pattern of collaboration in order to determine whether a particular set of functional assignments makes sense. And herein you find the key to enterprise architecture: patterns.

Patterns

A pattern is a style of describing a solution to a problem. In the words of Christopher Alexander, "Each pattern describes a problem which occurs over and over again in the environment, and then describes the core of the solution to that problem, in such a way that you can use the solution a million times over, without ever doing it the same way twice."[3]

If you examine the business processes in your enterprise, you will find that the majority of the collaborations in these business processes follow a relatively small number of patterns. For example, a customer uses a web browser to interact with an application server and execute a transaction in a particular back-office system. Any number of business processes might use this pattern. Enterprise architecture amounts to identifying those patterns and defining the structure, functional organization, and collaboration to be used when implementing those patterns.

You will find patterns at many different levels of abstraction in your enterprise architecture. High-level collaboration patterns that define business processes are refined through the application of lower-level patterns. This book is essentially a walk through the family of patterns needed to address distributed systems design in the enterprise. For enterprise business systems, it provides the equivalent of Alexander's

---

3. Alexander, Christopher, Sara Ishikawa, and Murray Silverstein. 1977. *A Pattern Language: Towns • Buildings • Construction*. New York, NY: Oxford University Press, p. x.

pattern language for characterizing towns, buildings, and construction.[4] The patterns in this book fall into the following categories:

- Collaboration patterns: Parts II and III
- Communications Patterns: Part IV
- Data Patterns: Part V
- Coordination Patterns: Part VI
- HA, FT, and LD Patterns: Part VII
- Security Patterns: Part VIII
- Monitoring Patterns: Part VIII

These patterns are presented in a suggested sequence of refinement. If you address the design issues in this sequence, it is most likely that you will be able to address each issue through refinement—using the selected pattern to add detail to the current architectural description. This sequencing will minimize the likelihood of having to alter a design decision after it has been made, and thus lead to an efficient design process.

Summary

Architecture is structure related to purpose. In the enterprise, this purpose is to support the business processes that make the enterprise work. Your understanding of the business processes is an essential prerequisite to creating an architecture. In fact, the business process itself defines the collaboration of peoples and systems required to execute the business process, and this collaboration definition is actually part of the architecture. It is through understanding of this collaboration that you become aware of the responsibilities of and the requirements for the people and systems involved. Understanding this collaboration also makes it possible to derive the nonfunctional requirements for the individual participants from those of the overall business process. This derivation ensures that the collaboration will be capable of satisfying the business process's overall nonfunctional requirements.

Architecture is high-level design. The goal is to specify that design in such a way that the design can be driven to implementation through a

---

4. Ibid. pp. xvii–xxxiv

process of refinement—adding detail without altering the design. To accomplish this, a total architecture definition must:

1. Identify all participants (distinct entities) involved in the business process, whether human or machine.
2. Specify each system component.
3. Specify component interactions with human participants.
4. Specify each communication and communication mechanism.
5. Specify the geographic deployment of the participants and the connectivity among them.
6. Specify how the participants collaborate to satisfy the business need.

Architectures evolve over time as changing business processes require new functionality and added capacity. Care must be taken to ensure that these changes are made in a coherent and consistent manner, and that the resulting architecture remains robust and flexible. This requires the maintenance of current-state architecture and business process definitions so that the architectural impact of proposed changes can be readily assessed.

The collaborations defined by business processes require added detail before they can be implemented. Design issues related to communications, data, coordination, fault tolerance, high availability, load distribution, security, and monitoring must all be addressed before the individual components and services can be implemented.

If individual projects are left to their own devices to address these design issues, the result is liable to be a hodge-podge of solutions and technologies that will drive up the complexity and cost of systems development. Avoiding this problem requires a proactive enterprise architecture group that defines enterprise-standard design patterns for addressing design issues.

Key Architecture Fundamentals Questions

1. Does your architecture documentation identify all participants in the solution, both human and machine?
2. Does your architecture documentation define the functional responsibilities of the participants and the manner in which they collaborate to satisfy the business needs?

3. Do you maintain current documentation of both your architecture and your business processes?

4. Are the nonfunctional requirements for participants derived from the nonfunctional requirements of the business processes they participate in? Is the derivation included in your architecture documentation?

5. Does your enterprise architecture group define, teach, and evolve the design patterns for high-level collaborations found in your business processes?

6. Does your enterprise architecture group define, teach, and evolve the design patterns to solve communications, data, coordination, fault tolerance, high availability, load distribution, security, and monitoring problems found in your enterprise?

Suggested Reading

Alexander, Christopher, Sara Ishikawa, and Murray Silverstein. 1977. *A Pattern Language: Towns • Buildings • Construction*. New York, NY: Oxford University Press.

Buschmann, Frank, Regine Meunier, Hans Hohnert, Peter Sommerlad, and Michael Stal. 1996. *Pattern-Oriented Software Architecture: A System of Patterns*. Chichester: John Wiley and Sons.

Gamma, Erich, Richard Helm, Ralph Johnson, and John Vlissides. 1995. *Design Patterns: Elements of Reusable Object-Oriented Software*. Upper Saddle River, NJ: Addison-Wesley.

Shaw, Mary and David Garlan. 1996. *Software Architecture: Perspectives on an Emerging Discipline*. Upper Saddle River, NJ: Prentice Hall.

Chapter 3

Service Fundamentals

A business process (or any process, for that matter) is an organized set of tasks. Executing the business process is a matter of coordinating the execution of these tasks. The idea behind a service-oriented architecture (SOA) is to have the individual tasks performed by specialized components called services. The work of these services is then coordinated to bring the business process to life. What differentiates the SOA approach is that each service is designed for convenient reuse. If another business process requires the same task to be performed, it employs the existing service—the same service that was used to support the original business process.

What Is a Service?

A service is a well-defined unit of work performed by a component and packaged for easy access. The idea is to implement the functionality exactly once, do it well, and then make it widely accessible. The extra effort involved in initially creating the service (and there is always extra effort) is paid for by avoiding future development costs either through the direct reuse of the service or by isolating the service user from ongoing internal implementation changes within the service.

Operations

The tasks performed by a service are its operations. You can think of a service as a bundle of closely related operations (Figure 3–1). The simplest operations are, in the mathematical sense, pure functions—they take inputs and produce outputs that are solely based on the inputs. For example, they take two numbers and add or subtract them.

However, addition and subtraction are so simple that they are actually not good candidates for service operations—at least when the service user is a computer. This becomes apparent when you realize that the operation is actually being performed by another component with communications involved (Figure 3–2). In the case of addition and subtraction, the overhead of communicating with the service provider to invoke these operations is so much greater than the service user's cost of executing the operations that it just doesn't make sense. So one of the tradeoffs in deciding what ought to be a service begins to emerge: the granularity of the work versus the communications costs.

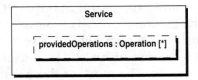

Figure 3–1: *Basic Service*

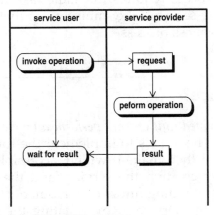

Figure 3–2: *Simple Service Utilization Example*

Service operations that are pure mathematical functions do exist, but they are not common. Two examples that often begin their lives as purely functional concepts are data transformations and rule evaluations. A data transformation takes one data structure and reorganizes its data elements into another data structure. A purely functional business rule takes in one or more data structures and generates output structures containing conclusions about the input data.

Referenced Objects

In reality, data transformations and rule evaluations commonly require some form of reference data. Data transformations frequently perform lookups and substitutions on the data. One system's identifiers in the input data structure need to be replaced with another system's identifiers in the output data structure. To support this, a cross-reference table is needed that maps one system's identifiers to the other system's identifiers. Data transformations often convert monetary values given in one currency to values in another currency. To support this, a currency exchange table is needed.

Rules often require reference data as well. Consider the rules governing the access to business banking accounts. A business rule might state, "Permission to perform operations on this account is granted if the person requesting the operation is either the person owning the account or a superior of that person." Executing this rule obviously requires some information about the placement of individuals within an organization structure. This is reference data.

To keep an operation in its purely functional form, the user of the operation would have to access the reference data prior to invoking the operation. The user would have to look up the other system's identifiers, map dollars to euros, and explore the organizational structure of the people involved in the transaction. Logically, however, these additional tasks belong with the operation. The operation now evolves beyond being a simple mathematical function to include the use of reference data.

The idea that operations can reference things goes beyond simply referencing data. Some service operations may reference physical objects as well: an individual person, an automobile, an aircraft, a package, or a building. In general, many service operations will reference *objects* in the process of performing their operations (Figure 3–3). But these objects are not part of the service. The service does not manage these

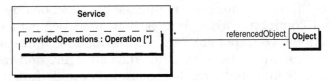

Figure 3–3: *A Service with Referenced Objects*

objects—it only references them. Thus, these objects lie outside the scope of the service.

Owned Objects

Some services exist specifically to manage objects. In fact, the core functionality of most business processes revolves around the management of objects such as sales orders, shipments, and warehouse inventory. If you want to assemble such business processes from services, then you need to organize services that manage objects. Management implies complete control, and the only way to guarantee complete control over an object is for the service to own it. Now you have services that own some objects and merely reference others. You need to clearly distinguish between the objects that the service owns and manages, and those objects that it merely references (Figure 3–4). And herein lies one of the major challenges in service design—clearly establishing the ownership of objects.

Consider an SOA approach to building an order-to-cash business process. Figure 3–5 shows some initial concepts for some of the services you might want. In this conceptualization, the `Sales Order Service` manages the information specifically related to individual sales orders, the `Product Information Service` manages the information about the products being offered, and the `Customer Information Service` keeps track of information about the individual customers. So far, so good.

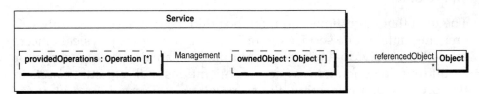

Figure 3–4: *Structure of a Service with Owned Objects and Referenced Object*

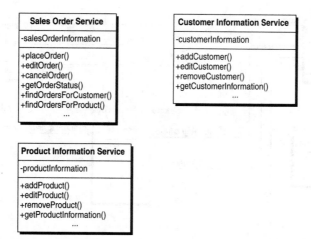

Figure 3–5: *Initial Service Concepts Supporting an Order-to-Cash Business Process*

Now take a look at the inherent structure of the data (Figure 3–6). Some of the classes clearly belong to a specific service. `Sales Order` and `Sales Order Line Item` obviously belong to the `Sales Order Service`. Likewise, `Product` belongs to the `Product Information Service` and `Customer` belongs to the `Customer Information Service`. But what about `Address` and `Phone`? Even more challenging, what about the relationship between `Sales Order` and `Customer`, and between `Sales Order Line Item` and `Product`? Which services own these?

Such questions are the crux of service design and comprise a major challenge in evolving from a design centered around a single monolithic database to a design involving distributed services, each managing a subset of the data. The ownership of `Address` and `Phone` is fairly straightforward. As a class (i.e., a concept), neither is uniquely owned by any specific service. Instead, each service owns specific instances of these classes that play particular roles with respect to the other objects that are owned by the service. For example, the `Sales Order Service` owns the `shippingAddress`, `billingAddress`, and `contactPhone`, while the `Customer Information Service` owns the `homeAddress`, `workAddress`, `defaultShippingAddress`, `defaultBillingAddress`, `homePhone`, `workPhone`, and `cellPhone`. In fact, each service may have different representations for these objects, although there are benefits to maintaining a uniform representation of

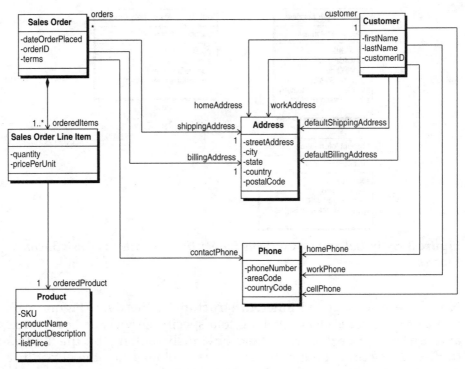

Figure 3–6: *Information Related to Sales Orders*

these objects across the services (i.e., a common data model), particularly in their interfaces.

Owning Relationships

Determining the ownership of relationships presents more of a challenge. Defining a relationship requires referencing the objects at both ends of the relationship. How do you represent a relationship when one of these objects is owned by one service and the other by another service? The `Sales Order Service` needs to know who the customer is for the order, but it is not the owner of the `Customer` object. How exactly do you do that?

One approach is to add some of the needed customer data to the `Sales Order Service` and have this service manage this customer data. However, now you've lost the advantage of having a `Customer Information Service` that manages all of the customer data. How do you update customer data and keep it consistent when there is customer data present in more than one service? This is exactly the type of problem you are seeking to avoid with a SOA.

Another approach is to keep a bare-bones reference to the customer— just the `customerID`—in the `Sales Order Service`. This is simpler and less risky, for identifiers are generally not edited after they have been created. However, this approach presents its own issues. First, if you want to print out or display the order with the customer name or other customer information, the `Sales Order Service` has to go to the `Customer Information Service` to obtain the information. From a performance perspective, the delays in such retrieval may not be acceptable, and it may not be practical for the `Customer Information Service` to support this type of query load. Second, you won't be able to delete a customer from the `Customer Information Service` without first determining whether there are any remaining references to that customer (i.e., instances of the `customerID`) in any other service. Otherwise, deleting the `Customer` would leave invalid references in the other services. Even worse, recycling the `customerID` would actually leave old `Sales Orders` referencing the wrong customer.

Don't get the wrong impression here. These issues do have eminently practical resolutions. The point is that you have to dig down into the structure and ownership of the data (and other managed objects) in order to clearly define the scope of each service. As you dig and define ownership, your concept for each service is likely to evolve. Continuing this example will illustrate the evolution.

Assume that, for performance reasons, the `Sales Order Service` must have the customer's name readily available. Also for performance reasons, it must have the product name available. Figure 3–7 shows the resulting logical data model for the `Sales Order Service`. Note that you need an understanding of the service's intended utilization to conclude that this information needs to be present in the `Sales Order Service`!

This data model clearly resolves the issue of owning the relationships: The relationship between the `Sales Order` and the `Customer` is owned by the `Sales Order Service`, as is the relationship between `Sales Order Line Item` and `Product`. But now you are left with copies of this data in the `Sales Order Service`—data for which the service is not the owner. How do you manage this data?

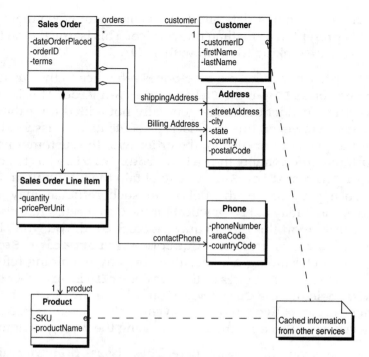

Figure 3–7: *Logical Data Model for Sales Order Service*

Managing Cached Information

The solution for maintaining the accuracy of replicated data is to treat it as a cached copy of the original. This involves establishing a single service as the system-of-record for the original data and adding subscription operations to notify others of changes to the original data. Services that maintain copies of the information subscribe to this service and update their local copies when the data changes.

Figure 3–8 shows the modified conceptualization of the services considered earlier. The `Sales Order Service` (the service containing the cached information) subscribes to the change notification service of each of the other services for which it holds cached data. The `Product Information Service` provides a `subscribeToProductChangeNotification` subscription operation and a corresponding `productInformation-HasChanged` notification operation. The Customer Information Service provides the `subscribeToCustomerChangeNotification` and `customerInformationHasChanged` operations.

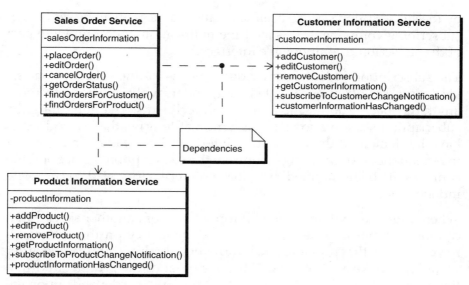

Figure 3–8: *Extended Services*

The placement of the `productInformationHasChanged` and `customerInformationHasChanged` operations may seem a bit strange at first. These are the operations that are called by the subscription service when changes occur. Intuitively, you would expect these operations to be on the service that receives the change notification (i.e., the `Sales Order Service`), since it is the one responding to the notifications. However, it is the subscription service itself that actually defines the operation interface, including the data that is passed when it is called. For this reason, the operation is shown as part of the subscription service. These notification operations are examples of the proposed WSDL `Out-Only` message exchange pattern.[1]

It may take a bit of thought to get comfortable with the `Out-Only` message exchange pattern, but it is an important one. The subscription service defines the interface (the notification interface), but this interface is not called by another component. Instead, the interface is called

---

1. W3C (World Wide Web Consortium). March 2004. "Web Services Description Language (WSDL) Version 2.0 Part 2: Message Exchange Patterns." W3C Working Draft 26. www.w3.org/TR/2004/WD-wsdl20-patterns-20040326.

by the subscription service itself and causes a message to be sent to the subscribing component. It is as if the notification operation were part of the subscribing component's interface.

The subscription paradigm provides a means for the subscription service to send notifications to other components without having to know anything specific about the notification recipients. The only thing the subscription service knows (or assumes, at least) is that all recipients have implemented the notification interface. This leads to a degree of independence—decoupling—between the subscription service and the components being notified, but does not necessarily lead to complete independence.

When a service contains cached information from another service that cannot be arbitrarily deleted, it has a dependency on the system-of-record service that provides the information. In this example, the order would not make a lot of sense if the customer or the product information were deleted. Thus the `Sales Order Service` depends upon the `Customer Information Service` and the `Product Information Service` not to delete information that it is currently using.

The existence of such dependencies usually becomes clear when you consider the impact of purging—permanently deleting—information. In a practical system, the removal of customer and product information requires coordination with the `Sales Order Service` so that orders don't end up missing customers or products. You may find yourself with a purge strategy that starts with removing old orders and then proceeds to remove old customers and old products. To ensure that you are not deleting customers and products for which there are still active orders, you may want to add operations on the `Sales Order Service` to find orders related to a particular customer or product. Alternatively, you may not want to delete old customers or products at all; instead, simply mark them as inactive in the system-of-record. Of course, eventually you are going to need to do a purge anyway as the accumulating information will degrade performance and stress physical storage limits.

As this example illustrates, defining services requires that you rationalize the structure and ownership of data as well as functionality. You can't just wrap a poorly organized database with services and expect to have well-defined and easy-to-manage services. Put lipstick on a pig and you still have a pig! Designing services requires teasing data apart for manageability and establishing clear ownership for both objects and relationships.

When one service references objects owned by another service, you will likely have to add operations to manage replicated data. The full lifecycle of referenced objects, from creation through modification and destruction, needs to be considered. If arbitrary purges of referenced objects cannot be allowed, then you must document this dependency, describe the required object management, and add the required operations to the services.

Service Interfaces

Service users need to be able to access the service operations in order to use them: The operations require interfaces. To achieve the expected benefits from services, these interfaces must facilitate convenient access. Your services should be accessible from any platform and location, and your service providers should be able to run on whatever platform is most appropriate. To accomplish this, you need to carefully consider the technologies you use for accessing the services and representing data. You also need to consider the potential benefits of refining the semantics of the data structures used by the operations and the operations themselves.

Common Access Technology

When a component directly uses the functionality of another component, it is tied to the design of that component's interfaces in a number of ways (Figure 3–9). First and foremost, it is tied to the technology of that interface. If the functionality being accessed is a CICS transaction on a mainframe, the user must be able to invoke a CICS transaction on a mainframe. If the functionality is in a Java subroutine, the user must be able to invoke a Java subroutine. This kind of dependency creates problems for services. If you want your services to be widely accessible, the technology used for accessing the service interface must be uniformly available on a wide variety of platforms. This is a fundamental requirement for all services.

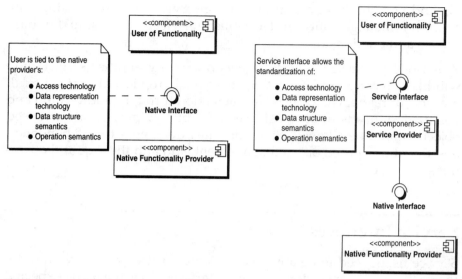

Figure 3–9: *Native and Service Interfaces*

Common Data Representation Technology

Most service operations require passing data back and forth. Native interfaces expect this data to be in the form required by the provider. Depending on the provider, this form might be a binary representation, text encoded in EBCDIC[2] (Extended Binary Coded Decimal Interchange Code) or ASCII[3] (American Standard Code for Information Interchange), or a serialized Java object. The variety of native representations is nearly endless.

Many of these representations are platform-specific. EBCDIC and its variants are the standard character representations on mainframes, while ASCII and its variants are the standard character representations on most other platforms. Text representations can also be specific to the native language of the people using the systems. The basic EBCDIC and ASCII encodings represent the Roman alphabet as used in English-speaking countries. They cannot represent the character sets used in

---

2. www-306.ibm.com/software/globalization/cdra/index.jsp, Appendix A. Encoding Schemes.

3. ANSI X3.4-1967, American Standard Code for Information Exchange.

other languages. More recent standards such as Unicode[4] are capable of representing the character sets used in many human languages.

Beyond the issue of simple character representations, applications often have rules regarding how the data is organized. Often these rules are ad hoc, specifying the format of individual records and the sequencing of records in a file or message. Understanding and complying with ad hoc rules is a time-consuming design process for both the provider and user of the data structures. Recent standards have begun to change this picture. MIME (Multipurpose Internet Mail Extensions)[5] organize the structure of e-mail messages and allow for multiple character sets (and non-character data as well) to be employed. HTML (Hypertext Markup Language)[6] and XML (eXtensible Markup Language)[7] provide standards for organizing data, and XML schemas provide standard representations for the rules governing the structure of the data. The use of these standards greatly simplifies the passing of data.

Binary data presents even greater challenges. Binary representations on different platforms can vary in the ordering of the bytes within a word, with some platforms placing the high-order (most significant) bytes first and others placing them last. The actual manner in which the data itself is represented in binary depends upon the type of data being represented (images, sounds, video, computer programs). Even for one type of data, there are often multiple binary representations in use. Some of these representations have become standards.

Too many variations in data representation complicate the exchange of data between the user and provider. Because of this, it is common practice in establishing a service-oriented architecture to standardize the technologies used to represent data being transported across service interfaces. XML has emerged as the representation of choice for

---

4. The Unicode Consortium. 2006. The Unicode Standard, Version 5. Upper Saddle River, NJ: Addison Wesley Professional.

5. MIME is defined by a set of standards from the Internet Engineering Task Force (IETF). Part I of these standards can be found at http://www.ietf.org/rfc/rfc2045.txt.

6. HTML is a joint standard of the International Organization for Standardization (ISO) and the International Electrotechnical Commission (IEC). The current version can be found at https://www.cs.tcd.ie/15445/15445.HTML.

7. XML is a specification developed by the World Wide Web Consortium (W3C). Information about the specification can be found at http://www.w3.org/XML/.

textual data, but only when the increased size of the data structures is tolerable. When the increased size is not acceptable, more compact proprietary formats may be preferable, but these carry with them the increased costs of custom code for assembling, parsing, and validating the data structures. In establishing your service-oriented architecture, you should standardize by selecting a preferred set of data representations.

While standards for data representations are important, you need to be careful not to inappropriately force these standards on every interface. If two components use the same native data representation (not one of your standards) and you are implementing a dedicated point-to-point interface between them, there is little benefit in converting the data to one of your standard representations only to convert it back to the same native representation.

Common Data Semantics

Selecting a data representation technology facilitates the exchange of data between the parties, but it still leaves quite a bit of room for variation. Specifying XML for text-based representations does not determine what information is being represented or how that information is organized. Yet both the user and provider of functionality need to understand what information is expected and how it is expected to be organized.

When you are using a native interface, the content and structure of the data is completely determined by the provider. The rules for organizing the information often have no formal representation. Consider the representation of a sales order shown in Figure 3–10. This is typical of the organization of sales orders found in many older systems, particularly file-based systems. This representation simply defines two record types, but does not tell you what the rules are for combining the two record types into a file or message. Common sense would tell you that there ought to be one instance of `Record Type 1` to represent the overall order and one instance of `Record Type 2` for each of the order's line items. But are you allowed to put more than one order in a file or message? Could the order record be the last one, after the line items, instead of the first record?

There are other issues as well. The concepts of customer, address, and phone are all blended together in `Record Type 1`, and the concepts of sales order line item and product are blended together in `Record Type 2`. There is no explicit representation of the complete sales order—just the collection of instances of the two record types.

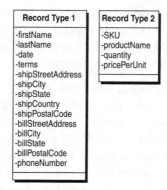

Figure 3–10: *Native Order Representation*

Such representations are often awkward. In traditional record format, the fields containing the data are present, but there are no labels identifying which field represents which piece of data. There may be rules regarding which fields are required and which are optional. To use these data structures, you have to know the format and the rules—if you can find them!

These types of issues motivated the development of data structures with machine-readable formal definitions such as the data description language (DDL) used to describe relational database structures and XML schemas for describing textual structures. XML schemas are defined using the XML Schema Definition (XSD) language.[8]

The logical data model you saw back in Figure 3–7 is an abstract example of this sort of data structure. If such a logical model is transformed into an XML schema with each object and attribute represented as an XML element, then you have achieved two benefits. From a human perspective, such data structures are generally easier to produce and consume, since the XML representation of the order is self-describing and easy to understand. From a machine perspective, standard software can be used to access the data and validate that the order representation complies with the schema definition.

Having gone to the trouble of engineering such a data structure, it would make sense to use that data structure (or the relevant parts of it) in other interfaces whenever the same set of information is required.

---

8. XML Schema Part 0: Primer Second Edition W3C Recommendation 28. October 2004. www.w3.org/TR/xmlschema-0/.

This gives rise to the notion of a common data model (CDM) or common object model (COM). Such models standardize the representations of specific concepts and relationships. Chapter 18 explores the engineering of these data structures in more detail.

While common data models sound like a good idea, you have to realize that there is work involved in their development. Developing representations that can serve multiple purposes requires understanding the variety of its potential usages. Furthermore, using a representation that is native to neither the user nor the provider requires that the data be transformed into this representation by the user and transformed from this representation by the provider. You want to be convinced that the representations will actually be reused before making the investment. There is little point in engineering an abstract representation for a dedicated point-to-point interface.

Common Operation Semantics

While there may be an exact 1-to-1 correspondence between the operations you want to provide for your service and the operations actually available in the native implementation, there may be times when you want the service to provide an operation that is actually a composite of underlying operations. For example, a common enterprise resource planning (ERP) application does not provide the ability to place an order as a single operation. Instead, it provides two operations. The first operation takes the order and places it in a temporary staging table. The ERP application periodically checks this staging table and tries to process any orders it finds. It then places the processing results in a second status table and provides a second operation to retrieve the status.

For ease of use, you may want your service to provide a single operation that, from the user's perspective, accepts the order and returns the results. The implementation of this operation would invoke the first native operation, wait the requisite period of time to allow processing to occur, retrieve the results, and return the results to the user. Of course, determining what the appropriate abstract operation ought to be will require some understanding of the intended utilization, and therefore more work.

Choosing the Level of Interface Commonality

It should be apparent by now that there are a number of standardization choices to be made in developing service interfaces. These choices are summarized in Table 3–1. Note that the standardization of the access technology and data representation technology does not require an in-depth understanding of the business processes—only a broad understanding of the type of information being used. Standardizing the data and operation semantics, on the other hand, requires a detailed understanding of the business processes that will use the data and operations, and is correspondingly more difficult and expensive to achieve.

Table 3–1: *Pros and Cons of Interface Standardizations*

Type of Standardization	Advantage	Disadvantage
Common Access Technology	Makes the functionality uniformly accessible on any technology platform.	Mechanisms to access the common technology must be provided for each technology platform.
Common Data Representation Technology	Simplifies data access when moving data between technology platforms.	• Mechanisms for reading and manipulating the representations must be provided for each technology platform. • Mapping to/from native representation technologies may be required.
Common Data Semantics	The use of well-engineered representations for business concepts and relationships simplifies the understanding and use of this information.	• Engineering data representations that can support multiple operations requires a good understanding of the business processes and a correspondingly greater development effort. • Mapping to/from native data representations may be required.
Common Operation Semantics	Providing a well-defined operation that makes sense in multiple business contexts makes the operation easier to use and thus promotes reuse.	Defining operations that can be used in multiple business contexts requires a good understanding of the business processes and a correspondingly greater engineering effort.

Because of this variability in effort, you probably don't want to try and standardize all of these for every service operation. In many cases, standardizing the access and data representation technologies alone is sufficient to provide significant business benefits. The additional benefits of standardizing the data structure and operation semantics should be carefully weighed against the costs before deciding to standardize them as well.

The effort required to achieve these differing levels of standardization is also the reason why you don't want to arbitrarily turn every interface into a service operation. If you have two applications on the same technology platform that are already interacting successfully and you can't demonstrate the need for a third application to use those interfaces, then there may be little business benefit in standardizing any aspect of the interfaces.

The Rationale Behind Services

What benefit do you derive from using services? Services obviously provide an abstraction mechanism that allows you to think about the use of the provided functionality without getting bogged down in the details of its implementation. They encapsulate the functionality into a separate component that can be independently tested, monitored, and managed. This abstraction makes it easier to design and understand higher-level designs, but this simplicity comes at a price.

Building services requires time and effort beyond simply implementing the required functionality, and there is a runtime cost to using abstracted service access mechanisms as well. So what are the specific benefits that justify the extra development and runtime costs? There are basically two: reuse and stability. While there are other benefits that accrue from building a service-oriented architecture, it is difficult to make a case that these other benefits justify the SOA investment. Reuse and stability are the economic drivers.

Service Reuse

The largest form of payback comes from the reuse of an existing service interface (Figure 3–11). This reuse typically occurs when a second or subsequent component utilizes an existing service interface. The initial payback comes in the form of cost avoidance. When the second

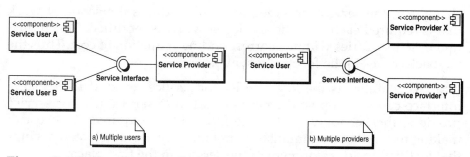

Figure 3–11: *Service Reuse Patterns*

and subsequent users are able to utilize the existing interface to access the same functionality, the cost of developing additional interfaces and/or modifying the underlying functionality is avoided. You can also get interface reuse payback when a single service interface masks the existence of two or more service providers, a situation that often arises as a result of mergers and acquisitions. Once again, the savings comes from avoiding the cost of modifying the service user(s) so that they can utilize the second service provider. The interface remains the same, and the rules for determining which provider to use under which circumstances are encapsulated in the service and hidden from the users.

When you are considering an interface's potential for reuse, you should take future plans into consideration. Today you may have only a single service user and a single service provider, but you expect to add another service user or service provider in the not too distant future. The new service user may be a consequence of adding another channel for doing business. The new service provider may be the consequence of mergers and acquisitions, or a technology decision to replace a custom system with a best-of-breed commercial system. Identifying these additional service users and providers establishes that there will eventually be payback for establishing the stable service interface. Of course, in making the final decision to build the service interface, you have to weigh the likelihood of these future changes actually occurring against today's investment in developing the service and its interfaces.

Interface Stability

Another form of payback occurs when the interface itself becomes a point of stability in an otherwise evolving service provider implementation. The stable interface isolates the service user from the ongoing changes in the service provider, and thus reduces the scope of work that is required each time the service provider is modified. This reduction in scope carries with it a corresponding reduction in cost. Thus the payback comes in the form of cost avoidance.

Interface stability is the key enabler for service reuse. If the existing interface cannot support the needs of a future service user or service provider, then changes to the interface will be required. The cost of making these changes diminishes or eliminates the anticipated savings that justified the development of the service in the first place.

Achieving interface stability requires extra work and contributes to the incremental added cost of developing services. Designing stable interfaces requires a broad perspective on the future business processes in which the service will be used, which in turn requires additional analytical effort. Generally when you first develop a service, only one use of the service clearly defined—its application in the current project. To achieve interface stability, you need to put additional effort into discovering and analyzing other future usages. Only then will you have confidence that the interface will support those future usages without significant modification. This additional effort not only drives up the cost of the service, but the exploration requires the expertise and experience of relatively senior people whose insight into the future plans for the business and the implications of those plans are required to fully understand the future service usages.

Service Evolution

Of course, no crystal-ball look into the future is going to yield the perfect service or the perfect service interface. You need to recognize that there are changes that are easy (and inexpensive) to accommodate and changes that are hard to accommodate. Additive changes are generally easy to accommodate, while structural changes are generally hard to accommodate.

Additive changes simply add to what is already there without altering the existing structure. The only components that are impacted are the ones using the additions. Adding a new operation to a service does not require any changes to the existing operations or the existing users of those operations. Similarly, adding a new field to an existing data structure does not need to force changes on the components that do not use the new field. Additive changes can generally be introduced gradually in an evolutionary manner at relatively low cost.

Structural changes, on the other hand, are expensive. Changing what an operation does immediately impacts all users of the operation. Changing the structure of data immediately impacts all users of the data. For example, consider the extent of the changes that would be required to the earlier sales order design if you wanted to extend your business to sell to companies as well as individual people (Figure 3–12). Now your customer is a legal entity that might be either a person or a company. Furthermore, if the order is placed by a company, you will want to know both the company and the individual who placed the order. You may even need to validate whether that person is authorized to make purchases on behalf of the company.

What is complex about this change is that a single concept—the `Person`—has evolved into three. Some of the existing relationships now point to different classes, a change that impacts every user of those relationships. Entirely new relationships have been added: `purchaser` and `authorizedPurchaser`. These new relationships must be created, managed, and communicated.

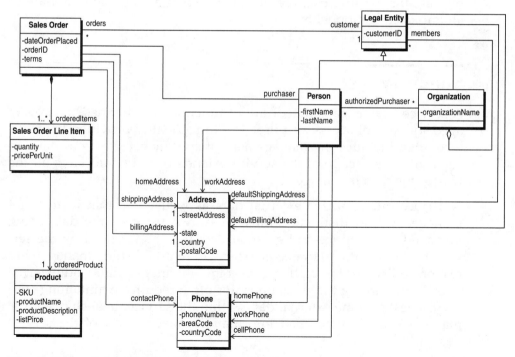

Figure 3–12: *Sales Order Information Model Extended for Business to Business*

Structural changes like this will cause many data structures and interfaces to change, with correspondingly high costs. Because of this, you want to make an effort when designing services to ensure that your information model is rich enough to accommodate the changes you can see coming down the pike without altering the structure. Some of the potential sources of such changes include changes in product or service offerings (often the result of mergers and acquisitions), changes to the supply pipeline (outsourcing, in particular), and the addition of new channels through which goods and services will be offered. Every needed data structure refinement that you can identify ahead of time is cost avoided—and thus increases the return on investment for your services.

At the same time, you have to be realistic in terms of your expectations. Despite your best efforts, some structural changes will eventually be required. To enable the graceful introduction of structural changes, you should ensure that your service infrastructure allows the simultaneous deployment of multiple versions of service operations. This will enable you to introduce the new operations and gradually migrate the existing users rather than forcing a "big bang" update of all impacted components.

Summary

A service is an encapsulated unit of functionality that has been packaged for ease of access and use. The functionality provided by a service often includes the management of specific categories of data. In such cases, the scope of the service extends from its interfaces all the way to the data it manages.

A service often utilizes external data as well—data that it does not manage. A clear distinction must be drawn between the data being managed by a service and external data being referenced by the service. Particular attention needs to be paid to establishing management responsibility for the relationships joining managed data and external data. Representing these relationships often requires maintaining copies (caches) of some external data within the service. In such cases, the maintenance of this cached information must be part of the service design.

Service interfaces are the means by which service users gain access to service functionality. The ease with which these interfaces can be used depends upon the choice of access technology. Ideally, the chosen access technologies should make it relatively simple to provide services on any platform and access them from any platform.

Most service operations require the exchange of data between the service user and the service provider. The use of a common data representation technology greatly facilitates the exchange of data between disparate platforms.

Beyond establishing common access and data representation technologies, service interfaces may also employ standardized representations of data (i.e., common data models). The considerations involved in deciding whether or not to use standardized representations are discussed in Chapter 23. The service interface may also standardize the semantics of the operations, abstracting them away from the details of the underlying functional implementation. The level of standardization for data representations and operation semantics does not have to be uniform across all services.

Implementing a service always costs more, both in terms of design effort and runtime resources, than simply providing direct access to native functionality. The payback for this additional investment occurs when the service is used a second or subsequent time—or when the service interface serves to isolate the service user from an evolving service implementation. In both cases, the stability of the service interface—its ability to support future usages without alteration—is essential for obtaining payback from this additional investment. The ability of the service to support future usage without interface alteration is the key consideration in deciding whether the investment in creating the service is warranted. The identification and evaluation of potential services is explored in Chapters 12 and 16.

Key Service Fundamentals Questions

1. Do your service definitions extend to identifying the data being managed by the service (i.e., defining the system of record for the data)?

2. Do your service definitions clearly identify external data (data for which the service is not the system-of-record) that is cached within

the service? Do your service designs include mechanisms for updating this cache?

3. Does the technology you use for accessing services make it convenient to implement services on any platform and access them from any platform?

4. Do your services employ common data representation technologies that facilitate the movement of data between disparate platforms?

5. In designing services, do you evaluate future service usages and design the service interfaces broadly enough to support these future usages without significant modification?

6. Are you able to evolve services by co-deploying old and new versions of services and gradually migrating service users to the new version?

Suggested Reading

W3C (World Wide Web Consortium). March 2004. "Web Services Description Language (WSDL) Version 2.0. Part 2: Message Exchange Patterns," W3C Working Draft 26. www.w3.org/TR/2004/WD-wsdl20-patterns-20040326.

Chapter 4

Using Services

Services, on their own, provide no benefit. To get benefit from your services, you need to employ them as an element of a larger process—a process that provides value to your enterprise. Other participants in the process need to interact with the service and benefit from the service results. Thus you need to be able to integrate the service with other services and nonservice functionality as well as to form your business processes. This chapter explores a number of choices that are available for integrating services into business processes.

Service Interaction Patterns

Synchronous Request-Reply

When you think of "using" a service, what probably comes to mind first is having the service user ask the service provider to perform the service—and then waiting for the result. This style of interaction is characterized by the synchronous request-reply pattern shown in Figure 4–1. It is perhaps the most common service interaction style.

The synchronous request-reply pattern is simple. The service provider only needs to supply a single operation interface (Figure 4–2). The service user calls this operation to submit the request, and this same operation provides the mechanism for returning the result.

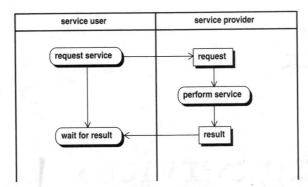

Figure 4–1: *Synchronous Request-Reply Interaction Pattern*

Figure 4–2: *Synchronous Request-Reply Interface*

Asynchronous Request-Reply

The synchronous request-reply interaction pattern is not sufficient to build most real-world business processes. Much as you (and the retailer) might like it, when you order a book online, the book does not arrive while you are still sitting at the keyboard! You don't wait for the book, to the exclusion of all other activity, until it arrives. Instead, you go off about your business for a few days until the book is delivered. This is the style of interaction represented by the asynchronous request-reply pattern shown in Figure 4–3.

Since the asynchronous request-reply pattern delivers the result at some future point, it requires a mechanism—a second operation—for the service provider to deliver the result. If the service provider is to initiate the delivery of the result, then the *service user* typically provides an operation and corresponding interface for this purpose (Figure 4–4). Note that for the service provider to use this interface, the original request must tell the service provider about the interface to be used to deliver the result.

Alternatively, the service provider could supply a result retrieval operation with its corresponding interface (Figure 4–5). With this approach,

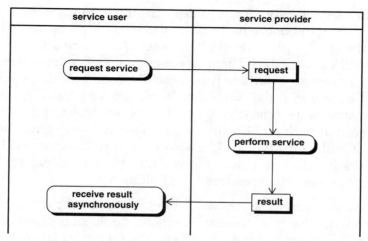

Figure 4–3: *Asynchronous Request-Reply Interaction Pattern*

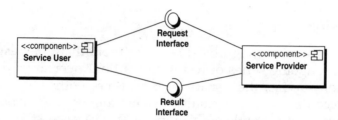

Figure 4–4: *User-Supplied Asynchronous Result Interface*

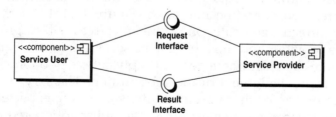

Figure 4–5: *Provider-Supplied Asynchronous Result Interface*

the service user invokes the result retrieval operation to determine whether the result is ready and retrieve it if it is. This is the style of interaction you use when you take your laundry to the dry cleaners. In the first interaction, you deliver the dirty laundry, and in the second you go back to pick up the cleaned items.

When the service provider supplies a result retrieval operation, the service user is the one who initiates the second interaction. For efficiency, the service provider typically specifies a time after which the results will be available. This response-time service-level agreement (SLA) is a promise, but there is no absolute guarantee that your laundry will be ready at that time. But if the service provider meets the promise most of the time (99%), it makes for an efficient interaction. In the absence of such an SLA, the service user can only guess at when the result will be ready. This guesswork leads to the repeated invocation of the interface to determine whether the results are ready—an inefficient process often referred to as polling.

Message-based service access, which involves a third-party communications intermediary, is inherently asynchronous. Thus message-based communications provides a convenient alternative for returning asynchronous results. Message-based approaches are discussed later in this chapter.

Subscription

Subscription services (Figure 4–6) deliver more than one result. They provide an ongoing series of results spread out over time. In using a subscription service, the service user registers with the service provider to receive a series of results—asynchronously. Your newspaper subscription is an example of this type of service, as are the stock market activity alerts delivered to your phone or computer.

Like the asynchronous request-reply pattern, the subscription pattern also requires two operation interfaces (Figure 4–7). If the parties are interacting directly, generally one of the interfaces will be provided by the service provider and the other by the service user. The service provider supplies a synchronous request-reply subscription interface that results in acknowledgment of the subscription. The service user provides an interface for the subsequent delivery of the expected results. As with asynchronous request-reply, the subscription request must indicate how the results are to be delivered.

Unsolicited Notification

The existence of the service user's delivery interface opens up the possibility for a fourth interaction pattern: the unsolicited notification (Figure 4–8). Once a service provider becomes aware of the presence of

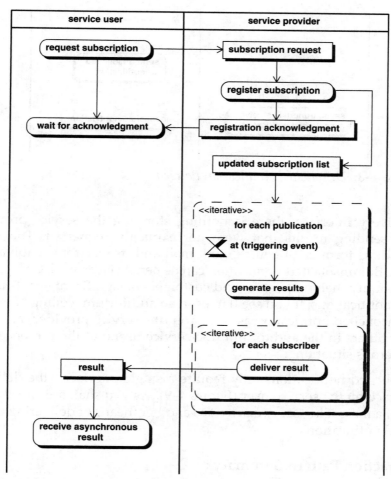

Figure 4–6: *Subscription Interaction Pattern*

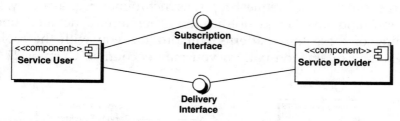

Figure 4–7: *Typical Subscription Interfaces*

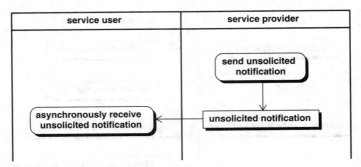

Figure 4–8: *Unsolicited Notification Pattern*

a delivery interface, there is nothing stopping the service provider from sending results that were not explicitly requested. The most obnoxious form is, of course, junk mail and its electronic equivalent, spam. But unsolicited notification can be beneficial as well. Companies often notify their employees and customers of significant events using such notifications. If you see flames in an auditorium, yelling "Fire!" is an unsolicited notification as well. You (the service provider) are notifying others in the auditorium (the service users) of the presence of a dangerous situation.

Unsolicited notifications only require a single interface—the delivery interface on the service user (Figure 4–9). As you shall see shortly, the use of a messaging service provides another means of delivering unsolicited notifications.

Interaction Pattern Summary

More complex interaction patterns than these are, of course, possible. But every interaction pattern can be assembled from these four basic patterns: synchronous request-reply, asynchronous request-reply, subscription, and unsolicited notification. Therefore, a detailed understanding of these four patterns will provide you with the tools to analyze any interaction pattern you may encounter. Chapter 27 will

Figure 4–9: *Unsolicited Notification Interfaces*

explore the properties of these patterns in more detail and will elaborate on some of the more common complex interaction patterns as well.

Service Access

On the surface, accessing a service sounds so simple—just call the interface! In reality, access can get very complicated as you try to control access to services and maintain flexibility concerning where service users and providers are deployed. The following sections explore a number of the design issues you will encounter and the design patterns that you can use to address them.

Direct Service Access

The most obvious way to use a service is to directly access the service provider's interface (Figure 4–10). While this is straightforward, it requires that the service user be aware of both the functionality provided by the service interface (which you would expect) and the location of the interface. If you are using HTTP to access your service, for example, then the service user needs to know either the IP address or hostname of the machine on which the service is running as well as the specific socket corresponding to the service's interface.

This requirement to know about the interface's location makes the design of the service user dependent on the deployment specifics of the service provider. If the service provider is moved from one machine to another, then the service user's configuration must be updated to reflect the change. If the service becomes very successful and has many users, such dependencies make it difficult to move the service provider. Such movement might be required to add capacity by moving the service to a larger machine or recover from a machine outage by moving the service to an alternate machine. While network-level solutions such as virtual IP addresses and virtual hostnames pro-

Figure 4–10: *Direct Service Access*

vide some relief, they have their own limitations and accompanying administrative costs as well.

Variations in Direct Service Access

Service Lookup

One means of avoiding this dependency between the service user and the location of the service interface is to employ a lookup service (Figure 4–11). The lookup service knows the actual location of the provider's service interface. In order for the service user to access the service, it first uses the lookup service to get the actual location of the service interface and then uses this information to access the service. The JNDI (Java Naming and Directory Interface)[1] is a service interface that is commonly used for this purpose. The advantage of this approach is that when a service provider changes location, only the lookup service needs to be updated. The service users will pick up the change from the lookup service.

When a lookup service is used, the lookup typically occurs just the first time a particular user wants to access the service. Once the service interface is located, the user continues to use that interface as long as it is operational.

Of course, the lookup service itself now presents exactly the same problem that it solves for other services: the service user must know the location of the lookup interface to be able to use it. But at least the problem is reduced in scope to just accessing the lookup service, which presumably will not change its interface location very often.

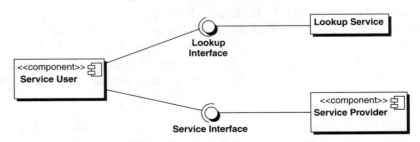

Figure 4–11: *Lookup Service*

---

1. http://java.sun.com/products/jndi/.

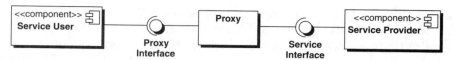

Figure 4–12: *Proxy Access Interfaces*

Proxy Access

Another approach that can isolate the service user from the details of the service provider's deployment is to employ a level of indirection— a proxy—for accessing the service (Figure 4–12). To the service user, the proxy presents what appears to be the service's interface without knowing that it is, in reality, a proxy interface. The proxy forwards all incoming requests to the real service interface and forwards replies from the service interface back to the service user through the proxy interface.

Direct Access Limitations

There are a couple of drawbacks to the direct access approach and its service lookup and proxy variants. One is that any change in the location of the service provider's interface requires changes to the configuration of some other component. In direct access, the component requiring update is the service user. With service lookup, it is the lookup service, and with a proxy it is the proxy. This dependency of other components on the physical location of the service provider's interface complicates changing the service provider's location. It adds administrative overhead and adds to the time it takes to implement such changes.

This administrative overhead affects more than just the normal deployment of services. It comes into play when you want to provide a fault tolerant or highly available service as well. In such cases, when something happens to the existing service provider you need to bring up a replacement copy of the service provider. This replacement copy will be in a different location, generally on a different machine. For local failover, this different machine may be in the same data center, but in the case of a site disaster it will be in a different data center. In such cases it becomes very difficult to maintain the appearance of the "same location" for the service interface with network-based virtual IP addresses and hostnames. Administrative changes to service users, lookup services, or proxy agents are generally required.

These administrative changes significantly complicate the design, implementation, and test of service failover. A failure to make any of the required administrative changes during a failover will cause the service to become unavailable just as surely as a breakdown in bringing up the backup service provider. The more administrative changes that need to be made, the greater the chance an implementation mistake will cause the failover itself to fail. Since testing failover is an arduous and risky activity, there are advantages to keeping the administrative changes as simple as possible—or eliminating them altogether.

This situation gets even more complicated when asynchronous request-reply, subscription, and unsolicited notification patterns come into play. These patterns often require delivery interfaces on the service user—interfaces that the service provider, lookup service, or proxy need to know about. This makes the administrative problem even more complex, since location information now needs to be updated when service clients move.

Message-Based Service Access

Messaging services provide an alternate means for service users and service providers to interact. We are all familiar with messaging services such as e-mail and instant messaging. At the systems level, messaging services such as the standards-based JMS (Java Messaging Service), IBM Websphere MQ, and TIBCO Rendezvous are in common use.

When using a messaging service, all communications between the parties is exchanged using an intermediary—the `Messaging Service Provider` (Figure 4–13). In contrast with the proxy approach, both sender and recipient are very much aware that they are employing a third party to send and receive messages.

Electronic messaging services differ from postal (physical mail) services in a subtle but significant way. Postal service mailboxes are physical entities that serve as the interfaces between the messaging service and its users. An address in physical mail systems designates the physical mailbox to which the letter or package is to be delivered. In other words, the address is location-specific.

In contrast, electronic messaging separates the concepts of destination and interface. The address now denotes a logical destination whose physical location is unknown to either the sender or recipient. The messaging service interface is no longer tied to a specific destination. Instead, the messaging service provides a generic interface for sending

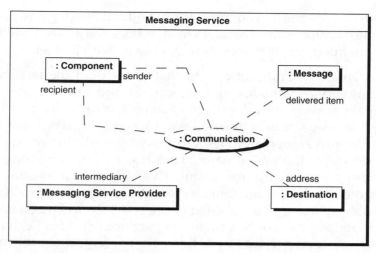

Figure 4–13: *Messaging Service*

and receiving messages regardless of the destination. This separation greatly simplifies the use of messaging services.

Abstract destinations provide location independence. The fact that the logical destination is no longer tied to the physical location of the recipient means that the recipient's location can change without impacting the sender—or the mail service. Thus, you can send an e-mail message to `jane.doe@messageservice.com` without having any idea where Jane Doe actually is. Furthermore, Jane Doe can retrieve her message from any machine that can access the messaging service, whether at home, at work, or at an Internet café in Istanbul!

The messaging service provides all the interfaces needed for communications (Figure 4–14). This simple shifting of interfaces to the messaging service greatly simplifies making deployment changes. None of the participants—sender, recipient, or messaging service—has any dependency at all on the location of the sender and recipient. In fact, the only location dependency that remains is that the sender and recipient must know the location of the messaging service interfaces. Consequently,

Figure 4–14: *Messaging Service Interfaces*

the sender and recipient can move freely without altering any configuration information—anywhere. As long as both can access the messaging service interfaces, they can communicate with each other.

There is another significant benefit that arises from the fact that the messaging service provides both the sending and receiving interfaces. Because the message recipient does not have to provide an interface to receive a message (it uses the messaging service's interface instead), it is easy for any component to receive a message. All that is required is an agreed-upon destination name. Thus it is easy for any component to be both a sender and a recipient. This communications flexibility enables the convenient implementation of the asynchronous request-reply, subscription, and unsolicited notification service interaction patterns. Therefore, the use of a messaging service provides flexibility in choosing whatever service interaction pattern seems most appropriate for the service being designed.

Access Control

The primary reason for creating services is to make it easier to access their functionality, but at the same time you need to exercise some control over who is using the services. You may need to control who can perform certain operations. After all, you don't want some stranger making withdrawals from your bank account! You may need to limit the volume of usage. Services have finite capacity, and an unbounded demand may cause undesired performance degradation or outright failure. For a variety of reasons, you often need the ability to control access to your services.

Access control can be thought of as a set of *policies* applied at one or more *policy enforcement points*. An access control policy is a rule governing the access to the service. These rules may specify actions that individual parties are either allowed to take or must take under specific circumstances, or they may specify conditions under which access may be granted. One of the access control policies governing access to your bank account from an ATM is that you must provide a PIN (a required action on your part), and that PIN must match the one the bank has associated with your bank account (a condition that must be satisfied).

A policy enforcement point identifies the specific place in the architecture (usually an interface) at which the policy is enforced. In the ATM example, the enforcement point may be in the ATM (which would require the bank to provide the real PIN for the account to the ATM), or it may be at the bank when the transaction request is approved (a safer alternative).

Access control policies can cover many topics. Authentication (validating your credentials), authorization (establishing that the supplied credentials give you the right to access this particular account), and encryption (protecting your PIN from unauthorized viewing) are common topics for access control policies, but there are many others as well. Digital signing of message contents, the non-repudiation of requests (making an undeniable record that a particular message was received), and the creation of an audit trail of service utilization are frequently found to be requirements in business processes.

Policy Enforcement Points

While it may be easy to state a policy, finding the appropriate place to enforce the policy is often not as straightforward as you might like. The enforcement of a policy requires the interception of the request, and possibly the reply as well. Setting up the system to intercept the request and reply requires a change to the architecture.

There are a number of places at which access control policies might be enforced. The choice of where to locate the policy enforcement point and which participant will initiate the policy enforcement depends very much upon the technique used to access the service. When services are being directly accessed, the enforcement point for these policies is generally the service interface, and the required functionality for enforcement is generally provided by the service provider (Figure 4–15). Of course, the service provider will likely employ other supporting services to aid in this enforcement, but it is the service provider that is responsible for intercepting the requests (and possibly the replies as well) and ensuring that the policies are checked and enforced.

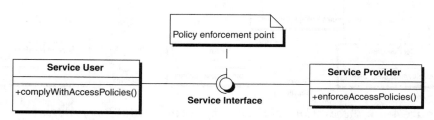

Figure 4–15: *Access Control Policy Enforcement in Direct Service Access*

While placing policy enforcement within the service provider may make logical sense, it does require a change to the service provider design. For some service providers, particularly purchased software applications, this may not be an option. Even when it is possible, changing the service provider design may be complex. From a software maintenance perspective, this can be an expensive option.

Access Control with Proxies

Proxies provide an alternative location for policy enforcement—one that allows access control policies to be added without altering the service provider (Figure 4–16). This style of access control is commonly used when services are being provided via HTTP interfaces. In many cases such proxies are introduced into HTTP-based systems specifically to provide access control. Proxies used for this purpose are often referred to as *policy agents*.

Moving policy enforcement into the proxy provides a nice separation of concerns from a software engineering perspective. With this approach, policy enforcement can be added or modified without altering the underlying service provider. The policies and policy enforcement can be tested and managed independently of the service provider.

The proxy approach has an access control weakness: In the strictest sense, the original service interface remains unprotected. Any component that can gain access to this service interface is in a position to use it—or abuse it. Because of this, when the proxy pattern is employed, the actual service provider is generally located on a physically secure private network protected by a firewall. To guard against unauthorized access, the proxy is placed in a demilitarized zone (DMZ), which is separated from the public network by another firewall, resulting in the configuration shown in Figure 4–17.

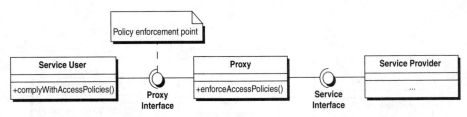

Figure 4–16: *Access Control Policy Enforcement with Proxy Access*

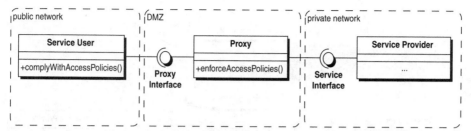

Figure 4–17: *Typical Proxy Deployment*

Beyond the access control weakness, there are other drawbacks to the proxy approach. The introduction of the proxy requires a configuration change on the part of the service users to redirect their requests to the proxy interface. The use of a proxy also introduces additional inter-process communications. In high-volume low-latency applications, the increase in latency caused by these additional communications can be an issue.

When asynchronous result delivery is required, there is additional work that must be done. To control access to the results delivery interface, either the existing proxy must be extended to also be proxy for the service user or a second proxy must be introduced. Since every proxy is dependent upon the location of the interfaces it is guarding, it becomes increasingly difficult to manage this approach as the number of services and service users increases. Every deployment change to every interface requires a proxy update.

Access Control with a Mediation Service

The use of a messaging service for communications between the service user and the service provider presents yet another possible location for policy enforcement (Figure 4–18). Because of the extended functionality, this expanded service is more appropriately termed a *mediation service*. The mediation service contains within it both the messaging service and the policy enforcement.

As with the messaging service, the mediation service provides the interfaces for both the service user and service provider. Since the mediation service provides both interfaces, there are no dependencies on the location of either the service user or service provider. The symmetric nature of the sending and receiving interfaces makes it easy to support all of the basic service interaction patterns.

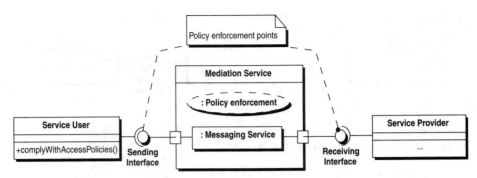

Figure 4–18: *Access Control Policy Enforcement with Message-Based Access*

The mediation service can enforce policies governing access to its own interfaces. It can authenticate the component trying to gain access and check that component's authorization to use the mediation service. Beyond this, it can check the component's authorization to send or receive from a particular messaging destination. It can require encrypted communications at both interfaces, perhaps using SSL. This ability to secure the connection to the service provider overcomes one of the shortcomings of the proxy approach, which cannot protect the service provider's interface from direct access.

Service Request Routing

The discussion thus far has talked about both messaging and mediation services as if each were a single monolithic entity. But in reality any physical component has finite capacity limitations, so the implementation of the mediation service may require more than one component to spread the load. The service user may not be at the same location as the service provider, so the mediation service must be present at each location. There may also be more demand than can be satisfied by a single service provider, so the mediation service must be capable of distributing service requests among multiple service providers. For all of these reasons, the mediation service must be considered a logical service whose implementation can involve more than one component.

Load Distribution

Perhaps the simplest routing task is simple load distribution (Figure 4–19). In this situation there are two or more service providers residing in the

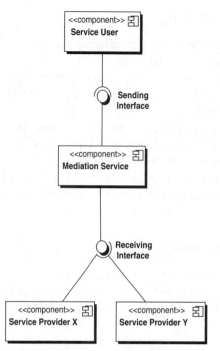

Figure 4–19: *Routing Requests for Load Distribution*

same location, and all of them are equivalent from a functional per-spective. The routing problem is to determine which service provider should get each request. But even this can get complicated. What criteria do you use to select the service provider for the next request? Consider IP-redirectors, proxies that distribute incoming requests. Early redirectors used a round-robin approach, feeding each request to the next service provider in a sequence. Unfortunately, with this approach a "dead" service provider still gets its fair share of requests, which thus go unserved. More recent IP redirectors employ some form of liveness testing to avoid this kind of problem.

With the proxy-based approach, the proxy must make the decision as to which service provider should get each request. Making an assignment to an inoperable service provider runs the risk of the request going unserviced. Message-based mediation services avoid this problem. Message-based services hold the requests in a queue until a service provider retrieves them. Since the service provider takes the initiative in retrieving the request, the service provider must be operational to some extent. Dead service providers will not ask for more requests!

Location-Based Routing

Another routing challenge arises when you have service users and service providers residing at different locations. A request originating at one location may need to be routed to a service provider at a different location (Figure 4–20). While this could be handled with a single mediation service component serving both locations, the result generally leads to some very inefficient communication patterns. Service users and providers at the remote location that need to intercommunicate must do so via the remote mediation service. From a communications perspective, it is far more efficient to have a local component of the mediation service and then let the mediation service take care of routing requests to other locations as required.

Content-Based Routing

A third routing challenge arises when there are multiple service providers of the same service at different locations. Now the mediation service must determine which provider should get which request (Figure 4–21).

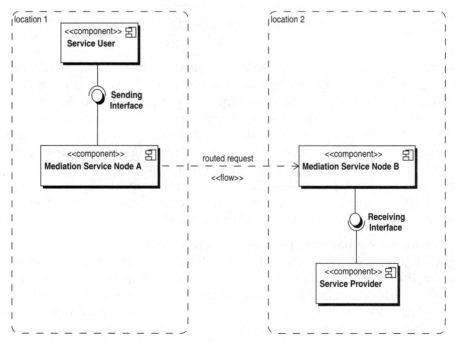

Figure 4–20: *Routed Service Requests*

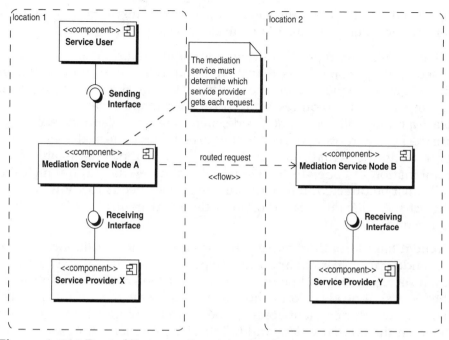

Figure 4–21: *Routed Requests Requiring Logic*

This routing can get complicated because different situations may call for different routing strategies.

The simplest situation is again the one in which the service providers are all identical. While you could leave the requests in a single queue and let both service providers pull from the same queue, this does not necessarily make optimum use of the bandwidth between the two sites. You may want to implement a strategy that weights requests for local servicing as long as the local service provider has the capacity. Only when the demand exceeds the local capacity and the other site has idle capacity would requests be routed to the remote service provider.

Life gets more complicated when the service providers are not all equivalent. You have your North American customer data in one database; your European, Middle Eastern, and African customers in a second database; and your Asian and Pacific-Rim customers in a third. Each database is located in the region it serves. For uniformity, you want to provide a single generic interface at each location through which all customer information can be accessed, regardless of where it is located. In this case, the mediation service must determine which service provider (database) can handle each request.

What makes this type of routing, commonly referred to as content-based routing, complex is that there is rarely enough information in the incoming request to do the routing. Determining the appropriate routing generally requires some form of reference data. When you place a phone call, the country code, area code, and telephone exchange are the keys to routing the call to the correct telephone exchange. However, to do the actual routing you need information that relates each combination of codes to the actual telephone exchange to which the call must be directed. Furthermore, the service needs to know how to extract the relevant data from either the message itself or its destination name.

Content-based routing makes the design of the mediation service dependent upon certain application-specific characteristics. The mediation service needs to know how to extract the key information from the request. It needs to know how to access the reference data and perhaps cache it for efficient access. It needs to know the correspondence between the reference data and the service providers. And it needs to know the rules for deciding which service provider gets which request.

The bottom line is that content-based routing is a service. As such, it needs to be treated with the same rigor as any other service. In particular, the stability of the interfaces to this service is a key concern. There is a tendency to think of content-based routing as being loosely driven by rules—rules that can easily be changed. But if changes to the rules require additional input data or reference data, interfaces change and there is a lot more work to be done. Thus any proposal for content-based routing must be evaluated in terms of its ability to support future as well as current needs.

Service Composition

Services are only of value when they are employed in a business process. While some value is provided when a service is first employed as part of one business process, additional value—the added value that justifies making the functionality into a service—is provided when the service is employed in other business processes as well. The service makes it possible to create, modify, or extend other business processes faster and at a lower cost than would be possible without it. The ultimate goal of a service-oriented architecture is to enable the low-cost assembly of business processes from existing services, and the process of combining the services together is referred to as *composition*.

Composition is often discussed as a technique for combining services together to form a new higher-level service. Such a service is referred to as a *composite service*. However, the idea of composing services together is distinct from the idea of turning the resulting composite into a new service. The majority of composites you are likely to encounter are not services—they are business processes. The core value provided by SOA is the ability to quickly and inexpensively create these composites. Turning a composite into a service is gravy.

Hard-Wired Composition

The simplest way to compose services is to hard wire them together so that the result of one service becomes the input to the next (Figure 4–22). This type of composition is termed hard-wired because there is no explicit embodiment of the overall process. To determine what this overall process actually is, you have to trace the sequence of interactions between the participants. While this type of composition may not strike you as being particularly service-oriented, it is the most commonly found composition technique in use today, although the participants in such compositions are often not designed as services.

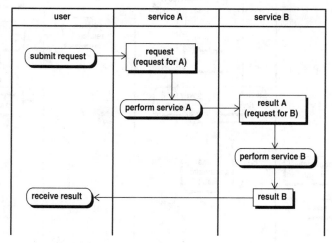

Figure 4–22: *Hard-Wired Composition*

In hard-wired composition, the result produced by one service may not be in the proper form to serve as the input to the next, or the component producing the result may not be configured to direct it to the next service. In such cases, intermediate components can be used to transform the results and deliver them to the appropriate destinations. Part IV of this book explores these components and their attendant design issues.

Nested Composition

Service-oriented architectures lead to a very natural style, modularizing functionality into request-response service operations and then building composites that invoke these services (Figure 4–23). This compositional style is an excellent first thought in terms of organizing functionality, but it must be examined from a performance perspective

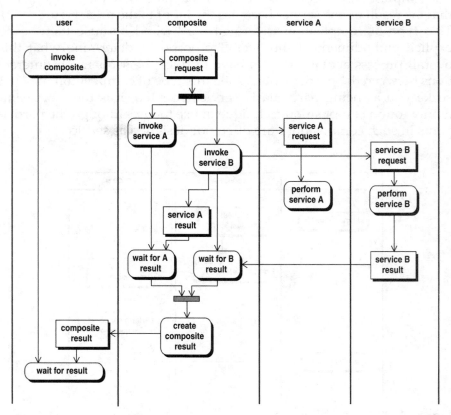

Figure 4–23: *Nested Composition*

to determine whether the modularization is adequate for the task. The performance examination must explore both response latency and the downstream service capacity limitations.

When requests are nested in this manner, the accumulated latency resulting from the nested request-response calls may result in unacceptable overall response time from the user's perspective. For each service call, there is a communication delay in each direction. On top of this, there is the time it takes the service provider to respond to the request, and the additional time it takes the service provider to perform the work. These delays add to the time required for the user to interact with the composite and the time it takes the composite to do its own work. When the underlying services are themselves composites, additional latencies are introduced. Depending upon the needs of the user, the accumulated composite latency may become unacceptable.

You also need to consider the load being placed on the lower-level service. The service may not have been designed to handle the volume of requests coming from the composite. One hotelier with multiple properties in the same location decided to change the service its customers use to locate hotel rooms in a city. Instead of having the customer first select from a list of hotels and then check room availability in that hotel, they implemented a new composite service that checked the availability of all hotels in the city for each customer request. The impact was that the volume of queries increased dramatically on all the hotels—by a factor of eight! During peak periods (the most important times for hotel bookings), the resulting demand exceeded the capacity of the individual hotel systems. As a result, the majority of the queries timed out and provided no response. Instead of delivering a new and improved service to customers, many room availability queries went unanswered.

Performance evaluation for any use of a service should be a routine part of the design process. Chapter 39 shows how to perform this type of analysis.

Cached Composites

The nested composition performance lesson is one that was first learned when businesses first started adding customer-facing web self-service front-ends. These web sites allowed customers to check the status of their orders and shipments. However, the underlying back-office production systems that processed these orders were never designed to handle this kind of dynamic query load. Early web site implementations that simply queried the back-office production systems not only performed poorly, but their query load often had an adverse impact on the back-office system's ability to perform its work.

To cope with this type of situation, an architectural style evolved in which status information is extracted from the production system and cached for convenient access by the web application server. In service-oriented terms, the style of interaction with the underlying service changed from a request-reply interaction to a subscription interaction (Figure 4–24).

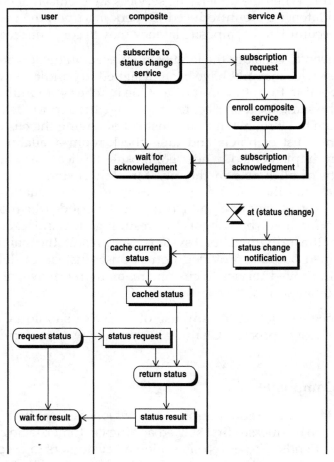

Figure 4–24: *Cached Composite*

Note that this architectural change impacted not only the composite, but the underlying service as well. Interaction with the underlying service changed from a request-reply to a subscription, and the composite changed from a nested composition to a cached composition. Once again, you can see the importance of understanding the intended utilization of a service—particularly the volume of activity and the required response times. This understanding will impact the architecture of both the composite and the service, and will deeply influence the operation interfaces.

Locating Services

You can't use a service unless you are aware of its existence. A significant challenge in SOA is helping architects and designers locate the services that are appropriate for their needs. UDDI registries provide a mechanism for sharing some information about services (primarily interface details and information about service providers and users), but there is a wealth of additional information required to support the use of services, including (but not limited to):

- Service requirements—how the service specification is derived from its intended utilization
- Service specification—the interface (WSDL), including operations and data structures, the information managed by the service, the externally observable behavior, the characterization of intended utilization, and supported SLAs
- One-line description of the service—for quick weeding out of services
- Abstract (paragraph)—for a second-pass weeding
- Service user's guide—everything a user needs to know to use the service, from an introduction to its capabilities and intended utilization to the details of best practices in employing the service
- Service operation and maintenance guide
- Service operational support procedures

This information must be created, organized, archived, and made accessible to the community of service users. Services need to be categorized and indexed for easy access (some of which can be done in the UDDI registry), and the one-line descriptions and abstracts should be searchable as well.

Enterprise Architecture for Services

Except in the most unusual of circumstances, you will not be constructing your SOA in one mammoth project. Instead, your enterprise will evolve its existing architecture in a series of projects. However, to reap the benefits of SOA, you must make sure that design decisions are made consistently from project to project. The role of maintaining this consistency is typically given to the enterprise architecture group. With respect to services, this group's responsibilities are:

- Selecting the service interface standards to be followed and selecting the supporting infrastructure to be used
- Defining service interaction patterns and their preferred technology implementations
- Defining the criteria to be used in determining when standardized data representations (common data models) should be employed in operation interfaces
- Defining the selection criteria for proposed services and the procedures for validating their appropriateness
- Defining the preferred architectural styles for implementing services and the criteria to be used in selecting a style
- Defining the service mediation architecture and selecting the supporting infrastructure to be used
- Establishing the preferred design patterns for content-based routing and the criteria to be used in selecting a pattern
- Establishing the capacity planning procedures for services and ensuring that these procedures are followed

As an enterprise architect, you should be aware that it is difficult to formulate an efficient and practical set of guidelines without a bit of trial and error. You must make every effort to observe the guidelines and procedures you have defined being put into practice. Are the guidelines easy to follow, or do they constantly require interpretation? Interpretation opens the door for variation and therefore inconsistency from project to project. Such variation may work against your SOA objectives. Observe the level of effort required for project teams to comply with the guidelines and weigh this effort against the benefit you expect from the guideline. Is the effort justified? Be particularly vigilant for signs of excessive administrative complexity, making records that are never used or whose accuracy is never validated. Such complexity not only increases the level of effort, but it can also be a significant source of error.

Summary

When incorporating services into a business process, there are a number of ways in which a service user and service provider may interact. The synchronous request-reply style is perhaps the most common, but many business processes require asynchronous responses, subscription services, and unsolicited notifications as well. Determining the appropriate style of interaction requires an understanding of how the service will be employed in business processes.

Your choice of service access mechanisms directly impacts the ease with which you can access services, your ability to provide the different interaction patterns that may be required by the business processes, and the amount of work required to change the location of both service users and service providers. While direct or proxy-mediated access to services provides good support for synchronous request-reply, it makes implementation of other interaction patterns complex. Direct and proxy-mediated approaches are always dependent on the location of the service provider, and the use of interaction patterns other than synchronous request-reply makes them dependent upon the location of the service user as well.

Message-based service access provides more flexibility for interacting with services. It has no dependency on the location of the service users and providers, and it provides simple support for all of the service interaction patterns. It provides the most flexible service access.

Many services require some form of access control to manage who has access to which service. Access control can be implemented by the service provider, but this approach requires the modification of the service provider and can be expensive. Alternatively, access control can be implemented by either a proxy or a mediation service (an extended messaging service). Once again, the proxy approach is convenient for synchronous request-reply, but awkward for the other interaction patterns. The mediation service approach works well for all interaction patterns.

Accessing services may require the routing of service requests. The need for routing may arise from the need to distribute load across multiple service providers, the need to route specific requests to specific providers, or the placement of users and service providers at different geographic locations. Routing may also require some introspection into the message, the access of reference data, and the evaluation of routing rules. A mediation service provides a convenient architectural home for this functionality. Geographic routing generally requires the presence of mediation service components at each geographic location.

Services provide value when they are actually utilized in business processes. Combining services to form business processes is referred to as composition. Optionally, the resulting composite may, itself, be offered as a higher-level service.

The architecture of composites must be carefully evaluated for performance. Nested synchronous request-reply interactions can lead to excessive latency and unacceptable loads on back-end services. In such cases, architectural alternatives such as caching information in the composite may be more appropriate. Choosing such alternatives may impact the architecture of the back-end service as well as that of the composite, transforming a synchronous request-reply interaction between them into a subscription interaction. Thus, to achieve the service interface stability that is required to justify the service development cost, potential service usages must be thoroughly explored before the service is specified and implemented.

Achieving the benefits of a service-oriented architecture requires consistent decision making across many projects. The enterprise architecture group plays a key role not only in establishing standards and best practices for building services but also in ensuring that these guidelines are practical for routine day-to-day usage by project teams.

Key Service Utilization Questions

1. Does your SOA infrastructure support the common service interaction patterns: synchronous request-reply, asynchronous request-reply, subscription, and unsolicited notification?

2. How does your SOA infrastructure control access to services? Does the access control work for the four common service interaction patterns?

3. How does your SOA infrastructure route requests to the service provider(s)? Does it support the routing of requests between geographic locations? Does it support content-based routing?

4. Who reviews the proposed architecture of new services from a per-formance perspective?

5. Has your enterprise architecture group established standards and best practices for the development of services and for the supporting infrastructure? Has the group followed up to determine whether these standards and best practices are practical and being used?

6. Do you have an archive for service-related information? Does it contain one-line descriptions, abstracts, and user documentation? Is it searchable?

Suggested Reading

W3C (World Wide Web Consortium). March 2004. "Web Services Description Language (WSDL) Version 2.0, Part 2: Message Exchange Patterns," W3C Working Draft 26. www.w3.org/TR/2004/WD-wsdl20-patterns-20040326.

Chapter 5

The SOA Development Process

What Is Different about SOA Development?

Scope differentiates SOA (and other distributed systems) development projects from conventional development projects. To achieve SOA goals, the services and other components being developed must fit smoothly into all the business processes they are intended to support. Thus, building a service (or any distributed system component) requires a certain level of understanding about those business processes. The challenge is that your current project is most likely focused on a subset of these processes. To create a widely usable service, you need to have an understanding of all of the business processes the service will participate in—both present and future. That understanding must encompass the patterns of interaction between the business process and the service, the volumes of activity that can be expected, and the response times that are required.

SOA development commonly involves multiple development teams—both present and future. Typically one team is developing the business service while another team implements the business process that uses the service. In the early stages of your SOA initiative, there may be a third team working on SOA infrastructure and infrastructure services. And, since the true benefits of SOA are realized when the service gets reused, the needs of future development teams using the services being developed must also be considered.

The companion book, *Succeeding with SOA*, explores these SOA development issues from an organizational perspective. This book, in the remainder of this chapter, explores SOA development from a technical perspective. It focuses on the critical development activities that must be performed to achieve a successful result.

The Overall Development Process

Most development projects are incremental in nature. You generally don't build an entire enterprise of systems from scratch, and only occasionally will you build or acquire a complete system. Instead, most projects make incremental improvements to one specific system. For the most part, such projects assume that the architecture of the system will remain untouched, and the typical development process looks something like that shown in Figure 5–1. In this style of project, there is generally an IT group dedicated to the maintenance of the system, and the development team is drawn from this group. The development team is either given a set of requirements or is asked to elicit those requirements from the business community. It makes the changes to the system, which are then tested and placed into production.

This incremental system-oriented development process falls short when it comes to SOA development—or any other form of distributed system design for that matter. It assumes that there is a single development team, which is rarely the case for SOA and distributed systems development in general. It assumes that the architecture has already been determined, when actually SOA is introducing architectural

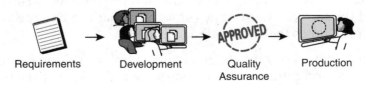

Requirements   Development   Quality   Production
                               Assurance

Figure 5–1: *Typical Incremental System-oriented Development Process*

changes. Finally, it assumes that a satisfactory business process definition already exists when in fact SOA requires rationalization and realignment of business processes in order to share services.

What is required for SOA development is a process that looks something like the one shown in Figure 5–2. The primary difference here is the presence of an explicit architecture definition step prior to development. This step determines both the business process and systems architecture changes that are required. It not only ensures that the business process and systems architectures blend to achieve the business objectives, but it also determines what each of the development groups needs to do.

This architecture step is not a new idea. In fact, it is a primary best practice for developing systems—from scratch. The problem is that this step has, in many IT shops, disappeared entirely. In many cases, if architects participate at all, they do an after-the-fact review of a design, often after the implementation is well under way. By then, significant changes have become cost-prohibitive. After-the-fact reviews will not suffice to evolve your systems to a service-oriented architecture.

The SOA development process in Figure 5–2 adds two additional steps: an explicit charter and an integration test step. The charter sets forth the business expectations for the project. It quantifies the

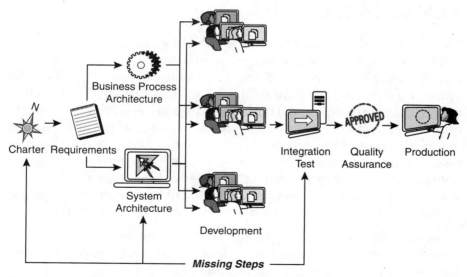

Figure 5–2: *SOA Development Process*

expected benefits and establishes the cost and schedule constraints for the project. This information provides objective criteria for determining what is important to the business, and thus provides an objective means of making architectural tradeoff decisions for both business processes and systems.

The integration test step is a concession to reality in building distributed systems. A service-oriented architecture is assembled from many components and services. Making changes to multiple components and then just turning them all on at once can lead to chaos. It is difficult to diagnose a distributed system until a certain level of working dialog has been established between the components and services. The integration test step simply executes a planned order of assembly for the components and services. With this approach, a few components are assembled and tested to ensure that they are interacting properly. After this has been established, a few more components can be added and interactions once again tested. This process is continued until the entire system has been assembled. Integration testing establishes that there is sufficient working dialog in place that you can monitor the execution of the business processes and effectively diagnose problems as they occur. At this point more complete testing of the business processes and systems can commence.

Architecture Tasks

The work within the architecture step breaks down into three major tasks: defining the business process architecture, defining the systems architecture, and finally specifying the components and services of the systems architecture (Figure 5–3). The business process architecture defines the participants in the business process along with their roles and responsibilities. For a new business process, this will be the first time that the architecture of the process has been defined. For an existing process, the task is to refine the business process architecture so that the revised business process produces the desired business results. Since some of the business process participants will be systems, the business process architecture essentially defines the systems requirements.

The systems architecture refines the business process view of systems, which is pretty coarse, into the structure of system components and services, culminating in the specification of those components and services and the physical environment in which they will be deployed.

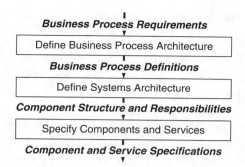

Figure 5–3: *Architecture Tasks*

For new components and services, these will be new specifications. For existing components and services, these will be revisions to the existing specifications.

For efficiency, the development of these specifications is decomposed into two tasks: defining the systems architecture and specifying the components and services. The architecture definition task identifies each of the components and services. It decomposes the systems activities defined by the business process into individual activities that are performed by the components and services. Finally, it identifies the communications between the components and services required to execute the business process.

The purpose of the systems architecture definition task is to efficiently explore possible architectural alternatives: alternative decompositions of systems into components and services, and alternative assignments of roles and responsibilities to these components and services. To make this process efficient, the architecture definition task intentionally stops short of fully specifying the components, services, and communications. It identifies the components and services and determines the categories of data that will be managed by each, but does not detail that data. It identifies the activities being performed by each component, along with their inputs and their results in terms of information content, but does not detail the interfaces or data structures. Finally, it roughly characterizes the level of effort required to execute each activity in terms of the system resources that will be required.

Completing the specification for a component or service is a painstaking and time-consuming task. By deferring this task and roughly characterizing the components and services, it becomes practical to explore different architectural alternatives. Only after an alternative is selected is the investment made in developing the specifications for the components and services.

Architecture in Context

If you insert these additional steps to the development process, you end up with a sequence of project tasks similar to the one shown in (Figure 5–4). You charter the project, clearly spelling out the expected business benefit and the cost and schedule guidelines. You embark on a requirements definition phase and a business process synthesis phase that result in well-defined business processes. You then architect the system and move on to specifying the individual components and services. These are then implemented, integrated, tested, and deployed. But there's a lurking problem here: efficiency.

The problem with this approach is that it does not deal well with the complex relationship between business process architecture and systems architecture. There are many possible business process designs,

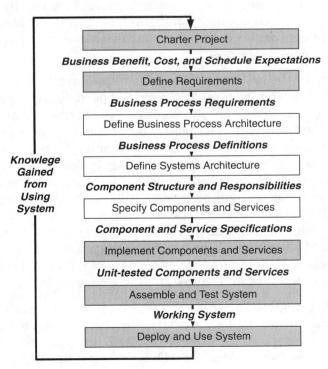

Figure 5–4: *Architecture in Context*

each of which will assign different responsibilities to the systems. There are many possible system component and service designs for each of the system responsibility assignments. Some of the business process designs will assign systems responsibilities that turn out to be infeasible or impractical in terms of being able to implement the design within the project's cost and schedule guidelines.

The dilemma this produces is that you will not know whether a given business process architecture is feasible (i.e., can be implemented within the cost and schedule guidelines) until you have designed the supporting system. That's a lot of throw-away work if the design turns out to be infeasible. Furthermore, if it ends up that you can't find any combination of business process and systems architecture that produces the expected benefit within the project's cost and schedule guidelines, you won't discover this until you are deep into the project lifecycle.

Total Architecture Synthesis (TAS)

From the outset of a project, you face the challenge of determining whether a project is feasible and having to define an appropriate architecture—all without burning up excessive time and resources. What makes this challenging is the combination of a large number of possible designs and the fact that you can't estimate cost and schedule until a design is at least partially completed. Deferring the specification of the components and services solves part of the problem, but you are still left with a large number of design alternatives to explore. You need a way to simplify this search through design alternatives.

The key to simplifying this search lies in a fundamental observation: Most business requirements are relatively easy to satisfy. Only a small portion of the business requirements will present real challenges to the architecture of your business processes and systems. Furthermore, these difficult business requirements will not present a challenge to *all* of the business processes and systems impacted by the project, only a few. So, if you concentrate your efforts initially on those difficult requirements, and confine your explorations to the specific business processes and systems whose architecture they challenge, you will have fewer designs to explore. This simplifies your search for suitable architectures. Since the remaining business requirements are, by definition, easier to accommodate, addressing them is less likely to require alterations to the architecture you have already established. In fact, whatever architecture you select that satisfies the challenging requirements will, most likely, be readily extensible to support the less-challenging requirements. This is the guiding principle behind *Total Architecture Synthesis* (TAS).

TAS takes an iterative approach to gathering requirements, defining business processes, and defining the systems architecture (Figure 5–5). The TAS approach is a variation of Barry Boehm's spiral development approach. The difference is that the TAS approach is narrowly focused on just the business process and systems architecture, whereas Boehm's spiral development addresses the entire development life cycle. TAS can be used for the architecture activities within a larger spiral development process.[1]

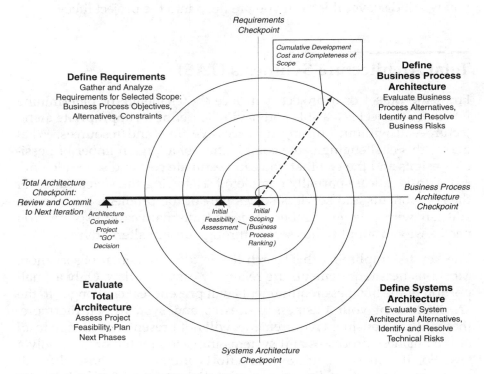

Figure 5–5: *Overview of Total Architecture Synthesis*

---

1. Boehm, Barry. 2000. "Spiral Development: Experience, Principles, and Refinements." Spiral Development Workshop February 9, 2000 Special Report CMU/SEI-2000-SR-008. Pittsburgh, PA: Carnegie Mellon University.

The technique begins with an initial breadth-first inventory of all the business processes that appear to be impacted by the project. This inventory is based on the business goals set forth in the project charter and is the first cut at defining the full scope of the project. A minimal amount of data is gathered in order to rank the business processes according to their perceived level of design difficulty and business importance. Once the initial ranking is complete, the iterations of synthesizing the architecture begin. The first iteration begins with a small number of what appear to be the most challenging business processes. Each iteration comprises requirements gathering, business process definition, systems architecture definition, and a concluding evaluation.

From the perspective of determining project feasibility, the first iteration is the critical one. You begin by selecting a small number of the most challenging business processes based on their difficulty and importance ranking. You gather the requirements for just these business processes, identifying the changes to business process results, benefits, and operating constraints that are required to achieve the business objectives. You next explore possible business process architectures and select one or two promising ones for further exploration. You then explore the possible system architectures that can support the chosen business process architectures. You select one or two of these system architectures, and then you evaluate which combination of business process and systems architectures best achieves the overall business benefit while remaining within the cost and schedule guidelines. If you have one or more combinations that work, you select the most promising as the basis for the next iteration. In this next iteration you select a few more business processes to be considered, and the process continues until you have completed the architecture of both the business processes and systems.

You must keep in mind that the first iteration may not produce a combination of business process and systems architectures that is capable of producing the expected benefits within the cost and schedule guidelines. Should this occur, it is clearly appropriate to try again and explore additional design alternatives, but you should keep in mind that you may be looking at an infeasible project—one that cannot produce the expected benefits within the project's cost and schedule guidelines. While this is not your preferred outcome, it is not exactly unusual either. The good news is that should you reach this conclusion, you have done so with the bare minimum of time and resources—which is the whole point of approaching the architecture in this manner.

Should you conclude that your project is not feasible, your work leading to this conclusion will most likely have given you some insight as to which aspects of the project charter have driven the cost or schedule out of range. Or, perhaps the goal of the project was not realistic. In any case, you can use this understanding as the basis for proposing changes to the project charter's goals, schedule, and budget—changes that would yield a feasible project.

Most importantly, if you conclude that the project is not feasible you should take this conclusion to the project oversight team. Your conclusion should be accompanied by some alternatives, such as less ambitious goals or an extended set of cost and schedule guidelines. If none of these alternatives is acceptable, the project oversight team may choose to abandon the project altogether and apply the resources to another project. Regardless of the outcome, you and the business have reached this conclusion with a minimum expenditure of time and resources, and have therefore maximized the time and resources available to pursue other opportunities.

Standing back from these iterations for a moment and considering how this activity fits into the overall project flow, you can see that TAS impacts the organization of the work in the earliest stages of the project (Figure 5–6). With TAS, requirements gathering is no longer a distinct activity, separated from business process and systems architecture. These three activities are now iteratively intertwined and must be executed by a cross-functional team consisting of business experts, business process architects, and systems architects. At the conclusion of TAS, there is still some architectural work to be done: finalizing the specifications for the various components and services whose design is impacted by the architectural changes. But this work is not undertaken until you have stabilized the architecture and determined that the project is feasible.

Figure 5–7 details the TAS approach. TAS begins with the assumption that the project has been chartered with clearly identified and quantified business benefits along with cost and schedule guidelines. The quantified business benefits provide objective criteria for deciding whether or not a proposed architecture can deliver those benefits. The cost and schedule guidelines allow the architects (along with the project manager) to select architectures that fit these constraints. The charter as a whole serves to focus the TAS efforts on those aspects of the project that are most important to the business. The details of the project charter are covered in the companion volume, *Succeeding with SOA*.

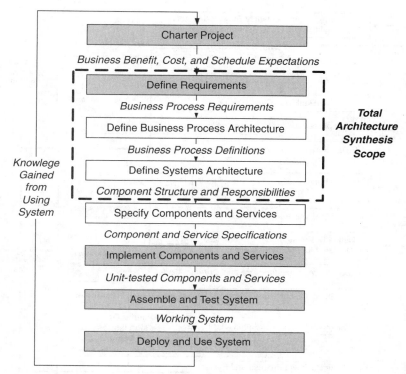

Figure 5–6: *The Scope of Total Architecture Synthesis*

Defining the Initial Scope

TAS begins by defining the initial scope of the project in terms of business processes. An inventory is made of those business processes that will clearly be impacted by the project based on the project charter's statement of project goals. Once these business processes are identified, a small amount of information is gathered about each process. The stakeholders involved in the business process are identified. A brief dialog with the stakeholders ensues to obtain a rough estimate of the peak rate at which the process executes and the volume of information being carried through each execution along with the business significance of the process. The degree of automation in the existing process is determined, and the level of automation required to meet the business objectives is identified.

This collection of information is sufficient to determine a relative ranking of the business processes in terms of their anticipated level of

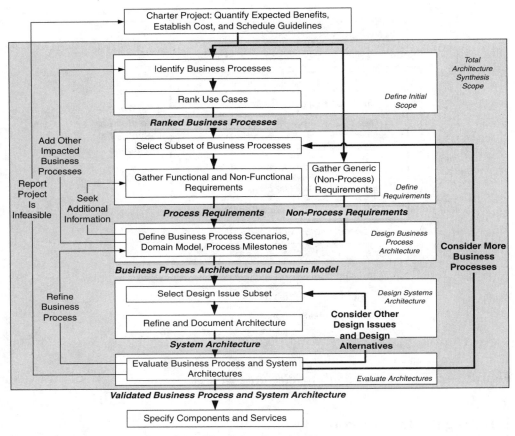

Figure 5–7: *Details of Total Architecture Synthesis*

design difficulty and business importance. Note that errors in rankings will not lead to an inappropriate architecture. They merely impact the efficiency of the process. The worst that can happen is for a less important business process to be considered before a more important one. The scoping task is detailed in Chapter 6.

Defining the Requirements

Once you have completed the initial scoping, the iterative part of TAS begins. To begin each iteration, you select a small number of business processes from the ranked list. These become the focus of the current iteration. In the first iteration you may only consider one or two business processes, anticipating that these will be challenging enough to motivate significant architectural exploration without adding the complexity of additional business processes.

Once the business processes have been selected for the current iteration, you gather their requirements by interviewing the stakeholders for each process. What you are seeking is a "black box" view of the business process, focusing on the inputs, results, milestones, and constraints. Functionally, what does the process accomplish? What results does the process produce for the business, and what inputs does it require from other processes? What are the constraints on the performance of the process? What are the key progress milestones?

It is essential that you relate the business process requirements back to the project's business objectives. You need to determine which requirements (or changes to requirements) will enable the process to produce the expected business benefits. Very often the key requirements will be the constraints on the business process execution: the length of time or the level of effort it takes to reach a milestone or produce a result. Identifying these requirements helps to keep the project focused on achieving the project goals.

In addition to gathering these business-process specific requirements, you will also be gathering more generic requirements. These usually take the form of compliance constraints on how business is conducted or how technology is to be used. Compliance with corporate security standards, audit requirements, and technology best practices are common examples. These compliance requirements are generally discovered during the requirements gathering for specific business processes, but they apply to all of the business processes in the project inventory. Requirements definition is covered in Chapters 9 through 11.

Designing the Business Process Architecture

Once the requirements have been gathered, you begin architecting the business process. This is the high-level design of the business process that focuses on identifying the participants in the process (people and systems), the activities being performed by the participants, and the dialog between them needed to bring the business process to life. Unless the requirements mandate that specific activities are to be performed by specific systems, the actual system that will perform the activity is intentionally left unspecified at this point.

It is now that you explore the various business process alternatives and business rules that can satisfy the requirements. You explore various combinations of participants in the proposed processes and various activity assignments, paying particular attention to the information being communicated between participants and the complexity of this communication. Your goal is to identify a simple and robust process architecture that is capable of producing the desired business benefit within the given constraints.

Some sources of information required by a business process may originate in another business process. In such cases you must identify the source business process. If the source business process requires modification and is not already in the business process inventory, you must add it. Such additions, of course, constitute a change in scope (or at least a growing awareness of the actual scope) for your project.

While you are defining these business processes and their alternatives, you are at the same time capturing the key concepts and relationships involved in the processes in a domain model. Some of these will be physical in nature (people, companies, products) while others will be information abstractions (orders, phone numbers, etc.). This domain model emphasizes the variability in relationships that can occur in the actual application domain and thus serves as a reference against which proposed data structure and schema representations can be evaluated. You also ensure that the milestone status is clearly identifiable in the business process design.

The explorations of business processes and the assemblage of the domain model may raise questions about requirements and thus require reengaging with the stakeholders to seek clarification. You will refine the requirements based on these discussions and modify the business process architecture accordingly.

As you conclude the design of the business process architecture, you explore the advantages and risks of the different business process alternatives and select one or two promising business process definitions for each process as input to the next step. The details of business process synthesis are discussed in Part II.

Designing the Systems Architecture

Once you have selected the candidate business processes, you can begin the design of the systems architecture. Here you are exploring various system design alternatives that could support the selected business processes. In defining the architecture, you will address a number of design challenges. Rather than tackle them all at once, it is more productive to take an iterative approach. You sequence the design issues so that later design issues are unlikely to require changes to decisions made regarding earlier design issues. You then tackle the design issues a few at a time. After refining each of the proposed architectural alternatives to address the selected design issues, you evaluate the overall results. This evaluation weeds out unsuitable alternatives early in the game and singles out the best candidates. If you find suitable candidates, then you consider additional design issues. If you do not find any suitable alternatives, you must explore alternative architectures. However, you must once again keep your mind open to the possibility that there is no suitable architecture that will yield the desired benefits within the cost and schedule guidelines. The details of systems architecture synthesis are discussed in Parts III through VIII.

Evaluating Architectures

As should be apparent from this discussion of TAS, evaluation is an ongoing process that tests the suitability of business process and system designs as needed. As with the design issues in systems architecture synthesis, there are a number of evaluation questions to ask about the overall design. These questions are also ranked, with the show-stopper questions such as performance feasibility placed high on the list. When the early design issues are being addressed, you consider only a few of the most fundamental evaluation questions.

As the design becomes more complete (with respect to the business processes being considered), you consider more of these evaluation questions. In the end, however, there is really only one question to be answered: Does it still appear feasible that you can achieve the desired business benefit within the cost and schedule guidelines? If the answer is yes, it is time to move on with the architecture and consider more design issues or business processes. If the answer is no, it is time to work with the business executive sponsor and project oversight team to rethink the project. Evaluation is discussed in Chapter 39.

Beware of Look-Alike Processes!

Iterative development processes and agile development have become quite popular in recent years. These techniques, TAS included, all seek to reduce risk by quickly trying out ideas as a means of validating them and obtaining feedback. But I must urge some caution here.

Agile development that attempts to quickly produce a working system often tackles the simplest aspects of a problem first. These aspects generally do not pose any particular architectural challenges. Consequently, in the early stages of the project, virtually any architecture may appear to be adequate. Yet if an inappropriate architecture is selected (by accident), by the time the difficult requirements are addressed, a considerable investment will have already been made in the inappropriate architecture. Changing the architecture at this point will be costly and time consuming—and may even be cost prohibitive. Whoops!

Barry Boehm sums the issue up nicely: "As in life, if you marry your architecture in haste, you and your stakeholders will repent at leisure."[2] Care should be taken in this methodology to consciously select the architecture and evaluate its suitability before making a commitment to that architecture. As you are considering it, you should interpret architecture broadly as being inclusive of the business process design as well. Total Architecture Synthesis aims to do exactly this for the design of distributed information systems, testing and reviewing the design of both the business process and supporting systems on paper before committing to an implementation effort.

The use of Total Architecture Synthesis is not necessarily inconsistent with agile development methodologies that seek early implementations. At any point in the TAS iterative business process and architecture development, a subset of the business processes and supporting systems can be driven to implementation. However, to maintain risk at acceptable levels, it is imperative that even if the more difficult business processes and supporting systems are not implemented in these early iterations, they are still designed to avoid accidentally implementing an inappropriate architecture.

Manage Risk: Architect Iteratively

A question you need to always keep in focus is whether the project is feasible. Can you actually deliver the expected project benefits within

---

2. Barry Boehm. 2000. "Spiral Development: Experience, Principles, and Refinements" Spiral Development Workshop February 9, 2000 Special Report CMU/SEI-2000-SR-008, Pittsburgh, PA: Carnegie Mellon University, p. 15.

the cost and schedule guidelines? The question may be easy to ask, but it is hard to answer truthfully—especially when you are well into the project. The problem is that the further you are into the project, the greater the investment and the more difficult it becomes to report that the project (at least as chartered) is not feasible.

Generally, by the time you have finished the design work in a project, it is too late. Promises have been made, career reputations staked; money has been invested, critical time has elapsed. But this problem is avoidable by restructuring the early phases of the work as just outlined. Instead of making a large investment in requirements gathering followed by a large investment in architecture (the point at which a definitive answer becomes possible), you focus instead on exploring only those business processes that are likely to pose a feasibility challenge. By focusing on those business processes and their associated systems architecture, you can provide an early answer to the feasibility question with minimal investment.

Total Architecture Synthesis can thus be seen as a risk management technique. In fact, it is entirely appropriate to introduce a few project oversight team reviews and project go/no-go decisions into TAS's iterative cycles of expanding business process coverage. This gives the oversight team the opportunity to identify, at minimal cost, the projects whose unfolding costs or schedules are becoming inconsistent with project expectations. This early exposure affords maximum flexibility in terms of re-scoping the project, increasing the budget, or reassigning the resources to more beneficial projects.

Total Architecture Synthesis provides an efficient means of attacking a business problem and delivering the desired benefits within cost and schedule guidelines. Its initial focus on the difficult aspects of a problem leads to a quick determination as to whether these benefits are, indeed, achievable within the given constraints. This focus also leads to the efficient exploration of design alternatives and thus a lower-cost development process. It also ensures that both the business process and system designs are up to the task before the detailed specification of system components and services is undertaken. The use of UML standard notation creates documentation that enables a common understanding of both business process and system design that can be shared between the business and technical communities.

Summary

Incremental IT development methodologies do not adequately address enterprise-scale projects or interdependencies between business process design and systems design. Waterfall-style approaches assume that the resulting business process designs will permit reasonable system designs, while in reality some give-and-take is required to arrive at effective business processes with reasonable supporting system designs. Agile development does not address the multiple-organization challenge of enterprise projects, and can lead to early commitment to an architecture before the challenging aspects of the problem have necessarily been addressed.

The Total Architecture Synthesis approach provides an effective alternative. Its iterative approach efficiently blends requirements gathering with business process and system design, and it provides an early assessment of project feasibility. It quickly identifies the business processes that are most likely to present feasibility challenges and addresses them first. Business process by business process, it guides the architecture team through gathering requirements, designing the business process and supporting systems, and evaluating the design. Its evaluations provide both cost and performance feasibility assessments before a commitment is made to implementation. Its artifacts, based on industry-standard UML notation, promote efficient and effective cross-communication between the business process and systems communities. TAS keeps the project focused on delivering business value.

Key Development Process Questions

1. Does your development process include an explicit architecture step that covers the design of both business processes and supporting systems? Is this design completed and reviewed prior to the start of any significant development?

2. Does your development process explicitly identify and resolve architectural challenges before a commitment to the architecture has been made?

3. Does your development process begin with an explicit charter that sets forth quantified business objectives along with cost and schedule constraints?

4. Does your development process have an explicit integration test step to promote efficient initial assembly of the completed system?

Suggested Reading

Boehm, Barry. 2000. "Spiral Development: Experience, Principles, and Refinements" Spiral Development Workshop February 9, 2000. Special Report CMU/SEI-2000-SR-008. Pittsburgh, PA: Carnegie Mellon University.

Part II

The Business Process Perspective

Chapter 6

Processes

Any discussion of processes must begin with a basic understanding of what a process is. The dictionary defines a process to be a series of actions leading to a goal. This definition, however, is a bit vague with respect to marking the beginning and ending of the process and the nature of the steps in between. Business processes, at least the repeatable ones supported by information systems, have discrete starting points and discrete ends. They have discrete steps, and produce discrete results. These processes fall into the category of processes known as discrete processes.[1]

A discrete process is a sequence of discrete activities whose performance is triggered by a discrete external event and whose execution produces (or attempts to produce) discrete countable results and may require one or more discrete countable inputs (Figure 6–1). Since all of the processes discussed

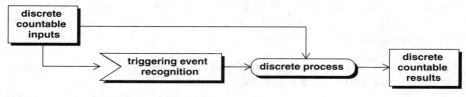

Figure 6–1: *Discrete Process*

---

1. Sowa, John F. 2000. *Knowledge Representation: Logical, Philosophical, and Computational Foundation.* Pacific Grove, CA: Brooks/Cole Publishing Co.

in this book are discrete processes, they will generally be referred to as just processes.

Triggers, Inputs, and Results

Processes begin with the recognition that some event has occurred that warrants the execution of the process. This recognition is really a determination that the process's expected results are desired. The triggering event for a process is most often the arrival of an input to the process. Consider the "Withdraw Cash via ATM" example shown in Figure 6–2. The triggering event for this process is the arrival of the transaction request from the customer (i.e., the customer entry indicating that Withdraw Cash is the desired type of transaction).

In addition to the trigger, other inputs to the process may be required as well. The PIN, the ATM card, the current account balance, the cash to be dispensed, and the paper to print the receipts are also required inputs. All inputs to a process, including those whose arrival constitutes a triggering event, originate outside the process. Anything that originates within the process should be considered an internal design detail of the process itself. The specification of the amount to be withdrawn, for example, is an internal detail of the process and not an external input. You might be tempted to place the PIN and ATM card in this category. What makes them inputs is that both originated outside the scope of this process.

There are many sources of inputs for triggering processes. The input may be a user input, a message arriving from a business partner, or the arrival of a result from another business process. Although you often don't think of time (i.e., the tick of a clock) as an input, time can also be used as a triggering input. The tick of the clock is used to update a timer, and the expiration of this timer becomes the triggering event that causes the execution of the business process.

It may seem a bit pedantic to talk about the details of triggering events, but the fact is that if you want robust business processes you must be aware of every aspect of the process that might cause a failure. The failure to recognize a triggering event (e.g., that the customer has requested a withdraw cash transaction) will cause that transaction to fail as surely as anything else that can go wrong with a process. From a design perspective later on, this recognition of the triggering event is an activity that must be assigned to a participant in the business process.

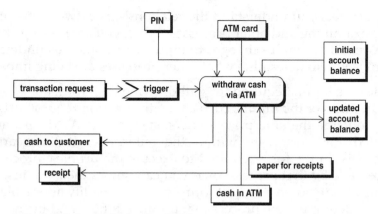

Figure 6–2: *Withdraw Cash via ATM*

The purpose of the process is to produce results. It is not unusual for processes to produce multiple results. The bank's Withdraw Cash business process produces cash, a receipt, and an updated account balance. The goal of the process is to generate these results, even if a particular execution of the process is unsuccessful in achieving the goal. The Withdraw Cash business process, for example, will not produce cash if there is an insufficient balance in the bank account. But regardless of the outcome, it is still the Withdraw Cash business process.

To bring closure to the execution of a process, the results of a process must be discrete and countable. Withdraw Cash is not some nebulous ongoing activity that distributes funds held in bank accounts to the account holders. It is a focused, repeatable process that takes a specific request for funds withdrawal and attempts to produce specific discrete countable results, namely the requested amount of cash, a receipt, and an update to the account balance. Requiring those results to be discrete and countable provides a clear means of determining, for each execution of the process, whether the process goal has been achieved and whether the process execution is complete.

Related Processes

Processes never live in isolation. The inputs to one process are actually the results from other processes, and the results of a process are inputs to other processes. Understanding the sources and destinations of inputs and results lets you understand the relationships between the process you are examining and other processes. When you are making changes to a process that require changes to inputs or results, this understanding allows you to determine what other processes are being impacted.

Consider the inputs required for withdrawing cash from an ATM (Figure 6–3). Some of the inputs, such as the transaction request, originate entirely outside the enterprise. Others, such as the ATM card and its associated PIN, originate within the enterprise. If these artifacts already exist in the form required to execute the primary process and are accessible by that process, then you can ignore their origins. But if these inputs are not in the right form or are not readily accessible, then you must determine the process that produced them and the nature of the required changes to those processes. This discovery process is the primary means of discovering the true scope of the project.

Process Maturity

Everything you do with information systems is in some way related to business processes. But the nature of the relationship between the systems and the business process varies greatly with the level of maturity of the process, as does the level of detail that you need about the process itself.

Paul Harmon suggests the process maturity levels shown in Figure 6–4, which are derived from the Software Engineering Institute's Capability Maturity Model.[2] At the Ad Hoc level (which Harmon calls Initial), each execution of the process is different. A marketing analysis of sales data looking for new trends or market opportunities might take this form as the analyst examines some initial data and then lets the findings drive the remainder of the analysis process.

From an information systems perspective, you don't care so much about the process itself as you do the kinds of information that the process will require, and the interfaces needed to retrieve and analyze this information. The difficulties in supporting such processes lie primarily

---

2. Harmon, Paul, "Evaluating an Organization's Business Process Maturity," *Business Process Trends*, Vol. 2, No. 3, March 2004, pp. 1–11. http://fac.ceprin.gsu.edu/welke/CIS9240/Papers/BPM/Business%20Process%20Maturity%20Assessment.pdf.

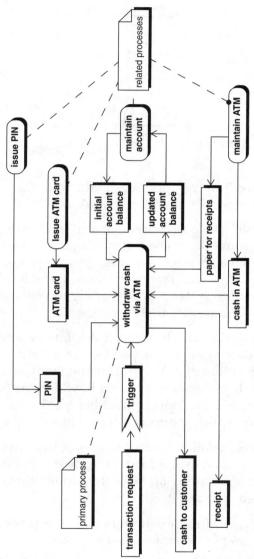

Figure 6–3: *Inputs, Results, and Related Business Processes*

117

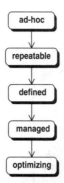

Figure 6–4: *Process Maturity Levels*

in their ad hoc nature. You can speculate about what the process might require, but you can never be completely sure.

At the repeatable level, the processes have a conscious organization to them, and there is some basic level of management that tracks cost, schedule, and functionality. Most business processes that have information systems associated with them are at least at this level of maturity. At this level, information systems are generally directed at assisting or performing individual activities in the process.

At the defined level, processes have been documented and standardized. In the information systems, the process (or significant portions of the process) may be automated. This automation may take the form of hard-wired relationships between systems in which the results of one system's activities become the inputs to another's activities, or there may be a component that explicitly directs the activities of other systems.

At the managed level, detailed measurements of the process itself and the quality of its results are being made. Information systems are generally involved in the gathering and dissemination of this data as well as the execution of the process itself.

At the optimizing level, the measurements of the process are themselves inputs to a separate optimization process that focuses on improving the basic process. This optimization process itself can be at any one of these maturity levels. Information systems may be involved in the analysis of the measurement data but may also be involved in the optimization response, such as the dynamic deployment of additional resources to handle increasing demands made of the basic process.

Understanding the level of maturity of the process will help you understand the kind of information that you need about the process. Also keep in mind that many projects seek to move business processes further up this maturity chain. As such, the level of information that you will need to achieve that next step is likely to exceed the level of information currently available about the process. If you are seeking to make a repeatable process into a defined process, the process definition has to be created, socialized, and approved. This is all part of the business process architecture task.

Continuous Processes

While most business processes are discrete by nature, you may be called upon to deal with real-world processes that are continuous. Managing the distribution of electrical power over the power grid and managing the operation of an oil refinery are examples of processes in which the process inputs and results are continuous, as are the activities of the process itself.

While the process being managed may be continuous, the information systems used to manage them are not. Computers are discrete machines, and the manner in which they interact with the continuous process is itself discrete. Information systems do not take measurements and read inputs continuously. Instead, they sample these values at discrete points in time. The measurements themselves are discrete digital representations (approximations) of the actual real-world continuous values. Systems take discrete actions changing the settings on controls and providing other outputs. The process itself is composed of discrete activities that take discrete inputs and produce discrete results. The control process is a discrete process.

So how does a discrete process manage a continuous process? The trick is to execute the management process frequently enough that the process being controlled does not have a chance to change significantly between executions of the management process. With this approach, the discrete management process actually simulates the operation of a continuous management process.

The design of this type of process follows most of the principles outlined in this text, but with a few significant differences. The biggest difference is that the ability to control the continuous process requires precise and predictable timing of the input→process→output cycle. A few milliseconds difference in response time can make the difference between a well-behaved system and one that vacillates wildly out of control. Thus the precise scheduling of work tends to dominate the technical design. The techniques for this type of design are the core topics of digital control systems design and are beyond the scope of this text.

The other major characteristic of control processes is that the consequences of a process failure tend to be catastrophic. Widespread power outages, oil refinery leaks and fires, and plane crashes are the kinds of consequences that can be expected. These consequences lead to investments in fault-tolerant design that are well beyond what is typically warranted for information systems. Failures must be compensated for within the sub-second response time required for control systems, which generally requires a significant degree of redundancy combined with a voting system to determine the final result. The space shuttle, for example, not only has four redundant control computers operating simultaneously and voting on the results, it also has a fifth computer of a different type that is programmed by a different team performing the same functions and alerting the crew to discrepancies between its results and those of the other four computers.[3] Such designs are extremely expensive and are warranted only when the consequences of failure are extreme. This type of fault-tolerant design is beyond the scope of this text.

Aside from these two areas (which are admittedly significant), the processes and techniques discussed in this text are generally applicable to the design of control systems. However, the criteria for prioritizing processes and the sequencing of design considerations require some adjustment to make them appropriate for control systems design.

Structured Processes

The characterization of a process in terms of its inputs, triggering events, and results is also applicable to the individual activities within a process. Thus you can view any activity as a process in and of itself.

---

3. Alfred Spector and David Gifford, "The Space Shuttle Primary Computer System," Communications of the ACM, Vol. 27, No. 9, September 1984, pp. 872–900.

In other words, every process that involves more than one activity can be viewed as a composite of subprocesses.

This view of activities as subprocesses sets the stage for the modularization of processes into subprocesses. This is an essential step in recognizing service opportunities, since the operations of a service must eventually be used as activities in a process in order to provide value. It also gives you some insight as to what is required in a service specification. To achieve reusability, the interactions with the service must be clearly defined and easy to understand. Defining the inputs, triggering events, and results of a subprocess, along with its operating constraints, provides the basis for specifying services.

Summary

A process, or more specifically a discrete process, is a sequence of distinct activities that produces (or attempts to produce) discrete countable results. Every discrete process requires at least one input, and the trigger for performing a process is the recognition of the arrival of one or more of these inputs. From an external perspective, a process can be characterized by these inputs and results, the triggering event, and the constraints under which the process operates.

The activities of a process can be characterized in the same manner as the overall process: inputs, triggers, results, and constraints. Recognizing this, it becomes clear that each activity is a process unto itself, and thus a process can be viewed as a composition of subprocesses.

When you employ services, the operations of the service are used as activities in a process. Thus the characterization of activities as subprocesses provides a sound mechanism for specifying the service operations in terms of their inputs, triggers, results, and constraints.

A process's inputs and outputs do not come out of thin air. Inputs are the results of other processes, and results are the inputs to other processes. This flow of inputs and results identifies dependencies between processes. When a project requires changes to inputs and outputs, these dependencies serve to identify other processes that are impacted by the project.

Processes exist at many maturity levels. Some are totally ad hoc: The required activities and their sequencing are determined as the process unfolds. As processes mature, their definitions become standardized and their executions become managed and then optimized.

The maturity level of a process significantly influences the manner in which information systems participate in the process. Ad hoc processes employ systems to perform individual activities. As the processes mature, systems become involved in coordinating activities and in measuring, managing, and optimizing the execution of the overall process.

Some real-world processes are continuous in nature, but discrete processes can be used to manage these processes. Real-time process management requires control system design techniques and fault tolerant design techniques that are beyond the scope of this text.

Key Process Questions

1. What is the maturity level of the process you are examining? What does the maturity level imply concerning the nature of the information system's involvement in the process?

2. What are the inputs and results of the process? What triggers the execution of the process?

3. What are the constraints on how the process executes? How do these constraints relate to the inputs, triggering event, and results?

4. What processes produce the inputs for the process you are examining? What processes consume the results of the process you are examining?

Suggested Reading

Ahern, Dennis M., Aaron Clouse, and Richard Turner. 2004. *CMMI Distilled: A Practical Introduction to Integrated Process Improvement.* Boston, MA: Addison Wesley.

Harmon, Paul, "Evaluating an Organization's Business Process Maturity." *Business Process Trends*, Vol. 2, No. 3, March 2004, pp. 1–11. http://fac.ceprin.gsu.edu/welke/CIS9240/Papers/BPM/Business%20Process%20Maturity%20Assessment.pdf.

Sowa, John F. 2000. *Knowledge Representation: Logical, Philosophical, and Computational Foundations.* Pacific Grove, CA: Brooks/Cole Publishing Co.

Chapter 7

Initial Project Scoping

It is day one for your new project. You have your project charter, and now you need to figure out exactly what needs to be done to meet the business objectives. This exercise is commonly referred to as scoping the project.

The intent of initial scoping is to identify those business processes that must be created or modified to realize the business goals. Once these processes have been identified, a small amount of information is gathered about each identified process to aid in understanding which of the process improvements is likely to present the greatest challenge. This information is used to then rank the processes by the anticipated difficulty, and this ranking is used to determine the sequence in which the process requirements will be gathered and the architecture of the process and supporting system defined.

To do this ranking you need to arrive at an overall understanding of the nature of the changes that must be made in order to achieve the business objectives. Your understanding needs to be broad enough to identify all of the work that will eventually need to be done, with just enough detail to ensure that there is no ambiguity concerning what is in scope or out of scope for the project.

Defining the scope of the project in terms of business processes enables iterative architecture development. Once you have the inventory, you gather a small amount of information about each process to help you understand which processes are likely to present the greatest architecture challenges at both the business process and systems level. This level of detail will not enable you to estimate the level of effort for the project, but it will steer you towards the processes that are the most likely to demand high levels of effort so that you can investigate them first. This will help you focus on those processes that are most likely to challenge the project's cost and schedule constraints, and thus lead you to an early understanding of project feasibility.

This focus on business processes also makes it easy for the business side of the house to understand and manage the scope of the project. Once the required time and level of effort for a project is well understood, it is not uncommon for the scope of the project to be altered to remain within the project's guidelines. Defining the scope of the project in terms of business processes makes it easy to understand the business impact of various scoping alternatives. This understanding simplifies the process of making scoping decisions, and it clarifies the impact of scoping decisions on the business benefits that can be expected from the project.

Assembling the Business Process Inventory

Assembling the process inventory is an iterative process (Figure 7–1). It begins by interviewing the key project stakeholders—generally the people who chartered the project. From these initial stakeholders, you discover some of the business processes that will be impacted and, equally important, discover other stakeholders that must be interviewed. Stakeholder initial interviews focus on seven key questions:

1. Which business processes will require changes in order to either directly achieve the project goals or to support the required changes in other processes that lie within the project scope?

2. For business processes that require changes, what is the nature of the change that is required? How can these changes be characterized in terms of inputs, results, process triggers, and operating constraints? Note that these questions apply to both newly identified processes and processes that have been previously identified.

3. For each business process requiring change, what is the consequence to the business if the process does not execute properly?

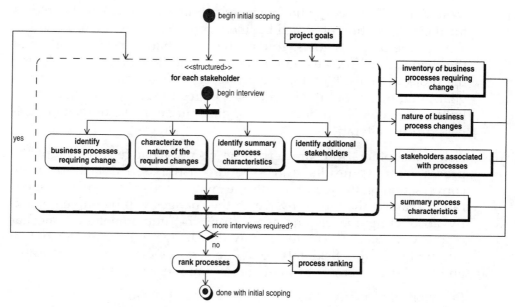

Figure 7–1: *Initial Scoping Process*

4. For each business process, what is the peak rate at which this business process must execute? What volume of data moves through the process? What is the required completion time for executing the process? These answers should take into consideration future growth plans.

5. For each business process, what is the current maturity level of the process? What is the desired maturity level upon completion of the project? What level of system participation is expected upon completion of the project?

6. For each business process, are there any variants of the process in the enterprise (i.e., different processes that achieve the same results)?

7. For each business process, who are the key stakeholders involved?

Conducting Interviews

The questions listed above comprise a discovery process whose purpose is to identify the processes that require change, roughly characterize their needed changes, and identify the stakeholders who can provide more detail. To discover the business processes, you ask stakeholders for their perception of which business processes must be modified to achieve the project's goals. You ask them to characterize the nature of the change they foresee and how that change contributes to achieving the project's goals. By tying the proposed changes back to the project goals, you will avoid the kind of scope creep that occurs when stakeholders perceive the project as an opportunity to make unrelated business process alterations.

Ask stakeholders to characterize the needed change in terms of the process's inputs, results, triggers, and constraints. This will focus the conversation on the requirements (i.e., what needs to be accomplished) rather than on the means by which the changes will be implemented. By abstracting the requirements from the implementation mechanisms, you retain flexibility in how the change will be implemented. You will need this flexibility to define services that are truly reusable and to adjust processes to share these common services.

Be aware that many stakeholders will find it difficult to separate the nature of the change from the mechanisms by which the change is accomplished. In such cases, adjust your interview style. Let the stakeholder describe proposed changes to the process. Then ask: What is there about the proposed process changes that achieves the business goals? This will lead to a discussion of inputs, results, triggers, and constraints. Remember that the more abstract the characterization of the process changes, the more flexibility you will have in considering business process and system design alternatives.

One of the goals of the interview process is to identify those business processes that are liable to present architectural challenges. Business significance is one indicator of potential design complexity since higher levels of business importance tend to drive designs towards high availability and fault tolerance.

You can arrive at an understanding of business significance by asking what the impact on the business would be if the business process failed to execute. There are primarily two cases of interest. In the first, you want to understand what would happen to the business if a single execution of the business process failed. In the second, you want to understand what would happen if the business process was unable to execute for some period of time. It is likely that the impact will vary with the length of time that the process is unavailable, so you should explore a range of outage periods.

In assessing business significance, try to quantify the impact of process failures, expressing it in terms such as the loss of revenue or the cost of regulatory penalties. This quantification will help to identify those processes that are most critical to business operations and are therefore likely to require fault tolerance or high availability.

Stringent performance requirements also contribute to complexity and cost. Ask about the peak rates at which the process will execute, their required completion times, and volume of data being moved through the process. This information will help you understand the demand for capacity that the business process will present on the people and systems involved in the process. Capacity demands that are large enough to require distributing load across multiple participants (whether people or systems) or scaling up system resources add complexity and cost to the project.

Another significant driver of complexity and cost is the degree of automation in the business process. Understanding the maturity levels of both the current and desired processes will help you understand the level of system participation in the process—i.e., the degree of automation involved. The more deeply involved the systems are in the collaboration, monitoring, and management of the business process, the more complex the design will be.

It is not unusual to find a variant of a business process in the enterprise—another business process that seeks to produce the same results. Since these processes require similar functionality, they represent opportunities for sharing services. Ask your stakeholder to identify process variants and add them to your inventory.

To assemble the information you need, you must talk to all the key stakeholders associated with a process. They are the sources of both requirements and current state knowledge for the project. In these initial interviews, they are helping you to define the scope and nature of the project. In subsequent interactions they will become both the providers of requirements and the reviewers of proposed changes.

You must make a conscious effort to identify all of the stakeholders with an interest in your project. You must ask each stakeholder you are interviewing to aid you in identifying other stakeholders. The consequence of failing to identify a stakeholder at this stage will be the delayed discovery of some requirements. If the discovery occurs after a substantial architectural commitment has been made and necessitates architectural changes, it will play havoc with the project cost and schedule. A bit of due diligence in stakeholder discovery up front will reward you with a smooth and predictable project execution.

Your understanding of the scope of your project will evolve during these interviews. Each stakeholder may identify new business processes that are impacted and additional stakeholders to be interviewed. You need to periodically consider these changes, assessing the completeness of your effort and revising your schedule of stakeholder interviews. The scoping process will be complete when you have interviewed all the identified stakeholders and are no longer uncovering additional business processes or stakeholders.

Your expectations about the discovery process need to be tempered with a dose of reality. Despite your best efforts, it is unlikely that you will discover all the business processes that impact your project. As you later dig into individual process requirements, you are likely to discover inputs and results that are associated with business processes that were not in your inventory. This is to be expected. A well-done scoping exercise will reliably identify all the primary business processes, those with changes that directly contribute to achieving the project's business goals. Many of the related processes will not be discovered until you begin the requirements gathering for the primary business processes.

Documenting the Inventory

You are going to gather a lot of information in the process of scoping your project. To aid in understanding what you have learned, it is good practice to summarize your findings in graphical and tabular form. These representations not only provide a quick overview of the project, but also serve to show the degree of completion of the scoping exercise.

Goals and Stakeholders

Table 7–1 provides a summary of the business processes. It is a quick overview of the project scope and goals along with a list of the stakeholders for each business process. Be sure to include variant processes even if you do not anticipate changing them. If your project is building a new variant, you will want to know about the existing process as well.

Table 7–1: *Goals and Stakeholders for the ATM Project Example*

Business Process	Required Change	Stakeholders
Withdraw Cash via ATM	Create the process	Marketing; Retail Banking Operations; Accounting; Enterprise Architecture; Project Team; System Operations; Account Management System Owner
Withdraw Cash via Teller	None	Retail Banking Operations; Accounting; Enterprise Architecture; System Operations; Account Management System Owner
Make Deposit via ATM	Create the process	(Same as Withdraw Cash via ATM)
Make Deposit via Teller	None	(Same as Withdraw Cash via Teller)
Transfer Funds via ATM	Create the process	(Same as Withdraw Cash via ATM)
Transfer Funds via Teller	None	(Same as Withdraw Cash via Teller)
Check Balance via ATM	Create the process	(Same as Withdraw Cash via ATM)
Check Balance via Teller	None	(Same as Withdraw Cash via Teller)
Maintain Retail Bank Account	Modify the process to incorporate issuing ATM cards and PINs	Retail Banking Operations; Accounting; Enterprise Architecture; Project Team; System Operations; Account Management System Owner
Issue ATM Card	Create the process	Marketing; Retail Banking Operations; Accounting; Enterprise Architecture; Project Team; System Operations; Account Management System Owner

continues

Table 7–1: *Goals and Stakeholders for the ATM Project Example (Continued)*

Business Process	Required Change	Stakeholders
Issue PIN	Create the process	Marketing; Retail Banking Operations; Accounting; Enterprise Architecture; Project Team; System Operations; Account Management System Owner
Maintain ATM System	Create the process, including triggering the installation and servicing of ATMs	New ATM Operations group; Marketing; Retail Banking Operations; Accounting; Enterprise Architecture; Project Team; System Operations; Account Management System Owner
Install ATM	Create the process	New ATM Operations group; Marketing; Retail Banking Operations; Accounting; Enterprise Architecture; Project Team; System Operations; Account Management System Owner
Service ATM	Create the process	New ATM Operations group; Marketing; Retail Banking Operations; Accounting; Enterprise Architecture; Project Team; System Operations; Account Management System Owner

Primary Processes

The scoping exercise focuses on identifying the business processes that must be changed to achieve the business goals. These constitute the primary business processes for the project. Their modification or creation directly contributes to generating the expected benefits.

Looking at the ATM example, the goal of the project is to reduce per-transaction costs from the present $3 per transaction to $1 or less. The primary processes involved are the transactions that the bank wishes to have performed through the ATM machine: withdraw cash, check balance, make deposit, and transfer funds.

A UML *composite structure diagram* provides a convenient graphical means of presenting an overview of the business process inventory

(Figure 7–2). It presents a concise at-a-glance summary of the project's scope—an overview of the details that have been gathered in the interview process.

In this overview diagram, each business process is shown as a UML *collaboration*, graphically represented by an oval with a dashed outline. It is good practice for the name of the business process to be a short descriptive phrase. This phrase should reference the most obvious result of the process (e.g., the "cash" in withdraw cash) and a verb that reflects the most obvious action being taken (e.g., "withdraw" in withdraw cash). You also want to make sure that your phrase covers the entire scope of the business process and not just the beginning of the process. For example, if you are describing a business process for selling goods, "place order" would not be a good descriptive term for the process, since it only describes the start of the process. "Sell goods" would be a more appropriate name.

An additional information element you must capture is the source of the triggering events that initiates each process. In the ATM example, the bank customer initiates each of the primary business processes by requesting a transaction. The relationship of this participant with the business process is indicated by adding the participant to the composite structure diagram and creating an association (represented by a solid line) between the participant and the collaboration. The importance here lies in clarifying that the full scope of the process includes the recognition of the triggering event. By identifying the source of the triggering event and referencing the primary result in the process name, you have provided an easy-to-understand overview of the complete scope of the process.

If you are familiar with UML notations, it may strike you that the diagram in Figure 7–2 looks very much like a UML use case diagram. This similarity is intentional, since both use cases and collaborations to represent

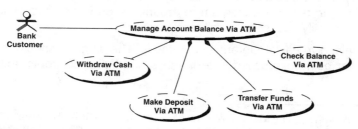

Figure 7–2: *Primary Business Processes for ATM Example*

units of behavior. In fact, the only observable difference in the diagram is that the oval representing the collaboration has a dashed outline instead of a solid outline. The difference, however, is more substantial. A use case represents the behavior of a single participant, whereas a collaboration represents the behavior of a group of participants. Since business processes are, by definition, collaborations between business process participants, the collaboration notation is the appropriate one to use.

Another observation that you may make is that the composite structure diagram is capable of representing the collaboration's relationships to other participants as well. While this is true, there is benefit in keeping these initial inventory diagrams as simple as possible. Their intent, after all, is simply to convey the breadth of scope for the project. The details will come later.

Keep Diagrams Simple

The diagrams you are creating are communications vehicles. Their primary intent is to help stakeholders understand the information being represented. To facilitate this, each individual diagram should focus on making a single point.

Avoid the temptation to create massively comprehensive diagrams. You have probably seen database schema wall charts—comprehensive diagrams that show dozens or hundreds of entities and their relationships. Such diagrams may be useful to someone already familiar with the database but present a daunting challenge to someone who is trying to learn about the database.

There is a venerable psychology study that points the way here: "The Magical Number Seven, Plus or Minus Two: Some Limits on Our Capacity for Processing Information."[1] This study shows that people are capable of distinguishing about seven items (plus or minus two) in short-term memory. The implication for diagrams is that you want to limit the number of major items in a diagram to around seven in order to make the diagram readily accessible to all readers.

To do this, give each diagram a clear focus. The diagram should make a particular point, expressed in terms of a handful of concepts and their

---

1. George A. Miller. "The Magical Number Seven, Plus or Minus Two: Some Limits on Our Capacity for Processing Information," *The Psychological Review,* Vol. 63, 1956, pp. 81–97.

relationships. If you need to make a different point, use a different diagram! You can still create your wall chart diagram if you wish—just don't expect people to use it as a learning tool.

Related Processes

Processes rarely live in isolation. The primary processes that you have identified are likely to depend on the results from other processes. Bank customers cannot use ATMs without ATM cards; some business process must have produced the ATM card as a result. The ATM will not be there at all unless it has been installed; there must be an installation process. The ATM cannot produce cash and receipts unless cash and receipt paper are routinely placed in the machine, and it will overflow if deposits are not regularly removed; there must be a servicing process. All of these *related processes* are necessary for the operation of the primary business processes.

Achieving the project benefits depends as much on the proper execution of these related processes as it does on the primary processes. For this reason, the related processes must be included in your business process inventory. This does not necessarily imply that these processes require changes—only that they must be examined to determine whether changes are required. In the case of the ATM example (Figure 7–3), many of these processes don't even exist, so their creation is clearly part of the project. Others, such as `Maintain Retail Bank Account`, do exist, but must be modified to incorporate the `Issue ATM Card` and `Issue PIN` processes.

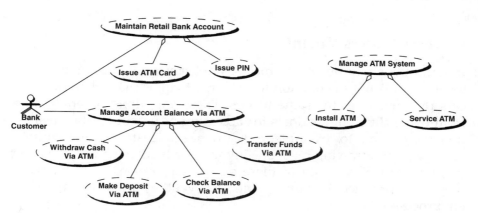

Figure 7–3: *Primary and Related Business Processes for ATM Example*

Unlike the primary business processes, the presence of and need for related business processes cannot be directly inferred from the business requirements. Instead, related processes are discovered through their exchange of inputs and results with primary processes. Many of these interactions will not be discovered until the requirements for the primary business processes have been explored. Nevertheless, if it is obvious during the scoping exercise that a primary process requires a particular input, the question should be asked as to what business process produces that input. Similarly, if the primary process produces a result that is used outside the process, you should ask what process (or processes) consumes that result. During the scoping exercise, let common sense be your guide. Later, in requirements gathering, you will become rigorous about identifying all of the related processes.

Primary business processes, by definition, always require project work. Related processes, on the other hand, may or may not require work. If the results that are being exchanged already exist in suitable form and the mechanisms for moving or accessing them are also suitable, then no related process work is required. On the other hand, if the related processes do not exist, the results are not in suitable form, or the mechanisms for transporting and accessing them are not suitable, then the related processes will require some work.

By the time you have finished gathering the requirements for the processes, you will have an understanding of the results-driven dependencies between the processes and will know which ones require significant work. By the time you have completed business processes and systems architecture, you will have identified all of the work that needs to be done and will truly understand the full scope of your project.

Business Process Variants

If you think about business processes in terms of the results that they generate, it is not uncommon to find that there is more than one process that generates the same results. These variations generally arise from using different channels for accessing or executing the business process. A bank, for example, typically has at least two different processes for withdrawing cash, one involving a bank teller and the other involving an ATM. Both of these business processes have the same intent and produce the same results, and yet they are distinctly different processes.

When you have variant business processes, understanding the variant process can be valuable. When you are creating an entirely new process (e.g., the `Withdraw Cash Via ATM` process) that produces the same results as an existing process, there is great benefit in understanding the existing process. For the most part, the new process will perform the very same activities as the existing process. What is likely to differ between the new and old processes are the participants that perform individual activities, the sequencing of the activities, and the communications mechanisms involved. In the existing teller-based withdraw cash transaction, it is the teller that identifies the customer, determines whether funds are available, disburses the cash, updates the account balance, and gives a receipt to the customer. In the ATM variant, the ATM machine will perform these functions.

The inputs to each activity and the results generated by the activity will generally be similar in both processes, even though they may differ in some details. Both the teller and the ATM must identify the customer, but the teller will do so using a driver's license or other identification, whereas the ATM will use the PIN associated with the ATM card. Despite these differences, understanding the existing business process will provide insight into what the new process must be capable of doing and what inputs and results are required.

In designing the new process, much time can be saved and many mistakes avoided by examining the existing process. For this reason, you must also include these related processes in the process inventory. The generalization relationship in the UML notation provides the means of indicating exactly this type of relationship. You create a collaboration that represents all processes seeking to achieve this common goal (e.g., `Withdraw Cash` from the bank), and then use the generalization relationship to indicate that the actual processes are specializations of this abstract process as shown in Figure 7–4. For clarity, you may want to color or otherwise indicate that the `Withdraw Cash via Teller` process is an existing process whose modification is not within the intended scope of the project.

There is another deeper benefit to identifying these related business processes: finding candidate services. If you create the two processes independently, you may well be duplicating functionality—and duplicating business rules as well. This will increase both development and maintenance costs. By examining both business processes, you afford yourself the opportunity to identify functionality that can be made common between the two processes. Common functionality presents a

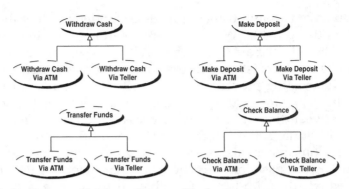

Figure 7–4: *Primary Business Process Variants*

service opportunity. At the same time, you may also identify a barrier to creating the service: In repackaging the functionality as a service, changes to the existing process may be required. If you decide to turn this functionality into a service to make it available to the new process, you may be increasing the scope (and cost) of the project. Of course, the modifications to the existing process may be postponed to another project, but they must eventually occur to obtain the expected service benefits.

When these service opportunities arise, a business decision needs to be made as to how to proceed. The decision will often depend on the position of the decision maker in the organizational hierarchy. If the decision maker has no authority over the existing business process and its underlying systems, the decision is likely to be to duplicate the functionality—that is, not build the service. The motivation behind making this decision is that the decision maker actually has control over all of the resources required to complete the project and can therefore control his or her own destiny. However, such decisions may not be in the long-term best interests of the enterprise. Here, in a nutshell, you find the core organizational problem underlying services: How do you get decisions regarding services made at an appropriate level so that the right decision for the overall enterprise is made? This issue is explored in depth in the companion volume, *Succeeding with SOA*.

Process Metrics

Much of the design challenge presented by business processes is related to achieving performance objectives. To understand which processes are liable to present such challenges, you need to gather some rough performance metrics for the processes in your inventory. These metrics are:

- The peak (maximum) rate at which the business process must produce results
- The variation in peak rate over time (i.e., when the peaks occur)
- The allowed completion time for the process
- The average rate at which the process will execute
- The volume of data that will move through the process

There is a subtlety in defining the peak rate that you need to carefully manage in order to get useful information. The numerical value for a peak rate is very sensitive to the time interval over which you measure the peak. Imagine that there are 1,000 ATMs and you want to know the peak rate at which withdraw cash transactions can occur. You might argue that it is possible for 1,000 customers to simultaneously initiate 1,000 transactions in the same second, giving a peak rate of 1,000/second. You might argue that 1,000 transactions could be initiated in one millisecond, giving a peak rate of 100,000/second. In fact, by choosing appropriate (or inappropriate) time intervals, you can make the peak rate nearly anything you want! That's not particularly useful, since you want to use this peak rate to determine the required capacity of machines and networks. How then do you arrive at a reasonable understanding about peak rate?

The key to solving this problem is to use the allowed completion time for the process as the time interval for peak rate measurements. The allowed completion time is the acceptable time interval between the process's triggering event and the production of its last result (i.e., the completion of the process). The peak rate you are after is the maximum number of business processes that can be initiated during this interval. The assumption is that it really doesn't matter when activities occur within this time interval as long as the results are produced on time. In other words, if the allowed completion time for a transaction at an ATM is 30 seconds and you have 1,000 machines out there, then the peak rate at which you need to be able to complete the transactions is 1,000 transactions in 30 seconds, or roughly 33.3 transactions/second. Even if 1,000 customers all initiate their transactions simultaneously, as long as you can complete those transactions within 30 seconds you have satisfied the requirements. Note that you still need to be able to accept 1,000 initiating events simultaneously—you just don't have to do the actual work that fast.

The peak rates for different processes often occur at different points in time. If all the peaks for all the processes occur simultaneously, then obviously you need the capacity to execute all of the processes simultaneously. But if the peaks occur at different times, you can get by with less capacity and still satisfy the business requirements. To take advantage of this, you need to ask when the peak rate occurs and how it varies over time. This understanding will enable you to more accurately determine the human, machine, and network capacities that will be required. This information will have a direct impact on the level of investment that you will make in operational staff, machines, and networks.

Many business processes accumulate data about each process execution. Knowing the average rate at which transactions will occur gives you an understanding of how rapidly this information will accumulate. The average rate, taken together with the volume of data, will then enable you to determine the required record storage capacity.

The volume of data moving through a process will give you a better understanding of the capacities required for machines, networks, and storage. Taken together with the peak rate, it will help you understand the network bandwidth required and the amount of work being done in the machines. Taken together with the average rate, it will help you understand the storage capacity required to support the business processes.

It is good practice to gather this data together in a form that is readily understandable. Table 7–2 summarizes the metrics for the ATM System example. Note that the metrics for the variant business processes involving human tellers have been included. This information will help you understand the capacities of the existing systems that are used to support those processes and will thus help you evaluate whether portions of those systems can be used (without modification) to support the new processes.

When you first ask the business community for answers to these metrics questions, you are unlikely to get very accurate numbers. You will get some initial "guesstimates," and then it will take some time for the business people to investigate and refine the values. That is OK. Since the initial use of these metrics will be to rank processes, and the ranking will be based on order-of-magnitude rates and data volumes, even these guesstimates will be sufficient. You will not need the more accurate numbers until you begin evaluating your systems architecture, and it will take you some time to get there. In the meantime, the business people can be doing their homework refining these numbers. This emphasizes the importance of asking for metrics right at the beginning

Table 7–2: *ATM Business Process Metrics*

Business Process	Variant	Peak Execution Rate	Variation in Peak Rate over Time	Allowed Completion Time	Average Sustained Rate	Volume of Data Moved per Execution
Withdraw Cash	Via Teller	61,000/hr	Peaks at lunch hour	3 minutes	160,000/ day	1KB
	Via ATM	104,000/ hr	Peaks during morning and evening commute	30 seconds	139,000/ day	1KB
Make Deposit	Via Teller	7,200/hr	Peaks at lunch hour	3 minutes	16,000/ day	1KB
	Via ATM	3,600/hr	Peaks during morning and evening commute	30 seconds	4,800/ day	1KB
Transfer Funds	Via Teller	360/hr	Peaks at lunch hour	3 minutes	1,000/ day	1KB
	Via ATM	3,600/hr	Peaks during morning and evening commute	30 seconds	4,800/ day	1KB
Check Balance	Via Teller	3,600/hr	Peaks at lunch hour	3 minutes	10,000/ day	1KB
	Via ATM	11,000/hr	Peaks during morning and evening commute	30 seconds	14,400/ day	1KB
Manage Retail Bank Account		200/hr	Peaks at lunch hour	15 minutes	1,600/ day	4KB

continues

Table 7–2: *ATM Business Process Metrics (Continued)*

Business Process	Variant	Peak Execution Rate	Variation in Peak Rate over Time	Allowed Completion Time	Average Sustained Rate	Volume of Data Moved per Execution
Issue ATM Card	Via Bank Branch	100/hour	Peaks at lunch hour	5 minutes	800/day	1KB
	Via Mail	10,000/day	Peaks during first month of rollout	8 hours	10,000/day	1KB
Issue PIN	Via Bank Branch	100/hour	Peaks at lunch hour	1 minute	800/day	1KB
	Via Mail	1,500/day	Mid-morning and mid-afternoon	8 hours	1,500/day	1KB
Manage ATM System		TBD	TBD	TBD	TBD	TBD
Install ATM		1 every 4 hours	Peak during first few weeks of rollout	4 hours	2/month	1.5MB
Service ATM		5/minute	Uniform during working day, gap at lunch	2 minutes	333/day	20KB

of the project, for it will take time to get accurate answers. Ultimately, inaccurate answers will result in under- or over-investment in capacity.

You may not get metrics (or at least accurate ones) for the infrequently executed processes. The less often a process runs, the less likely statistics are gathered for it. That is not a problem. Unless the infrequent process uses an extraordinary volume of data (like a slice-and-dice analysis of data in a data warehouse), it will not demand significant system resources and therefore will not be a factor in your capacity estimates. For these processes you don't care about the actual rate as long as you know that it is low! However, when large volumes of data are involved, then you do need to press the business for some rate numbers and, at the same time, make them aware that their answer will directly impact investment.

For business processes that are already in existence, it is tempting to go immediately to the systems that support these business processes and begin to extract rate information. While this is not a bad place to start, it does not provide the complete picture you need. You must know whether the data is truly representative of peak periods. Furthermore, the measured data will not tell you what to expect in the future, especially when there are mergers and acquisitions afoot. For this understanding, you must go to the business side of the house and ask for future projections. These projections need to include both organic growth and step changes (like acquiring your biggest competitor). It will also help the business people to understand why you are asking these questions. You need to make it clear that the questions are not really about the numbers. They are a means of determining the level of capacity investment that needs to be made.

Ranking Business Processes

Once you have created your initial business process inventory, you need to start diving into their details, understanding their individual requirements, and architecting both the processes and the systems that will support them. To make this exercise efficient, you want to first explore those business processes whose implementations are expected to be the most difficult. To do this, you need to make an initial assessment of each process in terms of its anticipated implementation difficulty and then rank them accordingly.

This ranking and iteration gives you two benefits. First, because you are examining the most difficult processes first, you get an early identification of infeasible projects—projects whose benefits cannot be achieved within the given cost and schedule guidelines. This gives you an early opportunity to re-scope the project when there are still many alternatives available. Second, you gain system design efficiency. Any architecture that is capable of supporting these difficult business processes will, most likely, be able to accommodate the remaining business processes without an architectural restructuring. It is unlikely that you will have to go back and revisit earlier design decisions when you are addressing later business processes. The ranking and iteration of the TAS methodology improves the efficiency of the overall development process.

To determine the ranking, you need some rudimentary information about these processes in four areas: the peak rate at which each process will execute, the volume of information it uses, the complexity of the interactions between its participants, and the business risks associated with process failure. Each of these areas is an indicator of potential design difficulty. You rank each business process in each category and then create an overall ranking that will determine the order in which they will be explored.

The Ranking Scheme

Process ranking involves two steps. First, you individually score the processes in four categories: peak rate, data size, complexity, and business risk. Then you combine these scores to obtain an overall score for the business process. The overall scores comprise the process ranking.

These rankings are not completely objective—they involve some judgment as to what will truly present a challenge when it comes to business process and system design. However, getting the ranking wrong will not affect the quality of the resulting business process or architecture—it merely affects the efficiency with which you arrive at the end result. The worst-case scenario is that you will consider a process that does not have significant impact on the architecture before a process that does have significant impact, and that when you address the latter process some of the design decisions will force some re-design of the former process. In practice, this rarely happens.

The first scoring, shown in Table 7–3, is driven by the peak rate at which the business process executes. The score reflects the order of magnitude of the rate. Processes that happen at a rate of once a second or less are grouped together with a score of 1—they are not very challenging, at least based on rate alone. Similarly, you group processes that happen 10,000 times a second or more with a score of 5—extremely challenging. Differences in rate above this are irrelevant for ranking purposes—the rank of 5 will push them towards the top of the overall ranking list, which is where you want them.

You next score business processes on data volume, as shown in Table 7–4. What you are after here is a characterization based on the volume

Table 7–3: *Peak Rate Scoring*

Peak Rate/Second	Peak Rate Score
1 or less	1
10	2
100	3
1,000	4
10,000 or over	5

Table 7–4: *Data Size Scoring*

Data Size (Bytes)	Data Size Score
1K or less	1
10K	2
100K	3
1M	4
10M or more	5

of information that is being moved through the business process. For example, an ATM transaction may involve 1 KB of data, and it would get a score of 1. Such data volumes present virtually no challenge by themselves. An online order for books moving through the complete process might accumulate 10KB of data when all of the stock, warehouse, shipping, and billing information is included, and it would get a score of 2. Processes involving large data sets—10MB or more—are grouped together with a score of 5. They will, by definition, be challenging, and this scoring will push them towards the very top of the overall ranking.

The third scoring is based on the anticipated complexity of the overall business process. You make your assessment of complexity based on the type of work that you expect the systems to do, specifically in terms of providing data, triggering processes and activities, monitoring the processes, and managing processes. The resulting rankings are summarized in Table 7–5.

Table 7–5: *Complexity Ranking*

Sources of Data	Source of Activity and Process Triggers	Monitoring of Processes	Management of Processes	Complexity Score
Users	Users	Users	Users	1
Users and Systems	Users	Users	Users	2
N/A	Users and Systems	Users	Users	3
N/A	N/A	Users and Systems	Users	4
N/A	N/A	N/A	Users and Systems	5

If the users are doing everything in the to-be process—providing data, triggering all the work, monitoring the process, and managing the process—the system gets a complexity score of 1. This does not imply that the individual systems are not complex—only that there is little complexity in the interactions between them, which is the focus of your distributed system design. At the other extreme, if systems are involved in managing processes (e.g., process automation or workflow) you assign the highest complexity score—5. If the systems are not managing the process, but are engaged in monitoring the process, the process is assigned the score of 4.

The final scoring reflects the business impact of the process, expressed in terms of what would happen to the enterprise should the process not execute properly (Table 7–6). At one extreme, the consequences of failure are catastrophic. An error in a medical information system, for example, might result in an incorrect dosage for a medication (or an incorrect medication), a mistake whose consequences might cause the loss of the patient's life. Similarly, a mistake in a $20 billion real estate transaction might well result in bankruptcy for the enterprise. Such catastrophic risks warrant a score of 5. As the consequences become less severe, you move down in score. Processes whose failure will cause significant impact on the enterprise's bottom line warrant a 4. Processes whose failure will significantly impact a departmental bottom line, but will only have a small impact on the enterprise bottom

Table 7–6: *Business Impact Scoring*

Risk Category	Impact on Business if Process is Not Successfully Executed	Business Impact Score
None	No measurable impact.	1
Minor	Barely observable impact on the departmental bottom line, no observable impact on the enterprise bottom line.	2
Significant	Significant impact on a departmental bottom line, barely observable impact on the overall enterprise bottom line.	3
Major	The failure of a single execution is survivable, but inability to execute or errors in the process will result in failure to comply with regulations and/or a major impact on the enterprise bottom line.	4
Catastrophic	A single process execution failure can result in unrecoverable business failure and/or physical injury or loss of life.	5

line, warrant a 3. Processes whose failure will only have a small impact on the departmental level and no discernable impact at the enterprise level get a 2. Beyond simply indicating the importance of the business process to the overall success of the enterprise, the business impact score also reflects the level of investment that the enterprise is willing to make to ensure that the business process is robust or that performance goals are achieved.

Combining the Scores

Once you have scored the business processes in each of the four categories, you obtain a combined score by multiplying together the individual rankings. Table 7–7 shows the combined scores for the ATM example. Highest scoring is the `Withdraw Cash Via ATM` process, as you might expect. The ranking reflects the relatively high complexity and business impact ranking. This would be the first business process you would address. Second in the scoring is the installation of the ATM, due to the combination of a large data volume with modest complexity and risk scores. Note that this is not one of the primary business processes that directly contributes to the business goal. This underscores the importance of identifying related business processes in the initial process inventory, as they may turn out to present some of the more difficult design challenges.

Table 7–7: *Summary Business Process Scoring for the ATM Example*

Business Process	Variant	Frequency Score	Data Size Score	Complexity Score	Risk Score	Overall Score
Withdraw Cash	Via Teller	3	1	1	4	12
	Via ATM	3	1	5	4	60
Make Deposit	Via Teller	2	1	1	4	8
	Via ATM	1	1	5	4	20
Transfer Funds	Via Teller	1	1	1	4	4
	Via ATM	1	1	5	4	20
Check Balance	Via Teller	1	1	1	4	4
	Via ATM	2	1	5	4	40
Maintain Retail Bank Account		1	2	1	4	8
Issue ATM Card	Via Bank Branch	1	1	3	4	12
	Via Mail	2	1	5	4	40
Issue PIN	Via Bank Branch	1	1	3	4	12
	Via Mail	1	1	5	4	20
Maintain ATM System		TBD	TBD	TBD	TBD	TBD
Install ATM		1	4	3	4	48
Service ATM		1	3	3	3	27

A wild card in this ranking is the maintenance of the ATM system. Not enough is known about this process at this point to even guess about its characteristics. In addition, what needs to be done in this process depends to a large extent on the resulting ATM system architecture. In such cases you should make a conscious effort to flesh out this process as your architecture emerges. After all, its costs are part of the success equation for the project.

Finally, note once again that mistakes in this ranking (if you can even call them mistakes) in no way affect the quality or capabilities of the business processes and systems you are architecting. You are simply using the ranking as a guide in determining the order in which you will address the business processes and their supporting systems. If you get the ranking "wrong," you might spend time exploring a less-important business process before you address a more challenging process. The worst that could happen is that a business process or architectural change that is needed to accommodate the more challenging process will cause you to do some re-work in the architecture of the less challenging process. Ranking is simply an efficiency issue.

Organizing the Remaining Work

Once you have ranked the business processes, you are ready to begin gathering requirements and developing the architecture. Total Architecture Synthesis (TAS) takes an iterative approach, with each iteration beginning with the selection of the business processes to be addressed and the organization of the stakeholder participation.

Your first iteration is likely to have an exploratory flavor to it as you organize your understanding of the requirements and the various architectures that might satisfy them. To keep the scope of this first iteration tractable, it is a best practice to select a very small number of business processes—often only one—for this iteration. In the ATM example, it would be reasonable to select just the `Withdraw Cash Via ATM` business process for the first iteration. You've already identified the stakeholders, so now you set up interviews with them, either individually or in a group.

When selecting business processes for an iteration, it is good practice to include the variant processes in the same iteration even if their score is significantly lower. The reason for this is that you want to avoid the duplication of functionality (i.e., create services) wherever possible, and variant processes are the most likely candidates for sharing functionality. Therefore, the variant requirements need to be considered when defining the architecture of the more challenging process. In the ATM example, this means that the `Withdraw Cash Via Teller` would also be included in the first iteration.

Your first iteration focuses on identifying the broad range of business process and system architectures that might be suitable for meeting the business process requirements. You determine which of these architectures are feasible from a cost and schedule perspective. You want to end this iteration with at least one viable architecture or the conclusion that the project is not feasible. If you have identified more than one viable architecture, you may want to keep two or perhaps three alternatives in the mix for the next iteration. While the choices between these alternatives may seem arbitrary when considering just the present business processes, the consideration of subsequent business processes will likely make the correct choice clear.

Your second iteration should once again focus on challenges, taking on two or three additional business processes. In the ATM example, the `Install ATM` and the undefined `Maintain ATM System` would be good candidates for this iteration. You have several alternatives for the architecture as candidates at this point, and now you can explore their implications in terms of their installation and maintenance. Once again, your focus is on feasibility and refining the architecture.

In all but the most complex of projects, by the end of your second iteration you should have one solid candidate architecture and a pretty good idea whether your project is feasible. Because you are now largely refining the architecture as opposed to considering architectural alternatives, it is reasonable to consider a larger number of business processes in each subsequent iteration. At this point the selection of business processes to be considered in each iteration is driven less by the business process rankings than by the convenience of organizing the stakeholder discussions. The requirements for the remaining business processes for the ATM example might all be gathered in the third iteration, for example, with the exploration of architecture within the iteration still being driven by the ranking and occurring one business process at a time.

Summary

Defining the scope of a project is a discovery process. You begin with the project goals and a few stakeholders who have an idea which business processes need to be changed to achieve those goals. From this starting point, you work with the stakeholders to characterize the nature of the change that is required, identify related business processes, and identify other stakeholders. Your exploration continues until you have talked with all the stakeholders and are no longer identifying additional business processes and stakeholders. At this point, you have identified the scope of your project.

During the course of your stakeholder interviews you gather enough information to get an idea of the challenges each business process will present. By asking about the rate at which business processes will execute and the volume of data moving through the process, you arrive at a rough understanding of the process's resource demands. By enquiring about the level of process maturity and the degree of automation expected in the process, you arrive at an understanding of the complexity of the process. Finally, by asking about the business consequences arising from a failure to execute the process, you arrive at an understanding of the degree of fault tolerance and high availability the process will require.

The information gathered is used to score each business process on a one-to-five scale in four categories: peak rate, volume of data, complexity, and risk. These scores are then combined to give an overall score for the process. These scores serve to rank the processes in terms of their likelihood of presenting architectural challenges.

The business process ranking is used to organize the remainder of the project in an iterative manner. The highest-ranking processes, those most likely to challenge the architecture (and therefore the project's feasibility), are addressed in the first iteration, which produces a small number of validated candidate architectures. Successive iterations take on additional business processes, down-selecting to a single architecture and refining it to support the additional processes.

Key Scoping Questions

1. What business processes need to be created or altered to achieve the expected project benefits? How can the required alterations be characterized in terms of inputs, results, triggers, and constraints?

2. What other business processes are related to the ones whose creation or alteration is required? These are processes whose results are needed (directly or indirectly) to enable the primary business processes or are consumers of primary business process results.

3. Who are the stakeholders for each process?

4. What are the current and target process maturity levels?

5. What are the key metrics for each process? These include the peak and average execution rates, the variation in peak rate with time, the allowed completion time, and the volume of data that moves through the process.

6. On a scale of 1 to 5, what is the business risk associated with a failure to execute each process?

7. On a scale of 1 to 5, how complex is the design of each process expected to be?

Chapter 8

The Artifice of Requirements

The intent of requirements is to specify the compulsory aspects of a design. The thought is that you first specify what your project's business processes and systems must do, and then you design and implement them. However, merely identifying these business processes and systems reflects a higher-level design. This design differentiates the design elements—the business processes and systems your project will build or modify—from the context in which they reside. It also defines the required interactions between the design elements and their context. Thus the requirements for the design elements are actually reflections of this high-level design. They define the existence of certain design elements and express the constraints on the design of those elements.

If you think about the ATM example, you can't specify an ATM without first defining the banking processes in which it will participate and the manner in which it will participate. That is design! You can't even express the business goal for the project (i.e., a lower cost per transaction) without talking about how the banking transactions participate in the profit and loss picture of the bank. That, too, is design. Even the existence of the bank itself is a reflection of a higher-level design (admittedly, an old one) in which people choose to keep their funds in a bank as opposed to keeping them under a mattress or in a safe at home. Requirements always reflect a higher-level design.

To write requirements, therefore, you must understand the higher-level design. It is this design that defines the design elements involved in your project and the roles they will play with respect to the context. The process of writing requirements is one of understanding the higher-level design and then understanding the constraints that this design places on the design elements that are the focus of your project.

The purpose of every project is to affect changes to the higher-level design. After all, if you can't see the effect of the changes, what is the point of the project? The project goals express the desired impact on that overall design. In a perfect world, the so-called requirements define the minimal changes to that overall design that are needed to achieve those goals. In the real world, the requirements more often reflect people's perceptions of the changes that will be required. You and your stakeholders must satisfy yourselves that these changes will, indeed, achieve the project's goals. In the ATM example, the project's goal is to reduce the cost of routine banking operations. The larger design characterizes the banking operations in terms of operational cash flow and the interactions between the bank and its customers. The design change is not just to replace human tellers with automated machines, but to do so in a manner that reduces the operating cost from $3 per transaction to less than $1 per transaction.

Requirements are design constraints. If those constraints completely characterize the relationships between the design elements and their context, they become the specifications for those design elements. But if these relationships are only partially characterized, the design elements are not fully specified. Partial specification may just indicate that you have not learned enough about the higher-level design to be able to fully specify the design elements—you have more homework to do. More often, it indicates that the higher-level design is not, in fact, complete.

In the ideal case, the higher-level design is, indeed, complete. Your requirements-gathering process is simply an effort to learn enough about this higher-level design to fully specify the design elements you are responsible for. Unfortunately, real projects are rarely this simple. More often than not, the higher-level design is not complete, and the design decisions your project makes will further change it.

Higher-level design changes arise when changes you make to design elements require corresponding changes in the interactions between these elements and elements of the context. The need for such changes alters the scope of your project, and this poses challenges at both the technical and organizational level. ATMs, for example, require the issuance of ATM cards. While the process for creating the ATM cards is obviously in scope for the project, the issuance of ATM cards will alter the business processes for opening and maintaining bank accounts. It may well be that changes to these processes were not anticipated in the original project concept. Thus, the ensuing design alters the design of the context and may even end up altering the original requirements. Understanding and managing this process is a significant project challenge.

Implementing changes is generally not a one-shot affair. After initial requirements gathering you probably won't design and implement all of the business processes and systems in a single step. Instead, you progress through a series of design refinements. Each refinement adds some structure to the activities, participants, and artifacts of the process being modified. You decide, for example, that the ATM system should consist of a number of ATMs and a central ATM server. In the process of defining this structure, you define the required interactions between the new structural elements. In the ATM design, you define the interactions between the ATMs themselves and the ATM server. These interactions comprise the requirements for these newly differentiated structural elements. This process of adding structural refinements, defining interactions, and defining the requirements for the new structural elements continues until you have defined structural elements that can be directly implemented. The design is complete.

With this evolutionary picture in mind, you can see that requirements are not a starting point—they are a waypoint in an unfolding design process. Requirements simply capture the implications of a larger design for an element of that design. If the requirements cover every aspect of that element's interactions with its context, they comprise a complete specification. If the requirements only partially specify those interactions, then they only provide a partial specification for the element. The remainder of the design has yet to be defined.

Differentiation

The essence of design is a concept that Christopher Alexander refers to as differentiation—making a distinction where previously there was none.[1]

---

1. Christopher Alexander. 1979. *The Timeless Way of Building*. New York: Oxford University Press, pp. 367–373.

Figure 8–1: *External View of the Manage Money Activity*

Think of the process a person goes through in managing his or her money. Taken as a whole and viewed externally, there is not much you can say about this process (Figure 8–1).

Differentiating Activities

However, if you differentiate the process into sub-activities, you have more to work with. You can, for example, differentiate between the activity of managing the cash flow (itself comprising the activities of making and spending money) and the activity of safekeeping the money in a repository (Figure 8–2). Once you differentiate these activities, it then becomes clear that there are interactions between these activities. The acquired money needs to be put into the repository. The money needs to be removed from the repository before it can be spent. Planning for expenditures will probably require checking the current inventory of funds in the repository. Note that there is not, as of yet, any structure to these interactions, that is, no indication of their possible sequences and the rules governing the interactions. That detail will

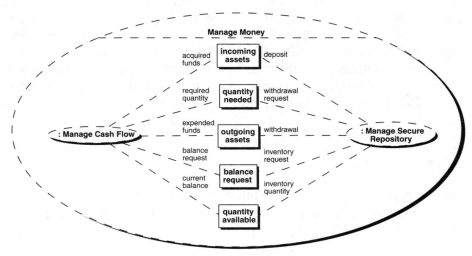

Figure 8–2: *Manage Money with Differentiated Sub-Activities*

come later. The point here is that differentiation exposes interactions, and there are no interactions without differentiation.

This example nominally differentiates two activities, but there are other differentiations present in the artifacts (represented as rectangles) exchanged in the individual interactions. The artifacts being exchanged between the activities are differentiated from one another: Different kinds of requests are distinguished from one another, and from incoming and outgoing assets and reports of available funds. Each of these artifacts plays a different part in the overall `Manage Money` activity, as indicated by the labeling of the artifact. Each of these artifacts in the `Manage Money` activity also plays its own distinct role with respect to each of the sub-activities. In other words, the artifact is also a part of each associated sub-activity. Figure 8–3 shows the artifacts as parts in `Manage Secure Repository`. Note that the part names shown in this figure are the same as the association labels in the previous figure.

The `Manage Secure Repository` activity is itself refined by differentiating between its sub-activities and the artifacts involved in their interactions. You'll notice that this example has one part, the `repository agent`, which plays an active role in the activity as a whole and in its sub-activities. From this you can see that parts being played in an activity may be either passive or active in nature. However, the UML

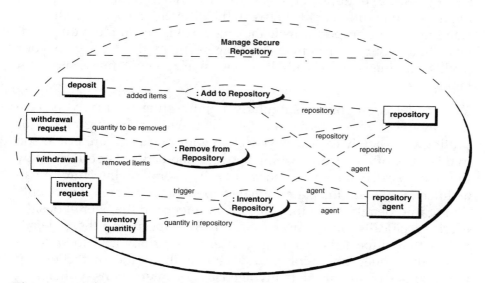

Figure 8–3: *Managing a Secure Repository*

collaboration notation does not distinguish between active and passive parts. This is because the same participant can play a passive part with respect to one activity and an active role with respect to another. For example, consider walking into a bank and deciding which teller to use for your transaction. In the activity of choosing which bank teller to approach, the teller plays a passive role, whereas in the subsequent banking transaction the chosen teller is an active participant.

Differentiating Participants

Differentiating between parts is a major focus of architecture. You are identifying the different kinds of passive artifacts and active participants involved in a process. In systems design, you are proposing new system components and services (i.e., active participants) and defining their roles with respect to activities. At the end of the day, you are seeking to define all the participants in a process and the activities that each is performing. These responsibility assignments determine the required interactions between the participants just as the required interactions between the assigned activities define the required interactions between the corresponding participants. All of this is differentiation at work.

Going back to the `Manage Money` activity, the example thus far has not said anything about the performers of the `Manage Cash Flow` and `Manage Secure Repository` activities. Making such a statement requires you to differentiate between the different ways in which these activities might be performed. Picking a trivial example, you might talk about your own personal management of the money in your pocket, and then end up with the money management model shown in Figure 8–4.

This model is, of course, singularly uninteresting because you have now modeled your internal mental dialog while spending money or putting your newly cashed paycheck in your pocket. There is a lesson in this. Very often, distinguishing between sub-activities performed by the same participant is unimportant to the overall architecture. As an architect, you want to be a minimalist about such differentiation, only diving into details when they make a difference to the overall design. More specifically, you want to refrain from specifying these details unless they impact the externally observable behavior of the participant—the sequencing of interactions, the timing of the interactions, or the qualities of the artifacts involved in the interactions. Otherwise,

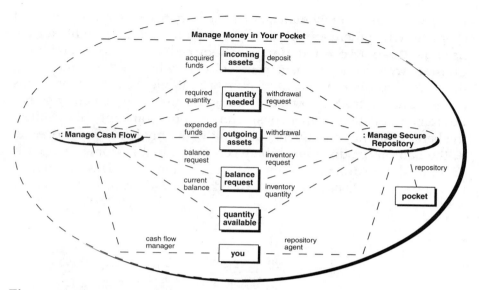

Figure 8–4: *Managing Money in Your Pocket*

leave the details to the designer of that system service or component, or to the individual participant if this is a person.

On the other hand, if you identify a single activity that has two or more active participants, it is important to further differentiate the activities being performed by the individual participants. Without such differentiation, you cannot specify the responsibilities of the participants. If one participant is the system being designed and the other is a system user, this differentiation defines what the system does and what the user does. The activity differentiation leads to the identification of the interactions between the activities, and hence between the participants. You need to understand what these interactions are before you can evaluate their reasonableness.

Design Is Differentiation

Differentiation—some would call it decomposition—is not unique. There are many possible ways the collaboration can be split into sub-activities, and many possible differentiations between parts and participants. Each alternative decomposition results in a different pattern of interactions between the sub-activities and between participants. Evaluating the alternatives and selecting a particular decomposition is design.

For example, the money management activity takes on a very different character when there are different participants acting as agents for the **Manage Cash Flow** and **Manage Secure Repository** activities. Consider what money management looks like when the party managing the secure repository is a bank (Figure 8–5). While the basic interactions of the **Manage Cash Flow** and **Manage Secure Repository** activities remain unaltered, other considerations now come into play. Unless the bank customer has a personal bank with only his or her money in it, the bank must distinguish between individual customer accounts. From this, the **Identify Account** activity emerges. This differentiation of participants has created the need for new kinds of activities.

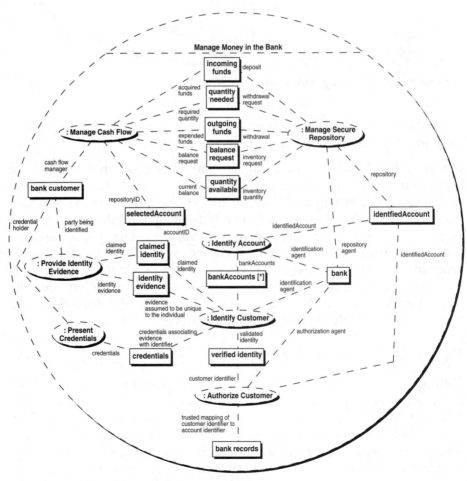

Figure 8–5: *Managing Money in the Bank*

Along these lines, the `Identify Account` activity is required so that the customer can identify the account to be accessed and for the bank to determine which of its accounts the customer has nominated for the transaction. The element of trust (or distrust) also enters into the picture. It also becomes necessary for the bank to determine whether the person walking into the bank is actually the person he or she claims to be, and to further verify that the person is allowed to access the account in question. This raises the need for the `Identify Customer` and `Authorize Customer` activities. The need for all these activities is a direct consequence of differentiating between the two parties—the customer and the bank. Differentiation drives design.

There are many additional activities—entire business processes—that result from the differentiation between the bank and its customers. Accounts must be opened and closed. Customers must be added to or removed from existing accounts. There needs to be a process for reconciling the bank's records of the account with the customer's record of the account. There must also be a process for resolving disputes between the customer and the bank. Exploring these activities identifies additional artifacts such as transaction receipts, monthly statements, and internal bank audit trails. All of this is driven by differentiation.

Characterizing Processes

Functional differentiation begins with the identification of the process to be modified or created. The scope of the process may be large or small depending on the nature of the project, ranging from reengineering an enterprise-scale business process to implementing a new process for moving messages from one system to another.

Each process is actually a behavior. Viewed from outside the process, this behavior comprises all the interactions between this process and other processes (Figure 8–6). This is the functional context for the process. Half of your responsibility as an architect is to make sure that behavior is well defined—and is the behavior that the business really wants. Viewed from within the process, producing this behavior is a collaborative effort on the part of the participants involved. The other half of your responsibility as an architect is to design this collaboration to ensure that it produces the expected behavior.

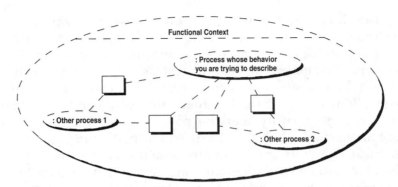

Figure 8–6: *Functional Context*

To define the behavior of a process, you have to describe its interaction with other processes. This collaboration itself comprises a larger process that we will refer to as the functional context. Fortunately, you do not need to define behavior of the functional context (i.e., its interactions with other functional contexts), nor do you need to define the functional context in its entirety. You only need to define the portion of the functional context that relates to the process or processes you are modifying.

Collaborations Represent Processes

In this book, a UML collaboration is used to represent each process. Because each process exhibits behavior, the name of the collaboration provides an identity for that behavior as well. The collaboration might characterize a complete business process, or it might characterize the simple exchange of a message between two parties. Just as importantly, it can characterize the functional context in which the processes being designed reside.

From a notational perspective, the collaboration is represented by a dashed oval with a dashed horizontal line across it (Figure 8–7). The name of the collaboration goes above the horizontal line. If this strikes you as being similar to the UML use case notation, the similarity is not accidental. Both identify behaviors. (Later in this chapter these similarities will be explored further.)

Figure 8–7: *Basic Collaboration Notation*

Collaboration Roles

UML collaborations enable you to provide more information about the process beyond its name. The collaboration enables you to identify the participants in a collaboration, as shown in Figure 8–8. Each role (called a part in UML) is represented by a rectangle containing the name of the role and/or the type of the participant.

Participants in collaborations may play either active or passive roles in the process. Consider the `Send Message` collaboration of Figure 8–9. Here, `sendingParty`, `receivingParty`, and `messageService` are all active participants in the process, while the message itself and the address are passive artifacts that are used in the process. As mentioned earlier, no notational distinction is made between active and passive participants, because a participant that plays a passive role in one collaboration may play an active role in another. The distinction is merely one of perspective.

Collaborations can be either abstract or concrete depending on whether or not you choose to specify the types of participants involved. The previous `Send Message` example is abstract: It does not specify the types of participants, only their roles. You can make the collaboration more concrete by adding the types of the participants. Figure 8–10, for

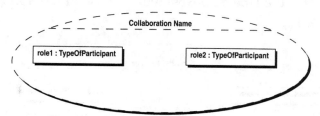

Figure 8–8: *Collaboration Roles*

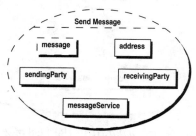

Figure 8–9: *Send Message Collaboration Roles*

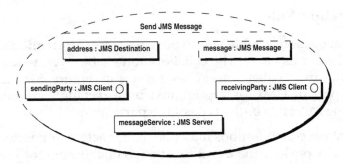

Figure 8–10: *Send JMS Message Collaboration Roles*

example, shows the more concrete `Send JMS Message` process. Specifying the types of the participants specializes the collaboration. It is no longer a generic `Send Message` process, but a more specific `Send JMS Message` process.

Abstract collaborations are useful for defining interaction patterns that can later be employed in concrete collaborations. Assume, for the moment, that the interaction pattern for `Send Message` has been defined (this will actually be done in the next section). You can then reference that pattern in the `Send JMS Message` collaboration as shown in Figure 8–11. The dashed lines connecting the `Send JMS Message` roles (the labeled boxes) with the use of the `Send Message`

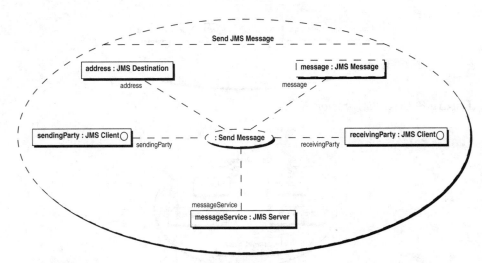

Figure 8–11: *Collaboration Incorporating the Use of Another Collaboration*

collaboration are labeled with the role names from the `Send Message` collaboration. In this particular case, the two sets of role names are redundant. However, in many cases you will find that the roles belonging to the outer collaboration are different than those associated with the collaboration being used.

Participants May Be Unaware of their Roles

One of the challenges you will face in identifying and defining business processes (collaborations) is that many of the participants (or the people that design them in the case of system participants) may be unaware of the larger process. Their view of the process extends only to the interactions they have with other participants, and they may be completely unaware of the larger purpose of these interactions.

This is particularly the case for shared infrastructure services such as a messaging service. From the service's perspective, it delivers messages. From the larger business process perspective, the service delivers orders in one business process and invoices in another. The same service can even play multiple roles within the same business process.

Your challenge then is to understand how the individual participants fit into the larger business processes. The messaging service may be called upon to deliver some small messages quickly and reliably and at the same time deliver other large messages slowly and efficiently. Only when you understand the various roles that each participant is called upon to play will you be able to determine the behaviors that are required to support those roles.

Patterns of Interaction

Once you differentiate activities, you must characterize the required interactions between the activities. But simply identifying the interactions is not enough. You need to describe the required behavior—the possible sequences—of these interactions. It doesn't make sense for a customer to obtain cash from an account before specifying the amount to be withdrawn, nor does it make sense to withdraw cash before any funds have been placed in the account. There are patterns of interactions that make sense, and others that don't. When you differentiate activities, you have to define the interaction patterns that can (and cannot) occur.

Use Case Descriptions

To define interaction patterns, you need a way to represent them. There are a number of techniques that can be used for this purpose. One well-established approach is the textual narrative of a use case description.[2] Use cases describe the pattern of interactions between a system user and the system itself while attempting to achieve a particular goal. The use case itself represents the overall interaction pattern, and the text describes the various scenarios that can occur under different conditions. Each scenario is an example of a possible interaction sequence that occurs under a specific set of conditions. The remaining information in the use case describes the constraints on these interactions. These constraints may include the timing of events, the rates at which events can occur, and the conditions under which particular scenarios will occur. They also characterize the artifacts that are exchanged during the scenario.

Use Case Limitations

While the use case approach can be generalized to discuss any interactions between any participants, they have several disadvantages. Their major drawback is that textual representations of interactions require a fair amount of study in order to attain an overall understanding of the interaction pattern, particularly if the pattern is complex. It requires an even greater effort to assess the completeness and correctness of the pattern's description. This level of effort presents a problem. The primary reason for documenting the interaction pattern is to ensure that it is complete and correct—prior to investing in implementing the pattern. To ensure completeness and correctness, the stakeholders need to review and understand the descriptions, and the effort involved presents a barrier.

Compounding these use case difficulties are the ambiguities associated with the use of human language. These ambiguities can render the understanding of a textual description somewhat dependent on the interpretation of the reader. Two different readers may arrive at two different perceptions after reading the same written description. Even worse, it may not be apparent that different people are interpreting things differently. This makes it even harder to reach consensus about the completeness and correctness of the interaction patterns.

---

2. An excellent reference on this approach is Alistair Cockburn's *Writing Effective Use Cases*. Boston, MA: Addison-Wesley (2001).

UML Activity Diagrams

The graphical languages of UML provide an alternative to human languages for capturing and representing design information. The UML notations have the advantage of being precise, thus avoiding the ambiguities of human language. The notations are easy to learn and, once understood, their graphical form makes it easy to quickly grasp what is being represented.

Up to this point, UML collaborations have been used as a means of identifying business processes and their differentiation into their constituent parts. Using this notation, Figure 8–12 characterizes the Withdraw Cash via Teller business process based on the earlier Manage Money example. In this collaboration you can see the roles being played by the customer and the bank along with a number of artifacts that are involved in the transaction. But this representation does not describe the possible sequences of activities and interactions.

The UML activity notation provides a precise graphical mechanism for describing participant responsibilities and interactions (Figure 8–13). The swimlanes (vertical or horizontal lanes in the activity diagram) represent the active participants in the collaboration. Activities (rounded rectangles) placed in the swimlanes represent responsibility assignments for the participants. Objects (rectangles) represent artifacts that are exchanged between activities and hence between participants. Note that the placement of objects in swimlanes has no meaning. It is the object flows (arrows) indicating the source and destination of the objects that are significant.

This particular activity diagram is a bit more concrete than the collaboration it represents, reflecting the results of some further design work. It provides more detail about the bank, differentiating it into a teller and a bank system. In keeping, the bank's activities have been differentiated into teller and bank system activities.

The activity diagram shows other refinements as well. While the collaboration depicts the amount, account identification, and signature as three discrete artifacts, the actual design (as reflected in the activity diagram) aggregates these elements into a single WithdrawalSlip. The information structure of the WithdrawalSlip is shown in the UML class diagram of Figure 8–14 along with some additional detail about the information content of a PhotoID.

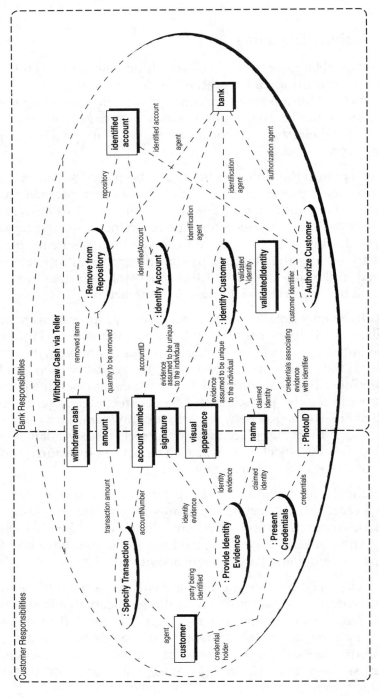

Figure 8–12: *Collaboration Diagram of Withdraw Cash via Teller*

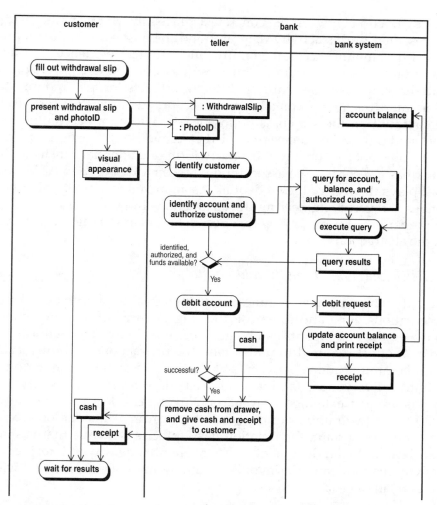

Figure 8–13: *Activity Diagram of Withdraw Cash via Teller—Normal Execution*

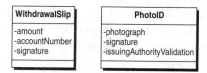

Figure 8–14: *Artifacts for Withdraw Cash via Teller*

The distinction between the concrete artifacts (the `Withdrawal Slip` represented in this activity diagram) and the abstractions they represent (the amount, account identity, and physical evidence) is often important when modifying a business process. The ATM version of withdrawing cash uses entirely different artifacts for the amount (the user enters the amount on a keypad), account identity (the user selects the account on the screen as opposed to providing an account number), and physical evidence (the ATM card and PIN). Furthermore, the ATM does not rely on any third-party form of credentials. Instead, the bank has a record of the association between a PIN and an ATM card that plays the role of the credential. As an architect, one of your challenges is reverse-engineering the abstractions from an existing design in preparation for modifying that design and maintaining the integrity of the abstractions.

Activity Diagram Strengths and Limitations

Activity diagrams have significant advantages over purely textual representations. First and foremost, the "big picture" of the interactions between the participants can be grasped at a glance. This reduces the level of effort required to understand the interactions and thus facilitates communications between stakeholders. Second, the notation is intuitive. Everyone is familiar with basic flowcharts, and activity diagrams are just extended flowcharts. Anyone can learn to read them with just a few minutes of explanation regarding the notation. Third, and most important, the notation has a precise semantic that is standardized and well documented. There is only one way to interpret an activity diagram, and this avoids the ambiguity issues associated with human languages.

The use of UML activity diagrams facilitates the discovery of related processes as well. By identifying all the inputs and results of activities, you are led to consider where those inputs came from and where the results go. In the case of the example, the `PhotoID`, the `cash` in the teller's drawer, and initial `account balance` have to come from somewhere. These are all clues about the interactions between this process and other processes—interactions that are easy to overlook early in the design process.

Activity diagrams also clarify when activities are performed, what their triggering events are, and the circumstances under which those triggering events can occur. This type of characterization is particularly important when you are trying to understand how activity in the "real world" is going to impact the system you are designing. Understanding that a particular user action will trigger the execution of a process will lead you to enquire about the real-world circumstances that will lead the user to take that action, and thus give you a better understanding of the rate at which those actions might occur.

However, UML activity diagrams are not a panacea. To begin with, they are not complete representations. While they characterize the big picture of interactions very precisely, they do not fully specify all of the details of the artifacts being exchanged. For this they require augmentation in the form of UML class diagrams. While the activity diagram can identify the type (class) of the artifact and the role it plays in the process, the definition of that class requires a class diagram.

You have to pay some attention to complexity as well when creating UML activity diagrams. While the notation is rich enough to represent all of the possible interaction variations in a single diagram, doing so can result in a diagram that is complex and hard to understand. This is a situation you should try to avoid. Avoiding this complexity begins with recognizing that interaction patterns vary depending upon circumstances. Instead of creating one large diagram, create a series of diagrams, each showing what happens under a particular set of circumstances. The activity diagram of Figure 8–13, for example, shows withdrawing cash under normal circumstances. If the pattern of interaction is significantly different under different circumstances, create a separate activity diagram showing what happens under those circumstances. With this approach, each diagram tells a specific story of what happens under a specific set of circumstances. This makes them easy to understand.

The Interface Perspective

Collaborations and activity diagrams present a broad top-down view of the participants in a process and the interactions among them. But there is another perspective you can take on these interactions—an interface perspective. You arrive at this perspective by defining a boundary between participants and then looking at the interactions from the perspective of the participants on one side of this boundary. From this perspective you see the interfaces of the participants on the other side of the boundary.

Figure 8–12 shows such a boundary in the division between customer responsibilities and bank responsibilities. You can see the same division in Figure 8–13 in the boundary between the `Customer` swimlane and the `Bank` swimlane. From the customer's perspective, it is clear that the bank has an interface (provided by the teller) that accepts a `Withdrawal Slip`, `Photo ID`, and `visual appearance`, and then returns `cash` and a `receipt` (Figure 8–15).

In describing participants, system components in particular, interface descriptions are often employed as a means of abstraction. The intent is to separate the externally observable behavior (the interactions defined by the interfaces) from the details of what goes on behind the scenes of those interfaces.

The intent of interface abstraction is noble, but the reality is that interfaces, individually, are rarely sufficient to fully characterize observable behavior. In most significant components (services in particular), there is internal state within the component that is implicitly or explicitly observable through the interfaces. That state is as much a part of the observable behavior as the interfaces.

The account balance is an example of this kind of state. If a bank customer attempts to withdraw more cash than is available in the current balance, the transaction will fail. You can't explain this failure without referring to this internal state information. Thus an understanding of the bank's observable behavior (from the customer's perspective) requires an understanding of the relevant internal state as well as the available interfaces.

The interface perspective also contains an implicit assumption: The participant providing the interfaces is passive, and all interactions with that participant are initiated by invoking one of these interfaces. While this may have been an acceptable assumption for systems of the past, it is in no way representative of the business processes and systems driving today's enterprise. The bank customer may take the initiative in obtaining a replacement ATM card, for example, but if the bank changes the design of the ATM cards it may choose to preemptively send replacement ATM cards to customers. It is no longer safe to assume that the service provider is passive.

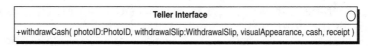

Figure 8–15: *Teller Interface*

Interaction Patterns Characterize Participants

The interaction patterns that a participant will engage in provide a complete external view of that participant. For completeness, these patterns must capture all possible sequences of interactions under all possible circumstances. They must also capture what a participant will *not* do as well—the order that can't be cancelled because it has already shipped, and the withdrawal that cannot take place because there are insufficient funds in the bank account. The patterns must also capture the interactions that are initiated by the participant as well as those that are initiated by other participants.

There is a branch of mathematics that can be applied to characterizing interactions called process algebras.[3] However, representation of interactions at this level of detail is complex and is generally used only for proving the correctness of communications protocols and parallel processing algorithms.

As a practical matter, interactions are usually presented by example. Such representations generally begin with the characterization of a "typical" scenario. Variations on this scenario are then developed, each representing a significant deviation from the typical scenario that occurs under a particular set of circumstances. The challenge you will face as an architect is to ensure that all of the meaningful variations have, indeed, been identified and captured.

Your reliance on interaction examples, however, does not mean that you have to abandon precision. The reason that the UML notations in this book are useful is that they have two important characteristics: They are both intuitive and precise. Once you are familiar with the notation, it is easy to grasp the meaning of a diagram employing the notation. Your intuition upon looking at the diagram will guide you to the correct interpretation. At the same time, the notation is precise. Every aspect of the UML notation corresponds to some statement about either the composition (or decomposition) of components or the interactions between those components. Each of these aspects and their relationships with one another can be uniformly expressed in terms of process algebras.[4] In fact, it is theoretically possible to

---

3. Brown, Paul C. 1993. "Constructive Semantics." In *NAPAW92: Proceedings of the First North American Process Algebra Workshop.* Stony Brook, New York. August 28, 1992. New York: Springer-Verlag.

4. Ibid.

automatically generate a process algebra representation from a UML model.

What does this have to do with your day-to-day work as an architect? It means that the statements you make using UML notation for the most part have one and only one possible interpretation. Unlike written text, there is little possibility of ambiguity. Other people working from your diagrams are much more likely to interpret them in the manner that you intended. UML notations thus provide a powerful, clear, and unambiguous communications vehicle for you to use in your work.

Requirements Reflect Design

When you are working on a project, the elements being modified by your project must fit in and interact with other elements in the context. Whether your project's elements are processes, participants, or artifacts, these interactions are part of some larger design, the design of the context. The requirements for the elements you are modifying are simply reflections of the larger design. The only difference is that you, yourself, did not create that larger design. You are simply bound by its constraints.

The scope of the context will vary from project to project. The ATM example represents a major change to a bank, adding an entirely new channel for customers to conduct their business. The context here is the overall operation of the bank, including all factors that drive its profit-and-loss position. A smaller-scale project might accommodate a new ATM machine design or add a new transaction type. The context here comprises just the business processes in which the ATM participates. An even smaller project might change some of the underlying implementation technology and leave the business process unaltered. The context here comprises the processes altered by the technology change. But regardless of the scope, the project's requirements reflect a design that exists (or is supposed to exist) at a scale larger than the project itself.

Requirements Specify Interaction Patterns

Every form of requirement is a statement about interactions. Requirements can specify particular interactions that are (or are not) allowed.

The circumstances under which interactions are allowed can be expressed either indirectly in terms of prior sequences of interactions or directly in terms of internal state that is the result of those prior sequences of interactions. Inputs and outputs are simply the artifacts that are exchanged during the interactions. Timing requirements reflect time intervals between different interactions. Quality requirements reflect the interactions you can have with the artifacts that are exchanged during interactions. Profitability reflects the relationship between the interactions in which money is spent and the interactions in which money is acquired.

The design of the context, expressed in UML collaboration, activity, and class diagrams, provides a consistent and unifying framework for expressing and understanding requirements. It is this design that actually determines the requirements. Requirements are reflections of constraints imposed by this design. Some of these constraints are existential in nature—they require the presence of certain activities, artifacts, or participants. Simply expressing the design in UML notation records the required presence of these elements.

Other constraints are qualitative in nature. These express such things as the rate at which an input arrives or a result is produced. They can constrain the duration between events, such as the time interval between the arrival of an input and the production of a result. They can constrain the quality of an artifact that is an input or output. Note that for both clarity and precision, qualitative constraints must actually be expressed in quantifiable terms.

In many cases, qualitative constraints can, themselves, be directly expressed in UML. But in all cases, the element of the design is the thing being constrained, and the UML documentation of this element and its interactions makes the expression of the constraint simple and straightforward.

For this reason, rather than focusing on requirements, this book focuses on the expression of designs and design constraints. It uses the same UML techniques for representing designs at any level of detail, from the context surrounding the highest level of business processes down to the details of bits and bytes moving across a network. These same techniques can be used to describe both the requirements (the existing design) and the development (the new design). This uniformity renders irrelevant the specific level of detail of a given project. You start at whatever level of detail is appropriate to establish the project's context (i.e., its requirements) and work your way down to the solution.

Requirements Are Rarely Complete

The design constraints that constitute the project's requirements rarely provide a complete characterization of the activities, participants, and artifacts that are involved. If they did, you would call them specifications instead of requirements. The consequence is that during the course of the project, completing the design will result in changes that are observable to the rest of the context. These changes may well require changes to the context that were not initially thought of as being within the scope of the project. Be on the lookout for this. It is a major source of scope creep.

The ATM cards in the ATM example are a good case in point. Going back to the basics of the ATM example, the goal of the project is to reduce the per-transaction cost from $3 per transaction to less than $1 per transaction. If you had never seen an ATM system, your initial statement of requirements would probably focus on replacing the human teller with an automated system as a means of reducing costs. You would specify the banking transactions to be provided by the system, and you would require account identification, customer identification, and customer authorization activities as part of those transactions. However, from a requirements perspective, it is unlikely that the concept of an ATM card itself would be part of the requirements. It is an artifact of design.

In fulfilling the ATM requirements, the design team would likely conclude very quickly that the current techniques for account identification, customer identification, and customer authorization are not practical for an automated system. With currently available technology (at least at the time ATMs were first conceived), the task of evaluating signatures and comparing the customer's actual appearance against a prerecorded image are impractical. Other approaches to the identification and authorization tasks are required.

The concept of the ATM card is a solution for customer identification. The combination of the physical card and the PIN (a secret supposedly known only by the legitimate card holder) serves to identify the customer. The activity of account identification then becomes a process that first associates the ATM card with certain accounts (at the time the card is issued) and then offers the customer a choice of those accounts on the ATM screen. This association of the ATM card with accounts also provides a solution to the authorization problem.

The decision to use ATM cards, however, has far-reaching implications that extend well beyond simply replacing a human teller with a machine in the banking transactions. ATM cards need to be manufactured or purchased. They need to be issued to bank customers and associated with bank accounts in the bank's systems. Procedures for issuing and changing PIN numbers need to be established, and the corresponding system changes need to be implemented. Procedures for handling lost ATM cards need to be established as well, again with corresponding system changes. All of these changes impact business processes other than the simple banking transactions the ATM is designed to handle.

Projects can introduce changes that have scope extending beyond the project's perceived boundaries. This is another reason why you want to understand and document the larger collaborations in which your project's elements play a role. Initially, this serves to help you, the architect, evaluate the reasonableness of the changes you are proposing. But beyond that point you need to seek understanding and approval of these changes from those responsible for the rest of the context. Towards this end, the at-a-glance readability of well-conceived UML diagrams (once people have become familiar with them) will greatly facilitate this communication.

Summary

Requirements are conditions that a planned process or system must satisfy. Abstractly, these conditions are design constraints that reflect the expected collaboration between the planned processes and systems and their context—the rest of the enterprise, its partners, and its customers. These collaborations are actually the enterprise's business processes, and understanding the requirements requires an understanding of these business processes.

A collaboration comprises the cooperative interactions between a group of participants collectively seeking to achieve a particular goal. The collaboration, as a whole, represents this collective activity. The structure within the collaboration—the identification of the activities, participants, and artifacts involved in the collaboration—is defined through the process of differentiation.

Differentiation is simply the act of making a distinction where previously there was none. You differentiate the act of managing money into the activities of managing cash flow and managing the secure repository of cash. You differentiate between the party managing the cash flow and the party managing the cash repository.

Differentiation involves more than simply distinguishing among the various activities and participants. To achieve the goals of the overall collaboration, the distinguished elements must interact with one another. Characterizing these interactions requires further differentiation of the artifacts that are exchanged in the interactions.

Differentiation is, in fact, design. There are many different ways in which activities, participants, and artifacts might be differentiated. Choosing a particular differentiation is a design decision. Choosing the particular pattern of interactions between the activities and participants is also a design decision. In fact, architecture can be viewed as a shell game in which the "shells" are the participants and the "peas" are the activities that are assigned to the participants. If two activities interact, their assignment to different participants creates a need for those participants to interact. The architect's task is to find a reasonable arrangement of participants and activity assignments.

Patterns of interaction are descriptions of observable behavior. Patterns can thus be used to specify behavior. Such behavioral descriptions comprise a significant part of what are conventionally referred to as requirements. However, it is important to recognize that these behavioral descriptions are the result of differentiations—design decisions. Fully understanding these behaviors requires an understanding of the design that gave rise to the interaction pattern.

Use cases and use case descriptions have traditionally been used to define and detail user-system collaborations. Characterizing business processes and large-scale systems architectures requires describing large-scale collaborations. Collectively, the UML collaboration, activity, and class notations provide a rich and effective means for describing these collaborations, capturing the structure of the business processes and its component activities, participants, and artifacts. These notations are easy to learn and, once understood, provide a highly effective mechanism for conveying an understanding of business process and system designs.

While requirements are the starting point for a project, their origin is always some larger design of which the project's elements are but a part. This larger design is the context for the project. Requirements are statements about the constraints that this larger design imposes on the project's elements. Fully understanding these requirements requires an understanding of this larger design—the manner in which the project's elements are expected to collaborate with other elements of the context.

The concept of requirements makes a tacit assumption that the design decisions made within the project will not impact elements outside the project. This is rarely the case in practice. Design decisions frequently impact other elements of the context. In such cases, the impact of design decisions on the larger design must be communicated, reviewed, and approved as part of the project efforts.

Understanding requirements and communicating the impact of design decisions both require an understanding of the larger design. Because of this, documenting the relevant aspects of the larger design is the right starting point for a project. Documenting this design makes clear the role that the project's elements are intended to play in the context and provides a framework for understanding the refinements to this context that are supposed to be created by the project. This approach can be uniformly applied regardless of their scope of the project—from massive business process reengineering efforts to tiny rewrite-this-algorithm code changes.

Key Requirements Questions

1. The requirements you have been given are the consequence of some larger design that forms the context for the project. What is this design?

   - What collaborations (business processes) are involved?
   - How are those collaborations differentiated into individual activities?
   - What interactions must occur between the activities?
   - What participants are involved? Which already exist in their final form, and which are the elements you are supposed to design or modify as part of your project?
   - What are the activity responsibility assignments of the participants?

- What participant interactions are implied by the activity assignments?

2. How would you restate the requirements as constraints on this design?

3. Requirements often define the expected behavior of the elements you are building as part of your project in terms of how they will interact with other participants. What are the interaction patterns that are implied by the requirements?

4. Behavioral descriptions in requirements are often incomplete. What portions of the interaction patterns have been left unspecified? Will the completion of these interaction patterns require changes that are perceived to be outside the scope of your project?

5. Interactions between the elements you are designing and the rest of the enterprise involve artifacts, including both information and physical objects. Are these artifacts defined in the requirements? If not, will the subsequent definition of these artifacts require changes that are perceived to be outside the scope of your project?

Suggested Reading

Christopher Alexander. 1979. *The Timeless Way of Building*. New York: Oxford University Press.

Alistair Cockburn. 2001. *Writing Effective Use Cases*. Boston: Addison-Wesley.

Chapter 9

Business Process Architecture

Business processes, like systems, have physical structure, functional organization, and a collaborative behavior that strives to achieve specific goals. In other words, business processes have architecture. The components of a business process architecture (henceforth referred to as *participants*) are the people and systems involved in the business processes. The participants have physical structure, which we tend to think of in terms of both organizational structure and physical location. The participants are functionally organized, each having specific functional responsibilities. In addition, the participants collaborate to produce the business process's expected results.

Depending upon how your project is organized, you may or may not be personally responsible for defining the business process. No matter. Whether or not you are actually designing the business process, you must understand its architecture to appropriately architect the supporting information systems. Part of this responsibility is to determine whether the business process architecture definition is complete. And what better way to assess the completeness of an architecture than to document it. Whether you are actually designing the business process yourself or merely evaluating a design that has been given to you, the techniques that follow are designed to ensure that you have a complete specification of the business process architecture.

What you will not find in the following sections is a methodology for designing business processes. Establishing a dialog between groups of people for the purpose of designing business processes is a topic unto itself and is beyond the scope of this book. If you wish to learn more about this topic, I refer you to Sharp and McDermott's *Workflow Modeling: Tools for Process Improvement and Application Development*[1] and Paul Harmon's *Process Change: A Manager's Guide to Improving, Redesigning, and Automating Processes.*[2]

Results

Business processes, by their nature, are courses of action designed to be repeatedly and consistently executed to deliver specific results. These results must, in some sense, be measurable or quantifiable, for it is only through such measurement that you can determine whether the process successfully reached completion. Most business processes produce discrete, countable results such as the cash from an ATM or the packaged goods from a store. Other processes produce results that, while not discrete, are still quantifiable. The gasoline you purchase for your car and the electricity and water you purchase for your home are common examples.

Understanding any business process begins with knowing the results it is supposed to generate. Figure 9–1 shows the multiple results produced by the `Withdraw Cash via ATM` process. As with this process, many business processes produce multiple results. To understand what constitutes the successful completion of the process, you need to make sure that you have captured all of the process's results.

In the `Withdraw Cash via ATM` example, delivering cash without updating the account balance, or vice versa, is a failure condition for the business process. Unless you understand all of the expected results, you will not be able to identify this type of failure. Consequently, you will not be in a position to even ask how this type of failure can be detected, let alone consider which participants might be in a

---

1. Alec Sharp and Patrick McDermott. 2001. *Workflow Modeling: Tools for Process Improvement and Application Development*. Norwood, MA: Artech House, Inc.

2. Paul Harmon. 2003. *Business Process Change: A Manager's Guide to Improving, Redesigning, and Automating Processes*. San Francisco, CA: Morgan Kaufmann.

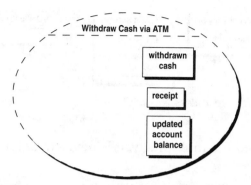

Figure 9–1: *Business Process Results for the Withdraw Cash via ATM Business Process*

position to observe the failure and what actions should be taken as a result. Since your business process must operate in the real world, the detection and handling of breakdowns has to be as much a part of the business process design as the sunny-day scenario.

Beyond simply identifying the results, you need some understanding of their types and quantities. Figure 9–2 shows the Withdraw Cash via ATM result augmented with this information.

The syntax for the information in the collaboration part rectangle is:

```
roleName : Type [multiplicity]
```

Generally, when the multiplicity is one, by convention the multiplicity expression is omitted. If you are concerned at all that there might be

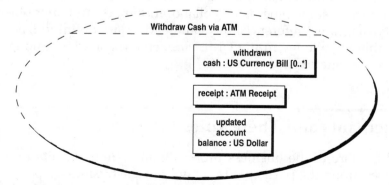

Figure 9–2: *Quantified and Typed Business Process Results*

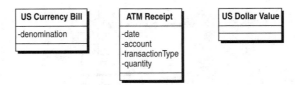

Figure 9–3: *Business Process Result Types*

ambiguity around the multiplicity, it is never wrong to explicitly state the multiplicity.

Each `Type` is actually a reference to a UML class, which gives you the opportunity to provide more detail about the type (Figure 9–3). Resist the temptation to be drawn into design details here. Ask yourself what is important in the business process and focus on that. Your primary task is to determine the nature of the artifact. You should only specify the details that are relevant to the participation of the result in the business process. The exact representation of a `US Dollar Value` is not relevant at this point—only the fact that the balance will be maintained in US dollars. The fact that the ATM will dispense US currency is relevant, and perhaps even the denominations that will be dispensed, but you don't care that bills have serial numbers and watermarks. Leave the details for the specification stage or later.

You should recognize also that the results of this process are inputs to other processes. In terms of requirements, what is relevant and important about these results will be determined by the role that these results play in those other processes. Thus, a full understanding of results requires investigating each business process that employs them. This accumulated understanding is added to the UML class defining the results. Since each collaboration part (and later objects in activity diagrams) references the same UML class definition, accumulating this knowledge in the UML class enables sharing among all of these representations.

Participants and Their Roles

There is more to the business process than results. Results produced are based upon the participants' activity in the business process. Thus the architecture of the business process must include the identification of the participants in that process (Figure 9–4). Note that the partici-

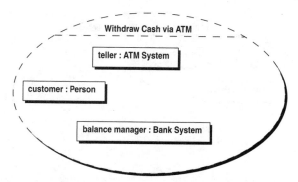

Figure 9–4: *Participants and Their Roles in the Withdraw Cash via ATM Business Process*

pants are identified in the same manner as the results, indicating both the role and the type of the participant.

Distinguishing between the role and the type of participant may seem a bit artificial at first, particularly in the early stages of conceptualizing a business process. However, the distinction is important. As business processes evolve, the role may stay the same, but the type of participant may change. This example illustrates exactly this point: In the old business process, the role of `teller` is played by a `Person`. In the new business process, the role of the `teller` is played by an `ATM System`. Although the type of participant has changed, the role remains much the same.

Differentiating Participant Types and Roles

Another reason for maintaining the distinction between role and the type of participant is that the same type of participant might play different roles, either in the same business processes or different business processes. Consider the `Withdraw Cash via Human Teller` example of Figure 9–5. In this variation of the business process, both the `teller` and `customer` roles are played by participants of type `Person`. A single person might even play both roles!

Understanding that the same type of participant might possibly play multiple roles, either in the same or different business processes, can be very important. In the previous banking scenario, understanding that the same person might play both the role of `customer` and `teller` provides insight into a potential source of fraud. Documenting

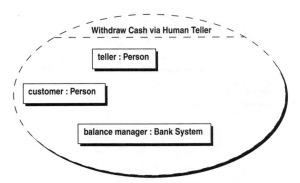

Figure 9–5: *Participants and Their Roles in the Withdraw Cash via Human Teller Process*

the participant type highlights this possibility, and thus promotes awareness. To avoid such fraud, banks usually have business rules prohibiting the same person from playing both roles.

Consider now the implications of requiring this rule to be enforced by a system. Enforcing the rule obviously requires (a) knowing the identities of both of the participants and (b) being able to correlate a customer identity with a teller identity. Beyond the information needed to support the rule, there are business process implications as well. Some participant must be responsible for enforcing the rule, and this activity itself must become part of the business process. The basic identify information itself must, in turn, have originated in other business processes (e.g., Add Customer or Add Teller). To be able to recognize that both participants happen to be the same individual, there must be a mapping between teller identifiers and customer identifiers (or they must be the same identifier). Accomplishing this may require changes to the bank's Add Customer and Add Teller processes. One of the goals of your business process modeling effort is to identify requirements like this while the business process is still in its formative stages. This will allow the supporting design changes to be incorporated in a cost-effective manner.

Aside from facilitating an understanding that an individual can play multiple roles in a business process, separating the concept of role from the concept of participant type gives you a richer understanding of the business process itself. The existence of a participant type makes it clear that you can have groups of people (or even groups of system components, for that matter) who are all capable of playing the same role. You generally don't find a single bank teller in a bank; instead, you have a staff of bank tellers, any one of whom can play this role. The same is true of ATMs.

Roles Often Require Role-Specific Activities

The role may determine a subset of participants or the specified type of participants who are allowed to play that role. Only people who have accounts at the bank are allowed to play the role of `customer`. Similarly, only bank employees with the appropriate permissions are allowed to play the role of `teller`. You can even have different categories of people who are allowed to play the same role. When the bank is busy, a branch manager may chip in and play the role of teller. A significant part of many business processes centers around authenticating and authorizing participants (both people and systems) with respect to the roles they are attempting to play. These activities require information—information that originates in other business processes. You want to identify these requirements while the architecture is still fluid and on paper so that the required design changes to both the business processes and systems can be gracefully accommodated.

Roles and Business Process Evolution

When business processes evolve you will often find that what remains constant is the role and what changes is the type of participant who will play the role. Today's human activity becomes tomorrow's system activity. You can see this in the ATM example: The `teller` role that is played by the `Person` in the existing business process will be played by the `ATM System` in the new process. While some of the details of the activities may change, very often the basic structure of the process will remain the same. Because of this, it is often beneficial to model an existing business process both when that process is being modified and when a completely new process with the same business goal is being created.

Identifying and Understanding Roles

Process modeling is an exercise in discovery. When you first model a process, it is unlikely that you will have crisp definitions for both roles and participant types. Consequently, when you begin you simply label the collaboration parts with whatever seems appropriate at the time, whether it is a role name or a participant type. For example, when you first model the existing `Withdraw Cash via Human Teller` process, you are likely to label the balance manager simply "bank." Later you will recognize that the activities being performed by this participant collectively comprise a `balance manager` role, and you will identify that this role is being played by the `Bank System`. Similarly, you are likely to label the other two roles as "customer" and "teller" without consciously differentiating between the role and the type of participant playing the role. After that, you will refine this to reflect that both roles are played by a `Person` (at least in the human teller version)—and potentially the same person! As you refine your process model, bear in mind that by the time you finish you want to have crisp distinctions between role names and participant types, and you want to take every opportunity to clarify this distinction as your design evolves. Toward this end, the use of a well-engineered UML tool will greatly facilitate making such changes. In such tools, changing a name or a type in one place automatically updates all the representations with the new information.

The ease with which you are able to find a simple and descriptive name for a role is itself a good test of the quality of your design. Complex names, or difficulties in coming up with good names, are often an indication that the roles are not particularly well defined. When this occurs, it is often the case that activities that properly belong to a single role have been distributed among two or more participants. Conversely, it may be that activities belonging to more than one role have been combined into a single role simply because both roles are (coincidentally) being played by the same participant.

Role names become increasingly important as business processes and systems evolve. Well-conceived role names not only summarize a participant's current responsibilities, they also indicate where future responsibilities ought to reside. Simple and well-defined role names are a good indication of a robust design that will gracefully evolve into the future.

Activities and Scenarios

A business process is a structured set of activities organized to produce specific results. To understand the business process, you have to know what these activities are and which activities interact. You need to understand which roles are responsible for which activities. Assigning interacting activities to different roles then requires interactions between the roles. Assigning the roles to individuals, in turn, requires communications among the individuals.

The previous chapter discussed differentiating activities and the resulting interactions among the activities. The activity differentiation you are interested in at the architecture level is among activities being performed by different participants and that require interactions among the participants. Interactions require communications, a major issue in any type of distributed design regardless of whether the participants are people or information systems. Communications take time, and thus can adversely impact the speed with which a process is able to execute. Communications require resources, which can adversely impact the operational costs associated with the process. And communications can fail, which of course can adversely impact the ability to complete the process. Ultimately, you need to be able to tie these aspects of communications back to the business process design and determine whether the entire package—the total architecture—satisfies the business need.

While you need to differentiate all activities performed by different roles, the level of detail required within a role is considerably less. A good guideline here is to look at the role from the perspective of its interactions with other roles. If from this perspective you can't tell when one activity ends and the other begins, then there is no need to differentiate between those activities.

Scenarios and Variations

Scenarios provide a simple and expedient means of exploring activities, their interactions, and their association with roles. A scenario is nothing more than an example of a possible business process execution under a specific set of circumstances. It describes the participants in the process (both people and systems), the activities of each participant, and the interactions between them. It provides a dynamic view of the business process architecture.

You generally capture business process scenarios by asking a business person or small group to give an example of how they envision their business process working. If the process has already been thought out, then you are just asking them to describe their vision of how it would work. If the process is being designed, then you are asking them for a first-cut operational concept of how the proposed business process might work. This first scenario then serves as a straw man for further discussions.

For the `Withdraw Cash via ATM Machine` process, this first scenario provides the basic operational concept for how a user would withdraw cash from a bank account using an ATM. If this were the initial exploration of the concept of using an ATM, at this point you would explore alternative operational concepts. One alternative concept might be that an ATM placed in a retail setting would not actually dispense the cash, but would instead dispense a receipt that would be taken to a retail cashier to obtain the cash.[3] The discussions around the alternatives serve to weed out the unreasonable ones and home in on a small number of viable candidates worthy of further exploration. In this way alternative scenarios can be proposed and explored quickly and inexpensively.

Once you have arrived at one or more viable primary scenarios for each business process being considered, you then ask the business people to envision variations in circumstances that might alter the business process. Each variation is then illustrated with an example scenario. For the ATM, these variations would include circumstances such as having insufficient funds in the account and the entry of an incorrect PIN. Again, the scenarios, their variants, and possible alternatives are discussed until consensus is reached about each one.

Finally, you ask the business folks to consider a different category of circumstances—breakdowns in the process. You ask what might go wrong in the process and what the scenarios would be for dealing with these breakdowns. In the ATM example you might consider a malfunctioning cash dispenser or the failure of communications with the bank while the transaction is in progress. These considerations may actually lead to the alteration of the primary scenario. In fact, the consideration of a communication failure in the middle of the transaction results in a primary ATM scenario involving not one but two interactions with the bank.

It is interesting to look at the actual evolution of ATMs in terms of business process scenarios. In some early ATM systems, if the customer entered his or her PIN incorrectly, the ATM kept the card! This required the customer to go to the bank in person to get a new ATM card. In other words, every time a PIN was incorrectly entered, some other business process had to be executed to obtain a new ATM card.

---

3. Some early ATMs actually worked this way.

Had the designers of those early ATM systems simply asked how often the PIN might be incorrectly entered, this design might never have been implemented. An understanding of the frequency with which customers would have to go through the inconvenience of obtaining a new ATM card would have emerged. This understanding might have led to the consideration of an alternative business process design that did not keep the card.

It is exactly this type of process variation discussion that you are trying to motivate through the exploration of circumstances and scenario variations. You want to make and then recognize design mistakes while the design is still just a concept and easy to change. You want to postpone making the investment in detailed design and implementation until you are reasonably sure that the operational concept and supporting system design are sound.

Project Efficiency

Does the postponement of design and implementation while scenarios are being explored make the project take longer? Definitely not. In fact, making and resolving architectural mistakes on paper actually reduces the time and cost required to deploy a working business process and reap the expected benefits. It leads to the early definition of a comprehensive, well-considered, and stable set of responsibility assignments and interfaces for each participant. Thoroughness here significantly streamlines the subsequent design, implementation, and testing, making the overall project shorter and more efficient.

You should recognize that everything you do in defining scenarios is work that would have to be eventually done anyway. At some point, every activity will have to be identified, defined, and assigned to a process participant. Every interaction will have to be identified and designed. Every variation in circumstances is going to have to be appropriately dealt with. By defining the scenarios up front, you are making the process more efficient, identifying the need for changes *while the design is still on paper*. As noted by Boehm and Basili,[4] "Finding and fixing a problem after delivery is 5 to 100 times more expensive than finding and fixing it during the requirements and design phase." They go on to note that "good architectural practices can significantly

4. Barry Boehm and Victor R. Basili, "Software Defect Reduction Top 10 List," *IEEE Computer*, Vol. 34, No. 1, pp. 135–137 (January 2001).

reduce the cost-escalation factor even for large critical systems. Such practices reduce the cost of most fixes by confining them to small, well-encapsulated modules."

This book is essentially a compendium of architecture best practices for both the business processes and the systems that support them. It would not be unreasonable to claim that you can't get to a working system faster. You should be aware, however, that you can quickly arrive at a system that does *not* work by avoiding the early consideration of important business process variations and design issues. In the end, such shortcuts are a foolish and wasteful (though not uncommon) practice. They give the illusion of quick project success while forcing the business to find an alternative mechanism for dealing with these unconsidered business process variations and design issues. Prudence demands that you consider these variations and issues while the architecture is still in its formative stages.

At the same time, you need to make sure that you do not get trapped in an endless analysis exercise. So when should you stop exploring scenarios? You should continue to explore scenario variations until you are no longer discovering either (a) new activities, (b) new interfaces, or (c) new patterns of interaction between the participants. At this point, you will have defined a candidate architecture for your business processes that characterizes its overall structure, organization, and dynamics.

Note that when the architecture has been defined, the business process will not be completely defined. There will still be design details to be worked out within each participant's role and within each communication. User interfaces will be identified along with the information being displayed and captured, but the details of those interfaces will not be fully specified. System interactions will be identified along with the general information content of each communication, but the system interfaces will not be fully specified. Business rules within individual activities will require further detailing, though the architecture will identify the information needed and generated by those rules.

In general, such incomplete definitions are expected and acceptable as long as you are satisfied that you have identified all the inputs and results that are required for each activity (including their interactions with other business processes in the architecture) and you are satisfied that there are no feasibility issues associated with implementing the activity. If you have done your job right, these details will be added later without altering the overall architecture of the business process. Thus you can safely leave these details to be worked out later.

Modeling Scenarios

Modeling a scenario begins with an abstract understanding the basic activity flow required to produce the results (Figure 9–6). There are no roles yet—only an understanding of the activities that are required, the inputs they require that originate outside the process, and the results they produce that are destined for other processes. Very often this abstract understanding results from analyzing other business processes that produce the same results, such as the `Withdraw Cash via Human Teller` example discussed earlier. This particular representation employs the UML 2.0 activity notation, which is an enhanced version of the familiar flowchart.

In this abstracted process view, the initial focus is on identifying the activities that must occur to complete the business process. For each of

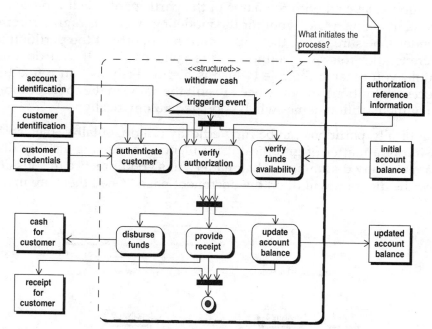

Figure 9–6: *Abstracted Withdraw Cash Process*

these activities, you need to determine whether it requires any inputs that come from outside the process and whether it produces any results that go outside the process.

You also need to determine the required sequencing of the activities and be very careful in doing so, for whatever sequencing is specified here must be preserved as the process is refined. Consequently, when it is acceptable for activities to occur at the same time, this should be clearly indicated in your process representation. The mechanism for doing this in the activity notation is through the use of fork and join nodes (Figure 9–7). The semantics of a fork node is that after the preceding activity has completed, then the subsequent activities are allowed to proceed in parallel. Conversely, a join node indicates that *all* of the preceding activities must complete before the subsequent activity can begin.

Differentiating Participant Roles

The next step in modeling the scenario is to introduce the participant roles into the activity as shown in Figure 9–8. Each role is represented by an activity partition (commonly referred to as a swimlane). Each partition is labeled with the name of the participant role it represents. If you are using a UML tool for the modeling (which is highly recommended), be sure to use the `represents` property of the partition to reference the role you defined in the collaboration. If you do this, should you rename the role (which is highly likely as you refine the process definition) you only need to edit the name in the collaboration. All of the partition names will be updated automatically.

Graphically, partitions can be run vertically or horizontally—the choice is simply a matter of graphical convenience. In creating activity diagrams (or any diagram, for that matter), it is good practice to consider how the diagram will fit on the document page. When there are many

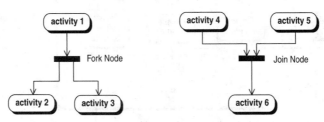

Figure 9–7: *Fork and Join Nodes*

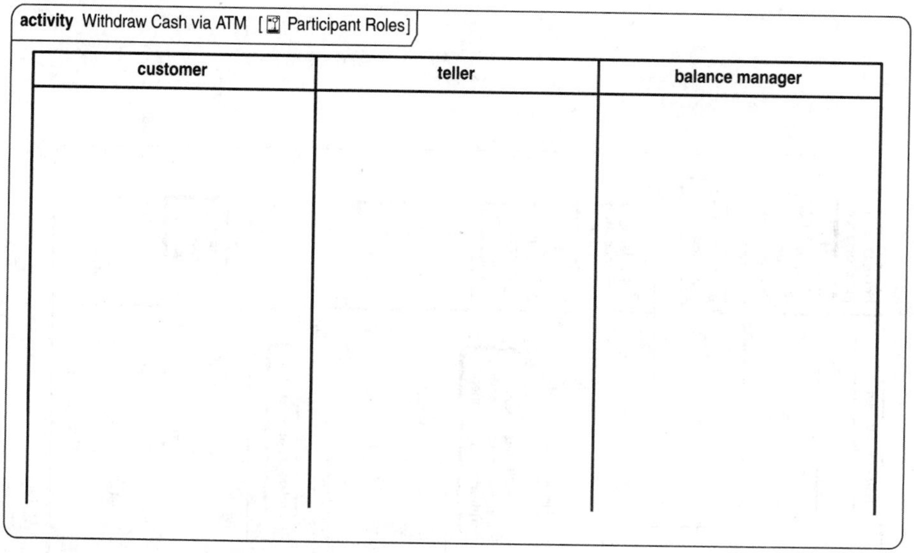

activity Withdraw Cash via ATM [▣ Participant Roles]		
customer	teller	balance manager

Figure 9–8: *Participant Roles*

interactions between a relatively small number of participants, generally vertical partitions will fit better on a portrait-layout page. Conversely, when there are many participants, each having relatively few interactions, horizontal partitions tend to fit better on portrait-layout pages.

Assigning Activity Responsibilities

The next step in modeling the process is to place the activities in the activity partitions. The placement of the activity in a partition is a responsibility assignment. It indicates that the participant playing that role is responsible for executing the activity. The act of placing activities in swimlanes forces you to be clear about what each participant is doing in the process. It forces you to differentiate abstract activities into the individual activities that individual participants can perform. These activity assignments identify the required interactions between the participants, and the artifacts involved in these interactions.

The successful withdrawal scenario for the `Withdraw Cash via ATM` process is shown in Figure 9–9. This design reflects a number of refinements from the abstract process. The ATM card, or more specifically the `cardID`, and the `PIN` together play the role of the `customer identification` and `customer credentials` in the abstract process.

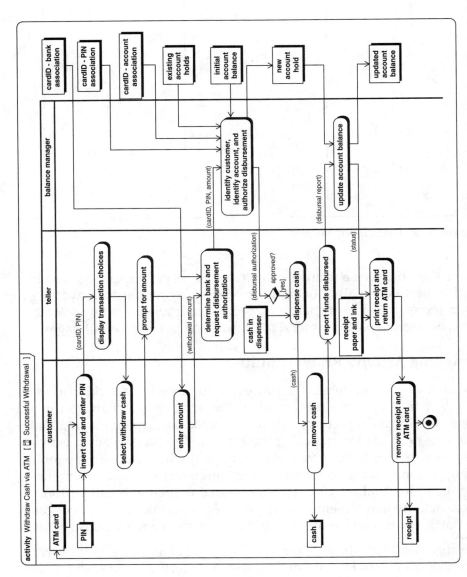

Figure 9–9: *Successful Withdrawal Scenario*

194

The abstract `authenticate customer` activity becomes a comparison of the `PIN` supplied by the customer with the `PIN` associated with the `cardID` in the bank's records. The abstract `verify authorization` activity becomes a lookup of the account associated with the card (this example makes the simplifying assumption that there is only one account associated with the card).

While the decision making associated with authenticating the customer and verifying the authorization are performed by the balance manager (i.e., the bank), there are related responsibilities for the other participant roles as well. The customer must provide the `cardID` (by inserting the ATM card) and entering the `PIN`. The teller (i.e., the ATM system) must aggregate this information and pass it on to the balance manager.

New activities and artifacts are introduced in this differentiation of roles as well. When a customer enters a bank in person and deals with a human teller, that teller is only acting on behalf of one bank. However, when a customer is using an ATM system that services many banks, the teller (i.e., ATM system) must determine which bank to interact with. This activity also requires some reference information—a `cardID–bank association`.

Another nuance introduced by the possibility of a breakdown either in the ATM system or the communications to it is the need for an `account hold`. With a human teller, the teller simply attempts to debit the account for the amount of the withdrawal. If the debit succeeds, then the teller takes cash from the drawer and hands it to the customer. Any breakdowns in the process after the debit transaction are handled by the human teller.

In the ATM variation, however, the reply to the debit request may get lost, or there may be a malfunction in the ATM after the debit occurs. To make these situations easier to deal with from a business process perspective, two interactions occur with the balance manager (Figure 9–10). In the first interaction, the disbursal of funds is authorized and a hold of the amount to be withdrawn is placed on the account funds. This hold keeps those funds from being withdrawn for some other purpose. After the funds have been successfully disbursed, a second interaction occurs in which the ATM system reports the disbursement and the balance manager updates the balance and removes the hold. Since there may be other holds on the account (from other transactions), the disbursal report must be associated with the specific hold to

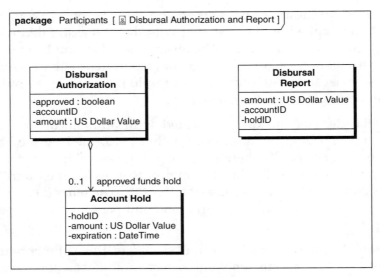

Figure 9–10: *Disbursal Authorization and Report*

be removed. In this design, information about the hold is returned to the ATM system with the disbursal authorization and the identifier of the hold is returned with the disbursal report. Note also that the account hold is intended to impact the execution of other business processes. It represents yet another interaction between processes.

Detailing the scenario has identified additional artifacts that originate outside the business process and additional artifacts that are produced by this process and used elsewhere. These artifacts should be added to the collaboration as shown in Figure 9–11.

The `authenticate customer` activity in this example illustrates that without assigning activities to participant roles, it is easy to create an activity that is actually a collaborative effort between two or more participants. Such collaborative activities tacitly assume that the dialog between the participants is both clear and feasible—an assumption that often turns out to be wrong. If you were designing an ATM system for the first time, such vague activity descriptions might leave the impression that traditional forms of identification (such as presenting a driver's license) could be used as the basis for identification.

When you assign responsibility for activities by placing them in partitions, you force yourself to differentiate activities. This makes you explore the nature of these collaborations, defining the individual participant

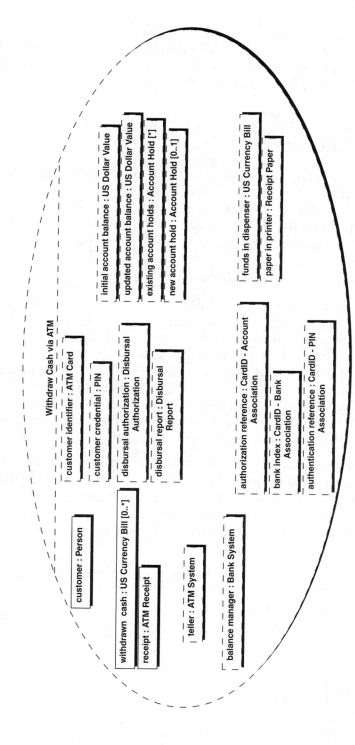

Figure 9–11: *Updated Withdraw Cash via ATM Collaboration*

197

activities and the required communications between them. This exploration is generally sufficient to surface and resolve any feasibility issues in the business process definition.

Modeling Interactions

The manner in which interactions occur has implications for both the sunny-day scenario execution of a business process and its execution under failure conditions. If your representations of processes are to precisely indicate their behavior under all conditions, it is important that you capture and represent interactions clearly in your designs.

Producer-Consumer Interactions

Virtually all interactions take the form of a *producer-consumer* interaction (Figure 9–12). In this interaction one activity produces an `artifact` (referred to as an *object* in the UML notation) that is then consumed by one or more activities. This artifact might be something physical, such as the cash or receipt that is produced by an ATM, or something abstract, such as a request for funds disbursement from a bank. Of course, when your design is implemented such abstractions will generally have some concrete manifestation in the form of a message, a database record, or even a spoken communication.

This notation identifies the activity producing artifact with an arrow (technically known as an object flow) drawn from the activity to the artifact (technically known as an object) it produces. Activities that consume the artifact (and there may be more than one) are identified with arrows from the artifact to each activity that will consume it. It is

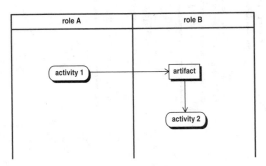

Figure 9–12: *Producer-Consumer Interaction*

important to note that the placement of the artifact itself has absolutely no significance in the notation. The meaning of the figure would remain the same even if the artifact were shown in the `role A` activity partition or entirely outside the partitions.

Strictly speaking, in a distributed system virtually all interactions between participants should be shown as producer-consumer relationships. This is because in real life, participants rarely interact directly with one another. Instead, they most often interact through some medium, be it paper, e-mail, system messages, files, databases, packages, pipelines, or some other means. The artifact then represents whatever is passed through the medium from the sender to the recipient. The ATM system, for example, produces a disbursement request, a message that is transmitted to the bank. The bank, in turn, generates a response, a message that is transmitted back to the ATM system.

Simultaneous Interactions

Occasionally there is, indeed, a direct interaction between the participants: a true simultaneous interaction between them. A handshake is an example of such an interaction: Both parties are doing complementary actions at exactly the same time. Figure 9–13 shows how a simultaneous interaction would be represented. In reality, it is very rare for the participants in a distributed system to directly interact simultaneously; for example, even when one person talks to another, his or her voice produces sound waves (the artifact) that the other person hears.

This distinction between interaction styles is important because they have significant differences in their possible failure modes. In simultaneous interactions, the entire interaction either happens or it doesn't—it is essentially a single atomic action. The completion of the previous

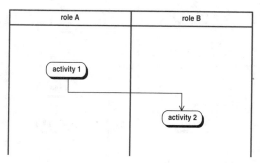

Figure 9–13: *Simultaneous Interaction*

activity coincides with the beginning of the subsequent activity; either both things occur or neither occurs. But if the interaction occurs via a medium, then the previous activity generates some artifact that is subsequently delivered to the subsequent activity. This interaction has a failure mode that is not shared by the simultaneous interaction: The delivery of the artifact might fail. The previous activity might actually generate the artifact, but something might go wrong with the delivery and the artifact might never be presented to the subsequent activity. This difference in failure modes is significant when you are trying to design a process that is robust with respect to failure.

Notational Shortcuts

Because of the differences in failure modes, it should be clear that if interactions between participants are producer-consumer interactions, then your process models should reflect this. The diagram should show the artifact being exchanged between the participants as well as the activities that produce and consume the artifact. But showing these artifacts can lead to very cluttered-looking activity diagrams. The graphical presence of the objects in the diagram can obscure the overall flow of the process. Consequently, shortcuts are often used when modeling a business process (as opposed to its technical implementation). The shortcut is to show a simultaneous interaction. Typical usages of this shortcut are illustrated in Figure 9–14.

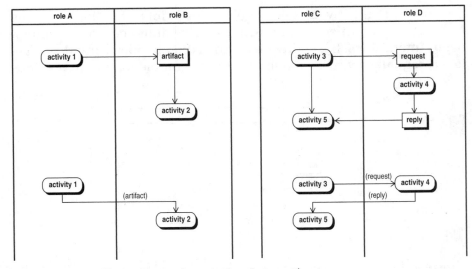

Figure 9–14: *Shortcuts in Annotating Interactions*

When you use this type of shortcut, you must do so with the full understanding that the simultaneous interactions that cross swimlane boundaries almost always represent producer-consumer interactions. You should use the shortcut notation only when you are documenting the business process. Do not use them when you document the systems design that supports the business process, because understanding and dealing with the mechanics of delivering the artifact and the related failure modes is an important aspect of the technical design.

Scenario Variations

A single execution scenario generally does not represent everything that can happen in a business process. To further increase your understanding of the process you want to consider the significant variations that can occur. You are looking in particular for significant variations, that is, variations involving new activities, new participants, new communications, new artifacts, and differences in communications patterns. For each significant variation, you create another activity diagram to capture this variation. Figure 9–15, for example, shows the insufficient funds scenario for the `ATM Withdraw Cash` business process. Note the absence of the second interaction with the banking system in this scenario and the absence of the account hold. The interaction pattern for this scenario is different than the primary scenario. Understanding these variations in interaction patterns will help you to better understand what the expected load will be on individual participants and upon the networks they use for communications. Different interaction patterns may also present different symptoms when breakdowns occur. Both considerations will influence your evaluation of the proposed business process.

Note that while the UML activity notation is rich enough to allow you to combine these alternatives into a single diagram, the resulting diagram will be more complex and difficult to read. While minor variations can be incorporated into a single diagram, significant variations warrant their own diagrams. With this approach, each diagram represents the behavior under a specific set of circumstances. Different circumstances, different diagram! Keeping each diagram focused on a single set of circumstances makes it easy for the business stakeholders to understand the circumstances and validate the desired behavior. To facilitate the identification of the differences, it is good practice to graphically highlight the differences between the variant scenario and the initial scenario.

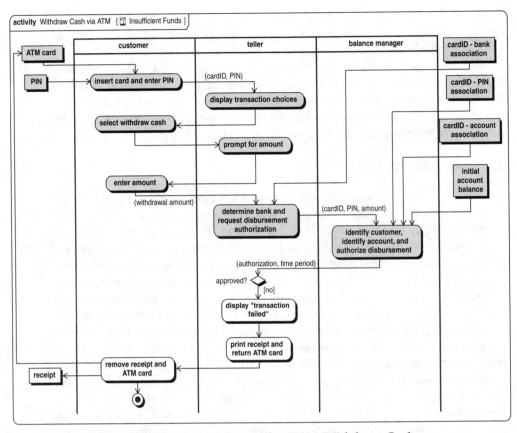

Figure 9–15: *Insufficient Funds Scenario for ATM Withdraw Cash*

While you are thinking through and documenting the business process scenarios, you may well think of alternate scenarios that could produce the same results. This is good! Activity diagrams provide a simple and inexpensive vehicle for comparing and contrasting alternative scenarios. They also give you a means of documenting the alternatives that you have considered and discarded—a record of the rationale behind the business process design. This type record—a design notebook, as it were—can help future maintainers of the business process and supporting systems understand why the design is the way it is.

At the end of the day, the goal of this entire modeling exercise is to eliminate any possible ambiguity as to how the business process ought to behave. Any ambiguity in the business process definition can easily lead to a system that inappropriately and unintentionally produces (or forces) the business process to diverge from this intent. Well-defined business process scenarios, documented in the form of activity diagrams, make absolutely clear what the expected business process behavior should be under various circumstances. If a sufficiently rich set of variations is considered, this approach provides the level of clarity required to get it right the first time. Ultimately, it averts the dreaded "that's not what I really wanted" reaction from the user community after the system has been built.

Exception Handling

One important category of business process variations that you must consider is exceptions. In these variations you want to explore what can go wrong with the business process and what the appropriate business process response should be. For each business process and each type of breakdown you want to determine what the symptoms will be and how (by what means) the participants in the process will recognize that something has gone wrong. You then want to consider whether an alternative design might improve the participant's ability to detect breakdowns in the process.

Beyond simply detecting the presence of problems, you need to consider what the follow-up actions will be after a problem has been detected. But you do not necessarily need to design a detailed process for recovering from each possible breakdown. Many breakdowns will be investigated and dealt with in an ad hoc manner by people participating in the process. In such cases you need to consider how they will investigate the problem and what system interactions they will require during investigation and recovery. These interactions may require additional or extended interfaces to systems. These interfaces then become requirements on the systems, even though the process that uses these interfaces may not be defined in detail.

Finally, you need to consider whether there might be alternate business processes employed—variations on the process—when things go wrong. If an order placement business process normally calls for a customer credit check and the participants cannot communicate with the credit service for some reason, is the business going to stop taking orders? Maybe not. Maybe it will have some alternate process for validating credit, such as checking the customer's recent credit history in the business's records. If the customer has a good track record, the business may want to accept the order without a new credit check. Alternatively, orders from customers for which the business does not have a history may go through some type of manual approval process, at least until such time as the credit service becomes available again. Clearly, if you are going to design the systems to support these alternate business processes, these alternates and the circumstances under which they are executed must be clearly understood and documented.

How Much Detail Is Enough?

It should be apparent by now that if you continue this design process you will eventually document every single detail required to actually implement the business process. But you don't want to go to that level of detail until you are satisfied that the overall architecture of the process is suitable. So where do you stop? Here are some guidelines.

When you are architecting the business process, you want to identify all interactions between participants, but you do not want to detail them—yet. Instead, you use the shortcuts to simply show that the interactions exist. Similarly, you want to identify the fact that there are artifacts (information, physical objects, etc.) being exchanged during these interactions. You do this by labeling the control flows to indicate that these artifacts are being passed. For example, Figure 9–15 shows the customer providing the teller with the card ID, the PIN, the transaction type, and the amount to be withdrawn. The actual mechanisms for this communication will be determined when you define the corresponding system architecture, but you will do this only after you are satisfied with the basic architecture of the business process.

This distinction in level of detail—showing the existence of something as opposed to characterizing it in detail—is a good example of the distinction between architecture and design. Architecture identifies the overall structure—the existence of the artifact, the need to convey it from one participant to another, and the dynamics of when this occurs. While you are doing this you also want to identify the characteristics of these artifacts that are most important to the business process, namely the identifiers and attributes upon whose values decisions are made. This understanding of concepts and their key attributes is captured in the domain model (which will be discussed in Chapter 13), in which you will accumulate this information as you are defining the business processes. But once again, you are just identifying the basic structure. You will defer detailing the physical form of these artifacts and the mechanisms by which they will be communicated until such time as you are addressing the system architecture and component and service specifications.

As you progress more deeply into the design process, through business process architecture, system architecture, component specification, and component design, you will find that this level-of-detail boundary moves. When you are architecting the business process, you are intentionally ignoring all system details below the level of simply identifying what the systems (as a whole) are expected to be doing and what people are expected to be doing. Later, when you are architecting the systems, you will be refining the structure of the systems. At that point you will be identifying the components and services, and choosing the technologies to be used both for their implementation and for the communications between them. But once again you will be intentionally ignoring some level of detail. You will not detail all of the data structures and interfaces, nor will you detail the internal design of the individual system components. Only after you are satisfied with the business process and system architecture will you invest in specifying the system components and services, including their interfaces. Following this, the internal design and implementation of the components will occur.

Returning now to the consideration of business process architecture, since you have not yet defined the architecture of the system, you do not yet know the details of which system components will be performing which activities (unless these responsibility assignments are, themselves, business requirements). Consequently, in your business process architecture you should treat the to-be-designed system as a single participant (partition) in the process. The component-level structural refinement of this system will be defined later in the system architecture.

There is one significant exception to this treat-the-system-as-a-single-participant approach. If it is a requirement that specific systems will perform specific tasks, then it is entirely appropriate to show those systems as individual participants in the business process. These are design decisions that have already been made, and there is little point in not showing them in your business process model.[5] You see an

---

5. One exception might be when you wish to illustrate that these preordained responsibility assignments are, in fact, inappropriate. In such cases, you might want to show the unconstrained business process and the alternate system architectures that might be used to implement the process.

example of this in Figure 9–4 in which the `Bank System`—an existing system with mandated responsibilities—is playing the role of `balance manager`. The remainder of the system activity (the non-bank functionality) is shown as the `teller` role being performed by the yet-to-be-defined `ATM System`. Bear in mind that at this point you have not yet decided what the architecture of that ATM system will be!

Guidelines for Using Activity Diagrams

Every business process should have a primary scenario—a common execution example—that is documented with an activity diagram. This diagram should show all the major participants in the process and all of the interactions between them. Even if you are narrowly focused on improving a fragment of the overall process (i.e., a single activity or small group of activities), this overall diagram will help you to understand the impact your work will have on the overall process. In particular, by including all of the major participants, you are identifying all of the participants who could, potentially, drop the ball and cause the process to fail. Major variations on this primary scenario should similarly be documented with activity diagrams that also show the full scope of the process.

These full-scope activity diagrams show all of the major participants along with their activities and communications between them. This gives you a view of the patterns of interaction among the participants and an understanding of how responsibility is handed off from one participant to another. This perspective is essential to understanding what might go wrong with the process and which participants are in a position to identify process breakdowns. This identification of breakdowns is the key to maintaining the process availability.

The high-level scenarios you assemble do not detail the mechanisms used to communicate between the major participants—they simply show that a particular body of information is communicated. This is appropriate when you are defining the business process, for the details of the communications have not yet been designed. Even if they were, adding swimlanes to represent communications intermediaries and objects to represent the exchanged artifacts would complicate these overview diagrams, obscuring the understanding of who the major participants are and what they are doing.

However, there will come a time in the design process when you will need to understand and document exactly how communication occurs. When you introduce additional participants to carry out the communication, these participants need to be identified and the details of their interactions documented. To accomplish this, you should document the communications details in supporting activity diagrams. Each diagram will document a specific pattern of communication. Once these patterns have been documented, the control flow on the high-level activity diagram can be labeled with the name of the pattern being used. This approach is detailed in Chapters 17 and 18.

Another form of top-level diagram simplification is to aggregate a number of a participant's activities into a single activity. The details of this composite activity are then shown in a supporting activity diagram. When you do this, however, you must be sure not to mask the existence of communications, for this will in turn mask potential sources of failure in the overall business process. All communications between participants must be shown in the high-level diagram, and it is desirable to show the decision making that affects communications as well.

When you are documenting a business process, you should continue to explore the details of the process until you are satisfied that you have identified all possible communications between participants. In particular, you want to identify any inputs that may be needed by activities that come from other processes. These other processes must be added to the inventory of collaborations that impact the project. In some cases these other processes must themselves be designed. In others, they will already exist but will need to be modified to make their results available. All of this contributes to a fuller understanding of project scope and of the work required to achieve project success.

Summary

Understanding a business process begins with knowing the results that the business process is intended to generate and the inputs the business process requires. You also need to understand the participants in the process and the roles that they play. Roles define the responsibilities of the participant in terms of the activities they are expected to perform. UML collaboration notation provides a means of documenting the business process and its constituent parts.

Differentiating a business process into its constituent activities exposes the interactions between the activities. Assigning the responsibility for interacting activities to different participants requires communications between those participants. Scenarios provide a useful mechanism for identifying activities, interactions, and roles. UML activity diagrams provide unambiguous and readily understood scenario documentation.

Comprehensive analysis of the business process requires exploration of all the important business process variations. Both normally expected variations and exception handling variations need to be explored. The exploration of variations should continue until new participants, artifacts, activities, interactions, and patterns of interactions are no longer being discovered.

The business process architecture should focus on identification and structure—not detail. Artifacts that are produced and consumed should be identified, but not necessarily detailed. Activities should be identified and roughly characterized but, again, not detailed. These details are dependent on the structure and organization of the business process. You don't want to make the investment in detail until you are somewhat comfortable with the structure and organization of the business process. Avoiding this detail in the early stages lowers the cost of exploring alternate business process designs.

Key Business Process Architecture Questions

1. Have all of the participants in the business process been identified? Have all of the artifacts that are produced or consumed by the business process been identified?

2. Has the primary (common case) scenario been defined for the process? This scenario illustrates the basic operational concept of how the business process is supposed to operate.

3. Have all significant variations on the primary scenario been defined, particularly those that introduce new participants, activities, artifacts, or communications?

4. Has the business handling of exceptions been defined for each process?

Suggested Reading

Harmon, Paul. 2003. Business Process Change: *A Manager's Guide to Improving, Redesigning, and Automating Processes*. San Francisco, CA: Morgan Kaufmann.

Rumbaugh, James, Ivar Jacobson, and Grady Booch. 2005. *The Unified Modeling Language Reference Manual, Second Edition*. Boston, MA: Addison-Wesley.

Sharp, Alec, and Patrick McDermott. 2001. *Workflow Modeling: Tools for Process Improvement and Application Development*. Norwood, MA: Artech House, Inc.

Chapter 10

Milestones

Whenever you have a business process, it is to be expected that people will want to know its status. Reporting status, particularly of complex processes, can be tricky. Generally, what people want to know is what business-meaningful state the process has reached. These are commonly referred to as the milestones in the business process. Unfortunately, simply reporting the last completed activity of the process may not provide this information.

Basic Process Milestones

In a simple process, there may not be a great deal of distinction between the individual process steps and the process milestones. But as process complexity increases, this distinction becomes more pronounced. Consider the `Catalog Sales Order Process` for a mail-order catalog business shown in Figure 10–1. The `New Order` milestone corresponds in a fairly obvious way to the actual receipt of the order.

The correspondence of the `Order Accepted` milestone, on the other hand, is less obvious. This milestone marks the formal commitment on the part of the business to fulfill the order. It reflects the fact that the items in the order have been verified to be known catalog items and that payment authorization has been received. In this process design, the activity whose completion marks the achievement of the milestone is the `obtain payment authorization`, but that correlation is simply

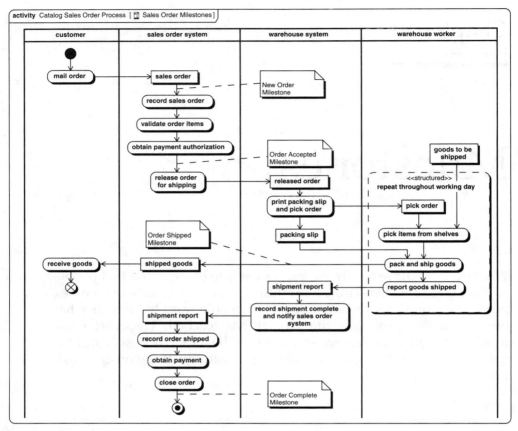

Figure 10–1: *Catalog Sales Order Process Showing Milestones*

an accident of the process design. Should the sequence of the `obtain payment authorization` and `validate order items` activities be reversed, it would be the completion of the `validate order items` activity that would mark the achievement of the milestone.

Technically, the `Order Shipped` milestone reflects the actual shipment of the goods. However, in the actual process design, this may be an event that cannot be directly observed. In such cases, a surrogate event such as the receipt of the `shipment report` by either the `warehouse system` or the `sales order system` may have to be used. In other cases, such as the `Order Complete` milestone, some of the events may not be observable at all. As shown, this milestone occurs after the `close order` activity, but one might justifiably question whether this truly marks the completion of the order when the receipt of the goods by the customer has not been verified.

The meaning of a milestone is a reflection of the conditions that must be met to reach the milestone. By using the UML state machine notation, you can represent both the milestones and the conditions under which a transition to the next milestone can occur (Figure 10–2). The states represent the milestones, and the transitions are labeled with the events and conditions that cause the transition to the next milestone. This diagram represents the typical lifecycle for a successful catalog order.

The syntax of the transition labeling is:

```
event[condition]
```

The meaning is that if the event occurs under the specified conditions, then the transition to the next milestone will occur.

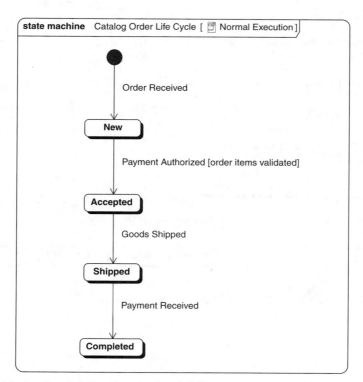

Figure 10–2: *Partial Catalog Order Lifecycle*

Variations in Milestone Sequences

The states and transitions shown in Figure 10–2 represent only the sunny-day scenario for an order. They do not, for example, represent the milestones associated with cancelled orders or what happens when payment is not authorized. To be useful, the state diagram must represent all the possible milestones and the events and conditions that lead to them. Figure 10–3 shows a more complete set of milestones for the catalog ordering process, indicating some of the alternative outcomes.

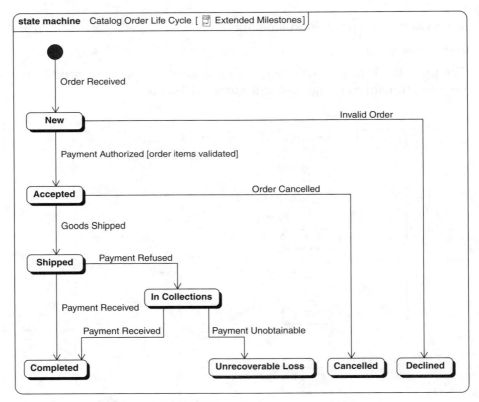

Figure 10–3: *Extended Order Lifecycle*

Grouped Milestones

While this lifecycle example provides a richer understanding of the process milestones, it still lacks a certain level of clarity surrounding one very high-level milestone, namely the completion of the order processing. While there is a `Complete` milestone that marks the end of a successful order, `Unrecoverable Loss`, `Cancelled`, and `Declined` also mark possible outcomes for an order. There is no single milestone that indicates that the order is "done," regardless of the outcome. The UML state machine notation provides a composite state for grouping states together. This grouping can be used to aggregate all of the outcome states together into a single `Closed` state, as shown in Figure 10–4. This type of grouping can greatly simplify the mechanics of reporting, monitoring, and managing processes.

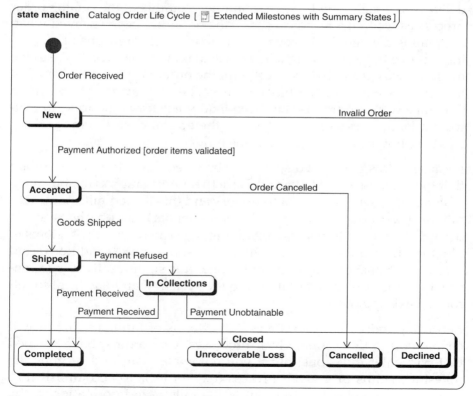

Figure 10–4: *Extended Order Lifecycle with Summary States*

Recognizing Milestones Requires Design

Milestones provide a useful abstraction of a business process. However, just because a milestone has been abstractly defined in terms of events and conditions, this does not mean it is readily observable in the actual business process. In fact, some milestones may never be observable. In the catalog business, one milestone the business would very much like to mark is the delivery of the goods to the customer. Depending on the delivery mechanism used and its reporting capability, this milestone may not be observable at all. As a result, the business may have to compromise on a related milestone that it can actually observe, such as the shipment of the goods.

Marking the achievement of a milestone requires both recognizing an event and determining whether specific conditions have been met. Sometimes the event itself is not readily observable, as in the package delivery just mentioned. There is another example in the catalog order process as well. In a technical sense, the order has been received when the mail is delivered. However, there is no practical means of observing this event, i.e., realizing that a particular order happens to be in the mail that was just delivered. Not until the order is opened and entered into the system does the business even become aware of the order. Once again, a compromise has been made. The New milestone, in reality, marks the entry of the order into the `sales order management system`, not the actual receipt of the order.

Because of this potential discrepancy between the milestone definition that the business would like and the actual information available in the systems, it is very important to understand the desired milestone definitions (events and conditions) before embarking on the systems design. Armed with this understanding, you can design the systems to identify the requisite events, check the appropriate conditions, and record the achievement of the milestone. It is significantly less expensive to design these capabilities into the system than to attempt to retrofit an existing design.

Recording individual milestones, however, is of limited value. It will enable you to determine which processes (e.g., orders) have reached that particular milestone, but it will not enable you to determine the milestone status of a given process (e.g., order). To accomplish this, you need to be able to gather all of the milestone information. If the achievement of different milestones is recorded in different systems, this involves a fair amount of work gathering the milestone information and correlating it. In other words, if milestone information is scattered, determining the status of processes is an expensive operation.

To be useful, milestone information needs to be readily available. It is good practice to designate a particular system as the holder of milestone status information. Since the achievement of individual milestones may still occur in different systems, this will require additional communications between the system recognizing the milestone and the system maintaining the record of its achievement.

Using Milestones to Reduce Inter-Process Coupling

Processes often need to know the status of other processes. This creates a design dependency between the processes, as one process must know enough about the other process to determine its status. Milestones provide a means of simplifying these interactions and keeping them stable over time as the underlying processes evolve. Milestones tends to be far more stable over time than the underlying business processes. Thus the milestone lifecycle of a process represents a point of stability in the design. This is exactly the type of stability you are looking for in service design.

Once you recognize that milestone lifecycles rarely change, you can create more stable designs by ensuring that milestone status information is readily accessible and using this as the basis for inter-process communications. The process that reaches the milestone updates the milestone status when the milestone is reached, and then the milestone status change is communicated to the other process. By doing this, you make overall system design independent from the design of individual business processes. This makes it easier to evolve those processes, and thus facilitates the evolution of the business. The business can, for example, evolve the process without having to modify process reporting. Service-level agreements and key performance indicators can also be defined with respect to milestones, rendering their definitions independent of the process design.

For all but the most trivial processes, the clear identification of process milestones is a basic requirement for each business process. It then becomes a process design requirement that these milestones are clearly identifiable. This approach also makes it possible to have common reporting on different business processes that produce the same results. This can be very useful in businesses that provide the same goods and services through different channels.

Summary

Milestones mark key events in a business process. The possible sequences of milestones and the conditions for transitioning from one to the next represent an abstracted lifecycle of the business process. Grouping milestones provides a means of identifying similarities among milestones while at the same time preserving their uniqueness.

A milestone represents an event that occurs under a particular set of circumstances. Recognizing a milestone therefore requires recognizing the event and determining whether the circumstances have been satisfied. Sometimes the actual event of interest is not observable, and some related event must be used as a surrogate.

There is design work involved in recognizing events, and the recognition of different events often occurs in different systems. When this occurs, the milestone status of a given process ends up being distributed across a number of systems. This makes the determination of process status an expensive activity.

To make status reporting convenient, milestone-level status must be gathered in a single system. This necessitates communications between the systems recognizing the events and the system aggregating the milestone status. These needs constitute additional design requirements for the systems.

Milestones present an opportunity to reduce inter-process coupling. Because milestones represent an abstraction of the underlying process, their use in communicating process status decouples the consumer of the process status from the details of the underlying process design. This facilitates the evolution of the underlying process without necessitating changes to the consumers of process status. It also makes it possible to have a common abstracted view of different business processes that produce the same results.

Key Milestone Questions

1. Have the business-relevant milestones been defined for the process? Have the events and conditions they mark been identified?

2. Have milestone similarities been represented with groupings of milestones?

3. Have the points in the business process that correspond to the milestones been clearly identified?

4. Has a process participant been designated as the repository for milestone status? Has the business process been updated with the communications between the participants recognizing the events and the participant recording the milestone status?

5. Are milestones being used for inter-process communications regarding business process status?

6. Are milestones being used for process status reporting and monitoring?

Key Adaptation Question

Chapter 11

Process Constraints

Almost all business processes have constraints that they must satisfy. The rate at which a process must be able to execute and the allowed completion time for its execution are two examples of constraints discussed in earlier chapters. These happen to be performance constraints, but there are other categories of constraints pertaining to availability, fault-tolerance, security, monitoring, management, and exception handling, to mention a few. To complete the architecture of a business process, you need to comprehensively specify its constraints.

The subject of constraints (often referred to as nonfunctional requirements) is somewhat open-ended. You should consider the categories of constraints discussed here, but you should not let your thinking be limited to these categories. Any constraint that the business process must satisfy is valid, regardless of whether or not it fits into one of these categories. You might need to specify the allowed error rates for decisions or the accuracy of a financial computation. In general, any characteristic of the business process is potentially subject to constraints.

It is essential that you understand the constraints on a business process before you undertake the design of its supporting systems. Accommodating the business process constraints will require certain system participants to satisfy derived constraints. Satisfying these constraints can significantly alter the systems architecture.

Discovering business process constraints after system design commitments have been made may require expensive and time-consuming architecture changes. Rest assured that eventually all important business process constraints will surface! The only question is when. To avoid expensive rework with associated cost and schedule overruns, you want to make a conscious effort to learn about constraints up front, when the design is still conceptual and can be easily altered. You certainly do not want to learn about constraints during user acceptance testing or, even worse, after the system is in production.

Business Process Constraints Drive System Constraints

System constraints are derived from business process constraints. If you have a 300-millisecond allowed response time for a business transaction and three system components are sequentially involved, the response times of the individual components combined with expected communications delays must add up to no more than 300 milliseconds. It is your responsibility as an architect to determine what combination of individual component constraints will be used to satisfy each business process constraint. Without such design thought, you may well end up with a set of components that, collectively, are incapable of satisfying the business process constraint. Sad to say, this actually happens in real projects.

Case Study

Case Study: Late Identification of Performance Requirements

A large multinational firm specified and purchased a very expensive document image management system. The system allowed the viewing of document images at workstations distributed over an entire continent. Any document could be retrieved and displayed anywhere within five seconds. Given the geographic distribution and the communications delays involved, the five-second system response time constraint seemed quite reasonable.

Unfortunately, the real business process constraint did not come to light until after the document management system had been purchased. It turns out that in the existing business process (the one being "improved" by the new system) the workers literally flip through piles of physical documents, spending less than a second on each one. This short time reflects the worker's familiarity with the document formats, that they are only looking at one or two data fields, and just the exceptional values in those fields. Essentially, they are browsing for exceptions.

What would a five-second response time do to these workers? Given that each worker examines thousands of documents every day, a five-second response time for retrieving each document would literally add hours of nonproductive wait time for each worker every day. The resulting productivity losses would have cost the business more each year than the purchase price of the imaging system! Not exactly a good business investment.

The result of this inappropriate system specification was that the user's workstations had to be redesigned to pre-fetch the needed documents and cache them locally. This work-around enabled the workstations to present the documents with sub-second response time. Unfortunately, the image viewers that came with the document retrieval system could not be adapted to utilize a local cache. New viewers had to be developed. Logic had to be added to guess what documents would be required and get them into the cache. More logic had to be added to retrieve needed documents when the guessing was wrong and they were not already in the cache. Still more logic was required to get late-arriving documents (a common occurrence) quickly into the cache.

All tolled, the update of the workstation turned out to be a complex and expensive undertaking. The cost of redesigning the workstations nearly equaled the cost of the document retrieval system, thus doubling the cost of the project. And all of this happened because the real business process constraints were not understood before the document retrieval system was specified! Had the real requirements been known, most of the functionality could have been built into the document retrieval system, and the overall project cost (not to mention schedule) would have been substantially reduced.

As this case study illustrates, before you design a system you need to first understand the business process constraints and derive the appropriate system constraints. Determining system constraints this way will also help you avoid over-engineering the system by putting more stringent requirements on components than are warranted by the business process. There is no point in implementing a high-performance printing system for occasional use in printing short reports that are not time critical. As you design the business processes and supporting systems, bear in mind that you are making investment decisions on behalf of the business. Every constraint you specify is a potential cost driver. You want to make sure that the level of investment you are requiring is commensurate with the business benefits and risks involved. In other words, you want to be confident that you are making sound investment decisions.

So with this goal in mind, let's take a look at some common categories of constraints. Keep in mind though that these categories are not exhaustive. Your business process may have constraints that do not fall into one of these categories—don't forget them. Talk to the business people and understand what constraints are truly important to their business process. Learn enough to make sound investment decisions on their behalf. And make sure *they* understand that constraints can drive cost.

Performance Constraints

One of the most common categories of constraint is that of performance. This type of constraint was touched upon lightly when discussing the ranking of business processes in Chapter 7. There the performance-related ranking focused on the allowed completion time for the process, its peak rate of execution, and the volume of data being handled. But these characterizations were rough approximations made before examining the business process in detail. As such, their correlation with the actual business process execution was unclear. In contrast, at this point in the design process you have a process definition to use as a framework. You can (and should) take advantage of the process definition to be far more precise about what the performance constraints really are.

Rates and Response Times

Activity diagrams provide a solid framework for clearly defining constraints. The business process ranking referenced the allowed completion time for the `Withdraw Cash via ATM` business process, but it did not precisely define the time interval referenced by the constraint. Figure 11–1 shows how the definition of this time interval can be made precise by referencing the specific interactions that mark the start and end of the time interval. It now becomes clear that the allowed completion time is the time interval between when the user provides the last piece of information required for the transaction and when the ATM dispenses the cash (assuming a successful transaction).

Using activity diagrams and other UML notations in this manner enables you to be very clear about constraints. The precision of these representations enables business people to verify that you have cap-

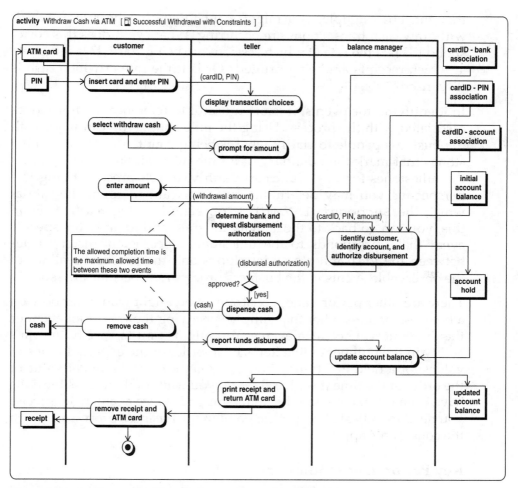

Figure 11–1: *Response Time Measurement Specification*

tured their expectations and gives the technical people their first clear look at the challenges facing them. Even at this point in the project cycle it is not too early to be sketching system architectures, doing research, and perhaps even performing feasibility experiments to determine whether the performance constraints can be realistically met. It is much cheaper to deal with issues now, before any design commitments have been made, than after investments have been made.

Performance measurements always reference events that are occurring in the business process. But identifying the event often requires a bit of thought. For example, you might want to specify the rate at which withdraw cash transactions are occurring. What event does this correspond to? Is it the rate at which sessions are being started? Is it the rate at which receipts are being printed? Or is it the rate at which cash is dispensed?

In identifying the events, it is often useful to reference the milestones associated with the process. Using the milestones, you can work with the business people to clarify what is being counted or the two milestones that mark the boundary of a time interval. Figure 11–2 shows the milestones for the `Withdraw Cash via ATM` process. Using this perspective you may determine that you want to count the rate at which the `Successful Completion` state is being reached. From this, you can go back to the activity diagram and identify the specific event that corresponds to the milestone. Once again, discrepancies between the ideal milestone definitions and the practical realities of the observable events in the business process may become an issue.

There are other performance constraints you might want to impose on a business process other that simply specifying the rate of an event or the time interval between events. You might want to specify the variability in the number of line items in an order or the expected range of values for a field in a transaction. Do you measure the dollar value of the order at the time it is placed, or do you wait until the possible edits have been completed and the items shipped? Once again, to be precise you need to indicate the specific point in the business process to which the constraints apply.

Key Performance Indicators

The existence of a performance constraint does not automatically lead to that constraint being satisfied. Ensuring that the constraints are being met often requires measurement not only during testing but during actual operation. A runtime measurement that is a leading indicator of the health of a business process is often referred to as a *key performance indicator* (KPI).

Implementing the required KPI requires capture of the raw data and the performance of the associated computation. Both of these activities must be performed either as a part of the business process being measured or by another process. In either case, architectural decisions are required. If the process being measured will implement the KPI measurement, then the data capture and computational activities need to

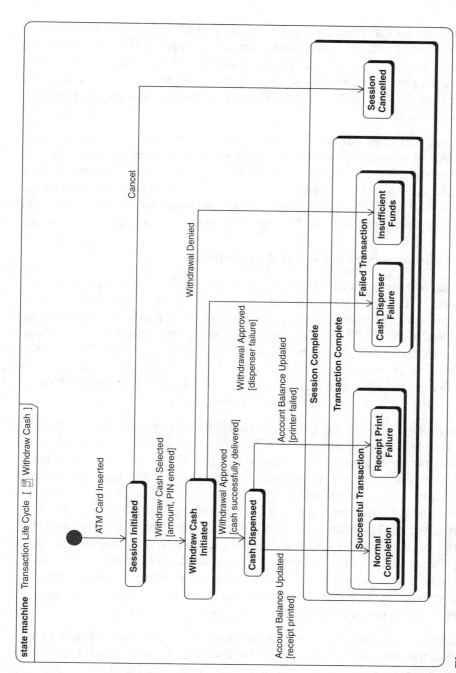

Figure 11–2: *Withdraw Cash Milestones*

be added to the process specification. If another process is to implement the KPI, then the mechanism for capturing the data must be determined along with the means of getting the captured data to that other process. In many cases, the raw data will be captured by the process being measured and then passed to the process performing the computations.

When a KPI goes out of tolerance, there is an ensuing process by which the out-of-tolerance condition is brought to the attention of some process participant and acted upon. In some cases the participant will be a person, and in others a system or service, but in all cases there is a process that defines the possible responses to these conditions. This is yet another process that needs to be added to the project inventory.

Performance Service-Level Agreements

A performance service-level agreement (SLA) is a key performance indicator that has been turned into a contractual commitment. This commitment requires that specific performance goals be attained with respect to that KPI. For example, consider the hotel chain's service promise that your room-service meal will be delivered within 30 minutes or your meal is free. This is a service-level agreement. The KPI is the length of time it takes to get your meal. The SLA contract states that if the KPI exceeds 30 minutes, your meal is free.

Generally service level agreements consist of three parts: (1) the specification of the key performance indicator (KPI); (2) the specification of the performance goal with respect to the KPI; and (3) the specification of some form of penalty or reward based upon whether or not the performance goals are actually achieved. In the room-service example, the KPI is the time interval between placing the order and receiving the meal. The performance goal is to keep the KPI under 30 minutes. The penalty is that if the meal is not delivered within 30 minutes, it is on the house. Note that some SLAs actually reward exceptional performance in addition to penalizing poor performance. In large construction projects, for example, it is not uncommon for a bonus to be paid if the project comes in significantly ahead of schedule or under budget.

As simple as the room-service example is, it illustrates some of the problems that can arise with service-level agreements. Each part of the SLA has its own potential problems. Which participant will make the actual KPI measurement, and what (exactly) are the events being measured? Which participant captures the time at which the room-service order is placed, and which one captures the time at which the order is delivered? The hotel guest? A hotel employee? The computer system that the hotel uses to manage room-service orders? Who will make the determination as to whether or not the SLA goal was achieved? And finally, who will actually implement the reward/penalty actions?

In the room-service example, there is not a lot at stake, and therefore such details are often not fully specified. For room service, the measurement and SLA compliance determination is often left up to the hotel guest, and the hotel manager makes the final decision as to whether the meal should be free. When the stakes are low, imprecision in gathering data and enforcing penalty/reward terms can be tolerated. But often the stakes are much larger. Let's look at another real-world example.

Case Study

Case Study: Failing to Monitor SLA Performance

A large telecommunications firm provides contracted telecommunications services to customers. These contracts include service-level agreements related to the time it takes to restore service once a problem is reported by a customer. There are cost penalties if the repairs are not accomplished within the specified time.

The company was losing money—many millions of dollars every year—due to failures to satisfy these contracted service-level agreements. Even worse, the company was unable to determine whether it was in compliance with its own service-level agreements!

The problem was that the complexity of the telecommunications operations made it nearly impossible for the firm to determine the actual status of a repair. There are many aspects to the firm's operations—long distance trunks, central switches, local switches, local loops to customer premises, and on-premise customer equipment and wiring. Each of these operational aspects is managed by a different organization, each with its own information systems and problem-resolution processes. Furthermore, the provisioning of many of the services is subcontracted to other companies—companies that have their own organizations, information systems, and processes. No system had ever been put into place to measure actual repair times. Customers would report outage times in excess of the SLA and demand compensation, and the company had no way of verifying whether or not the SLA had been met.

Fixing this—making it possible to measure actual performance and compliance with the SLA—required three distinct steps. Interestingly, these are the same exact steps used for evolving business processes and systems: model, measure, and evolve. The first step is to map out the process—in this case, the overall report-diagnosis-repair process—with a particular emphasis on understanding the interactions between the organizations and the milestones of the process. When this first step was completed it became very clear why the company could not determine whether it was meeting its service-level agreements. The relevant status information was distributed all over the place in different organizations, systems, and companies. Milestones were not well defined. Status feedback was poor. There was no monitoring of work-in-progress, and in particular there was no ability to identify that intermediate milestones had been missed—a leading indicator that the SLA was in jeopardy. Making this task even more difficult was that the recovery process for a particular problem could not even be defined until the problem was diagnosed, which was itself a hard-to-track distributed activity! All this analysis led to the definition of diagnosis and recovery milestones that provided a consistent view of the process despite the variability.

The second step was to determine which of these milestones could be identified in existing systems. Where milestone information was present in systems and actually available (many of the systems were not under the control of the communications company), it was captured and brought to a centralized site. Here the progress of the process was compared against standard deadlines for the intermediate milestones. A failure to meet one of these early deadlines then indicated a need for action to avoid missing the SLA. Even though many of the milestones were still not measurable (either because they were not easily identified in the current design or the status information was located in subcontractor's systems), the improved visibility into the existing process was sufficient to enable the company to begin to identify major problem areas, take corrective action, and reduce the resulting losses due to SLA noncompliance.

The third step was to begin to improve the process itself, beginning with improving the ability to recognize the occurrence of milestones. Much of this improvement was accomplished by simply adding responses to requests—responses that improved the visibility of the process status. The process was further improved when subcontractors were required to provide promise dates for completing requested work and timely feedback on actual progress. Further improvements were made in aggregating fragmented status information to determine when milestones were actually reached. All of these improvements enhanced the ability to understand how the process was behaving, and thus set the stage for continuous process improvement—finding and fixing the real problems with the process.

This case study illustrates the risks associated with SLAs that have business processes for which progress cannot be readily observed and measured. This company lost many millions of dollars because it could not manage its own processes, and then it spent many additional millions fixing the problem. But these costs were avoidable. Had management of the business process been thought out when the service-level agreements were established, the necessary reporting and feedback mechanisms could have been put in place from the start. This is the point of seeking out SLA requirements as you design the business processes. You want to ensure that the relevant milestones are identifiable and measurable when the process is deployed.

High Availability and Fault Tolerance

Availability and fault tolerance are a means to an end, and that end is to limit the risk to the enterprise arising from breakdowns in the business process. The real constraint is the level of risk that is acceptable in the business process. It is the acceptable level of risk that determines the required levels of fault tolerance and high availability.

Definition of Terms

A process is *highly available* if it has a high probability of being able to provide its functionality on time, but interruptions in the availability of the process are acceptable—within limits. With high availability, there are two distinct service-level agreements. One SLA specifies the percentage of time that the process is available for use—the *availability* of the process. The other SLA specifies the maximum amount of time that the process can be out of service. This limit is the *maximum allowed outage time* or *recovery time objective*. When you specify high availability, you need to specify both of these SLAs.

A process (or service) is *fault tolerant* if it continues to function properly within its service-level agreement (SLA) even when one of its participants ceases to function. Such an event is known as a *fault*. What the definition implies is that the process is (a) completed on time as specified by its service-level agreement, and (b) there is no loss of any work in progress at the time of failure. If you were to examine the detailed execution of the process, you might be able to observe a pause in the execution, but as long as the process completes on time, the process is considered to be fault tolerant. Thus when you are considering fault tolerance, it is very important to understand the service-level agreement specifying the allowed completion time for the process. This represents the time available for failure recovery.

When you are considering fault tolerance and high availability, you need to consider the fate of the work in progress at the time a failure occurs. Implicit in the definition of fault tolerance is that this work will not be lost. The process will continue as if nothing happened. The definition of high availability, on the other hand, does not tell you what happens to the work in progress when a failure occurs. You thus have three possible strategies for handling participant failure:

1. Fault tolerance
2. High availability without loss of work in progress
3. High availability with loss of work in progress

Note that these definitions characterize a process or service, not an individual participant in the process. This is because handling the complete failure of a participant involves more than just that lone participant. Fault tolerance and high availability both involve coordinating the failed participant's work with the rest of the process and redirecting communications to the participant taking over the role of the failed participant. Achieving fault tolerance and high availability is a process architecture issue, not a component design issue. This is why you must consider it as part of your architecture.

It's All Relative

Adding fault tolerance or high availability to an architecture yields an incremental improvement over an architecture that makes no special provisions for increasing these measures. As such, it is important to have some idea of what can be expected of the individual components in your architecture with respect to their availability and fault tolerance.

The best way to do this is to collect data. One (admittedly old) study found that certain Internet hosts were available 92.6 percent of the time, with a recovery time (mean time to repair) of 1.2 days.[1] Chances are that your operations center collects similar availability statistics on

---

1. D. Long, A. Muir, and R. Golding. September 13–15, 1995. "A longitudinal survey of Internet host reliability," *14th Symposium on Reliable Distributed Systems*. Bad Neuenahr, Germany. Proceedings, IEEE Computer Society, 1995, p. 2 (ISBN 0-8186-7153-X).

the systems in your environment. For fault tolerance statistics (data loss, in particular), it is sufficient to keep track of the rate at which disks (or other persistent storage devices) fail. While it is theoretically possible to analytically compute expected availability, such computations are complex, tedious, and error prone. It is generally simpler and more accurate to use measured statistics.

This component availability and failure data provides a basis for your thinking about fault tolerance and high availability. It tells you what you can expect if you do not take any extraordinary measures with respect to fault tolerance and high availability. You can then evaluate the risks and make a determination as to whether an investment in improving availability and fault tolerance is warranted.

Investment versus Risk

When you consider fault tolerance and high availability you must begin with two concessions to reality. You must first recognize that there are no guarantees. No process is ever 100 percent fault tolerant, and high-availability percentages and maximum outage intervals can never be guaranteed. No matter what investment you make, there will always be some combination of participant failures that will result in these reliability and availability objectives not being met.

Second, you must realize that fault tolerance and high availability require investment—they are not free at either design time or runtime. A comprehensive fault tolerance solution that encompasses site disaster recovery (failover from one data center to another) can increase the investment in hardware and software by a factor of four and require significant communications bandwidth between data centers. These are not inexpensive solutions.

Taken together, these two observations lead to the practical conclusion that you must weigh the contemplated investment in fault tolerance or high availability against the business risks associated with the non-availability of the business process. The result of this tradeoff will likely be different for different business processes. You are likely going to treat the business process that takes online customer orders differently from the process of generating monthly office supply inventory reports. If you can't take orders, you immediately impact the cash flow and profitability of the enterprise. This warrants at least considering some level of investment in fault tolerance or high availability to mitigate these risks. On the other hand, if the office supply inventory monthly report is delayed by the amount of time it routinely takes to restore a failed participant, who would notice? The delay would most likely have no measurable impact upon the enterprise. In such cases, no investment in fault tolerance and high availability is warranted.

So how should you go about determining what the business process availability and fault tolerance constraints ought to be? You need to determine the risks (costs) arising from different types of failure scenarios, including:

- The failure of a single execution of the business process
- The failure of a number of process executions
- The unavailability of the process for various periods of time
- The delay of process completion beyond its SLA

The impact of these different scenarios will vary according to the type of business and the specific business process. A more detailed discussion of this risk assessment can be found in Chapter 12 of the companion volume, *Succeeding with SOA*.

Business Process Design Impacts Systems Investment

It is tempting to say that a fault-tolerant process requires the underlying systems to be fault tolerant, but that is not necessarily true—and it is a very expensive thought. Consider how the phone company deals with the risk of not getting paid for its services.

Case Study

Case Study: Fault Tolerance through Process Design

Consider how a phone company collects payment for its services and the impact of breakdowns in this process. There is certainly an impact if the company does not get paid—it loses part of its revenue stream. But you do not receive your phone bill via an expensive registered mail or courier service, nor do you make payments using such services. Instead, the process employs the inexpensive standard mail service, despite the fact that this service can (and does) misdirect or lose a small percentage of the bills and payments.

How is this loss risk mitigated? Through clever but simple process design. If one month's bill is not paid, the amount overdue is simply added to the next month's bill. This simple, elegant, and low-cost solution does not place extraordinary fault tolerance and high-availability requirements on any of the participants in the process except for the system that keeps track of the payment status. Clever process design has eliminated the need for expensive infrastructure.

As this case study illustrates, achieving a fault-tolerant business process does not necessarily require reliance upon fault-tolerant systems. Consequently, once you understand the risks, you need to consider different design alternatives—combinations of business process design and systems design—for reducing these risks.

Availability can also be impacted by process design. Availability is simply the percentage of time that a business process (or whatever you happen to be talking about) is available to perform its task. You can express availability in terms of the time that the process is operating normally and the time taken to restore the process to normal operation. In terms of statistics that you can gather, the normal operation time can be represented by the mean time between failures (MTBF), and the time to restore normal operation can be represented by the mean time to repair (MTTR). Thus availability can be expressed as:

$$availability = \frac{time_{normalOperation}}{time_{normalOperation} + time_{restoreNormalOperation}} = \frac{MTBF}{MTBF + MTTR}$$

From this formula, you can see that there are two ways to increase availability. One is to increase the amount of time that the process is operating normally, that is, decrease the probability of failure. This is generally accomplished by increasing the investment in the system components, potentially employing fault-tolerance techniques so that a failure of one system component does not impact the availability of the business process. The other approach is to reduce the amount of time that it takes to restore the system to normal operation. This may be as simple as bringing the failure of the process to someone's attention in a timely manner. Either approach results in increased availability, but there may be a significant difference in cost between the two. An effective recovery process may turn out to be less expensive and more effective than an increased investment in system components.

Focus on Risk

The cost implications tell you that you need to be careful when you are determining what the availability requirement should be for a business process. In particular, you have to be careful how you phrase the question. Ask a business person what the availability of a critical business process ought to be and you are liable to get an answer like "24 × 7, 365 days a year"—in other words, continuously available with no interruption. Or you'll get an answer like "99.999 percent available"—down less than six minutes a year. Achieving goals like these can be very expensive—often more than the business is willing to invest. On the other hand, if you ask "How much extra are you willing to invest to improve the process availability from 99 to 99.999 percent?" you are liable to get a very different answer—one that more realistically reflects the needs of the business.

How you ask this question can have a huge impact on the success of the project. If you ask the availability question in the naive way and get an answer that does not reflect an understanding of costs, you are (most often) in for a rude awakening. You will take the availability specification and design a system to support it. You will manage somehow to achieve the required availability (whew, was that tough!) and proceed with the design and implementation—until the resulting cost of the system becomes apparent. At this point sticker shock and rage are often followed by an audit (a.k.a. a witch hunt) of the project and system costs. This audit culminates in an ultimate reckoning in which you will be challenged to justify the cost of the system. In defense, you reference the specification, which is now re-examined in a more realistic light. The result is often a relaxation of the availability requirement and a directive to redesign the system in order to lower costs—but it may be too late! Depending upon how far you are into the project lifecycle, a redesign at this point may actually *increase* costs—not to mention introduce further delays into the project.

This unpleasant scenario arises from a failure to realistically consider the cost of meeting availability and fault tolerance requirements at the time that availability and fault tolerance are specified. You absolutely need to consider these costs when you are determining what the availability and fault tolerance constraints ought to be for the business process. The prudent level of investment should reflect the enterprise's risk exposure. Bear in mind that a fully fault-tolerant infrastructure with a no-loss-of-data site disaster recovery capability can easily require four times the investment in hardware, software, and network capacity. You need to be a good business person and ask whether and when such investments are warranted.

As the telephone billing example illustrates, reducing the impact of failures does not necessarily require reliance upon expensive system infrastructure. Clever business process design can often create a process that is tolerant of such failures without requiring expensive infrastructure. Such designs reduce business risk without calling for extraordinary system investments.

Risk-Related Service-Level Agreements

Ultimately what needs to be constrained for each business process is the level of risk resulting from various process breakdowns. The level of risk is determined by the business's tolerance for risk. Your task as an architect is to combine this level with your understanding of the investment required to increase availability and reliability to establish three service-level agreements for the process: the recovery point objective, the process availability, and the recovery time objective.

Recovery Point Objective

Data loss is a significant contributor to risk. The recovery point objective (RPO) establishes the point in time to which you want to restore data after a failure occurs. This is specified as a time interval before the moment of failure. An RPO of one hour means that the data would be restored to the state that it was in one hour before the failure occurred. The most stringent RPO has a time interval of zero, meaning that the data would be recovered to its state at the exact moment of failure—that is, no data loss. Less stringent requirements might allow for a few seconds or minutes of data to be lost. Very relaxed requirements might allow the loss of a day or a week's worth of data.

The time period for the recovery point objective will drive the strategy for duplicating the data for safekeeping. A 24-hour or 7-day recovery point objective can be met by making daily or weekly backups of data and keeping them in a safe place. Shorter time periods require increasing investments in replicating the data.

A recovery point objective in the seconds-to-minutes range requires a near-real-time replication of stored data. Because some loss is allowable, the replication of data can be asynchronous. The entries in the transaction log of one database instance can be used to update another copy of the database with a short time lag. Similarly, changes to a disk in one file system can be used to asynchronously update a disk in another file system.

The moment-of-failure recovery point objective requires the concurrent update of two or more copies of the data. No longer are you storing the data in one place and then updating another: You have to update both before the business process can conclude that the data has been successfully stored.

Business processes often have two different recovery point objectives: one covering recovery within one data center and the other covering recovery at a remote data center. Typically the in-data-center recovery point will be the moment of failure, while the between-data-center recovery point will allow for some amount of data loss.

Regardless of what the recovery point objective is, the strategy for recovery relies on the duplication of data. In this, there is a tacit assumption that the duplication renders the likelihood of data loss—losing all copies of the data—very remote. But for business processes in which the failure of a single execution can cause grave damage to either the enterprise or an individual, you should invest some time in analyzing the probability of total data loss and convincing yourself that the likelihood presents an acceptable risk.

Availability

Another risk the business faces is that the business process will not be available when needed. The availability SLA specifies the percentage of time that the business process must be available in order to meet the business need.

Recovery Time Objective

Once a failure occurs, there is risk associated with the length of time it takes to restore service. In many business processes, the risk associated with nonavailability increases as time goes on. A five-minute outage for a web site might just annoy a customer, while a one-hour outage might lose the order to a competitor, and an eight-hour outage might lose the customer altogether. The recovery time objective (RTO) establishes the length of time allowed to restore the process after a failure occurs. As with the recovery point objective, it is not unusual to have different SLAs for in-data-center failover and between-data-center failover.

Security

Your consideration of security must begin with an understanding of the business rules regarding the handling of information in your enterprise. Most enterprises have a corporate security policy that categorizes information and specifies the business rules for handling each category. Generally there are at least three information categories. At the low end of the spectrum lies unrestricted information. This is typically information about the products and services offered by the enterprise and public information about the enterprise itself. There are generally no restrictions on either accessing or transporting information in this category. In other words, there are no security requirements for information in this category.

At the other end of the spectrum lies a category of extremely sensitive information. Typically this is information regarding sensitive intellectual property, pending mergers and acquisitions, or private information about individuals and companies. The inappropriate disclosure of this type of information potentially has serious implications for the enterprise or individual. To guard against such consequences, information in this category generally has very stringent handling requirements. In the extreme, every access to such information must be authorized and logged. The business rules often require such information to be encrypted in transit or on disk, even in a database. Compliance with such requirements is expensive, impacting the design of every system that comes in contact with the information.

Between these two extremes there are generally one or more intermediate categories of information that require some level of protection, but not to the extremes required by the sensitive information. These somewhat relaxed requirements may, for example, allow information to remain un-encrypted within enterprise data centers, but still require encryption when information is moved across a public network. The rules may allow trusted systems to access the data using their own system credentials rather than the actual end user's credentials. But even though the requirements are less stringent, they still impact every system coming in contact with the information in these categories, and there is cost involved.

Since security requirements potentially impact every system involved in the business process, it is essential that you identify the category of information being used in each business process. Based on the category, you can then determine what the security requirements are. To do this, you must first acquaint yourself with the enterprise security policy that categorizes information and specifies the handling rules. After you have understood the categorization and handling rules, you can then determine their impact on the business process. You can determine whether you need to authenticate and authorize participants in the process, both human and system, and decide where in the business process you are going to do this. You can understand which data requires encryption and where in the business process encryption and decryption need to occur. And you can understand the requirements for audit logs and the specific points in the business process at which log entries need to be made.

You should also take this opportunity to document other audit and logging requirements that must be met even though they are not strictly the consequence of security policies. You need to update the business process design to reflect these decisions and document the requirements so that you are appropriately prepared to design the underlying systems.

Reporting, Monitoring, and Management

The reason you implement business processes is to standardize how particular things are done in the enterprise. The goal is to create a manageable and predictable means of achieving the desired end. People in the enterprise are going to want to know how well the business process is executing. Determining this requires information about the business process execution and a process for reporting on the process. The processes for reporting must, themselves, be designed. Even an ad hoc query regarding process status requires a user interface with access to process status information.

Reporting

We have already discussed some aspects of the process that may be involved in reports—milestones, key performance indicators, service-level agreements, availability, and so on. Now it is time to broaden the question and ask what other kinds of information are needed. What you are looking for is an understanding of the operational characteristics of the business process that are important to the enterprise. Does the enterprise need to measure error rates or decision outcomes? Does it need to track response times or throughputs? Does it need to know about (and act upon) processes that have broken down or been delayed?

Once you understand the information that is required, you need to determine how to go about capturing it. You want to make sure that what is being captured is well-defined—and actually available in the systems. Such information requirements are more easily accommodated if they are understood prior to designing the systems. They are often cumbersome and expensive to retrofit onto an existing implementation.

As part of the process design, you need to determine which participant will be responsible for capturing each required data element and at what point in the process. You need to determine which participants will accumulate, report, and act on the data. This reporting and reaction may itself be a new business process, requiring its own process design. If so, you need to update the business process inventory to reflect these decisions.

Monitoring

Reporting is an after-the-fact activity. Reporting will not fix a problem that is occurring right now. Reporting will not warn the enterprise that a deadline related to a service-level agreement is about to be missed so that action can be taken to correct the situation. For that you need to actively monitor the process.

Monitoring generally involves at least three activities: gathering information (as with reporting), comparing that information against benchmark standards to identify out-of-tolerance conditions, and then triggering the response to the out-of-tolerance condition. You need to ask yourself what this means for the business process design. You need to decide which participant will perform each of these activities. You must determine what measurements to make and what benchmark values to compare them against.

The purpose of monitoring is to trigger an appropriate response to out-of-tolerance conditions. Often that response is outside of the normal business process. It is a separate and distinct exception handling process. These exception handling processes are discussed in the next section.

Management

Note that when you treat an out-of-tolerance condition as an exception, you are basically saying that the business process is not designed to handle this condition. On the other hand, there are times when you want to monitor a process and use that monitoring information to actively manage the process. In such cases, both the measurements and the responses to various measurement conditions become an actual part of the business process. Here you need to add the measurement and comparison activities to the main business process and explore the management responses through additional scenarios. In other words, you need to enrich the process design to show how the monitoring and response actually occurs.

Process management involves many of the same activities as process monitoring. You need to gather information about the process as it is executing. You need to evaluate those measurements in order to decide what needs to be done. And you need to execute the appropriate portion of the business process—which may, itself, require management! All of these activities need to be added to the business process design, and responsibilities for them assigned to the appropriate participants.

In summary, meeting reporting, monitoring, and management requirements all require business process design. You need to consider them and factor them into the design of the business process and the supporting system architecture. This is particularly critical when the process is to be managed, as will be discussed in more detail in Chapters 29 and 42.

Exception Handling

An exception is an unusual situation for which the response has not yet been determined. As with reporting, monitoring, and management, there are responsibilities that must be assigned to participants in the business process. What kinds of exceptions are to be reported, and which participant is responsible for reporting which exceptions? To whom are these exceptions reported? Who is responsible for taking action when an exception occurs?

Exception handling is one of those areas in which the stated requirements often encompass a good deal of wishful thinking. A requirement to report business exceptions to one participant and component (system) exceptions to another presupposes that a clear distinction can be made between these two types of exceptions. Which category does a database update failure belong in? The answer depends upon the nature of the database error and its root cause. The conundrum is that this type of determination typically occurs *after* the error has been reported! Leaving the requirements in this wishful state can create a situation in which it is either impossible or impractical to comply with the requirements.

Again, before you embark upon the implementation of the business process, you want to be clear about how exceptions are to be handled and ensure that the thinking in this area is practical. You want to be clear about how each participant will go about reporting exceptions. You want to ensure that there is a process in place for responding to these exceptions, even though that process itself may be outside the scope of the project. You want to be clear about what kind of information needs to be reported to effectively execute the exception handling process.

Whatever the level of detail you have about the exception handling process, there are some basic things you must know about it. You need to know how reporting an exception triggers the exception handling process. You need to know what user interactions might be required during the investigation and resolution of the problem so you can ensure that those interfaces actually exist. Very often there is additional design work associated with these interfaces, and this work must be included in the project scope. If there is a detailed exception handling process design, you need to consider whether it needs to be modified to handle the exceptions you are now considering. You need to make clear who the first-, second-, and third-tier responders are going to be for various exceptions. This is particularly important for services, whereby the ownership of the service itself is often a topic of organizational debate.

Exception handling should be treated like any other process. You should represent it in the business process inventory. You need to explore the design of the process even if you are not responsible for its design. This exploration is necessary to reveal the required interactions with the business processes and systems you are responsible for so that you can incorporate them into the design. If you do not consciously do this as part of the design process, you are liable to end up with a design that is difficult to diagnose and repair. This, of course, will have an adverse impact on business process availability, and thus increase the risk for the enterprise.

Test and Acceptance

Before your business processes and their supporting systems go live, they are going to have to go through some level of user acceptance testing. This testing is the means by which the business process owners and users of a system gain confidence in the new design. Successfully passing these tests is a strategy for reducing the risk associated with the deployment of these changes.

It is useful for you to have some insight into the nature of these tests that will be performed. For one thing, this will help you to better understand the use to which the system will be put—that is, the larger design. Each test is an execution scenario. If you have been thorough in the business process design, you should already have incorporated these scenarios into the business process architecture. Asking about the testing scenarios is then a means of validating the completeness of the scenario coverage.

Testing Can Impact System Design

Aside from simply validating scenarios, there is additional value in understanding the nature of the tests that will be performed. Acceptance testing generally requires that specific information be captured during the test and made available for later analysis. If this information is understood at the time that the business process and systems are designed, it is generally a fairly straightforward process to ensure that the correct information is easily captured and readily available during the test. This information is often closely related to the monitoring already planned for the process. Understanding the measurements required for user testing may even help you refine your thinking about how to monitor the process under normal conditions!

Retrofitting monitoring capabilities onto an existing system is always more costly and time-consuming than designing them in from the beginning. In the worst case, the exact information that is required might not be available at all without a significant system re-design. You want to avoid these kinds of problems and factor in these requirements right from the beginning.

Testing Can Require Additional Components

Aside from capturing the required test information, you also need to consider how these tests will actually be performed. Specifically, what supporting components will be required to run the tests? Will test components be required to generate inputs? Will test components be required to capture and/or report on the data? Will the test data be examined manually, or will test components be evaluating the results? You need to keep in mind that whenever there are additional components involved, there is design work as well. Their design and construction must be factored into the project plan.

Testing Requires an Environment

The environment in which testing will be performed also needs to be considered. It is good practice to make tests repeatable. Then if you fix a problem, you can re-run the exact test to verify that the problem was, indeed, corrected. But to repeat the test, you need to be able to restore the test environment to the same initial state. This can be particularly challenging when the systems include mainframes or complex server applications sitting on top of databases. Establishing such a testing environment, if one does not already exist, requires significant effort. Obviously, this will impact the project scope.

While the actual development of test scenarios is typically the responsibility of an independent testing team, the architects need to know what the system must be capable of doing in order to support these tests. Where additional components are needed for testing, the requirements for these components must be identified and their design and implementation included in the project plan. Thus, it is prudent to define the testing requirements for each business process at this point in the project lifecycle.

Compliance Constraints

Business processes are often subject to constraints imposed by corporate, government, and regulatory policies as well as contractual agreements with other parties. Many of these constraints manifest themselves in terms that we have already discussed, such as mandated response times and security requirements. But policies, regulations, and contractual agreements can impact anything from the quality, pricing, and availability of products and services to the generation of unintended results (pollution, aggregated demographic data, etc.) and the timing of business activities (e.g., restricting stock trading around the time of reporting quarterly results).

Compliance with such constraints almost always requires some level of data gathering and measurement, and very often requires process extensions for active monitoring and management to ensure compliance with the constraint. As with other measurement, monitoring, and management requirements, they are most readily incorporated into a process while the process is being conceptualized.

Summary

To effectively support the enterprise, business processes must satisfy a number of constraints. These constraints, often referred to as nonfunctional requirements, reflect various ways in which the project's business processes and systems interact with the other business processes both within and external to the enterprise.

One major class of constraint addresses the performance capabilities of the business process itself. They specify the rate at which the process must be capable of executing, the volumes of data it is expected to handle, and the response time of the process. Closely related are key performance indicators—measures of process performance that are indicators of process health. The commitment to achieve specific performance goals is often formalized as a service-level agreement (SLA).

Another class of constraint seeks to limit the risk exposure of the business resulting from failures in executing business processes. These constraints specify limits on the amount of data that can be lost (the recovery point objective), the availability of the business process, and the length of time it takes to recover from a breakdown. The values assigned to these constraints should reflect a balanced compromise between the risk resulting from breakdowns and the investment required to lower that risk.

Enterprise security policies are another source of constraint. These policies categorize information and specify the rules for accessing and handling different categories of information. Satisfying these constraints actually requires changes to the process design, introducing activities such as authentication, authorization, encryption, and decryption. Enhanced record keeping in the form of logging and audit trails may further alter the business process design.

Reporting, monitoring, management, and exception handling also require extensions to the business process design. These requirements either reflect required interactions with external reporting, monitoring, and management processes or required extensions to the business process to take on these responsibilities. Either way, they impact the design of the business process.

The testing process may impose its own requirements on the business process design, requiring specific information to be captured and made available. Testing may also require additional components to execute the tests—components that must, themselves, be specified, designed, and implemented. Testing also requires a controlled environment that must, itself, be designed if it does not already exist. For best results, this environment must be readily restorable to known states so that problems can be diagnosed and fixes verified.

Corporate and government policies and regulations are another significant source of process constraints. Complying with the constraint may require data capture, monitoring, or proactive management—all impacting the process design.

Key Process Constraint Questions

1. Have the performance goals for the process been clearly defined? Have the measurements required to establish whether these goals are being met also been defined? Have they been incorporated into the process design?

2. Have the risks associated with failures of the business process been identified and quantified? Have the process's availability, recovery point objective, and recovery time objective been established? Have the strategies for mitigating these risks been defined? Have the strategies been incorporated into the process design?

3. Has the security classification of the information used in the business process been established? Have the business rules for the handling of this class of information been incorporated into the process design?

4. Have the reporting, monitoring, and management requirements been defined? Have these requirements been incorporated into the business process design?

5. Have the exception handling requirements been defined? Does the exception handling process exist? Has exception reporting been incorporated into the business process? Has the exception handling process been examined to determine how it will interact with the business process and systems? Have the requirements implied by such interactions been captured?

6. Has the testing approach been established? Have the appropriate information capture points been identified? Have the mechanisms for information capture and evaluation been defined? Has the test environment been defined? Are there supporting components required? How will tests be repeated in this environment?

7. What are the compliance constraints that are being placed on the project? Are there requirements related to technology selection, standards compliance, regulatory compliance, or policy compliance? Does the business process design satisfy these constraints?

Suggested Reading

Cockburn, Alistair. 2001. *Writing Effective Use Cases*. Boston, MA: Addison-Wesley.

Sharp, Alec, and Patrick McDermott. 2001. *Workflow Modeling: Tools for Process Improvement and Application Development*. Norwood, MA: Artech House, Inc.

Chapter 12

Related Processes

Business processes rarely live in isolation. Most processes depend upon artifacts generated by other processes or produce artifacts upon which other processes depend. For the enterprise to operate properly, all of these business processes must be operating and all of the interactions between them must be executing properly. To ensure proper operation, you need to understand these interactions—these dependencies between processes.

For the most part, you will discover dependencies between business processes by determining the artifacts required by each activity in the process you are designing. For those artifacts that originate outside the process, you determine the business process that generates the artifact. You have now identified a required interaction between the two processes. A similar examination of the results that are produced and their destinations will reveal other process interactions.

Beyond identifying these interactions, you need to determine whether the related processes will require work, and thus impact the scope of the project. The work required may be the creation of the entire process, or it may be the modification of the process to generate the required artifact and make it accessible. This analysis will guide you in determining the true scope of the project.

For example, the `Withdraw Cash via ATM` process (Figure 11–1) needs to determine which bank it should communicate with, and therefore there must be an association between the bank and the ATM card. Where does this information come from? In the proposed design, this information is produced by the process that issues the ATM card along with an association between the card and the account (Figure 12–1).

Some of these business processes are new and will be created as part of the project. The issuing of ATM cards and PINs and the installation and servicing of ATMs are examples of this. But other processes already exist and will require modification. The `Manage Account Balance` process is already in place and is used routinely by the human tellers in the bank branches. This process will require some modification to support the ATM processes. Not only does the ATM system require access to this process, but it also requires a new concept—an `Account Hold`—to deal with the possibilities of breakdowns during a withdrawal transaction. If it does not already have this capability, the process of managing the account balance will have to be modified to add it.

For some artifacts, the related business process may not be obvious at first. The initial account balance, updated account balance, and funds reservation are examples. Intuitively, their scope of utilization extends beyond this business process. The account balance will be impacted by deposits and funds transfers. The account hold will impact funds transfers as well as ordinary withdrawals. And the updated account balance will affect other processes as well. Such situations are not only indicators of the existence of another process (whether or not it is recognized at this point), but that other process is often a candidate to be a service. This will be discussed further in the next section.

It is important that you actively seek out process interactions early in the design process. In a project there is a natural tendency to focus almost exclusively on the main business processes, since they are the ones that provide the value to the enterprise. Unfortunately, this narrow focus tends to overlook the related processes that provide required inputs. A failure to identify these processes can create situations in which the need for inputs and the processes that generate them is not even identified until the project is well into the development phase. In the worst case, you will not discover the missing work until you are ready to test the primary business process for the first time—at which point you realize that you are missing a needed input. Such late identification of dependencies can play havoc with both the cost and schedule for a project, often leading to less-than-optimal quick-fix solutions because of the time pressure—pressure that could have been avoided!

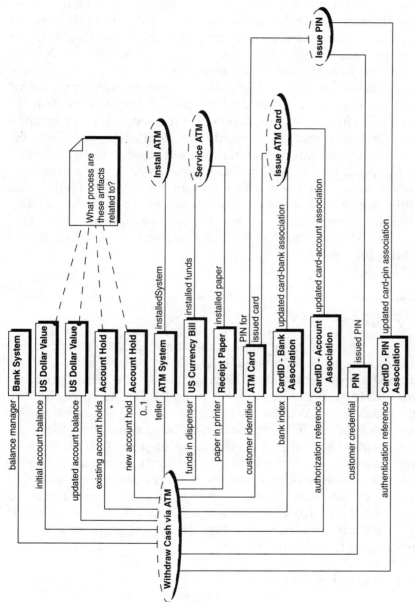

Figure 12–1: *Interactions with Related Processes—Partial*

There is another benefit from actively looking for these interactions while the project is still in its formative stages. Many times the true complexity of and feasibility issues related to the project lie not in the creation of the mainstream business processes at all, but in the number and complexity of the related business processes. Such situations can arise when you are conceptualizing a workflow system in which work will be assigned to individuals based on their skills or other qualifications. Where does this skill and qualification information come from? Does it already exist somewhere, and in a form that can be used? If the enterprise has thousands of employees and the inventory of employee skills is not in a form that can be used in the workflow (i.e., the information is in a paper folder), then the process of getting this information into the proper form and maintaining it accurately may turn out to be more trouble than it is worth. If you do not chase down the need for this information and seek out the process that generates it, you may end up building a workflow that assumes the availability of this information, only to discover much later that it is impractical to obtain and maintain this information.

Identifying Services

There are four artifacts in the `Withdraw Cash via ATM` example that have not, as of yet, been related to other processes: the `initial account balance`, the `updated account balance`, the `existing account holds`, and the `new account hold`. If you think about it, the relationship between these particular artifacts and other business processes is not simple. The `new account hold` is consumed by both this process and by any other process attempting to withdraw funds or check funds availability. The `existing account holds` might originate in another instance of this process or from any other process that places holds on account funds. The `initial account balance` comes from whatever process last altered the account balance, and the `updated account balance` is an input to any other process requiring knowledge of the account balance.

Managing Shared State

What is different about these artifacts is that they are not simply values that are being passed around. These artifacts denote the states of the

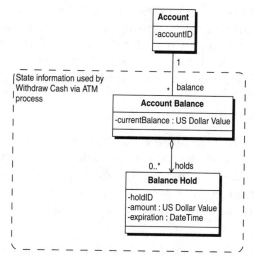

Figure 12–2: *State Information Used by Withdraw Cash via ATM Process*

account balance (Figure 12–2).[1] Each of the holds on the account reserves some of the funds in the account for some purpose. In the `Withdraw Cash via ATM` process, the hold is used to ensure that the funds about to be delivered are not used for some other purpose between the time the disbursal is authorized and the time the successful disbursal is reported.

It is not unusual for a business process to examine state information, make a decision based on that information, and then update the state. As Figure 12–2 illustrates, that state information is often more than the state of a single object—it is a set of self-consistent information. In authorizing the disbursal of funds, the `currentBalance` is retrieved and the `amount` from each `Balance Hold` is subtracted. If the remaining funds are sufficient to cover the requested withdrawal, the withdrawal is approved and a new hold is added to the balance in the amount of the withdrawal.

In this sequence, there is a tacit assumption that the state will not change between the time the available balance is computed and the

---

1. An account may have more than one balance associated with it. For example, a credit card account might have a purchases balance, a cash advance balance, and a payment due balance.

time the new hold is placed on the balance. If some other business process were to modify the state during this time (e.g., withdraw all the available funds), the result might be incorrect. For correct operation, the access and manipulation of this state information must be managed. You have identified an opportunity for a service.

Refining the Service Definition

Based solely on the `Withdraw Cash via ATM` business process, a sketch of an `Account Balance Management Service` begins to emerge (Figure 12–3). This service is responsible for the `Manage Account Balance` process, which in the present state of the design is defined by the interactions required for the `Withdraw Cash via ATM` process.

Reexamining the `Withdraw Cash via ATM` process with the proposed service in mind (Figure 12–4) leads to other questions: Should the proposed service perform the additional operations of identifying the customer and account and checking to see whether that customer is authorized to access the account? Should the proposed service be the actual interface between the bank and the ATM system?

Based on this single scenario, the answer to these questions is not obvious. Furthermore, there is more to managing an account balance than just withdrawing funds. To resolve these questions and determine the full scope of the proposed service, you need to examine other scenarios (a hacker trying to access the bank via the ATM interface, for example) and other business processes. Through such explorations you will

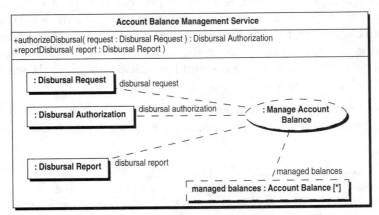

Figure 12–3: *Partial Account Balance Management Service*

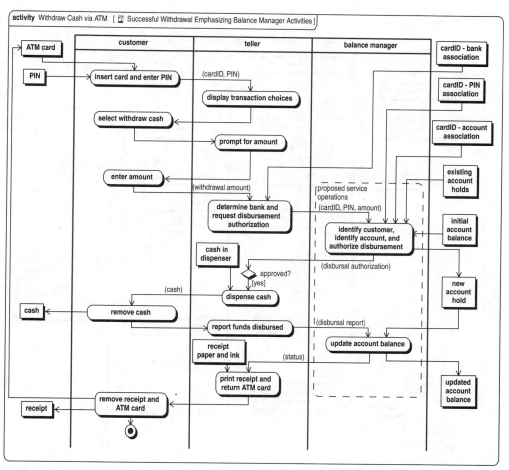

Figure 12–4: *Proposed Service in the Withdraw Cash via ATM Process*

be able to propose and test various ideas about the scope of the proposed service and the balance of responsibilities for the bank.

It is clear that the other primary business processes of the ATM example must be examined to determine the scope of the `Account Balance Management Service`. The `Make Deposit via ATM`, `Check Balance via ATM`, and `Transfer Funds via ATM` business processes all interact in obvious ways with the account balance.

But there are other business processes that interact with the state of the account balance as well, specifically those involving a human teller. Figure 12–5 highlights the activities in the `Withdraw Cash via`

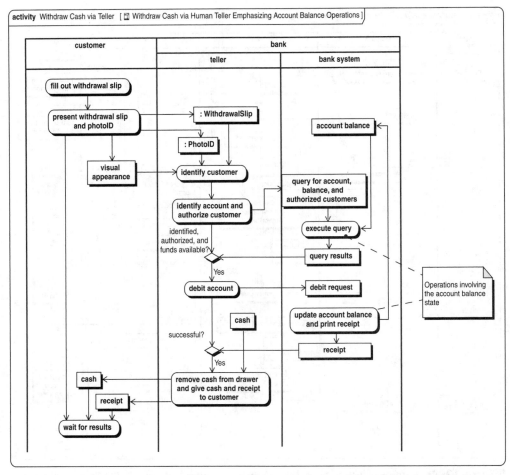

Figure 12–5: *Fragment of Withdraw Cash via Human Teller Showing Bank System Activities*

Human Teller process that involve the account balance state. Examining these activities raises some interesting questions. One very interesting question is whether the update **account balance and print receipt** activity of the existing bank system could be modified to play the role of **update account balance** in the ATM scenario. In other words, can you reuse existing functionality as the basis of the service and thus avoid implementation costs?

Whatever the final service ends up as, it is clear that the **Withdraw Cash via ATM** process interacts with that service. This factoring of the

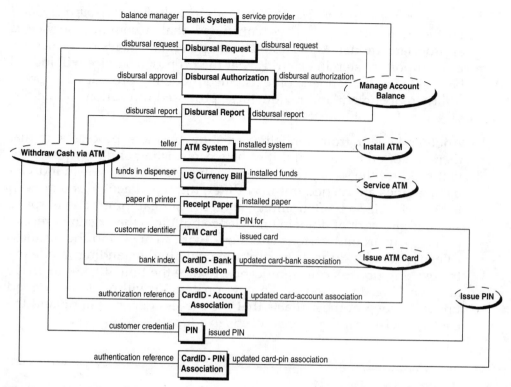

Figure 12–6: *Interactions with Related Processes—Completed*

service out of the business process leads to a different set of artifacts being involved in the interactions, as shown in Figure 12–6.

Modeling Existing Processes

As this example illustrates, when there are existing business processes that produce the same results as new business processes, it is often useful to model the existing processes. One benefit is that such modeling will help you understand whether there are portions of the existing process that might be reused in the new process. This type of analysis is essential when building a service-oriented architecture. Modeling both the new and existing processes helps you to identify opportunities for sharing functionality between the old and new processes. In other words, it helps you identify potential business services. While you need to investigate further to determine whether a common service could indeed be used in both processes, if you do not model both processes *you will not even be able to identify these service opportunities!* Furthermore, once you have concluded that a common service is appropriate, modeling these and other potential usages of the service is an important step in ensuring that the proposed service will indeed be usable in all intended contexts. Such modeling provides an opportunity to document and review these proposed utilizations of the service and thus validate its utility.

Another benefit from modeling existing business processes is that there are often many similarities between existing and new processes that produce the same results. Although the means by which individual activities are carried out may differ, the actual activities that need to be performed are often similar, and have similar inputs and outputs. There is also a lot of domain knowledge built into the existing process, particularly around various situations that can arise and the business rules for handling them. In capturing this understanding, modeling the existing process can significantly reduce the time it takes to arrive at a working definition of the new process. It will give you a good understanding of the artifacts that the process depends upon and the contingencies that the process needs to address.

Triggering Events

Business processes and their individual activities do not start spontaneously. There is always some event that triggers execution. Sometimes this triggering event marks the arrival of a required input. When you are playing catch, for example, you catch the ball when the ball arrives. The arrival of the ball (or, to be more precise, your observation of its approach) is the event that triggers your catching of the ball. And if you are not trying to detect the event—not watching for the ball— you won't perform the required action.

While some triggering events correspond to the arrival of needed inputs or the completion of previous activities in the process, other triggering events may be totally unrelated to the process. What triggers your reading of the mail is not necessarily the arrival of the mail. You may choose to read it when you come home from work or when you take a break. While you obviously cannot read the mail prior to its arrival, the actual event that triggers your reading of the mail does not have to be related to the delivery of the mail.

You commonly find both types of triggering events in business processes. When a result needs to be moved from one system to another, the actual transfer of that result might be triggered by its creation, or it might be scheduled to occur at some arbitrary point in time—unrelated to previous activities. Consider the movement of purchase requests from a production planning system to a purchasing system (Figure 12–7). Depending upon the process design, the movement of the purchase request might be triggered by the generation of the purchase request or by some unrelated event.

Batch transfers provide a common example of unrelated events. With batch transfers, the purchase requests are created and saved in the production planning system. The triggering events for the transfer are timers—unrelated to the process flow. At 12 a.m. a batch job is run that queries the production planning system and generates a file containing the previous day's purchase requests. At 2 a.m. this file is transferred (probably along with many other files) to the purchasing system (and possibly transformed as well). At 4 a.m. another batch job is run that reads the file and inserts the purchase requests into the purchasing system.

The antithesis of the batch transfer is the real-time transfer driven by business events. In this approach, the creation of the purchase request in the production planning system triggers the sending of a message announcing the new purchase request. The arrival of this message in the purchasing system, in turn, triggers its entry and subsequent processing. Here the result of one activity serves as the trigger for the subsequent activity.

This distinction between the arrival of inputs and the triggering event may seem to be a small point, but it can be very significant. The

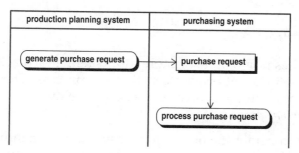

Figure 12–7: *The Movement of Purchase Requests*

absence of a triggering event will cause a business process to fail just as surely as the lack of a needed input. Consequently, you must pay as much attention to triggering events and their sources as you do to the required inputs for each activity. If there are steps in a business process that have triggering events originating in another process, you must consider the design of that other process and the interactions that convey the triggering event. In other words, you need to treat triggering events as just another form of required input.

Independent Processes

Let's now take a step back and look at entire processes and their interactions with other processes. Some business processes are completely self-contained—they have no interactions with other processes during their execution. Once the process has been triggered, the activities within the process generate all of the inputs required for the remaining activities in the process, both results and triggering events. Once the initial triggering event occurs, everything else that happens in the process is completely determined by the process itself. These are called *independent processes* to emphasize that that they do not depend on any other processes for successful execution.

The closed nature of an independent process makes it easy to document in a single UML activity diagram. For example, consider the consumer in-store check-out process shown in Figure 12–8. The process has one initial triggering event, the arrival of the `customer` at the head of the check-out queue. The triggering event for subsequent activities is the completion of a previous activity in the process or the arrival of an artifact from another activity. You can see that this process is completely self-contained, dependent only upon the activities within the process. Its execution is thus independent of the execution of any other process.

Dependent Processes

Many processes rely on one or more inputs (either artifacts or triggering events) that do not originate within the process. These processes are dependent upon the processes that generate these artifacts and are termed *dependent processes*.

For example, consider the online purchasing of merchandise shown in Figure 12–9. The triggering event for this process is the customer's deci-

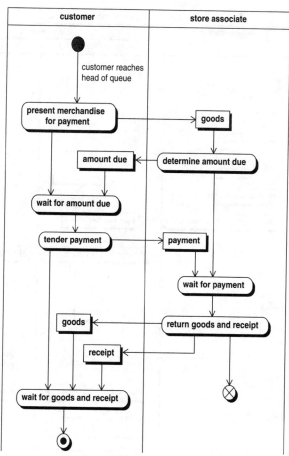

Figure 12–8: *An Independent Process*

sion to purchase. The process proceeds as if it were an independent process from this point up until just after the `pick order` is printed in the warehouse. But at that point, the process waits for a warehouse worker to `decide to get next assignment`. This decision is the triggering event for the `get next order` activity, but this event does not originate within the process. The actual triggering event may be the worker's completion of another order, the end of a coffee break, or the beginning of the work day. In any case, this triggering event is completely unrelated to the previous steps of this particular purchase. Since the purchasing process is dependent upon this unrelated event, it is a dependent process.

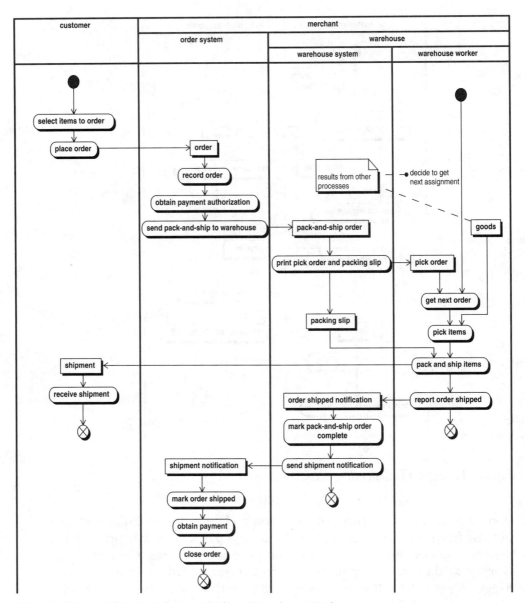

Figure 12–9: *Basic Catalog or Online Merchant Order*

The source of this dependent triggering event may seem like a small point, but when you are trying to actually manage the process this event is extremely important. You cannot, for example, make this process execute quickly without having some control over the timing of when a worker decides to get the next assignment. A lazy or absent worker can delay shipment, which may cause the shipment to occur later than promised, resulting in an unhappy customer and possibly a service-level agreement violation with an associated financial penalty. Every process that depends upon human participation is a dependent process.

This example contains another external dependency as well: It depends upon the availability of the goods to be shipped. The presence of these goods is itself the result of another process—one that is not shown in the diagram in Figure 12–9. If these goods are absent, no product can be shipped. Furthermore, if the goods are not present, then the order becomes a back order, which has a different execution scenario. The back-order scenario includes activities that trigger the ordering of missing items and activities for subsequently shipping the goods. These shipment activities are triggered by the eventual arrival of the goods, another external dependency.

External process dependencies can have a significant impact on the execution of a business process. Even if there is no design work involved, these dependencies represent possible sources of failure. Thus, when you find external dependencies, you should consider whether the design of the process should encompass mechanisms for detecting the absence of expected inputs and alerting people to their absence. In the case of the warehouse worker, an alert might be generated by the warehouse system if a shipment notification is not generated within eight hours after the generation of the pick order. In the case of the back order, if the merchandise is not in stock, a notice might be sent to the customer, with a copy to the stock-ordering system as well. Further action might be required if the goods have not arrived within 30 days.

Towards Event-Driven Processes

Completely independent processes are relatively uncommon in practice. Most business processes coordinate the work of autonomous entities, whether they are individual people or entire organizations. Autonomous entities generally decide, on their own, when to perform work. The overall business process is thus dependent upon these decisions.

Much of today's innovation in business process design lies in rethinking the interactions between processes. In older designs, the ordering process and the pack-and-ship process may well have been completely independent, each being driven by a daily schedule. The order system might have accumulated the pack-and-ship orders in a batch file, which would be transferred each night to the warehouse system. The daily schedule of the pack-and-ship process would trigger the printing of those pick orders, which would then be taken to the supervisor for distribution to warehouse workers.

This old-style process design relies on many triggering events that are unrelated to the actual processing of an order. A more modern event-driven process design might move individual orders, as they are received, through the warehouse system and to workstations on the warehouse floor. Wherever possible in the event-driven style, the completion of one activity in the process serves as the triggering event for the next. Such designs eliminate the delays associated with waiting for unrelated events, and thus make it possible to provide services such as the same-day shipping of merchandise.

Note that when you are reengineering processes in this manner—from batch-oriented to event-driven—virtually all of the activities from the original process remain intact. They still require the same inputs and produce the same results. What changes are the triggering events for some of the activities and, to a lesser extent, the performers of those activities. Because of the similarities, an analysis of the as-is process will yield a great deal of information about the to-be process.

This distinction between dependent and independent processes may seem like a nuance at first, but it has a great impact on the way you go about monitoring and managing processes. If a process is independent, then you can manage (control) each execution of the process as an independent entity. The management begins with the initial triggering event for the process and can actively direct all work, telling each participant which activity to perform and when to perform it. The management is providing the triggering event for each activity and is thus relatively straightforward. But if the process is dependent on events from other processes, then all the process manager can do is to observe whether or not the event actually occurs. Furthermore, unless a service-level agreement (SLA) has been established regarding the timing of this external event, the process manager has no basis upon which to decide whether or not a problem exists. These issues will be discussed in more detail in Chapters 41 and 42.

Summary

Most business processes interact with other business processes. They provide inputs to those processes and consume results from those processes. These processes collaborate, and the proper operation of the overall collaboration requires the proper execution of these interactions. Because of this, the processes that are the sources of all inputs and the destinations of all outputs must be identified.

Sometimes the input to a process is not an artifact but is instead the current state of an artifact, and the result of the process is a change in state to that artifact. When the state of that artifact can be modified by another process instance, some control must be exercised over the artifact to ensure proper execution of the process. This control is actually another process that is being executed by a service, a service that manages the state of that artifact. This service not only provides the state information and makes the state changes, but it provides transactional control over these activities as well.

When a state management service interacts with more than one process, every process it interacts with needs to be modeled in order to fully specify the service. Existing processes that use this state information must be examined as well as new processes that are being created.

Some process inputs are simply events that trigger the execution of an activity within the process. When a process requires such triggering events, its execution becomes dependent upon the process that generates those events. A process that does not require any input triggering events is an independent process.

Independent processes can still be consumers of artifacts generated by other processes, but the movement of those artifacts is unrelated to their creation. This introduces delays in the movement from one process to another, and thus retards the overall business process. Using the creation of the artifact as the triggering event for its movement to the other process creates a real-time, event-driven business process that minimizes processing delays.

Key Related Process Questions

1. Have the business process sources for all required input artifacts been identified? Have the business process recipients for all result artifacts been identified?
2. Have the sources of all triggering events been identified, particularly those that arise outside the business process?

3. With respect to each identified process interaction, are the interactions driven by the creation of the artifact or by some external event? Would the process be improved by using the creation of the artifact as the trigger for the interaction? Would the receiving process be improved by using the arrival of the artifact as a triggering event for an activity in that process?

Chapter 13

Modeling the Domain

Thus far, the consideration of business processes has focused primarily on their procedural aspects. But as you are discussing the process, you are inevitably learning about the domain itself. You hear references to information used in the process—withdraw cash requests, sales orders, and so forth. You hear discussions about the results being generated, such as cash, receipts, and goods shipments. You hear about other things related to the process, such as bank accounts, ATM cards, and credit reports. And you hear about the participants in the process: customers, bank tellers, banks, and, of course, the system you are designing.

Virtually all of these things that are discussed in reference to the business process will have some form of representation in the system you are building. So it is in your own interest to begin capturing an understanding of what these things are. As you learn about the business process, you need to keep track of the different types of things that you have come across. As you learn about their important characteristics you need to keep track of them as well. This is the purpose of the *domain model*.

The reason you want to put a domain model together is to get an accurate big-picture understanding of what can actually happen in the application domain. You want to capture a working understanding of the types of things that your systems will need to deal with, so you need to be aware of their existence. If you need to be able to reference individual entities—whether they are people or products—then you need to know how those individuals will be identified. If the business process makes decisions based on their characteristics, then you need to know what these characteristics are.

Many of these concepts have relationships to one another. Bank accounts are related to specific customers and to specific banks. Shipments are associated with specific orders. These relationships are as important as the things to which they relate, so you want to capture an understanding of them in your domain model as well.

Your understanding of relationships, and in particular their multiplicity, will have a profound impact on the design of your data structures and the way systems interact with them. Is a bank account associated with a single customer, or can there be multiple people associated with a single bank account? The answers to such questions will directly impact the way in which you design data structures and database schema, and these things are extraordinarily difficult and expensive to change once they have been implemented. Consequently, you want to make sure that you have an accurate understanding of what can really happen in the application domain so that your systems are fully capable of handling this variety.

Domain modeling does not strive for completeness. You are not trying to capture every single attribute associated with every concept, nor are you trying to decide what the representations (data types) of the attributes should be. You are simply trying to understand what concepts are relevant, what relationships can exist between them, and which of their attributes play a major role in the business processes.

The domain model not only helps you understand the information involved in the business processes, but it also serves as a guide for partitioning the information and assigning system-of-record ownership responsibilities. As discussed in Chapter 3, the ownership of relationships is a major issue when the related concepts are "owned" by different components or services, inevitably necessitating the replication of some information about the related concepts. A good domain model will help you quickly understand the implications of partitioning the data in various ways.

UML Class Notation

The UML class notation provides an excellent means of representing a domain model. The concepts in the domain—bank accounts, ATM cards, customers, orders, and the like—are represented as UML classes. Classes[1] represent types of things. A class is depicted as a rectangle divided into three regions, called compartments (Figure 13–1). The first compartment contains the name of the concept, such as `Person`. The second compartment contains attributes that characterize the concept, such as a person's `name`, `date of birth`, `height`, and `hair color`. Some of these attributes may be fixed for any given individual, such as a person's date of birth. Others, such as height or hair color, may change with time. The third compartment contains operations— things that instances of the concept can *do*. A person can, for example, `sleep`, `eat`, and `walk`.

For some passive objects, such as bank accounts, the notion of operations may not be meaningful. But for other objects, such as the active participants in the business processes, operations may be quite appropriate. The display of the attribute and operation compartments is optional in any given diagram, as is the display of individual attributes and operations. In other words, you can be selective about the attributes and operations you wish to display in any given diagram.

For the most part, you will not be paying much attention to operations in your domain modeling, particularly early in the business process analysis. Operations generally reflect design decisions and become relevant relatively late in the design process. During the process design,

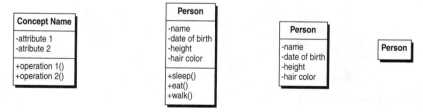

Figure 13–1: *Basic UML Class Notation*

---

1. Also referred to as Classifiers in UML 2.0.

the responsibilities of participants are reflected in the activity diagrams. So, during process design you should focus primarily upon concepts and their important attributes.

As important as concepts are, the relationships between them are equally important. Relationships between concepts are called *associations* in UML and are depicted as a line drawn between the two related concepts (Figure 13–2). An association can be annotated at each end to indicate the *role* that the concept plays in the relationship. The example indicates that a `Person` may be an `employee` of a `Company`, and a `Company` can be the `employer` of a Person.[2] You can also annotate each end of the association to indicate the possible multiplicity of the relationship. The example indicates that a `Company` can have 0 or more `employees` (the asterisk represents an unbounded value), and that a `Person` can have 0 or more `employers`.

Your understanding of multiplicity is crucial to creating a flexible and stable design, for it will determine the basic organization of your data structures. Changing the organization of data structures is an expensive and time-consuming process—one that should be avoided wherever possible. As such, it is prudent to explore multiplicities with the business community to understand what can *actually happen in the application domain*. By seeking an understanding of the multiplicity possibilities in the domain rather than the possibly more restricted multiplicity implemented in the current business process, you will be designing flexibility into the data structures that will allow the enterprise to evolve.

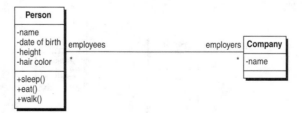

Figure 13–2: *Basic UML Association*

---

2. If you are familiar with the Chen Entity-Relationship (E-R) notation, note that the role names in UML appear at the opposite ends of the association as compared to the E-R notation.

Imagine that you are designing a database for a business's online phone directory. What is the relationship between a person and a phone? Consider the relationship shown in Figure 13–3. What are the appropriate multiplicities for the association? If any given person either has a work phone or does not, and each phone is assigned to exactly one person, then the multiplicity of each end of the association is 0..1. You might then represent a phone book entry as a single record containing the person's name and the phone number, reflecting this one-to-one relationship between person and phone. The user interfaces for updating and querying the phone book would be designed with this 1:1 relationship in mind.

Now consider what would happen if the system were designed with this 1:1 multiplicity, and then somebody got a second phone line, or two people started sharing a phone, or both. Not only would the database need to be changed, but all the components that interacted with the database would need to change as well. This would be an expensive change to say the least.

So as you explore the business process, you want to make every attempt to be sure that you get the relationships and their multiplicities right. The time to explore the possibilities and make mistakes is now, when the design is still on paper and before you have begun investing in detailed design and implementation. Changing your mind now is inexpensive. The later you make the changes, the more expensive they become.

When you have an association between concepts, there is often information related to the association that you wish to capture. Consider the Employment relationship shown in Figure 13–4. When a person works for a company, there is information associated with each instance of this relationship, such as an `employeeID`, a `salary`, and a `title`. The presence of such information is represented with an association class, which is a class connected to the association itself by a dashed

Figure 13–3: *Phone Directory Example*

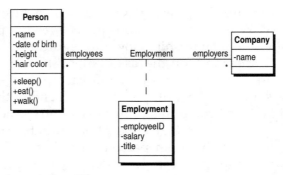

Figure 13–4: *Association Class*

line. In this class you place the attributes that are relevant to the association. The semantics of the association class is that one set of this information exists for each instance of the association.

It takes some time and practice to become adept at modeling. One of the more common modeling mistakes is to blur the distinction between the role that a class plays and the class itself. The result is that the two are represented as a single concept. The roles of `Employee` and `Customer` are two common examples, as shown in Figure 13–5. Here each class contains a mixture of information about the person (e.g., the `name`) and information related to the role that the person is playing (e.g., `employeeID`). From this representation it is difficult to recognize that the same person could potentially be both a customer and an employee.

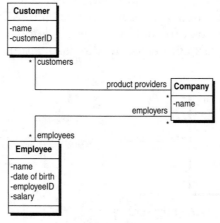

Figure 13–5: *Merged Concepts and Roles*

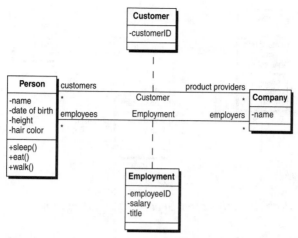

Figure 13–6: *Employment and Customer as Association Classes*

Contrast this with the model shown in Figure 13–6, which shows the concept of `Person` explicitly, and shows `Employment` and `Customer` as relationships between a `Person` and a `Company`. When you are having difficulty in modeling, the first question you should ask yourself is whether you have accidentally merged a concept and a relationship into a single class. If this is the case, separating the class from the relationship (i.e., explicitly showing the relationship) will resolve the difficulty.

These modeling difficulties usually arise when you are trying to show relationships between the "combined" class and other concepts. Let's take the combined employee/person class and look at two relationships, both of which are relevant to an employment situation (Figure 13–7). One of these relationships is the supervisor/direct report relationship,

Figure 13–7: *Relationship Difficulties with a Combined Concept/Role Class*

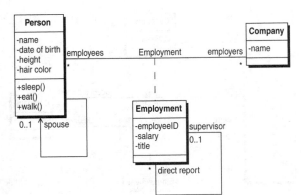

Figure 13–8: *Relationships after Separating Concept and Role*

and the other is a spousal relationship (this might be required for insurance purposes, for example). The problem with this model is that it implies that the spouse is also an employee, which is most likely not the case.

Contrast this with the representation shown in Figure 13–8. Here the concept of `Person` has been separated from the concept of `Employment`. Now the spousal relationship from person to person can no longer be confused with the supervisor/direct report relationship between employees. The overall model is much clearer.

ATM Example Domain Model

Building a domain model is an iterative process. You capture your current understanding, examine the implications (often reviewing the model with key stakeholders), and then refine the model. Figure 13–9 shows an initial cut at the domain model for the ATM example. It represents some of the basic concepts in the domain: `Person`, `Account`, `Bank`, `Bank System`, `ATM Card`, `PIN`, and `ATM System`. It also represents the relationships among them.

There are a couple of problems with this model as it stands. `Account` is shown as an association between `Person` and `Bank`. While this captures the idea that a person can have many accounts, it also implies that there can only be one person associated with an account. This is a restriction that is not consistent with real bank accounts, and the

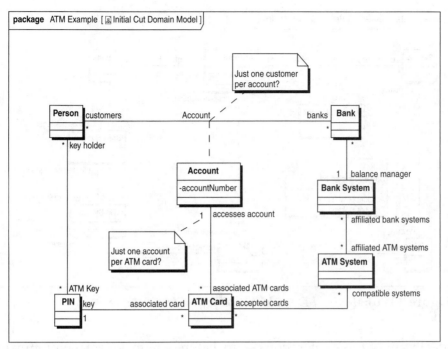

Figure 13–9: *Initial Cut Domain Model for the ATM Example*

model is, therefore, incorrect. The model also shows that there is exactly one `Account` associated with each `ATM Card`. This would make it impossible to perform funds transfers between accounts and is therefore incorrect as well.

Figure 13–10 presents a refined domain model for the ATM example. `Account` is now a concept on its own and can have multiple `account holders`. The `ATM Card` can now be associated with more than one account—which actually creates a design complexity: Since the card can be associated with multiple accounts, the person using the card will have to specify the accounts to be involved in the transaction.

The refined model also raises an additional question: Should the `ATM Card` be associated with the `Account` or with the `Account Holder`? If the card is associated with the account and there are multiple cards on the account, then it may not be clear which person is using the card. This is the appropriate time to explore such questions—before any design commitments have been made. Ask the business people whether it makes a difference, and help them explore the implications.

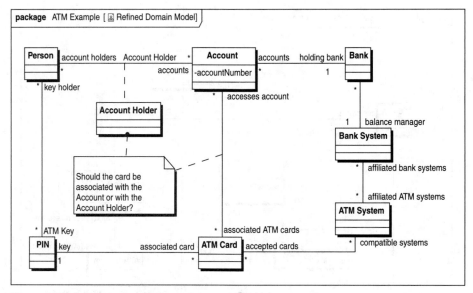

Figure 13–10: *Refined Domain Model for ATM Example*

Ideally, all of this exploration occurs before you make any commitment to data structures—messages, file formats, and database schemas. But even if these data structures already exist, your domain model will help you understand any limitations in these data structures—real-world situations that the existing data structures cannot adequately represent. These are limitations in the enterprise's ability to cope with real-world situations and thus represent risk for the enterprise. It is prudent then to have a discussion with the business community regarding these limitations, the business risks they present, and whether these risks warrant investing in changes to the systems.

Reverse Engineering the Domain Model

While you can learn a lot about the domain model by talking about business processes, you can learn a lot about existing processes by examining the data structures in their databases and communications. This is a relatively straightforward exercise when these data representations have formal representations such as the data definition language (DDL) used to define SQL database schemas or the XML schema definition (XSD) used to define XML data structures.

When reverse engineering data structures, however, you need to do some interpretation to determine the overall domain model. Each individual schema generally represents only a fragment of the whole. Furthermore, many schemas contain partial data about concepts and relationships, and other schemas contain additional data about these same concepts and relationships. Because these representations evolved independently, they may not be consistent in their representations. You need to determine how these fragmentary representations relate to one another as you assemble the domain model.

Another issue you will face is that the natural structure of the data may be somewhat obscured and flattened in these representations. A single record may contain both customer and person information, perhaps with a smattering of phone and address information as well. Some analysis will be required to recover the true structure, particularly with respect to roles.

Some of the data you will encounter may be design artifacts that are not properly part of the domain model at all. A record sequence number that gives a unique identity to each record in a file, for example, is just a design artifact related to the structure of that file and has no significance in the domain model itself. One of the challenges you will face is distinguishing such design artifacts from the relevant domain data.

Despite these shortcomings and challenges, reverse engineering existing data structures can save you a lot of time. It will also raise the visibility of data that might not be otherwise mentioned in the discussion of the business process. It is a good practice to look at existing data structures while you are building your understanding of the business processes. This will afford you the opportunity to ask about the significance of the data and how it relates to the business process.

Domain Modeling Summary

Concepts and relationships play a major role in the design of both business processes and their supporting systems. They represent the information on which business processes operate. This information will be stored in databases, communicated between participants, and displayed and edited in user interfaces. It drives the decision-making logic of the business process itself. To effectively design business processes and systems, you need to understand this information and how it is being used. You must also decide where this information will reside and how it will be accessed and maintained. The more you understand about these concepts and relationships, the better you will be able to design the business processes and the systems that support them.

Although you need to understand the overall structure of this information, namely the basic concepts and relationships, along with a few key attributes, you do not need all of their detail at this time. What you need to understand in order to architect the business processes and systems is the following:

- What concepts exist, and the relationships that exist among them
- The multiplicity of the relationships
- The attributes used to identify instances of concepts and relationships in situations in which the identity is important in the business process
- The attributes that are used for decision making in the business process

These things have deep implications for the design of the system. If the ATM card can be associated with more than one account, then every user interaction that starts with an ATM card must in some manner ask the customer to identify the account that is the target of each transaction. If you design a system for a single account, this dialog will be absent. If you later decide that you want to add support for multiple accounts, many portions of the design will be impacted. Thus, it is important at this stage of the design process to understand what might be possible in the application domain and consciously decide how much of that variability should be accommodated in the business process and system design. You want these to be conscious decisions, not accidents of design.

If there is no cost impact associated with handling this flexibility, then you should obviously build the flexibility into the design. It would be foolish not to do so. But if there is a cost impact, part of the decision-making process should be to acquaint the business stakeholders with the relative costs of changing the design at some point in the future as opposed to incorporating the flexibility into the current design. Again, multiplicities of relationships are of particular interest. If you design the ATM system to only work with a single bank (the one that owns the ATM system) and later decide that you want to provide services for other banks as well, there will be many changes required to the design. It is prudent, therefore, to spend time with the business stakeholders early in the design process to explore such possibilities before any design commitments have been made. Since they are the ones making the investment in the system, they should be the ones balancing short-term investment decisions against long-term risk for the business.

This discussion has only scratched the surface of modeling. Modeling is an art—one that requires some experience in order to develop proficiency. There is often more than one way to represent a situation, and one representation is not necessarily "more correct" than another. For guidance in modeling, refer to *Object-Oriented Modeling and Design with UML, Second Edition*[3] and similar books. For proper use of the notation itself, refer to *The Unified Modeling Language Reference Manual, Second Edition.*[4]

Key Domain Modeling Questions

1. Have the major concepts and relationships involved in the process been added to the domain model?
2. Has the possible multiplicity of all relationships been established?
3. Have the key attributes involved in identification and decision making been identified?
4. Has the model been validated and reviewed with the business community?

Suggested Reading

Blaha, Michael and James Rumbaugh. 2005. *Object-Oriented Modeling and Design with UML, Second Edition.* Upper Saddle River, New Jersey: Prentice Hall.

Rumbaugh, James, Ivar Jacobson, and Grady Booch. 2005. *The Unified Modeling Language Reference Manual, Second Edition.* Boston, MA: Addison-Wesley.

---

3. Blaha, Michael, and James Rumbaugh. 2005. *Object-Oriented Modeling and Design with UML, Second Edition.* Upper Saddle River, NJ: Prentice Hall.

4. Rumbaugh, James, Ivar Jacobson, and Grady Booch. 2005. *The Unified Modeling Language Reference Manual, Second Edition.* Boston, MA: Addison-Wesley.

Chapter 14

Enterprise Architecture: Process and Domain Modeling

Unless you are creating an enterprise from scratch, your projects are generally not starting with a clean slate and building entire business processes and their supporting systems. Each project is making incremental changes to existing business processes and systems, operating in areas where other projects have been before.

There is considerable overlap in projects with respect to business processes and domain models, and therefore an opportunity to share information and reduce the amount of work required for each project. If one project has developed a model of a business process or part of a domain, subsequent projects should be able to build on that work, extending and refining it. One of the key responsibilities of the enterprise architecture group is to develop this shared understanding of business processes and their related domain models.

For one project to build upon the work of another, there must be consistency in how things are done from one project to another. Standards are required for representing business processes and domain models as well as for the mechanics of archiving and versioning these models. The enterprise architecture group is responsible for this archive and the quality of its contents.

Skills are also required—skills in process modeling and domain modeling. The enterprise architecture group will contain the greatest concentration of these skills in the enterprise, but it is generally impractical for this group to directly do the modeling for each project. Instead, this work must largely be done by project architects. However, these project architects must have the appropriate skills to do this work, and it is the enterprise architecture group's responsibility to ensure that they do. Toward this end, the enterprise architecture group must determine (and often deliver) appropriate training, mentor project architects, and review their work.

As a whole, the process and domain modeling group will have two interrelated streams of work. One will focus on assembling the overall model for the enterprise and organizing that information to make it accessible to those who need it. The other stream will focus on the needs of individual projects, both transferring knowledge to them and specifying common process patterns and data models as required. For the sake of project efficiency, it is important that the enterprise group be proactive in both of these activities. Helping the project team get the process and domain models right the first time, and ensuring that they are using the appropriate business process patterns and common data representations will be far more efficient than showing them their mistakes after the fact. Late reviews and feedback will make the project teams reluctant to adopt the changes, and small changes may not be made at all due to schedule pressures. For a quality result, the process and domain modeling group needs to be aggressively involved in project activities.

Process and Domain Modeling Responsibilities

Process and domain modeling are skills that can only be acquired with practice. The number of people who are truly adept at modeling is relatively limited, so you must consider how the needed skills will be provided for individual projects. The basics of modeling can be taught relatively easily, but novices require support as they encounter complex and unusual situations. Review and feedback regarding their work will be required to ensure consistent quality. The question is, how can you organize your limited resources to accomplish this?

A common practice for sharing a valuable but limited skill set is to organize the people with the needed skills into a center of excellence. In this case, we are talking about creating a process- and domain-modeling group comprising the most skilled process modelers in the enterprise. Logically, this group is part of the enterprise architecture group. What does this group do? Well, a variety of things, including:

- Establish standards and best practices for process and domain modeling
- Manage process and domain knowledge transfer to project teams
- Review process and domain models from projects
- Maintain a repository of business process and domain models
- Establish models of common process patterns
- Establish common data model representations

Establishing Standards and Best Practices

Because the enterprise architecture group contains the most skilled process and domain modelers, it must assume the responsibility of providing leadership with respect to the tools and techniques for modeling. There is real need for leadership and guidance in this area, as the techniques for process modeling, in particular, are still in flux, and tools for supporting both process and domain modeling are evolving rapidly.

The modeling of domains with UML class diagrams is relatively mature. Graphical domain modeling has been around since the 1970s in the form of Chen Entity-Relationship (ER) diagrams. The Object Modeling Technique, first published in 1989, provided a richer notation with more refined representations of relationships. In 1997 it became the basis for the UML class notation. It is now a very mature notation that is widely used.

Process modeling, on the other hand, is still evolving. The leading notations for modeling the flow of activities in a process are the UML activity notation (used in this book) and the closely related Business Process Modeling Notation (BPMN). There are efforts under way in the industry to reconcile the differences between these notations.

While the representation of the flow of activities is very similar in the two notations, UML activity notation has linkages to other UML notations that are absent in the BPMN notation. For example, activities frequently produce artifacts (objects in the UML notation) that are inputs to other activities. In information systems these artifacts are, more often than not, communications that embody data structures. In the UML activity notation, the type of an object (i.e., the type of the data structure) can be identified as a UML class. This class, in turn, can be defined using the UML class notation.

Fully characterizing business process and system architectures requires multiple perspectives: process and component structures, activity flows, concepts and relationships, state transitions, and implementations. Just as importantly, the elements of these different perspectives must be related to each other in a precise and unambiguous manner. This is the intent of the UML notations and is noticeably absent in the BPMN notation.

However, in contrast to UML's stable class and state notations, the structure, activity, and implementation notations are still in flux. UML 2.x evolved significantly from UML 1.x, and although the rate of evolution appears to be slowing, refinements in the notation can be expected to continue for some time into the future.

These ongoing UML refinements are not just niceties. They occur because architects continue to identify important concepts that do not have convenient and precise representations in the existing notation. The most striking example is the introduction of structure notation in UML 2.x. This notation now makes it possible to describe the performance of work as a collaboration of participants. It provides a mechanism for identifying the roles in the collaboration. It also allows the structure of that collaboration to be defined in terms of other collaborations, and it paves the way for the precise characterization of patterns and their usage.

Because of this ongoing evolution, the enterprise architecture group, as part of its leadership role, must track the state of maturity of these notations (and their supporting tools) and make a determination as to when notational changes and the corresponding tool support should be introduced into the enterprise. As the keeper of the skill base for process and domain modeling, the enterprise architecture group must be responsible for establishing standards for how business processes and domain models will be represented. These standards comprise the selection of notations and the tools for creating these representations.

When standards for process and domain modeling are established, it is important to keep in mind that they are part of a larger enterprise architecture effort. The models and tools need to integrate smoothly with the models and tools used for the remainder of the architecture at both the enterprise level and the individual project level. Process and system structure, milestone lifecycles, and implementations all need to be defined and clearly related back to the business processes, concepts, and relationships being captured.

Complementing these standards are the best practices regarding the use of process and domain modeling. These best practices establish conventions regarding the handling of certain situations. For example, complex business processes frequently require views at different levels of detail: a high-level view presenting the overall structure of the business process and a series of more detailed views presenting the details of portions of the business process. The high-level view is needed to keep the big picture in focus, while the details are required to support systems development. While reference materials (such as this book and its references) offer a number of possible alternatives for dealing with various situations, maintaining consistency choosing these alternatives can be as important as the alternative itself. Establishing the best practice requires an evaluation of the available alternatives and the selection of a preferred alternative along with the identification of the circumstances under which it is applicable. The enterprise architecture group must also document the best practices so that they can be readily shared and provide training in their use.

Managing Process and Domain Knowledge Transfer

Perhaps the most important responsibility of the enterprise architecture group is knowledge transfer. The expertise of the group must somehow be effectively applied at the project level. In most organizations, the number of projects is large enough that direct staffing by the enterprise architecture group is not practical. In such cases the project architect, who is not a member of the enterprise architecture group, will do the process and domain modeling for the project. The key question is, how do these architects obtain the needed skills?

Some level of skill can be obtained through direct training. This training may be delivered by the enterprise architecture group or an external party; this is a matter of choice. However, the enterprise architecture group must be responsible for the training curriculum and for the quality of the training.

Training must be augmented with a structured mentoring program. Training alone is not sufficient to give the project architect the skills necessary to do process and domain modeling. Training will convey a basic understanding of the techniques, but only through practice will the project architect truly develop the skill. During this practice period, the architect will require guidance. Real-world modeling will present the architect with situations that require clarification in the use of the modeling techniques or were not covered in the course at all.

There are a couple of variations on mentoring programs. The strongest one is an apprenticeship program, in which the project architect works under the direct guidance of an enterprise architect on common projects. This affords ample opportunity for the enterprise architect to observe and guide the project architect. Alternatively, an enterprise architect may be assigned to mentor one or more project architects, but not work directly on the projects. The mentor periodically reviews the work of the project architects and is on call to answer questions that the project architect may have.

Part of this knowledge transfer is conveying an understanding of how the enterprise shares process and domain models between projects. Individual projects rarely, if ever, develop complete process or domain models. They work on fragments of the models. For both efficiency and consistency, these fragments need to be merged into a cohesive whole so that they can be referenced and extended by future projects. Since the enterprise architects are responsible for maintaining these merged models, they must show the project architects how to access, refine, and extend these models.

Reviewing Project Models

As the owner of process and domain models, the enterprise architecture group has a quality control responsibility with respect to individual projects. Apart from the training and mentoring responsibilities, the enterprise architects must review the work being done on the individual projects to ensure that it is both correct and done in a style that is consistent with the shared process and domain models. This review should take place prior to any implementation commitment and prior to its merger with the overall enterprise models.

These reviews also provide a means for the enterprise architecture group to evaluate the skills of the project architects and thus evaluate the effectiveness of the knowledge transfer program.

Maintaining the Business Process and Domain Model Repository

Since individual projects generally work on fragments of the business process and domain models, the project work needs to be assembled into a coherent whole. This will let projects build upon the work of other projects and, over time, assemble a complete enterprise business process and domain model. Establishing and maintaining this repository is the responsibility of the enterprise architecture group.

A repository must be organized so that people can find the content that is relevant to their work. Toward this end, the enterprise architecture group should look beyond the current projects and identify as many of the enterprise's key business processes as possible. The level of information that should be gathered is that required for ranking business processes, as discussed in Chapter 7. This inventory can then be used to establish a framework for organizing and storing business process models for easy access. A similar organization of the domain models can be achieved by grouping related concepts and relationships into topic areas.

As business process and domain models are created, whether as part of a project or part of other enterprise architecture activities, they should be added to this repository. The enterprise architecture group should make this repository readily available to the enterprise. Business people, enterprise architects, and project teams will all need to access this information.

Don't use the creation of a repository as an excuse for a technology project! Your goal is not to build the world's greatest archive of business process and domain knowledge. Rather, it is to establish a practical means for documenting and sharing business process information. Keep it simple.

Defining Business Process Patterns

While a process model reflects the dialog between participants in a specific business process, you will find that many processes follow very similar interaction patterns. For example, customer queries coming in through a front-end web site and hitting the same back-end systems will likely all share the same interaction pattern between the participants involved regardless of the nature of the query. Abstracting even further, it is likely that queries coming in via the same type of channel (i.e., web browser access) and hitting the same type of back-end system (i.e., a mainframe) will all follow the same pattern.

In such cases it is beneficial to document the interaction pattern and establish a repository of such patterns. Once a pattern is identified, the enterprise architecture group can then define a corresponding system architecture. The combination of business process pattern and corresponding system architecture then provides a standard cookie-cutter template that project teams can use to streamline their work. Once they have modeled the business process and identified the pattern, they can find the corresponding architecture template and apply it, saving time and money. This approach provides an effective means of broadly sharing architectural expertise (always in limited supply) and achieving consistency among projects.

Defining Common Data Model Representations

The data structures that are exchanged between process participants are all derived from the domain model, that is, an understanding of the inherent structure of the information. This derivation requires some time and thought, and the quality of the result is dependent upon the skill of the architect designing the data structure.

It is common to find different participant interactions requiring similar sets of data. In such cases, it makes sense to define one data structure that can support these different interactions. Such data structures are called common data models, and their engineering is discussed in Chapter 23.

Since the enterprise architecture group has the highest level of skill, it make sense for this group to actually do the engineering of common data models, organizing them and placing them into a repository.

Many of these will originate as data structures proposed by the individual project teams. The enterprise architecture group should routinely be reviewing these data structures as part of the project architecture review. If the group has not been involved in the engineering of these data structures and it appears as though their content, conceptually, is appropriate for a common data model, the review is an appropriate time for the group to modify the data structures into their more general form.

Summary

Even though the bulk of the work occurs within individual projects, process and domain modeling are part of an overall enterprise architecture effort. Consequently, the enterprise architecture group must take responsibility for this overall effort from a number of perspectives.

The enterprise architecture group needs to establish the standards, techniques, and best practices for creating business process and domain models. It needs to ensure that project architects have the training to do this modeling and support them in their efforts, and it needs to ensure that the modeling done on individual projects is done in a consistent manner, both by mentoring project architects and by reviewing their efforts.

To avoid different projects remodeling the same processes and information, the enterprise architecture group must collect the work of individual projects and merge them into an overall enterprise process and domain model. These models must be kept in a repository that is readily accessible by business and technical personnel alike.

There are structural patterns to be found in the enterprise model, patterns in both the structure of business processes and the structure of the information that is communicated between process participants. These patterns represent opportunities to pre-engineer their implementations. These pre-engineered implementations simplify projects, reducing much of their work to recognizing the presence of the pattern and borrowing the predefined implementation. The net result saves time and effort. To achieve these benefits, the enterprise architecture group must be proactive in identifying these patterns, engineering their solutions, and making this information available to the project teams.

Key Enterprise Process and Domain Modeling Questions

1. Has the enterprise architecture group established standards and best practices for modeling business processes and the information they use?

2. Does the enterprise architecture group oversee the training of project architects and provide mentoring support for them?

3. Does the enterprise architecture group routinely review the process and domain models produced by individual projects?

4. Has the enterprise architecture group established a repository for process and domain models? Does it manage the incorporation of individual project models into the repository? Is the repository readily available to both business and technical personnel?

5. Does the enterprise architecture group look for patterns in the process models? Does it document the patterns and define standard implementations for these patterns?

6. Does the enterprise architecture group look for commonalities in the information exchanged between process participants? When commonalities are found, does it define common data models for the exchange of this information?

Part III

The Systems Perspective

Chapter 15

Systems Architecture Overview

We turn our attention now to the architecture of the systems underlying the business processes. When you are designing business processes, for the most part you are treating the "systems" as a single participant in the process. The only exceptions occur when the use of a specific system is mandated for specific activities. The focus of the business process is on determining what systems need to do in the process, not on their architecture and design. But to complete the implementation of the business process, you need to architect and then implement those systems.

Before diving into the design issues, it is worth stepping back to take a look at how to create the architecture from a methodology perspective. There are two major activities in putting an architecture together: defining the architecture and evaluating its suitability for supporting the business processes. When considering how you are going to accomplish these steps, there are two questions you must address. First, given that there are many possible architectures for any solution, how are you going to explore those possible architectures and find the right one? Second, given that you have a real project with a real deadline, how are you going to make this architecture selection process efficient?

The Challenge of Architecting Distributed Systems

Explicitly architecting large-scale distributed information systems is a relatively new phenomenon. Historically, the majority of IT architectural efforts have focused either on the structure of client-server, 3-tier, or n-tier applications, or on establishing their underlying hardware and communications infrastructure. These application-oriented architectural styles provide guidance in the vertical partitioning of functionality within an application, but provide no guidance whatsoever in horizontal partitioning—deciding which business process activities belong in which applications.

In distributed information systems, the major systems are peers. No one system is in charge. In such systems, rationalizing the allocation of responsibilities to the individual systems can be challenging. The placement of some functionality may be clear; for example, the sales order management system is obviously responsible for functionality directly related to the management of sales orders. The placement of other functionality may not be as obvious. Business processes span multiple systems. Where should functionality reside that is related to business process monitoring, management, and reporting? If individual systems provide individual services, where should a composite service reside that involves services from multiple systems? When data is replicated between systems, which system should manage that replication? When interactions require data transformation, where should you put that functionality?

Learning from the CORBA Experience

The architectural placement of functionality must take into consideration both the logical organization of that functionality and the dynamic performance implications of that placement. Experiences in using CORBA provide some object lessons in this regard. The purpose of CORBA is to establish a standardized foundation for distributed system design. It provides the ability to define objects in such a way that any one object can use the services of another object, regardless of the object's physical location. The nature of CORBA encourages you to modularize your distributed design into objects (each bundling data and related operations) without worrying about how and where the objects will be deployed.

Unfortunately, as many an architect has discovered, it makes a great deal of difference where those distributed objects actually reside. When objects are co-located in the same environment, the overhead of communicating between them is low. Interactions occur in a matter of microseconds. Latency is so low that it can be safely ignored and there is no traffic that impacts the network. But the story is different when two interacting objects reside in different machines. Communications delays and operating system context-switching can easily increase communications latency a thousandfold, making the delays noticeable. Communications also requires network traffic, and therefore requires network bandwidth. The consideration of latency and network load often demands rethinking placement of the objects, and often requires changing the granularity of the object's operations. The following case study illustrates this point.

Case Study

Case Study: Credit Card Fraud Investigation

A bank is implementing a system to investigate credit card fraud. The bulk of the business process consists of examining information associated with the account. The investigator pokes around in the information, looking for suspicious patterns of activity. After an initial examination, the investigator makes contact with various parties, commonly the cardholder, merchants, and law enforcement agencies. Ultimately the investigator determines which transactions are legitimate and which are fraudulent. The investigator then creates a new account and transfers all legitimate activity to the new account, leaving the old account with just the fraudulent transactions.

This investigative work and the ensuing account modifications require the display of detailed account information. This information resides in the Credit Card Account System, an existing system that is separate from the new Fraud Investigation System. Part of the project is to define the services that the credit card account system will provide.

A simplified view of the credit card account information is shown in Figure 15–1. This figure represents a logical model of the information, and it is proposed that this logical model be directly implemented as CORBA objects in the Credit Card Account System. Each class has a set of attributes (the actual data stored in the credit card account system) and a set of operations that provide access to this data. For simplicity, the operations that would be required to create and modify these classes and their attributes have been omitted.

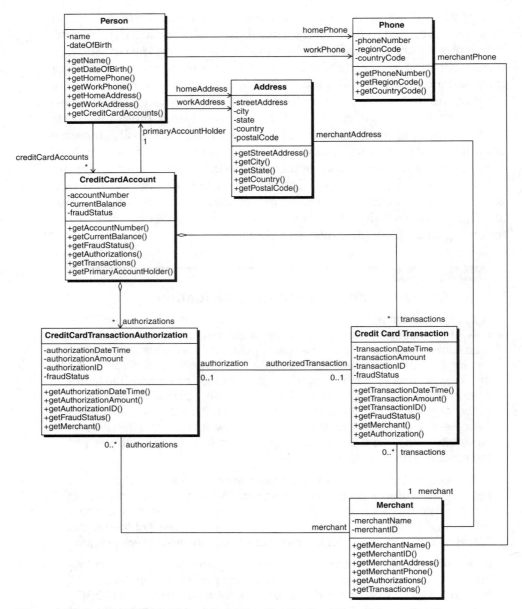

Figure 15–1: *Simplified Class Model for Credit Card Fraud Investigation*

Now consider the design of the Fraud Investigation System. Assume for the moment that the Credit Card Account System has its account information represented by CORBA objects in the manner just described. When an investigator wants to work on an account, the Fraud Investigation System must display a window containing virtually all of this information in a tabular representation so that it can be easily scanned.

To populate this table, the Fraud Investigation System needs to retrieve the account information. The mechanics of this retrieval seem straightforward: Use the account number to locate the Credit Card Account and then use a sequence of get<attributeName>() calls to retrieve the remaining information. Figure 15–2 shows the resulting dialog between the Fraud Investigation System and the Credit Card Account System.

Figure 15–2 immediately highlights the problem with this design: The retrieval of each attribute requires a round-trip communication with the Credit Card Account Server. Each exchange will take several milliseconds or more and require a few hundred bytes of network traffic—all to retrieve a dozen bytes of information. A page displaying 40 transactions along with 10 fields of data (including fields from their corresponding authorizations and merchants) will require 400 interactions between the two systems and will generate over 100KB of network traffic.

Optimistically, if the server stands ready to instantly respond to each request, it will still take more than a second to assemble the data. More realistically, it will take a number of seconds to display the table, and that is to display only 40 transactions. Many accounts have hundreds of transactions, and the fraud investigator needs to flip back and forth through the transactions looking for suspicious activity. Multi-second delays in retrieving the data will be very annoying to the investigators and will seriously degrade their efficiency.

Moving the responsibility for field-by-field data retrieval to the Credit Card Account System greatly simplifies the interactions between the systems (Figure 15–3). With this approach, the Fraud Investigation System sends a single request, and the Credit Card Account System accumulates all of the required information. Latency is now reduced to less than a second, and network traffic is reduced from more than 100KB to around 5KB. The downside, of course, is that doing this requires changes to the Credit Card Account System. Unfortunately, that system belongs to a different organization and has a different IT group maintaining it. That group doesn't have the resources to make the changes in the time frame required for the Fraud Investigation System project. Welcome to the realities of distributed system design!

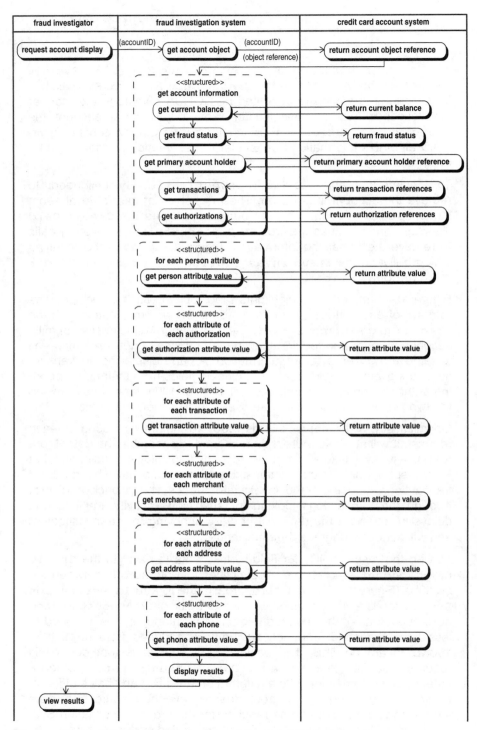

Figure 15–2: *Client-side Assembly of Account Data*

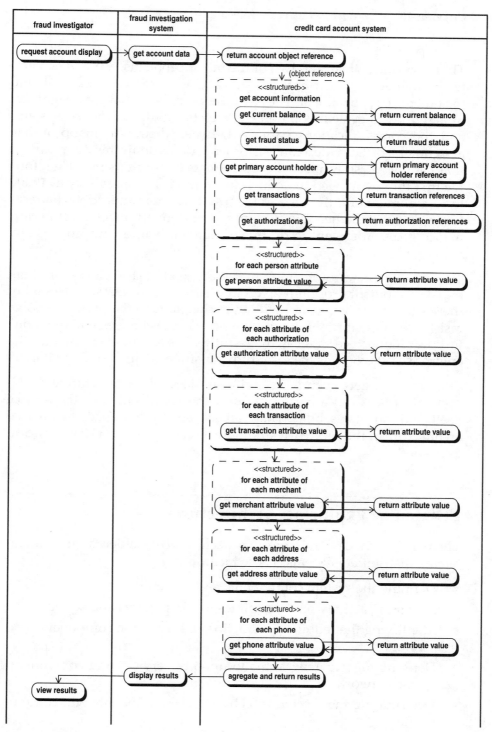

Figure 15–3: *Server-side Assembly of Account Data*

This case study illustrates two of the major problems you will encounter in architecting distributed systems. One of these is technical, and the other is organizational. The technical problem is that the assignment of activities to system components affects the design of the systems and the communications patterns between them. An inappropriate assignment of activities can easily lead to a communication pattern that cannot possibly meet the performance requirements. Therefore, the first thing you need to do in your design is to consciously evaluate the assignment of activities and the resulting communications patterns to determine whether this design can reasonably meet your performance goals. You want to do this evaluation before you proceed any further with the design.

The organizational problem is that there is almost always more than one development group involved in distributed systems. Unless all of these groups are active and willing participants in the project, passive resistance in the form of unwillingness to make changes will often distort the architecture. At best, the result will be less than optimal for the enterprise. At worst, as the case study illustrated, it just won't do the job.

This problem gets even worse with services. Non-cooperative development groups can adversely impact the specification of the service itself, and thus its usability. They can also adversely impact the internal architecture of the service, resulting in a service that just can't perform as needed.

Efficiently Exploring Architectures

There are many design issues that need to be considered when architecting distributed systems. These include:

- Defining the system components and services
- Assigning activity responsibilities to components and services
- Identifying the required interactions between the components and services
- Determining the geographic location of services and components on the network
- Determining the mechanisms by which components will communicate
- Defining common data models where appropriate

- Determining the need for data replication and the mechanisms for managing the replicated data
- Deciding how to coordinate the activities of components and services
- Determining how error detection and handling will be done
- Deciding whether high availability, fault tolerance, and load distribution are needed and the mechanisms that will be used to provide them
- Determining how security requirements will be addressed
- Determining the need for business process and component/service monitoring and the mechanisms that will be used
- Determining how repeatable testing will be supported and how performance and failure-mode testing will be conducted
- Evaluating the architecture to determine its suitability

Sequencing Architecture Issues

The sheer number of architectural issues mandates that some order be brought to their investigation. One of the challenges you face here is that the decisions you make with respect to one issue may alter the decisions you make addressing another. You don't want to end up in a situation in which you have to go back and revisit design decisions. Such situations can be avoided by considering the sequence in which you address the issues. A sequence that has worked well for architecting distributed information systems is the following:

1. **Top-Level Architecture**—identifying the major components and services, assigning responsibility for individual activities, identifying the needed communications between the components, and determining where the components will live on the geographic network

2. **Communications**—determining the mechanisms to be used for communication transport and the need for adapters, identifying the required data representations and the need for content transformation

3. **Data**—determining systems of record, how identifiers will be mapped, whether common data models are needed, whether information will be replicated, how replication will be managed, and where results will be validated

4. **Coordination**—determining how the execution of activities will be coordinated and how coordination choices will impact business process breakdown detection, determining whether and how processes

will be monitored and managed, and determining the coordination patterns to be used for the business process

5. **High Availability, Fault Tolerance, and Load Distribution—** determining the need for these capabilities and the mechanisms by which they will be carried out

6. **Security**—determining the need for authentication, authorization, encryption, and audit logs, and assigning the responsibilities for these activities to components

7. **Monitoring**—determining what needs to be monitored and how it will be monitored both at the business-process and component level

8. **Testing**—determining how the business process and system will be tested and modifying the design to facilitate this testing

Field experience has shown that if these topics are addressed in this sequence, it is unlikely that decisions made in earlier steps will have to be revisited when later issues are considered. Thus security and monitoring are late in the sequence not because they are unimportant, but because they are heavily impacted by decisions in the other areas.

Periodic Architecture Evaluation

Noticeably absent in the previous sequence is evaluation of the architecture. Evaluation consists of determining whether the chosen architecture can perform adequately, can be built within the cost and schedule guidelines, has adequate provisions for future growth and change, and complies with standards and best practices.

Doing evaluation once requires performing the evaluation last. This placement can lead to serious inefficiencies. If you spend time addressing all of these architectural issues only to find through evaluation that you have made some bad design choices, you have wasted a lot of effort on the bad design. To avoid this, you want to stop and evaluate your architecture at key stages in the architecture development, as discussed in Chapter 5.

The first key evaluation point comes immediately after you have sketched out the high-level architecture for the first business process. At this point you want to do a preliminary performance evaluation. The major components are known, and their responsibilities and patterns of interaction have been captured in the form of activity diagrams. If you combine the understanding of these interaction patterns with an understanding of the peak rate at which these interactions occur, you can determine how often each component needs to perform its tasks. Adding an understanding of the deployment topology and the volume of information exchanged in each interaction allows you to determine the volume of communications traffic within and between locations. Given this understanding, you can then assess the feasibility of components doing work at this rate, and make an initial assessment of the class of machines and networks that will be required. After that you can make a preliminary assessment of the feasibility of implementing the architecture within the cost and schedule guidelines.

Once you have convinced yourself that this initial architecture is feasible, you can then proceed to considering the remaining architectural issues and round out the architecture for that business process. Since each of the architecture issues has at least the possibility of adding new components, activities, and communications to the evolving systems architecture, you need to repeat the performance analysis and cost assessment once you have completed the architecture for the first business process.

From this point on, after each iterative round adding new business processes and refining the architecture to accommodate them, you will want to once again evaluate the expected performance and reassess anticipated costs and schedules. This periodic reevaluation will give you an early indication as to whether you are moving in a direction that might not provide a suitable architecture. This will drive you to consider alternate and more suitable architectures while minimizing the level of effort required.

Summary

Distributed systems present design challenges not present in client-server and n-tier application design. The responsibility for individual business process activities must be assigned to specific systems, and the resulting interaction patterns must be evaluated. The evaluation must consider both the logic of the functional organization and the performance of the overall architecture.

There is additional functionality that must also be considered, functionality that is not strictly a part of any individual business process activity. The coordination of activities, the monitoring and management of the overall business process, and the transport and transformation of information in motion from one system to another must all be considered.

There are many architectural issues that must be addressed, and the choices made with respect to one issue frequently impact the choices for others. To avoid continual rework as issues are addressed, it is prudent to sequence these issues so that decisions made regarding early issues are unlikely to be altered by decisions made about later issues. The sequence in which issues are presented in this book is that which is used for architecting distributed information systems.

For efficiency, there is one issue that must, intentionally, be repeatedly addressed: architecture evaluation. It is risky to postpone evaluation until the architecture is completed. Should the evaluation indicate that the architecture is inadequate, you have squandered much of your effort. To make the overall architecture effort more efficient, you should perform an evaluation early in the development cycle that is focused on the most challenging business process and just the basic high-level architecture. Only with a favorable evaluation will you then invest time in addressing other architectural issues. Evaluations should be repeated periodically as the architecture evolves to ensure that the architecture remains viable.

Key Systems Architecture Overview Questions

1. Is your systems architecture work structured so that decisions regarding one architectural issue are unlikely to require altering previous decisions regarding other architectural issues?

2. Does your architecture approach explicitly determine the placement of responsibility for business process activities assigned to the systems?

3. Does your architecture approach explicitly determine the placement of responsibility for supporting functionality? Does this encompass business process monitoring, management, and reporting? Does it encompass transaction management as well as the transport and transformation of information between systems?

4. Does your architecture approach periodically evaluate the evolving architecture, and address both the performance feasibility and the cost and schedule feasibility of the architecture?

Chapter 16

Top-Level Systems Architecture

The first step in determining an architecture is to define the major system participants in each business process being considered. Some of these system participants may have already been identified as part of the business process definition since their participation is mandated. Their presence and the role they will play have already been established. The remainder of the functionality to be provided by systems was intentionally assigned to a single swimlane representing the systems as a whole. Your task at this point is to determine which components should be involved and what role each will play.

First-Cut Structure

Defining a component structure is a creative activity and inherently a trial-and-error process. You propose a set of components, assign responsibility for activities, determine the required communications between the components, and then evaluate the result. For example, in the Withdraw Cash via ATM Machine business process, the teller functionality was assigned to a yet-to-be-defined ATM System. One possible architecture for this system (but not the only one) is to have a number of ATMs at various locations and a centralized ATM server acting as an intermediary between the ATMs and the bank systems.

The participants in the business process would then consist of the `Person` (the customer), an `ATM Machine`, an `ATM Server`, and the `Bank System` (Figure 16–1).

Note that the `ATM System` is shown to be an aggregation of an `ATM Server` and a number of `ATM Machines`. By doing this, you are making a clear statement about the relationship between the `ATM System`, which played the `teller` role in the business process diagrams, and this more detailed decomposition of the system participants. Clearly documenting this relationship is important for follow-on projects. Without it, future projects will not know which components are involved in a given business process, nor will they know which business processes could be potentially impacted by changing specific components.

Simply identifying the system components is not very interesting. It tells you nothing about what each component is doing—or why they even exist. You must define how the components participate in the business process. You do this by extending the activity diagram of the `Withdraw Cash via ATM` scenario to indicate what each component is doing in the process (Figure 16–2). The `teller` swimlane in the business process is relabeled with the more specific `ATM System`, whose decomposition into its constituent `ATM Machine` and `ATM Server` components is indicated with nested swimlanes. Note that this diagram accomplishes several things. It indicates the activity responsibilities of each participant, identifies all required communications, and identifies the types of communications (more on this shortly). What this diagram documents is how the system components collaborate with the other participants to bring the business process to life. Remember, that's the purpose of the architecture. Thus, it makes sense to explore this collaboration even when the architecture is in its formative stages.

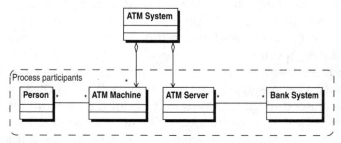

Figure 16–1: *Top-Level Architecture for Withdraw Cash from ATM Machine*

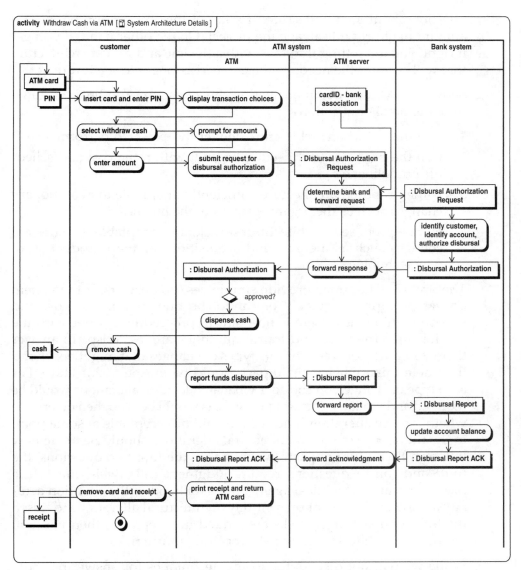

Figure 16–2: *Withdraw Cash Showing Top-Level Architecture Participants*

Initial Evaluation

Once you have sketched this collaboration, the next question in your mind ought to be, "Is this a good architecture for the solution?" This may not be a simple question to answer, yet it is the most important question about an architecture. If you get the architecture wrong, no amount of effort will salvage the project. On the other hand, if you get it right, you are setting the stage with a flexible and robust architecture that will support the needs of the enterprise long into the future.

So how do you go about answering this question? You break it down into four smaller questions:

1. Can the proposed architecture deliver the expected performance?
2. Can the proposed architecture be built within the cost and schedule guidelines?
3. Is the proposed architecture sufficiently adaptable to evolutionary changes such as the organic growth of the business?
4. Is the proposed architecture sufficiently adaptable to stressful changes such as mergers and acquisitions or the introduction of new technology?

The first two questions provide simple yes/no answers. If the system cannot perform adequately or cannot be built within the cost and schedule guidelines, there is no point in proceeding further with the architecture. The third and fourth questions are less crisp. To answer them you must consider various types of changes that might occur and then determine what their impact would be on the architecture. For each type of change you consider what architectural alterations would be required and what the corresponding costs would be. You then determine whether those alterations and costs would be acceptable at some point in the future, or whether architectural alterations should be made now to lessen this future impact. In contrast to the first two questions, the third and fourth questions require judgment calls, weighing future risks (costs and schedules) against the likelihood of the situation actually arising or the cost of present-day architectural alterations to lessen the future impact. If the risks are judged unacceptable, then you will modify the architecture now to lower those future risks.

While we will not discuss the formal techniques for answering these questions until Chapter 39, it is worth pausing to consider some of the questions you expect that architecture evaluation to answer. One question is, "What class of hardware will be required to implement each component?" To answer this question you need to understand what each component needs to do and how often it needs to do it. Unless you are trying to do something very difficult from a performance perspective, this usually boils down to a cost question: Does the class of machine required fit within the cost and schedule guidelines for the project?

Another question you expect the evaluation to answer is "What network bandwidth will be required?" Again, unless you are asking the impossible in terms of performance, this usually boils down to a cost question, particularly with respect to wide-area-network (WAN) bandwidth. WAN connections are typically leased and represent an ongoing expense during the lifetime of the system. Once again, you are seeking to understand whether these costs fit within the guidelines for the project.

While there are formal approaches to answering these questions, there is an informal question you can ask that generally weeds out bad architectures without going through the formalities: Is the overall pattern of activities and communications simple and easy to understand? Generally, the simpler the interaction pattern, the easier it will be to implement, monitor, and manage the business process and system. Complex patterns usually translate into higher costs.

Communications and Modularization

One of the things you are trying to decide as you formulate the top-level architecture of your solution is how you want to modularize the design. Modularization allows you to divide functionality into smaller units that are easier to manage. The basic unit of modularization in distributed systems is the operating system process—the running program in a computer. When you separate functionality into different operating system processes, the resulting processes need to communicate with each other. As an architect, you need to factor this communication into your thinking. In particular, you need to consider the performance overhead in terms of both latency and bandwidth.

Communications Latency

Communications latency is the time messages spend in transit between sender and recipient processes (Figure 16–3). For distributed systems in general and service-oriented architectures in particular, latency becomes a factor when the provider of functionality resides in a different operating system process than the user of the functionality. In such situations, you must weigh the time it takes to perform the actual work (T2) against the time it takes to communicate between operating system processes (T1 + T3). If the work to be performed only requires a few microseconds and the inter-process communications

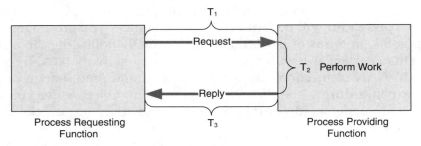

Figure 16–3: *Communications Overhead in Process-Based Modularization*

delays require milliseconds, it does not make a lot of sense to place that functionality in a separate process. You don't, for example, place addition in a separate process even though it is a commonly used element of functionality. The communications overhead would be prohibitive.

The consideration of latency leads to a rule of thumb for modularizing functionality into separate processes: *At a minimum, the time required to perform the work should be at least as great as the time it takes to communicate between the processes.* Preferably the work time will exceed the communications latency by a significant margin—an order of magnitude or more. Anything less and the execution of a business process requiring many such interactions will be noticeably slowed by the latency. In other words, the act of modularizing the functionality is going to degrade systems performance.

Communications Bandwidth

Communicating between operating system processes requires resources. When these processes are executing on different machines, the resource required is communications bandwidth. The information required to perform a modularized function must come either directly from the requesting process or indirectly from some other process, a database, or some other persistent data store. Either way, communications bandwidth is required to move this information.

Bandwidth may not appear to be a significant issue when you are just considering the modularization of a single function. However, if that functionality is, in turn, broken down into a number of modules, the cumulative effect can be significant. Modern communications technology has actually made the problem worse by making it easy (from a development perspective) for one module to communicate with another. It is now so easy to separate functionality into communicating processes that this capability is often overused. The resulting communication demand can easily increase network bandwidth requirements by an order of magnitude or more.

Data Marshalling

The form in which data is moved between components is rarely the form being used internally by components. In such cases, the internal data representations need to be transformed into a representation that can be communicated (a process known as *marshalling* the data), and the receiving component needs to perform a corresponding transformation into its required internal representation. The work involved in these transformations adds overhead to the communications and requires computational resources, particularly for large data structures and when encryption is involved.

Geographic Distribution

Communications latency and bandwidth become serious issues when the functionality is geographically distributed. Long-distance communications introduces increasing latency as messages are passed from node to node in the network. In addition, the cost of these long-distance connections is usually proportional to the bandwidth required. Unlike local communications costs, which tend to be dominated by the investment in network hardware, long distance communications costs tend to be ongoing monthly expenses. Thus your modularization decisions can significantly impact both near-term capital investments and ongoing operational costs.

Consider Other Modularization Approaches

Finally, you should remember that partitioning functionality into another process is not the only modularization option open to you. You can factor common functionality into code libraries (or similar design artifacts) that can then be incorporated into the components wishing to use the functionality. While this is often an internal design issue within a component, as an architect you need to keep an eye open for functionality that may be more appropriately shared in this manner.

Service Identification and Performance

At this point in the development of your architecture you should once again pause to identify potential services. Similar operations identified in different business processes (or used more than one place within the same business process) should be considered a candidate for a service. Operations requiring coordination, such as the various operations on a common data structure, are also good candidates for services. Note that this, too, is sharing: The rules regarding the coordination of the operations are being shared.

Before you consider creating a service, you must first ask one question: Does it even make sense to partition the proposed functionality into a separate operating system process? Based on consideration of both communications latency and network bandwidth, is this partitioning warranted? Only if the answer is yes does it make sense to pursue the service approach. If the answer is no, but the functionality still needs to be shared, other avenues of sharing, such as shared code libraries, should be considered.

Modeling System Interactions

As with modeling business processes, the UML activity notation once again provides a powerful mechanism for showing how the top-level architectural components participate in the business process. You saw an example of this in Figure 16–2. The notation makes it easy to show the activities of each system component and the required interactions between them, along with some detail about the artifacts conveyed in the interactions.

A significant difference between the use of activity notation here and the way business processes were represented is that shortcuts are not being used to represent the interactions between the system participants (Figure 16–4). Instead, each interaction is represented as an object (typically a message, database record, or file). The type of that artifact is indicated, represented as the name of a UML class. The association of this type with the artifact is indicated by following the artifact name with a colon and the type name. This association indicates that the artifact is an instance of the type—a relationship known as *instantiation* in UML.

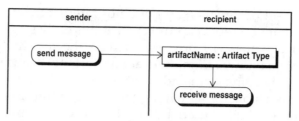

Figure 16–4: *Representation of a Communications Artifact and its Associated Type*

The type, at this point, has no definition other than a name. You should begin sketching the type now using the UML class notation. Identifying key attributes (including identifiers) will stimulate you to think about the information needed to support the business process and the origins of that information. It is good practice to create a diagram containing all of the data structures used in each business process or collection of related business processes (Figure 16–5). You don't need to detail the entire data structure—at least not yet. In fact, you want to avoid getting bogged down in such details because the architecture is still tentative, and the interaction artifacts will come and go as you rearrange the component structure and activity assignments. You don't want to make the investment in details until you are confident that you are headed in the right direction with the architecture.

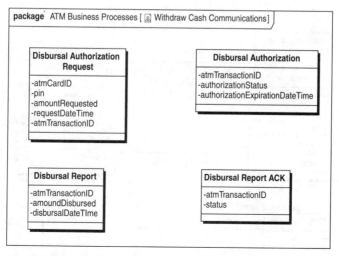

Figure 16–5: *Withdraw Cash Communications Data Structures*

While the full set of details may not be of interest this time, there are some details that you must capture even at this early stage. Any identifiers used in the business process, such as the identity of the bank account, must be known. Identifiers are important because you need to know where they come from and what component (and what business process) is responsible for managing them. Other important details are data elements explicitly used by the business process, such as the amount being withdrawn from the bank account. Any essential piece of information, particularly information being used to support decision making, should be identified in your model. Note, however, that you only need to identify the information—you don't need to detail its representation.

Let's look at another example. Consider the sales order process in a catalog retailer. The sales order management process obviously must involve sales orders, the individual line items in the order, and the catalog item being ordered on each line (Figure 16–6). Catalog orders involve a shipping address and billing information, but at this point you do not necessarily need the details of how addresses and billing information are represented. Orders must also be related to shipments, which require their own information.

If your proposed system design involves an `Order Management System`, a `Fulfillment System`, and a `Warehouse Management System`, these systems must obviously communicate information about orders and shipments related back to the sales orders (Figure 16–7).

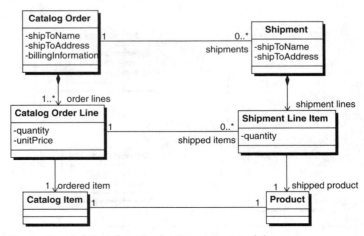

Figure 16–6: *Partial Catalog Order Domain Model*

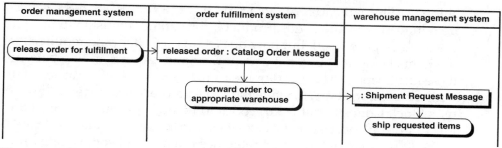

Figure 16–7: *Fragment of Catalog Sales Process*

In defining this architecture, you need to identify the collection of information that is being exchanged in each interaction. Again, you don't want to worry about the details, but you do need to consider the source of the information. A first-cut model identifies the subset of the domain information that is exchanged in each of the interactions (Figure 16–8).

Defining the information content of these interactions raises a question: Where did the `Product` information come from? Somehow the catalog items in the order must be mapped to the products that are actually

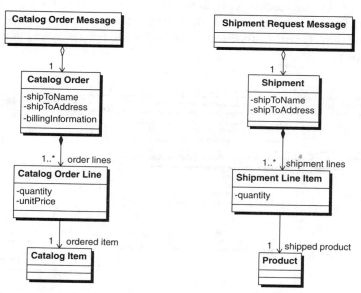

Figure 16–8: *First-Cut Model of Information Exchanged in the Catalog Sales Process*

shipped. Since the `Order Fulfillment System` receives catalog item information and sends product information, it must map one into the other (Figure 16–9). But how does it do this? Mapping requires that the items being mapped have identifiers and requires a map between those identifiers. The `Order Management System` identifies catalog items with a `catalogItemID`, while the `Warehouse Management System` uses Stock Control Unit (`SKU`) codes to identify products. The `Order Fulfillment System` uses a cross reference to map the `catalogItemID` to the `SKU`. Note that the cross reference is a result of some related process that must now be brought into scope for the project.

Other identifiers may be required by the business process as well. For example, while exploring the handling of returns you are likely to discover a need for a reference to the order in the shipping paperwork. Since this paperwork is generated by the `Warehouse Management System`, the `Shipment Request Message` must contain such a reference. This is easily accommodated by adding an `orderID` to the `Catalog Order` and having the `Order Fulfillment System` pass this information on in the `Shipment Request Message`.

As a result of these considerations, you need to add the identifiers to the information being exchanged between the participants (Figure 16–10). The `Catalog Order`, `Catalog Item`, and `Product` all now require identifiers. Furthermore, you have to determine what information is required in the cross-reference data structure, which business process will maintain it, and how the `Order Fulfillment System` will gain access to it.

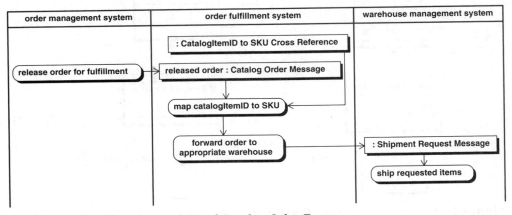

Figure 16–9: *Refined Fragment of Catalog Sales Process*

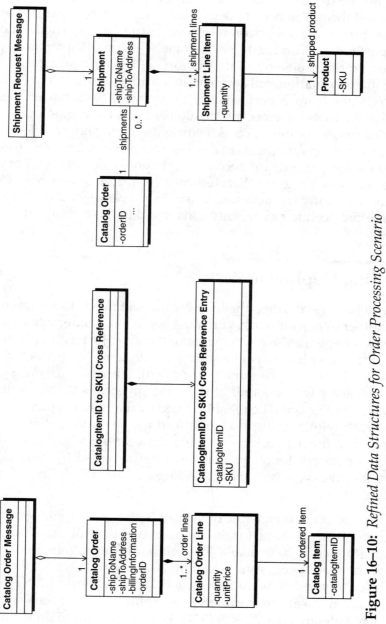

Figure 16–10: *Refined Data Structures for Order Processing Scenario*

The maintenance of cross-reference information can have a significant impact on the design of both the business processes and the systems that support them. You need to determine when (at which point in which business processes) the cross-reference entries are created, and by which participant. You need to determine which participant is responsible for storing reference information and how participants that require the information will access it. In addition, you need to evaluate your decisions from a performance perspective. It is not enough to know that the cross-reference information exists. If the component requiring the information cannot access it efficiently, it may not be able to meet the performance requirements of the business process. Chapter 16 examines the design patterns for accessing reference information. For now, you just need to recognize that decisions regarding reference information can potentially impact many business processes and participants, and therefore need to be carefully considered in the architecture.

Modeling Deployment

Once you have established that one component needs to communicate with another over a network, you must begin to consider where on the distributed network the participants will reside. Just as it is easier for you to interact with a colleague sitting at a desk next to yours than one in another room, state, country, or continent, it is easier for one system to communicate with another at the same physical site than with one located at another site. The reliability and availability characteristics of the network within a site also tend to differ from the reliability and availability of the network connections between sites. An understanding of the network topology that must be traversed by communications will give you an understanding of the reliability of those communications.

What you need to consider at this point is the geographic location of each component. Assume for the moment that the full bandwidth of a local area network is available for communications between components within each geographic location. As a result, you treat each geographic location as if it were a single local area network (LAN) (Figure 16–11). Communications between geographic locations then needs to traverse a wide-area network (WAN). What you want to do is propose a coarse topology of LAN and WAN connections, locate your top-level components on the topology, and evaluate the demand this will place on the various network elements.

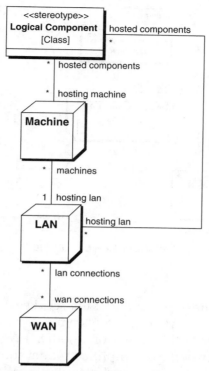

Figure 16–11: *Deployment Metamodel*

The motivation for this exercise is simple. Bandwidth over a wide-area network between physical sites is more expensive than bandwidth within a physical site. You want to understand how different deployment alternatives will impact bandwidth demands, and thus relative cost. At this stage of your design, the analysis will be simple. You simply want to know if the bandwidth requirements are reasonable. Have you overloaded a LAN by trying to move information at a rate greater than the readily available network can handle? Are you moving information across the WAN at a rate that will push you into a more expensive communications technology? What kind of WAN connections (in terms of bandwidth) are available in the locations you are considering? Satellite links? Dial-up phone lines? DSL or cable modem connections? Trunk lines? How sensitive is your solution to the costs of these connections?

The initial modeling of deployment is often crude—intentionally so. In the interests of efficiency, you want to do a simple analysis to determine whether a more detailed portrayal is warranted. So, for example,

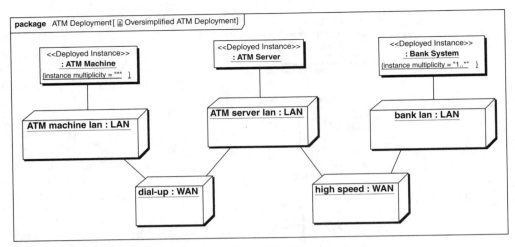

Figure 16–12: *ATM Example: Oversimplified Deployment*

you might model the deployment of the ATM system as shown in Figure 16–12. Here every ATM in the system is located on a single LAN, and every bank server is located on another LAN. Obviously, this is not realistic! However, if this simplified model shows that there are no issues with LAN loading or, more importantly, WAN loading, a more detailed deployment model is not required to determine the viability of the proposed architecture. This is an important approach to efficiently designing an architecture: Do a simple analysis to determine whether a more extensive (and therefore more costly and time consuming) analysis is warranted.

Let us pause for a moment to examine the UML implementation notation being used. The box-like elements in the diagram are called nodes. In this deployment modeling, nodes are being used to represent three different types of infrastructure elements: machines, LANs, and WANs. Each of these has been defined as a type of node. A solid line between two nodes represents a communications path between those nodes.

While the solution infrastructure is represented with nodes, the logical components of the design are represented with UML classes.[1] These

---

1. UML components are not used as they represent "physical replaceable parts," and the intent here is to represent logical components. The physical structure of these logical components will be defined later in the architectural process.

classes are the logical components of the top-level architecture defined previously (Figure 16–1). In the deployment diagram, instances of those logical components are represented with UML instance specifications. Links (lines) between the instance specifications and nodes represent hosting relationships. It is permissible to have more than one instance of a component type, indicated either with multiple-instance specification icons in the diagram or, as in the example, an explicit instance multiplicity. This example shows many ATMs and many Bank Servers.

There is one bit of nonstandard UML that is being used here that warrants some explanation. The `Instance Specification` of UML 2.0 does not make provisions for indicating the number of instances. However, UML does allow for the definition of user-defined stereotypes. Stereotypes can have properties and can be applied to other UML constructs. Through this mechanism, properties can be added to UML constructs. In this case, a `Deployed Instance` stereotype has been created with an `instance multiplicity` property (Figure 16–13). As the stereotype indicates, it can be applied to any `Deployed Artifact`, which includes the subclasses `Instance Specification` and `Artifact`. This stereotype has been applied to the instance specifications shown in Figure 16–12, allowing the multiplicity of the individual instances to be specified.

While software components must eventually be hosted on machines, it is quite likely at this point in your design that you haven't yet figured out what machines will be needed and where each component will be hosted. To allow flexibility in modeling component deployment and communications early in the architecture development, the metamodel used here allows component instances to be deployed either on a `Machine` or on a `LAN`. This model is rich enough to evaluate the communications load on the LANs and WANs. Then, as your design progresses and you make deployment decisions, you update the deployment model to indicate the machines and the component instances that will be deployed on each machine. You may even begin

Figure 16–13: *Deployed Instance Stereotype Specification*

to refine the network topology by showing interconnected LANs within a physical site, particularly when firewalls are involved.

When you are modeling deployment, it is important to keep in mind the purpose of the exercise: You are simply trying to determine whether the communications bandwidth requirements are reasonable. To do this, your network model does not have to be very sophisticated. Keep it simple for the architecture phase. In general, don't partition the local LAN until bandwidth demands indicate that you will actually need to divide the traffic. Of course, if there are major partitions of the physical network that already exist, there is no harm in modeling them, but the intent of the model at this point is to identify potential problems, not define the detailed deployment of the system.

Addressing Performance

Once you have sketched how the major architectural components will functionally support the business process, you need to assess the feasibility of meeting throughput and response time requirements. The ATM example stipulated a 30-second response time for the transaction to complete, and Figure 11–1 identified the events that mark the start and finish of that interval. Now it is time to determine the performance requirements that each individual component must meet to achieve the overall performance goal.

When you have overall process-level performance requirements, you must derive the requirements for the individual components. When you have an expected peak rate of activity for the overall process, you need to determine the implied peak rate of activity of each component. When you have a response time requirement, you need to budget that time, determining how much will be spent in each participating component—that is, a response time requirement. Keep in mind that those response times must be met while the components are experiencing the peak rates!

Peak Loads

The techniques for determining peak rates and evaluating the feasibility of meeting those load requirements will be discussed in Chapter 39. What those techniques will give you is a means of transforming the peak rate for the overall business process into the corresponding peak rates that will be experienced by each of the individual components. It will also provide some guidelines for determining the horsepower that will be required to execute the work at those rates.

Response Times

In addition to evaluating peak rates, you need to determine the response time budgets for each component as well. When you are establishing these response time budgets, you need to consider that communications delays will contribute to the overall response time. Not only do the individual participants take time to do their work, but communications takes time as well. You need to take this into account when you establish the response time budgets for each component, and you need to take care that the specification for each component is unambiguous. What exactly do you mean when you say that the response time budget for a component is 5 seconds?

The need for clarity around this specification becomes apparent when you look at a component in the middle of a chain of activity as shown in Figure 16–14. What does it mean when you specify a 5-second response time for component B? Are you talking about T_1, the total amount of time that elapses between the time B receives a request and the time it provides the reply? Or are you only talking about $T_3 + T_4$, the time that B actually spends doing work (note that this is the same as $T_1 - T_2$)? You need to be clear what you mean when you specify response times.

You also have to recognize that the response time specified for B will not be the same as the delay seen by component A, for there are communications delays between the two components. T_1 is the minimum amount of time that A might have to wait, but you can expect that T_5 will in fact be greater than T_1. Consider the ATM example. If A is the `ATM Machine`, B is the `ATM Server`, and C is the `Bank System`, how

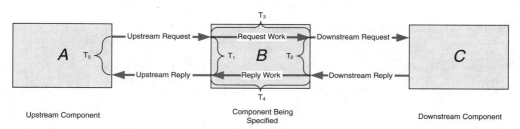

Figure 16–14: *Measuring Response Time*

long does it take the ATM machine to get disbursement approval from the bank? The wait will be longer than the time it takes the ATM server to get the approval, particularly considering that most ATM machines (at least at the time of this writing) use dial-up phone service to access their networks. It takes a few seconds to place the call and establish communications before the request can actually be submitted. You need to budget for these delays when you determine how you are going to meet response time requirements.

When you have response time requirements, you should record the response time budget decisions for each component and each communication. For the components you are going to build or modify, these budgets become requirements for the components. For components that already exist, these budgets become assumptions about those components, assumptions whose accuracy needs to be verified with the system owners. You also need to record the budgets for communications delays and verify these with the communications infrastructure providers. Table 16–1 shows an example time budget for the `Withdraw Cash from ATM` scenario.

The ATM example has a relatively straightforward process structure for which it is relatively simple to assign response time budgets. When the pattern of component interactions becomes complex, particularly when there is branching logic that alters the communications pattern, it may require some thought and effort to determine what the response time budgets need to be.

When complicated situations arise, it's tempting to conclude that it is just too complicated to figure out—it's not worth the effort. Resist this temptation! What you are really saying is that you'll figure it out after you have built and deployed the system. A production environment is not exactly the best place to discover that your architecture is infeasible, nor is it the best place to finally determine what the individual component and communications time budgets need to be to meet over-

Table 16–1: *Response Time Budget Summary*

Business Process	Required Total Response Time (Seconds)	ATM	Machine-Server Communications	ATM Server	ATM Server - Bank Server Communications	Bank Server
Withdraw Cash via ATM	30	5	10	3	1	5

all process response time requirements. Do your homework now. Make sure each component and service provider knows exactly what their component needs to be doing.

Response Time Test Specifications

If a response time is important, it is not enough to simply specify what the response time ought to be. You need to measure the actual response time before you will know whether you have achieved the goal. These tests warrant consideration at this point in the design process because response time measurements require some design work. Each measurement requires capturing time stamps to mark the beginning and end of the time intervals. These time stamps need to be correlated, and the time difference calculated. This is not necessarily a big deal, but it is often awkward and expensive to retrofit these capabilities into an existing design.

Because response time measurement requires design work, you need to specify the needed measurements early in the design process. You should also give some thought to when these measurements will be made—in testing, in production, or in both. You should also consider what your next steps might be if a response time measurement turns out to be out of specification. You might need to make additional measurements on other components to determine which component is really at fault. And, once again, you need to consider whether these additional measurements will be made in test or in production.

For now your task is just to define the measurements that need to be made and when they need to be made. The mechanics of making these measurements are covered in Chapter 38, which considers various choices about which components will be responsible for the capture, correlation, computation, and recording of the information. The performance impact of making these measurements will also be considered; you need to make sure that the measurement itself does not distort the data.

Early Architecture Evaluation

At this point in the architecture development you have arrived at a high-level understanding of the pattern of communications that will be required to execute the business process. This gives you enough information to perform an initial evaluation of the architecture.

The first question you want to consider is whether the communications pattern looks reasonable. Is it overly complex? Back in Figure 15–2 you saw an example of one component communicating with another many times to assemble some data, and in Figure 15–3 you saw an alternative design in which there was a single exchange between the same two participants. The latter approach is the simpler of the two, and in general the simpler the design the better. Simple designs are easier to understand. Fewer communications require less design work and less run-time activity. Simpler systems are easier to monitor and diagnose—and there are fewer things that can go wrong with them! So you want to look for simpler design alternatives. If you have complexity, you want to make sure that you have a justifiable reason for the complexity.

If the complexity of the communications pattern looks reasonable, you then want to estimate the network and component loading using the techniques of Chapter 39, and ask whether the loading looks reasonable. From a component perspective, you want to understand the machine resources that will be required for each component to handle the peak rate of incoming communications and perform the work that it needs to do. You want to determine whether that level of resource is reasonable given the project's cost constraints. At this point you may even perform some feasibility experiments to determine whether or not it is even practical to do things at the rates you are contemplating and achieve response time goals.

From the network perspective, you want to determine the volume of communications that will occur over each network segment, again using the techniques of Chapter 39. You need to determine the network resources that will be required to make that volume possible and determine whether those resources are available. If they are not, you need to determine whether the costs of upgrades fall within the project cost constraints.

Finally, you need to consider whether you can actually implement the proposed architecture within the project's cost and schedule guidelines. At this point, you have an inventory of both components and communications data structures, and you have at least a cursory understanding of the complexity of each. From this, you can make an initial estimate (using conventional estimation techniques) of the level of effort required to implement the design. The key question, of course, is whether that estimate lies within the project cost and schedule guidelines. You need to remember, particularly in the early iterations, that you are only looking at a partial design, and you have yet to consider many design issues that will add components and complexity. Considering this, for a feasible project you would expect your initial estimate to be well within the project guidelines. If you are anywhere near the limits on this first pass, you have a problem!

Early architecture evaluation helps you determine whether you are headed in the right direction. If you like the evaluation results, then you can proceed with the consideration of other design issues. If you do not like the evaluation results, you should consider whether there are alternative architectures or possibly alternative business process designs that would lead to a better result.

If you don't like the evaluation results and there do not appear to be any viable alternatives, then you have reached a difficult conclusion: You can't solve the problem within the given cost and schedule constraints. In other words, the project is not feasible within the limits set forth in the project's charter.

When you conclude that a project is infeasible, there is little purpose in proceeding further without a reevaluation of the project. The best course of action at this point is to estimate what it will actually take to solve the problem and then gather the project manager and executive sponsors together and share the bad news. Ideally, it should be the business executive sponsor's decision as to what to do next—politics permitting, of course. If you end up in the unfortunate position of continuing with the project under the original cost and schedule constraints, it's time to consult Ed Yourdon's *Death March*.[2] You've got a problem!

Key Top-Level Systems Architecture Questions

1. Have all top-level architecture components been identified?
2. Do the top-level architecture components play clearly identifiable roles in each of the business processes?
3. Have the functional responsibilities been assigned to the top-level architecture components?

---

2. Edward Yourdon. 2004. *Death March, Second Edition*, Upper Saddle River, NJ: Prentice Hall.

4. Have all the required communications between components and their associated data structures been identified?

5. Have reference information and other activity inputs that originate in other business processes been identified? Have their source business processes been identified and added to the business process inventory?

6. Has the deployment of the architecture been modeled?

7. Has the required level of machine resources been determined for each component? Does that level of resource fit within the project cost and schedule guidelines?

8. Has the required level of network resources been determined? Is that level of resource available within the project cost and schedule guidelines?

9. Have potential business services (or the usage of existing business services) been identified?

10. Have the throughput requirements been established for each component in each major scenario?

11. Has a response-time budget been established for each component in each major scenario? Does it account for communications delays?

12. Have the required response time measurements been defined that are needed to demonstrate that the response time requirements are actually being satisfied? Have diagnostic measurements been defined that are needed to identify the offending component when response time requirements are not being satisfied?

Suggested Reading

Edward Yourdon. 2004. *Death March, Second Edition*. Upper Saddle River, NJ: Prentice Hall.

Part IV

Communications

Chapter 17

Transport

At this point in developing your architecture you have explored the business processes, proposed the high-level system architecture components, and identified all participant interactions that are required. Now it is time to turn your attention to the mechanics of the interactions. You need to determine all of the transports that will be required for communications, from carrier pigeon to high-speed data networks. You need to determine the physical nature of all content, from paper to electronic data structures. You need to determine the form that the content will take, from the spoken word to an XML representation of a purchase order. And you need to determine the event that the arrival of the content represents, whether it is the announcement of a previous result, a request for something to be done, or a response to such a request. All of these considerations fall under the broad brush of communications.

To be more precise, you need to consider the technology being used for the transport and the content representation. The transport technology establishes the mechanism by which the communications content will be delivered. This content could be sent as a JMS message, an HTTP communication, an e-mail, a fax, inter-office mail, or a courier service. But each transport is only capable of delivering certain types of content.

The selection of a transport technology constrains the content technology: You can't send physical paper over the phone. But specifying the transport technology does not completely define the content technology. IP networks support electronic content as streams of bytes, but the content technology defines how those bytes are organized. IP-compatible content technologies include various image representation schemes such as JPEG, structured (XML representations) and unstructured (ASCII text) data representation schemes. Service technologies have introduced even more highly structured representations such as SOAP. In contrast, the audio signal transport of an analog phone connection supports content technologies such as raw audio data, the encoded image of a fax, or the encoded data from a modem.

Transport Technology

Defining the transport starts with the consideration of the physical aspects of communications. You are addressing, in a physical sense, just how the content of the communications will be transported from one party to the other. If you want a reliable business process, you need to be thorough in the exploration of all transports involved in the process, even the interactions between people. A failure in a human-to-human interaction will hurt the business process just as surely as any technical failure in the systems. Consequently, from the architecture perspective you need to examine all transports involved.

Your interest in transport encompasses two tasks: selection and evaluation. Some of the selection may have already been done as part of the business process design. For example, the business process may call for the customer to phone the customer service representative. In other cases, specifically in system-to-system interactions, it is your task to select the transport mechanism. In any case, for every interaction you need to ensure that the transport mechanism has been clearly identified.

The second task you have is to evaluate the suitability of the selected transport from the perspectives of functional capability, capacity, reliability, and cost. Is the transport mechanism appropriate for the task? You are probably not going to move terabytes of data over a dial-up phone line. Does it promote effective information transfer? You are probably not going to verbally convey a graphic design for a magazine cover over the phone. Is it sufficiently reliable? You are probably not going to use the postal service to transport large sums of cash. Is it sufficiently auditable, that is, does it provide a record of interactions and their content? Is it scalable, both in terms of capacity and cost? For each interaction in the business process you need to decide which questions are relevant and then answer them.

Pragmatically, an exhaustive analysis of all transport options and all of the possible design considerations associated with each is not only impractical but would also be boring. To keep it practical, the following sections focus on two things: the key questions that you should be asking yourself as you make these choices and the techniques you can use for capturing the design decisions. Along the way, some techniques will be provided for answering some of the common questions, particularly those related to performance feasibility and capacity planning. But your primary focus is on ensuring that you have thought through the mechanics related to all communications and specified a clear and unambiguous design pattern for each interaction to follow.

Person-to-Person Interactions

The transports available for person-to-person interaction are quite varied. This should not be surprising, as people have been inventing new means of interacting with each other for some time now. Phone, intercom, radio, instant messaging, e-mail, fax, inter-office memo, and letter are but a few examples of transports used for human interaction. Even air, the transport for direct conversation, needs to be considered in some contexts. While you may normally think nothing of this, the absence of air in the vacuum of space makes even the availability of this common transport an issue for astronauts.

Although you may not spend a lot of time on the human-to-human communication aspects of your process design, you at least need to understand what is being communicated, the medium that is being used, and the appropriateness of the medium for that particular type of information. This is particularly important when you are modeling an existing process that will be partially or completely automated. What is actually communicated, and the mechanisms used to do it, are often known only to the participants in the process. If you are to automate these activities, you must first understand them.

Scalability of the person-to-person transport is of particular concern when there is a large workforce involved. Techniques that work well with a small team may break down badly as the number of people increases. Unstructured face-to-face interactions may be fine for a small team, but hundreds of people communicating with each other by simply yelling across the room might not be such a good idea. On the other hand, the near-chaos of an equities trading floor demonstrates just how much communication is possible in such a chaotic environment! When all is said and done, you need to make sure that these human-to-human interactions are appropriately organized. You also need to determine what supporting technology is required and ensure that if it is not already available, its provisioning is included within the scope of the project.

Human-to-System Transport

When people need to interact with systems, there are many vehicles available. Some are fundamentally designed as human interfaces: generic web browsers, dedicated application interfaces (fat clients), and custom hardware devices such as ATMs and hand-held devices are common examples. Increasingly, however, media that were originally intended for person-to-person interactions are being adapted to become system interfaces. The telephone (via voice response systems), e-mail, and faxes have all been adapted in this manner, and this is an area in which there is constant innovation. Cellular phones in particular, with integrated text messaging, text paging, touch screens, audible alerts, and web browser capabilities, are rapidly evolving into personal portable system terminals.

When you look at human-to-system interactions, you need to evaluate the choice of medium from the perspectives of both human usability and technical feasibility. The complexity of the technical design work and anticipated performance challenges must be evaluated along with the cost of acquiring and using the technology. The bottom line is that you need to determine whether the approach is practical within the cost and schedule guidelines of the project.

System-to-System Transport

When it comes to system-to-system interactions, at least within a physical site, physical IP networks are generally the medium of choice,[1] but there are many other options that might also come into play. Terminals and peripheral devices may use serial interfaces such as RS-232, USB, or IEEE 1394 (firewire). They may use parallel interfaces such as the Centronix parallel printer or IEEE 488 interfaces. When distances

---

1. Strictly speaking, an IP network is not a medium but rather a low-level communications protocol that can itself be provided over lower-level protocols and media. However, the availability of IP fabric has become so ubiquitous that at the application level it is not inappropriate to view it as a medium, at least within a physical site.

increase, various types of voice and digital switched wide-area networks and satellite links may come into play.

Wide-area and satellite connections have cost and performance characteristics that you need to be very aware of in your design, as they can be major contributors to ongoing operations costs. The cost of wide-area communications is usually proportional to the bandwidth required, so your design choices that impact bandwidth requirements directly determine the associated operational costs. For a remote connection, a portion of that IP network (the last-mile drop to the premises) might be built on top of a dial-up analog telephone network, a Digital Subscriber Line (DSL) service, or a CATV service. Higher-bandwidth links such as T1 and T3 connections will cost proportionally more. Satellite communications can be priced in data increments as small as 60 bytes.[2] You need to consider these cost implications in your projects.

Another communications issue to consider is latency—the time it takes for the interaction to occur. This is a problem you always have to face for wide-area connections. At least as of this writing, the speed-of-light problem has not been overcome, and there may be further (and more significant) delays associated with traversing the network components (switches and routers). The use of satellite links contributes further delays, as will the use of encryption/decryption, data compression/decompression, and other types of encoding/decoding techniques. While no one delay may seem particularly large, the cumulative effect of many delays can have an adverse impact on the overall process. You need to determine whether the delays are acceptable. Of course, to do this, you need to understand what delays are acceptable, so you are once again referring back to the requirements associated with the business process itself.

In addition to picking the medium for system-to-system interactions, you also need to select the application-level communications protocol that will be used over the medium. The protocol determines the actual mechanism for information exchange between components. A web browser, for example, typically uses the Hyper-Text Transport Protocol (HTTP) or its secure cousin, HTTPS, to communicate over an Internet Protocol (IP) based network. Java Messaging Service (JMS) or other messaging service might be employed. You might even end up selecting

---

2. An increment of bandwidth utilization known as a Message Transmission Unit (MTU).

an e-mail or ftp protocol. The list of available choices continues to grow as new technologies are introduced and evolving service standards have begun to add additional protocol layers. SOAP (the Simple Object Access Protocol), for example, is a protocol that can operate over different transports such as HTTP, e-mail, and JMS.

Selecting Transports

Within the space constraints of this book it is not possible to go into all the details of physical media and the layers of communications protocols that can be built upon them. That, in itself, is enough material for a book nearly as large as this one![3] However, at this point in your architecture you do need to establish the transport mechanisms that the architectural components will use to communicate regardless of how much research that requires. With respect to the chosen transports, you need to know what to expect in terms of availability, performance, and cost. Even though you may not be responsible for the design, implementation, or provisioning of the transport, you as the architect are ultimately responsible for determining the adequacy of the choice with respect to the application. Overloaded networks, excessive latency, or exorbitant costs will kill the application just as surely as a poorly designed participant. Your job is to ask enough questions so that you understand the available communications approaches, evaluate them, and select the right ones.

In choosing the transports, you need to be practical as well. While it may be desirable to uniformly employ a single communication protocol throughout the system, there are many valid reasons for employing more than one. In fact, the different behavioral properties of various communications protocols often makes it attractive to employ more than one protocol in the enterprise. For example, socket-level protocols such as HTTP (and HTTPS) might be the preferred protocols for external-facing interfaces that the enterprise presents to other enterprises since their use requires no specific technology footprint at the other end. On the other hand, a messaging service such as JMS might be the

---

3. Ray Horak 2000. *Communications Systems and Networks, Second Edition.* Foster City, CA: M&T Books.

preferred protocol for communications within the enterprise since it enables asynchronous interaction and load distribution.[4]

There are other considerations as well. Socket-level protocols such as HTTP are tied to the host names and IP addresses (either physical or virtual) of the participants in the communication. When communication is required, a connection is established to the system hosting the application, either directly or indirectly.[5] Once this connection has been established, it is used to conduct subsequent communications. This dependency on a specific connection to a specific host means that both parties must be active at the same time for communications to occur. It also presents specific design challenges with respect to high availability, fault tolerance, and load distribution, which we will discuss in Part VII.

In contrast to socket protocols, which are inherently point-to-point connections, messaging services (such as JMS) introduce a communications service that acts as an intermediary between the parties. The originating party sends a message to the communications service, which in turn delivers the message to the intended recipient. With this approach, the sender and recipient no longer need to be active at the same time for communications to occur. The message service can accept the message from the sender, and then deliver it to the recipient at a later time. In addition, the sender and recipient no longer need to be aware of one another. Messages are sent to and from abstractions known as destinations (topics and queues in JMS). This level of indirection allows the actual recipient of the message to be moved from one machine to another without requiring any change to either the sender or the messaging service. It also allows multiple applications to subscribe to the same message, again without the knowledge of the sender. Multiple subscribers with JMS topics allow the same message to be delivered to many parties. Since messages in JMS queues are delivered to exactly one recipient, the use of multiple subscribers allows the processing load to be distributed across the subscribers. These capabilities can significantly reduce system maintenance costs in the ever-changing world of enterprise systems.

---

4. Strictly speaking, JMS is a standardized Application-level Interface (API) written in Java and not a true communications protocol. The actual protocol is hidden under the covers.

5. Indirect communications can occur through an IP-redirector, proxy, or both.

One issue you will have to face is that not every end-point system will be capable of utilizing the chosen protocols. The presence of legacy systems and commercial off-the-shelf components that happen to employ different protocols mandates that these protocols be at least minimally supported to enable communications with these components. This may drive you towards the use of adapters (Chapter 18) to limit the extent to which these noncompliant protocols pervade the enterprise. In any case, it is certainly reasonable to restrict the use of these noncompliant protocols to these special cases.

Once you have selected the communications mechanisms, you update your activity diagrams to reflect the choices you have made, as shown in Figure 17–1. Here the `ATM Machine` is using JMS (the JMS1 label will be explained in a moment) to send `message 1` to the `ATM Server`, that in turn is using HTTP to send `message 2` to the `Bank System`. You are now making the activity diagram more specific, reflecting the design choices you are making.

If you are employing messaging servers, in addition to annotating the communications in the activity diagrams, you also need to update the deployment diagram to show where these messaging servers reside. Figure 17–2 shows the placement of a `JMS Server` in the ATM example deployment. This placement is important in helping you understand what the network load will be. Knowing the location of the sender, recipient, and communications server, you can trace the path of the communication. This will enable you to determine the load that the

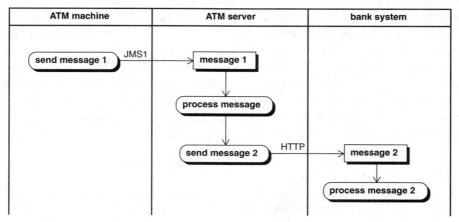

Figure 17–1: *Annotating Activity Diagrams with Communications Mechanism Selections*

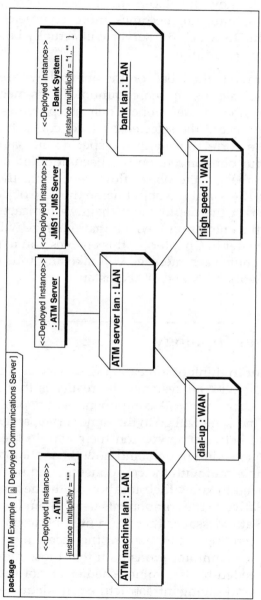

Figure 17–2: *JMS Server Deployment*

communication will present on each LAN and WAN instance (more on this in Chapter 39). When you initially locate the messaging server, you will probably only show the placement of the server on a network LAN. Later, as the architecture becomes more complete, you will determine the machine to which the server will actually be deployed, updating the diagram accordingly.

You should note that while the labels on the object flows are standard UML, their use to indicate the chosen communications mechanism is simply a convention, albeit a useful one. Their use provides you with the ability to not only record the selected protocol choice but can also be used to establish a correlation with the specific messaging server being used. Here a further convention has been adopted such that a match between the label on the object flow generating the message (e.g., JMS1 in Figure 17–1) and the object name (not the object type) of the messaging server in the deployment diagram indicates that this messaging server is the one through which that message will be delivered. As we shall see later in Chapter 39, this enables you to determine the precise network route each message will take and thus determine the load on each network LAN and WAN instance.

Messaging Server Topology

While it is convenient to think of a messaging service as a ubiquitous fabric equally accessible by all systems, the reality is that messaging services are provided by physical components—and possibly more than one. Not every message will go to the same server, and some messages may be routed between servers on their way to their destinations. As a result, you need to understand how those components will interact with each other and with the components sending and receiving messages. You need to know their location on the network relative to each other and relative to the components using them for communications. When there are messages that are routed between servers on their way from the sending component to the receiving component, you need to know the communications path that those messages will take. All of this is needed to determine whether or not the proposed communications and messaging infrastructure can adequately support the application. Even when you are not responsible for the actual design of this messaging or communications infrastructure, you must still do this evaluation.

The simplest case for messaging servers is to have exactly one server. To be clear, the reference to a server here is a reference to the logical component and not the physical machine it resides on. You could, potentially, have two or more messaging servers residing on the same machine. In any case, when you have only one server, the evaluation is pretty straightforward. You simply need to determine the peak rate at which the server needs to handle messages (as determined by your application), and then determine whether the proposed (or existing) server can handle that number of messages per second while meeting the latency requirements for message delivery. You also need to consider the network locations of the sender and recipients of these messages and the availability of the network bandwidth to and from the messaging server. All in all, the analysis involving a single messaging server is relatively straightforward. But a single messaging server is not always the right solution.

There are generally two types of situations that will drive you towards the use of multiple messaging servers. One arises when the total messaging load exceeds the capacity limitations of either a single server or a single network LAN. The other arises when there is a geographic distribution of components involving two or more physical sites. Either type of situation can lead to the use of multiple messaging servers.

Coping with Capacity Limitations

When the total message load exceeds the capacity of a single messaging server or network LAN, you will need to split that load. One solution is, of course, to redesign to reduce the amount of traffic. But for the moment let's assume that you need to deal with the volume of traffic as-is. If a LAN is overloaded, it is likely that this LAN is the one on which the messaging server is located. To relieve the overload, you must split the network traffic across two or more LANs. This may lead you to add additional messaging servers as well, splitting the traffic between the servers. If the messaging server itself is overloaded, then you must split the traffic across two or more messaging servers. Although the details are not discussed here (the design patterns and other considerations for load distribution are covered in Chapter 35), *it is at this point in the design process that you would identify the need for load distribution and choose the appropriate design pattern.*

Let's pause for a moment here to reinforce just how important it is to determine whether an overload situation exists, regardless of whether the overload occurs at the communications level or at the application-component level. Time and again enterprises build and deploy systems without stopping to consider whether the capacity actually exists to handle the load. Not only do these systems fail, but their failure is predictable early in their design and with a very modest amount of work. One company in particular was in the process of architecting a system for archiving and retrieving emails. They got so caught up in figuring out the pipeline of activities required to process these emails that they never even calculated the overall communications load. The architecture they were defining would have resulted in a single LAN communications load exceeding 10 Gbits/second, which was (at the time) an order of magnitude greater than available network components could provide. A simple back-of-the-envelope calculation was all it took to reveal that this was not a practical architecture, yet they were several months into working out its details. The message (pardon the pun) is clear: A few simple questions early in the design cycle can avoid months of wasted effort and millions of dollars in wasted development costs. Do your homework!

So what do you do if the communications turns out to be infeasible from a performance perspective? You need to consider alternate architectures until you can find a satisfactory solution—or conclude that the problem cannot be solved within the project cost and schedule guidelines. Alternatives can run the gamut from choosing different communication mechanisms, relocating system components on the network, up through redesigning the overall business process so that it requires a lower volume of communications.

Coping with Geographic Distribution

When the components requiring messaging services are geographically distributed across multiple sites, you must consider how those components will access the messaging servers. The seemingly simple solution is to have all of the components connect to a single messaging server, but this requires each remote component to make its own connection over the WAN. This presents a number of potential design issues related to the use of the WAN, including the number of socket connections, provisioning the credentials used to establish and secure those connections, and the total bandwidth demand placed on the WAN connection to the server.

If each remote component establishes its own WAN connection, then the number of sockets required on the messaging server will be equal to the total number of components. One issue this raises is that there is a finite limit to the number of connections that can be practically supported by a messaging server. Another issue is that each of the connecting components must be configured with all of the information necessary to establish the connection, including the network address (hostname or IP address) and required security credentials. This provisioning can make the administration of the system complex, particularly when the messaging server needs to be re-hosted as part of a failover or site disaster recovery scheme. A third issue is that each of the components must be designed to deal with the breakdowns typically associated with WAN connections. They must be capable of handling dropped connections, reestablishing connections, and restoring the application to the correct state. A fourth issue is that when the same message needs to be sent to multiple recipients at the same remote site, it will be sent multiple times over the same WAN connection. This increases the bandwidth requirements for the WAN connection and may have significant cost implications for the project.

There is an alternative worth considering if the chosen messaging servers are capable of routing messages from one to another. In this alternative approach, a messaging server is placed at each physical site. Components local to each site connect to the on-site messaging server. The messaging servers then route messages to the correct site, where they are delivered to the appropriate recipient. This approach has a number of advantages. First, only the messaging servers need to deal with the WAN connections and their associated configuration, credentials, and breakdowns. Second, it limits the number of connections that each messaging server needs to handle. And third, this configuration may provide a means of reducing WAN bandwidth requirements for the case in which a single message is delivered to multiple recipients at a remote site. Assuming an appropriate delivery semantic is used for the message (i.e., a JMS topic), the message will only be sent once across the WAN. The local messaging server will then distribute it to each recipient.

If you choose this type of distributed messaging server topology, you can extend the annotation convention to cover these routed messages. You do so by labeling each of the object flows with the name of the messaging server involved from the perspective of each participant.

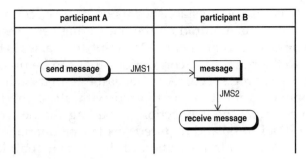

Figure 17–3: *Labeling Messages with Routed Communications*

Thus in Figure 17–3, `participant A` sends a `message` using the `JMS1` server, while `participant B` receives that message from the `JMS2` server.

Continuing on with the convention, you show both servers on the deployment diagram (Figure 17–4). You also show the logical connection between the JMS servers, indicating that the two servers are aware of each other and capable of routing messages between them. These logical connections determine the sequence of servers that the message will traverse through on its way to its destination. This, in turn, will enable you to determine the network LANs and WANs each message traverses on its way to its destination.

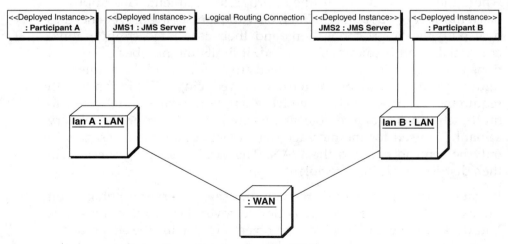

Figure 17–4: *Geographic Distribution of Messaging Servers*

Capacity

As an architect, you are ultimately responsible for the choice and adequacy of the communications mechanisms you select for the solution. These mechanisms may not be something you design and create as part of your project—they are often services that are already in place in the systems environment. Nevertheless, you must ensure that the service is actually capable of doing the job you expect. You cannot assume that these services are infinite in capacity and provide instantaneous response. Every service has finite limitations, and you need to factor those limitations into the design. If you are trying to move data at the rate of several gigabits per second between a pair of participants, then a 1-gigabit network service is not going to do the job. Furthermore, if the service is already in use for other applications, you need to determine whether there is sufficient capacity remaining to support the application. Once you understand the needed capacity, you must then interact with the service provider to determine whether that capacity is available and obtain a commitment to provide it.

When you are asking capacity questions, you need to bear in mind that communications services may be built, in turn, upon other communications services. To understand the overall limitations, you need to understand the capacity limitations of each service. A messaging server, for example, will utilize a network to interact with the message senders and recipients. Therefore, you need to understand the capacity limitations both of the messaging server itself and of the underlying network. You will learn how to determine the needed capacity in Chapter 39, but for now let's assume that you have already made these calculations.

Simply understanding the needed capacity is not sufficient. If you are obtaining communications services from a service provider, whether in-house or external, you need to obtain a commitment to provide that capacity. Be forewarned that there is often a long lead time (measured in months) required to establish new telecommunications services. You also need to determine what the cost will be, particularly of wide-area network connections, keeping in mind that the solution must be implementable within the project's cost and schedule guidelines.

A note of practicality is in order here. If another organization (not part of your project team) is responsible for communications services, you must make some judgment calls in terms of how you deal with that organization. At a minimum, you need to present them with the load requirements and obtain a commitment to provide that level of service. You might even go so far as to negotiate a service-level agreement (SLA) for providing the needed services. But, much as you might dislike admitting it, you also need to make a judgment call as to whether or not you can trust the commitment.

This does not necessarily imply that the organizations providing the services do not have the skills required or are insincere in their commitments, for this is rarely the case. But the fact is that many infrastructure groups simply do not know how much of their capacity is truly available under worst-case conditions. Yes, they routinely observe and measure current activity, and they have a pretty good understanding of the resources that will be available on a day-to-day basis. They probably have an understanding of when predictable periods of peak activity occur and what the available capacity is during those times. *But the core problem is that the true peak periods, the disaster scenarios, very rarely occur!* How often does the stock market crash? In the absence of direct observations, how are you to know what the true remaining capacity is during exceptional peaks? How can you know what the available network capacity will be in a stock exchange during a market crash?

The reality is that the demands on the communications and messaging infrastructure during true peak load situations can only be determined analytically. That analysis requires an understanding of the business processes that are using the infrastructure and the behavior of those processes during these periods. If the infrastructure is shared, this analysis must include the other business processes as well. It is highly likely that this analysis has not been done for those other business processes. Therefore, you need to make a judgment call. Is your application mission critical, that is, a category 4 or 5 in the business process impact ranking from Chapter 10? Do you therefore need to guarantee performance even under these extreme peak load conditions? If the answer to both of these questions is yes, then you must pursue the understanding of capacity until you are satisfied that the answers reflect reality. Whether that means using a separate communications infrastructure or analyzing the other business processes (or teaching the service organization how to do this), you must do whatever you feel necessary to ensure that the business processes will meet their service-level agreements. Don't forget that this might include concessions on the solution side, renegotiating the SLAs to make them less stringent during disaster scenarios.

Point-to-Point Interaction Patterns

The simplest form of communication is for the two parties to interact directly with one other using the selected communications protocol. This interaction can employ one of two interaction patterns: batch (the reason for this name will become apparent in a moment) or event-driven (Figure 17–5). In the batch style, a triggering event that is generally *unrelated to the execution of the business process* (usually time-based) causes `participant A` to generate a `dataset`. A second triggering event, generally time-based and unrelated to the arrival of the dataset, then causes `participant B` to retrieve this `dataset` and process it. This pattern is typical of the nightly batch-processing that often goes on in data centers.

The triggering events for batch communications are usually time-based and are not directly related to the participants' generation of business process results. Even when a management utility is used to orchestrate the transfer, the triggering of the utility itself is usually

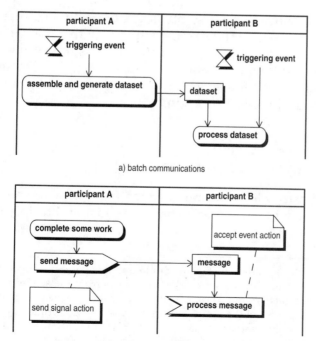

a) batch communications

b) event-driven communications

Figure 17–5: *Point-to-Point Communications Patterns*

based on time or some other event unrelated to the business process execution. This lack of correlation between the business process's generation of results and the communication of those results leads to an interaction style that is commonly known as batch processing. In this style, when the triggering event occurs in `participant A`, all of the business results that have been generated since the last triggering event (or, alternatively, all of the business results that are available) are collected and placed in a dataset. This set of results is the "batch," and all subsequent activity in the communication pattern uses this batch as the unit of work: hence the term *batch processing*.

The alternative to batch processing is an event-driven interaction. In this style, the completion of an activity acts as the trigger for the communications. When this trigger occurs, the participant gathers the relevant information, packages it up as a message, and sends the message to the recipient. The recipient's activity is, in turn, triggered by the arrival of the message. Here all the events driving the communication are directly related to the meaningful events in the business process—hence the term *event-driven*.[6]

The fact that a message is intended to act as a trigger is so significant that UML provides special symbols for the activities that send and receive such messages. The messages that play this role are referred to as *signals*, the action of sending such a signal is represented by a *send signal action*, and the recipient is an *accept event action*. The use of these symbols emphasizes the special role that such messages play in the overall business process execution.

Point-to-Point Intermediaries

As you begin to select communications mechanisms, one of the first dilemmas you will encounter is that the sender and recipient in a com-

---

6. The term *real time* is often mistakenly applied to this pattern of interaction. In reality, there is some time lag as the message propagates from the sender to the recipient and the recipient gets around to processing it. This time interval, although generally short, tends not to be rigidly controlled. In contrast, it is the rigid control of timing work performance that is the hallmark of truly real-time systems. Thus the term *real time* is not precisely appropriate for most business applications. The term *near-real-time* might be employed to emphasize that information is moved and processed as quickly as is practicable.

munication do not share a common communication protocol (or you choose not to use a protocol they do share for policy reasons). Assuming that you don't wish to modify the participants, you must employ a communications intermediary to facilitate the interaction (Figure 17–6). This intermediary uses protocols that are available on each of the participants and performs whatever additional work is required to transform one participant's information into a form suitable for the other participant.

As with point-to-point communication, the intermediary typically operates in either batch or event-driven styles. In the batch style, management

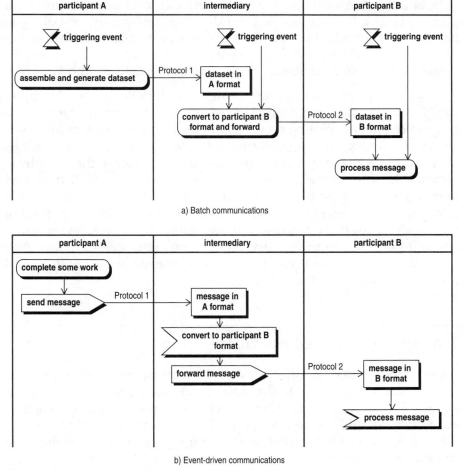

a) Batch communications

b) Event-driven communications

Figure 17–6: *Point-to-Point with Intermediary Communications Patterns*

utilities are often used to generate the triggering events for all participants and verify the correct creation and processing of the data sets.
These management utilities, however, can be hampered by an inability
to generate the required triggering events. The recipient system, for
example, may not have an interface that allows the management utility to trigger the consumption of a data set. The trigger for this must
come from some other source, such as a human operator or a schedule
contained within the application.

An important design consideration with the point-to-point intermediary
approach is that the construction and maintenance of the intermediary
can become quite complex. There are three responsibilities embodied
in the intermediary: interacting with `participant A`, converting the
dataset into a form suitable for `participant B`, and interacting with
`participant B`. This requires the developer of the intermediary to
become familiar with both communications protocols, both data representations and their related representation technologies, and the techniques available for mapping one representation into another.

The point-to-point intermediary design problem becomes even more
complex when the two participants reside on different machines (possibly on different operating systems) and the end-point system interfaces
are programming language interfaces (APIs) and not communications
protocols. Use of the API often requires that the user of the API physically reside on the same machine as the end-point system. If both end
points have this type of interface, it is not possible to create a single
intermediary. When such situations arise (as they frequently do), the
intermediary itself needs to be split into two components, one residing
on each machine, and these two components now must interact with
one another. These split components are referred to as *adapters*, and
they are the subject of the next chapter.

Transport-Supplied Services

As service-oriented architectures evolve, transport mechanisms are
being extended to facilitate the interactions between service consumers and service providers. These extensions provide features such as
access control and request routing. These features were discussed in
Chapter 4, but this is the point in the design process at which their use
should be determined.

Summary

The interactions you have defined in your architecture must occur over some physical transport, and the artifacts being exchanged must have a physical representation as well. You need to identify the specific transport to be used for each interaction and update your architecture documentation accordingly. Your choice of transport technology constrains the possible physical representations of the artifacts, particularly the technologies available for representing information. The representation of data requires the definition of its syntax and semantics, so you need to identify (though not necessarily define) the particular syntax and semantics to be used in each exchange. You must also identify the semantics of the interaction itself as representing either a request, a reply to such a request, or an announcement.

In architecting a solution, all interactions need to be considered, even those between people. In every case, you need to determine whether the transport chosen is adequate to the task, and whether the parties can operate on the same physical artifact and share an understanding of its syntax and semantics. The available capacity of the transport needs to be evaluated and a commitment secured to provide the required capacity to support the solution.

When the selected transport involves communications servers, the architecture of those servers needs to be considered along with their capacity. If the solution is geographically distributed, you must determine the location of the various servers and the routing of communications between them. Once this topology is understood, you need to reevaluate the load that will be placed on network LANs and WANs as well as the load on the individual communications servers.

Finally, you need to identify the events that trigger the interactions. Some interactions will be triggered by activities that are a part of the business processes, while others will be triggered by external events. The sources of external events must be identified.

Key Transport Questions

1. Have communications mechanisms been identified for all interactions between participants? Have the transports and protocols

been identified? Have the activity diagrams been appropriately updated?

2. If messaging is being used, have the locations of the messaging servers on the network been defined? If there are multiple messaging servers, has the messaging server topology been defined? Have the deployment diagrams been updated?

3. Has the performance feasibility of the network and messaging infrastructure been established? Has the analysis been documented? Is the required capacity available within the project's cost and schedule guidelines? Have commitments been obtained to provide the required communications services?

Suggested Reading

Ray Horak, 2000. *Communications Systems and Networks, Second Edition.* Foster City, CA: M&T Books.

Chapter 18

Adapters

In an ideal world, once you have selected the protocol for each interaction, each of the participants would simply use the selected protocol. You could then turn your attention to other aspects of the system design. Unfortunately, in the real world a lot of existing functionality is embodied in components that cannot directly employ the protocol you have selected. Such participants require intermediaries to map their existing interfaces into the chosen protocol, which is generally one of the protocols on which the enterprise has chosen to standardize. These intermediaries are commonly referred to as *adapters* (Figure 18–1). While the enterprise's long-range goal may be for all participants to directly employ a standard protocol for their interactions, in the short term the bulk of the participants (mostly those that already exist) will require the use of an adapter to employ these protocols.

When an adapter is required, you need to look at how the adapter is going to interact with the end-point system, and you need to consider this for both inbound and outbound communications. In both inbound and outbound directions you need to determine (a) what event will determine that action is required, (b) how that event will be recognized, and (c) how the action will be implemented.

In general, you will find that the interfaces on end-point systems break down into four categories:

- Application programming interfaces (API)
- Databases

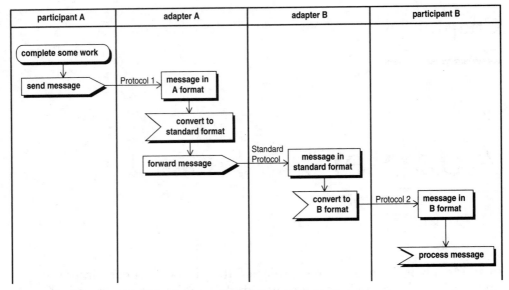

Figure 18–1: *Standardized Protocol and Adapters Pattern*

- Files
- Protocols

Each category differs with respect to event identification and triggering, and each has certain strengths and weaknesses. Let's take a look at each type of interface from the perspective of event identification, event recognition, and action implementation.

API-Based Adapters

APIs are programming-language interfaces that are provided by the end-point systems. They are generally intended to be a means for an external piece of programming language code to invoke functionality in the end-point system. As such, they tend to provide a fairly straightforward means for an adapter to translate an inbound message into specific actions in the end-point system as long as that functionality is made available through the API. Upon receipt of a message (the trigger), an API-based adapter un-bundles the information in the message and invokes the appropriate APIs.

Unfortunately, most APIs do not provide an event-recognition capability that will allow adapter code to be called by the end-point system when specific events occur in that end-point system. When these mechanisms do exist, they are generally referred to as *callbacks*. The use of a callback, if available, involves a two-step interaction between the adapter and the end-point system. In the first step, the adapter registers the callback (the code to be called) with the end-point system. This registration associates the callback with a particular type of event. Depending upon the specific mechanisms offered by the end point, this registration may be accomplished through the static configuration of the end-point system, or it may occur dynamically at runtime. In either case, once the registration has taken place, subsequent occurrences of the specified event will result in the invocation of the call-back code in the adapter, which can then generate an outbound message.

In the absence of callbacks, the only means that an adapter has for identifying events in the end-point system is to periodically call APIs to determine whether any significant changes have occurred—a practice referred to as *polling*. Depending upon the available APIs, polling can range in complexity from very simple to practically impossible. Polling may also present an unacceptable performance demand on the end-point system. The reality is that most systems that have APIs are not designed for efficient polling. Consequently, it is very difficult to identify the occurrence of triggering events in the end-point systems. Thus, APIs tend to be good for inbound communications and poor for outbound communications.

Database-Based Adapters

It may seem a bit strange to think of a database as an interface, but the reality is that many applications reside (logically) on top of a database. Furthermore, significant changes in the application, particularly those marking the occurrence of significant events, generally result in updates to the database. When an order is placed, for example, the new order is saved in the database. The entry of the order in the database can then be taken as a signal that a new order has been created. Most databases support triggers that initiate the execution of stored procedures. These triggers can then be used as a means for recognizing application events. This, of course, assumes that you understand enough about the database to determine which changes correspond to meaningful events.

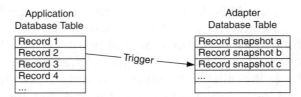

Figure 18–2: *Using Triggers for Database Adapters*

The availability of triggers can then be used to architect an adapter. The technique is to identify an application table of interest, create a second table whose structure replicates the original, and implement a trigger that takes a snapshot of each application record that changes (Figure 18–2). A simple query of the `Adapter Database Table` will reveal any changes that have occurred. The adapter is set up to periodically query this table, retrieve the event information, and publish messages. In general, the combined use of triggers and queries of the event table, coupled with a reasonable time interval for querying the event table, puts far less of a burden on the database than would a broader query of the `Application Database Table` that seeks to identify the records that have changed since the last query was performed. It is efficient.

While database triggers often provide an effective means of triggering outbound communications, direct database updates generally do not provide a good means for handling inbound communications. The reason for this is that the application owning the database almost always contains business logic that governs the use of the database. A direct update of the database bypasses this business logic and is therefore unacceptable from the applications perspective. A secondary issue is that the schema of the database is likely to be proprietary and subject to change between application releases. Therefore, an adapter that works with one version of the database may need to be modified when the application owning the database is upgraded.

Combining API and Database Approaches

Many end-point systems are applications that have both publicly supported APIs and underlying databases. Such systems present an opportunity to combine both the API and database techniques when implementing an adapter. In the inbound direction, the adapter accepts a message and uses the API to interact with the application. In the outbound direction, the adapter uses the database trigger technique to capture events. The combination can be further leveraged to minimize the dependency on the database schema, which is likely to be proprietary. This is accomplished by using the trigger to just capture the bare-bones identification information about the event, perhaps as little as an identifier (i.e., primary key). The adapter then uses this identifier in conjunction with the (presumably standard and publicly supported) API to retrieve the rest of the relevant information. Many commercial adapters are built using this technique.

File-Based Adapters

The oldest style of interface typically found on applications is based on the production and consumption of files. In the outbound direction, the application either periodically or on command generates (or updates) a file containing the needed information. The adapter can then recognize (via operating system polling) that the file has been created or changed. This recognition of change serves as the triggering event, at which point the adapter opens the file and publishes the needed information as a message. The adapter may, in addition, delete, rename, or move the file to indicate that the file has been processed.

In the inbound direction, the adapter reverses these operations. It receives the inbound message and either creates or updates a file with the content of the message. Optionally, the adapter may invoke an application operation (generally through a command line interface) that causes the application to then consume the file.

The primary problem with most file-based interfaces is that they are unable to recognize actual business process events and use them to trigger the generation of files. Consequently, the triggering event that causes the generation of a file tends to be either a scheduled time or the interaction of a user with an interface. In either case, this lack of correlation between the real business events and the generation of the files tends to make this type of adapter more suitable for the "batch" style of interaction than the event-driven style.

Protocol-Based Adapters

Many applications are beginning to appear on the market with protocol-based interfaces. Newer applications are providing web services access to their functionality via SOAP over HTTP. These protocol-based interfaces are very similar to API interfaces, except that the operations are invoked over a communications protocol rather than directly through a programming language API. As such, they also tend to have similar strengths and weaknesses: good in the inbound direction and weak in the outbound direction.

Documenting Adapter Usage

Once you have determined that adapters are required, the architecture needs to be updated to reflect this decision. One approach is to simply add swimlanes to the high-level activity diagrams to represent the adapters. Unfortunately, this makes those activity diagrams larger and more complex, so it obscures the fundamental pattern of interactions among the top-level components.

Preferably, you create an activity diagram that shows the details of a single interaction and identifies the adapter patterns for the two end points (Figure 18–3).

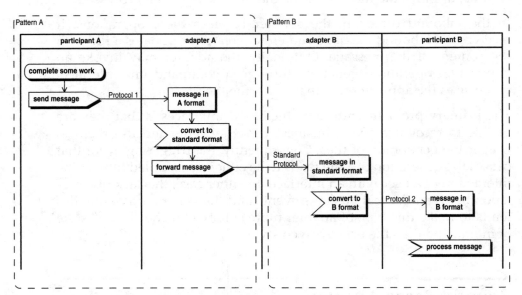

Figure 18–3: *Adapter Patterns*

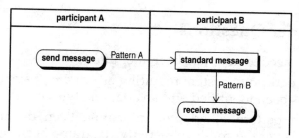

Figure 18–4: *Documenting Usage of Adapter Patterns*

Once the adapter patterns have been identified, you can then update the top-level diagrams by labeling them with the patterns being used (Figure 18–4). With this approach you have a precise design for the details and preserve the simplicity of the top-level diagrams. If the adapter pattern is used in many places, you can define it once and then reference it wherever it is used.

Summary

When you have decided to use a protocol that an end-point system cannot use directly, you need an intermediary to map the chosen protocol to and from the available end-point interfaces. Such intermediaries are referred to as adapters.

The design of the adapter is heavily influenced by the nature of the interfaces available on the end-point systems. These interfaces generally fall into four categories: API, database, file, and protocol. API and protocol interfaces tend to make it easy to take inbound messages and initiate activity in the end-point systems. These interfaces generally do not provide mechanisms for recognizing end-point system events and triggering the sending of messages. Database adapters tend to work well in the outbound direction, but are weak in the inbound direction. Many adapters combine the API and database techniques to create an adapter that works well in both directions.

The use of adapters in the architecture must be documented. The preferred mechanism for doing this is to detail the patterns of adapter usage independent of the top-level architecture diagrams, name those patterns, and then reference the usage of the pattern in the top-level diagrams.

Key Adapter Questions

1. Have the needed adapters been identified?

2. For each end-point system requiring an adapter, have the available interfaces been identified and an adapter style chosen?

3. Has each pattern of adapter utilization been documented and named? Have the top-level activity diagrams been updated with these pattern names to indicate where each pattern is being employed?

4. Have the network locations of the required adapters been determined? Have the deployment diagrams been updated?

Chapter 19

Enterprise Architecture: Communications

The need for communications and adapters becomes apparent at the project level, but there is value in achieving consistency from project to project in terms of how these decisions are made. The benefits range from minimizing investments in software, hardware, and training to making it easier for people to move from project to project. The following sections explore the enterprise architecture responsibilities associated with communications.

Defining a Communications Strategy

It is a good practice for an enterprise to establish a well-defined communications strategy. The strategy identifies the preferred communications protocols and the conditions under which each should be used. It also categorizes other protocols as being either (a) acceptable for existing usages (generally with no new usage permitted) or (b) deprecated, with the admonition that deprecated protocols should be migrated to preferred protocols at the earliest opportunity.

The establishment of preferred protocols does not imply that a project should be undertaken whose primary purpose is simply to replace old protocols with new ones. Such projects typically do not provide a positive return on their investment. Instead, adopt a policy directing that when noncompliant interfaces are being worked on (for reasons that truly do have an ROI associated with them), the opportunity should be taken to upgrade the protocol as well. Note that, over time, the execution of such a strategy may eventually lead to a situation in which a project could be justified to migrate a small number of remaining interfaces from a deprecated protocol to a standard one. Here the ROI comes from completely retiring the deprecated protocol and its supporting infrastructure.

Simply documenting a communications strategy, however, is not sufficient. There must be governance processes in place to ensure that projects actually comply with the chosen strategy, and there must be a group (generally the enterprise architects) that is responsible for the evolution of the strategy as well.

Keeping the communications strategy current and relevant requires more than just a periodic review and update. When project teams are having trouble selecting a communications protocol for an application from the approved list, the enterprise architecture group must get involved quickly to determine whether the selection problem lies in the articulation of the strategy or in the strategy itself. It may be that none of the "standard" protocols will satisfy the requirements of the project. The hypertext transport protocol (HTTP), for example, does not support asynchronous communications. Emerging requirements, such as those surrounding the evolution towards event-driven service-oriented architectures, will often provide the first indication that the current strategy may not be adequate. Active involvement in the application of the communications strategy will keep this guidance team in touch with the evolving needs of the business. You need to bear in mind that the strategy will not be particularly useful if its evolution lags behind the actual business needs.

Interaction Standards

In the IT community the complexity of designing, implementing, and maintaining point-to-point intermediaries resulted in the development of architectural styles and supporting technologies that standardize the interactions between participants. Examples include e-mail[1], fax, the Open Software Foundation's Distributed Computing Environment (DCE), Microsoft's COM/DCOM, the Object Management Group's Common Object Request Broker Architecture (CORBA), IBM's MQ-Series, TIBCO's Rendezvous, HTTP (HyperText Transport Protocol), JMS (Java Messaging Service), and SOAP (Simple Object Access Protocol).

When you consider the use of standards for interactions, you need to be clear about precisely which aspects of the interaction you are establishing standards for: transport technology, content representation technology, or both. Each of the examples just mentioned establishes a standard for communications transport, and most establish a standard for the technology of content representation as well.

The bottom line is that the identification of a standardized technology for use in a given interface only partially specifies that interface. In general, application teams will still need to specify the operation and data structures associated with each interaction. The drive towards standards in this area is the impetus behind common data models, which are discussed in Chapter 23.

Standardizing Adapters

Architecting an adapter requires a significant effort and a deep understanding of the end-point system architecture. Because of this, and the repeated need of different projects to access the same end-point system, it is good practice to standardize the adapter approach for each end point. It takes a fair amount of research to explore the different interface capabilities of a given end point and decide upon the best approach for providing adapters. The approach must define the design patterns to be used for both inbound and outbound communications.

Standardized adapter patterns provide a cookie-cutter approach for implementing interfaces to the application. The design of these patterns should take into consideration the volume of the data involved in each exchange, the frequency with which interactions will occur, and the latency that is acceptable in the communications. When there are

---

1. This is actually a collection of standards that include various choices for the transportation interface and for the content representation.

significant variations in these requirements, it may be appropriate to provide two or more patterns in each direction along with design rules for selecting the appropriate pattern. Note that these patterns encapsulate the end-point system functionality as a service, and thus define at least part of the internal architecture of that service.

Summary

There are many communications protocols available today. To avoid chaos, it is good practice to standardize on a few protocols and restrict or prohibit the use of others. The enterprise architecture group is responsible for selecting these protocols and overseeing their usage. Part of this oversight responsibility includes an ongoing evaluation of the suitability and adequacy of the preferred protocols as technologies and enterprise needs evolve.

It is likely that some end-point systems will be unable to directly use the preferred protocol. In such cases an adapter will be required to act as an intermediary between the end point and the preferred protocol. The architecture and design of adapters requires a deep understanding of the end-point system. To avoid repeating this effort, the enterprise architecture group should standardize the design for each end-point system requiring an adapter. The design must specify the usage patterns for both inbound and outbound traffic. Significantly different utilization patterns (i.e., time-critical request-response versus large batch interactions) may require different design patterns.

Key Enterprise Architecture Communications Questions

1. Have the enterprise's preferred communications mechanisms and patterns been identified and documented? Is the documentation sufficient to guide application teams in the proper use of the selected mechanisms? Does the documentation provide guidelines as to when each mechanism should be used? Does the documentation tell application teams how to proceed if none of the chosen mechanisms seem suitable for the application?

2. Have standard adapter patterns been identified and documented for end-point systems? Is the documentation sufficiently detailed to guide application teams in the proper use of the patterns? Does it tell application teams how to proceed if there is no documented pattern for a given end point or if the documented pattern does not appear appropriate?

3. Is there a governance process in place that ensures compliance with transport and adapter policies?

4. Is there a procedure in place that enables an application team to engage the enterprise architecture group when the communications or adapter policies do not appear to provide appropriate mechanisms for the application? Is the time it takes to engage the group and resolve the issue appropriate given the project schedules?

Part V

Data and Operations

Chapter 20

Data Challenges

At this point you have chosen the mechanisms for interaction. Now you need to consider the data being exchanged in those interactions. This data is as fundamental to the business processes as the processes' activities. A sales order, for example, must include the identification of the merchandise being purchased, a method of payment, and a shipping address. In reality, most of the activities in business processes do nothing other than acquire, manipulate, and deliver data. Only at key points in the process is physical action taken. The goods are not shipped until after the order information has been entered, the availability of the goods has been checked, and the credit has been checked.

Business process data is expected to reflect what is going on in the real world. The customer's name, address, and billing information are expected to be correct and current. Inventory numbers are expected to reflect the actual count of goods on the shelf. Inaccuracies, inconsistencies, and ambiguity in the data all can result in business process errors. Thus you need to pay attention to the handling of data. You need to look at the activities that are the touch points between the data and the real world—points at which the data is synchronized with reality. These are the points at which the warehouse ships the order and then updates the inventory, or the bank teller gives cash to the customer and updates the account balance. For robust business operation, the design of these activities must minimize the likelihood of errors. Wherever data is used in the business processes, it must be current and accurate.

If all of the enterprise's data were stored in a single database, data-related design activities would largely focus on the data representations in that database and the business rules governing the update of that data. But most enterprises have multiple systems. Each system manages data associated with some aspect of the business. The sales order management system manages the lifecycle of orders, while the warehouse management system manages the inventory of goods in the warehouse. These systems share data, and the systems architecture must manage this sharing. Customer information is present in the order management system, but some customer information is also present in the warehouse system. Each movement of data provides opportunities to create data inconsistencies. This is where you need to focus your attention.

There are a number of key issues related to the management of data in the enterprise:

- The semantics (meaning) of data both in communications and at rest
- The representation of data and the transformation between representations
- The consistency of data
- The management of identities
- The validation of results

Data semantics tells you the meaning of the data—what it actually represents. The data representation clarifies the structure of the data, and the presence of different representations usually requires transformation between those representations. Data consistency deals with maintaining a single version of the "truth" throughout the enterprise. Ideally, no matter where you look, you want to see the same information. Identity management ensures that customers, accounts, orders, and claims can be clearly and unambiguously identified across multiple systems. Results validation ensures that the results generated by business process activities make sense and are consistent with other information in the enterprise.

Chapter 21

Messages and Operations

The selection of a communications protocol establishes the technology that will be used to transport the data and perhaps the technology that will be used to represent the data. It generally does not establish either the semantics (meaning) or syntax (structure) of the message itself. When interacting components differ in their expectations concerning the semantics or syntax of the messages they exchange, some form of transformation is required as part of the exchange.

Message Semantics and Operation Names

When you look at a message, there are two relevant semantic questions: What does the content of the message represent? And what does the message as a whole represent? One does not necessarily imply the other.

Message Semantics

The meaning of a message is not necessarily implied by its content. Consider a message containing a representation of a sales order. What does this message actually represent? It might be a request for the order to be placed, the result of a query for the order, or an announcement that the represented order has been placed. Just looking at the data, you can't tell the difference.

It is not always obvious how to discern the meaning of a message. Many messages do not contain explicit indicators of the message intent. While protocols such as SOAP have an explicit `soap action` header to indicate the meaning of the message, the meaning of many messages is indicated by the destination to which the message is sent rather than the message itself. One of your responsibilities as an architect is to ensure that the meaning of each message is clear.

Broadly speaking, any given message plays one of three roles:

1. It is a request for some action to be taken.
2. It is a response to a request.
3. It is an announcement that some event has occurred.

The first two are the communications commonly associated with a request-reply exchange. The third is the basis of broadcast-style event-driven notifications.

Messages are exchanged between components, and are sent either to or from specific operations being provided by those components. The meaning of the message is thus closely related to the semantics of the operation. A `placeOrder request` message might be the input to the `placeOrder` operation, whose reply might be a `placeOrder reply` (Figure 21–1).

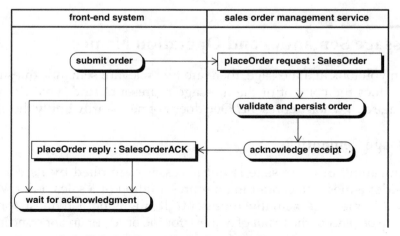

Figure 21–1: *Labeling Messages to Indicate Their Roles*

Operation Naming

At this point in assembling the architecture you should begin thinking about naming the operations and identifying the roles that the various messages are playing. It is good practice to place this information in the name field of the object representing the message in the activity diagrams. One test of your naming is to try to read the diagram as a sentence, for example, "The `front-end system` submits a `placeOrder request` (of type `SalesOrder`) to the `Sales Order Management Service`. The service validates and persists the order and sends a `placeOrder reply` (of type `SalesOrderACK`) to the front-end system that is waiting for this acknowledgment. Use this as an opportunity to refine the terminology that you are using so that what is going on is clear even to someone not familiar to the system. With appropriate terminology, these diagrams provide an easy-to-understand introduction to the systems.

At the same time that you are updating the activity diagram, you should add the operations you are identifying to the class model of the component (Figure 21–2). The parameters of the operations are the data structures being passed in, and the return types of the operations are the data structures being returned.

When the transport and representation technology such as SOAP provides for an explicit representation of the operation name, then the name you give to the object in the activity diagram becomes an explicit reference to the operation. However, in many message-based systems there is no explicit operation name. The message sender directs a message to an abstract destination name (e.g., a JMS topic or queue name). The operation provider subscribes to that destination and processes the messages, possibly sending other messages in response. In such situations, the message name should be the name of the destination, and the name of the destination should reflect the semantics of the messages.

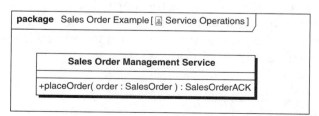

Figure 21–2: *Adding Operations to the Sales Order Management Service*

The syntax and semantics of the content define what the content is and how it is organized. It might be a purchase order from a customer represented in a particular XML schema, or a list of customers and their credit history in a file format, or the description of a product as free-form ASCII text.

Transport Destinations and Operation Bundling

When a messaging service is being used to deliver operation requests, it is common practice (though not always a good idea) to use a common messaging service destination for different kinds of requests. This is particularly the case with SOAP services defined with the Web Services Description Language (WSDL): All of the operations defined in a single WSDL interface[1] are usually provided through a single destination. Such bundling can provide advantages, but it needs to be approached with caution.

Bundling Advantages

Bundling is attractive for two reasons: administrative simplicity and sequencing. From a messaging administration point of view, bundling definitely makes life simpler. Having a single destination for all operations provided by a single service interface makes the setup of the communications infrastructure straightforward: Each interface corresponds to a messaging system destination.

A more compelling argument in favor of bundling is the issue of sequencing. When different operations impact a common shared state, the sequence in which these operations are applied is usually important. If you perform a credit operation followed by a debit operation, it is important that these operations be performed in the correct order. This is not usually an issue when the operations are performed in a synchronous request-reply, since the party invoking the transaction will wait for the first transaction to complete before invoking the second. However, when there are asynchronous interactions involved, preserving the sequence is important.

---

1. Called a `portType` in WSDL 1.x.

Messaging systems, in general, guarantee the ordering of messages between pairs of components. By bundling together the operations requiring sequencing and using a single destination, the messaging system will preserve the required sequencing. Thus, it is beneficial to bundle the CRUD (create, read, update, and delete) operations for a given entity.

Bundling Disadvantages

There are a couple of disadvantages to bundling related to change management and tuning. From a change management perspective, bundling the operations together can complicate adding or altering operations. Bundling effectively requires a logical case statement to take the incoming requests, determine which operation has been invoked, and direct the request to the appropriate implementation. Adding a new operation or altering the implementation of an existing operation requires the modification of this case statement. Depending upon the implementation technology, this can make it awkward for different people to make changes to different operations at the same time. Furthermore, the fact that this logic has been altered may require a complete retest of all operations—an expensive and time-consuming task. Finally, changes that actually alter the interface definition now impact all users of all operations in the bundle.

Another disadvantage of bundling is that it may make it difficult to tune the service provider. In many implementations, tuning is done at the interface (bundle) level. If the same interface happens to contain both small operations requiring a quick response time (e.g., a status request coming from an interactive user) and large resource-intensive operations (e.g., a batch submission of 10,000 insurance claims) it may be a practical impossibility to optimally tune the service provider for both operations.

Compromises

As the architect, it is your responsibility to sort out the bundling dilemma and decide what approach should be taken for the solution. You might, for example, segregate short-response-time operations and resource-intensive operations into separate interfaces (Figure 21-3). This achieves some of the administrative simplification while preserving the ability to tune the resulting implementation. Of course, to make

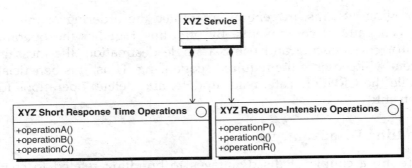

Figure 21–3: *Bundling Operations*

such decisions you need to be familiar with the likely implementation technologies along with their strengths and limitations. As much as you would like the abstraction of services to mask such underlying implementation details, the reality is that they often show through in the form of observable differences in performance.

As you define the interface bundles, you need to define the destinations associated with each bundle (Table 21-1). If this turns out to be a SOAP service, this information will eventually end up in the WSDL defining the service interfaces. Bear in mind that you may want to have multiple destinations (representing multiple transports) for each interface to facilitate access.

Mediated Transports

There is a trend towards increasing levels of abstraction in the interactions between service consumers and service providers. The Java Business

Table 21–1: *Service Interfaces and Destinations*

Service	Interface	Destination
XYZ Service	Short Response Time Operations	MyCo.Sales.XYZService.interactiveOperations
XYZ Service	Resource-Intensive Operations	MyCo.Sales.XYZService.batchOperations

Interface (JBI) specification is an example of such an abstraction.[2] These abstractions seek to hide transport details, allowing service consumers to simply indicate the desired operation and interface without having to specify a destination for the request. The mediated transport then determines the actual destination and routes the request.

While mediated transports relieve the service consumer (and provider) from the necessity of indicating the destinations for messages, the actual destinations still need to be determined—now by the mediating transport. Far from eliminating operation bundling as an architectural concern, you must now understand enough of how the mediating transport determines destinations to determine the impact of operation bundling upon the performance of the solution.

Content Representation

At this point in defining the architecture you identify the data representations that will be used for each interaction. This consists of identifying the schema of the representation along with any constraints on the data content. For example, if the component is presenting a SOAP interface, the defining WSDL schema defines all of the interface's operations. For a particular interaction, you want to identify not only the WSDL, but also the specific operation involved in the interaction.

In some cases you will have no choice in the data representation being used. The data structures involved in existing end-point system interactions are generally defined by the interfaces of those systems, and you have to use them as-is. Similarly, many commercial adapters produce data structures that are automatically derived from the end-point system's data structures. However, for all other interfaces you must determine the data representation.

When you are determining the data representations, your goal at this point is simply to identify the schema that will be required. The actual definition of the schema will come later after you are satisfied with the architecture. In some cases a suitable schema already exists and you

---

2. Sun Microsystems Inc. *Java Business Integration (JBI) 1.0 Final Release* http://jcp.org/aboutJava/communityprocess/final/jsr208/index.html (2005).

just need to reference it. In all other cases you need to identify the type of the schema and give the yet-to-be-defined schema a name.

The purpose of the exercise is primarily to determine whether the sending and receiving components in an interaction are using the same schema or different schemas. In particular, you need to identify those cases in which the interacting components are using different schemas, for these cases require an additional activity to transform the content from one format to the other.

Content Transformation

If two interacting participants differ with respect to the data representation, you need to introduce a content transformation to convert the message from the form supplied by the sender to the form required by the recipient. This activity might be performed by one of the existing components or by a separate component dedicated to this task. Figure 21–4 shows the content transformation being performed by a dedicated `content transformer`.

The content transformation could just as well have been incorporated into one of the two adapters and there are valid arguments for architecting the solution either way. The data structures produced and consumed by many adapters are determined by the end-point systems and tend to be relatively fixed. The content transformation, on the other hand, is driven by the solution's need for one end-point system to interact with another. Placing the transformation in its own component means that transformation changes are isolated from the adapters, simplifying the lifecycle of the change. This approach also allows the same adapter (or end-point system) interface to participate in many different transformations. On the other hand, making the content transformation part of the adapter eliminates one interaction and therefore simplifies the overall design. This approach is often used when the data structure being produced is a common data model representation (discussed in Chapter 23). Note that if you are using commercial adapter and transformation components, their design may dictate which approach is used.

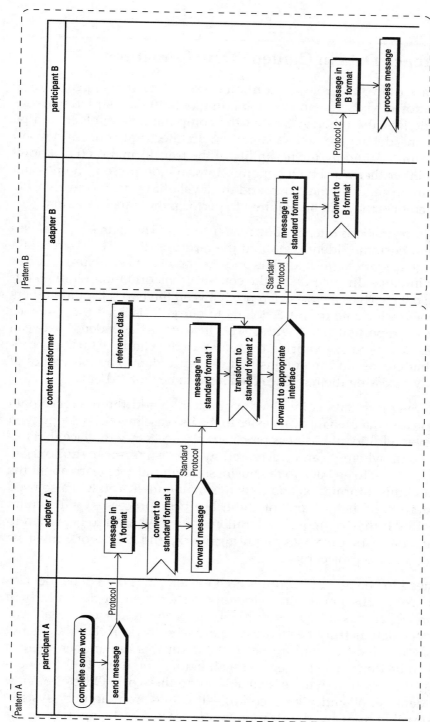

Figure 21–4: *Standardized Protocol and Content Transformer Communications Pattern*

Reference Data in Content Transformation

On the surface, the role of `Content Transformer` appears to be straightforward: Given an understanding of both data structures, convert one into the other. Although the computations involved can be messy, the details are generally not an architectural concern beyond simply understanding the feasibility of the transformation (i.e., knowing whether there is actually enough information present in one data structure to generate the other) and the level of resources (mostly CPU and memory) that will be required to perform the transformation.

But transformations often require reference data. The source system uses different customer identifiers than the target system. The source data structure has prices in US dollars and the target data structure requires prices in euros. In such cases, the content transformation requires reference data such as a cross-reference between the two sets of identifiers or a conversion rate from US dollars to euros. This need for reference data is an important architectural issue. It creates a dependency between the business process requiring the reference data and the business process that creates and maintains that reference data. The mechanics of actually accessing the reference data need to be worked out.

When reference data is involved, you have to add the reference data creation and maintenance processes to the use case inventory along with whatever additional business processes are necessary to place that reference data where it can be accessed by the `Content Transformer`. You may have to go back to the business community to learn about the origin of this information and how it is maintained. You will also need to determine whether any of these business processes will require alteration. If they do require alteration, then they need to be added to the inventory of processes requiring work, and that work must be included in the project plan.

You need to be vigilant in your search for reference data dependencies and make a conscious effort to identify these dependencies as early in the project as possible. Every one of these dependencies is real—the reference data is truly needed to perform the work. If that data is not already in a location and format suitable for this usage, then there is work to be done. The longer you wait before you identify the dependency, the less time will be available to do the work. Often the reference data is not under your control—it comes from another system, and possibly from an organization that is not presently involved in the project. It will take calendar time to negotiate with that organization, even if the work to be done is trivial. Early identification of these dependencies can avoid fire-fighting later in the project. It will also reduce project costs, as fire-fighting tends to consume more resources than properly scheduled work.

Summary

A message can play one of three roles: It can be a request for some action to be taken, it can be the response to such a request, or it can be an announcement that some event has occurred. Indicating the role being played by each message brings clarity to the overall design and serves as a guide to the naming of the operations. As you identify these roles, you also identify the operations being performed by the components and thus begin to build an understanding of the required component interfaces.

Component operations must be accessed via the transport, and the association of transport destinations with operations requires careful consideration. Associating bundles of operations with a single transport destination may make it difficult to tune the component implementing the operations when some operations require rapid response times while others are time-consuming resource hogs.

The data structures being produced and consumed by interacting components need to be identified along with the schemas that define those structures. When two interacting components employ different data structures, the content of one must be transformed into the form of the other for the interaction to occur. The responsibility for this content transformation activity must be assigned to a component and may result in the addition of a new component dedicated to this task. Content transformation may also require reference data for lookup and substitution of values. The business process origin of the reference data must be identified.

Key Messages and Operations Questions

1. Has each interaction been characterized as a request, a reply, or an announcement?

2. Have the operations of the components been identified? Have the associated data structures been identified?

3. Is there a need for content transformation? If so, has this responsibility been assigned to a component?

4. Do any of the content transformations require reference data? If so, what business process is creating this reference data?

5. Have the bundling of operations and the associations between operation bundles (interfaces) and transport destinations been established?

Chapter 22

Data Consistency: Maintaining One Version of the Truth

When you look at data elements in the business processes, you want to see the same values regardless of where you look. If you look up the shipping address in the warehouse management system, you want to see the same shipping address that is in the order entry system, even if the customer just went online to the order entry system and changed it. Discrepancies in values are, in fact, errors—errors that can cause mistakes in business processes.

Since data inconsistencies can cause errors in business processes, you would naturally want to avoid such inconsistencies. But actually the siloed systems that typically populate the enterprise IT landscape were never designed to coordinate their information updates with those of other systems. In addition, the geographic distribution of the enterprises and the latency and less-than-perfect availability of wide-area communications often make it impractical to guarantee 100 percent consistency across all systems at all locations all of the time. Therefore, to some extent, you have to live with some level of inconsistency in business processes. But this does not mean you can afford to ignore the issue. Shipping goods to the wrong address or shipping the wrong goods costs the enterprise money. While you may not be able to guarantee complete consistency, you can design the business processes and manage the data updates so that you minimize the likelihood of inconsistencies and the impact they have on the business processes.

Approaches to Maintaining Data Consistency

The simplest way to achieve data consistency is for each data element to reside in exactly one system. This system is then the *system of record* for that piece of data. If you need that piece of data, you must go to that system to obtain it. But there are three problems with this approach. One is that some level of data sharing between systems is unavoidable. It is not possible for an order to be in the order management system (the system of record) and to have the shipment information in the warehouse management system without the warehouse management system having at least a reference to the order. Therefore, the order identifier must be present in both systems—and now you have duplicated a piece of information.

The second problem with the single system of record approach is performance. If the data is frequently used, it may be impractical for the system of record to support a high rate of access to the data. Imagine the impact on an online bookseller if every time a customer ordered a book the system queried every warehouse in the enterprise to determine whether that book was in stock! The query load on the warehouse system would vastly exceed the capacity required to support the normal warehouse operations. In addition, the latency incurred in aggregating all of this data together would slow down the response to the customer, thus degrading the customer experience. Better to support the customer queries with a central inventory cache and update that cache when items are actually shipped from the warehouse. Once again, this results in replicated information.

The third single system-of-record problem is availability. If you have to go to each of the warehouses to get inventory information, then each of those systems must be available and every communications link has to be operable in order to obtain the inventory. All of that for just one piece of information! In distributed systems, the strategy of obtaining every piece of data from its system of record can create so many inter-system operational dependencies that the availability of the overall business process—the percentage of the time that the process is working properly—suffers. Maintaining a high-availability business process would then require extraordinarily large investments in high-availability systems and communications links—investments that eat into (or overwhelm) any benefits the enterprise might realize from the single system of record.

For all of these reasons, you often need to replicate data. But replication immediately raises the specter of data inconsistency, so now you need to determine how to go about maintaining consistency. What strategy should you employ, and how should you go about implementing that strategy? Your choice of strategy will be heavily influenced by both the design of the business process and the impact that a data inconsistency will have on the business process. Conversely, your consideration of available data management strategies might lead you to alter the business process design to minimize the business impact of data inconsistencies. Let's explore the possibilities.

There are three basic strategies available for maintaining replicated data. The first involves a single system of record for each data element combined with managed replicas (caches) of that data. The second abandons the notion of system of record and seeks to simultaneously update all copies of the data. The third, also abandoning the system-of-record notion, allows the data to be edited anywhere it appears and then attempts to reconcile the discrepancies. As we shall see shortly, the first and second options can guarantee data consistency (if you ignore the time lag in updating the cache), while the third can never provide such a guarantee. So why should you even consider this third possibility? Because, unfortunately, it is the one you most commonly encounter in existing systems. You must learn how to deal with it.

Cached Data with a Single System of Record

The simplest strategy for maintaining data consistency across the enterprise is to establish a single system of record for each piece of data. This system is the only place that the data may be altered, whether it is being created, modified, or deleted. All other instances of the data in other systems are read-only copies of the system-of-record data.

Cached copies only work if they are kept consistent with the system-of-record data. Accomplishing this requires two things: an event-recognition mechanism that recognizes changes in the original data and a data update mechanism to get the revised version of that data into the data caches. Generally, the recognition of the change event presents the greatest design challenge. The design issues surrounding this event recognition are the same as those of the communications adapters that were discussed in Chapter 18. Ideally, the system-of-record application would be designed to recognize the change and immediately announce changes to the data (Figure 22–1). It would send a message out each time a new order was entered, modified, or cancelled. This message would then serve as the triggering event for updating the cached information in other systems. Problem solved.

Unfortunately, in the real world you rarely find systems that are either designed to announce such changes (in standard form via standard protocols) or to receive such generic notifications and update local copies. In such cases you must employ adapters (Figure 22–2). You might, for example, employ an adapter using database triggers to capture the change to the original data. On the receiving end, another adapter is used here to accept the standardized change notification and invoke the necessary interfaces on the caching system to update the cache.

If you are unable to capture the change events associated with altering the source data, you can employ the batch approach (Figure 22–3). This approach, commonly referred to as ETL (Extract, Transform, and Load), is frequently found in older batch-oriented architectures. Depending upon the circumstances, it can have some significant draw-backs. In many systems it is difficult to identify exactly what information has changed. In such circumstances, all of the system-of-record data (regardless of whether or not it has changed) must be extracted

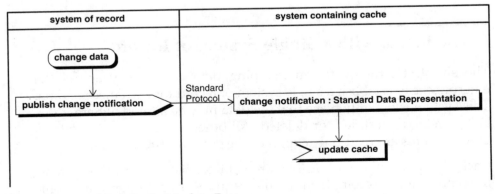

Figure 22–1: *Ideal Cache Update Pattern*

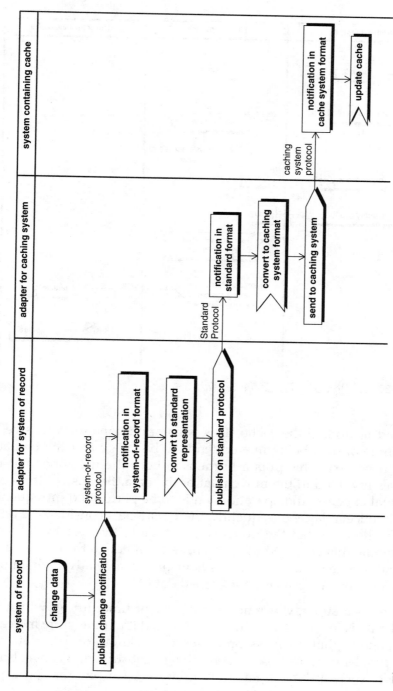

Figure 22–2: *Typical Event-Driven Cache Update Pattern*

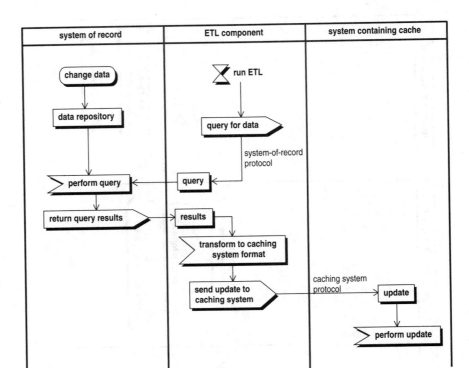

Figure 22–3: *Typical ETL Cache Update*

and used to update the cache. This is computationally expensive, as the volume of data being moved tends to be far greater than what is strictly necessary. This puts a burden on both the networks and the machines involved in the movement of the data. Because of this computational expense, the operation tends to be performed infrequently, typically once a day. Consequently, there may be a considerable delay between the time that the updates are made to the system of record and the time that corresponding changes are made to the cached data. During this time the cached data is in error and may adversely impact the business processes using the cached data.

Batching, as a strategy, extends the period of time during which the cached data is inconsistent with the original data. It therefore increases the likelihood that business processes will use out-of-date data and cause problems. For this reason, the event-driven, near-real-time update of cached data is generally preferred. Despite that on a per-item basis the computational cost for event-driven updates will likely be greater than for batch updates, fewer items will need to be processed, and the processing will more than likely be distributed over time. The peak load will therefore be lessened, and less machine and network capacity will be required. The combination of quick update and lower peak-capacity requirements makes a compelling case for event-driven updates.

Regardless of which approach is taken to updating the cache, caches are not perfect. There will always be a lag between the time the original data is edited and the time the cache is updated. During that period, the cached data will be inconsistent. You must therefore examine the business processes that are using the cache and determine whether the business risks arising from such inconsistencies are tolerable. Ultimately this is a judgment call that can only be made by the business community. Therefore, you must engage the business community to attain an understanding of these consequences, and then let that understanding guide your actions.

Another issue you need to consider with cache updates is the impact of communications failures. If nothing else, the loss of communications will lengthen the period of time during which the cache will be out of date. But you also need to ensure that all of the needed cache updates are applied after communications is restored. Another kind of communications failure is the outright loss of a cache update message. You need to understand the consequences of such a loss. If the consequences are serious enough, you must determine how you will know when the cache is in error, how will it get refreshed with the latest data, and what level of effort is warranted for these activities.

One simple thing you can do to minimize the impact of losing a cache update message is to avoid sending updates in the form of incremental changes. Rather than sending a message indicating that one book has been removed from inventory, send a message giving the latest total inventory for that title. With this approach, even if one inventory update message is lost, the next inventory message related to that title will automatically correct the error.

The same type of thinking can be applied to sending collections of related data rather than individual data element updates. When a customer moves, instead of sending a billing address update followed by a phone number update, it is better to wait until the editing has been completed and then send a full set of customer data. This not only makes the updates more efficient, but it will correct any previous breakdowns in updating other information related to this customer. Of course, it does introduce another kind of problem: How do you know when the editing is "done"? You need to understand what defines the boundaries around a given transaction so that you can ignore the activity going on within it and only capture information when the transaction has been completed.

Coordinated Updates via Distributed Transactions

A second alternative for maintaining data consistency is to allow multiple copies of the data, but to update them all at once. There are some characteristics of this distributed transaction approach (the mechanics of which are discussed in Chapter 28) that may make it unsuitable in some business processes:

1. All participants must be designed to participate in a distributed transaction, and many of the participants are likely to be existing systems that do not have this capability.

2. All of the participants must be operational at the same time in order to perform the update. Thus if any participant is unavailable, no update can occur and the business process grinds to a halt. Operational interdependencies such as this make it difficult to maintain a high level of business process availability, particularly when the participants are geographically distributed and communications are unreliable.

3. The time it takes for all of the communications and updates to occur may introduce unacceptable delays into the business process.

For these reasons, distributed transactions are rarely used for coordinated data updates: They are complicated to implement; most existing systems lack the support for the needed protocols; no update can occur if any participant is unavailable; and the time it takes to do all the updates slows down the overall business process. Taken together, this unattractive set of circumstances explains why you generally do not see distributed transactions used to maintain data consistency.

Edit Anywhere, Reconcile Later

The third alternative for maintaining data consistency is to allow the editing of information in more than one system and then attempt to reconcile the information after the fact. The major problem with this approach is that it is literally impossible to guarantee that you end up with the correct value in every system. The reason for this is that while you may be able to detect a difference in values, you don't know which value is correct. Intuition may suggest some approaches, such as time-stamping the updates, but what do you do if both values have the same time stamp? You could spend a lot of time trying to develop approaches to guaranteeing consistency, but such efforts are futile—and provably so! No matter what you do, there will always be circumstances that will lead to ambiguity. If you are interested in understanding why this is so, Lamport, Shostak, and Pease provide an elegant proof in their paper "The Byzantine Generals Problem."[1]

So if this approach can't guarantee consistency, why are we even talking about it? Because you are often forced into this approach by the design of existing systems. Customer data is all over the place. It is in the order entry system, the warehouse system, and the billing system. Product information is in the manufacturing system and in the online catalog system. Each of these systems has its own mechanisms for entering the data, and none of them have been designed to coordinate their updates with those of other systems.

There is another source of data inconsistency that you must consider as well, and this is an inconsistency between the data you have in the system and the physical reality it is supposed to represent. The inventory level in the warehouse system is supposed to reflect the actual number of items on the warehouse shelf, but there is no guarantee that the two are consistent. Loss, breakage, theft, and human error can all result in inconsistencies. These are realities that you will encounter in business processes, and you must design accordingly at both the business process and system level.

Dealing with Data Inconsistencies

Given that you are going to encounter data inconsistencies, you need to think about how they are going to be managed. Managing inconsistencies

---

1. Leslie Lamport, Robert Shostak, and Marshall Pease, "The Byzantine Generals Problem," ACM Transactions on Programming Languages and Systems, 4(3):382–401, July 1982.

boils down to looking for inconsistencies and then reconciling them. The reason companies do physical inventory is to check the consistency between the records and the actual on-shelf stock level. When there are discrepancies, the company may just correct the records (writing off the losses) or may start a search for the missing items. Similarly, you can compare the data in different systems and begin a process of reconciling their differences. Whether checking and reconciliation are manual or automated, they constitute yet another business process that you need to add to the inventory.

When you consider the design of a checking and reconciliation process (or whether it should be done at all), the starting point has to be an understanding of the consequences of an inconsistency. What is the risk if your checkbook balance differs from the bank's record? What is the risk if the enterprise promises immediate delivery to a customer and later finds out that the inventory is in error and there is nothing to deliver? What is the risk if the wrong dosage of medicine is delivered to a patient? Once you understand the risk, you will have a better understanding of the level of effort that is warranted in detecting and resolving inconsistencies. You have already acquired some insight into this—it was part of the business process ranking when you asked about the business impact of each business process. You simply need to augment this with an understanding of whether the specific inconsistency you are considering is likely to cause a breakdown in the business process.

If an inconsistency warrants action, what action can you take? Basically, you have three choices: change the data management strategy, manage the way the systems are used to avoid inconsistencies (e.g., restrict editing to just one system), or detect and fix the discrepancies. To alter the data consistency strategy, you change the design of the business process and systems to either avoid replication at all or adopt a replication strategy that *can* guarantee consistency. This is often more easily said than done for existing business processes and systems. The extent of the systems impact can make this is a relatively expensive approach. Such changes often end up as a long-term goal rather than a short-term solution.

The second option is to impose business process policy on the use of the systems to avoid creating inconsistencies in the first place. This is actually a poor-man's approach to achieving a single system of record. You identify one system as a de-facto system of record and (by policy) avoid using the editing interfaces on the other systems to make changes to the data. The only time those interfaces are used is to enter updates that originate in the newly designated system-of-record. Unfortunately, while such a policy may reduce the likelihood of inconsistencies, it does not prevent those interfaces from being used. Implementing such policies is a business process design issue. Whenever the information needs to be updated, the business process must be altered to use the newly designated system of record, and a cache update scheme must be implemented. The challenge lies in finding *all* of the business processes that may update the information—particularly during exception handling!

The third option is to find and fix discrepancies. Despite the fact that you cannot tell which of two differing values is correct, you can always tell whether they differ! A simple comparison of the data will identify whether or not the values are the same. Of course, there is work involved—both design work and runtime computations, and you need to factor these into your thinking. But there are also options. Rather than comparing every data element of two data sets to discover a discrepancy, you might compute a check-sum from each and compare the check-sums. This is less expensive (particularly with respect to communications costs) and more easily done. Of course, it doesn't tell you which data elements are different. That would have to be part of a follow-on reconciliation process.

Once a discrepancy has been identified, you need to determine what the reconciliation process will be. This reconciliation process may involve some form of assumption (the data in system A is in error less often than the data in system B, so system A's data will be considered correct) or it may involve a human investigation. Regardless of the reconciliation strategy, you need to determine what the reconciliation process is.

Data Management Business Processes

One thing that has become clear in this discussion of data consistency is that if you have replicated data, there is extra work to do. If you have a data cache, the cache needs to be updated when the source data is changed. If you are using distributed transactions, the transaction itself needs to be designed and probably offered as a service. If you allow editing of the data wherever it appears, you need a process that detects and reconciles data discrepancies.

Each of these data management tasks is yet another process that needs to be performed so that the primary business processes work properly. Some, such as the distributed transactions, may only be services and not complete business processes. Nevertheless, they are all processes on some scale—even the service. As such, you need to treat each as you would any other process. You need to identify the collaboration, add the process to the inventory, understand its business risks and required performance metrics, and rank it. You need to design it along with its supporting systems, deploy it, and operate it. The existence of a data management process alters the scope of the project and must become part of the project plan.

Summary

There are a number of approaches to maintaining data consistency. The simplest is to have only one copy of the data, but that is often impractical. The next simplest is to have a single system of record for each data element but allow cached copies in other systems. The use of caching, however, requires a cache update mechanism. Distributed transactions can be used to keep multiple copies in synch, but this approach has drawbacks that limit its use. The worst case is to allow editing of the data wherever it appears, a common situation when there are legacy systems involved. In such cases, data consistency can never be guaranteed.

When data inconsistencies are a possibility, the business risks arising from the inconsistencies must be assessed. Higher risks may warrant investments in detecting and reconciling inconsistencies.

Key Data Consistency Questions

1. Is there a clearly defined system of record for each concept and relationship involved in the business process?
2. If there is no single system of record for a concept or a relationship, do discrepancies pose a significant business risk? If there is significant risk, have processes been defined for detecting and reconciling data discrepancies?

3. Is data being replicated? If so, have the processes been defined for managing the replicated data? Is auditing required to detect discrepancies in the replicated data?

Suggested Reading

Bernstein, Philip A., and Eric Newcomer. 1997. *Principles of Transaction Processing for the Systems Professional.* San Francisco, CA: Morgan Kaufmann.

Lamport, Leslie, Robert Shostak, and Marshall Pease. "The Byzantine Generals Problem," *ACM Transactions on Programming Languages and Systems*, 4(3):382–401, July 1982.

Chapter 23

Common Data Models (CDM)

When information is moved from one system to another and those systems organize that information differently, the information originating in one system's representation must be transformed to that of the other. When such transformations are required, you have a design choice to make: Should you simply transform this information directly from one system's format to the other, or should you transform it first to a system-neutral data format and then to the recipient's format? Such a system-neutral format is generally referred to as a *common data model*. Designed properly, common data models can make the information more accessible. Their power increases further when they become the data representations that end-point systems actually work with.

What Is a Common Data Model?

A common data model is simply a well-engineered and standardized representation of a set of information. It is a standardized view of some aspect of the enterprise. But do not be confused by the term "standard." The standardization required is relative to the enterprise and does not need to be an industry standard. Calling it a standard just means that the enterprise has decided to use it (as opposed to some other representation) universally within the enterprise.

A brief comment on industry standards is in order here. Even though industry standards are very useful as the basis for common data models, they are rarely used in their industry standard form. In most cases, some data needs to be added to support internal business policies and practices. Some industry standards allow for variations within their schema definition, but even so, the schema extension must be formalized to accurately represent the required information as needed by the enterprise. Other industry standards do not allow for such extensions at all. In either case, these standard schemas must be augmented to incorporate the information required to support the enterprise's proprietary way of doing business. Consequently, industry standards are usually used as a starting point for defining common data models.

The actual representation you choose for a common data model will have a significant impact on how much benefit will result from its use. If you choose an obscure binary format, it will be difficult for people to understand what the data structure represents. Mapping between this format and the formats of the end-point systems will be a miserable task. While you may have established a standard, the enterprise will not derive any benefit from its use. What you want instead is a format that is easy to understand and work with. A good common data model is a representation of information that is both standardized and easy to understand.

So let's consider data models and data structures. Figure 23–1 is an example of the information you might expect in a monthly bank statement. The statement includes a set of transactions and an address. An individual transaction or an individual address is represented by a well-structured set of fields—a structure that can be readily understood and reused in other contexts. When information is organized this way, the meaning of each field in the data structure is clear. Of course, in the formative stages of the architecture you most likely will not have this level of detail, but you would have its basic structure. Regardless, for clarity, Figure 23–1 shows the full structure as it will appear after the component and service specifications have been completed. This detail will help to illustrate the points about common data models.

Now consider a couple of choices for the physical representation of this information. First, look at the simplified XML representation of a bank statement shown in Listing 23-1. It has the same structure as the class diagram of the statement, and it is easy to identify each individual data field and each block of data. This is an example of a self-describing

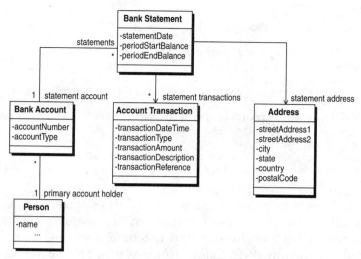

Figure 23–1: *Information Model of a Bank Statement*

data structure. Self-describing structures are easy for people to work with. Using them greatly reduces the likelihood of errors in defining mappings to other data structures. XML data structures are equally easy for systems to work with. Not only are standard parsers readily available, but standard software is available to check the correctness of the data structure using the referenced schema definition. Using XML simplifies programming all around.

Listing: 23–1: *Simplified XML Statement Representation*

```
<?xml version = "1.0" encoding = "UTF-8"?>
<BankAccountStatement
    xmlns:xsi = http://www.w3.org/2001/XMLSchema-instance
    xsi:noNamespaceSchemaLocation = "BankStatement.xsd"
    StatementDate = "2007-01-31"
    PeriodStartingBalance = "4375.22"
    PeriodEndingBalance = "7078.56" >
    <BankAccount
        AccountType = "Checking"
        AccountNumber = "1239854639">
        <AccountHolder
            AccountHolderRoleType="PrimaryAccountHolder"
            <Person Name="John Q. Smith" />
        </AccountHolder>
    </BankAccount>
    <Address
        StreetAddress1 = "123 Anywhere Drive"
        City = "MyCity"
        State = "New York"
```

```
        Country = "USA"
        PostalCode = "10000"/>
    <Transaction
        dateTime = "2007-01-15T08:05:13-05:00"
        TransactionType = "Deposit"
        Amount = "2743.34"
        Description = "Payroll Deposit - XYZ Manufacturing Inc."/>
    <Transaction
        dateTime = "2007-01-14T13:20:04-05:00"
        TransactionType = "Withdrawal"
        Amount = "40.00"
        Description = "ATM Withdrawal - 14th St. Garden Center"
        Reference = "123067843"/>
</BankAccountStatement>
```

However, despite their advantages, XML data representations are not a panacea. While they present information in a manner that is readily understandable by both human and machine, they are a bit verbose. They tend to consume three to four times as much space as just the raw data, and thus impact network bandwidth utilization and storage requirements. The parsing and assembling of the data structures takes more machine time than straight string manipulations, at least in simple cases. However, the advantages of XML are so strong that as long as the expanded size and performance impact do not actually jeopardize the feasibility of the project, it is a good practice to employ such representations.

Now contrast the XML representation with the more traditional file format for the same information shown in Listing 23–2. Take a look at the listing first before you read the explanation of its structure.

Listing: 23–2: *Comma-Separated Value (CSV) Representation of a Bank Statement*

```
01,John Smith,2007-01-31,123 Anywhere Drive,MyCity,New York,10000
02,4375.22,7078.56,Checking,1239854639
03,2007-01-15T08:05:13-05:00,2743.34,Payroll Deposit - XYZ Mfg.
04,2007-01-14T13:20:04-05:00,40.00,ATM 14th St. Garden Center,123067843
```

This file format has four types of records, with the first two characters of the record indicating the record type. The rest of the data in the record consists of fields separated by commas. There is no indication of the meaning of any of the fields contained in the record. You have to know, from some other source, that the position of each field in a given record type (first position, second position, etc.) indicates the meaning of that field. This requirement to have knowledge from some source other than the data structure itself in order to interpret (or construct) the data representation is the biggest drawback to this approach. Furthermore, the interpretation of this external knowledge, usually written in plain text, and the verification of the data structure conformance are two design time activities that need to be performed by every developer generating or consuming this data structure. It is difficult to maintain consistency with imprecise textual descriptions and so many people involved.

In this particular example, record type "01" contains the account holder's name, statement date, and address. Record type "02" contains the starting and ending balances, the type of account, and the account number. Record type "03" is a credit to the account, with the date-time, amount, and description. Record type "04" is a debit against the account, with the date-time, amount, description, and an optional transaction reference number.

There is more to the structure of this file than just the structure of the individual records. A set of rules governs the overall structure of the file—the order of the different record types. For example, in order to have a valid bank statement you must at least have both a record "01" and a record "02." Records "03" and "04" are optional, as there may not have been any transactions in the period. However, when transactions do occur, they may be more than one of each type. Are there rules governing the organizations of these transaction records? Are they grouped by type and then ordered chronologically, or are they ordered chronologically regardless of type? Producers and consumers of the data structure need to know what is allowed and what to expect.

This file-based representation gets even more complex if you allow more than one statement in a file. When you do this, you must adopt a convention that the transaction records ("03" and "04" records) appear immediately after the appearance of the header records ("01" and "02" records) for an account. The occurrence of a header record after a transaction record then marks the end of one account and the beginning of the next.

The problem with this type of representation is that you have to read and understand these rules in order to know how to construct or read it. When the data structures become complex, so do the rules. It becomes increasingly difficult to ensure that the rules are self-consistent and unambiguous. Developers need to write custom parsers and generators to read and write the representation with the rules for interpreting the data embedded in the parsing logic.

Sometimes handwritten parsing logic accidentally embeds rules that were never actually defined! For example, the rules may not state that record "01" must appear before record "02." Common sense tells us that it does not matter as long as both records appear together. However, when you are writing a parser it will take more work for it to accept the records in either order. Developers are likely to simply assume that record type "01" occurs before record type "02." Such parsers will break when presented with the records in the opposite order regardless of the fact that the rules do not require this ordering. The more complicated the rules, the more complicated the parsing logic. The more complicated the logic, the less likely it is that the logic will be correct. Every time the data structure changes, the parser has to be rewritten. Seemingly simple changes, such as the introduction of a third transaction type (for bank fees), may require major changes to the parsing logic. Because of this, designs using this type of data representation tend to be fragile and expensive to change. It is exactly this set of circumstances that led to the development of XML.

You obviously have many data structure choices, but it should be clear from this discussion that self-describing data structures (such as XML) with standard parsers and generators offer some significant advantages. Systems can produce and consume these data structures without special programming. People can understand the data without first studying reference material, and this can greatly speed up development, testing, and troubleshooting. Overall, self-describing data structures yield lower development costs and systems that are more robust. Thus, they are the preferred choice for common data models.

CDM Relationship to the Domain Model

One of the things you strive for in designs is stability—but not the stability of an arbitrary declaration that there will be no further changes or the "cast in concrete" stability that arises from the encumbrance of inflexible systems. You want your design to be able to evolve gracefully as the business needs change, adapting business processes to those changing needs. The kind of stability you want is for the basic building blocks of the business processes, systems, and data structures to remain relatively unchanged as they are recombined into new or modified business processes to suit new purposes. This is the goal of a well-designed service-oriented architecture, but this same stable building block principle also applies to the design of data structures in general and common data models in particular. In fact, stability at this level is an essential prerequisite for a stable service-oriented architecture.

The key to data structure stability lies in the use of a well-considered domain model as a guide for its construction. The domain model captures the concepts and relationships as they inherently are found in the application domain. As long as this world remains stable, the domain model will remain consistent. You gain stability in the CDM data structures by first deriving their building blocks from the concepts and relationships of the domain model, and then by ensuring that the structure of the information in the domain model is preserved and obvious in the CDM.

In the account statement example, every concept and relationship in the account statement information model is explicitly represented in the XML example. In contrast, many of the relationships are only implicit in the record sequencing of the file example (hence the discussion about the complicated rules governing the structure of the file).

The bank account statement information model in Figure 23–1 is obviously not a complete domain model. Take a look at the more complete domain model for accounts and statements in Figure 23–2. Note that a `Bank Account` can have many `account holders`, with each `Person` playing a specific `Account Role`. The `Bank Statement` representation in Figure 23–1 contains only one account holder, namely the `primary account holder`. A well-engineered common data model represents a strict subset of the domain model and preserves the structure of the domain model. While the domain model represents the full set of transactions belonging to the account, the `Bank Statement` common data model in Figure 23–1 only represents those transactions associated with the current statement. Are these deviations from precise correspondence between domain models and CDM representations? The answer is no, but we need to refine what we mean by "representation" to understand why.

The representation of a bank statement in Figure 23–1 does not include all of the information from the domain model. Instead, the domain model serves as a reference, providing a means of being clear about what information is actually contained in the bank statement. The transactions that are included are clearly definable in terms of the domain model: They are the transactions associated with the specific bank statement. The account holder in the bank statements is the

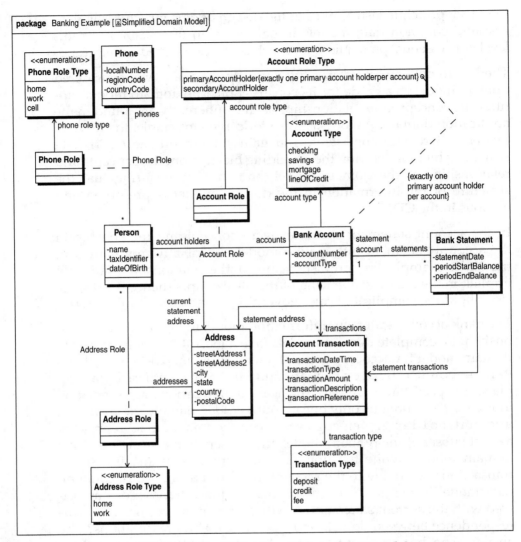

Figure 23–2: *Simplified Domain Model Showing Accounts and Statements*

account holder playing the `primaryAccountHolder` role. It is a best practice to always relate common data models back to the domain model in this manner.

There are any number of possible common data model representations—different subsets of the domain model. Which one(s) should be used? What information should be included, and what should be excluded?

The Need for Multiple CDM Representations

The intent of a common data model is to establish a singular common representation of a concept. In the example being discussed, this concept is an account statement. However, a bank statement in printed form contains information from several related concepts: the account statement, the account transactions related to the statement, the statement address, the account to which the statement belongs, and the primary account holder for that account. These concepts have additional relationships with concepts such as the people, addresses, and phone numbers associated with the bank account. Just how many of these concepts and relationships should be carried along in the CDM representation of a bank statement? The answer is—it depends! *The amount of detail carried in the representation of an individual concept depends upon the intended use of that representation.* Conversely, different uses may warrant different levels of detail.

From the perspective of a bank statement, even though the statement references the associated bank account, it clearly does not make sense to drag the entire set of attributes and relationships associated with that bank account into a communication that is focused on a single bank statement. The reader of a bank statement will not need to know about all of the account holders, addresses, and phone numbers, nor will he or she need to know about the transactions that are not directly related to the current statement. Thus for the bank statement, it seems appropriate to have a simplified representation of a bank account. On the other hand, there will be times when someone will, indeed, want to see the full set of account information. For example, when a customer has a question about his or her bank account, the customer service representative will need to see this full set of information. Such situations call for a more complete representation of the account.

This leads to an understanding that for each major concept in the domain model you will most likely need not one but several representations of that concept. Typically, you will need at least four:

1. *The Basic Concept:* the representation of just the concept and its attributes, excluding any related concepts. In the bank statement example, this would be just the `Bank Statement` object and its attributes.

2. *An Inclusive Representation:* a comprehensive representation of a concept including at least a minimal representation of all related concepts.

An example would be a representation of a `Bank Account` that included all of the `People` who are `account holders`, the `current statement addresses`, the `transactions` and the `statements`. *An inclusive representation includes a representation of every concept directly related to the core concept and all relationships to those concepts.* Where one of these relationships has an unbounded multiplicity, such as the `transactions` relationship for the `Bank Account`, the representation should allow for the inclusion of an arbitrary number of instances of the referenced concept. The inclusive representation does not, however, require an inclusive representation of each related concept.

3. *A Pure Reference:* the simplest possible representation of a unique instance of a concept. A pure reference is simply a unique identifier for that instance. The `accountNumber`, for example, is a pure reference to a `Bank Account`.[1] In database terms, a pure reference is a primary key for the record representing the concept.

4. *A Minimal Representation:* a minimal representation is a pure reference augmented with the most commonly required information about the concept. The reason you need a minimal representation is that the pure reference is generally not very helpful to a person viewing the information. When the intended use of the representation is to present information to people, you need to augment the pure reference with enough of the inclusive representation so that people can understand just what is being referenced. In the case of the `Bank Account`, this minimal representation might augment the account number with the type of account, the name of the primary account holder, and the current statement address.

Different circumstances call for different representations. The goal of a common data modeling effort, therefore, should not be to define a singular representation for each concept. Rather, you should seek to minimize the number of representations and then standardize them. Given the characterization of different representations above, the complete representation of a bank statement (Figure 23–1) comprises:

• An inclusive representation of the `Bank Statement`
• A basic representation of each `Transaction` directly related to the statement

---

1. In a context that included multiple banks, you would need to augment the account number with a unique identifier for the bank, for example, the routing number on a check.

- A basic representation of the `current statement address`
- A minimal representation of the `Bank Account` that includes a minimal representation of a `Person`

To summarize then, a common data model is *a standardized representation of a concept found in the domain model*. In other words, it is a view of the domain model. In defining common data models, you seek to avoid re-inventing representations every time there is a need to communicate. It is a best practice to minimize the number of representations used in an architecture.

Planning for CDM Changes

Despite your best intentions and best efforts, you will never produce the perfect common data model. Inevitably, some business process will come along that needs a field that is not in the current representation, or some business process change will require the addition of a new field, concept, or relationship. However, if you plan properly all you will need to do is add the new information without altering the rest of the structure. For example, the business might want to associate a bank branch with an account and then include a minimal representation of the bank branch in the statement.

It is relatively easy to accommodate the addition of a new field or relationship into a data structure. Aside from changing the schema definition, the only changes required to the applications using the data are directly related to the creation or use of the new data. In contrast, the type of change you want to avoid is a restructuring of the existing data representation. Since applications must navigate through data structures to find the fields of interest, changing the structure will require changes to every application navigating the affected portion of the data structure. If typically you only have to add a field or a relationship when you need to make changes, you will have achieved the business objectives in the design of common data models.

Regardless of whether you are simply adding fields or altering the structure of the data, you still need to revise the schema that defines the data structure. Making schema changes is a complex problem. Every component using the schema needs to be altered to utilize the new data structure. The more components using a data structure, the more complex it becomes to introduce the change. Yet, at the same time, your goal is to have as many components as possible use the same common data model! Unless you make provisions in the design for gracefully introducing schema changes, you will force the modification of all of these components at once. Such big-bang approaches to change are complex to orchestrate and risky to execute. The more components that need to be changed at once, the greater the likelihood at least one of them will experience a problem.

The last thing you want is for your efforts at improving and standardizing communications through the use of common data models to result in a situation that actually makes it difficult for the enterprise to evolve. Consequently, you need to make provisions in the design for changing common data model schemas. There are basically two approaches you can take. One is to allow for two versions of the schema to be in use at the same time so that components can be migrated gradually from the old to the new. The other is to design the schemas to allow for additive changes.

Schema Versioning

Allowing two versions of a schema to be in use at the same time is actually an issue of interface design more than schema design. How you go about introducing the change depends upon the pattern of communication. The two basic patterns of concern are a targeted point-to-point request (possibly with a reply) and a broadcast to many recipients. The evolution strategies for these two patterns are different.

Versioning with Point-to-Point Communications

For point-to-point requests, you can evolve to the new schema as follows:

1. Modify the recipient of the request to accept the new schema as well as the old. Depending upon the communications technology in use, this either requires the modification of one interface to accept both versions of the data representation or it requires the versioning of the interfaces and the simultaneous deployment of both the old and new versions.

2. Modify the senders of the request to use the new version.

3. Modify the recipient of the request to retire the old version of the data representation.

Versioning with Broadcast Communications

For broadcast requests, the sequence is slightly different:

1. Modify the sender to broadcast both the old version and the new version of the data representation. The broadcast channels for the two versions will be different. Note that initially there will be nobody "listening" to the new version.

2. Migrate individual recipients from the old version to the new version.

3. After the last recipient has been migrated, modify the sender to cease broadcasting the old version.

Both of these approaches accomplish the transition one change at a time, thus lowering the risk associated with each individual change. Note that executing these transition plans requires a significant level of organizational discipline, particularly in the broadcast case. You cannot eliminate the old version from the design until the last user of the old version is retired. If the owner of that system is short on budget or has other priorities, their reluctance to change will create a situation that perpetuates the use of multiple versions. This not only complicates the maintenance and support of the overall system, but it also effectively foregoes the business benefits expected from the use of common data models.

Versioning with Additive Changes

When you are making additive changes, you can use a simplified variant of these migration strategies. The simplification requires the ability to initially add information to the representation (not modify what is already there) without having to alter any of the recipients. This can be accomplished with XML, for example, through the use of wildcards. The trick is to make provisions for the addition of new fields (called attributes in XML) and new elements. You can make provision for new attributes for an element by including an optional `anyAttribute` to the list of each element's attributes. Similarly, you can make provision for new sub-elements by including an optional `any` element in the sequence of sub-elements for an element.

If you have made these provisions, then the following approach can be taken for additive data structure changes:

1. The creator of the message adds the new attributes and elements to the data structures in the wildcard locations. The change is placed in production.

2. The consumers of the message that require the changes are modi-
    fied to use them and are placed in production. Functionally, the
    change is complete.

3. The formal schema definition of the representation is then updated
    to include the new attributes and elements. When components
    using the schema are subsequently updated, they will pick up the
    revised schema definition. The sequence in which the components
    are modified does not matter.

This strategy for evolution does carry with it some level of risk, but the
risk can be managed with suitable governance. The risks are twofold.
First, because there is no formal checking of the extensions during the
transition (prior to completing step 3), it is possible that there will be
errors in the modified portions of the data structures that will not be
caught until runtime. This risk can be mitigated by keeping changes
simple and performing adequate testing. The bigger risk, however, is
that the final updating of the schema will never occur. This leaves portions of the data structure unchecked by the schema. The danger is not
so much in the first change, but in the cumulative effect of multiple
changes that are never formalized with schema updates. The result
will be that significant portions of data structures are no longer being
formally defined. In other words, you are foregoing the very benefits
you sought in using common data models with formal schemas.

Schema Migration Governance

This risk of incomplete schema migration can be mitigated with a simple governance process that involves two steps.

1. Projects wishing to use the schema extensions must first obtain
    permission from the enterprise architecture group. The request
    must include a formal specification of what the ultimate data struc-
    ture will look like (i.e., the revised schema) and a release plan for
    all components involved, including the final incorporation of the
    updated schema. Note that this release plan must, by definition,
    include at least two releases for each component using the new
    data—one for the data change and one for the schema update. The
    enterprise architecture group approves both the technical aspects
    of the extension and the migration plan.

2. Each component production release review incorporates a check
    against the in-progress release plans for schema migration. For the
    first release (including the data without the schema extension), the

review checks to ensure that the actual data representation modification conforms to the intended schema. This can be accomplished by validating data structures in the test environment against the revised schema. The production release review for the subsequent schema update simply checks to see that the revised schema has, indeed, been incorporated.

The importance of this governance in the migration of schemas cannot be emphasized enough. Without the governance, development groups are liable to get sloppy and fail to update the formal schemas. Over time, the quality of the data representations will deteriorate, and the benefits of a common data model will be lost.

A final note on schema migration: It is not unusual to take one of the end-point system data formats and "bless" it as being a common data model, even though this representation may not be structured for long-term stability. This eliminates the need for a transformation between that end-point system and the common data model—at least initially. But what happens if the next release of that end-point system changes its data representation? Unless you take precautionary steps, this change would force an immediate change to the common data model, and hence to all systems and transformations involving that common data model. Because of this, it is wise to incorporate an architectural "placeholder" for a transformation between the end-point system with the "blessed" data structure and the common data model. This placeholder will initially be a simple pass-through of the unmodified data structure, but its presence now makes it architecturally possible to alter the end-point data format and map this revised format into the original common data model without any other modifications. This will make it easier for the overall enterprise to evolve its common data model schemas.

When to Use Common Data Models

While common data models can provide some significant benefits, they have some drawbacks as well. In particular, the use of common data models requires extra work, both at design time and runtime. The diagram in Figure 23–3 shows the transformations required to convert data from the format of one system to the formats of a number of other systems both with and without common data models. The left-hand side of Figure 23–3 shows the pattern that emerges when each consumer

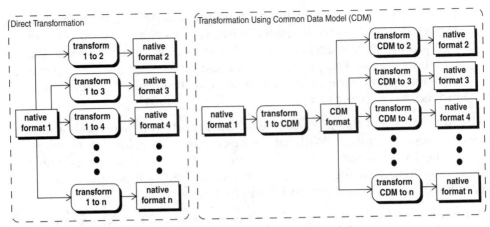

Figure 23–3: *Transformations and Common Data Models*

of a data structure requires its own unique format. This is not an unusual situation in the enterprise when systems have evolved independently. In such situations, the number of transformations required equals the number of data structure consumers. If there are n participants, one being the producer and the others being the consumers, then you need n−1 transformations.

On the right side of the figure is the pattern that emerges if a common data model (CDM) is used. The initial structure is first transformed into the common data model and then into the formats required for each consumer. The number of transformations required is equal to the number of publishers plus the number of consumers. In other words, if there are n participants, you need n transformations. Comparing these two patterns, the use of the common data model obviously involves more work, so why would you ever want to do this?

Well, to begin with, you must first dispel a myth that is often used to present an argument in favor of the use of common data models. The myth is that if you are using the direct transformation approach and you have n participants, the number of transformations required is n(n−1), which is often approximated as n^2. While this is, strictly speaking, correct, this situation only arises when each participant in the process is both a producer and a consumer of the data structure, which hardly ever occurs in practice. In fact, as Chapter 22 discussed, such situations lead to intractable problems in data management! Most of the time, any given system is either a producer or a consumer of the data in question, in which case you need n−1 transformations for direct transformation or n transformations using common data models.

So why would you choose common data models? The answer is simplicity. If the common data model is a self-describing data structure, the task of defining mappings is simpler and less prone to error. If structures with formal schemas (e.g., XML) are used, then the data structure can be checked for correctness on the producing side, making error handling simpler. Furthermore, many modern components and systems are now directly producing and consuming XML data structures, which provides the potential for eliminating at least some of the transformations altogether. If you specify that new systems are required to produce or consume the common data model structure, then transformations are also eliminated.

The common-data-model style of data representation, backed by formal schema definitions, lies at the heart of service-oriented architectures. The ability to both specify the universe of acceptable data structures (through the schema) and independently validate the compliance of any given data structure against the specification makes it possible to completely define an interface independently of any specific implementation. The down side, of course, is that there may be transformation work required on both sides of the interface if the participants do not natively use this form.

Criteria for Choosing Direct Transformation

Returning to the tradeoff discussion, direct transformation makes sense when:

1. There are only two participants involved in the communication
2. The participant interfaces are stable (unlikely to change)
3. No other participant will ever need to use that particular set of data

When these circumstances exist, it does not make much sense to use a common data model. There is a dedicated communication between the two participants, and inserting a common data model will simply cost more at both design time and runtime and provide no benefit.

However, before you reach the conclusion that a common data model is actually unwarranted, you need to validate the assumptions. If you look into the future, are there truly only two systems involved? Is it likely that some other system will, at some point, need to either produce or consume that data set? Is it likely that one of the two systems being considered will be replaced in the not-too-distant future? Is it likely that the data structures used by the participants will change over the next few years? If any of these conditions exist, it is worthwhile to at least consider the use of a common data model.

Criteria for Choosing a Common Data Model

The benefits of the common data model generally accrue when the CDM becomes a point of stability in a world of ever-changing systems. This emphasizes the importance of having an active enterprise architecture group participate in the specification of the common data model. If the common data model *is significantly less likely to change* than the data structures of the participants, then its use will reduce the level of effort required to accommodate changes in the data structures of the participants. It's a pay-me-now-or-pay-me-later type of situation. Spending more now (and it *will* cost more!) to design the common data model and the extra transformation that goes with its use will not only save you money in the long run, but it will shorten the time it takes to accommodate the change. The more systems that are involved, the greater the potential savings. But there is another issue you need to consider before you make a final decision: performance.

As has been mentioned a number of times, the use of a common data model usually carries with it a runtime performance penalty—an extra transformation and an extra inter-process communication. Before you decide to use a common data model, you must assess whether that penalty is acceptable. There are three aspects of performance you need to consider:

1. The network bandwidth required
2. The resources required to perform the extra transformation
3. The increased latency caused by the extra hops in the communications chain

Starting with the network bandwidth, the common data model itself must be exchanged between the first data transformation and the second. If the two transformations are in separate components, as they normally would be, this communication will generally occur over the network. As a result, an exchange between two parties in the network will increase the network bandwidth requirement somewhere around 50 percent. This increase will be proportionately less as the number of message consumers increases. In most cases, this increase is acceptable as long as it does not push the demand for bandwidth over the edge in terms of either feasibility or cost.

If, on the other hand, a single component provides all of the transformations, then the common data model becomes an internal data structure within that component. While this avoids the network cost, it renders the data structure inaccessible without modifying the transformation component. This presents a problem. There is a significant benefit to making the easy-to-understand common-data-model data structure readily accessible to other components. When it is moved via a transport (such as a messaging protocol) that enables easy access, this promotes the sharing of information. Furthermore, the actual movement of the data itself often indicates the occurrence of a business meaningful event such as the placement of an order. Making the movement observable in the CDM form makes it possible to observe and understand these business events. This makes it possible to monitor business processes, which in turn makes it possible to detect business process breakdowns and measure business performance. It also makes it possible to trigger other work based on the occurrence of events. For all of these reasons, it is a best practice to make the movement of these common data model representations as widely observable as possible. CDM representations provide little value when they are buried inside components.

Beyond network bandwidth, you also need to consider the processing power required to execute the extra transformation and the increase in latency (delay) caused by its introduction. Obviously, if the increase in processing power or latency makes it impossible to satisfy the business process requirements within the cost and schedule guidelines, you cannot use the common data model approach. However, if you are able to achieve the required performance and do so at a reasonable cost, you should not let these increases deter you from using a common data model.

Summary

A common data model (CDM) is a system-neutral data representation used for the exchange of information between components. A well-engineered CDM derives its structure from the domain model and represents a point of stability in the design.

Each common data model represents a subset of the concepts and relationships in the domain model. Different common data models (different subsets) will require different levels of detail about individual concepts and relationships. It is good practice to standardize and limit the number of concept and relationship representations used to construct common data models.

Despite the best of analysis and planning, it is inevitable that eventually changes will be required to common data models. The process of adding new information can be facilitated by introducing "wildcard" placeholders for new information in the CDM data structure representation. However, in all cases, changing these representations requires versioning and an associated governance discipline.

The use of common data models introduces some additional overhead into the interactions between components. For some dedicated point-to-point interfaces, the use of CDM does not make sense. But when there are three or more participants in the exchange, there are significant benefits as long as the overhead is tolerable.

The true benefit of a common data model is the flexibility it brings to the overall enterprise architecture. It makes information more widely available and makes it possible to observe the events that drive the business. It lowers the cost of accommodating future changes in the participant's data structures. Therefore, as long as you can arrive at a common data model that will be relatively stable over time (as compared to the rate of change in the participant's data structures), and as long as the performance and cost penalties are acceptable, it is good practice to use common data models when exchanging information between systems.

Key Common Data Model Questions

1. Which interactions will use common data models?

2. Are the common data models derived from a domain model? Did the enterprise architecture group participate in their design?

3. Have the extra transformation components required for CDM been incorporated into the architecture?

4. Have provisions been made for evolving and versioning the CDM?

Chapter 24

Identifiers (Unique Names)

Many business processes require distinguishing one individual from another. When you place an online order, the business needs to be able to distinguish you as an individual from your next-door neighbor. Similarly, the business needs to distinguish the order you place today from the one you placed yesterday. The way this is approached is to give a unique name to each object—each person or order. Such unique names are called *identifiers*.

Identifiers are simply unique numbers or strings that are created and assigned to individual objects. These identifiers are then used to represent individual objects in the systems. When a customer places an online book order, he or she creates an account (if one doesn't already exist). As part of creating the account, the system generates a unique identifier for the account—an account number. This account number then becomes a surrogate to represent the customer in the order management system. Since the customer is not physically present in the system, the system cannot associate orders directly with the customer. Instead, the system associates the account number with each order, implying that *the customer* placed each of those orders.

This association of identifiers with the individual objects they represent is as much a part of the identity game as are the identifiers themselves. You can generate as many identifiers as you want, but until you associate them with individual objects, the identifiers have no meaning. So when you consider identity, you must consider both the creation of the identifier and its subsequent association with the object it is supposed to represent. The goal, of course, is for each identifier to uniquely designate a specific object.

This goal of maintaining a unique mapping from identifier to object is difficult to achieve in practice. There are often data quality issues, and these quality problems can have a significant impact upon the enterprise's business processes. You need to understand what these quality problems are so that you can manage them. But before you can explore the sources of these problems, you must first understand the process of creating identifiers and associating them with objects. This is the job of the *identity authority*.

Identity (Unique Name) Authorities

An identifier, by definition, uniquely represents a single object. This means that the value you come up with for the identifier must be unique (there can be no other objects with the same identifier). Most identity systems impose a second requirement: Each object can only have one identifier. This is how driver's licenses are supposed to work. Your driver's license has an identifier on it, and you are the "object" that the identifier is associated with. Of course, it is always possible to have more than one type of identifier for a given object. In addition to your driver's license identifier, you probably also have a national income tax identifier, and you may even have a passport with a passport number on it as well. So the uniqueness properties of an identifier are with respect to a particular type of identifier.

The only way that the uniqueness properties can be guaranteed is to have a central authority managing them—an *identity authority*. This authority keeps track of the identifiers that have been issued and the objects they are associated with. Each type of identifier requires a corresponding identity authority. In the case of your driver's license, the authority is your state's Department of Motor Vehicles. More than likely, the authority employs a system that maintains the driver's license records. This system keeps track of which driver's license numbers have already been issued and identifying information about the people they have been issued to. When a new license is issued, the system issues a new[1] number, checks to ensure that the person does not already have a driver's license (at least in this state), and associates the person's identifying information (name, hair color, height, picture, etc.) with the driver's license.

Thus the identity authority has two primary responsibilities:

1. To issue unique identifiers.
2. To uniquely associate identifiers with the objects they are supposed to identify.

The basic issuing of unique identifiers is a relatively straightforward task. The common approach is for the naming authority to maintain a list of identifiers in a repository (generally a database) and simply ensure that each new identifier issued is not already in the repository. But sometimes it is impractical to have one central identity authority. In such cases, you have to use hierarchical identifiers.

Hierarchical Identifiers

Some identifiers are actually composed of a hierarchy of smaller identifiers. The familiar Internet host names such as `www.ieee.org` are an example. The overall identifier is actually a name for a specific computer and is associated with the specific Internet protocol (IP) address assigned to that computer. Thus, instead of remembering the IP address of the machine (`www.ieee.org` is associated with `209.18.36.42` as of this writing) you can use the more easily remembered host name.

This host name actually comprises several identifiers organized into a hierarchy. The right-most field is a top-level identifier that is (literally) globally unique. The Internet Corporation for Assigned Names and Numbers (ICANN) serves as the identity authority for this top-level domain. It establishes the allowed values for the names in the domain (`.com`, `.org`, `.net`, etc.), and for each value assigns an identity authority to manage the next-level domain. For example, the Public Interest Registry serves as the identity authority for names within the

---

1. Some identity authorities recycle old identifiers under the assumption that the objects they identify no longer exist. This violation of the uniqueness assumption can lead to errors in business processes.

.org domain while Verisign Global Registry Services serves as the identity authority for the .com and .net domains.

The identifiers issued by the second-level identity authorities are not globally unique—they are unique only within the scope of the top-level domain. The identity authority that owns the .org domain does not have to check the uniqueness of its identifiers with the identity authority of any other top-level domain. Instead, it simply appends its own identifier to those it generates. Since its own identifier is guaranteed to be unique, the identifiers it issues will be similarly unique. Thus both the .org domain and the .com domain can (and have) issued the identifier ieee. However, ieee.org remains a separate and distinct identifier from ieee.com.

The identity authority for the second-level domain assigns allowed values for the third-level domain and designates the identity authority for managing that domain. In this example, the Public Interest Registry assigned the .ieee domain name and gave the responsibility for its management to the organization known as the Institute for Electrical and Electronics Engineers (IEEE). The IEEE then assigned the name www in its .ieee.org domain and designated an authority (more than likely itself) to manage fourth-level values. It also associated www.ieee.org with a specific machine having the IP address 204.2.160.14.

In the case of Internet host names, the naming authorities do not attempt to make host names the unique representatives of the entities they are associated with. The machine being referred to as www.ieee.org can also be accessed using the hostname www.ieee.org.edgesuite.net. The host-naming scheme also allows multiple domain names to be assigned to one identity authority and even to the same IP address. For example, the IEEE manages the domains ieee.net and ieee.com as well as ieee.org. As of this writing the hostnames ieee.org, ieee.net, and ieee.com are all associated with the same IP address!

Hierarchical Identifiers within the Enterprise

As the IEEE example illustrates, a structured namespace with a hierarchy of identity authorities makes it possible to have unique identifiers without requiring a central identity authority. This approach becomes essential when there are multiple organizations involved. Hierarchical namespaces with separate identity authorities for each level in the hierarchy make it practical to uniquely identify objects without introducing the bottleneck of a central identity authority.

Hierarchical identifiers are of particular interest to enterprises comprising relatively independent organizations. A central organization (such as the enterprise architecture group) is still required to establish the overall structure of the namespace and directly manage the first level of the hierarchy. In this role it assigns top-level values and, for each value, designates the organization that will be the identity authority for the next tier in the hierarchy. The designated organization then assigns the next-level values and, for each value, may designate yet another organization (or project) to administer the third-tier values, and so on. Note that if the enterprise itself is designated by an Internet domain name, appending that domain name to the identifiers it issues guarantees that those identifiers will be globally unique! This approach can be used to uniquely name Java objects, Eclipse plug-ins, JMS topics and queues, XML schemas, SOAP services, or anything that requires unique names.

UUIDs and GUIDs

While it may not seem so at first glance, a Universally Unique Identifier (UUID)[2] is actually a hierarchical identifier. Each identifier is a 128-bit value comprising two parts, one identifying the issuer of the identifier and the other being an identifier locally assigned by that issuer. The combination is then used to uniquely identify a specific object. In this scheme, the issuer is acting as the identity authority for the second part of the identifier. Assuming that the identity of the issuer is unique, and the identifiers it issues are also unique, then combination of the two parts constitutes a unique identifier for a specific object.

One common implementation of this UUID standard is the Globally Unique Identifier (GUID) shown in Figure 24–1. A GUID[3] uses the 48-bit MAC address of the computer's network interface card (NIC) as a unique identifier for the issuer. The MAC address, itself, is composed of two 24-bit parts. The first part identifies the manufacturer of the NIC card, and the identity authority that manages these values is the

---

2. ISO/IEC 9834-8:2005 Information technology—Open Systems Interconnection—Procedures for the operation of OSI Registration Authorities: Generation and registration of Universally Unique Identifiers (UUIDs) and their use as ASN.1 Object Identifier components.

3. This is actually a description of a Version 1 Microsoft GUID; there are other versions as well.

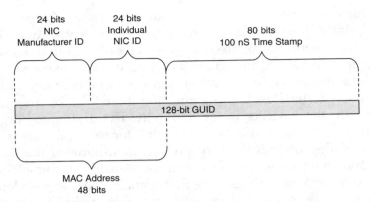

Figure 24–1: *GUID Structure*

IEEE Registration Authority.[4] The remainder of the MAC address is assigned by the manufacturer to uniquely identify the NIC card. Thus the manufacturer becomes the identity authority for the second part of the MAC address.

The remainder of the GUID, the part that uniquely identifies the object, is the elapsed time (measured in 100-nanosecond intervals) between the adoption of the Gregorian calendar and the issuance of the identifier. This serves as the individual object identifier. As long as the machine designated by the MAC address is not generating identifiers within 100 nanoseconds of each other, this will result in a unique identifier for each object.

You can see then that a GUID (as it is described here) involves three hierarchical naming authorities:

1. The IEEE Registration Authority issued the identifier for the manufacturer of the NIC card, which became the first part of the MAC address assigned to the NIC card

2. The manufacturer issued the identifier for the individual NIC card, which became the second part of the MAC address assigned to the NIC card

3. The component running on the computer with the NIC card that issued the GUID. The component used the MAC address to uniquely

---

4. This description applies to universally administered MAC addresses, so indicated by the first (most significant) bit of the address being a "0". MAC addresses may also be locally administered, in which case the first bit is a "1".

identify itself.[5] This becomes the first part of the GUID. It then used the clock to determine the value for the second part, which it then used to uniquely identify the object.

There are other schemes for creating UUIDs besides this particular GUID approach, but they all share the same general pattern: The first part of the UUID uniquely designates the component issuing the identifier, and the second part uniquely designates the specific object.

Note that while the UUID approach seeks to generate unique identifiers, it does not absolutely guarantee uniqueness. Two processes running on a multi-CPU machine might invoke two independent GUID libraries at exactly the same time and thus generate the same GUID. Resetting the clock on a computer might also result in a duplicate being generated. Admittedly, the likelihood is low, but if you need an absolute guarantee then you must use an identity authority that actually keeps track of which identifiers have already been issued so that identifiers can never be duplicated.

Coping with Identity Errors

The goal in using identifiers (unique names) is to have each identifier designate exactly one object. Often, you want to further require that each object have exactly one identifier (of a particular type). Unfortunately, in the real world, you often cannot guarantee that this ideal state will be achieved. Consequently, you must design systems and business processes to be tolerant of such errors. At a minimum, you want to design systems so that if the uniqueness assumption turns out to be false, the system at least handles the situation in a graceful way—it doesn't crash. Beyond that, you might want to design the systems to actually recognize and report a violation of the uniqueness assumption (or at least a potential violation). Going even further, you might want to design the business process that will resolve the discrepancy should one be found. All of this, of course, requires work. The amount of work that is justified will depend on the business impact of the error.

---

5. Here there's a potential flaw in this particular system, as there could be more than one component running on the machine and generating GUIDs.

Consequences of Identity Errors

Companies that prepare tax returns long ago learned that tax identifiers, which are supposed to uniquely identify a single individual, occasionally end up being used by more than one person. But assume for a moment that this possibility for non-uniqueness has not yet been recognized and accounted for in the systems design. The database of tax returns might well put a "unique" constraint on the field containing the tax identifier in the customer record. In fact, it would be tempting to use this field as the primary key for this record. This design would then throw a database error if a second person was entered with the same tax identifier. Uncaught, this would cause a failure of the process attempting to enter that second person's information. *The recovery from this error would require nothing less than a redesign of the database and the systems using it to remove the "unique" constraint and generate new identifiers for all individuals.* Not a happy prospect!

Recognizing that the non-uniqueness of the tax identifier is a possibility, the system might be designed to catch the duplicate tax identifier error while the data is being entered. This would allow the employee entering the data to be alerted that the tax identifier is already in the system and associated with another person. However, while this would avoid an outright crash of the system, it would not enable the processing of the new tax return. The presence of a "unique" constraint would still prevent the data for the second person from being entered with the same tax identifier. Once again, the design would have to be changed before this tax return could be processed.

Sources of Identity Errors

Assumptions about the uniqueness of identifiers can turn out to be erroneous, and designs can easily fail as a result. To help you identify such situations, let's take a look at how such errors can arise. There are actually three types of identifier error:

1. The identifier may actually be associated with the wrong object (i.e., a different object than the one it is supposed to identify)

2. The same identifier may be associated with more than one object

3. More than one identifier may be associated with the same object (this may or may not be an error depending upon the intent of the identifier).

Figure 24–2: *Using Identifiers to Associate Information with Objects*

The reason that these errors cause systems problems is illustrated in Figure 24–2. Systems use identifiers as surrogates for the real-world objects they are supposed to represent. When you want to associate information with real-world objects, you associate the information with the identifier within the system, with the assumption that this identifier uniquely designates the real-world object. Thus a name and address become associated with an identifier that is supposed to represent a unique person.

When there are errors in identifiers, the result is that there are errors in associating the information in systems with the real-world objects.

Associating an Identifier with the Wrong Object

When an identifier is associated with a real-world physical object, you generally cannot be absolutely sure of the actual identity of the physical object. Sometimes this occurs through fraud, as when false identity papers are use to obtain a driver's license. Sometimes it occurs by accident, as when a radio-frequency ID (RFID) tracking tag or bar-code label is accidentally placed on the wrong pallet of goods.

This type of error does not generally pose a problem with respect to system design. The existence of the error will not cause a breakdown in the system itself. However, the error may well cause problems for the enterprise and its business processes. A false name and address on a driver's license may cause problems for law enforcement. A wrongly placed RFID tag may result in the goods being shipped to the wrong destination.

You need to think about the impact of such errors on the enterprise, and then let the severity of that impact guide your efforts. At a minimum, if such situations can arise and they are serious, you need to include the facilities in the system to correct the error once it is recognized. Otherwise, the enterprise will be stuck with the error and unable to correct it. If it is discovered that the RFID tag has been placed on the wrong pallet, the system needs to provide the interfaces to edit this relationship. At a minimum, this will require an interface that allows such editing, but the changes may be more extensive if the identity information has been replicated in other systems. You now have to design mechanisms for updating the replicas. This is a serious design issue, for you tend to think of identity information as being immutable, and thus overlook the modify and delete operations with respect to identifiers.

Beyond simply making provisions for correcting the error, if the consequences are serious enough, you might want to reexamine the business process that first associated the identifier with the object and determine whether an alteration of that process might reduce the likelihood of such an error occurring. Similarly, you might want to alter the business processes that rely on the accuracy of the object identity to re-verify that identity before taking actions that might expose the enterprise to the risk. When a loan is about to be made, for example, the bank may well ask for additional forms of identification to verify that the customer is, indeed, the person he or she claims to be. Similarly, the shipping clerk might verify the actual content of the pallet before it is shipped. In any case, you want to let the level of risk that the error poses guide the level of design effort you put into mitigating that risk. And do not forget to include the design of the business process itself in your thinking.

Associating an Identifier with More than One Real-World Object

Associating more than one real-world object with the same identifier is an error—one that presents greater system challenges than simply associating the identifier with the wrong object. The systems now have information from two or more real-world objects all associated with a single identifier. When it is discovered that the same identifier is actually associated with more than one real-world object, the recovery can be very complicated. The easy part is to create a new identifier for the second object. The difficult part is correcting the associations between the information elements and the identifiers. This involves determining which of the information elements currently associated with the original identifier now should be associated with the new identifier, and then correcting the associations. The correction requires editing facilities for making those changes. If any of the information has been replicated, additional facilities are required to propagate the changes to the replicas.

There are a number of ways this type of error can arise. The recycling (reuse) of identifiers, mistakes made in merging information, and identity theft are a few examples.

Recycling Identifiers

The recycling (re-use) of identifiers, whether intentional or accidental, can cause a single identifier to become associated with multiple objects. The reason that the identifiers are recycled is usually because there is a finite size for the identifier and this limits the number of possible identifiers. Perhaps the best known example is the infamous "Y2K" problem that occurred at the end of the last century. Years were being represented in many systems with just two digits, so the "1/1/00" identifier for January 1, 2000 could not be distinguished from January 1, 1900. The same identifier represented two different dates.

Because of this possibility, when you consider the design of the identifier you need to consider the likelihood that the finite representation will result in the *inadvertent* reuse of the identifier. Even the timestamp used in the low-order 80 bits of a GUID will eventually roll over to all zeroes so that they begin to be reused. The good news is that this will not happen until around AD 3400, by which time it is unlikely that any of the systems being designed today and the objects being identified will still exist! However, these two examples illustrate the thought process you need to go through in evaluating such situations:

1. Is there a circumstance that will result in identifiers being reused? In both examples, the answer was yes.
2. Is that circumstance likely to present itself in reality? In the Y2K example, the answer is yes. In the GUID example, the answer is no.
3. If the reuse is likely, does it pose a risk? In the Y2K example, the answer was yes.
4. What level of effort is warranted by that risk? In the Y2K example, many systems were modified because the business processes they supported would not execute properly once the reuse began.

Mistakes in Merging Information

Mistakes made in joining information can cause more than one real-world object to become associated with one identifier. Many enterprises with multiple lines of business are today trying to assemble a unified picture of their customers across all of their lines of business.

Others are merging customer records from acquired businesses with their existing customer records. These synthesized customer views are assembled from the information available in different systems. You might find two John Smiths, both with the same address and phone number, in two different systems. Based on this, you might design the process that merges the data to conclude that they are the same customer and give that customer an identifier. Unfortunately, at a later date, a customer service representative, looking at this information while talking with John Smith, discovers that there are, in fact, two John Smiths in the household: one is the son of the other! Now a second identifier needs to be created, and the correct information associated with each identifier.

Design Considerations

You need to consider the business impact arising from having more than one real-world object associated with an identifier and let the level of risk determine the commensurate level of design-time and runtime effort. The task of determining which data belongs to which identifier is non-trivial, and it is generally difficult to completely automate. If the editing involved is relatively simple and the situation does not arise very frequently, a completely manual editing procedure may suffice, but this still requires the design and implementation of the editing interfaces.

If there is a lot of information involved, some level of automation may be required with human input identifying the required changes. In extreme cases, when the amount of editing is large or the frequency with which it must be performed makes it impractical to involve people, a fully automated solution may be required. But before you decide to do this, you need to determine the technical feasibility of such automation. Just because you would like to automate this editing activity does not necessarily mean that all of the information needed to carry out the operation is present in the system. Nor does it necessarily mean that you can, in a practical sense, write down all the rules needed to cover all of the possibilities. Feasibility is a key consideration in automating this type of error recovery operation. Even if you conclude that automation is feasible, you also need to keep in mind that the more automation that is included, the greater the design effort and runtime performance impact. You may encounter cost issues as well as feasibility issues.

Multiple Identifiers for the Same Object

The third type of situation you may encounter is multiple identifiers for the same object. Depending upon the context, this may or may not actually be an error. In the case of the Internet hostnames we discussed earlier, it is perfectly acceptable to have multiple hostnames for one machine. On the other hand, it is generally not acceptable for you to have multiple driver's licenses from the same state or multiple tax identification numbers from the same country.

When having multiple identifiers is not acceptable and you actually find such an error, you need to be able to merge the two identifiers into one. Basically this requires removing one of the identifiers and re-associating all of its information with the other identifier. Once again, you need to determine how this will be accomplished, whether through manual editing, partial automation, or complete automation. And, once again, the feasibility of complete automation needs to be determined. One common problem that occurs in this merger of information is that con-flicting information may be associated with the two identifiers. Each identifier may have a different address or phone number associated with it. When this occurs, there is generally insufficient information in the systems to determine which one is correct. The term "correct" is used somewhat loosely here, as there is often judgment involved. It may be the case that both addresses are valid. One just happens to be the residence, while the other is the work address. Unraveling such sit-uations usually requires human assistance.

Mapping Identifiers

There are many real-world situations in which different identity authorities have each issued identifiers for the same object. One indi-vidual person may have a tax identification number, a driver's license number, and a passport number. You find this in systems as well: It is not unusual for an object to be assigned different identifiers by differ-ent systems. This poses some interesting problems when these systems need to exchange information.

A real example of the identifier mapping problem is found in the auto-motive industry. An automobile manufacturer has two computer sys-tems: one used by its dealers and the other used by the factory. Customers are present in both systems. If a potential customer goes to the manufacturer's web site and requests information about a car, he or she ends up with an identifier in the factory system. If a customer walks into a dealership and orders a car, this person ends up with an identifier in the dealer's system. Each of these systems acts as its own identity authority.

In the normal course of doing business, these two systems need to interact with each other and exchange customer information. The dealer system, for example, needs to move the order into the factory system so that the car can be built. During this movement, the factory system needs an identifier for the customer. Which identifier should it use?

Answering this question is not simple. You might consider using the dealer system's identifier, but it was issued by a different identity authority and might not be unique in the factory system. You might consider using the identifier in the factory system that was created when the customer went to the web site, but you might not even know that this identifier exists. You might create a new identifier in the factory system, but now you would have a duplicate in the factory system. If there are different identifiers in the different systems, you need to determine which component will keep track of the correspondence between the identifiers.

These types of identifier-mapping questions arise all the time in enterprise systems. Even in this example, there is a second set of identifiers associated with the order itself. The dealer system needs an identifier for the order, and so does the factory system. Where will these identifiers come from, and how will they be managed? These questions bring you back to the data consistency questions discussed in Chapter 22.

The simplest solution, of course, is to have a single system of record for all identifiers. In fact, there has been such a system in place for identifying individual automobiles since 1978—the Vehicle Identification Number or VIN system.[6] The VIN is another example of a hierarchical identifier. Part of the VIN identifies the manufacturer, who then becomes the identity authority for issuing the remainder of the VIN number. The International Standards Organization (ISO) serves as the identity authority and system-of-record for the manufacturer's ID, which is known as the World Manufacturer's Identifier (WMI).[7] The

---

6. The standard for VIN numbers is specified in ISO Standard 3779 first issued in February 1977 and was last revised in 1983.

7. The standard for the WMI is defined in ISO 3780.

manufacturer then serves as the identity authority and system-of-record for the VIN number itself.

The single system-of-record approach to creating identifiers is the only way to avoid the possibility of duplicate identifiers.[8] Thus when the business consequences of duplicate identifiers are significant, this approach should always be taken. In fact, it was the business consequences of not being able to accurately identify automobiles (for ownership records, insurance, and theft purposes) that motivated the world-wide automobile industry to establish the VIN system.

Unfortunately, much as you might like to have a single system-of-record for identifiers, you are often faced with situations in which different systems, each acting as an identity authority, end up generating different identifiers for the same object. Since scrapping or modifying these systems is often not a viable option (at least in the short term), you must come up with real-world approaches for coping with this situation.

Correlating Identifiers

When you have different identifiers for the same object in different systems, you are faced with the problem of matching them up, particularly when you are creating new identifiers. Figure 24–3 illustrates a typical scenario involving two systems and a cross-reference manager. The cross-reference manager is a role that might be played by either one of the systems or by a third component. `system A` creates a new identifier and notifies the `cross-reference manager` about its creation. This notification includes both the new identifier and sufficient information to allow the `cross-reference manager` to determine whether a corresponding identifier already exists in `system B`. If the `system B` identifier is not found, one is created using the information that came along with the `system A` identifier. In either case, once the `cross-reference manager` has a `system B` identifier, the two identifiers are added to the cross-reference table. This table is used in subsequent interactions between the systems to substitute one system's identifier with that of the other.

For performance reasons, it is desirable to reduce the two interactions between the `cross-reference manager` and `system B` to a single

---

8. The formal proof of this is again the Byzantine General's problem referenced earlier in Chapter 22.

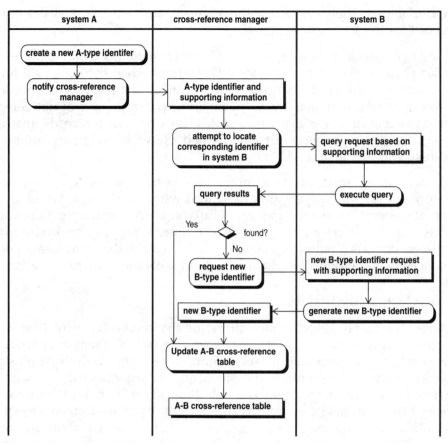

Figure 24–3: *Correlating Identifiers between Systems*

interaction. However, this requires moving the logic of checking for an existing identifier and conditionally creating a new one into `system B`. Often, for technical and/or organizational reasons, this option will not be available. You may find, for example, that `system B` already provides search and identifier creation operations but does not provide a combined operation.

The process described here seems straightforward on the surface, but there is a potentially serious problem that can arise. The information used to perform the identifier lookup in `system B` may not exactly match the information currently present in `system B`, particularly when identifying people. The address might not match exactly, or the phone numbers in the two systems might be different. One system contains a person's given name while the other contains a nickname. As a result, the search may fail to locate the correct identifier. The consequence is that a second identifier for the same person will be created in `system B`, and you will have multiple identifiers for the same person.

Data quality problems are common in the enterprise, and duplicate identifiers are a common consequence. So what should you do about them? You must once again be guided by the level of business risk associated with duplications. That understanding should then guide the level of effort that the enterprise expends in detecting and removing duplicates. These efforts will manifest themselves as new business processes for duplicate detection and removal, supported by new operations on the systems to "merge" the entries associated with the duplicate identifiers. And even here you must recognize that a guaranteed 100% clean-up is impossible.

Summary

Identifiers are intended to uniquely identify individual real-world objects. Identifiers are issued by identity authorities whose responsibility is to ensure the uniqueness of the identifier and that the identifier is only associated with one real-world object. Some identity authorities further ensure that no more than one identifier is associated with a single real-world object.

The identity authority is a potential bottleneck in the issuance of identifiers. Hierarchical identifiers provide a means of avoiding such bottlenecks. The hierarchical identifier consists of a series of fields, each issued by a different identity authority. The value in the first field identifies the authority for assigning values for the second field, and the value in the second field identifies the authority for assigning values for the third field, and so on. This hierarchy distributes the work of assigning identifiers while maintaining a guaranteed uniqueness of identifier values.

Different types of errors can arise with respect to identifiers. The identifier might be associated with the wrong real-world object, or with more than one real-world object. There might be more than one identifier associated with one real-world object when there is not supposed to be more than one.

Identifier errors can cause both business and systems problems, and the possibility of such errors needs to be taken into consideration in designing both business processes and systems. Detecting and correcting such errors requires additional design-time and runtime work. The level of effort that goes into detecting and correcting errors should be guided by the business consequences arising from the errors.

Key Identifier Questions

1. Are identifiers present in the systems? Have the corresponding identity authorities been clearly identified?

2. Is there a potential for identity errors? What are the associated business risks? What level of design-time and runtime effort is warranted for detecting and correcting these errors?

3. Is identity mapping required in the business process? Which component is responsible for maintaining the map? Have the business processes for managing the mapping been defined and implemented?

Chapter 25

Results Validation

When you do work, it is good practice to check the quality of it after you have finished. The same is true in systems. When an activity generates a result, you should consider the extent to which the system should perform quality checks on that result. The problem that you run into, however, is that validation is potentially a very open-ended activity. To perform a full quality check on the result may actually take more computational resources (and time) that it took to create the result itself. So once again, you must ask yourself what is prudent and reasonable.

Start by considering what might be checked in the results, at least for data sets. The things that might be checked are:

1. The syntactic correctness of individual fields; that is, does the date field actually contain a well-formed date?

2. The syntactic correctness of the overall structure: Is the structure itself correct in form; that is, are all required fields present and are all optional fields in the correct places?

3. The internal semantic correctness of the result; that is, if the result is an order, is the requested ship date for the order later than the order placement date?

4. The external semantic correctness of the result in the context of the enterprise; that is, if the result is an order cancellation, does the order being referenced actually exist?

As you progress down this list, the work involved in performing the validation checks increases. The syntactic checking of individual fields is relatively straightforward except for the issue of enumerated values (which will be discussed in a moment). Checking the overall structure gets a bit more complicated because it involves the allowed variations of the data structure. Checking the internal semantic correctness requires the comparison of values of various fields according to some rules. Finally, checking the external semantic correctness requires access to data outside the data structure. In a distributed system, such data access can be very expensive and will almost certainly have a performance impact. From a practical perspective, the complexity and performance impact of any check is usually the limiting factor in how much "correctness checking" is actually implemented.

Checking Enumerated Values

Enumerated values are the list of allowed values for a given field. A commonly enumerated value in order entry systems is a unit of measure—how the quantity is to be interpreted. The unit of measure might be `kilograms`, `tons`, or `gallons`. Gender is another common example of an enumerated value, with the allowed values of `male` and `female`.

The problem presented by enumerations is simply finding the list of allowed values. Modern schema representations such as XML can include the list of values, and some designs use a database table to hold the list of allowed values; however, in many cases there is no centralized list of allowed values. In these cases, the allowed values end up being embedded in the code that does the checking. This makes value checking complex to implement and requires changing the code to add new values. Placing values in databases is more flexible, but accessing those values for checking purposes requires extra design and has performance implications.

XML has changed the picture for enumerations. XML schemas make it possible to include the list of allowed values as part of the schema. Standard XML validation code can then compare an XML data structure against the schema to determine whether it is correct. Furthermore, since the schema itself is an input to the validation process, adding a new value to the enumeration does not require code changes to the components providing validation. Yes, you still have to worry about rolling out the change across multiple components, but at least you have avoided making code changes. And you have removed the need to access an external data source in order to validate the data structure.

Where and When to Validate

The question as to where and when to validate data usually spawns a lengthy debate—and rightfully so. It is not a simple question to answer. The issue is that validation requires work, both at design time and runtime. To answer the question, you must turn once again to the pragmatic question—what is the risk resulting from incorrect data in the data structure? Once you understand the consequences of error, then you can let this understanding guide the decision.

If you have decided that a validation check is warranted, you need to determine where the validation should be performed. In general, the closer the validation is to the source of the error, the easier it will be to handle the error. Just imagine an online catalog-ordering process that does not validate the type of item being ordered until the order reaches the warehouse. What can the warehouse do if it does not recognize the type of item that has been ordered? The warehouse would have to notify the order entry people, and someone there would have to contact the customer for clarification. Contrast this with a validation that is performed by the order entry system at the moment the order is entered and before the customer is told that the order has been accepted. If the validation check fails here, the customer can be told immediately and the error can be readily corrected.

As part of this discussion, you should also consider the difference in computational cost between syntactic checking and semantic checking. When you are using XML, the availability of standardized libraries for validating the XML against its schema makes syntactic checks almost trivial to implement and the computational cost is generally a few milliseconds or less. If you implement a syntactic check each time an XML data structure is generated, you will have an effective means of isolating the source of the error. Since determining the source of errors in a distributed system is notoriously difficult, implementing syntactic checks at the source is good practice, provided that the small computational cost is tolerable.

Semantic checks, on the other hand, tend to be more costly than syntactic validation. They require explicit design effort to define what is acceptable, and the runtime effort often involves data lookups that require cached data for efficiency. Recovery from these errors almost always requires some form of process design as well. For these reasons, it is good practice to indicate the location and nature of semantic validation checks in the process design itself. If there is reference information involved, its access should be designed and treated the same way as any other required input to a process.

Summary

Data errors can be disruptive to the business process. Explicitly validating results raises the visibility of errors at known points in the process, making it easier to design error recovery. The potential impact of the disruption should guide the level of effort (both design-time and runtime) expended on validation.

Validation checks fall into four categories: syntactic validation of individual fields, syntactic validation of the overall data structure, semantic validation within the data structure (i.e., self-consistency), and semantic validation with respect to external reference data. In general, the level of effort required for validation increases as you move down this list. XML schema validation is relatively inexpensive and covers the first two types of checking.

The location of the validation checks should be carefully considered. In general, the closer the validation check is to the source of the error, the easier it is to design the business process to recover from the error. It is good practice to routinely validate XML data structures, as this functionality is readily available in most environments. Semantic checks, however, require design work. They frequently involve accessing reference data as well. As such, the semantic validation activities should be explicitly added to the process flow and treated like any other activity in the business process.

The bottom line is that data validation cannot be treated as an afterthought. The location of the check, the need to access reference data, the performance impact, and the process of recovering from errors must all be taken into consideration in the basic process design.

Key Data Validation Questions

1. What is the business consequence of data errors in the business process? What level of effort is warranted in mitigating these errors?

2. Where are data validation checks being performed? What type of check is being performed? Is access to reference data required?

3. What is the business process response to data errors discovered in validation checks?

Chapter 26

Enterprise Architecture: Data

Many data issues are strategic in nature. Decision making on these issues requires a perspective that extends well beyond the bounds of any single project. The enterprise architecture group, on the other hand, exists specifically to provide this broad perspective. Thus, the enterprise architecture group should both make these strategic decisions and see that they are appropriately applied in day-to-day project designs. This participation is necessary to achieve consistency across the enterprise, for it is only through the consistent application of the decisions that the benefits accrue to the enterprise as a whole.

Naming Schemes

Many things in an architecture require names: message destinations, operations, services, and schemas to name but a few. Names are identifiers, and to avoid the identifier problems described in Chapter 24, they require a naming authority or, more appropriately in the enterprise, a hierarchy of naming authorities.

The enterprise architecture group, with its enterprise-scale charter, is the appropriate group for managing the approach to naming. These responsibilities include:

- Establishing the hierarchical naming structure for message destinations, operations, services, schemas, processes, and whatever else requires consistent naming across the enterprise.

- Acting as the naming authority for the top-level values in this hierarchy, possibly interacting with external parties (e.g., ICANN) to obtain top-level values that will make the names globally unique. This is particularly important for external-facing services, operations, and data structure schemas.

- Establishing the policies for identifying naming authorities within the enterprise for lower-level names in the hierarchy.

- Identifying the naming authority to be associated with each name the enterprise architecture group issues.

For example, if the enterprise is using SOAP over JMS for its services, it needs to name the services, interfaces, operations, and JMS destinations. A consistent naming scheme across these elements will make it easy to understand the purpose of each item and the correspondence among them. A general naming scheme such as the following can provide a common framework for these names:

```
<Company>/<Domain>/<Service>/<Interface>/<Operation>/<Version>/<Format>
```

The specific character separating the fields will be dependent upon the particular usage. The "/" used here is typical of URL (universal resource locator) designators, but a decimal point (".") is common in other usages.

The enterprise architecture group would be responsible for defining this overall structure, obtaining the `<Company>` designator from ICANN (or some external authority), assigning values for the `<Domain>` field, and designating the naming authority for fields below the `<Domain>` field. The `<Company>` field is a hedge against mergers and acquisitions to ensure that the names remain unique after two companies are combined.

Of course, the enterprise architecture group could choose to remain the naming authority for the `<Service>` and `<Interface>` levels as well. Typically the authority for naming the `<Operation>` and below is temporarily delegated to the project team.

Taking this approach for the ATM example and its underlying services, the specific service operation used to acquire authorization for disbursing funds might be named:

```
//MyBank.com/Retail/Account/BalanceMgmt/DisbursalAuthorizationRequest/10
```

Note the presence of the version number as the last field. This sets the stage for evolving this operation should that become necessary.

When namespaces are used to identify message destinations, it is good practice to explicitly identify the role the message is playing and the format of the message. Thus the JMS destination for requests invoking the operation would be named:

```
MyBank.com.Retail.Account.BalanceMgmt.DisbursalAuthorization.Request.10.SOAP
```

The response destination would be named:

```
MyBank.com.Retail.Account.BalanceMgmt.DisbursalAuthorization.Reply.10.SOAP
```

If notifications of new disbursal authorizations were being provided for some reason, the destination for that would be named:

```
MyBank.com.Retail.Account.BalanceMgmt.DisbursalAuthorization.Notify.10.SOAP
```

The message format field at the end serves to disambiguate related messages that happen to be in different formats but use the same transport. If the SOAP request had to be transformed into a legacy format and delivered over JMS, the information content would be the same, but the format would be different. The resulting message would be named:

```
MyBank.com.Retail.Account.BalanceMgmt.DisbursalAuthorization.Notify.10.TargetFormat
```

Here is a final but important note on names. As much as possible, try to avoid using organization names and system names. These names tend to be arbitrary and subject to change without notice. Changing names in a namespace tends to be a lengthy and time-consuming process. For stability, use names from the domain model that represent the generic roles and concepts.

Architecting Content Transformation

One of the roles of the enterprise architecture group is to establish standard patterns for solving common problems. One of these common problems is content transformation. Looking narrowly back at the communications pattern shown in Figure 21–4, it would be tempting to identify `content transformer` as a type of architectural component and then standardize the technology to be used for its implementation. In fact, you might even consider content transformation a candidate to become a service. However, the context of this figure is too narrow to support such conclusions. In it you are not seeing

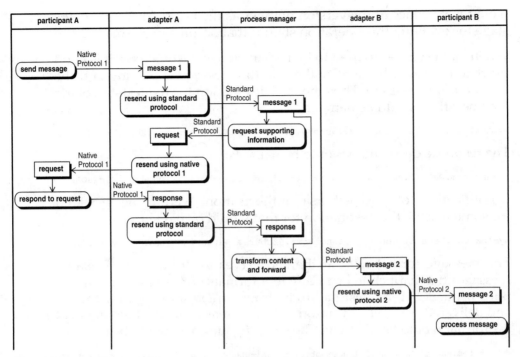

Figure 26–1: *Process Management Communications Pattern*

enough of a typical overall process to decide whether this architectural partitioning is appropriate.

Consider the slightly larger slice of a business process shown in Figure 26–1. This process involves a **process manager**—a component that is orchestrating at least some portion of the process. In this particular scenario, the initial message being received by the **process manager** triggers the retrieval of some additional data. The results of this retrieval are combined with information from the initial message, transformed into a form suitable for the target system, and sent.[1]

What you see here is a typical systems integration scenario involving a **process manager**. The content transformation is but one of a number of activities being performed by the **process manager**. If you make

---

1. If you are thinking that the need for the request reflects a poor design decision (i.e., the information ought to have been in the initial message), consider instead that this request might have been directed to a third system.

the `content transformer` a component (service) of its own, then you will add another communications round-trip between the `process manager` and the `content transformer` every time a content transformation is required.

In practice (and this has been done many times), making the `content transformer` a separate component has, for the most part, turned out to be a poor architectural decision. Most transformations are relatively simple, and the data marshalling, communications overhead, and data un-marshalling required by this architectural partitioning adds significant cost (not to mention delay) to the transformation operation. Furthermore, it significantly increases the network load. Most successful architectures tend to treat content transformation as a functional feature of a more broadly capable `process manager` component.

Systems of Record

Establishing a system of record is an enterprise-wide decision that impacts every project and system using the information. The Enterprise Architecture group should establish a policy regarding defining systems of record for each concept and relationship found in the domain. As appropriate, this policy must take into consideration the realities of operating over a wide geographic area and the impact of communication interruptions. This may require strategies for continuing business operations when the system of record is either unavailable or inaccessible. The enterprise architecture group should also establish a policy regarding the replication of data, stating a preferred approach (e.g., single system of record), the allowed alternatives, and the conditions under which the use of the alternative approaches are acceptable.

You should note that these decisions involve more than just an understanding of the domain model. They must take into consideration the dynamic usage of the data in different business processes and under different operational circumstances. A data modeling group, by itself, is not in a position to make these decisions and establish policies. The broader perspective of the complete enterprise architecture group is required.

These policy statements should be accompanied by a description of the preferred patterns for the maintenance of data, including the preferred patterns for updating data caches. These patterns will serve as guidelines for project teams and will ensure consistency across projects. Where it is expected that a pattern will be repeatedly implemented in a particular set of technologies, the enterprise architecture group should document a reference architecture for that pattern showing the use of those technologies.

In a practical sense, it is impossible for the Enterprise Architecture group to foresee every possible data management issue. Therefore, the group must establish procedures by which project teams can quickly engage group and resolve open issues.

Common Data Models

As discussed back in Chapter 23, when you employ common data models it is likely that you will need more than one representation of each major concept. Determining the number of representations that will be needed and the required information content of each representation presents a design challenge—one that requires broad understanding of the potential usages of the representations. Without this broad perspective, it is unlikely that you will be able to design a stable and reusable data structure. It is the enterprise architecture group that has this perspective, and therefore defining common data models should be an enterprise architecture group responsibility. This group should establish policies regarding the use of common data models covering:

1. The circumstances under which a common data model should be used and where the use of one would be inappropriate.

2. The preferred approach to implementing common data models and the acceptable alternatives along with the criteria for deciding which approach to use in a given situation.

3. The operational approach to making changes to the common data model. This policy must allow for a graceful transition to the new form rather than a big-bang update of all affected components.

4. Who will define common data models (generally the enterprise architecture group).

5. The mechanisms by which common data models will be defined and their relationship to the domain model will be documented.

6. Where common data model definitions will be stored and how they will be accessed.

A word of caution is warranted here. Do not become entrapped in the search for a technology solution for the management of common data model information. The management of metadata is a very complex problem, encompassing the definition of all data structures (including common data models and database schema) and the mappings between these metadata structures. There is a lot of research going on in this area in both academia and industry. As of this writing, there are no comprehensive solutions available for the management of all of the different types of metadata typically found in the enterprise. The good news is that you do not absolutely need such a tool, as nice as it might be to have such a thing. What you need is a readily accessible and managed repository of metadata information whose organization is well understood. In many cases, a source code control system will suffice. This is the essential requirement. The rest is gravy!

The common data model policies should be accompanied by a set of design patterns showing how the common data models will actually be employed in communications, particularly when the end-point systems do not natively use this format. When individual patterns will be frequently implemented with a specific set of technologies, the enterprise architecture group should create an accompanying reference architecture for that pattern detailing its implementation with those technologies. These patterns and reference architectures should be placed in a readily accessible managed repository.

Since it will be the enterprise architecture group that actually designs the common data models, it is important that this group define the procedure by which a project team requiring a common data model can engage the group. Since the group must get involved in a timely manner, the procedure must include the allocation of enterprise architecture resources and the prioritization required to provide a timely response.

Identifiers

Identifiers are another area in which the decisions being made impact the entire enterprise. The enterprise architecture group should manage all identifiers whose scope of usage extends beyond a single system. The group should:

1. Maintain a catalog of the different types of identifiers in use

2. For each type of identifier, specify the structure of the identifier to be used and the identity authority (or authorities in the case of structured identifiers) responsible for the creation of the identifier

3. Specify the logic of how identifiers will be mapped when identifiers in one system must be mapped into the identifiers of another system

4. Specify the patterns for managing cross-reference information and utilizing that cross reference in exchanges between systems

5. Define a reference architecture for implementing the design pattern in specific technologies when those technologies will be commonly used

6. Participate directly with project teams to resolve issues when the project team is having difficulty incorporating the cross reference into an exchange between components

Data Quality Management

No discussion of data would be complete without considering the quality of the data itself. Erroneous, improper, and absent values are a fact of life in real information systems. Earlier chapters discussed the impact of such errors on the enterprise and the detection of such errors through validation checking, but did not discuss what to do when an error is actually found.

The only situation in which you can automatically and correctly resolve data inconsistencies occurs when there is a single system of record for the data. Then, and only then, can you know definitively which copy of the data is correct (the one in the system of record) and which copy is in error (any other copy of the data that is different from the one in the system of record). In all other cases, an investigation is required to determine which copy is correct. While there may be a small number of cases in which data discrepancies can be automatically resolved, these are usually the exception, not the rule.

This raises the question as to how data discrepancies should be resolved. The answer is that it requires a process, and that process involves people. These people investigate the discrepancies, determine which value is correct, and correct the data. They should also, where possible, determine and document the root cause of the discrepancy and determine whether changes to business processes and/or systems might eliminate or reduce the likelihood of such errors in the future.

Data quality management is so closely related to the activities of the enterprise architecture group that the personnel involved in managing data quality should either be a part of that group or operate under the auspices of the group. In either case, the enterprise architecture group should establish the policies regarding data quality management. The data quality policy should:

1. Define the approach to be taken towards data validation, both syntactic and semantic. Guidelines should be provided as to when and where data validation should be included in processes.
2. Define the approaches to be taken in identifying data quality problems, including conducting system-based audits and providing mechanisms for personnel to report suspected data quality problems.
3. Define the approach for prioritizing the correction of data quality problems based on perceived business impact. The limited number of personnel available to resolve discrepancies will make this necessary.
4. Define the process(es) for reconciling data discrepancies and keeping track of the resolution status for each reported discrepancy.

If audits will be conducted as part of the data management activity, the audit itself should be treated in the same manner as any other business process requiring design work. This is not to say that implementing an audit should necessarily require a major design effort. On the contrary, available interfaces should be used wherever appropriate. But the audit process does need to be implemented, and the project implementing the audits should have focus. Priority needs to be given to the data issues that pose the biggest risks to the enterprise. The execution of the audit will have a performance impact on the components involved and must be taken into consideration. In fact, any one of the full set of design issues affecting a project might come into play. Auditing is simply another business process, and should be treated that way.

Summary

There are a number of data-related issues whose resolution requires a perspective extending beyond the scope of any particular project. Resolving these issues and setting forth the policies for dealing with these issues is one of the enterprise architecture group responsibilities. These responsibilities include:

- Establishing naming schemes for services, operations, message destinations, and other architectural elements requiring names
- Establishing architectural patterns for content transformation
- Establishing systems of record and policies regarding data replication and cache management
- Defining common data models and the policies for their use
- Establishing the authorities for identity issuance and management
- Establishing the policies and procedures for maintaining data quality

Key Enterprise Architecture Data Questions

1. Are there well-defined data policies with respect to defining and enforcing systems of record?
2. Are there well-defined policies for creating and using common data models?
3. Are there well-defined policies for managing identities? Have the identity authorities been established for each type of identifier?
4. Are there well-defined policies regarding data validation?
5. Is there a governance process in place that ensures compliance with these policies?
6. Is there an organization responsible for maintenance of the policies?
7. Are processes in place for an application team to engage the relevant policy group when the data policies do not appear to be appropriate for the application?
8. Are there processes in place for detecting and resolving data and identifier discrepancies?

Part VI

Coordination

Chapter 27

Coordination and Breakdown Detection

Enterprise architectures are composed of many interdependent moving parts. To bring a business process to life, the work that is being performed by one participant needs to be coordinated with the work being performed by others. It is this coordination that integrates the individual participant activities and defines the structure of the business processes.

The participants in a distributed system are autonomous. Each participant manages the execution of its own activities. Some activity management patterns involve interactions with other participants. These activity management patterns form the basic building blocks of coordination. These patterns are composed to form coordination patterns between pairs of participants. These pair-wise patterns are further composed until eventually the coordination pattern for an entire business process emerges.

Styles of overall process coordination emerge when there is consistency in the use of coordination patterns in a process. Some business processes are tightly controlled by a process manager: Its interactions with other participants serve, directly or indirectly, as the triggers for the performance of activities by those participants. Other processes have no management at all: The arrival of inputs from other participants serve as the triggers for performing activities.

What makes the choice of coordination patterns so important is that these choices not only define the structure of the process, they also directly impact the ability to detect breakdowns in the process. The simplest and most efficient coordination patterns (and therefore the ones you might be inclined to first consider using) are not capable of detecting breakdowns at all! In contrast, the patterns that add feedback make it possible to detect breakdowns also require additional design, communications, and participant resources. Your job as an architect is to select the appropriate balance for each business process.

If you are wondering why the term orchestration is not being used, it is because this term implies the existence of a leader, a process manager. While this is, indeed, one approach to coordination, it is not the only approach. Most end-to-end business processes, for example, do not have an overall process manager. So you need to consider all the coordination patterns, not just orchestration. On the other hand, orchestration is so important that two chapters are devoted to process management.

Activity Execution Management Patterns (AEMPs) Involving Interactions

Any discussion of coordination has to begin with an examination of the role that interactions play in activity execution management. The five basic activity execution management patterns (AEMP) are illustrated in Figure 27–1. In pattern AEMP1, the performance of activity A is triggered by the arrival of the input. The `participant` is responsible for observing the arrival of the `input` and, as soon as possible, commencing the execution of the activity. AEMP2 is similar, except that a previous activity must be completed before the `input` can trigger the performance of activity A. Here the design must accommodate the early arrival of the `input`, holding it until the previous activity has been completed. In AEMP3, it is the completion of the previous activity that triggers the performance of activity A. Here the `participant` design must account for the possible absence of the required input. In AEMP4, the occurrence of some `External Event` (unrelated to the execution of this process) serves as the trigger for executing activity A. The `participant`

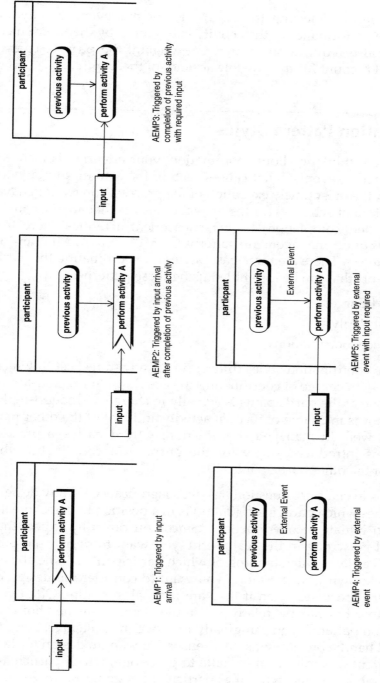

Figure 27–1: *Activity Execution Management Patterns Involving Interactions*

is responsible for detecting the occurrence of this event. Finally, in AEMP5, the performance of the activity is triggered by the `External Event` but also requires an `input`. Once again, the `participant` design must account for the possible absence of the `input`.

Coordination Pattern Styles

When you are thinking about coordination, your attention is focused on the triggering events: what causes each of the activities to be performed. For the most timely execution of the process, you want to have the completion of activities (or the arrival of results that are the consequence of their completion) trigger subsequent activities. Here the activity execution management patterns AEMP1 and AEMP2 are of primary interest. There are three basic styles for coordinating the work of participants that can be assembled using these patterns:

1. Fire-and-Forget
2. Request-Reply
3. Managed Coordination

These three coordination styles differ primarily with respect to which participant is in charge of coordinating the activities. In fire-and-forget pattern, none of the participants is actually in charge. In request-reply, the requestor is in charge of its own activity and that of the other participant as well. In managed coordination, a third party—a process manager—is introduced solely for the purpose of coordinating the activities of the other participants.

The "Who's in charge?" question has deep significance for any design. It determines which participant (if any) is in a position to detect breakdowns and initiate recovery actions. Since you can fully expect that things will go wrong in the real world, you want to design the processes with a clear understanding of which participants will be able to detect breakdowns. Furthermore, you want to consider the design of the recovery processes, even if they are manual in nature. Often you will find that by making relatively simple changes in the choice of coordination patterns, you can greatly improve the system's ability to detect and handle breakdowns. In a sense, you want to design for failure. You want to know what is liable to go wrong, which participant will know about it, and what that participant is going to do when it happens.

Fire-and-Forget Coordination Patterns

Event-Driven Two-Party Fire-and-Forget

Fire-and-forget is the simplest possible interaction between two participants. The event-driven two-party fire-and-forget pattern consists of a single one-way communication between the two participants (Figure 27–2). The `sending participant` produces an `artifact` that is received and acted upon by the `receiving participant`. The `receiving participant` is employing the AEMP1 or AEMP2 pattern (this and the ensuing discussions will ignore the differences), and the artifact serves as both the input and the trigger for the action.

You see examples of the fire-and-forget pattern all the time. Every piece of mail you place in your mailbox is a fire-and-forget artifact. E-mail messages are fire-and-forget artifacts as well. In fact, any message for which the recipient is not actively waiting for an immediate reply is a fire-and-forget artifact.

The use of fire-and-forget coordination does not imply anything in particular about the semantics of the communications. The artifact might represent a request, an asynchronous reply to a previous request, or an announcement of some event that has occurred.

Event-Driven Multi-Party Fire-and-Forget

The fire-and-forget pattern has an obvious extension to multiple parties, as illustrated in Figure 27–3. Here the basic two-party pattern occurs twice, once between the `sending participant` and the `receiving participant`, and again between the `receiving participant` and the `third participant`. This type of pattern is often found in systems. The first participant generates a file or message that triggers work in a second system. The work in that second system generates a file or message that is passed to a third system, and so on.

Breakdown Detection in Fire-and-Forget

Fire-and-forget is simple to design and inexpensive to implement, but it has one significant drawback: None of the participants are in a position to detect a breakdown in the process. A recipient has no way of knowing that there is supposed to be an artifact coming, and therefore it cannot detect a breakdown in either the sender or communications

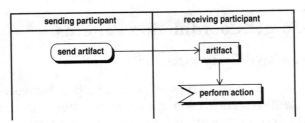

Figure 27–2: *Event-Driven Two-Party Fire-and-Forget Pattern*

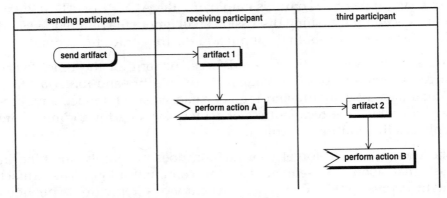

Figure 27–3: *Multi-Party Fire-and-Forget Pattern*

channel. Similarly, a sender has no way of knowing whether the recipient got the artifact or did the work. There is no overall process coordinator in the fire-and-forget pattern. Breakdowns will go undetected.

Despite the inability to detect a breakdown in the fire-and-forget pattern, it can be effectively used within the scope of a larger process that is tolerant of an individual message loss. The phone company's use of the mail to obtain its payments is a good example. The bill is sent via the mail—a fire-and-forget communication. The customer sends the payment back via the same fire-and-forget mechanism. Either might be lost in the mail, yet the system as a whole works! Why? Because the billing system is tolerant of failure. If the payment is not received (for whatever reason), the past-due amount is simply added to the next month's bill. Thus you can see that simple and inexpensive fire-and-forget communications can be used to implement robust business processes—but only if the overall process is designed to be tolerant of breakdowns and those breakdowns do not happen often enough to cause additional problems.

As a side note, when you are considering communications services, you must be careful not to be misled by the claims the service provider might make regarding the communications quality of service. Many communications services offer a "guaranteed delivery" option. Regardless of the claim, it is still a fire-and-forget service. To begin with, there are no guarantees in the real world. However the service operates, it is always possible for the message to be destroyed. In addition, even if the message is delivered, the communications service does not guarantee that the recipient will act upon the message once it has been delivered. The coordination pattern is still fire-and-forget.

So if communication is still fire-and-forget, despite the use of enhanced qualities of service, why would you use the enhancements? The answer is that they reduce the likelihood that the message will not be delivered. Just because the business process may be able to tolerate and recover from a communications breakdown does not mean that the recovery is without cost. If the recovery cost is significant, an investment in an increased quality of service may be justified.

Improving the quality of service in message-based communications usually involves extra work. In electronic communications, this usually involves making a persistent record of the message one or more times while it is in transit. You need to consider these cost and performance implications when you choose to specify the use of these enhancements. Extra disk capacity or a high-performance disk may have to be purchased. The act of writing a message to disk takes more time than simply sending it over a network. All of these things need to be factored in to your decision. When you decide to employ an enhanced quality of service, your goal should be to balance the probability and business impact of lost messages against the increased cost and decreased performance of the enhancements. In other words, you need to make a sound business decision.

Non-Event-Driven Fire-and-Forget

The event-driven fire-and-forget pattern assumes that the recipient triggers work when the artifact arrives. In other words, it assumes that the recipient is using activity execution management patterns AEMP1 or AEMP2. A variation on fire-and-forget is that the receiving participant is using AEMP3, AEMP4, or AEMP5 (Figure 27-4). In other words, it is not event driven: The arrival of the input does not itself serve as the triggering event for the action. The completion of some other activity, the arrival of another input, or the occurrence of some external

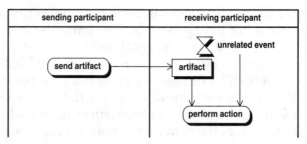

Figure 27–4: *Non-Event-Driven Fire-and-Forget*

event is what actually triggers the performance of the activity in the recipient. This dependence upon an unrelated event is yet another potential source of process breakdown. As such, the source of the unrelated triggering event should also be shown in the activity diagram. You want to ensure that all potential sources of breakdowns are readily observable in the activity diagrams so that you can fully evaluate all possible sources of breakdown.

Request-Reply Patterns

Event-Driven Two-Party Request-Reply

The second fundamental coordination pattern is the event-driven synchronous request-reply pattern (Figure 27–5). In this pattern one party requests that another perform a service *and waits for a response*. There are two interactions involved. The `requestor` sends a message to the `service provider` that triggers the performance of the service. Once the service has been completed, the `service provider` returns the result to the `requestor`. The `requestor` is waiting for the result, and its arrival triggers the continuation of its work. As with the two-party fire-and-forget pattern, each communication is both an input and a triggering event.

The synchronous request-reply pattern is more than just two fire-and-forget interactions. The requesting process is waiting for the result and, when that result arrives, correlates it with the request. This correlation can be used to determine whether or not the service was performed as requested. This additional functionality distinguishes the synchronous request-reply pattern from a simple combination of two fire-and-forget patterns.

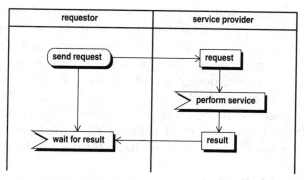

Figure 27–5: *Event-Driven Two-Party Synchronous Request-Reply Pattern*

Reply-Time Service-Level Agreements

The request-reply pattern is the simplest pattern capable of detecting a breakdown in a process. The `requestor` not only knows that something is supposed to happen (since it sent the service request), but it can also verify whether or not it actually did happen (via the service result). In sharp contrast with the fire-and-forget pattern, the use of the request-reply pattern eliminates communications breakdowns as a potential source of undetectable failure. Because of this, when you use request-reply you can generally use lightweight communications mechanisms and avoid the performance penalty of persisting messages in transit.

However, there is an important caveat regarding the ability to detect breakdowns: The absence of a reply is inherently ambiguous. The `requestor` does not know whether the `service provider` has simply not yet completed the work or whether something has truly gone wrong. The only way to resolve this ambiguity is to establish a service-level agreement (SLA) for the service. This agreement establishes a time frame within which a response is expected. Once this time has been established, then the breakdown detection criteria become clear: Before the expiration of the SLA time interval, no conclusion can be drawn; after the expiration, the absence of a reply clearly indicates the existence of a problem, if nothing more than the violation of the service-level agreement itself.

Because of the inherent ambiguity of an absent reply, it is a best practice to establish a response-time SLA for every request-reply activity—even when you are asking another person to perform a task. The time frame clarifies the expectations for both parties and eliminates a significant source of misunderstanding. This thinking carries forward into the specification of components and services as well. You want to ensure that both the user of the service and the provider of the service understand the SLA expectations. This gives the provider of the service a clearly defined performance goal and the user of the service sufficient information to decide whether the service will actually satisfy the needs of the process in which it will be used. The establishment of such time frames also makes it easy to recognize potential performance issues while the design is still in its formative stages.

Event-Driven Multi-Party Request-Reply

Multi-party request-reply is a generalization of the basic two-party synchronous request-reply (Figure 27–6). Here the `service provider` asks a `third party` to perform some or all of the service and waits for the `result`. When the `result` is returned, a final `result` is returned to the `requestor`.

The essential feature of the pattern is that breakdowns in the process at any level are detectable by the `requestor` as long as response-time service-level agreements are in effect. It does, however, have a drawback: Its synchronous nature ties up all parties until the work is completed. Depending upon the length of time involved, this can have an adverse impact on the level of resources required for a solution.

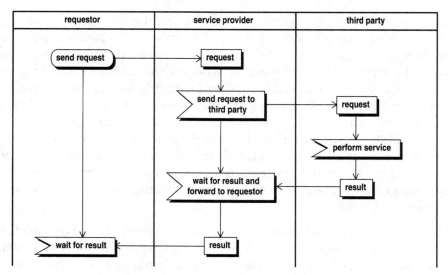

Figure 27–6: *Multi-Party Synchronous Request-Reply*

Event-Driven Asynchronous Request-Reply

In the event-driven synchronous request-reply pattern, the requestor waits for the reply. In its asynchronous variant (Figure 27–7), the `requestor` goes off and does something else after sending the request rather than just wait for the reply. This pattern is common in real business processes. For example, when you order a book online, you don't just sit idly and wait for the book to arrive! You go off and do other things while you wait.

The asynchronous request-reply pattern is useful when the performance of the service takes a long time, as in the shipment of the book. It is also useful when the request itself does not serve as the triggering event for the performance of the work, that is, when the `service provider` is using the AEMP3, AEMP4, or AEMP5 patterns to trigger the work. This can cause additional delays, as when the pending work rests in a queue. When you take clothing to the dry cleaners, your request goes into a queue (even if it is a 1-hour turnaround queue) behind other requests. You then go on about your business and come back later to pick up the cleaning.

Complexities in Asynchronous Request-Reply

In the synchronous request-reply pattern, the `requestor` is waiting for a response to a particular `request`: There is no ambiguity about the relationship between the `request` and the `result`, and the `requestor` can easily correlate the `result` with the state of the work in progress and continue the work. In the asynchronous variant, however, the

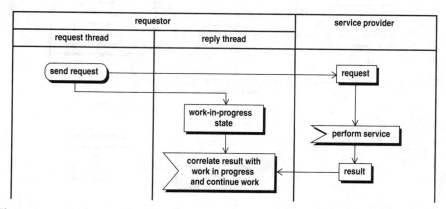

Figure 27–7: *Two-Party Asynchronous Request-Reply Coordination Pattern*

`requestor` has been off doing other things, and the `result` is logically handled in another thread of control. In order to process the `result`, the state of the work in progress must first be recovered. Furthermore, there may well be a number of outstanding requests and work-in-progress states. Additional work may be required to correlate the result with a particular work-in-progress state. These activities add extra design-time and runtime work.

Detecting the absence of an expected result also requires extra work. In the synchronous model, the `requestor` is waiting for the result, and can easily time out on that wait. In the asynchronous model, some event in the `requestor` must trigger a check (yet another control thread) to see whether any results are overdue. This, too, adds extra design-time and runtime work.

Synchronous Promise with Asynchronous Result

While the asynchronous request-reply pattern is eventually capable of detecting overall breakdowns in the process, the breakdown may not be detected until after the allowed time period for returning the result has passed. A variation on this pattern returns a promise in an initial synchronous request-reply exchange, with the eventual result being returned asynchronously. This pattern in shown in Figure 27–8, and is

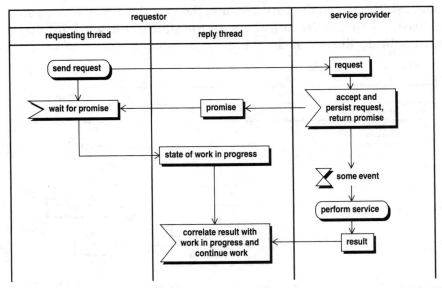

Figure 27–8: *Synchronous Promise with Asynchronous Result*

essentially a combination of a request-reply pattern returning the promise followed by a fire-and-forget return of the service result.

This pattern characterizes the basic online ordering paradigm that you find in many e-commerce businesses. The customer goes online to order a book and while waiting, the order is confirmed. This confirmation is essentially a promise to fulfill the order and often includes a promised delivery date (this is the SLA for the result) that may vary depending on the transportation mechanism chosen for the delivery of the order. The advantage of this pattern is that the customer learns immediately if there are any problems with the initial request. It also affords the customer the opportunity to review the promise (including the SLA) and take corrective action if required.

Delegation

Sometimes when a service is performed, the result service is not returned to the `requestor`—it is actually delivered to a third party. The intent here is to delegate the responsibility for the performance of the service to a `service provider`, who will then deliver the `result` to the third party. The simplest form of delegation is the multi-party fire-and-forget pattern of Figure 27-3, but this pattern is subject to undetected breakdowns. Generally, when you delegate responsibility you want some confirmation that the responsibility has been accepted. In other words, you want a promise that the work will be done. You can accomplish this by replacing the fire-and-forget delivery of the `request` with a request-reply exchange that returns a `promise`. This yields the delegation pattern of Figure 27–9.

In the delegation pattern, the `requestor` does not receive the actual work result—only a `promise` that the service will be performed. This, of course, renders undetectable any breakdowns that occur after the promise is returned. Because of this, to ensure that the service request is not lost, the `service provider` generally makes a persistent (fault-tolerant) record of the request before returning this promise to perform the service. This is not a guarantee that the service will be performed, but it reduces the likelihood that the `request` will be lost—at the expense of persisting the request and designing a restart of the `service provider` to recover the list of outstanding requests.

In the delegation pattern, triggering the service work and handling the result are exclusively the responsibility of the `service provider`.

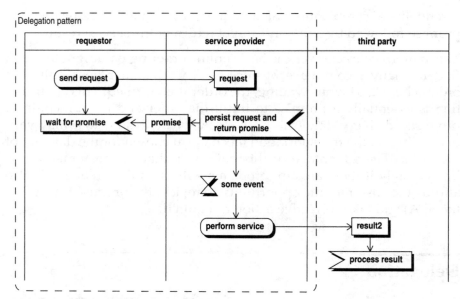

Figure 27–9: *Delegation Pattern*

The service performance may be triggered by the arrival of the request, but it might just as well be triggered by some other event. The service result can be sent to the third party using any one of the protocols discussed. The communication of the result is not, strictly speaking, part of the delegation pattern.

One of the benefits of the delegation pattern is that the use of request-reply for the exchange between the `requestor` and the `service provider` eliminates the communications channel itself as a potential source of undetectable failure. This allows the use of inexpensive light-weight communications for the request-promise exchange. However, once this exchange has been completed, a breakdown in the service provider cannot be detected by any of the participants. Thus, there is no overall process monitoring inherent in the delegation pattern. Despite this shortcoming, this pattern is often used to transfer responsibility between major systems involved in different parts of a business process. When a customer orders a book online, for example, the customer has a request-reply exchange with the order entry system in which the customer receives a promise to ship the book. The customer has delegated the responsibility for the order to the order entry system. It, in turn, will pass the order (at some point) to the warehouse system for fulfillment.

Delegation with Confirmation

The inability of the basic delegation pattern to detect breakdowns after the promise can be a serious problem. You can overcome this problem by adding an eventual asynchronous status feedback after the service has been successfully performed, as shown in Figure 27–10. This feedback allows the original requestor to confirm that the requested service was actually performed and thus detect breakdowns in the performance of the work. The status feedback gives the requestor greater visibility into the business process.

In this pattern, the feedback is provided after the service has been successfully performed, but does not necessarily indicate that the result itself was successfully delivered to the third party. If the performer uses fire-and-forget to pass on the service result, then the confirmation only indicates that the result was sent, not that it got to its destination. You can see the use of this pattern in the online book ordering example: When the book is eventually shipped, the customer receives an e-mail saying that the book is on its way.

One problem with this pattern stems from the use of fire-and-forget coordination with the third party. Once again, the use of fire-and-forget renders undetectable any breakdowns that occur in the delivery of

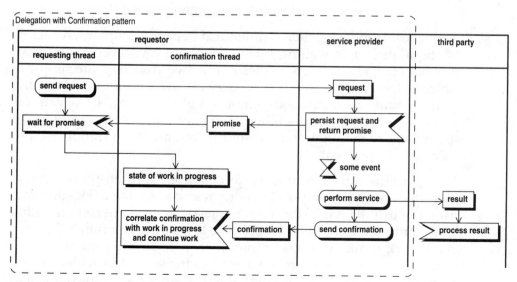

Figure 27–10: *Delegation with Confirmation*

the service result and subsequent processing. However, you can remedy this situation by using request-reply or delegation with confirmation to deliver the service result. If this pattern is used recursively by all recipients, then the original requestor can detect breakdowns anywhere in the process. When there are a number of parties involved in such exchanges, the overall pattern of result delivery and its relationship to status reports must be clearly understood to interpret the status reports correctly.

Summary

To form a structured process, the activities of the participants in a distributed system must be coordinated. The basic coordination patterns for pair-wise interactions between participants are fire-and-forget and request-reply. Fire-and-forget is simple, but it does not provide the ability to detect breakdowns. Request-reply can detect breakdowns, but it requires more work and may tie up resources.

Differences in how the work is triggered in these patterns provide many pattern variations. When the arrival of inputs triggers the work, the result is an event-driven pattern. When the triggers arise from other sources, the result is a non-event-driven pattern. In these patterns, it is important to understand the sources of these other events, as their absence will cause breakdowns in the process flow.

The request-response patterns differ also depending upon whether or not the requestor is waiting for the response. Synchronous request-reply patterns, in which the requestor is actively waiting, are simple to implement, but they tie up the resources of the requestor while waiting for the result. Asynchronous request-reply patterns, in which the requestor goes off and does other things until the result arrives, make efficient use of the requestor's resources but are more complicated to design and implement.

These patterns can be composed to characterize multi-party interactions. One common composition is represented by the delegation pattern, in which the requestor has a request-response interaction with a service provider but receives a promise to do the work rather than the actual work result. The service provider then executes the work at a later time. A variation on this pattern has the service provider returning an asynchronous confirmation that the work has been completed.

This puts the requestor in a position to detect breakdowns in the work performance.

Key Coordination Questions

1. What coordination patterns are being used in the business processes currently being designed? Do they afford the opportunity to detect breakdowns in the process?

2. Which participants in the business process are in a position to detect breakdowns?

3. Would the use of a different coordination pattern improve the ability to detect breakdowns?

Chapter 28

Transactions:
Coordinating Two or
More Activities

The coordination patterns in the previous chapter focus on the execution of a single activity, but there are times when you would like to treat the execution of two or more activities as if they were a single operation. In other words, you want to make these activities part of a transaction.

An ideal transaction is characterized by four properties, commonly referred to as the ACID properties, an acronym constructed from the four property names:

1. Atomic: Either all of the activities complete successfully or none are performed. The collection of activities appears to be a single operation.

2. Consistent: The changes made by one activity are consistent with the changes made by another. All of the changes related to a single transaction appear at the same time.

3. Independent: None of the changes that are in progress can influence other works in progress until the transaction has successfully completed. Changes that are being made are not visible until the transaction successfully commits.

4. Durable: Once the transaction has completed, the changes become permanent. Changes cannot get lost.

These properties represent an ideal for transactions—an ideal, as it turns out, that is not actually achievable in physically distributed systems. The good news is that you don't necessarily need to achieve the ideal. Once you understand the situation, you can design the processes in such a way that they are tolerant of the non-ideal behavior.

Let's begin the exploration of the issues by first examining the two-phase transaction commit protocol, a well-established approach that attempts to achieve this ideal. The uncontrollable communications delays on this protocol will highlight exactly why the ideal cannot be achieved. Then the failure modes of the two-phase commit protocol will be examined to highlight why the failure-mode behavior may not be what you want for the business process. Finally, alternative approaches such as the use of compensating transactions will be explored. While these approaches do not come as close to achieving the transactional ideal, they nevertheless prove to be very practical in real process designs.

Two-Phase Commit Distributed Transactions

One of the most widely studied families of patterns for coordinating activities is the family of distributed transaction protocols such as the two-phase commit protocol.[1] Figure 28–1 illustrates how this protocol can be employed to coordinate the updates of two participants. The scenario begins with the `application` interacting with a `transaction coordinator` to obtain an identifier for the transaction that is about to be executed. The `application` then interacts with both `participant A` and `participant B` to initiate the changes, passing along the transaction identifier as well as the information needed to actually make the changes. Each of the participants checks to see whether it is already participating in this transaction and registers itself with the coordinator if it is not. It then makes the changes in a manner that is not visible outside the transaction. After the application has finished initiating the

---

1. A more thorough description of the two-phase commit protocol can be found in Philip A. Bernstein and Eric Newcomer. 1997. *Principles of Transaction Processing for the Systems Professional*. San Francisco, CA: Morgan Kaufmann.

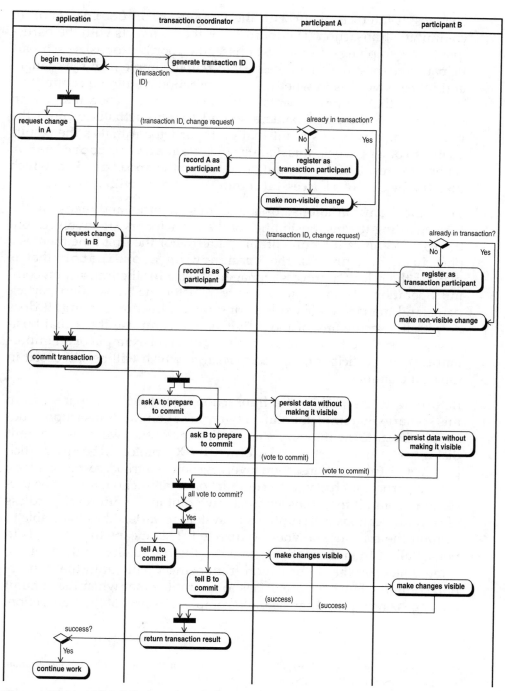

Figure 28–1: *Simplified Two-Phase Commit Scenario*

changes, it interacts again with the `transaction coordinator` to commit the transaction. The coordinator then interacts with the participants in two phases. In the first phase, the coordinator asks each participant to persist the data necessary to actually implement the changes and return a vote as to whether the transaction should be committed. Assuming that all participants vote to commit, the coordinator then interacts with the participants a second time to actually commit the transaction. It is at this point that each participant makes the results visible to other participants. Finally, the `transaction coordinator` reports the result of the commit operation to the `application`, which then (in the case of a successful commit) continues with its work.

There are many variations possible in this scenario, and many subtleties regarding the responsibilities of the participants are involved. But there is a significant feature of this pattern: For the first time there is a participant in a process, the `transaction coordinator`, that is playing the role of a process manager, at least for the transaction commit operation. Its sole purpose is to register the transaction participants and manage their work during the transaction commit. It does not, itself, execute any of the activities that comprise the actual business process. The `transaction manager` is an example of an important class of participant, a *process manager*, which will be discussed in the next chapter.

Returning to the notion of a transaction, it should be apparent from this scenario that implementing a two-phase commit transaction is not simple. Despite the industry standardization of the two-phase commit dialog between the parties in the form of the XA protocol,[2] being a participant in a distributed transaction involves some nontrivial responsibilities. Once a participant has voted "commit" on a transaction, it must be prepared to commit that transaction at any point in the future. Regardless of communications interruptions or system restarts, it has to be able to commit the transaction when so directed. This means that it needs to persist all of the information related to the transaction and yet at the same time keep that information from being visible until the transaction commits. Furthermore, it has to guarantee that when the commit message is received, it can actually complete its part of the transaction.

---

2. X/Open Company Ltd. 1991. *Distributed Transaction Processing: The XA Specification*. Reading, Berkshire UK: The Open Group.

Limitations of Two-Phase Commit Protocols

Much as you might like to take advantage of the ideal ACID benefits from a distributed transaction, there are several factors that limit the use of such transactions in practice:

1. Many systems do not support distributed transactions and thus cannot participate in a distributed transaction.

2. Consistency cannot always be guaranteed since communications and execution delays will make different participant's transaction results visible at different times.

3. Some real-world operations simply cannot be part of a two-phase commit transaction. These are operations whose actual execution cannot be guaranteed to always work. One example is the dispensing of cash from the ATM. The cash cannot be dispensed (i.e., the transaction results made available) until after the commit is received, yet according to the protocol must be dispensed reliably once the commit is received. How can you do this with a physical system since a mechanical failure of the cash dispenser can cause the commit operation to fail? Some operations are just not well-suited to be part of a distributed transaction.

4. The all-or-nothing atomicity of the transaction may not be appropriate for the business process. When one of the transaction participants becomes unavailable, no transaction can commit. This means that the portion of the business process following the transaction cannot execute until all parties are back online. From a business perspective, work halts.

This all-or-nothing behavior is generally not the desired behavior for most business processes. Most business processes call for some alternate course of action when one of the participants is temporarily unavailable, actions such as keeping track of what that participant was supposed to be doing and then playing catch-up when the participant comes back online.

Such alternate courses of action must be guided by a coordinator, but these courses of action are beyond the scope of the two-phase commit `transaction coordinator`. The mechanism commonly used to deal with participants that are unable to perform their required activities is the compensating transaction.

Compensating Transactions

You will be challenged to coordinate the activities of multiple participants without using two-phase commit transactions. Compensating transactions provide a useful alternative technique. A *compensating transaction* is simply a transaction that reverses the net effect of some previous transaction. If your bank accidentally deposits your paycheck twice, it does not correct the error by deleting one of the transactions: Instead, it executes a third transaction that debits your account by the amount of the excess deposit. This debit is an example of a compensating transaction.

Figure 28–2 is a scenario showing the use of compensating transactions. Here the application is doubling as the transaction manager for the transaction. To be clear, you have marked the logical boundaries of the transaction with begin and end activities even though these activities involve no work. The scenario begins with the application applying changes to both participants and getting a success/fail result from each in return. Note that with this approach these changes become immediately visible! Next, the application (in its role as transaction manager) checks to see whether all of the changes have been successful. If they are all successful, then the transaction is done. If any of them fail, however, then the compensating transactions need to be applied to any of the participants that previously reported success. After these compensating transactions have been applied, the net effect will be as if the transaction had never executed in the first place. At this point, alternative actions can be taken if needed.

Working around the Limitations of Compensating Transactions

As attractive as compensating transactions might be, not every action has a compensating transaction. Once you print a page, you can't take the ink back! However, compensating transactions can still be used even when there is one participant (but no more than one) that is incapable of performing a compensating transaction for its activity. This is accomplished by leaving that action for last. After all the other activities have been executed, the one without the compensating transaction is executed. If this action succeeds, then the work is done. If the action

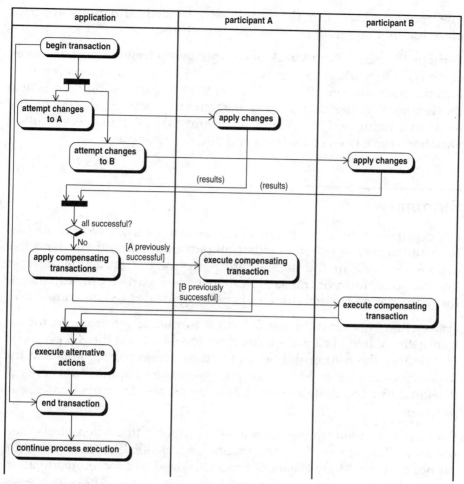

Figure 28–2: *Example Compensating Transaction Scenario*

fails, then the compensating transactions for the other actions can be executed.

The use of compensating transactions is not without its drawbacks. For one thing, participants expose the results of their actions immediately, even though they might need to be compensated for almost immediately. Therefore, the sequence in which the actions are performed must be carefully considered to minimize unwanted side-effects. Another drawback is that the compensating transactions themselves may fail—particularly if the root cause of failure is a communications breakdown.

The recovery logic can be complicated in such situations—a good place to rely upon manual recovery procedures.

Perhaps the biggest drawback of compensating transactions, however, is the need to actually design the coordination logic and incorporate it into the management process—that is the price of flexibility. It is also the reason that the design of management processes should be the focus of careful design reviews to ensure that all possible execution variations have been considered and addressed appropriately.

Summary

Conceptually, transactions coordinate the activities of two or more participants in such a way that either all parties perform their respective actions or none of the actions are performed. Transactions always involve some form of transaction manager—a participant responsible for coordinating the activities and ensuring the desired outcome.

Transaction coordination can be either formal or informal. In formal transactions, there is a well-defined protocol (such as the XA protocol) that defines the responsibilities of the transaction participants and the dialog between them. Many existing systems and applications are not designed to participate in such transactions, which limits their use in practice.

Formal distributed transactions have a property that often limits their use as well: If any of the participants are unavailable, the transaction cannot execute. Many business processes need to proceed using alternate logic when some participants are unavailable. These processes must employ other techniques as alternatives or supplements to formal distributed transactions.

Compensating transactions provide useful alternatives to formal distributed transactions. The compensating transaction undoes the net effect of a previous action and is invoked by the transaction coordinator to roll back the transaction after some other participant in the transaction fails.

Some actions, such as printing a page, do not have compensating transactions. It is still possible to include one such participant in a transaction when all the other participants have compensating transactions. The action without the compensating transaction is simply executed last: If it succeeds, the transaction is complete; if it fails, the compensating transactions on the other participants are executed to roll back the transaction.

Key Transaction Questions

1. Are there activities in the process whose execution must be treated as a transaction?
2. What type of transaction coordination is supported by the participants in the transaction? Do they support distributed transactions? Do they support compensating transactions?
3. Which component is playing the role of the transaction coordinator?

Suggested Reading

Bernstein, Philip A., and Eric Newcomer. 1997. *Principles of Transaction Processing for the Systems Professional*. San Francisco, CA: Morgan Kaufmann.

X/Open Company Ltd. 1991. *Distributed Transaction Processing: The XA Specification*. Reading, Berkshire, UK: The Open Group.

Chapter 29

Process Monitors and Managers

In the previous chapter, you saw that every transaction has a transaction coordinator—a participant whose job it is to manage the performance of activities by the transaction participants. This transaction coordinator is a specialized example of a *process manager*, a participant that coordinates the execution of activities. Generally, the manager also monitors the execution of the activities as well, determining whether they are executing as directed. A related role is that of the process monitor, a participant that monitors the execution of activities and compares the execution against an expected plan but does not manage the execution.

Regardless of whether the participant is managing or monitoring a process, it must have knowledge of the process structure. The process manager actually *defines* the portion of the process that it is managing by telling participants what to do and when to do it. A process monitor, on the other hand, has a model of the process against which it can compare the observed actions of the participants. The manager and monitor roles differ further when there are observed differences between the actual and desired behavior. The process manager, by virtue of the fact that it is directing the activities, can initiate recovery actions. The process monitor, on the other hand, can only announce the existence of a discrepancy. However, in either case, the observation of a discrepancy can be used to trigger activity that can improve the overall reliability and availability of the process.

Process managers and monitors provide an effective solution to a surprisingly complex and difficult problem in distributed systems: determining what is actually going on. This seemingly simple task can be astonishingly difficult to perform. An example will help to explain.

Figure 29–1 shows a simplified ordering process involving a customer, an order management system, and a warehouse. The customer is in a position to monitor the status of this process and detect breakdowns, assuming that response-time SLAs are in place for receiving the order acknowledgment and shipped goods. The problem is that from the enterprise perspective, none of the enterprise participants (i.e., the order management system or the warehouse) are in a position to detect breakdowns. The enterprise won't know anything has gone wrong unless the customer complains.

This lack of visibility into the status of business processes is a problem faced by many companies. In a highly competitive situation, it is not good practice to rely on customers to inform the enterprise that something has gone wrong with their business process. To manage the customer experience, the enterprise needs to be able to determine whether or not the business process is executing properly and to take corrective action if it is not. Let's take a look at how the enterprise could employ

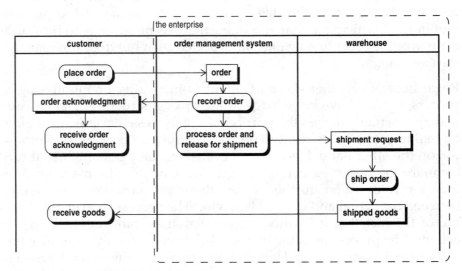

Figure 29–1: *Simplified Order Process*

process monitoring and process management to provide greater visibility into the process status.

Process Monitoring

One approach to improving process status visibility is to add a participant to the process whose sole responsibility is to monitor the process (Figure 29–2). The `process monitor` observes the events that trigger the start of activities and mark the completion of activities. The first event, the arrival of the `order`, causes the process monitor to note the beginning of a new process execution, noting its initial state. Subsequent events update the `order state`, and the monitor periodically checks to see whether there are events that should have occurred but have not. Any variation of the actual execution from the process model that indicates a problem results in the generation of an `exception alert`.

One of the challenges in monitoring is capturing the events—recognizing that meaningful things have happened to other participants. The monitor has to either retrieve status information from each of the participants (assuming that they even retain the appropriate status information) or directly recognize the events that mark status changes in the overall process. Consider the mechanism by which the `customer`

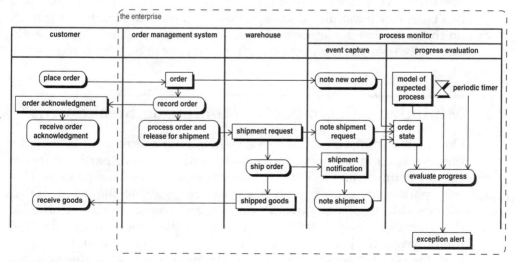

Figure 29–2: *Monitoring the Order Process*

places the `order` in this example. If the `customer` employs a user interface built into the `order management system`, there is no direct way for the `process monitor` to observe this event. Some means for recognizing this event will have to be added, perhaps involving an adapter (Chapter 18) monitoring the database underlying this application or the `process monitor` periodically polling the system to identify new orders. There is a similar problem with respect to the actual shipment: There is no way for the `process monitor` to directly observe the goods going onto the truck. The warehouse management system will have to be modified, perhaps through the use of an adapter, to either send a `shipment notification` or allow the `process monitor` to query for the status of the shipment.

Another issue of concern is the relationship between the tracking events and the details of the process itself. If you use events that are too tightly tied to the details of the process structure, then every time the process is modified you will have to update the process monitor as well. To avoid this problem, it is good practice to use abstracted process milestones for monitoring (these were discussed back in Chapter 10).

Regardless of whether you choose event recognition or periodically query for status, there is both design-time and runtime work involved in process monitoring. Status retrieval requires an interface, and the use of that interface will have an impact on performance. Event recognition has its own set of design problems and performance implications that were discussed in Chapter 18. The lesson here is that you can't just tack a monitor onto a process: You have to plan for its impact on the overall architecture and design. A failure to plan appropriately can easily result in a process that, literally, cannot be monitored.

Minimizing the Impact of Monitoring Breakdowns

One of the things you need to consider with monitoring is that the monitor itself and its communications with the other participants are subject to the same kind of breakdowns as the rest of the process. This is of particular concern with respect to recognizing the event that is supposed to trigger the overall process and trigger the monitoring of the process as well. If this event is missed (i.e., not recognized), then not only will the process not execute but the monitor will not be aware that it was supposed to execute. For this reason, it is good design practice to use the delegation pattern (or other request-reply exchange) for process initiation, and to include within the scope of this interaction both the initiation of the process and the initiation of the monitoring. With this approach, the party initiating the process (the `customer` in the case of the ordering process) will be able to tell that the process did not start correctly and take appropriate action.

Once monitoring has been initiated, it proceeds independently of the main process. At this point it will take a failure of both the business process and of the monitor for business process failures to go undetected. Because of this, you want to avoid failures that will bring down both the business process and the monitor. For critical processes, you may want to go so far as to host the monitor on a different machine than any of the other process participants, thus avoiding a single point of failure for the process and its monitor.

The Process Manager as a Monitor

It is not unusual to have one or more of the participants in a process actively manage the activities of other participants. In such situations, it is not difficult to extend the manager to become a monitor as well. After all, since the manager is directing the process (or at least a portion of it), it already knows what the process is supposed to look like.

For the manager to also be a monitor, the manager's knowledge of what is happening must be complete. This may require altering the coordination pattern being used to interact with the other participants to add synchronous or asynchronous feedback. Figure 29–3 shows the `order management system` extended to play both the role of process manager and process monitor. The primary modification is that the fire-and-forget interaction with the warehouse has been replaced with an asynchronous request-reply. This provides the `order management system` with feedback about the `warehouse` activities. The `order management system` also needs to be extended to periodically evaluate progress and check for activities that should have been completed, but have not.

One of the advantages of having the process manager also serve as the process monitor is that it can do more than simply announce the presence of an exception. While the example here shows the process manager only sending an alert, it could just as easily have taken an alternative course of action. In the previous chapter you saw an example of a possible alternative action in the form of the execution of a compensating

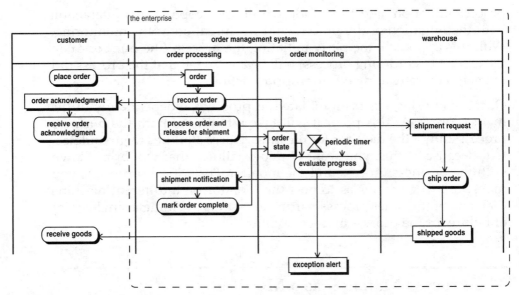

Figure 29–3: *Order Management System as a Process Manager*

transaction, but more constructive alternatives might be employed as well. For example, if processing of the order normally involves an interaction with a credit checking agency and that service is presently unavailable, the `order management system` might use alternative logic involving the customer's locally stored history to decide whether or not to accept the order. The presence of a process manager offers you as much flexibility as your imagination.

Extending a process manager to be a process monitor does involve some extra work—but significantly less work than adding an independent process monitor. Much of this work is simply choosing appropriate coordination patterns so that the manager is aware of the status of other participants' activities. Remember, however, that in order to interpret the absence of a response, a response-time SLA must be established for the performance of the work, and the process monitor must check to see whether the work is actually completed on time.

Process Management Limitations

Ideally, a management process's span of control would cover an entire business process from start to finish. Its coverage would begin with the recognition of the triggering event for the overall process and end with the confirmation of delivery of the final result. It would actively control all of the activity in between. But this assumes that the manager is actually in control throughout the entire process—an assumption that is rarely valid in practice.

To begin with, the process manager is typically not in control at the beginning of the business process. There is almost always at least one handoff of responsibility among participants before the manager even gets involved. For example, when an ATM is being used (which we will envision as the process manager for the moment), the machine is not initially managing the withdraw cash process—the customer is! The customer decides what PIN to enter and when to do it. The customer decides what transaction is desired and how much money is involved. In fact, up to the moment that the customer enters the amount to be withdrawn, the customer is managing the process.

At the moment that the customer hits "Enter" after specifying the amount to be withdrawn, there is a handoff of responsibility from the customer to the ATM. The machine now manages a portion of the withdraw cash process, getting approval from the bank for the withdrawal, dispensing the funds, notifying the bank that the funds were delivered, and printing the receipt. But once these activities have been completed, the responsibility for managing the remainder of the process is once again up to the customer. Nobody is going to force the customer to remove the cash from the slot in the machine or take the receipt. The customer is, once again, in control.

In situations such as this, you often find that the participant managing a portion of the process is also monitoring more of the business process than it is actually managing. The ATM is very aware that the customer is setting up a transaction and knows whether or not the customer has actually removed the cash. It is an observer of those portions of the process that the customer is managing as well as those portions over which it has direct control. So when you are specifying this component, you need to be clear about both the management and monitoring responsibilities. Based on these responsibilities, you need to determine the required interactions between the management/monitoring component and the other participants in the process in order to execute these responsibilities.

Summary

Process managers and process monitors play important roles in the overall business process. Not only are they key participants in terms of their responsibilities, but they are the source and destination for much of the communications traffic involved in the execution of the business process. Because of the importance of these roles, whenever a process manager or monitor is added to a process, it needs to be added to all top-level activity diagrams that characterize the operation of the business process at the technical level. In addition, any process manager needs to be added to the business process activity diagrams as well. This reflects the fact that the assignment of management activities to the process manager is actually a business process design decision—one that needs to be understood and evaluated by both business and IT personnel.

There are many design issues associated with the use of process monitors and managers. A few have been touched upon in this chapter, but only lightly. The discussion of these roles will continue further in Chapter 38, which considers process monitoring in more detail, and in Chapter 42, which considers the complexities of process management and workflow design.

Key Process Monitoring and Management Questions

1. Is a process monitor or manager being used? Which portions of the process are being managed and which portions are being monitored? Do the coordination patterns being used to direct or observe the work enable it to reliably detect breakdowns?

2. What actions will the process monitor/manager take when a breakdown is detected? Are these actions adequate and appropriate given the business consequences of the breakdown?

Chapter 30

Detecting and Responding to Breakdowns

Earlier chapters examined a number of coordination patterns, ranging from simple fire-and-forget up through the use of process monitors and managers. Now it is time to stand back and evaluate the overall process design and determine which combinations of these coordination patterns should be employed. Since you have already considered the normal operation of the process in bringing the design this far, the primary remaining consideration is breakdown detection.

Selecting Coordination Patterns to Improve Breakdown Detection

Up to this point, although you have arrived at some business-level understanding of what can go wrong with the business process, you have pretty much been focusing on the "sunny day" scenarios. For the most part, your choices of coordination patterns have been driven by the simple need to get a result from one participant to another. Now you want to explore the robustness of the design. In particular, you want to ask yourself whether selecting alternative coordination patterns might improve the system's ability to detect, report, and respond to breakdowns in the process.

The use of activity diagrams to represent scenarios makes this exploration of breakdowns a fairly straightforward process. The thought process is as follows:

1. For each participant in the process, consider what would happen if that component ceased to function. What would the symptoms be? Which participants, if any, are in a position to detect the breakdown?

2. For each communication in the process, consider what would happen if that communication failed. Again, what would the symptoms be? Which participants, if any, are in a position to detect the breakdown?

3. Would changes to the coordination patterns improve the ability to detect breakdowns in the process and otherwise monitor the overall process? Do the consequences of undetected breakdowns warrant making such changes?

Take a look at the example in Figure 30–1. There are five possible failures in this scenario: the loss of any of the three participants and the loss of either communication. A quick examination of this activity diagram will lead you to recognize the multi-party fire-and-forget coordination discussed in Chapter 27. This type of coordination cannot detect any breakdowns in the process. If this is an important business process, undetectable breakdowns are probably not acceptable—so you need to consider how to alter the coordination to improve the breakdown detection.

One of the things you can do to make breakdown detection possible is to add some feedback in the form of a `status report` as shown in Figure 30–2. Here, `participant C` sends the `status report` after it has finished handling the `result`, and `participant A` is waiting for that report. Now there are six possible failures in this scenario: the loss of any of the three participants and the loss of any of the three communications. In examining the diagram, it should be readily apparent that the loss of `participant A` still cannot be detected (at least by any of the participants in the scenario). So there is still a weak spot in the design, but one that might be mitigated by the addition of a component monitor that can determine whether `participant A` is alive and well.

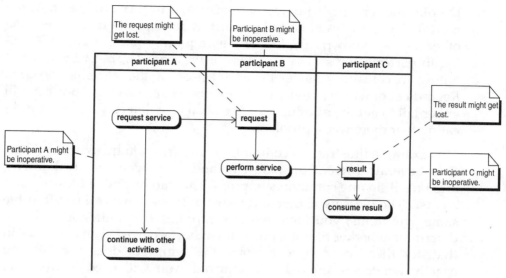

Figure 30–1: *Breakdown Analysis of a Simple Process*

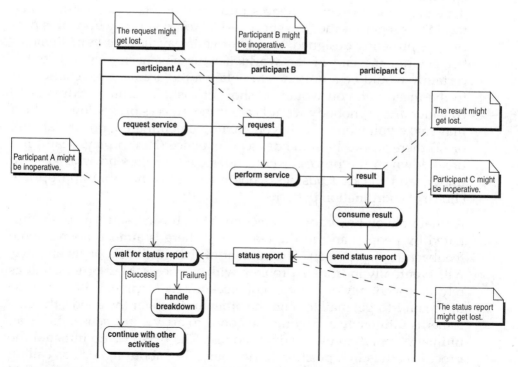

Figure 30–2: *Modified Process to Improve Breakdown Detection*

Despite the inability to detect a breakdown in `participant A`, the modified process puts `participant A` in a position to detect the other five breakdowns: the loss of the `request`, `participant B` failing to perform the service, the loss of the `result`, `participant C` failing to consume the result, or the loss of the `status report`. Regardless of which of these breakdowns occurs, `participant A` will either fail to get the `status report` at all or will receive a report indicating that there was a problem.

This example illustrates a common phenomenon in breakdown detection: Several different breakdowns, and even types of breakdowns, often result in one common symptom. This can be both a blessing and a curse. The blessing is that since several breakdowns all result in the same symptoms, you have fewer symptoms to monitor in order to determine whether or not a breakdown has occurred. The curse lies in that, for these very same reasons, the symptom does not tell you exactly where the breakdown occurred. You will need to do more investigation to determine the root cause of the symptom.

Determining the right coordination patterns to employ largely depends upon the consequences of a breakdown. One useful litmus test in this regard is the "paycheck test": Would you rely upon this process, as presently designed, to deliver your paycheck to you? Remember, it's not the end of the world if your paycheck gets lost, but it certainly would be a nuisance to obtain a replacement paycheck, and in the meantime you would be short of cash. Two other extremes to consider are: (1) nobody would care if the process broke down (which may make you wonder why you are implementing the process at all!); or (2) there would be some dire consequence (bankruptcy, death) if a breakdown in the process went undetected. In the end, you need to understand the true business consequences to make an appropriate choice of coordination patterns.

A final note on breakdown detection: Most business processes are initiated by people, and in the real world there is almost always some feedback to that person. The content of that feedback, or its absence, will eventually indicate a problem with a process. Mail-order catalogs rely almost entirely on this form of breakdown detection. Despite the use of fire-and-forget mail to send the order and deliver the goods, the customer is ultimately expecting the goods to arrive. In a sense, this is an ultimate "reply" to the original request. The person who initiated the process is thus in a position to do something about it, such as calling customer service. But in the competitive environments businesses find themselves in today, it is generally not a good practice to rely on your customers to tell you that your business process is broken! You want to build breakdown detection into the portion of the business process over which you have control in order to manage the customer experience.

Responding to Breakdowns

The discussion up to now has focused on detecting breakdowns; now it is time to consider what you ought to do when one occurs. There are many possibilities, ranging from completely ignoring it, recording it, or announcing it, to recovering from it either manually or automatically. The possibilities are nearly endless—but whatever you do a cost will be associated with it, both at design time and runtime. Once again, you must let the consequences of the breakdown guide you in deciding what to do.

Recording Breakdowns

Since you have gone to the trouble of detecting the breakdown, it is good practice to at least make a record of it. Of course, this will require some runtime resources, and the use of those resources will have a performance impact. Thus, you need to understand what that impact will be and determine whether it is acceptable. To understand the impact, you will need to know how much information will be recorded and the rate at which breakdowns are likely to occur. Let's look at a couple of examples that illustrate the possible extremes in this regard.

Consider the loss of a low-level data packet in a network TCP/IP protocol. While this is not something you would normally have to worry about at the application design level, it illustrates the extreme of high-volume breakdowns very nicely. Packet losses can happen at extremely high rates if there is noise on the network. Typically the network interface card (NIC), which is the hardware in the computer that handles its interaction with the network, detects and recovers from this particular type of breakdown automatically. It detects the loss of a packet and requests that the missing packet be retransmitted.

If the NIC card is automatically recovering from the error, why would you want to make a record of the breakdown? Because the packet loss may be an indication of network problems, ones that will require additional action to resolve. So what kind of record should you keep for these particular breakdowns? In practice, the computer doing the communications counts them and holds this count in memory. The operating system can be configured to periodically log the error count.

In this particular instance, the breakdowns (losses of individual packets) can occur at a relatively high rate, perhaps caused by a modem operating over a noisy phone connection. If you were to record a lot of information about each breakdown, the potential high rate of breakdowns could potentially consume system resources at a high rate. But this particular breakdown is of relatively little consequence unless the error rate gets very high. As a result, systems typically record only the minimal amount of information regarding each breakdown—a count. The information of interest here is not about the individual breakdowns, but the rate at which they are occurring.

Consider now a different extreme—one in which detailed information about each breakdown must be recorded. In the course of daily business, banks routinely transfer funds to other banks. A single inter-bank funds transfer can involve billions of dollars. When a breakdown is detected in this process, you need to know a great deal about the breakdown, for you will want to recover from this breakdown by completing the disrupted transaction. To do this, you need to know how much money was being transferred, what bank it was coming from, and what bank it was going to. You may also need transaction identifiers, time-stamps, and other pieces of data. The systems will need to record enough information so that you can recover from the breakdown as if it had never occurred (except for the time lag in completing the operation).

Once you decide to make a record of the breakdown and determine what information needs to be recorded, you must then design that portion of the process that does the actual recording. You must determine which components are involved, what their individual responsibilities are, and what communications will be required to execute the recording. *A significant factor to consider in the design of breakdown recording is that you expect to be recording breakdowns in the presence of system failures!* In particular, disruptions in communications are to be expected at least some of the time. Because of this, you do not want the breakdown recording to be totally dependent upon the proper operation of the communications infrastructure. You want the component that detects the breakdown to make a record of the breakdown using as few moving parts as possible. This usually boils down to having the component itself recording the breakdown, as illustrated in Figure 30–3. Then, if

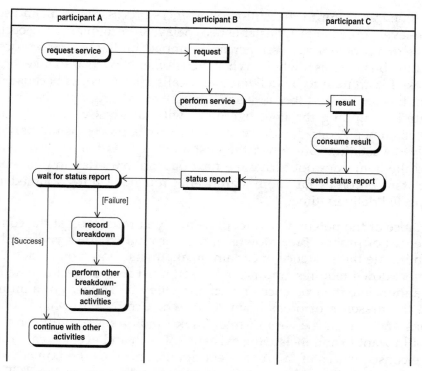

Figure 30–3: *Preferred Breakdown Recording Pattern*

communications permits, a notification of the breakdown can be sent to interested parties.

Annunciating Breakdowns

Simply recording the fact that a breakdown occurred is often not enough. Many times you will want to bring the breakdown to someone's attention so that something can be done about it. Logging a breakdown in a file will not, in and of itself, accomplish this. Unfortunately, there is a design tendency to log lots of information about breakdowns but not consider what ought to happen next. The data languishes in log files until someone suspects the existence of a problem, usually after some larger breakdown occurs that happens to be observable. At that point, a forensic search of log files begins as you seek an understanding of the nature and location of the problem.

The problem with simply recording breakdowns is that it may be a long time before someone becomes aware of the existence of a breakdown.

As time frames for the execution of business processes shrink and service-level agreements are established, delays in recognizing the occurrence of a problem have an increasing impact on the business process and the business as a whole. When a customer expects it to take 4 to 6 weeks for an item to be delivered and calls after 6 weeks because the item has not arrived (because something went wrong), you can remediate by shipping the item overnight without greatly disappointing the customer. A one-day delay in a 4- to 6-week process is not particularly devastating. But when the customer expects next-day delivery and the item does not arrive the next day, an extra day in delivering the item becomes far more significant. You have now doubled the expected delivery time.

Because of the potential impact of delays, you must look at the consequences of process breakdowns and determine whether you need to annunciate the existence of certain breakdowns. Once you decide that a breakdown requires annunciation, you must further decide whether to annunciate the existence of each and every breakdown or annunciate the presence of breakdowns only when certain threshold conditions are met. In the case of inter-bank funds transfer, you certainly would want to annunciate the existence of each and every breakdown. The consequences of failure are enormous, and must be immediately and individually addressed. By contrast, in the case of the TCP/IP packet loss, you don't want to annunciate the existence of packet losses unless they are happening frequently. Since the protocol itself recovers lost packets (under most conditions), you don't really need to take any additional action until the frequency of packet loss begins to impact the overall efficiency of the communications infrastructure or the packet losses become unrecoverable. Consequently, while you might be recording the existence of packet losses, you would probably not annunciate the existence of packet losses unless the rate of packet loss exceeds some threshold or packets become unrecoverable.

Responding to Breakdown Annunciations

The intent of annunciation, of course, is to make someone aware of the existence of a problem. This is often mistakenly viewed as purely a technical design problem, but you need to be aware that it is a business process and an organizational design problem as well. Someone needs to respond to the annunciation, and you need to look beyond simply determining who should be notified and how. You need to understand what these people will be doing once they have been notified. As they investigate and recover from the problem, they will need interfaces to the system components to examine and modify information.

Understanding what people are doing in the recovery process will help you to determine what information they need in order to investigate the problem. This can impact the information content of the announcement itself. If you are recovering from a failure of an inter-bank funds transfer, you may need the transaction identifier so that you can locate the specific transaction record in a system and update the transaction status. This may impact the design of the breakdown announcement to include sufficient information to determine (directly or indirectly) the transaction identifier. Interfaces to perform the system status update and to update the account balances will also be required. Recovery may need to re-initiate all or part of a larger business process to recover from the breakdown. The funds transfer, for example, may be part of a stock trade settlement, and the remainder of the stock settlement must be completed as well.

All of these activities have implications for both the business process design and the system design. The breakdown recovery is, itself, a business process. This process may consist of just one activity, `Find and Fix the Problem`, but it is nonetheless a process that must be executed. You need to understand the requirements surrounding this business process. Do you need to track this process and note the ultimate resolution? Are there key performance indicators and service-level agreements related to the recovery process? Recall the case study in Chapter 11 in which the telecommunications company was losing money because its breakdown recovery process was itself breaking down. Recovery processes themselves may need to be monitored and managed.

From a technical perspective, you need to understand what activities are being (or might be) performed in the recovery process, particularly when these activities involve people interacting with systems. You need to understand whether the system interfaces already exist to support these activities, and whether those interfaces are suitable for the intended purpose. From a purely technical perspective you may think that a generic SQL user interface can be used to update the database, but will this unfettered access satisfy the audit requirements for a banking system? Do you instead need to implement an interface with controlled access and audit trails to support this recovery? Do the risks warrant the development of these specialized interfaces? These are all questions you must consider, and to be cost-effective you need to do so while the design is in its formative stages.

Before going deeper into the recovery process, let us return for a moment to consider the basic annunciation of the breakdown. In contrast with the basic recording of breakdowns, which is best done by the component recording the breakdown, it makes a lot of sense to centralize the annunciation of breakdowns. The alternative requires that people monitor each system individually for breakdown reports, and this quickly becomes impractical in large-scale enterprise systems. Typically you will end up with a breakdown-reporting pattern similar to that shown in Figure 30–4.

Once you have decided that you need a common breakdown reporting service, you must consider its design. Which participant will provide this service? What vehicle will be used for communications? What will the information content of the communication be? What type of coordination and breakdown detection should be used in the interaction between the component reporting the breakdown and the breakdown

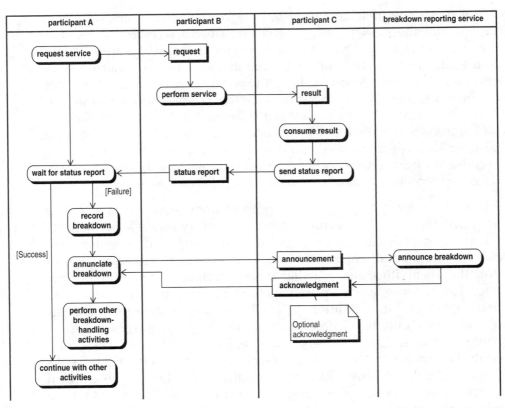

Figure 30–4: *Breakdown Reporting*

reporting service itself? Sound familiar? It's the same design approach already being discussed. Annunciation is just another process with which this process happens to interact. Once again, you need to be guided by the business impact of breakdowns in deciding what approach is reasonable.

A side note is in order here regarding documenting the handling of breakdowns. If you update every activity diagram to show the handling of every possible breakdown by every component participating in the process, the diagrams will quickly become cluttered with the interactions between the participants and the breakdown reporting service. On the other hand, the design for reporting breakdowns needs to be absolutely clear and requires this level of detail—somewhere. The practical compromise is to document, for each type of participant, how that participant type will interact with the error reporting system. Figure 30–5 presents an example of documenting the breakdown reporting pattern. You need to do this for each type of participant because the pattern will likely vary depending on the technology used to implement the participant. Thus for each specific combination of technologies involved, you will need to document the details of how the general pattern will be implemented.

Once the pattern for recording and reporting breakdowns has been documented, you can simplify the activity diagram that employs the pattern, as shown in Figure 30–6. Now, instead of showing the entire pattern each time it is used, you simply include an activity that indicates which pattern is being invoked. You are essentially showing the invocation of a service.

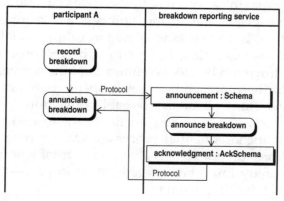

Figure 30–5: *Record and Annunciate Breakdown Pattern for Participant A*

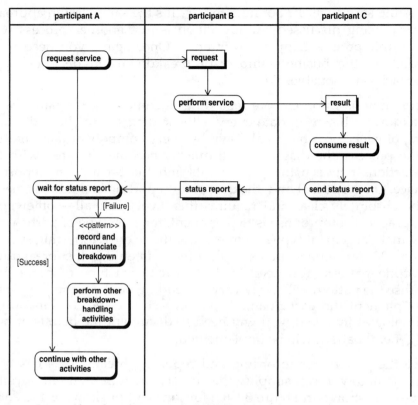

Figure 30–6: *Shorthand Notation for Breakdown Recording and Reporting*

Recovering from Breakdowns

Beyond simply making a record of breakdowns and annunciating their existence, in most cases the business process will require taking some additional action. But what kind of action is appropriate? This is an open-ended design question, to be sure. The response to a business process breakdown can be more complex than the normal execution of the process! Furthermore, you can easily spend more time considering how to recover from all of the possible breakdowns than you do designing the core process. You do not want to make this kind of investment for inconsequential processes. On the other hand, when there are billions of dollars involved in a transaction, breakdown recovery is a pretty important consideration in process design. How do you go about deciding what to do?

There are several questions you can ask yourself to help in this decision making:

1. Is the process, as presently designed, already resilient to the breakdown? At what point will this resiliency itself fail?
2. Is the recovery of work in progress required?
3. Should breakdown recovery be automated or manual?

Resiliency

Many processes are, by design, somewhat resilient to short-term breakdowns. Often this resiliency takes the form of buffering in the communications infrastructure. One participant is communicating with another via a Java messaging service (JMS), but the recipient of the messages goes offline for some reason. The messages destined for that recipient accumulate in the JMS server until the recipient comes back online. At this point, the recipient can catch up with the backlog of messages.

Of course, whether or not this buffering offers any benefit depends upon the design of the overall process. If the backlog of messages represents requests from users who are sitting at workstations waiting for responses within a few seconds, then this resiliency only offers benefits for a second or two. At the other extreme, you must consider that any form of buffer has a finite capacity. If the breakdown persists long enough, you will exceed that capacity. The resiliency will, itself, break down.

The TCP/IP communications protocol provides an example of another form of resiliency—an automatic retry. When a TCP/IP communications packet gets lost, the sender and intended recipient work together to redeliver the lost packet. However, if the communications channel is noisy enough or communication is lost altogether, it may not be possible to redeliver these packets. Again, the resiliency itself will break down.

What both of these examples illustrate is that even resilient designs have limits beyond which some action must be taken. When buffer limits are about to be reached, when communications channels become noisy enough, some form of action must be taken to prevent even greater problems. Thus when there is resiliency in the design, you must determine the practical limits of this resiliency. You must then determine how to detect the breakdown of the resiliency (or preferably anticipate the breakdown), who will be notified, and what actions will be required. For example, it may be better to shut down the upstream message publisher than to overwhelm the communications intermediary and lose data. It may be better to tell the bank that you can't perform the requested funds transfer than to lose a $20 billion transaction in progress!

Recovering Work in Progress

When a breakdown occurs, there is likely to be work in progress. What should be done with this work in progress? Should an attempt be made to complete it, or should it be written off? The answer will vary, depending upon the business process. Some process results only have value if they are delivered in a timely manner. Stock-market ticker information becomes obsolete the moment the next transaction involving that stock occurs. If this information is being delivered to a casual investor, is there any value in recovering the obsolete ticker entries? If there are interactive user queries in progress but the user is no longer waiting for the reply, is there any value in completing the query?

The reason you want to ask this question is that recovering work in progress after a breakdown is not free. There is real cost associated with designing, implementing, and testing the recovery process, and there is a runtime cost associated with the actual recovery. Furthermore, the recovery process is, itself, subject to breakdown. How much of this should you consider? The design changes needed to accommodate breakdown recovery will most likely require the persistence of information that would not otherwise have been persisted. This will have a performance impact on the business process. Before such costs are incurred, you want to ensure that the investment is warranted.

Once you have decided that some form of work-in-progress recovery is desirable, you can then embark upon the design of the recovery process. While the variations are endless, there are a couple of work-in-progress recovery strategies that are worth mentioning. One is to log the operations that need to be performed by the offline participant and then execute those operations once the participant is back on line. When you consider this approach, you must remember that this logging and replay is itself a process that is subject to breakdown. This can lead to complex recovery designs that are more trouble than they are worth.

Another recovery strategy is to use an alternate process that simply bypasses the failed operation, possibly employing alternate logic. If an order entry process calls for a credit check and the credit checking service is offline or unreachable, the business may want to employ alternate business rules rather than wait for the credit-checking service to come back online. The business might want to employ a business rule saying that for customers in good standing, the order will be accepted without the credit check, and for the rest a supervisor will be asked to make a judgment call as to whether the order should be accepted. Note that this is not a technical decision, but a business decision. You must get the business people involved in the discussion to determine which business processes warrant such alternate strategies.

Automated versus Manual Recovery Implementation

By and large, architects are technically oriented and tend to favor automated solutions. But when it comes to error recovery, automation should be approached cautiously. There are two reasons for this caution. First, a fully automated recovery from all possible errors is a notoriously complex design problem and is rarely worth the effort. You can easily spend much more time designing the automated breakdown recovery than you spend on the proper operation of the business process. It is unlikely that this will be a good investment. Second, and perhaps more telling, is that your ability to predict the breakdowns that actually occur in practice tends to be very poor. The number of relatively independent components found in distributed systems present so many possible combinations of failures, including combinations of shutdown and startup sequences, that it is virtually impossible to identify them all, let alone consider their consequences.

Given this complexity, it is generally not a good idea to automate error recovery based solely on speculation concerning what might go wrong. Instead, the initial design focus should be on the detection and appropriate annunciation of the problem and on the requirements for supporting a manual recovery processes. Even the manual recovery process itself will impact the design. It may require information that is not normally presented to users, such as primary keys for database records. It may require user interfaces to examine and modify information. Even though the manual recovery process involves some degree of speculation, it tends to be far simpler (and thus less costly) than automating breakdown recovery. Your initial focus should be on understanding the manual recovery process and making sure it is practical.

Once you have the tools to support a manual recovery in place, you can then complete and deploy the system. With the system in operation, you will be in a position to learn the types of breakdowns that actually occur in practice. Furthermore, you will gain experience in diagnosing such problems and recovering from them. Over time, as experience builds up handling real errors, you will learn which errors occur frequently enough to be annoying and how to diagnose and recover from those errors. In other words, you will learn enough to automate the recovery from those errors.

Of course, this strategy assumes that the volume of breakdowns can, in fact, be handled by support personnel, and further assumes that the delays involved in manual recovery are acceptable. If neither condition is met, then you will have to consider some form of automated assistance in the recovery process. But you must keep in mind that whatever you do needs to be practical and cost effective.

Summary

The coordination patterns you select directly impact the ability of participants to detect breakdowns in the business process. Simply adding one feedback communication can add the ability to detect breakdowns and thus preserve the integrity of the process. It is good practice to add sufficient feedback within the enterprise's business processes to detect breakdowns without relying on input from customers and business partners.

Simply detecting a breakdown does not provide any benefit. The existence of the breakdown has to be made known to those who must take action. Annunciating the existence of breakdowns requires design work as well as some understanding of organizational responsibilities for handling breakdowns.

Breakdown recovery, whether manual or automated, also requires design work and an understanding of the actions required to execute the recovery. For manual recovery, the requirements generally focus on the needed user interfaces. For automated recovery, the logic of diagnosis and the specific recovery action sequence must also be known. Automated recovery can be expensive, time consuming, and error prone. It is good practice to begin with manual recovery (where feasible), and then use the knowledge gained through the repeated diagnosis and recovery from specific breakdowns to automate just those specific recoveries.

Key Breakdown Detection and Recovery Questions

1. What coordination patterns are being used in the business processes currently being designed? Do they afford the opportunity to detect breakdowns in the process? Would the use of different coordination patterns improve the ability to detect breakdowns?

2. Which participants in the business process are in a position to detect breakdowns? What actions will they take when a breakdown is detected? Is the action appropriate given the business consequences of the breakdown?

3. If breakdown recovery is a manual process, is sufficient information being provided in the breakdown announcement to identify the work in progress that was impacted? Are the user interfaces sufficient to support diagnosis? Are they sufficient to support the needed recovery actions?

Chapter 31

Enterprise Architecture: Coordination

While every project and process design needs to consider coordination issues, there are a number of these issues that are best addressed by the enterprise architecture group rather than by individual projects.

Preferred Coordination Patterns

When coordination patterns are selected, the choice of pattern will determine the responsibilities of the individual participants with respect to the detection, recording, annunciation, and recovery related to breakdowns. Selecting different coordination patterns results in different responsibility assignments. Selecting different patterns for different business processes involving the same participants can create somewhat of a problem: The breakdown-related responsibilities of each participant will differ depending upon the business process. There will be no consistency in the roles that the participants play with respect to breakdowns, and you will not be able to broadly state what the breakdown-related role of a given participant is.

Such variability makes it very difficult to understand the behavior of a distributed system under adverse conditions. Since this is already a complex problem, you don't want to make matters worse. Consequently, it is in everyone's best interest to achieve a level of consistency from one process to another in terms of the specific breakdown-related responsibilities of each participant.

So how do you achieve consistency? You start by recognizing that, most likely, different business processes will be addressed in different projects. If you leave the decision making related to coordination and breakdown detection up to individual project teams, you are very likely to end up with different coordination patterns, and thus different breakdown-related responsibility assignments.

The way to go about achieving consistency is to have the enterprise architecture group participate in the establishment of coordination patterns. This group establishes the preferred patterns of coordination between the participants in business processes (both human and system). These patterns actually constitute the definition of an architectural "style" that indicates how these participants will interact. The style is documented by taking representative business processes and architecting them in the manner we have been describing. These style definitions are placed in a central repository.

When a project team needs to implement a new business process, it can determine what basic communications pattern is required by the business process and then locate the corresponding coordination pattern in the central repository. This approach assumes that similar patterns will be found in multiple business processes, but this is indeed the case for a large percentage of the business processes in a given enterprise.

To make this approach work, the enterprise architecture group must be prepared to quickly engage any project team that cannot find a suitable coordination pattern in the existing collection. This engagement may either review a coordination pattern proposed by the project team or it may actively design the required pattern. The end result will be a properly engineered and reviewed pattern. If it appears that this pattern will be used again, it should be appropriately documented and added to the coordination pattern library. In this way, the library can grow organically rather than having its creation be a project in and of itself.

In defining these coordination patterns, you need to make practical concessions to reality. One reality constraint is that there are liable to be a lot of legacy business processes out there that will not conform to the defined coordination patterns. You cannot afford, in the literal sense, to immediately modify all of these business processes to conform to the chosen coordination patterns. Instead, treat the coordination pattern as an ideal end-point design. If a project happens to be working on a particular business process, it should take every available opportunity to evolve that process's coordination pattern towards this ideal.

The other concession to reality is that many of the participants in the processes are liable to be software processes that are commercial off-the-shelf (COTS) products. You have little or no control over the design of these products. Thus you have little control over the coordination patterns they are designed to use on their interfaces. The selection of coordination patterns must take these limitations into account.

Breakdown Recording

Breakdown recording is one of those things that every participant in every process will most likely have to do. Rather than have project teams constantly reinvent this wheel, it makes sense to standardize the mechanisms that will be used for breakdown recording. This standardization extends to defining the formats that will be used for these records. Once again, the responsibility for establishing such standards belongs to the enterprise architecture group.

In standardizing the recording of breakdowns, you need to keep in mind that you want to do this recording with a minimum number of moving parts. This generally means that the actual recording of the breakdown needs to be implemented in a technology-specific manner. For each implementation technology in use, you will need to design and implement the recording mechanism. The enterprise architecture group should specify this mechanism and oversee its implementation and testing. A library of technology-specific breakdown recording implementations should be maintained.

The enterprise architecture group should also provide guidelines indicating when breakdowns should be recorded and what information should be included. In specifying this information, some level of standardization in the recording is beneficial, but you want to preserve the flexibility to record varying amounts of process-specific information as well. Each process will have its own unique requirements in terms of the data needed to understand the nature of the breakdown and recover from it.

In recording breakdowns, some concessions to reality are again required when COTS products are employed. Choices regarding when log entries are made will be limited to those provided by the product, and the information content and format are similarly limited. Thus while there may be a desire to establish a globally uniform format for log entries, pragmatics dictate that you will have to deviate from this ideal when COTS products are involved.

Breakdown Annunciation

While breakdown detection is generally done by the participant in a technology-specific manner, you generally want to provide one common mechanism through which multiple participants can annunciate the existence of breakdowns. As this is a common service that spans multiple projects and participants, its specification and architecture must be the responsibility of the enterprise architecture group. This group should also oversee the implementation, testing, and operation of this breakdown annunciation service.

While the annunciation service itself can be standardized, its invocation must, by definition, be technology specific. The mechanisms for sending an announcement to this service from a Java program running on a UNIX server will be different than for sending it from a COBOL program running on a mainframe. Thus, complementing the annunciation service, you need a library of technology-specific invocation mechanisms. The specification of these mechanisms is also the responsibility of the enterprise architecture group, as is the oversight of their implementation and testing. More often than not, this functionality will be bundled with the technology-specific breakdown recording library that has been developed for the technology.

Again, concessions to reality may be required when it comes to using COTS products. Generally these products will not have the ability to send this type of alert message. In such cases, you may want to monitor the log created by the product and have this monitor send the alert. The enterprise architecture group should specify the manner in which this should be done for each COTS product and provide a reference implementation that projects can use to guide their own implementation. As part of this, the enterprise architecture group should specify the specific technologies to be used for monitoring the log and sending the alerts.

Recovery Processes

While recovery processes are the most variable and open-ended aspect of coordination and breakdown handling, there is generally a lot of basic commonality in recovery processes. Who gets notified initially (first-tier support), how problems are tracked, how resolutions are recorded, and how problems are escalated (second- and third-tier support) are generally standardized in the enterprise (or at least ought to be). You don't want each project team to have to go through the learning curve of unraveling these questions and understanding the answers.

You also have to recognize that the recovery from breakdowns involves more than systems—it involves people, and typically people in multiple organizations. The passing of responsibility from organization to organization and the decisions about how to track and measure recovery operations are business considerations, not IT decisions. There is process design work here, and it needs to be treated like any other process design.

While the enterprise architecture group is generally not responsible for all the decision making that drives the design of these generic recovery processes, it is very much responsible for the resulting process design and its implementation. As such, it needs to make sure that the recovery process is well-defined and well-understood. It then needs to specify the technical underpinnings of the breakdown handling process and oversee its design, implementation, and operation. This is a business process that needs to be handled like any other.

Summary

The choice of a coordination pattern determines which participants in the process are in a position to detect breakdowns. Different choices result in different breakdown detection responsibilities. When the same participant is involved in multiple business processes, such differences make it difficult to understand how the architecture, as a whole, responds to breakdowns. For consistency and clarity, the enterprise architecture group should establish standard coordination patterns as a means of standardizing breakdown detection responsibilities.

Breakdowns need to be recorded and annunciated. Generally, at least a portion of these activities must be performed in the technology used to implement the participant. For consistency, it makes sense for the enterprise architecture group to specify and oversee the implementation of a standard set of recording and annunciation mechanisms.

Manual recovery processes involve organizational responsibilities as well as technical design. It is not efficient for each project to have to determine what these responsibilities are. The enterprise architecture group should document the manual recovery process and the corresponding organizational responsibilities. It should also design and oversee the implementation of the technical interfaces to the annunciation and tracking systems being employed in this process.

Key Enterprise Coordination Questions

1. Has the enterprise architecture group established standard coordination patterns with standardized breakdown detection responsibilities? Are projects being reviewed for compliance?

2. Has the enterprise architecture group established standard breakdown logging and annunciation practices? Is there a library of technology-specific logging and annunciation implementations? Are projects being reviewed for compliance?

3. Have manual recovery procedures been documented? Have the interfaces to the annunciation and tracking systems associated with these procedures been defined and implemented? Are projects being reviewed for compliance?

Part VII

High Availability, Fault Tolerance, and Load Distribution

Chapter 32

High Availability and Fault Tolerance Fundamentals

Earlier chapters have broadly considered the subject of detecting and responding to breakdowns in business processes, and they have touched upon some of the recovery actions that might be taken when breakdowns occur. This chapter narrows the focus to one particular type of breakdown and one specific type of recovery action. The breakdown is the loss of a participant in the business process, and the recovery action is the automatic replacement of the failed participant with another participant.

There are actually two closely related but subtly different strategies for the automatic replacement of a failed component. One is termed *fault tolerance (FT)* and the other *high availability (HA)*, and there are significant behavioral differences between the two. It is worth spending a little time exploring these concepts and their differences for several reasons. One is that an understanding of the behavior is required to understand the resulting behavior of a business process employing these strategies. The second is that there is usually a substantial cost differential between high availability (lower cost) and fault tolerance (higher cost). You need to understand this difference as well as the behavioral difference in order to make the right choice for your solution. The third reason is that in much of today's sales and marketing literature, products claim to be fault tolerant when they really provide high availability. You need to understand how to recognize what the product truly offers so that you know what you are actually getting and can design accordingly.

Fault Tolerance Strategies

A fault-tolerant process is a process that continues to function properly without interruption despite the failure of one of its participants. This obviously requires at least one additional participant capable of playing the role of the failed participant. There are two general strategies regarding how the backup participants get involved when the failure occurs: voting and failover. In the voting strategy, multiple participants continually perform the same identical service. Each generates tentative results, and these results are then compared (voted on) by other participants to determine what the ultimate result ought to be. Although very effective, this strategy is extremely complicated to design and expensive to implement. As a result, it is generally employed only in applications in which human life is immediately at risk: aircraft flight controls and industrial safety systems. It is rarely applicable to the design of enterprise systems except in the design of infrastructure components such as network components and storage-area networks, and will therefore not be discussed further.[1]

The failover strategy, like the voting strategy, also requires two or more providers of the same service. In the failover strategy, these providers are configured in such a way that when one provider fails, another takes over. This involves detecting that the primary provider has failed, activating a backup provider, and switching users of the service over to the new provider. This approach is the one generally used for both fault tolerance and high availability in commercial business systems. The differences between fault tolerance and high availability then boil down to the time frame in which the failover occurs and whether or not work in progress is lost during the transition. For fault

---

1. Nelson, V. P. 1990. "Fault-tolerant Computing: Fundamental Concepts," *IEEE Computer*, Vol. 23, Issue 7, pp. 19–25.

tolerance, the failover occurs within the SLA for delivering the service, and there is no loss of work in progress. For high availability, the failover takes longer than the normal SLA for providing the service, and whether or not work in progress is lost becomes a design decision.

Failure Detection Strategies

The cornerstone of any failover strategy is failure detection—determining that a participant is no longer providing its intended service. In a failover strategy, it is failure detection that triggers the action of bringing a backup component into service.

Unfortunately, it is rarely possible to unambiguously observe the failure of a participant. The problem is that the observations themselves are subject to failure. You might observe a symptom, such as the absence of a response to a request, and infer that a failure has occurred—but unfortunately a loss of communications could yield the same observation. The absence of an expected result is an inherently ambiguous situation, and in the case of a communications failure the conclusion that the participant is no longer operating properly would be erroneous. When you consider failover, you must take into consideration the reliability of the failure detection itself.

The following sections explore various ways in which a participant might be monitored. They address both the symptoms that might result from a participant failure and other sources of failure that might produce the same symptoms.

Direct Component Monitoring

A simple approach to detecting a component failure is to directly observe it as an operating system process—assuming that the service is being provided by a single operating system process. This type of monitoring is essentially checking to see whether the process exists. If the expected operating system process is absent, the service is obviously not being provided. Unfortunately, the presence of the operating system process does not necessarily indicate that the service is being properly provided. It cannot, for example, detect a hung process. For that you need to monitor some form of action that the component is taking.

Heartbeat Monitoring

Some components are designed to provide a periodic output, often referred to as a heartbeat, that indicates the component is alive. The intent is to make it possible for some other component, either the backup component or a separate monitor that will ultimately activate the backup component, to determine the health of the primary component. The absence of a heartbeat for some period of time is interpreted as an indication of a problem with the primary component.

There are a couple of issues related to heartbeat monitoring that impact the reliability of the conclusions you can draw from monitoring heartbeats. One has to do with the impact of communications availability on the monitoring and the other with the design of the component itself.

The Ping-Pong Effect (Split-Brain Syndrome)

Heartbeat monitoring requires operational communications between the monitor and the primary component. A communications failure will result in a failure to receive the heartbeats—the same symptom as a true component failure. This becomes an issue when the network can become overloaded and the monitor requires network communications to receive the heartbeats. In this situation, when a network overload occurs, the monitor will lose the heartbeats and conclude that the primary is no longer operational. As a result, the backup component will be activated and will begin performing the function of the primary component even though the primary is still, in fact, operational. This can yield duplicate results (one from the primary and one from the backup) or out-of-sequence results (the backup finishes processing the second transaction before the primary finishes the first transaction). Of course, when the network overload ends, heartbeats will again become visible, and one of the components will presumably revert to a backup role. Unfortunately, by then the damage has been done. This activation-deactivation phenomenon is variously referred to as "split-brain syndrome" and the "ping-pong effect."

Because of this phenomenon, you have to pay special attention to the possibility of network overload when you choose to use heartbeats as a failure-detection mechanism. This is such an important issue that most hardware clusters, which routinely employ heartbeats as part of their health monitoring, use one or more separate and dedicated networks purely for the exchange of status information. This approach guarantees that there will never be a network overload.

Brain-Dead Failures

The heartbeat monitoring strategy assumes that a failure of the component will actually result in the loss of the heartbeat. While a total failure of the component will certainly result in the loss of heartbeats, in a multi-threaded process the presence of a heartbeat may or may not be an accurate indicator of the component's health. If the heartbeat is being generated by one thread, and there are other threads in the component that are blocked or hung, then the component will still be generating heartbeats even though it is not operating properly. Despite the presence of the heartbeat, the component is "brain dead." Therefore, you have to pay close attention to the design of the component itself to ensure that the presence of a heartbeat accurately reflects the health of the component.

Liveness Checks

Yet another form of monitoring is the liveness check. With this approach, the monitor periodically invokes a component operation and checks the response. The return of a correct response is then assumed to be an indicator of proper operation, and an incorrect or absent response is assumed to be an indicator of failure. This strategy is employed in some of the more advanced IP-redirectors, devices often used to distribute IP traffic among a number of web servers for load-balancing purposes. These devices periodically issue HTTP "get" requests to each of the web servers in the group to determine whether they are still operational. Servers that test negatively are then removed from the list of machines to which requests are directed.

Liveness checking requires that the component being monitored provide an atomic request-reply operation that can be used for the check and assumes that the proper execution of the test operation is a good indication of the overall health of the service. These assumptions are often not valid when the service being provided is a long-running process or involves the collaboration of two or more components.

Failover Management

Failover requires a manager—a component whose responsibility it is to determine whether failover is required and then initiate the actual failover process. This component may be the backup component itself, or it may be an independent third party. If the manager is a "smart" backup component, it decides on its own when to take over the operation of the service. If it is a third party, it must communicate with one of the backup components and direct it to take over.

Each of these strategies has its strengths and weaknesses. The smart backup strategy requires backup components to be actively running. Even though they are not actively doing the work, they are still monitoring the primary component for failure. Smart backups get complicated when there is more than one backup component. This situation requires the backups to monitor each other (most often with heartbeats) and a distributed algorithm for determining which of the backup components will take over for the failed primary. Communications problems (i.e., overloaded networks) can create significant confusion in these situations. When you employ this type of strategy, you need to understand the decision-making process in sufficient detail to understand what will happen should communications become disrupted. You then need to make a determination as to whether that behavior is acceptable in the business process.

The third-party manager strategy has its own set of issues. On the plus side, it does not require that the backup components be online, although having the backup components already running can speed up the failover. However, the manager now becomes a single point of failure, although for the service itself to actually fail, both the service provider and the manager would have to fail at the same time. To compensate for this, the manager itself is often deployed as a fault-tolerant or highly available component using the smart backup strategy to manage the failover of the manager role. Another potential problem with this approach is that the manager needs to be able to communicate with the backup component to direct its operation. Communications problems can complicate this.

Redirecting Clients

When a component fails over, you need to consider how the clients using the service will be able to access the replacement component. Figure 32–1 illustrates the three basic approaches that are available. One approach is to configure the service client to be able to directly access both the primary and backup components. When the primary component becomes inaccessible, then the client accesses the backup

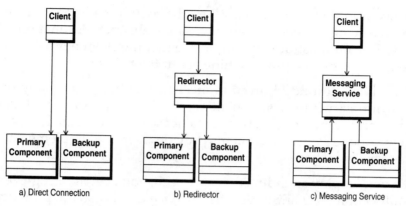

Figure 32–1: *Patterns for Accessing a Failed-Over Service*

service provider. This requires the service client to have the logic to switch between components and the connection information for both the primary and backup components. The mechanics of detecting the primary failure and switching to the backup component are specific to the communications mechanism used to access the service, as are the configuration details. As the number of clients and services increases, these factors conspire to complicate the administration of this type of failover. For this reason, the use of some form of intermediary has become popular.

One style of intermediary is a redirector: a component that accepts requests from the client and directs them to the appropriate component. With this approach, the client configuration does not change when a failover occurs. The nature of the indirection mechanism is generally specific to the communications protocol being employed. There are a number of mechanisms, for example, that provide IP redirection. The client uses the same IP address all the time, and the indirection mechanism directs the traffic to one of the providers. Alternatively, the primary service provider may be using a virtual IP address, and when the secondary takes over it uses the same virtual IP address. You can accomplish a similar level of redirection through the use of Internet domain names. The Internet domain name service (DNS) associates the domain names with Internet addresses, and can associate one domain name with more than one IP address. These strategies can be used when the client accesses the server directly using a domain name or IP address.

Another style of intermediary is a messaging service. The client sends requests to an abstract message destination, and the primary receives requests from that destination. When the backup takes over, it simply starts receiving requests from the same abstract destination. This approach is administratively simple: Neither the client nor the messaging service needs to know anything about the failover.

You are likely to find indirection mechanisms built into many of the system infrastructure components as well to support their failover: Storage area networks, network database access mechanisms, and even telephone switching systems provide their own implementations of these mechanisms.

When you employ an indirection approach, you need to recognize that the indirection mechanism itself is a service that is usually provided in some form of fault-tolerant or high-availability configuration. When it is, you have the same question all over again: How do users of the service switch over from the primary to the secondary provider? The same principles apply here as well.

Summary

Fault-tolerant processes continue to provide uninterrupted service despite the failure of one of the process participants. High-availability processes restore service after a short interruption in the event of a participant failure and may or may not (depending upon the process design) lose work in progress.

There are two strategies for implementing fault tolerance, one involving multiple active components that "vote" on the desired results and the other involving a failover from one component to the other. The voting approach is rarely used in the design of business applications—failover is the commonly used strategy.

Failover requires the detection of the active component's failure. There are several strategies that can be applied to failure detection: direct observation of the operating system process, listening for "I am alive" heartbeats, and executing explicit liveness checks. Each of these strategies has failure modes of its own that must be understood before a strategy is selected.

Failover requires a manager that determines when the primary component has ceased to function and initiates the backup component's activation. The manager may be a "smart" backup component or it may be a third party.

When components fail over, their clients need to be redirected to the replacement component. If the client communicates directly with the component, then the client must have the configuration information necessary to connect directly with the replacement component as well. Alternatively, the client can communicate with an intermediary such as an IP redirector or a messaging service. In this case the failover is transparent to the client. However, the intermediary itself will likely need to be highly available or fault tolerant.

Key High-Availability and Fault Tolerance Questions

1. What is the risk to the enterprise if this process is not available? How long can the process be unavailable before serious risk occurs?

2. What is the risk to the enterprise if a failure of the process results in a loss of information?

3. What is the risk to the enterprise if work in progress is lost?

4. Do these risks warrant making the process fault tolerant or highly available?

5. If the process warrants high availability or fault tolerance, which components need to be highly available or fault tolerant? Could modifying the coordination patterns simplify the design and/or lower the cost?

6. For failover, what is the recovery time objective (RTO) required by the business process?

7. What strategy will be employed for detecting component failure? What would the impact of a network overload on this strategy be?

8. Which component(s) are responsible for monitoring component failure and initiating failover? Do these components themselves need to be fault tolerant or highly available?

9. How will clients reconnect to the component after a failover? If an intermediary is used, is it also fault tolerant or highly available? What is the SLA for its failover?

Chapter 33

Stateless and Stateful Failover

Stateless and Stateful Components

When you want a business process to be fault-tolerant or highly available, at least some of the components must be implemented in such a way that should they fail to do their job, a backup component can take over that responsibility. There are two distinct cases to be considered:

1. Stateless component: A component that performs stateless atomic operations that use no reference data (data that is not provided as an input) and save no data. The operations simply take an input and return an output—like an addition operation.

2. Stateful component: A component that performs an operation that saves information and uses that information in subsequent operation invocations. An example is a service that manages records of inventory levels.

Stateless Failover

Stateless component failovers are relatively simple. A stateless component is one in which each invocation of each operation is completely independent from any other invocation. With a stateless component, failover requires only three things:

1. Detecting the component failure
2. Bringing the backup component online
3. Redirecting clients to the backup component

The previous chapter discussed various ways in which the first two tasks can be performed. What remains is to determine how to accomplish the third.

Saving Work in Progress through Coordination

Although a component may be stateless, there may be work in progress at the time that the failure occurs. In other words, the component might have received a request and been in the middle of producing the result when the failure occurred. What happens to this work in progress? Well, in stateless failover the service provider does not pass any information on to the backup component when it fails over. Therefore, there is no way that the backup component can even know that there was work in progress, and therefore the failover, in and of itself, will not preserve the work in progress. However, this does not necessarily mean that you have to lose the work in progress.

The fate of the work in progress ultimately depends on the coordination pattern you choose when invoking the operation. If you use fire-and-forget the work in progress is lost, for none of the participants is in a position to even detect a breakdown. On the other hand, if you use request-reply the client knows that the request has failed. The client can then, as one of its recovery options, resubmit the request, presumably after the failover is complete. This resubmission preserves the work in progress, although the responsibility for this preservation belongs to the client and not the failed component.

When the component sends results elsewhere, preserving work in progress gets a little more complicated. If you use a nested request-reply, then the original requestor is still in a position to observe the breakdown and take action to preserve the work in progress. If you use fire-and-forget or delegation, none of the participants will be able to detect the breakdown and the work in progress will be lost. But there is a variation of fire-and-forget involving persistent messaging that will preserve work in progress.

If a messaging service with persistence is being used for the communications, a hybrid of delegation and asynchronous request-reply can be used that will preserve work in progress (Figure 33–1). Many messaging systems (such as JMS) offer two capabilities that you can combine to preserve work in progress: message persistence and message acknowledgment. Using message persistence ensures that the messaging service makes a durable record of the message that will survive the failure of the messaging service itself (the failover of this stateful process is discussed in the next section). The use of a deferred message acknowledgment allows the delegation and asynchronous request-reply patterns to be combined to ensure that the request will persist until the component has completed its work.

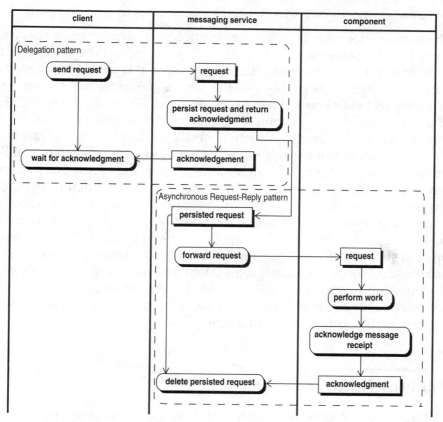

Figure 33–1: *Preserving Work in Progress with Delegation, Persistence, and Asynchronous Request-Reply*

Because the `client` is using delegation, it knows whether or not the `messaging service` actually got the message and can take appropriate recovery action if the acknowledgment is not received. Because the `component` is responding to the receipt of the request in a request-reply manner, the `messaging service` knows whether or not the message was successfully delivered. It can redeliver the message and, in particular, deliver it to the backup component if needed after that component has taken over from the primary. Work in progress in the component is preserved, at least as long as the messaging service does not lose the request.

Note that you can also daisy-chain this pattern to involve more participants in a larger process. As part of doing its work, the `component` can use this same pattern to deliver its results to yet another component, and so on. In fact, this is a common systems integration pattern.

The combination of delegation, persistence, and asynchronous request-reply may be common, but it does have some limitations. First of all, from an application-to-application perspective, it is still fundamentally a fire-and-forget pattern. Neither the service requestor nor the service provider will ever know if a message gets lost. Secondly, the reliability of the message delivery is only as good as the reliability of the messaging service itself. Careful attention needs to be paid to the failover characteristics of the messaging service and, in particular, the reliability of the underlying persistent storage. Finally, the use of this pattern can make distributed system troubleshooting very difficult. None of the major components is aware of the status of any requests. Once a request has been handed off, it lives in the messaging system until such time as it is delivered. Locating a work in progress to determine process status (without some kind of a process monitor) thus requires poking around in the messaging system looking for and interpreting the meaning of specific messages. Since most messaging systems do not provide an indexed retrieval mechanism, this kind of troubleshooting can be difficult and time-consuming.

Stateful Failover

Failing over a component with state requires a mechanism for the backup component to know what the state of the primary was at the moment of failure. There are two basic techniques that can be used for this. One is to keep the backup component up-to-date by having it actively monitor the primary component. In this approach the backup is commonly referred to as a *hot standby*. The other technique is to save the active component's state in a reliable manner (generally on disk) and have the backup component ready to retrieve that state when the primary component fails. In this approach the backup is commonly referred to as a *warm standby*. A variation on the warm-standby approach is to not have the backup already running, in which case it must first be started before it can retrieve the state and take over operation. The backup in this case is commonly referred to as a *cold standby*.

The hot-standby approach tends to be complex due to the active monitoring required. In the simplest case, when each operation is a single monolithic activity that produces a single result, all the backup component needs to do is be aware of what operation invocations have occurred and whether or not each invocation successfully generated its expected result. But many components are more complex than this. They are actually executing processes involving more than one interaction, and these processes tend to produce more than one result, a mix of database updates, files, and messages. In such cases the hot-standby monitoring not only gets more complex, but the details of the monitoring become highly dependent upon the process design. The backup component needs to know, in detail, which intermediate results have been generated, which have not, and exactly where in the process the primary left off.

Achieving this level of active process monitoring is nontrivial. Reliably monitoring a separate process (remember, this monitoring has to work right up to the moment of failure even when things are in the process of going wrong) can require more work than executing the process. In addition, the backup component needs to be able to resume the process at any point within that process. These design challenges are so daunting that the monitoring approach to fault tolerance is rarely implemented in practice—with one important class of exceptions: storage components that persist information in a fault-tolerant manner.

The other approach to state sharing is the warm (or cold) standby. With this approach, the state information that needs to be shared is stored in a fault-tolerant manner by the primary, most commonly on disk. When the failover occurs, the backup reads this stored state and then resumes operation. For this to work, sufficient information has to be persisted to allow the backup to determine the exact state of the primary at the moment of failure. Note that with the exception of reading the state information, the warm- (or cold-) standby approach is no different than the stateless failover discussed earlier.

While warm standby makes switching to the backup component easier, it does so by pushing the difficult part of the problem into the persistent storage. There is no magic for making persistent storage fault tolerant. It boils down to replicating—making copies of—information and determining when the primary copy is corrupted. When the primary is corrupted, the information is then recovered from the backup copy. It is not unusual for high-end storage subsystems and databases to provide this type of facility.

Storage Replication

There are two information replication approaches employed by storage subsystems, one for handling failures within a component and the other for handling the complete loss of a component and failing over to another component. The other component may be within the same data center (generally another fire-isolated location within the data center) or at another physical site (to guard against a site disaster). Some databases also employ in-component replication.

Synchronous Replication within a Component

Information replication within a component is generally accomplished through the use of a Redundant Array of Inexpensive Disks (RAID).[1] In a RAID array, sufficient information is replicated across the disks in the array to make it possible to recover that information despite the total loss of a disk.

There are a number of ways information can be distributed in a RAID array, but two basic strategies dominate: RAID 1 and RAID 5. RAID 1 duplicates the information in its entirety on two different disks (a technique known as mirroring). This obviously doubles the disk space required to store the information. It is usually used in conjunction with another technique known as "striping," which spreads the data across multiple disks for performance. Performance is improved because

---

1. David A. Patterson, Garth Gibson, and Randy H. Katz. "A Case for Redundant Arrays of Inexpensive Disks (RAID)," *Proceedings of the 1988 ACM SIGMOD International Conference on Management of Data* (ISBN: 0-89791-268-3).

multiple disks can be accessed simultaneously, thus increasing the performance of the array over that of a single disk. Striping is often referred to as RAID 0, and the combination of striping and mirroring is called RAID 0+1. There will be more discussion of striping when performance is addressed in Chapter 39.

Another common configuration, known as RAID 5, uses error detection and correction techniques rather than complete duplication. It spreads the information across a number of disks along with sufficient error correction information to recover from the loss of any one disk. If the data is spread across n disks without error correction, the equivalent of one more disk will be needed to contain the required error correction information.[2] Thus while RAID 0+1 would require 2n disks, RAID 5 only requires n+1 disks. RAID 5 requires fewer disks than RAID 0+1.

This space savings of Raid 5 comes at the expense of a potentially significant decrease in write throughput for small blocks of data. The block size at which write speed begins to deteriorate is the size of a disk sector (typically 512 bytes) multiplied by the number of disks the data is spread across. Thus for a 9-disk array (8 data, 1 error correction), this critical block size would be 4KB. Writing (not reading) blocks smaller than this incurs a significant performance penalty when compared with RAID 0+1. When the data block size is the same as the size of a single sector (e.g., 512 bytes), this can reduce the throughput by 50 percent.[3] Note also that this is a theoretical minimum deterioration, and the actual measured degradation of real RAID arrays when comparing RAID 5 to RAID 0+1 configurations have reported substantially larger relative throughput degradations.

The bottom line here is that you need to pay attention to the RAID configuration, particularly when you find applications using persistence, small data bocks, and high throughput. This combination is commonly found in messaging services, making them particularly sensitive to RAID configurations.

The two RAID configurations discussed are the ones most commonly found, but there are other variations that will be encountered in practice. The burden is on you, as the architect, to understand the performance

---

2. In RAID 5, the error correction information is actually spread across all the disks, but the space required is the capacity of a single disk.

3. The definition of "small" will vary depending upon the sector size for the disks and the number of disks in the RAID array, but is typically in the 2KB–10KB range.

characteristics of the proposed storage subsystem and determine its adequacy with respect to the needs of the business process.

The RAID performance problem (and the problem of disk performance in general) has not gone unnoticed by the vendors of storage subsystems. Some storage subsystems now include a redundant battery-backed memory-resident buffer. Write operations simply update the buffer, not the disk. This reduces the time for a write operation from milliseconds to microseconds and allows the storage subsystem to optimize the subsequent disk write operations. Fault tolerance is attained through a combination of redundancy (replicated data in two buffers) and using batteries to maintain the data in memory in the event of a power failure. While somewhat expensive, these storage subsystems offer a viable approach to improving storage performance.

Determining whether the storage subsystem is adequate can be difficult when it is owned by another organization. The economics of purchasing storage space tend to drive organizations towards the use of RAID 5 or similar configurations. They may be reluctant, for cost reasons, to even discuss alternate configurations. Nevertheless, if your application requires high throughput, is sensitive to the time it takes to write to disk, and involves small writes you need to investigate the actual configuration of the storage subsystem and determine the actual performance it will deliver. This is particularly important for messaging components handling a high volume of small messages. If the performance is not adequate, you need to negotiate a different storage configuration or your process will not be able to meet its performance requirements. This is one place where an appeal to executive sponsors may be required to resolve the situation.

Synchronous Replication between Components

Regardless of the investment in storage within a storage component (or subsystem), no amount of investment is going to protect against the physical destruction of that component. Fires, floods, explosions, and earthquakes can destroy the storage component and result in the loss of the information stored within it. To protect against this type of disaster, you need to make copies of the data in another component, possibly at another physical site.

Replicating data across components and keeping the data up-to-date in real time is similar to using RAID 1, but with the second copy of the data in another component. If you want to absolutely eliminate the possibility of data loss, both the local and remote writes must occur synchronously (Figure 33–2). Data at both sites must be saved before the application relying on the survivability of the data moves on to other activities.

This remote-component update has some drawbacks. The communications to the remote component will take time, particularly if that component is at a remote site. The application writing the data must wait for this communication to complete before it can proceed. Thus, synchronous update has a performance impact on the process requiring the storage. Minimizing the latency requires high-bandwidth low-latency communications between the sites—capabilities that typically carry significant costs. Because of these communications delays, storage subsystem vendors generally recommend a physical site separation of 50 miles or less. These factors combine to make the synchronous update of information at remote sites a relatively expensive choice, and one that requires a significant infrastructure investment.

Two operating characteristics of commercially available synchronous replication must be considered when you are designing the business processes. One is that the inter-component replication is rarely a symmetric process. While information from the primary component may

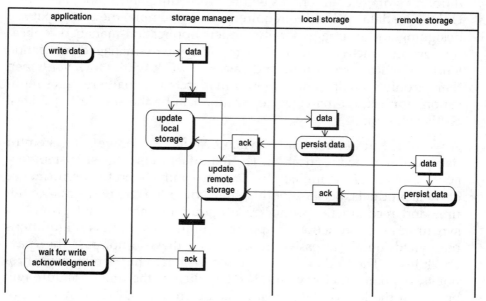

Figure 33–2: *Synchronous Write to Local and Remote Storage*

be replicated synchronously to the backup site, after a failover the updates at the secondary site may not be applied to the primary site. Instead, a list of the needed changes is accumulated and will be applied to the primary site upon command. From an operational perspective this makes sense, as the primary site is most likely inoperative at this time. However, the net result is that you no longer have two sites in synch with each other. If the secondary site is lost before these changes are applied to the primary site, data will be lost.

The other operating characteristic you need to consider is that when communications is lost between the primary and secondary storage components, synchronous replication will again no longer take place. Instead, the primary site will accumulate a list of the changes that need to be applied to the remote site. Generally, a manual intervention is required to bring the sites back into synchronization. If the primary site is lost before these changes are applied, once again, data will be lost.

Obtaining synchronous updates across storage components does not necessarily require a storage subsystem that can manage the replication of the data. Some databases, for example, provide an option for the database manager itself to manage the replicated storage. When the storage involved is simple, the application itself can manage the replication of the data, explicitly writing data to two files or databases on different storage components before proceeding on to other activities. Unless the data replication requirements are simple, the complexity of designing and testing generally renders application-managed replication an unattractive option. Storage- or database-managed replication tends to be less error prone and easier to work with. However, when there is only a small amount of information that actually requires replication, application-managed replication can be the simplest and least costly solution.

A word of caution is in order when evaluating storage subsystem or database-managed replication. The manufacturers of these systems are acutely aware of the impact that latency can have on the performance of their products. Because of this, they will often cite performance figures and recommend product configurations that do not provide a synchronous (transactional) update of both sites. Such configurations may yield more impressive numbers, but they do not pass the "paycheck test." The update of the remote system is happening asynchronously. Updates that have not been applied at the time of failure will be lost. If the loss of data must be completely avoided, then synchronous update is the only option.

Asynchronous Replication and Data Loss

Providing synchronous updates across multiple components, particularly at multiple sites, can be an expensive option. As a result, you may not want to apply this technique to all information. When you consider the risk to the enterprise that would result from the loss of the data, it may be appropriate to select a different alternative—one that might actually lose a small amount of data under certain circumstances, but is less costly to implement.

When going down this road, you have to begin by considering just how much data loss is acceptable. You also need to be very careful how you phrase this question. If you ask the business community whether data loss is acceptable, you will most likely get a simple "No!" What you need to do first is make clear that there are never any absolute guarantees against data loss, ever. No matter how many copies of the data are made, there will always be some disaster of a large enough scope that will destroy all of the copies. After making this clear, you can then ask some more pointed questions:

1. What is the business risk that would result from the data loss?
2. Does the risk warrant an investment in data replication within a storage component (e.g., a RAID array)?
3. Does the risk warrant an investment in data replication across two storage components within the same data center?
4. Does the risk warrant an investment in data replication across two storage components at two different data centers?
5. Is some level of data loss acceptable during an inter-site failover? If so, how much loss (measured in terms of time) is acceptable. The answer to this question is commonly termed the *recovery point objective* (a point referring to a point in time).

These questions will arise in virtually every business process you consider. It is good practice to develop guidelines for answering these questions so that you get consistent answers from different projects. And rather than engineer a solution each time, it is good practice to develop standard solutions for various combinations of answers. The result will be something like Table 33–1. With such a table and the guidelines for answering the questions, the task for individual projects simplifies to simply categorizing the information used in the business process. Don't lose sight of the fact that different pieces of information within the same business process may end up in different categories.

Table 33–1: *Example Enterprise Standard Data Loss Categories*

Data Loss Category	Local Failover Recovery Point Objective	Local Technique Examples	Remote Failover Recovery Point Objective	Remote Technique
6	No loss	RAID arrays	No loss	Synchronous replication
5	No loss	RAID arrays	Last few seconds of data	Asynchronous replication
4	No loss	RAID arrays	Last few minutes of data	"Tail" database transaction logs
3	No loss	RAID Arrays	Last few hours of data	Backup tapes, periodic file copies
2	Last few minutes of data	"Tail" transaction logs	Last few minutes of data	"Tail" transaction logs
1	Last few hours of data	Backup tapes stored off-site	Last few hours of data	Backup tapes, periodic file copies

In this example, Category 6 loses no data, but it is also the most expensive option. It requires up to twice as much storage for the RAID array and requires the same investment at the remote site along with a high-bandwidth, low-latency communications link between the sites. It also carries with it an unavoidable application performance penalty as the application waits for the confirmation of the remote site write.

Category 5 relaxes the constraints for remote site failover just a little bit, allowing the last few seconds of data to be lost. This allows the use of asynchronous updates in the interaction with the remote site as shown in Figure 33–3. The difference between this and the synchronous update is that the storage manager does not wait for the remote component storage confirmation before returning control to the application. This speeds up the application's performance and lessens the peak bandwidth demand to the remote component. The downside is that if the data in transit to the remote storage component does not make it successfully (perhaps due to communications problems) and the local storage should also fail, then that update will be lost. While

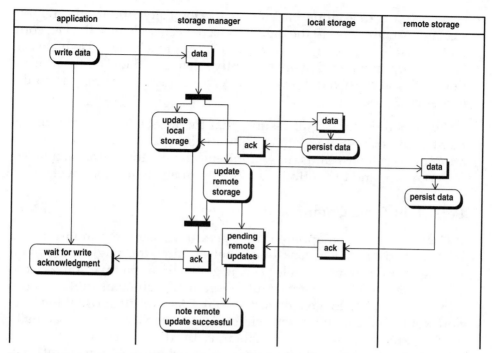

Figure 33–3: *Asynchronous Write to Local and Remote Storage*

this scenario involves multiple failures, it is precisely the type of failure that can occur during a site disaster.

Returning to the data loss categories, Category 4 employs a common technique in which changes to the database transaction log (the "tail" of the log) are periodically copied to the remote site. Some storage subsystems have a similar log that can also be used for remote update. These updates are subsequently applied to the remote storage component (or to the database on top of it) to bring it up to date. This technique runs the risk of losing the transactions that have occurred since the last copy took place.

There is a variation of this technique in which the remote site is periodically updated with local storage snapshots, but incremental updates are also sent asynchronously. In this variation, the incremental updates are not actually applied unless an actual site disaster occurs. While the data loss is minimized, it may take a considerable amount of time to apply the updates and get the remote storage ready for use.

Category 3 uses routine backups to periodically update the remote storage. Any updates to the data that have occurred since the last copy will be lost in the event of a disaster. This approach may also have difficulties copying files that are presently opened and locked by applications. On the other hand, it is relatively inexpensive compared to the earlier categories.

Categories 6 through 3 all assume that the local site failover requirement is to not lose any data at all. Categories 2 and 1 reflect a relaxation of these constraints, now applying the database transaction-log tail approach and the periodic backup approach to local failover.

Persistent-State Component Failover

By now it should be apparent that persisting state in a fault-tolerant manner is a nontrivial task—one that requires thorough design and testing in order to be reliable. This is generally not a task you want to take on each time you want a fault-tolerant or high-availability component that happens to have persistent state. As a result, most of the time you want such a service, you will design it so that its state is actually stored externally in a file or database. By doing this, you can take advantage of existing storage services and the robust persistent-storage failover mechanisms they provide. This approach leads to the persistent-state component failover pattern shown in Figure 33–4.

A fault-tolerant or highly available component with persistent state requires a storage replication and a failover mechanism for the storage of its state. Typically the component will be designed to access its persistent storage through some type of storage manager. The storage manager plays the role of an indirection mechanism and isolates the service from the details of the persistent state failover.

The storage manager (which is, itself, a fault-tolerant component) provides access control to the component's persistent state that is being stored. To maintain integrity, when a service is writing to the storage subsystem or database, the storage manager places locks on the files or tables.[4] When the primary component fails, these locks need to be reliably released before a secondary or backup provider can access the persistent state. The reliability of this lock release is an issue when NFS is used to provide the storage-management service. NFS can leave file

---

4. Some databases may employ low-level locking, but the issue remains the same.

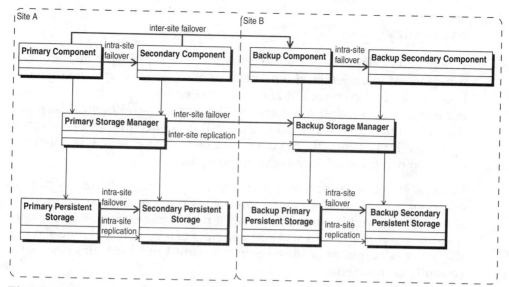

Figure 33–4: *Typical Failover Pattern for Persistent-State Component*

locks in place when the process holding the lock terminates abnormally.[5] This is an issue you need to pay attention to or your failover itself will fail. Whatever means you use for managing access to the storage, you need to ensure that locks are reliably released so that the secondary service provider can access the required storage.

Using a storage manager to save the component's state generally works well only when the component and the storage manager are both within the same physical site. Because of the latency and reduced reliability of inter-site communications, it is generally not a good idea to operate a component at one site with its persistent storage located at another site. This requires the replication of both the component and the storage manager at the remote site to maintain a high level of performance and reliability. Note that this requires an inter-site failover capability for the storage manager itself. Consequently, when an inter-site failover occurs, it is typical to fail over the component, the storage manager, and the persistent storage all as one unit. In other words, the entire site fails over.

---

5. When NFS Version 4 is used in conjunction with an operating system configured for synchronous disk writes for file operations, it does not exhibit this problem. However, this is not a commonly found configuration.

Summary

When a component needs to be failed over to a backup component, it is important to understand whether that component is stateful or stateless. A stateless component is one whose result depends solely upon the inputs provided: It requires no other inputs or reference data and does not retain any information that will influence the results of other operation invocations. To fail over a stateless component, it is only necessary to bring the backup component on line.

When a stateless component fails over, any work in progress in that component is likely to be lost. However, if the work in the component is being triggered by messages from a messaging service that persists the messages, the loss of work in progress can be avoided by delaying the acknowledgment of message receipt until the work has been successfully completed.

Failing over a component with persistent state requires that the state be restored in the backup component. While this can be done by having the backup component closely monitor the primary component and maintain a copy of the current state, this approach is complicated and rarely used. Instead, the component typically externalizes the state information in a reliable persistent storage. When a failover occurs, the backup component reads this persisted state and takes over operations.

For reliability, the persistent storage must, itself, be fault tolerant. This is accomplished through partial or total replication of enough information to be able to recover from the loss of a disk. This replication can occur both within and between storage components, and within or between physical sites.

To ensure that no data will be lost with the loss of one disk, data replication must occur synchronously. However, synchronous replication, particularly between sites, can be expensive and can have an adverse impact on performance. Where some data loss is acceptable, lower cost asynchronous replication techniques can be used.

When a stateful component fails over and its state has been externalized, the mechanism by which the backup component obtains access to the state needs to be considered. Some form of storage manager is required. The storage manager and stateful component need to be at the same physical site for best reliability and performance, which means that both must fail over together to the remote site when inter-site failover is required.

Key Failover Questions

1. Does the component that needs to be fault tolerant or highly available have persistent state?

2. If the component is stateless, does work in progress need to be preserved? If so, how will this be accomplished?

3. If the component is stateful, how will the backup component acquire the needed state information?

4. Is the choice of storage replication consistent with the business requirements regarding the loss of data and work in progress? Is the incremental investment in storage replication warranted by the business consequences of data loss?

Suggested Reading

Marcus, Evan, and Hal Stern. 2000. *Blueprints for High Availability: Designing Resilient Distributed Systems.* New York, NY: John Wiley & Sons.

Patterson, David A., Garth Gibson, and Randy H. Katz. 1988. "A Case for Redundant Arrays of Inexpensive Disks (RAID)." *Proceedings of the 1988 ACM SIGMOD International Conference on Management of Data* (ISBN: 0-89791-268-3).

Ramakumar, R. 1993. *Engineering Reliability: Fundamentals and Applications.* Upper Saddle River, NJ: Prentice Hall.

Nelson, V. P. 1990. "Fault-tolerant Computing: Fundamental Concepts." *IEEE Computer,* Vol. 23, Issue 7, pp. 19–25.

Chapter 34

Multiple Component Failover

Intra-Site versus Inter-Site Failover

Looking beyond the failover of a single component, larger patterns begin to emerge when you begin to consider the failover of services and their clients as shown in Figure 34–1. While you might, theoretically, allow clients at one site to access services at the other site, this requires the service access mechanism to act as a router for service requests. To route properly, the router would have to know how to access all instances of the service as well as their current status. The router would also have to be configured with appropriate rules governing routing within and between sites. Finally, the router itself would require an instance at each site and its own failover strategy.

Further complicating the consideration of inter-site failover are differences in policies regarding data loss during inter-site failover. The performance penalty associated with synchronous updates between sites usually limits the use of synchronous updates for only selected services and applications. Other services and applications will generally employ some form of asynchronous update.

Asynchronous updates often require some form of persistent state reconstruction before the service or application can be started at the remote site. Disks may need to be restored from backup tapes, or incremental

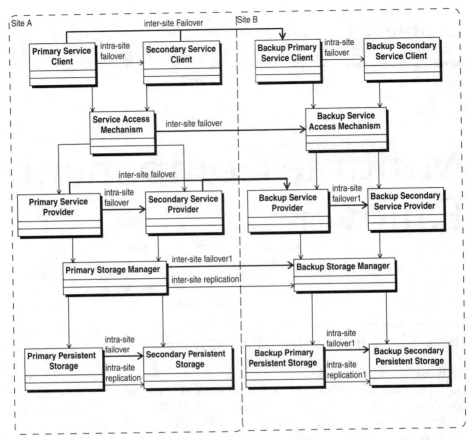

Figure 34–1: *Typical Intra-Site and Inter-Site Failover Pattern*

changes may need to be applied to older database snapshots to bring databases up to date. Unless each service and application has independently managed persistent storage, this recovery activity will span multiple services and applications.

Finally, synchronous persistent storage updates typically work only in one direction. Once a failover has occurred to the backup site, subsequent changes to the backup site are not being synchronously applied to the primary site. Instead, lists of pending changes to the primary site are accumulated. These changes must be applied to the primary site before services and applications can be switched back to the primary site.

The combination of these factors generally means that automated inter-site failover is not practical on a service-by-service or application-by-application basis. Consequently, you end up with two different failover strategies, one for intra-site failover and another for inter-site failover. For intra-site failover, the use of indirection mechanisms for service and storage access makes it practical to employ service-by-service or machine-by-machine automated failover strategy. Inter-site failover, however, tends to be a wholesale process that is manually initiated. Because of the complexity of communications, routing, and storage update issues cited above, it is generally simpler to fail over entire blocks of services, storage, applications, and indirection mechanisms together as a unit.

Clustering: An Intra-Site Failover Technique

One of the complicating factors in making business processes fault-tolerant or highly available is the variety of ways in which different services fail over and the variety of ways in which clients switch between service providers when they do fail over. Each technique has its own special configuration requirements and must be administered accordingly. Any given component might be both a fault-tolerant or highly available service provider and at the same time be a client for some other fault-tolerant or highly available services that use different access techniques. Without some constraints on the usage of these techniques it can be very difficult to even understand how a distributed system is expected to operate when failovers occur, let alone verify that the overall business process will continue to execute after such failovers.

One way to manage this complexity is to provide a high-availability environment for components to run in. With this approach, rather than fail over individual applications and services, the entire environment fails over. The environment being discussed here is essentially an entire computer, including the operating system and all processes running under the operating system. This machine may be physical, in which case it fails over to another physical machine. Alternatively, the machine may be virtual, in which case it fails over to another virtual machine either in the same physical machine or another physical machine.

Although environment failover can be accomplished manually, it is most often managed by a cluster manager, with the set of machines being managed referred to as a *cluster*. When a failure occurs in a machine, the entire machine is failed over to a backup machine. The storage subsystem that was mounted on the failed machine is remounted on the backup machine. A script is then run on the backup machine to initialize all of the components on the machine.

What makes the cluster approach work is that the backup machine and all of the components running on it assume the identity of the components on the failed machine. The identity of the machine itself is transferred by using a virtual host name and one or more virtual IP addresses. The components themselves start up with the same configurations and identities as their counterparts on the failed machines. This is accomplished by keeping all of this identity information in the storage subsystem that is switched over from the failed machine to the backup machine.

Clustering provides a significant level of uniformity when it comes to indirection mechanisms. The storage subsystem provides a uniform indirection mechanism for all persistent storage associated with the components running on the machines. The virtual host name and virtual IP addresses provide uniform indirection for all direct-socket connections. Higher-level indirection mechanisms such as messaging services fail over in their entirety, with their lower-level socket connections being made through the virtual IP addresses.

All in all, clustering provides a straightforward means of providing high-availability components with fault-tolerant underlying storage. It can be readily configured and is easy to test. But this convenience does come at a price. Since an entire machine is failed over, it will take time to start up all of the components running on the machine. Failover may well take longer than the simple failover of a single component. You must be sure that this failover time provides an acceptable level of service for the business processes.

Coordinating Peer Application Failover with Asynchronous Replication

When there are two related components, each with persistent state, these components may interact in a synchronous way to ensure that their respective states are mutually consistent. If these component states are being synchronously replicated, then the replicated states will also be mutually consistent. However, if the states are being replicated asynchronously, the replicated states may no longer be mutually consistent.

The potential problem is easily illustrated. Consider an `Order Management System` and a `Warehouse Management System` (Figure 34–2). When the `Order Management System` releases an order for shipment, it does so via a synchronous interaction with the `Warehouse Management System`. This synchronous interaction ensures that the state of the order in the two systems is consistent.

If each of the systems replicates its persistent storage synchronously, then after a failover the state of both applications will still remain consistent. However, if the storage replication is happening asynchronously, there is a potential problem. The timing of the replicated storage updates may not be coordinated. Consider what would happen if the `Order Management System` update of the order release is applied to its backup but the `Warehouse Management System` update has not been applied when a site failover occurs. The backup `Order Management System` thinks the order has been released to the `Warehouse Management System`, but the `Warehouse Management System` has no record of the order. The business process is now broken.

Unless the asynchronous updates of different applications are coordinated, consistency between application states can never be guaranteed. The implications are far-reaching. At the application design level, you have to design the applications to be tolerant of these inconsistencies. For example, after the failover, an `Order Management System` query of the `Warehouse Management System` to obtain the status of the lost order will result in an error because the order does not exist in the `Warehouse Management System`.

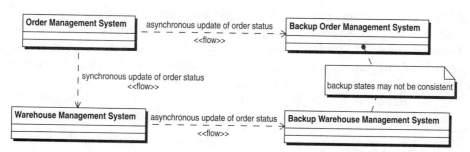

Figure 34–2: *The Problem with Peer Application Failover after Asynchronous Updates*

Beyond simply designing components to be tolerant of such errors, you have to determine what level of effort needs to be put into detecting and resolving inconsistencies after a site failover. This is a fundamentally hard problem, for it essentially requires an audit of all the systems to determine whether the information they contain is mutually consistent. To appreciate the complexity, recognize that there are three possible error states that might arise just from these two pieces of information:

1. The order management system update arrived, but the warehouse management system update did not.
2. The warehouse management system update arrived, but the order management system update did not.
3. Neither update arrived.

These are just the combinations for two pieces of information! For n independently replicated pieces of information, there are n^2 possible replicated states—only one of which has all n pieces of information in the correct states. The remaining n^2-1 states all represent various levels of information loss from the uncoordinated asynchronous replication.

From a practical perspective, there is little you can do to detect and resolve such situations. The choice to use asynchronous replication is, to begin with, a choice to accept some level of data loss. The best you can do is to design the applications to be tolerant of such inconsistencies and report them. The operations staff must then decide what action, if any, to take in resolving reported discrepancies.

Making a Business Process Fault-Tolerant

Making a business process fault tolerant—ensuring that it does not lose work in progress—does not necessarily mean that each of its participants needs to be fault tolerant to avoid losing state. Clever use of coordination patterns as discussed in Chapter 33 can reduce the number of components that need to maintain their state. This will reduce the performance demands on the persistent storage infrastructure, creating a lighter-weight and higher-performance business process.

When you employ a request-reply coordination pattern, the service provider does not need to be fault tolerant. Assuming there is an SLA in place for returning the reply, the requestor can detect a communication breakdown as well as a breakdown in the performer. If the activity of the performer can be safely repeated, all you need to do is fix the problem and then have the requestor resend the request. With such a configuration, you don't need a fault-tolerant implementation for either the communications infrastructure or the service provider. You do, however, require a fault-tolerant requestor so that it remembers what work needs to be requested and the status of completing that work.

A variation on this approach that utilizes a fault-tolerant messaging service was presented back in Figure 33–1. There the requesting component uses the delegation pattern to deliver the request to the messaging service. The messaging service then delivers the message to the service provider. Since the messaging service expects an acknowledgment from the service provider, its delivery of the request is essentially a request-reply exchange with the service provider. Because the messaging service will retain the message until the acknowledgment has been received, the request will survive a breakdown in communications with the service provider or the loss of the service provider itself. Note that this requires the service provider to delay sending the acknowledgment until the work has been completed.

While this pattern brings a level of robustness to the performance of the work, it is not without its limitations. Most message delivery services do not provide the ability to specify an SLA for message delivery and will simply wait indefinitely for the acknowledgment. Typically they will not redeliver a message until the socket connection with the recipient (in this case, the service provider) is broken. Thus in the case of a "hung" service provider, no action will be taken. Work will simply stall. This serves as a reminder that despite the persistence, this is still a fire-and-forget exchange between the requestor and service provider.

As long as the activity in the business process can be safely repeated, you can extend this principle to encompass larger portions of the business process. As long as the original requestor can detect a breakdown and re-initiate the request, the downstream participants do not need to be fault-tolerant. If you are employing a process manager, and all of the activity initiated by the process manager involves this type of request-reply interaction, you can make the entire business process fault-tolerant by simply making the process manager fault tolerant. Designing processes in this manner can significantly reduce the cost of achieving overall process fault tolerance and high availability.

By now it should be readily apparent that there are many choices available for making overall business processes fault tolerant or highly available. You can build a process in which every participant is fault tolerant, but this requires every participant to persist its state, and the resulting implementation may not perform as well as you would like. At the other extreme, you can build an end-to-end request-reply business process with a human being as the requestor. If all of the activity of this process is repeatable, then none of the participants need to be fault tolerant. If the process fails to return the expected result, the person simply submits the request again. In between, any number of combinations of fault-tolerant components will yield the robust business process you seek.

Summary

Failovers within a site and between sites often require different failover strategies. Within a site, the use of intermediaries to route requests and the availability of reliable high-speed communications make it straightforward to fail over individual components and services as needed. Between sites, however, communications latency and reliability make it unattractive to fail over components to the other site that still need to interact with components that are still at the original site. For this reason, it is common practice to fail over collections of related components between sites.

Clustering is a style of failover in which an entire execution environment is failed over, with the storage that had been attached to the original environment now attached to the replacement environment. The use of virtual hostnames and IP addresses makes the replacement environment appear identical to the original. This makes it easy for other components to resume interacting with the recovered environment and makes the use of clustering a popular choice for intra-site failover.

The use of asynchronous data replication between sites can cause inconsistencies in the data between applications at the backup site. Because of this, applications and business processes must be tolerant of these inconsistencies, and some loss of data can be expected. Because of the number of possible inconsistencies, it is generally not practical to attempt an automated reconciliation of states. Manual procedures may be required to reconcile states as much as possible.

Making an entire business process fault tolerant does not require all of the components to be fault tolerant. The use of request-reply coordination patterns makes it possible to detect breakdowns and retry operations that have failed. Only the component performing the request-reply needs to be fault tolerant. If there is a process manager that interacts with all the other participants via request-reply, it may be the only component that needs to be fault tolerant.

Key Multi-Component Failover Questions

1. What storage replication and failover techniques are being used within the site? What techniques are being used between the sites?

2. Is asynchronous replication being used? If so, are the asynchronous updates coordinated so that all changes are applied at the remote site in the exact order in which they were applied at the original site?

3. If asynchronous replication is being used without coordinated updates, are the components tolerant of the resulting potential state inconsistencies? What are the business implications of such inconsistencies? Are manual procedures required for recovery?

4. For each business process that must be fault tolerant, what combination of fault-tolerant components and coordination patterns is being used to make the process as a whole fault tolerant? Could the fault-tolerant requirements for the components be reduced by using different coordination patterns?

Chapter 35

Workload
Distribution

It is not unusual for a service demand to exceed the capacity of a single component. In such cases the work must be distributed across two or more components. The following sections discuss the architectural issues associated with workload distribution.

Work Assignment Strategies

When work must be distributed among multiple components, you need to select a strategy for assigning work to individual workers. There are three common strategies:

1. Blind algorithmic assignment
2. Weighted assignment
3. Work pull

Blind algorithmic assignments choose workers based entirely on a formula. Common blind algorithms include round robin (sequential) and pseudo-random assignments. Blind algorithmic assignments have a number of weaknesses: They are blind to the current state of the workers; they assume that the workers all have equal capacity; and they assume that the amount of work required for each request is the same.

Weighted assignments seek to bias the assignments based on weighting factors. These factors are commonly related to the capacity of the worker. There are two common variations, one in which the weights reflect the expected (not measured) capacity of the workers, and the other in which the weights reflect the current measured capacity of the workers.

The history of IP redirectors is an interesting study in the limitations of blind algorithmic and weighted assignments. Early IP redirectors employed a basic round-robin assignment. In practice, when some workers were no longer functional or were overloaded, they still received their share of requests. The next generation employed weighted assignments based on the measured CPU utilization of the workers. The CPU utilization of each worker was periodically measured, and incoming request assignments were biased towards the workers with the lowest CPU utilization. Unfortunately a "hung" worker doesn't use any CPU, but ends up getting a large portion of the requests. Third-generation IP redirectors added liveness tests (executing an HTTP "get") to determine which workers were still operational.

As the IP redirector example illustrates, liveness testing is an important part of any work assignment strategy. Continuing to assign requests to workers that are experiencing problems simply ensures that there will be problems in handling these requests.

One solution to the liveness problem is not to pre-assign work at all, but instead let each worker come and ask for the next task. This is the work pull strategy, and it has the advantage that it has a built-in liveness test: A worker with problems will likely never go back for the next task. This, of course, does not ensure that the tasks that worker is presently performing will be successfully completed, but it does ensure that no further work is assigned to that worker.

Distribution Management and Work Completion

At the core of load distribution lies one dominant requirement: Each request should be handled once—and only once. This is a responsibility that must be managed by a component. Some distribution mechanisms have an explicit distribution manager such as an IP-redirector. Others rely on the characteristics of the underlying communications transport, such as a JMS server. A JMS queue, for example, delivers each message to exactly one recipient. The queue itself (or more properly, the server upon which it resides) acts as the distribution manager.

As important as it is to understand the intended message delivery behavior, it is equally important to understand what happens under failure conditions. If a message has been delivered and the worker dies, is the message lost? JMS, for example, expects the message recipient to acknowledge receipt of the message. Once the message has been delivered, the JMS server will wait indefinitely for the receipt acknowledgment. Most JMS servers, however, stop waiting if the socket connection to the worker is broken (Figure 35–1). When the connection is

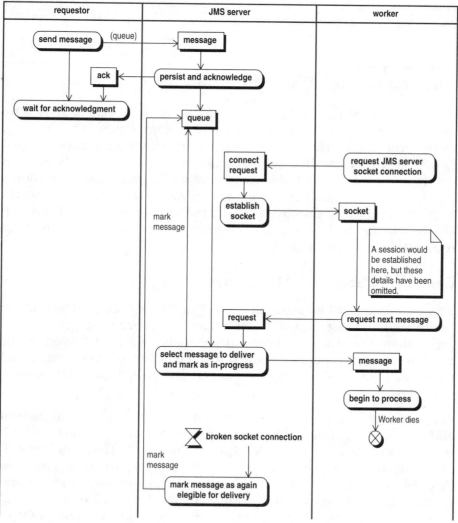

Figure 35–1: *Typical JMS Failed Message Delivery Scenario*

broken, the server marks unacknowledged messages as being once again eligible for delivery. When another worker requests a message, the previously delivered message will again be delivered.

In addition to understanding message delivery under failure conditions, you also need to understand the relationship between the message delivery and the actual worker activities. As Figure 33–1 showed, this relationship can depend as much upon the design of the process and its implementation in individual components as it does on any features of the underlying technology. As an architect, your job is to ensure that this behavior is both well understood and appropriate for the business process at hand.

The Sequencing Problem

When work is distributed among a number of participants, there is no guarantee that the order in which activities complete will be the same as the order in which they were begun. If there is a requirement that two messages be handled in a particular order (e.g., the sequencing of debits and credits in a bank account must be preserved), additional measures must be taken to preserve the message sequence when workload distribution is employed. These measures must extend through all participants in the process all the way to the delivery of the final result at the final destination.

Centralized Sequence Management

There are two strategies that can be applied to sequence preservation: centralized and distributed. In centralized sequence management, one component plays the role of sequence manager. Each participant in the process, when it is about to perform some action, obtains permission to proceed from the sequence manager. The participant may have to wait until other activities have been completed.

The centralized sequence manager strategy is complex to implement and prone to parallel processing problems such as deadlock. It requires a centralized understanding of the overall flow, yet it is neither a process manager nor a process monitor. All participants must be designed to interact with the centralized manager and must be prepared to hold the work in a pending state until permission to proceed is received. The centralized manager also becomes a single point of failure. For all these reasons, the centralized approach is not commonly used.

Distributed Sequence Management

Alternatively, sequencing can be preserved by having each participant in the process preserve the required sequencing. For workers, this means that the workers must be single threaded, that is, will complete the processing of one message before beginning the next. This presents a dilemma for the distribution management component, as it appears to require that all work be sent to the same worker!

Fortunately, the real business requirement is rarely that all messages need to be processed in the order received. More commonly, the requirement is that all messages associated with a particular entity (e.g., a particular bank account) be handled in sequence. In such cases, load can be distributed across multiple components as long as (a) all the messages associated with a particular entity are handled by the same worker, and (b) each worker handles the requests in the order delivered.

Access to Shared Persistent State

Another challenge in workload distribution arises when the workers require access to a common set of information. In such cases, scaling the access to that shared information is often a problem. One approach is to increase the performance of the singular component providing the information. A faster database or a faster SAN can improve matters, but the total capacity of any singular component is ultimately limited by the available technology. These limits may not provide the capacity required to support the demand.

One alternative is to partition the shared information so that different components are managing different subsets of the information. This partitioning requires, first of all, that the data be cleanly separable so that any given request only needs the services of one component. It further requires that the client (the worker, or an intermediary between the worker and the component managing the data) be able to determine which component should handle each request. While complex, this is the only practical approach when the shared information is being updated.

When the shared information is primarily read-only, the replication of the information becomes a viable alternative. Any of the load distribution mechanisms can then be applied to direct information requests to one of the replicated copies. Updates, however, become a problem with the replication approach. Simultaneous updates of all of the copies will require locking, which will adversely impact the high-volume read activity that is going on. Simultaneous updates may be totally impractical when the copies are geographically distributed. Another approach to updates is to apply the updates to one copy and allow the changes to propagate to other copies. This is what LDAP, the lightweight directory access protocol, does. Replication, however, introduces transient inconsistencies between the various copies. You need to determine whether such inconsistencies will present a problem to the business processes.

Geographic Workload Distribution

In a geographically distributed enterprise, it is not unusual to have workers distributed at different geographic locations. In such situations, it is often desirable (for performance reasons) to direct messages to workers in the same geographic region as the client sending the message. When this is a requirement, one of the challenges you will face is determining the information that will be used to associate the clients and workers. You need to determine the nature of this information, its source, and the component(s) that will use this information to direct the work. Note that this is just another type of request routing. As an architect, you need to determine whether the proposed routing scheme is practical from both a technical and administrative perspective, and whether it will perform adequately.

Summary

When the demand for a service exceeds the capacity of a single component to provide the service, more than one worker component is required and the requests must be distributed among those workers. A number of strategies can be employed to distribute the requests. Blind strategies ignore the actual state of the workers and just allocate the work. These strategies suffer when some (or all) of the workers are not functioning properly. Work distribution is best when the actual state of the workers is taken into consideration, including worker liveness tests. Pull strategies inherently incorporate liveness checking, as the workers themselves initiate the retrieval of the work requests.

The relationships among the delivery of work requests, the acknowledgment of the delivery, and the performance of the work have a substantial impact on the behavior of the business process when failures occur. It is important to choose coordination patterns that are appropriate for the business process.

Load distribution and sequencing are fundamentally incompatible concepts: When messages are processed in parallel, there is never any assurance that the work will be completed in the same sequence in which it was begun. In practice, absolute sequencing is rarely required. Usually sequencing is only required with respect to some entity, such as an account. Load distribution can still be used as long as all work associated with the sequence-relevant entity is sent to the same worker.

When load distribution workers require access to common information, the scalability of the component providing that information needs to be taken into consideration. While that component can be scaled vertically (increasing its individual capacity), it may become necessary to either partition or replicate the information among several components and then apply workload distribution techniques to accessing the information.

When workers and clients are geographically distributed, it may be desirable to route requests to workers in the same geographic region. This routing requires reference information, logic to direct the routing, and components responsible for directing the work.

Key Workload Distribution Questions

1. Is workload distribution required for any of the components involved in the business process? If so, what workload distribution strategy will be employed?

2. How does the workload distribution behave under failure? Do the selected coordination patterns preserve work in progress?

3. Are there sequencing requirements for the stream of messages being distributed? How will that sequencing be preserved when the load is distributed?

4. Do the workers involved in the load distribution require access to common information? How will the ability to provide information access be scaled to support the required number of workers?

5. Are the workers and clients geographically distributed? Is there a need to affiliate clients with workers within a geographic region? How will that affiliation be implemented?

Chapter 36

Enterprise Architecture: Fault Tolerance, High Availability, and Load Distribution

The components of the enterprise's systems do not live in isolation, especially those that are service providers. They interact with each other in a variety of ways, and these interactions result in design dependencies. The fault tolerance and high-availability design choices you make for a service (or for any component, for that matter) determine the mechanisms by which that service can be accessed. This, in turn, impacts the design of any component using the service. Every single interaction between components carries with it this type of design dependency.

On the enterprise level, the enterprise architecture decisions made regarding network, storage, machine, and messaging infrastructure will (and are intended to) constrain the options that are available to service developers. However, at the project level, there is still a lot of choice. The impact of these choices extends far beyond the boundaries of the present project. The fault tolerance, high availability, and load distribution decisions made by the project for the services it implements will impact every other project utilizing these services.

The potential complexity of these interaction design dependencies is not to be underestimated. Allowing each project to choose its own strategies for fault tolerance, high availability, and load balancing will likely result in enterprise-scale chaos. Variations in strategy from project to project and service to service will require the detailed study of each individual component and service in order to understand how it responds to failure and how it will be accessed. This not only presents a severe learning challenge to potential service users, it also makes it nearly impossible to broadly understand the overall behavior of a collection of components and services.

The implications are severe for business continuity (site disaster recovery) planning. A rigorous analysis of a data-center failover becomes so complex as to be impractical. Futhermore, the likelihood of a site-to-site failover actually working as planned is vanishingly small without repeated (and expensive) testing. Worst of all, any subsequent changes or additions will require this testing to be repeated.

The solution to this problem lies in establishing an across-the-board simplicity and uniformity in fault tolerance, high-availability, and load distribution approaches. This does not mean that every component and service needs to employ exactly the same strategy. It does mean that the choices need to be narrowed to a few well-chosen and well-engineered alternatives from which individual projects may choose. Guidelines need to be provided for the selection and use of these alternatives as well.

The enterprise architecture group should take the lead in establishing consistent and serviceable approaches to fault tolerance, high availability, and load distribution across the enterprise. This can be accomplished through establishing policies in a number of areas, including:

1. The categorization of information with respect to data loss (Table 33–1)

2. The categorization of business processes with respect to required availability and data loss

3. The establishment of standard information storage patterns

4. The establishment of standard component failover patterns

5. The establishment of standard load distribution patterns

6. The establishment of standard patterns for incorporating fault-tolerant, high-availability, and load distributed services into a process

7. The establishment of standard high-level design patterns for creating scalable, fault-tolerant, and highly available business processes

8. The establishment of the infrastructure needed to support these patterns

Business Process Categorization

To determine whether either fault tolerance or high availability is warranted in a business process, you must first understand the business impact of a business process breakdown. This understanding will help you decide whether the business process itself must be provided in a fault-tolerant or highly available fashion and whether work in progress must be preserved when a breakdown occurs.

This analysis and the interpretation of the results can be somewhat simplified if the enterprise architecture group establishes a business process classification policy. This policy defines the criteria for classifying business processes into categories similar to those shown in Table 36–1. The policy establishes the categories, gives the rationale for determining which category the business process should be in, and illustrates the rationale by giving examples of actual enterprise business processes that belong in each category.

Two of the terms in Table 36–1 warrant explanation. The *recovery time objective (RTO)* is the target length of time for restoring service. The *recovery point objective (RPO)* is the point in time relative to the moment of failure from which data is recovered. The RPO provides a way to define the amount of data that is allowed to be lost in the event of a failover.

Table 36–1: *Business Process Categorization*

Business Process Category	Business Process Availability	Hours of Allowed Downtime/Year (24×7 usage)	Intra-Site Failover		Inter-Site Failover	
			Recovery Time Objective (RTO)	Recovery Point Objective (RPO)	Recovery Time Objective (RTO)	Recovery Point Objective (RPO)
5	FT (100%)	0	0	Moment of failure	1 hour	Moment of failure
4	99.90%	8.76	5 minutes	Moment of failure	1 hour	Moment of failure
3	99.90%	8.76	5 minutes	Moment of failure	1 hour	30 seconds prior
2	99%	87.60	1 hour	1 hour prior	4 hours	1 hour prior
1	99%	87.60	24 hours	24 hours prior	24 hours	24 hours prior

Information Storage

Standardization of the enterprise's approach to fault tolerance and high availability has to begin with the storage of information. The enterprise architecture group should establish data loss categories similar to those in Table 33–1 along with the business rules for placing information in each category. Since higher categories mean higher costs, these categorization rules should, by default, assume information is in the lowest category and establish the criteria that would justify moving the information into a higher category.

Once these categories have been established, the enterprise architecture group should then define the acceptable design patterns for storing and replicating information in each category. These patterns show how the enterprise's storage infrastructure should be employed.

Individual Component and Service Failover Patterns

The enterprise architecture group should establish standard design patterns for intra-site and inter-site failover. These patterns should cover the failover of both fault-tolerant and high availability components, and should be specific to the technology used to implement the component. These patterns employ the information storage design patterns discussed earlier. Using these patterns ensures a consistent failover approach from component to component.

Most of the components that you will be concerned with provide some form of service. Because of this, the enterprise architecture group must also provide failover patterns for the clients accessing service. If the client directly accesses the service, the pattern must indicate what the service client needs to do in the event of a service failover. If the infrastructure is handling the failover, the pattern must indicate what the infrastructure is doing to make this possible. If an indirection mechanism (e.g., a messaging service) is used to access the service, the pattern must indicate the nature of the indirection mechanism and the requirements for its configuration. Patterns for both intra-site and inter-site failover must be provided.

While this approach will establish the design patterns for the most commonly used technologies, you must recognize that technology evolution makes it practically impossible to provide a predefined pattern for every possible combination of technology and fault tolerance, high-availability, and load distribution requirements. Consequently, the enterprise architecture group must be prepared to support project teams facing situations in which the required design patterns do not currently exist. Regardless of whether the project team or the enterprise architecture group actually proposes the solution, the enterprise architecture group must approve the proposed pattern and add it to the inventory of available patterns.

Composite Patterns for FT and HA Services

Making a service highly available or fault tolerant requires the application of at least four design patterns: an intra-site fail-over pattern, and an inter-site fail-over pattern for both the service and its clients. These four patterns must be combined to create a composite fault tolerance or high-availability pattern for each service.

There are often a number of ways in which these patterns can be combined. In such cases, it is advantageous for the enterprise architecture group to standardize the combination and minimize the variations. This standardization greatly simplifies the project work, and further simplifies the operational monitoring and first-tier support for services. This standardization obviates the need to study each individual service in order to understand how it is supposed to fail over and how to monitor its status.

To maintain consistency, the enterprise architecture group must establish preferred composite patterns and associated architectural implementations for various combinations of technologies used for service client implementations, service access, and service provider implementations. These should be summarized in a table similar to Table 36–2 and widely disseminated to project teams. Realistically, however, you are likely to have quite a variation of technologies in your enterprise, accompanied by varying inter-site fail-over requirements. Trying to populate this table for all possible combinations will consume resources defining some solutions that are unlikely to be used in practice. Your initial efforts should focus on defining the patterns that you know will be used. Beyond that, the enterprise architecture group should stand ready to engage and define additional patterns as the need arises.

Table 36–2: *Example Composite Service Failover Pattern Reference Table*

Service Client Technology	Service Access Technology	Service Implementation Technology	Inter-Site Failover Strategy	Failover Pattern
J2EE Application Server	JMS	Mainframe	Synchronous update	Pattern X
Unknown (External user)	HTTP	Application server	Asynchronous update	Pattern Y
Workflow Engine	JMS	COTS customer relationship management system	Overnight backups	Pattern Z

The conclusions about inter-site failover strategies for applications and components should be summarized in a readily available reference table similar to the one shown in Table 36–3. The table itself is the simple part. Your challenge lies in determining the appropriate entries for this table. This can be accomplished by examining business processes that involve two or more of these components. For each business process, you need to examine the coordination between the storage updates in the various components involved in the business process.

Table 36–3: *Example Application/Component Inter-Site Failover Strategy Reference Table*

Application/Component	Storage	Inter-Site Failover Strategy
Mainframe order management system	Database	Nightly database synchronization accompanied by copying transaction log entries as transactions are executed
COTS customer relationship management system	Database	Nightly synchronization
Web site application servers supporting customer order entry	Files (pages)	Nightly file synchronization
Warehouse inventory management system	Database	Synchronous updates (managed by storage subsystem)

Composite Patterns for FT and HA Business Processes

Defining standard failover patterns for individual service clients, services, and their underlying storage is not enough to ensure a consistent multiple-application failover between sites. As Chapter 34 explored, when one application expects another to be in a particular state, the failover strategies for both must be coordinated so that after a site failover the state of each is consistent with the other's expectations.

The enterprise architecture group must evaluate the major stateful components of the enterprise and the manner in which each fails over its persistent state to the backup site. Particular attention needs to be paid to the coordination (or lack thereof) of the replication for the individual applications. The potential for inconsistencies between these states after failover must then be evaluated. This evaluation must determine whether the inconsistencies comply with the business's guidelines regarding data loss. It must also examine the potential for system errors in the ensuing dialog between the systems and determine whether this potential warrants modifying the interfaces to render them more tolerant of errors.

Summary

Most of the decisions surrounding fault tolerance, high availability, and load distribution have an impact that extends beyond any single project, component, or service. Consistency in these decisions is essential to ensure that the enterprise business processes behave in a predictable manner after failover, particularly inter-site failover. Ensuring this consistency is the responsibility of the enterprise architecture group.

Ensuring consistency begins with categorizing information in terms of the allowed data loss and failover times. Based on this categorization, patterns for failing over individual services can be defined based on the categories of information they manage and the technologies they are based upon. Failover patterns for clients using these services and the access mechanisms they use for interacting with the services can also be defined.

Finally, business processes as a whole can be categorized, again based on the allowed data loss (now loss of work in progress) and failover times. Standard patterns can then be defined. These patterns can then be used as guidelines by individual projects.

Key Enterprise Fault Tolerance, High-Availability, and Load Distribution Questions

1. Have standardized categories of information been established in terms of acceptable data loss and recovery time during failover?
2. Have standardized categories of business processes been established in terms of acceptable loss of work in progress and recovery time during failover?
3. Have standard patterns for implementing service fault tolerance, high availability, and load distribution been established based on the categories of information they manage?
4. Have standard patterns for implementing service client failover been established for each service implementation pattern?
5. Have composite patterns been established showing how combinations of services and service clients fail over both within and between data centers?
6. Have standard fault tolerance and high-availability patterns been established for high-level business processes based on their categorization?

Suggested Reading

ISO Public Available Specification ISO/PAS 22399:2007. "Societal security— Guideline for incident preparedness and operational continuity management." International Standards Organization (www.iso.org) (2007).

Part VIII

Completing the Architecture

Chapter 37

Process Security

Business processes often encounter a number of issues related to trust—or the lack thereof. Comprising the subject of security, these issues include authenticating the credentials of a participant, checking that the participant is authorized to access a particular piece of information or a service, and encrypting information where required so that it cannot be observed by unauthorized participants. Security is an issue when either the participants must be sure who they are dealing with or there is activity that must be kept secret from unauthorized parties.

The enterprise's security policies specify the manner in which security is addressed with respect to a given security topic. These policies set forth rules and conditions for interactions between participants with respect to the relevant topic. As an architect, your responsibility is to understand these policies and ensure that the business process implementation is in compliance.

For clarity, the discussion of security in this chapter utilizes the notion of a *trust zone*. A trust zone defines a security boundary. All parties and all interactions within a trust zone are considered to be trusted and do not require any special security precautions. External interactions with the trust zone may require the enforcement of specific security policies depending on the type of information being exchanged and the nature of the other parties in the interactions.

Security Information Classification

The basis for all decisions regarding security is a set of enterprise security guidelines. These guidelines classify the information in the enterprise from a security perspective and specify the security policies that must be followed when dealing with information in each classification. An example summary of these guidelines is presented in Table 37–1. As an architect, you need to be familiar with these classifications and the corresponding security policies, because you are responsible for ensuring the systems you build are in compliance with these policies. Enterprise architects are responsible for establishing standards for the system implementation of each type of policy. Project architects are responsible for ensuring that the business process information has been classified by the appropriate parties and that the implementation complies with the appropriate enterprise architecture standards.

Identity and Authentication

When there is a potential lack of trust between participants in a business process, the identity of interacting parties needs to be understood. In some cases only one of the parties in an interaction needs to know the identity of the other. In other cases, both parties need to know the identity of the other party.

Unfortunately, it is nearly impossible to establish the absolute identity of any party. Instead, each party presents a claimed identity (e.g., a username) and some evidence that they are, indeed, the party that is supposed to be associated with the identity (e.g., a password). The process of verifying that the evidence matches the claimed identity is known as *authentication*.

The Authentication Process

The authentication process involves three elements: the claimed identity, the evidence provided by the party claiming to have that identity, and some reference information that is used to validate the evidence. In the case of a username/password authentication, the username is the claimed identity, the password is the evidence, and the local record of the password associated with the username is the reference information used to authenticate the user. Note, however, that there is no guarantee

Table 37-1: *Example Security Classification Scheme*

Classification Level	Examples	Applicable Security Policies
4—Extremely sensitive	Employment information, financial and health information; corporate merger and acquisition information	All parties must be authenticated and authorized; information in transit and in storage must be encrypted; an audit trail must be kept for all access (read and modification); all records must be digitally signed
3—Secret	Aggregate sales information sufficient to reveal enterprise financial performance	All parties must be authenticated and authorized; information in transit must be encrypted and may not be stored except in systems with the appropriate security provisions
2—Confidential	Individual retail sales transactions, inventory levels	Information within enterprise facilities may be stored in the clear, and its access from within the enterprise does not require authentication and authorization; information in transit outside the enterprise must be encrypted, and its usage outside the enterprise requires authentication and authorization
1—Public	Product catalog information; general information about the enterprise	No security restrictions

that the party being authenticated is the intended party: A stolen user-name and password will allow anyone to claim that identity.

There is also an element of trust involved in establishing the reference data. The party issuing the identifier and associating the password (or other reference data) with the identifier is being trusted to establish, by some unspecified means, who that party really is. They are also being trusted to ensure that the reference data is appropriately protected. A violation of this trust compromises the integrity of the authentication process.

Reference Data for Authentication

Reference data for authentication generally falls into one of two categories: secrets and direct evidence. A secret is a piece of information that is supposed to be known only to the party claiming the identity. Passwords and certificates are examples of secrets. The reference data for secrets is a record of the secret associated with a particular identity. Authentication consists of determining whether the correct secret was provided. To maintain security, this reference information must be appropriately protected against unauthorized access.

Direct evidence is derived from some physical characteristic of the party that is presumed to be unique to the party and difficult to imitate. Photographic images, fingerprints, and retinal scans are examples of direct evidence. The reference data for direct evidence is a copy of the expected evidence, and authentication consists of determining whether the actual evidence presented at the time of authentication matches the reference data. The use of the direct evidence approach is pretty much restricted to the identification of people and other living organisms whose physical characteristics vary sufficiently from individual to individual to uniquely identify the individual. Systems generally rely on the secrets approach.

Authorization

Once the identity of a participant has been authenticated, the next question is usually whether that participant has permission to access the information or operation. The act of determining whether they have this permission is referred to as *authorization*.

The Granularity Problem

One of the challenges in authorization lies in categorizing the things that require permission. Many systems require usernames and passwords for system access. Here the granularity of the permission is the system itself, granting the user the right to access the entire system and its contents. However, many systems use the user identity to further restrict access, limiting it to specific operations that the system provides. The granularity here is the operation.

The problem you face is a practical one. In the enterprise there can be thousands of systems, millions of operations, and trillions of data elements. Authorization policies seek to restrict access to these things, and, furthermore, these restrictions may depend not only upon the identity of the individual seeking access but also on the access channel being used. The sheer number of systems, operations, data elements, users, and access channels makes the administrative task of specifying who is authorized to access what, and under what circumstances, very complex.

Groups and Roles

Two concepts have emerged to help simplify the task of specifying who is allowed to access what: roles and groups. A role specifies a part that a participant might play in a business process. To play that role, the participant requires access to certain systems, operations, and data elements. The use of roles splits the administrative tasks in specifying authorization, allowing access rights to specific systems, operations, and data to be associated with specific roles, and then separately specifying which participants are allowed to play those roles.

While roles provide one level of simplification, defining who is allowed to play which role can still be complex when there are many individuals and each individual is allowed to play a number of roles. In such cases, it is often convenient to define groups of participants and then associate groups with roles. This is particularly useful when roles are specific to a particular system and a participant needs to interact with multiple systems. Consider a call center with thousands of individuals, each requiring access to multiple systems to support customers. Placing the call center workers in a common group and associating that group with the multiple system roles simplifies the administration.

Group and Role Limitations

While groups and roles simplify the administration of access rights, their use is not well suited to some situations. As commonly implemented, the association of participants with groups and groups with roles is usually assumed to be relatively static information that is accessed far more often than it is changed. A reference data manager such as LDAP is used to store these associations, which are then referenced each time a participant attempts access to a restricted resource.

Now consider the following situation. Employees in a large company carry company credit cards as part of the company's expense management system. The business rules for administering these credit card accounts stipulate that the employee and anybody in the organizational hierarchy above the employee (up to and including the CEO of the company) are authorized to administer the account. They also stipulate that anybody in the bank who is currently assigned to support any organizational unit containing the employee is authorized to administer the account as well. In this case, every account defines a unique role, and every organizational unit above the employee defines a unique group. There are additional groups in the bank assigned to support each organizational unit, and these assignments, themselves, change from time to time. This structure is so complex, and the organizational assignments in both the company and the bank so fluid, that pre-computing roles and groups does not provide an effective solution to the authorization problem.

Another complex example is also to be found in banks. Many banks have varied lines of businesses, including retail banking (checking and savings accounts), mortgage, insurance, and investment banking. These banks often want to assemble a consolidated customer view across these multiple lines of business. However, each of the bank's lines of business is generally a distinct legal entity. There are complex national and state regulations governing the sharing of information between legal entities. Access rights may vary depending upon the specific type of data, the type of account, the jurisdiction governing the account, the jurisdiction in which the customer resides, the jurisdiction of the party attempting to view the information, and the purpose for which the information is being used. Once again, a simple group-and-role model is not adequate to describe these rules.

The bottom line here is that in these days of increasingly tighter regulations regarding information access, the traditional group and role models often turn out to be inadequate for the task. The onus is on you, the architect, to understand the authorization requirements and determine just how these requirements are to be met. The result can be a significant design challenge in and of itself.

Encryption

Encryption protects information from being observed by unauthorized parties. Encryption is commonly applied to data in transit from one participant to another, but may also be applied to data being stored. When data is in transit, one participant (or a designated agent) encrypts the data prior to its transmission, and another participant (or designated agent) decrypts the data upon receipt. In the case of stored data, it is generally the same participant (or agent) that encrypts and decrypts the data.

Encryption and decryption use keys to encode and decode the information. When the same key is used for both encryption and decryption, the encryption is said to be *symmetric*. Symmetric encryption is usually efficient, but a compromise of the key renders the data vulnerable. Since the key must be exchanged between the parties, the movement of the key itself may create opportunities for its compromise.

Asymmetric encryption uses pairs of keys, generally referred to as a private key and a public key. The private key is held only by one party, and thus constitutes a relatively well-kept secret. The public key is generally available to all parties. When some party (other than the private key holder) wishes to send encrypted data, it encrypts the data using the public key. At this point, only the holder of the private key can decrypt the data. If the private key is used to encrypt the data, then anybody holding the public key can decrypt the data. One nice property here is that since only the holder of the private key could have encrypted this data, the successful decryption with the public key certifies the private key holder as the originator of the data.

While powerful, asymmetric encryption is computationally expensive and its use has a significantly greater performance impact than symmetric encryption. On the other hand, asymmetric encryption is widely considered to be the more secure approach. These two techniques can be effectively combined to yield a secure and effective encryption mechanism. The SSL (secure socket link) protocol is perhaps the best known example. It uses asymmetric encryption for an initial handshake, at which point one of the parties creates a symmetric key, encrypts it with the other party's public key, and passes it to the other party. The other party uses its private key to decrypt and recover the symmetric key, and now the two parties use this symmetric key to exchange data for some period of time. When that time expires, the parties revert to the asymmetric keys, generate and exchange a new symmetric key, and then use this new key for some period of time.

From an architectural perspective, you need to understand the performance impact of the encryption. You also need to understand the manner in which keys are generated, transmitted, and stored both from a process perspective and from a security perspective. Any compromise in this process or in any environment containing either a symmetric key or a private key is a potential source of a security breech.

Digital Signatures

Besides supporting asymmetric encryption, public and private keys can also be used to digitally sign data. A publicly known algorithm is used to derive a value from the source data that uniquely depends upon the data. Checksums and hash keys are simple examples of this kind of information. This generated information is then encrypted with the private key, and the resulting encrypted value constitutes the digital signature. The original data and the digital signature are sent as a unit.

On the receiving end, the recipient can use the public key to retrieve the generated value and then use the well-known algorithm to re-generate this value from the received data. If the two values match, then the recipient concludes that the data, as received, is the same as the data that was used to generate the signature.

Other Security-Related Requirements

Security is a somewhat open-ended topic, and many other requirements may be considered to fall under its umbrella. Among these are non-repudiation (the ability to record a message in such a way that the sender cannot deny its origin or timing) and assertions (signed statements that specific conditions have been met). Audit trails (records of who did what and when) are often considered part of security, particularly when they pertain to the modification of reference information used for authentication and authorization.

One topic that is very different in kind is often placed under the heading of security: denial-of-service attacks. A denial-of-service attack occurs when unauthorized parties attempt to access an interface at such a high rate that, even though the access is unsuccessful, valid access by authorized parties is adversely impacted. Avoiding adverse impacts from a denial-of-service attack is as much a performance issue as it is a security issue.

Reference Data Servers and Performance

Authentication and authorization both require access to reference data. The components that maintain this information and the communications with them are always potential performance bottlenecks. Consequently, the frequency and manner in which this reference information is accessed is a significant architectural issue.

One way to lessen this impact is to have the components using the reference data cache it for future reference. This, of course, only provides benefit if there is a statistically significant chance that future authentications and authorizations will require the same reference information. The likelihood of this occurring must be one of the factors influencing the architectural decision to employ such caching. The ability of the caches to update quickly in the event of access being revoked should also be a consideration. A disgruntled ex-employee can do a lot of damage in a short time if the revocation is delayed.

Another approach is to employ tokens. A token is a digitally signed list of authorizations and other security assertions. When tokens are employed, the first exchange with the authorization server returns a token containing the authorizations for the party being authorized. The token is then passed on in interactions with other participants. These participants can use the authorizations in the token instead of conducting their own interactions with authentication and authorization servers. The use of tokens thus reduces the frequency of interactions with authentication and authorization servers. However, in order to take advantage of this approach, the token must be carried forward in interactions, and the participants receiving the tokens must be capable of utilizing the information they contain.

Trust Zones

At its core, security is about who is to be trusted—and who is not. In any environment, there are always boundaries within which the parties and their interactions are trusted. Those regions are here termed *trust zones* (Figure 37–1). If everything within a process lies within one trust zone, then there is nothing to discuss in terms of security.

The security discussion gets more interesting when communications are required between trust zones, as shown in Figure 37–2. From a security perspective, the world outside the trust zone is not to be trusted. It then becomes necessary to determine, from a business perspective, what this lack of trust requires of the interaction. The security classification of information plays a key role here. Based on that classification, does the interaction require that the identities of the participants be authenticated? Does it require authorization checks? Does it require the encryption of communications between the participants? What other security requirements are there?

The answers to these questions will determine the security policies that need to be applied. As an architect, your task is to determine how these policies will be implemented, how they will be enforced, and at what point they will be enforced.

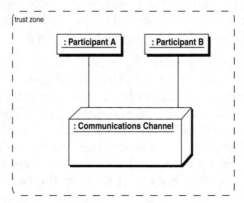

Figure 37–1: *Trust Zone*

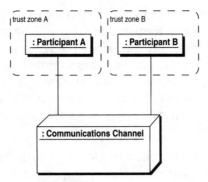

Figure 37–2: *Two Interacting Trust Zones*

If a policy is to be enforced, you need to define the location of the policy enforcement point. Will the policies be enforced by the participants at their interfaces, or will the policies be enforced by the communications channel itself? At first glance, it would appear that the participants provide the better home for this functionality. Since they are already trusted participants within their own trust zones, it would make sense that they would control the access to the trust zone.

Unfortunately, while it makes logical sense for the participants to be the enforcing parties, the practical reality is that enterprise environments are populated with many systems that have only limited security policy enforcement capabilities, particularly with respect to encryption. At the same time, some common communications transport mechanisms are available with at least some capability for authentication, authorization, and encryption, primarily through the use of secure socket links (SSL). The implementation of security is often a compromise between what the policy requires and what is feasible with the available technology.

Channel Enforcement

Some commonly used communications transports provide limited security policy enforcement capabilities, including HTTPS (secure hypertext transport protocol) and JMS (Java message service) accessed with SSL.

HTTPS provides the infrastructure for authentication and encryption in the form of a code library embedded in the participant. It provides the facilities for one or both of the parties to authenticate the other party. It also provides mechanisms for encrypting the ensuing communications. Authorization, on the other hand, must be dealt with outside the code library by the participants themselves. Each must decide, using its own logic, whether or not to accept a connection from the other party. Once the socket connection is established, further authorizations associated with individual interactions over the socket are also up to the participants.

JMS servers accessed via SSL can provide authentication, authorization, and encryption services depending upon the JMS vendor. The JMS server can authenticate JMS clients and offer the client the ability to authenticate the JMS server instance. The JMS server can control which parties are authorized to connect to the server and may provide authorization checks down to the level of which participants are allowed to publish or subscribe to specific JMS destinations. SSL also provides the ability to encrypt communications between the JMS server and its clients.

The administration of security with HTTPS is done on a participant-by-participant basis. Since the HTTPS code library executes as part of the participant code, its configuration is logically part of the participant configuration. Each participant is thus configured independently.

JMS security administration, on the other hand, impacts the configuration of the JMS server, although the client may be configured to authenticate the credentials of the JMS server to which it connects. The authentication and encryption are again provided by the underlying SSL library, but the authorization is managed entirely by the JMS server. Typically, the association of destinations with roles is maintained within the JMS server. The association of JMS client credentials with those roles, however, may typically be maintained either within the JMS server itself or in an external authorization server such as LDAP. When an external authorization server is used, there are typically a number of options available for either dynamically querying the server or replicating its authorization information within the JMS server.

JMS channel enforcement has its limitations. The authorization checks do not directly check the authorization of one participant to interact with another. Instead, they control access to destinations. Since most JMS servers allow destinations to be routed to other destinations, an understanding of the JMS configuration is required, in addition to the authorization information, to understand exactly who can talk with whom. Furthermore, even these authorization checks are relatively coarse grained. Destinations usually equate to operations or groups of operations, and it is at this level that they provide access control. Encryption is also a coarse-grained, all-or-nothing proposition.

While the use of a single JMS server provides a useful central point for security administration, geographically distributed enterprises typically employ routed networks of JMS servers. When this happens, the administrative simplicity vanishes, as each JMS server must be configured with respect to the participants who will connect to it. The JMS servers also need to be authorized with respect to one another, and again the routing of messages between servers must be understood as well as the participant authorizations with respect to each server.

Zone Enforcement and Policy Agents

The alternative to channel enforcement is to have policies enforced within the trusted zone. If the participant is connecting directly to the communications channel, this means that the participant itself becomes the policy enforcement point. Unfortunately, the majority of participants found in the enterprise today have limited capabilities in this regard.

An increasingly popular alternative is to employ a policy agent as an intermediary between the participant and the external communications channel (Figure 37-3). A policy agent is a specialized component designed to play this intermediary role specifically to enforce security policies (and other forms of policies as well). The agent acts on behalf of the participant, enforcing security policies as necessary. Of course,

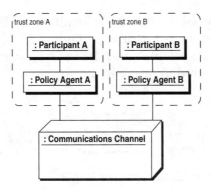

Figure 37–3: *Policy Agents*

the communications between the agent and the participant are now unregulated, and therefore must occur within a trusted zone. In this regard, some agents actually operate within the same operating system process space as the participant, reducing the scope of the trust zone to the operating system process.

There are a number of advantages to the policy agent approach. These agents are designed specifically to enforce policies and thus tend to offer a much broader range of capabilities than typically found in participants. They are generally capable of caching reference information, and thus provide performance efficiencies, and many are capable of using tokens as well. Agents tend to be designed to work with a centralized policy administrator so that they are relatively easy to administer. Finally, and perhaps most significantly, their use completely separates the lifecycle of policy development from the lifecycle of the participant development. This significantly reduces the cost and time required to implement or change security policies.

Multi-Zone Security

The number of participants in enterprise business processes frequently present even more complex security problems. For example, consider the three-party interactions illustrated in Figure 37–4. `Participant A`, who may be a user, submits `request X` to `Participant B`, which may be an application server. `Participant B`, in turn, submits `request Y` to `Participant C` on behalf of `Participant A`. The challenging question then becomes what credentials should accompany `request Y`—the credentials of `Participant B` or those of `Participant A`?

Historically, this problem has been dealt with largely by merging `Trust Zone B` and `Trust Zone C` (Figure 37–5). `Participant B` becomes a "trusted system," and `Participant C` simply accepts `Participant B`'s credentials and performs the work. There is no

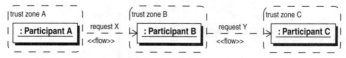

Figure 37–4: *The Three-Zone Security Problem*

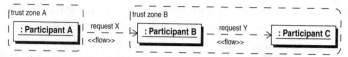

Figure 37–5: *Weakened Multi-Party Security*

deeper security, and if any information about `Participant A` is carried along, it comes in the form of data that is carried in `request Y`.

Concerns about internal security within the enterprise are increasingly making the expanded trust zone approach unacceptable at the business level. Ideally, `Participant C` would like to have the credentials of `Participant A`, since the transaction is really being performed on behalf of this participant. It may also want the credentials of `Participant B` to simply verify that the request is originating from a trusted location.

Working with these complex relationships requires more complex rules and a regularized scheme for expressing and enforcing these rules. The SOAP-related WS-Security and WS-Security Policy standards represent a significant and well-engineered step in this direction. You should become familiar with these standards and their application, as they not only provide well-structured solutions to this kind of security challenge, but they also form the emerging basis for policy agents as a class of component.

Summary

Security begins with the understanding that access to certain classes of information and functionality needs to be managed. The starting point for the enterprise is a classification scheme that defines the different classifications of information and specifies the business rules for the access and handling of this information.

Controlling access to information requires that the identity of parties be authenticated, and that their authorization to access or use the information be verified. Reference data and the logic for performing the authentication and authorization checks are required in both cases. The concepts of roles and groups can greatly simplify the administration of authorization, but they are not always adequate to the task.

Encryption prevents the unauthorized access of information. Symmetric and asymmetric encryption each provide different degrees of security and efficiency. Selecting one or the other, or using them both together, is an exercise in trading off performance against security. Digital signatures provide a mechanism for authenticating the origin of information.

Accessing the reference information required for authentication and authorization can create performance problems. The caching of this information or the use of tokens can significantly lessen the performance impact.

Security comes into play when participants in different trust zones need to interact. Enterprise rules, based on the classification of the information being exchanged, define the security policies that must be enforced. The actual enforcement point for these rules can be in the trust zone itself or in the communications channel connecting them. Both the communications components and existing participant systems tend to have limited capabilities with respect to implementing security policies. Policy agents, acting as intermediaries, provide an effective mechanism for policy enforcement as well as a means for separating the policy lifecycle from that of the participants in the process.

The presence of multiple participants in a business process presents even more complex challenges. The challenge lies in deciding what credentials to use in back-office systems when intermediaries take action in these back-office systems on behalf of front-office users. Carrying the user's credentials through to the back-office system is both administratively complex and technically challenging. SOAP, in conjunction with WS-Security and WS-Security Policy standards, provides the building blocks to make this problem manageable.

Key Security Questions

1. Is there an established security classification scheme for enterprise information? Does it specify the business rules for handling information in the different classifications?

2. Have preferred mechanisms for authentication and authorization been established in the enterprise? Have approved design patterns been established for systems and technologies that cannot utilize these preferred mechanisms?

3. Is the group-and-role paradigm sufficient to handle the authorization requirements of the business process? If not, what approach will be used?

4. Where are authentication, authorization, and encryption required in the business process? Have the activity diagrams describing the implementation been updated to reflect these activities and their responsibility assignments?

5. What credentials are being used to access back-office systems when front-office requests are being handled by intermediary components? Does this approach comply with enterprise security policies?

Suggested Reading

Cabrera, Luis Felipe, and Chris Kurt. 2005. *Web Services Architecture and its Specifications: Essentials for Understanding WS-**. Redmond, WA: Microsoft Press.

Weerawarana, Sanjiva, Francisco Curbera, Frank Leymann, Tony Storey, and Donald F. Ferguson. 2005. *Web Services Platform Architecture: SOAP, WSDL, WS-Policy, WS-Addressing, WS-BPEL, WS-Reliable Messaging, and More*. Upper Saddle River, NJ: Prentice Hall.

Chapter 38

Process Monitoring

Traditionally, monitoring has focused on determining the status of individual components such as databases and application servers. While that type of monitoring continues to be important, it needs to be augmented with the monitoring of the business processes that are executing across the enterprise environment. This monitoring is important for a number of reasons:

1. Detecting breakdowns (outright failures) in business processes. This enables the enterprise to determine the health and availability of the processes. Viewed after the fact, this information enables the enterprise to determine whether the processes are actually providing the levels of service that the enterprise requires. Monitored in real time, this information can be used to dynamically detect breakdowns and initiate their correction. Done properly, this can not only improve process availability, but also can be used to dynamically get an errant process back on track so that it satisfies its KPIs and SLAs in spite of breakdowns.

2. Measuring key performance indicators (KPIs) and their compliance with SLAs. These measurements will enable an enterprise to determine whether it is meeting its own performance objectives and satisfying its contractual service-level agreements.

3. Measuring the achievement of process improvement goals. This is the critical information needed to determine whether projects are actually successful in providing the business value that motivated them in the first place.

4. Comparing actual usage rates and data volumes for comparison against critical architectural assumptions and deployed component capacities. The purpose of this monitoring is to identify trends in the process and anticipate the need for future action, such as increasing capacity.

As enterprises grow, their business processes grow as well, involving increasing numbers of system components and increasing execution complexity. The complexity of monitoring these processes increases as well, which makes process monitoring an attractive target for automation. However, before doing any design work associated with this automation, the reasons for doing the monitoring must be clear so that the design work can be efficiently focused. The monitoring goals will dictate what needs to be monitored and what needs to be done with the monitoring results.

Performance Monitoring

Many needed process measurements are related to performance. During testing, you want to ensure that the business process and its supporting components are capable of providing the required level of service. Performance requirements without corresponding actual measurements are simply wishful thinking. Performance requirements demand performance monitoring.

You also need to make performance measurements during operation. These measurements will establish whether the business process is continuing to perform as designed. They will also determine whether the business process demand remains within the limits of the design and currently deployed capacity.

Monitoring at One Point

The simplest form of performance monitoring is to gather data at a single point. By monitoring communications at a single point, you can gather data about the rate at which interactions are occurring, the volume of data moved in each interaction, and the time distribution of these rates and sizes. These measurements clearly reflect the profile of demands that are being placed on components.

The problem with monitoring at one point is that you can't draw many conclusions about whether business processes are executing properly.

You may be able to identify an overloaded machine or component, but you can't draw any conclusions about lower levels of activity. This is because you don't know whether the activity level is low because something upstream in the business process is broken or whether there is simply low demand at the moment.

Uncorrelated Monitoring at Two Points

Nearly as simple as monitoring at one point is the collection of data at two or more points. Unfortunately, while these measurements tell you a lot about the demand profile at these different points, they again tell you very little about whether things are operating properly. The lack of correlation between the data samples at one point and the data samples at another do not allow you to draw conclusions about the portion of the process in between. While you might expect to see a rise in the upstream rate followed by a rise in the downstream rate, variations in the amount of work required to handle each communication and processing delays in intermediate components make it difficult to draw any definitive conclusions from these measurements.

Correlated Monitoring at Two Points

The best possible monitoring is to correlate the activity observed at one point with the activity observed at another. Interactions observed at one point are correlated with those observed at another so you know that this particular downstream interaction was the direct consequence of some particular upstream interaction.

If you can make this type of correlation, you can now measure response times. In addition, if you have an SLA for the intervening portion of the process, you can also detect process breakdowns. The absence of a downstream interaction within the SLA-allotted time of the upstream interaction indicates a breakdown in the process.

While powerful, these measurements require design work. The individual interactions must be observed and the observations brought together at a common correlation point. Furthermore, the observations must capture enough data to be able to correlate the observations. Fortunately, many message-based communications components make it relatively simple to capture all or part of a message, which simplifies this form of measurement.

As complex as correlated measurements are, they are the only nonintrusive way to measure response times. For this reason, it is good practice to identify the need for such measurements early in the design cycle, as the capture of this data can often be built into the system components at little additional cost.

Monitoring Process Status

When it comes to monitoring the overall status of a business process, you have a choice to make: Should you be monitoring the detailed status of the business process, or should you monitor the achievement of the process milestones that were discussed back in Chapter 10? The answer depends upon the monitoring goals, and the choice has substantial implications for the flexibility of the resulting monitoring.

Recall that the milestones reflect the state of a business process independently of the actual process details. Monitoring milestones generally provides all of the information that a nonparticipant in the actual process would want to know. At this level of abstraction you can establish how often a process is executing and how long it takes the process to reach a particular milestone.

While milestone monitoring provides less information about the process than might be gathered by direct monitoring, it has a distinct advantage: The measurements and their interpretation tend to be relatively stable over time. While business processes are continually being improved, the process milestones tend to remain stable. The milestones also tend to be the same across different business processes attempting to achieve the same goal. The milestones in ordering and shipping a product (order placement, credit approval, obtaining payment, and product delivery) do not change when the order is placed online versus over the phone. Thus monitoring that is focused on milestones will not require updating when the process itself changes, nor will the consumers of the monitoring information. This reduces the cost of making business process changes, and thus facilitates the evolution of business processes, making the overall enterprise more flexible.

Milestone monitoring, on the other hand, may not provide sufficient detail to fine-tune the individual steps of a business process. When there is more than one activity required to progress from one milestone to the next, milestone monitoring will not capture how long it took to perform each of these activities. Neither will it capture information about the resources expended at each step in the process: who did what work and how much effort was required. Gathering this type of information requires direct monitoring of the business process itself.

The design of direct process monitoring, however, is highly dependent upon the actual process design and must be updated each time the process is changed. But even though process-level data must be collected to meet some monitoring goals, other monitoring goals can still be met through milestone monitoring.

To keep milestone-level data analysis and progress evaluation independent of the process design, it is good design practice to abstract milestone-level status from the detailed process design and then use milestone monitoring wherever possible. Thus, a process change will only require the regeneration of the milestone status and will not impact the consumers of the milestone information.

Supervisory Processes

Simply identifying that the progress of a business process is unsatisfactory accomplishes nothing: It is the actions triggered by the monitoring that provide value to the enterprise. These actions comprise the supervisory processes—the processes that monitor and manage other processes.

Unfortunately, supervisory processes are all too often overlooked in the design of business processes and systems. An understanding of these supervisory processes is just as much a part of monitoring design as the capture of the data. A failure to consider how the monitoring results are to be used in these supervisory processes, even if those processes will not be implemented until a later phase of the project, can lead to the generation of monitoring results that simply cannot support the supervisory processes.

Monitoring results can either be delivered to supervisory processes as they occur or accumulated and delivered in batches. The style in which these results are delivered affects the choice of delivery mechanism, the design of the supervisory process, and the timeliness with which the supervisory process can respond to monitoring results. If the monitoring results are to be used for an after-the-fact analysis, then the batch delivery of the results in a file or in the form of a report may be appropriate. Here the supervisory process (whether manual or automated) runs periodically, picks up the results, and decides what action to take.

If the monitoring results are to be acted upon in near-real-time, then there is little choice other than to deliver them as they are produced. This always requires some form of automation. If the supervisory process is a manual one, requiring human action, then the automation consists of alerting someone of the need for action. If the supervisory process is automated, then the result must trigger supervisory activity when it is produced. In either case, the design of the interaction between monitoring activities and the supervisory process is a key element of the monitoring design.

Finally, you should note that process monitoring is often undertaken as the first step towards the eventual management of that process using a workflow engine. The intent is to ultimately combine process monitoring with active process management. In such cases, the full set of design issues discussed in Chapter 42 should be considered as part of the initial process monitoring effort in order to make this evolution as smooth as possible.

The Impact of Monitoring on Performance

Monitoring, as with any form of activity, requires resources. Data needs to be captured and analyzed, and resources are required for both. This resource utilization needs to be carefully considered in the design of monitoring. As much as possible, you want to design the monitoring so that it has little if any impact on the performance of the business process. It is a best practice to use components and machines for monitoring that are not actively involved in the business processes to minimize this impact. The impact on storage and network bandwidth needs to be taken into account as well.

Summary

Business processes need to be monitored for a variety of reasons, ranging from detecting process breakdowns to measuring their performance and achievement of business goals. Monitoring requires resources and must be carefully designed so that the performance of the monitored process is not adversely impacted.

Performance monitoring requires measurements. Throughput and data rate measurements can be made by monitoring interactions at one point, but the measurement of response times and the detection of breakdowns requires the correlation of measurements made at two or more points.

Process status can be monitored at either the milestone level or the detailed process activity level. Milestone monitoring is suitable for most business purposes, and this level of monitoring is not impacted by the evolution of the business process. Milestone monitoring, on the other hand, may not provide sufficient information to fine-tune the business process.

Monitoring results are the inputs to supervisory processes. The needs and design of those supervisory processes need to be taken into account when designing monitoring to ensure that the needs of these supervisory processes will be met.

Key Process Monitoring Questions

1. What are the monitoring objectives for the business process? What measurements are required to support those objectives?

2. What performance measurements are required? How will the data be captured? How will it be correlated? What component will analyze the data and generate monitoring results?

3. Which monitoring objectives can be achieved through milestone monitoring? Which require direct process activity monitoring?

4. Which supervisory processes will consume the monitoring results? How will the results be delivered? Is the delivery done in real time?

5. Is the use of process monitoring the first step towards process management? If so, have all process management design issues been considered?

Chapter 39

Architecture Evaluation

"Are you a good witch or a bad witch?"
—Glinda to Dorothy after Dorothy's
house landed on and killed the Wicked
Witch of the East in *The Wizard of Oz*

Just as Glinda in the Wizard of Oz could not determine whether Dorothy was a good witch or a bad witch (or a witch at all!) simply by taking a look at her, just looking at a system architecture does not provide sufficient information for determining whether the architecture is good or bad. You need to examine the architecture in the context of its intended usage to draw such conclusions.

The purpose of architecture evaluation is to determine the suitability of an architecture before a commitment is made to the design. Partial evaluations, performed frequently during the architecture development process, serve to ensure that the evolving architecture is and remains satisfactory. For distributed information systems in general and service-oriented architectures in particular these evaluations are typically performed in at least seven categories:

1. Usability
2. Performance
3. Cost and schedule feasibility

4. Observability
5. Ability to evolve
6. Ability to handle stress
7. Compliance with standards

This list represents a somewhat minimalistic evaluation, and should not be considered by any means to be either closed or complete. Use it as a starting point for your evaluations, and add to it any additional evaluation criteria that are relevant to your solutions.

Usability

Usability is the ease with which the architecture can support its intended purpose. It is, fundamentally, the most important requirement for any architecture. Fortunately, if you have been following the methodology outlined in this book, you have already addressed usability. You have defined the usage of the architecture in terms of the business processes it is intended to support. The variety of behavior required for the business processes has been expressed through a variety of scenarios. These scenarios have been the basis for developing the architecture. You have considered the functional support, communications, data, coordination, availability, fault tolerance, workload distribution, security, and monitoring—all with respect to the specific business process scenarios. A more thorough exploration of the architecture's usability would be hard to find.

Performance

To be successful, the architecture needs to support the volume of expected business process activity while also meeting business process expectations in terms of response times. Determining whether this is possible requires determining the rates at which individual components are required to respond to inputs, determining the required response times, determining the level of system resources required to support this activity, and making a judgment call as to whether those resource requirements are reasonable.

Much of the groundwork has already been laid for this evaluation. The rate metrics gathered for each scenario together with the activity diagrams and deployment diagrams provide sufficient information to determine the rate at which individual components need to perform their work and the load that will be placed on the network segments. These same activity diagrams provide the information required to take business process response time requirements and derive response time budget assignments for the individual participants in the process. This information can then be used to determine the computing and network resources required to support the business processes and determine whether these resource demands are reasonable.

This analysis process can (and should) be used throughout the lifecycle of the project. It should be applied to the very first business process analyzed as a means of determining whether it is even feasible to support these processes. As the architecture development continues, it should be applied to the small number (in most systems) of scenarios that account for the bulk of the system activity. This analysis will provide a rough estimate of the overall machine and network resources that will be required to support the architecture. These results can then be used to evaluate the reasonableness of the resource demands given the project cost constraints and can be used to compare the relative costs of two architectures. Finally, as the architecture nears completion, the analysis should be extended to encompass all scenarios that occur frequently enough to present significant system demands. This analysis can then be used to support the final hardware and network sizing for capacity-planning purposes.

Component Resource Demand Analysis

Each business process scenario depicts what happens for a single execution of the scenario. Figure 39–1, for example, shows the successful execution scenario for withdrawing cash from an ATM machine.

At the very beginning of the project, when you did the business process inventory, you determined the peak rate at which the scenario is expected to execute. By adding a little bit more information, you can directly obtain the rates at which different participants need to respond to interactions and perform their activities. The required information is the number of times each interaction occurs for each execution of the scenario. Most interactions occur once for each scenario execution. Each of the messages in this scenario, for example, occurs exactly once per scenario execution. However, in other scenarios, some of the interactions may be conditional or may occur a number of times. Repeated interactions can occur, for example, when a participant is iterating

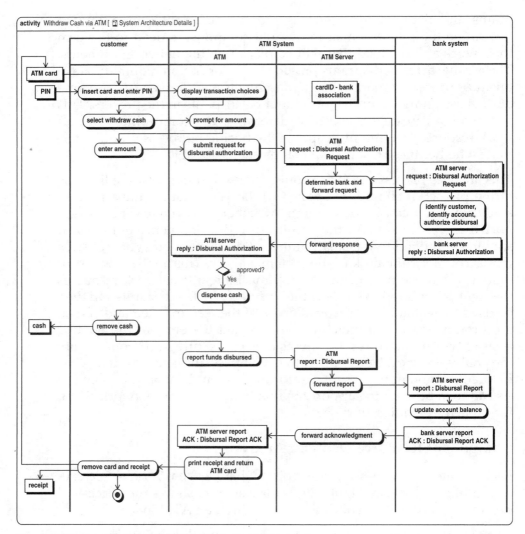

Figure 39–1: *Successful Withdraw Cash Scenario*

through a set of orders and interacting with another participant once for each order. When you combine this occurrence information with the scenario's peak rate, you can calculate the peak rate at which each participant needs to respond to each interaction.

The results of this analysis should be placed in a spreadsheet (Table 39–1). This table gives the details for each of the scenarios and totals the rates for each component at the top. In this example, the scenario executes at a rate of 29 executions/second (from Table 7–2). Each of the messages appears exactly once per execution. The Bank server and ATM each need to handle two incoming messages per execution, yielding a total rate of 58 messages/second for each. The ATM server handles four incoming messages a second, yielding a rate of 116 messages/second.

Table 39–1: *Component Load Analysis Results*

Business Process/ Scenario	Scenario Peak Rate (per Second)	Message	Component Sending Message	Number of Messages Processed by Component per Second		
				ATM	ATM Server	Bank Server
Totals for All Scenarios and Messages				58	116	58
Withdraw Cash via ATM/ Successful Withdrawal	29	ATM request	ATM		29	
		ATM server request	ATM Server			29
		bank server reply	Bank Server		29	
		ATM server reply	ATM Server	29		
		ATM report	ATM		29	
		ATM server report	ATM Server			29
		bank server report ack	Bank Server		29	
		ATM server report ack	ATM Server	29		

Once the peak rates for the individual participants have been determined, you can take a look at the work being done by the participant in response to the interaction. By roughly estimating the required computational complexity and disk utilization of the work done in response to each message, you can make a rough estimate of the number of CPUs and disk spindles it will take to support this role in this scenario.

Estimating CPU Requirements

Table 39–2 provides some guidance for determining the number of CPUs that will be required to support the level of activity. Be careful how you use this table, however. It only gives order-of-magnitude estimates, and an order-of-magnitude range can have significant cost implications for your project. Use Table 39–2 to guide you as to whether or not you need to investigate the CPU requirements more deeply. If your message rates are substantially below the numbers in the table, it is safe to assume that one CPU or less will be able to handle the load. If your numbers are within or near the order-of-magnitude range in the table, you probably should be doing some resource utilization experiments on the class of hardware you intend to use in order to determine more accurately how many CPUs it will take to support the business process. These experiments need to mimic the resource utilization, not the functionality, of your business process. If your numbers are at the high end of the range or above, you have a serious load distribution challenge. If you have not already incorporated load distribution into your design, it is time to go back and do so.

Table 39–2: *Single CPU Capacity Guidelines*

Computational Complexity	*Disk Utilization*	*Rough Order-of-Magnitude Single-CPU Capacity (messages/second)*
Low	None	10^3–10^4
Moderate	None	10^2–10^3
High	None	10^0–10^2
Low–Moderate	Low	10^1–10^2
High	Low	10^0–10^1
Any	Moderate–High	10^{-1}–10^0

Note that, at this point, you have not made any decisions as to how these CPUs will be provided—concentrated in larger machines or distributed across smaller machines. You are simply trying to determine whether the machine requirements are reasonable.

This component resource demand summarization process is straightforward if all the peak loads occur at the same time, but this is often not the case. Different business processes tend to peak at different times of the day, week, month, or year. When the peaks for different scenarios occur at different times, the analysis becomes more complex. You must identify the different time periods in which significantly different patterns of activity occur and perform an analysis for each of these time periods. This will yield an understanding of the peak resource demand for each component during each time period. This information from the various time periods can then be summarized for each component by finding the maximum demand for that component across all the time periods. This will provide an overall understanding of the peak computational resources required to support the application.

Messaging and Disk Performance

Some messaging services, such as JMS, are capable of persisting messages on disk. This feature is provided as a means of ensuring that messages in transit will survive the crash of a machine or the communications server running on it. This feature can be very useful, but you need to recognize that its use has performance implications. Without persistence, the messaging server performance is generally limited by CPU performance or available network bandwidth. With persistence, the performance of the disk becomes the critical factor and can easily reduce the throughput of the server by several orders of magnitude.

Estimating Disk Performance

To understand this, let's take a look at the factors that determine the performance of a disk. A disk is a physical device with platter-shaped surfaces upon which the data is written (Figure 39–2). The surface is divided into a number of tracks (rings), and each track is divided into a number of sectors. Each sector contains a block of data (typically around 512 bytes). A movable head reads and writes data to the disk. The head is mounted on an arm, which pivots to move the head across the disk. To access data in a given sector, three things need to happen: the disk needs to rotate so that the sector is under the head, the arm

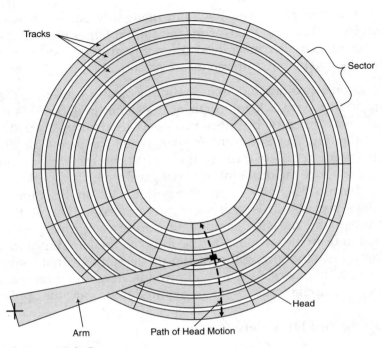

Figure 39–2: *Disk Geometry*

needs to move the head to the correct track, and finally the data itself needs to be transferred. Let's examine each of these activities in terms of its impact on performance.

First, consider the disk rotation. The disk is rotating at a constant speed. When data needs to be accessed, the disk drive must wait until the rotation of the disk brings the sector containing the data under the head. This time is referred to as the rotational latency. On average, you can expect that this will take a half a disk revolution. Thus the average rotational latency in seconds will be:

$$avgRotationalLatency_{sec} = \frac{1}{(diskSpeed_{RPM} / 60) \times 2} = \frac{1}{diskSpeed_{RPM} / 30}$$

For a disk rotating at 10,000 RPM, the average rotational latency is 3 milliseconds.

The second factor you need to consider is that the disk arm must move the head over the proper track. The time it takes to do this is called the seek time. The seek time for the disk is normally specified by the manufacturer who provides either an average value or maximum and minimum values. For the estimation here, the average seek time is the desired value. A typical seek time would be around 4.7 milliseconds.

The third factor you need to consider is the time it actually takes to transfer the data to the disk. The specification that will enable you to compute this time is the transfer rate. You have to be careful in reading this specification, as the rate at which the external interface to the disk drive can transfer the data (typically called the external transfer rate) may be significantly higher than the rate at which the data can be physically written to disk (called the internal transfer rate). Also, the internal transfer rate may be specified for both unformatted and formatted disks. For the analysis here, you want to consider the use of formatted disks. To be conservative, you should use the lowest transfer rate specified.

To compute the time that it would take to transfer the data, you need to know both the data transfer rate and the size of the message. Given this, you can compute the time required for the transfer as follows:

$$dataTransferTime_{sec} = \frac{messageSize_{bytes}}{transferRate_{bytes/sec}}$$

A typical transfer rate is around 50MB (megabytes) per second. If the typical message size is 1KB, then the time it would take to transfer this data would be about 20 microseconds. Note that for small messages, this time is so small with respect to the rotational latency and seek time that it can usually be ignored. Only when message sizes begin to approach a megabyte will the transfer time become significant.

These values can now be put together to approximate the rate at which a disk should be capable of accessing data. If you assume that the head will move while the disk is rotating to the correct position and then the data will be transferred, you can approximate the average access rate as:

$$avgAccessRate_{sec} = \frac{1}{\max\left(avgSeekTime, avgRotationalLatency\right) + dataTransferTime}$$

For the disk being used as an example, a 1KB message size yields an average access rate of 212 accesses/sec. This is a somewhat pessimistic estimate, as it assumes one access must complete before the next begins.

There are a number of factors that typically will speed actual disk performance. High-end disk controllers can schedule multiple accesses during a disk rotation, and messaging servers may batch updates to the disk. On the other hand, a message that is persisted on disk must subsequently be removed from the disk, which requires another disk access.

Considering all of these factors, the best practice is to look at this access rate as a conservative estimate of the rate at which the disk will support messages. If the peak message rate you are contemplating is less than this number (and there is not a lot of other disk activity going on), you can safely assume that the disk can support the message rate. If, however, the projected message rate is near or above the average access rate for the disk, you have more work to do. Your throughput exceeds the performance expectations for a single disk.

Achieving Throughputs in Excess of Estimated Single-Disk Capacity

At this point it is prudent for you to perform an experiment to measure the actual message throughput using the actual message server, machine, operating system, and disk configuration you are considering. When performing this experiment you need to pay careful attention to the interactions between the messaging server and the disk. *Unless message loss in the business process is acceptable, disk writes should always be synchronous.* What this means is that the messaging server will wait for confirmation of a successful disk write before acknowledging receipt of the message. While this reduces throughput, it is the only way to ensure that messages cannot be lost regardless of the failure scenario.[1]

If the measured message rate is still less than what you need, you have several options. One option is to split the traffic between different messaging servers, each using a different disk to persist its messages. Another option is to use a RAID array of disks (multiple physical disks working together to provide what appears to be a single disk) in a striped configuration. This spreads the data being stored across a number of disks. The net effect is that the throughput goes up by a factor approximately equal to the number of disks. Thus if the data is striped across 4 disks, the throughput would go up by approximately 4×.

Some high-end storage subsystems offer another alternative—a battery-backed and redundant buffer for the data. In these systems, the

---

1. The techniques for making persistent storage fault tolerant were discussed in Chapter 33.

data is not physically written to disk before the storage subsystem acknowledges the "writing" of the data. Instead, the data is simply placed in memory, an operation that is several orders of magnitude faster than physically writing to disk. The storage subsystem will later write this data to disk, but will optimize the writing so that, overall, it is much faster than random disk writes. This approach is "safe" from a data loss perspective because the memory is battery-backed (i.e., the data will survive a restart of the machine) and redundant (the loss of one buffer will not cause data loss). The use of this type of buffering can yield message throughputs that begin to approach the throughput the messaging server could achieve if messages were not persisted at all.

In summary, when you propose a messaging mechanism, you need to determine whether its performance will support the intended utilization. To do this, you will need an understanding of the message rate needed to support the business processes (and a rough understanding of the message sizes as well) and whether or not those messages need to be persisted. Armed with this understanding, you can then evaluate the ability of a particular combination of communications server, machine, operating system, and disk subsystem to support the business process needs. If the analysis indicates that the message rate can be supported, you can continue with the architecture development. If not, it's back to the drawing board.

Deployment Load Analysis

Once you are comfortable that the aggregate resource demands for the system seem reasonable, the next step is to analyze the proposed architecture deployment discussed in Chapter 16. Given this deployment model, you can add some additional information to the scenarios and obtain a further understanding of the design's impact on the network and communications components. The intent here is to ensure that the architecture's demands on the network are reasonable, particularly when there are WAN segments involved.

To determine the actual network load, you need to first determine the size of the data sets being moved in each interaction. This can be accomplished by either modeling the information in the data (yielding a precise size) set or simply approximating the expected size based on a rough count of the number of fields. Eventually you will need to do this for all scenarios, but to start with, you begin with only the scenarios you are currently considering. Remember that in the business process ranking scheme, you placed the most demanding business processes high up in the rankings, so the scenarios you consider first will likely be the ones that account for the largest portion of the network load.

Since the deployment model already specifies where each of the component instances resides on the network, you can use this information to determine which network segments need to be traversed by each data set. If there is more than one instance of a component type, you must make some assumptions about how the load is distributed across the instances, with an even distribution being the most common scheme. You then multiply the rate information from the component load analysis by the data set size information to obtain the network load presented by the interaction. Once you have determined the load presented by each individual interaction, you sum up these loads to determine the total network load. Table 39–3 is an example based on the Withdraw Cash via ATM example.

Once again, if the peak occurrences for the different interactions occur at different times, then you must perform a separate analysis for each time period. This will give you the network load demand for each network segment in each time period. You then determine the peak capacity required for each segment across all the time periods. This is the required network capacity for that segment.

You must be aware that the modeling you have done does not account for all of the network traffic that will actually occur, nor does the modeling take into consideration the fact that it is difficult to actually utilize the full available bandwidth of the network. Experience has shown that a conservative design rule-of-thumb is to plan for the computed bandwidth demand to be no more than 20 percent of the nominal network bandwidth available, and in no case should exceed 30 percent. Should circumstances indicate that a higher bandwidth utilization ought to be possible, a prototype should be undertaken to validate that this utilization can actually be achieved. To produce meaningful results, the prototype must include all traffic on the network segments, not just the one interaction that accounts for the high volume.

Evolving the Load Model

In the later stages of the architecture development, the deployment model will become more sophisticated and so will its analysis. The model will have the individual component instances located on the appropriate machines, and these machines will be located on the appropriate network segments. At this point you will be able to determine the aggregate

Table 39–3: *Network Load Estimates for the Withdraw Cash via ATM Example*

Business Process/ Scenario	Scenario Peak Rate (per Second)	Message	Message Network Size (bytes)	Component Sending Message	Bandwidth Requirement (Bytes/Second)				
					ATM LAN	ATM-ATM Server WAN	ATM Server LAN	ATM Server-Bank WAN	Bank Server LAN
Totals for All Scenarios and Messages					33,640	33,640	67,280	33,640	33,640
Withdraw Cash via ATM/ Successful Withdrawal	29	ATM request	290	ATM	8410	8410	8410		
		ATM server request	290	ATM Server			8410	8410	8410
		bank server reply	290	Bank Server			8410	8410	8410
		ATM server reply	290	ATM Server	8410	8410	8410		
		ATM report	290	ATM	8410	8410	8410		
		ATM server report	290	ATM Server			8410	8410	8410
		bank server report ack	290	Bank Server			8410	8410	8410
		ATM server report ack	290	ATM Server	8410	8410	8410		

CPU loads for each of the individual machines and the loading on their network interfaces.

The use of an analysis tool is very helpful when performing load analysis. While in the early stages of the design the numbers of scenarios and communications are small and the analysis can be done by hand (using a spreadsheet), it becomes increasingly complex as the numbers of components grows and the patterns of activity differ from time period to time period.

Cost and Schedule Feasibility

One of the challenges of architecture development is that you not only need to solve the problem, but do so at a cost that is consistent with the project expectations. Fortunately, the architecture model that you have been assembling provides enough information to produce a detailed and accurate cost estimate for the project. It enumerates all the required components, interfaces, and data structures, so you know exactly what needs to be built (for those things that don't already exist). It provides a description of what each component must do after each interface is invoked, so you know how complex the design task is for each interface. From this information you can readily estimate the development effort.

The performance analysis in the previous section provides you with an estimate of the machine and network resources required to support the system, so the required capital investments can be estimated as well as the operational costs of leasing equipment, space, and network bandwidth. This same analysis also indicates how often people must interact with the system, thus providing the basis for determining the staffing level required to execute the business processes and keep the system operating.

Putting this all together, you can now assess the capital investment, the development cost (which is often capitalized as well), and the operational expenses required to bring the business processes to life with this particular architecture. These estimates can now be compared to the budgetary estimates that the project started with to determine whether or not the current architecture is consistent with those expectations. If it is, you can proceed with the design. If not, it is back to the drawing board to find a more cost-effective solution.

Observability

At various points in this book there have been discussions about breakdowns and breakdown detection. These discussions focused on choices being made at various levels of abstraction, ranging from the design of business processes and systems architecture to the selection of coordination patterns. At other points there have been discussions about monitoring business processes and the benefits of abstracting process milestones from the details of the process design.

Each of these discussions has addressed some aspect of a broader concern: observability. When work is distributed among many participants (whether human or machine), it becomes increasingly difficult to determine exactly what is going on. Thus, it is prudent to evaluate a proposed architecture in terms of the ability to determine just what is going on. Is there sufficient monitoring in place to determine whether all components are up and running, and all business processes are executing properly?

These questions are best asked and answered early in the architecture process. Very often simple alterations in business process design and the choice of coordination patterns will greatly enhance the ability of business process participants to observe the execution of the process, and thus be able to report proper operation and the presence of breakdowns. Monitoring strategies are most easily integrated in the early stages as well. The further you get into the architecture, the more changes you will have to make to improve observability.

Ability to Evolve

Change is constant in business. Whether it is the organic growth of the business, the addition of new products, or the replacement of old technologies and systems, every enterprise faces changing needs that require corresponding changes to its systems. One of the things you need to evaluate about the architecture is its ability to accommodate change. You accomplish this by hypothesizing a number of changes that the architecture might have to undergo. These are termed change scenarios. For completeness, the full range of stakeholders must be involved in the exercise of developing this list of change scenarios, as each will represent a different source of possible changes to the architecture. The scenario definition must include not only the description of the change but also an assessment of the likelihood that the change will be required. It must also include an assessment of the benefit to the business arising from successfully accommodating the change and the risk to the business arising from not being able to accommodate the change.

What you need to understand for each of these change scenarios is the extent to which the architecture would need to be modified to accommodate the change. Ideally, you would like to know how much it would cost (capital investment, development cost, and operational expense) to modify the architecture, but it is generally impractical to develop that level of detail. In lieu of that, you sketch out the changes to the architecture that would be required and simply inventory the number of components and interfaces that must be altered—assuming, of course, that you have found a way to accomplish the needed change.

To draw conclusions from this analysis, the ability of the architecture to accommodate the change must be weighed against the probability of the change being required and the benefit/risk consequences associated with the change. For those scenarios in which the degree of change required seems reasonable given the benefit/risk associated with the scenario, you can conclude that the architecture can gracefully accommodate the change. Those scenarios in which the degree of change is excessive indicate potential problem areas—risks to the enterprise. For these scenarios, the likelihood of their occurrence must be weighed against the risks and a judgment made as to whether the risk is acceptable. It must be emphasized here that this is a business decision, not a technical decision! If the risk is not deemed acceptable, then the architecture must be modified to make it easier to accommodate these changes.

Ability to Handle Stress Situations

Beyond the evolutionary changes discussed in the previous section, enterprises are from time to time subjected to more sudden and radical forces for change. Mergers and acquisitions, the addition of entirely new lines of business, dramatic changes in business conditions, major changes in regulatory requirements, site closures, and physical disasters can all stress the architecture way beyond its original design parameters. You evaluate the architecture's ability to accommodate these stresses in a manner similar to that for the evolutionary scenarios, proposing the stress that might occur, the likelihood of it occurring, and the benefits and risks associated with being able to accommodate the stress.

To develop a realistic list of stress scenarios, it is again important to have all stakeholders involved, and it is absolutely essential that the business side of the house participate. Many of the potential stress scenarios are a direct consequence of strategic business decisions or concerns that the IT community may not be aware of. At the same time, it must be appreciated that some of these scenarios potentially represent very sensitive information, and the manner in which the scenario is expressed must reflect the business sensitivity. It may be inappropriate (illegal, for that matter) to tell the IT organization that the enterprise is in the process of acquiring another company, but it may be entirely appropriate to tell the IT organization that a 75 percent increase in business volume is something that the architecture must be able to handle. Each scenario is characterized in terms of the type of stress, the likelihood of its occurrence, and the benefits and risks associated with accommodating or not accommodating the stress.

As with the evolutionary scenarios, the changes required to the architecture are assessed. In contrast with the evolutionary scenarios, some of the stress scenarios may result in conclusions that the architecture simply cannot survive the stress. For example, a single computing center cannot continue to support the business after a site disaster.

Once the scenario-by-scenario assessments have been performed, the results must be evaluated to determine whether the present architecture is acceptable or requires some alteration to be better able to accommodate the stress scenarios. This evaluation is primarily a business evaluation of the risks inherent in the current architecture proposal. As such, it is essential that the business side of the house make the ultimate decisions as to whether the risks are acceptable. Where this risk is deemed unacceptable, the architecture must be modified to lower the risk.

Summary

Before proceeding with the implementation of an architecture, its suitability for its intended purpose needs to be evaluated. It must be able to provide the required functionality and perform adequately. It must be implementable within the given cost and schedule guidelines. It must be able to evolve gracefully to support the enterprise's changing needs and may be required to accommodate significant changes, such as merger and acquisition activities.

One of the key determinations is whether the architecture will be able to perform adequately. The business process scenarios characterize the collaboration between the components needed to bring the business process to life. Coupled with the peak rates at which these scenarios execute, there is enough information to determine the loads on the individual participants in the process. From these loads you can then determine the level of resource required to support that load and make a determination as to whether those resource demands are reasonable given the project's cost and schedule guidelines.

To be practical, it must also be possible to implement the architecture within the cost and schedule guidelines. The architecture has identified all components, interfaces, and data structures required to implement the business processes. This is sufficient information to derive a fairly accurate cost estimate and make a determination as to whether the current architectural approach can, indeed, be implemented within the cost and schedule guidelines.

The architecture may also be called upon to accommodate evolutionary changes and extreme stress situations. To perform these evaluations, you have to seek input from stakeholders concerning potential change scenarios, their likelihood of occurrence, and the business impact of being unable to accommodate the scenarios. This information is then used to evaluate the ability of the architecture to handle the scenarios. Whether or not the inability to handle a scenario justifies changes to the present architecture is ultimately a business decision.

Key Architecture Evaluation Questions

1. What is the peak load that will be placed on each component and each network segment? What level of resource will it take to handle this load? Are these resources available within the project's cost and schedule guidelines?

2. Can the proposed architecture be implemented within the project's cost and schedule guidelines?

3. How can the proper operation of the business processes and systems be observed? Is appropriate monitoring in place to determine whether systems and business processes are operating normally? Are appropriate processes in place to detect and handle breakdowns?

4. What evolutionary changes must the architecture be able to accommodate? Has the ability to accommodate these changes been established?

5. What revolutionary changes must the architecture be able to accommodate? Has the ability to accommodate these changes been established?

Suggested Reading

Clements, Paul, Rick Kazman, and Mark Klein. 2002. *Evaluating Software Architectures: Methods and Case Studies*. Boston, MA: Addison-Wesley.

Chapter 40

Testing

While testing occurs long after the architecture and design, testing itself requires design, and its requirements may influence the design of the components and services themselves. Individual components must be unit tested, and special test harnesses will be required for each component. Components must be assembled together and tested to determine whether they are interacting properly, and this integration order-of-assembly and the test harnesses that will be required must be designed. Many designs interact with existing end-point systems, and test versions of those systems may be limited in availability—or not available at all. In such cases "dummy" versions of these end-point systems will be required to support testing.

Full functional and system tests require the presence of all components, including end-point systems. These test environments also require realistic data and the ability to restore the entire system, including end-point systems, to a known initial state. This initial state must include the original initial data so that fixes to identified problems can be properly verified with the same data. Performance and failure mode testing require test environments that permit the full and exclusive utilization of machine and network resources and the intentional disruption of these resources. All of this requires design.

Unit Testing, Test Harnesses, and Regression Testing

To test a component, it is necessary to both exercise its functionality and evaluate the results. If component functionality is being exercised from a built-in user interface and all of its results are available through this interface, then no design work is required. However, if the inputs are provided through a system interface or the results cannot be observed from an existing user interface, then mechanisms must be established for providing the inputs and observing the results.

When the functionality of a component is invoked through a system interface and/or its results are only accessible through a system interface, then some other component must be employed to invoke the functionality and/or retrieve the results. This component is referred to as a test harness. Test harnesses can run the gamut from standard tooling (e.g., commercially available test tools) to fully custom components that, themselves, must be designed. The requirements for the test harness include the definitions of inputs to be exercised, the results to be retrieved, the manner in which the test will be conducted, and the manner in which results will be evaluated.

Sometimes the information needed to verify the proper operation of a component is not accessible through its existing interfaces. In such cases, additional interfaces may have to be added to the component or data added to existing interfaces to make this information accessible. In any case, the manner in which the component's functionality will be exercised and its state examined during unit testing must be considered before the component is implemented, as these considerations may well affect its design.

While the initial testing of a component is often conducted manually, it is often desirable to be able to automatically repeat the same tests after changes have been made to verify that behavior that was not supposed to change, indeed has not changed. This places significant additional demands on the test harness and upon the test environment itself. The test harness must be extended to automatically apply the test cases to the component, retrieve the results, evaluate the results, and report the evaluation conclusions. This obviously requires a significant level of design in and of itself. Regression testing also requires a degree of automation in the test environment. To execute each series of tests, the appropriate component and its associated test harness must be deployed in the test environment, the test sequence initiated, and the overall test results captured.

As should be obvious, regression testing requires a significant investment, and not just in the purchase of a testing tool. An investment in time is required to configure that tool to execute and repeat the tests. Not every component (or every element of functionality on a component) warrants this additional investment. The risks associated with the failure of the component (or the particular function on the component) must be weighed against the investment required for regression testing to determine what warrants regression testing. Generally speaking, it is shared services and mission-critical functionality that warrant this type of investment.

Depending upon the nature of the interfaces to the component and the degree of test automation required, test harnesses can vary from the simple to the complex. Components that will be manually tested and that utilize standardized communications interfaces can often be driven by off-the-shelf tools that are readily configured to simulate the inputs and retrieve the outputs. At the other end of the spectrum, fully automated testing requires a complex and sophisticated set of tools. It is generally not cost-effective to build a custom regression testing environment for each component. The use of standardized frameworks for this type of testing is generally necessary to bring the costs in line with the benefits. When considering frameworks, the diversity of interfaces that will be encountered must be taken into consideration. Testing modern distributed systems typically involves the use of a wide range of interface technologies, including user interfaces on thin and fat clients as well as system interfaces involving databases, files, socket connections, and various types of messaging.

Integration Testing and Order of Assembly

Once the proper functioning of individual components has been established, those components need to be assembled into a working system. In a large-scale distributed system, simply deploying all the components and turning them on in a "big bang" integration generally leads to a lengthy and unwieldy debugging process. What makes debugging difficult is that while it may be obvious that something is wrong, it is often very difficult to pinpoint the cause. The symptom may appear in one component, while the root cause is in another component—possibly several interactions away from the one exhibiting the symptoms.

To avoid initial integration problems, the integration should be performed in planned stages, with small groups of components being added and tested in each stage. Test harnesses are again employed to simulate the portions of the system that have not yet been integrated. *It is your responsibility, as the architect, to define an order of assembly that makes testing reasonable and minimizes the requirements for the test harnesses.* In many cases and with proper planning, the same test harnesses that were used for unit testing can be reused in integration testing.

One of the biggest challenges in integration testing lies in interacting with the existing end-point systems. Many of these are complex systems in their own right. They run in environments that are expensive to duplicate, and their proper operation often relies on further interactions with other systems and people. Because of these complexities, it may be impractical to do initial integration testing with the actual end-point system. Test harnesses simulating these end points may be the only recourse during integration testing.

Environments for Functional and System Testing

Functional testing looks for discrepancies between the system's functional specifications and actual behavior. System testing seeks to determine whether the system, as a whole, satisfies its original objectives. While the intents of functional and system testing are somewhat different, both require an environment that contains all of the actual system components. This presents a challenge when existing end-point systems are a part of the design being tested. Ideally, both the functional and system testing environments will contain test versions of the real systems with sufficient data in them to support the full range of testing. It also requires these systems and their data to be readily returned to their initial state so that tests can be identically repeated. Deviations from this ideal represent risk to the project and the enterprise.

Using a test harness to represent the actual end-point system during functional and system testing carries with it two risks. The first risk is that the initial deployment of the system may fail due to unknown differences between the test harness and the actual end-point system. The second risk is that problems that arise in production (due to differences between the test harness and the actual end-point system) will have to be diagnosed in the production environment and (by definition) the fixes can only be tested in the production environment. Not having a broad range of test data in the test environment carries with it exactly the same risks.

The inability to return the system and data to a known state makes it impossible to exactly repeat any given test. This may make it difficult to accurately diagnose a problem (particularly an intermittent problem) that occurs in testing, and makes it impossible to verify after the fix that the actual conditions that caused the initial failure will no longer result in a failure.

The inability to provide versions of the actual systems with realistic data and to reset these systems and data to a known state is a risk both to the project and the overall enterprise. The risk to the project is that the project itself will fail to achieve its cost and schedule objectives. The risk for the enterprise is that the deployment of a system that has not been fully tested may have an adverse impact on existing systems and thus disrupt the operation of the enterprise! These risks must be weighed against the cost of providing a full and complete testing environment for the overall system.

Performance Testing

Expecting a system to meet a performance requirement without testing to verify that the requirement has been met is wishful thinking. Whether the requirement involves response time, latency, or volume, the ability of the system to meet the requirement must be established through testing. Furthermore, it is prudent to test the actual operational capacity limitations of the system. This will enable the enterprise to monitor actual usage in production, anticipate reaching these imitations, and plan accordingly.

Performance testing requires two things: (1) an environment in which the required system resources (machine, disk, and network) can be 100 percent dedicated to the test, and (2) the capture of the measurement data required to determine the actual performance. Both of these require some design work.

To be able to interpret performance measurements properly, the resources required to perform the work must actually be available. To ensure this, ideally, there should be no other activity on the machines, disks, and networks being used for the test—otherwise the performance measurements may be adversely impacted by some other activity's use of the resources. Conversely, the performance of other applications and their users may be adversely impacted by the performance test. For these reasons, it is a good idea to do performance testing in an isolated environment.

The availability of equipment for running performance tests may also be an issue, especially if the production machine is costly. In these cases, performance tests can often be run on smaller-scale versions of the same type of hardware as long as the performance results can be reasonably extrapolated to predict the performance of the larger machine. Note that if any type of load distribution is being employed, it is not sufficient just to measure the capacity of one of the components, as the load distribution mechanism itself will impact the performance to some extent, and this impact must be measured.

As was discussed in Chapter 38, the measurement of any form of time interval requires design work. In general, it is easier for a component itself to measure a time interval between its input and its output than it is to perform this measurement externally. If these measurement needs can be identified before the component is actually designed and implemented, the lowest cost option for making these measurements is usually to design the measurement capability right into the component along with the ability to turn the measurement on and off as required.

Making Capacity Measurements

Making performance measurements and establishing the operating capacity of a component must be approached with some care, as the relationship between the input rate and output rate for most components and systems varies non-linearly with increasing input rates. Figure 40–1 shows a typical input-output relationship for a component (or an entire system, for that matter). Note that as the input rate increases from zero, the output rate exactly tracks the input rate over some range of input values. At some point, however, the output rate begins to fall behind the input rate. This point is the *operating capacity* of the component. Beyond this point, unprocessed inputs are accumulating. Further increases in input rate result in smaller and smaller increases in output rate, until a point is reached at which an increase in the input rate results in no increase in the output rate. Beyond this point, further increases in input rate actually result in a decrease in the output rate. The component (or system) is overloaded.

It is important to realize that as soon as the output rate begins to lag behind the input rate, the work in progress piles up in the component,

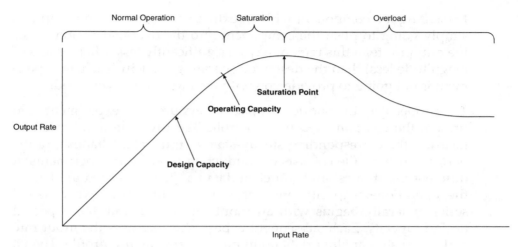

Figure 40–1: *Component Performance Profile*

and will continue to pile up until the input rate drops below the operating capacity and the accumulated work in progress has been completed. Continuous operation beyond the operating capacity will place increasing demands upon system resources as the work piles up. *Unless checked in some manner, such operation will always lead to the eventual catastrophic failure of the component.* Mechanisms available to avoid such catastrophic failures include refusing to accept additional inputs and the discarding of some work in progress.

Most components can tolerate operation in the saturation and even overload regions for a short period of time. If the input rate has not exceeded the saturation point and the input rate stays below the operating capacity long enough, then the component will be able to clear out the backlog of work in progress and be able to resume normal operation. If the input rate has gone beyond the saturation point into the overload region, the operation of the component becomes far less predictable. Generally, once a component has reached overload, the output rate is no longer just a function of the input rate, but is impacted by the size of the backlog as well. Thus, even if the input rate drops to zero, it may be some time before the output rate begins to actually improve. In general, operation in the overload region is unpredictable. Where possible, the system should be designed to ensure that no component ever operates in this region.

This profile of component behavior has a significant impact on how you go about experimentally determining the component capacity.

Presenting the component with an extremely high volume of input is simply going to push the component into the overload region. Since the output rate in this region may be significantly less (often orders of magnitude less) than the design or operating capacity, such an experiment is not going to provide you with the information you need.

The proper way to conduct a capacity measurement experiment is to present the component with a controlled steady-state input rate and measure the corresponding steady-state output rate. Establishing the performance profile consists of conducting a series of experiments at different input rates until sufficient data has been collected to identify the operational capacity and saturation points. This experimental series generally begins with an input rate well below the expected design capacity. Each subsequent experiment increases the input rate and establishes another data point on the performance profile. Then a final experiment is conducted at a very high rate for the express purpose of determining whether the component exhibits catastrophic behavior in the overload region.

It is a best practice to establish the operating capacity for each component for at least a representative example of its major operations. This operating capacity can then be compared to the design capacity required to support the current system. Of course, you should expect that the measured operating capacity will be above the design capacity (otherwise the component will not support the load!). The difference between the two represents the room for growth in the system. It is often convenient to design these experiments (and the components themselves) in such a way that response time measurements can be made at the same time, since the capacity experiments generally create the very load conditions required for the response time measurements.

System Capacity Testing

Simply establishing the capacity of individual components is often not sufficient to establish the actual capacity of the overall system. One reason for this is simply the delays inherent in inter-component communication and context switching. Another is competition for shared resources, such as network bandwidth and shared storage subsystems. A third is the phenomenon of emergent behavior: dynamics in interactions that cannot be predicted by simply examining the characteristics of the individual components. The cyclical speed-up and slow-down behavior of automobiles on a congested highway is an example of emergent behavior.

For these reasons, the actual operating capacity of the system as a whole should be measured in the same manner that you established the operating capacity of individual components. The testing should also include transient overloads. This will serve to determine the types of overloads from which the system is capable of recovering and those that push the overall system so far into the overload range as to render the system unrecoverable. The "fix" for this type of behavior is usually some form of throttling. Highway entrance gating using stoplights is an example of such throttling.

In summary, when you are testing distributed systems, you need to be on the lookout for emergent behavior, and go out of your way to create conditions that might trigger such behavior. This means that you need to (a) test systems at normal peak volumes, (b) test systems at excessive volumes, and (c) test the system's response to the failure and recovery of components.

Failure Mode Testing

An often neglected aspect of testing is failure mode testing. In this type of testing, failures of individual components, machines, and networks are simulated. This testing verifies that the symptoms exhibited are the symptoms that were anticipated in the design and that the recovery procedures work as intended. *Failure mode testing is mandatory for any process that has high-availability or fault tolerance requirements.*

Failure mode testing requires an isolated test environment that can tolerate the killing of applications, machines, and networks. This environment may well be required for an extended period of time as this type of testing is likely to uncover situations that require some redesign and retesting. While an ideal environment for failure mode testing would resemble the actual production environment as closely as possible, it is often not practical to assemble such an environment and dedicate it to this type of testing. Since performance is not normally an issue in this type of testing (except perhaps in measuring recovery times), an acceptable alternative in many cases is to assemble an environment of older equipment with similar hardware architecture running the same operating system(s).

Summary

There are a number of aspects of testing that require the attention of the architect. Unit and integration testing often require test harnesses, and these need to be specified and designed along with the system components. It is the architect's responsibility to establish a reasonable order of assembly for integration testing that minimizes the need for additional test harnesses.

The environments for functional and system testing are also a concern. End-point systems may not be available in some or all of these environments, in which case simulators will be required for these systems. These simulators will also have to be specified and designed.

Performance and failure mode testing also have special requirements. Performance test environments must provide unloaded machines and networks to produce unambiguous test results. Failure mode test environments must be tolerant of machine and network disruptions.

Performance testing requires carefully controlled experiments that characterize the components under both normal and overload conditions. In addition to testing individual components, the system as a whole must be tested as well. Emergent behavior may lead to overall system behavior that cannot be predicted from the behavior of the individual components, particularly under overload conditions.

Key Testing Questions

1. How will each component be unit tested? Does the component require additional interfaces to support testing? Is a test harness required?

2. Is automated regression testing required for this component? Are the component interfaces compatible with the regression testing framework? How will the results be evaluated?

3. What is the planned order of assembly for integrating the components?

4. What test harnesses will be required for integration testing?

5. Are end-point systems available in the test environments? Does the test version of the system contain a sufficiently rich data set to

support a full test? Can the system be readily reset to a known state? If the answer to any of these questions is no, are the resulting risks acceptable both to the project and to the business?

6. What risks would the project or the business face if performance testing did not occur and a performance-related failure (which might well be a catastrophic failure of the system) occur in production?

7. What environment will be used for performance testing?

8. What set of experiments is required to determine the capacity of each component? Have any required design modifications been made to the component and the test harness to support this type of testing?

9. For components that have response time requirements, have the experiments been designed that will establish the actual response time? Have the required design modifications been made to the component itself and the test.harness to support this testing?

10. For each business process that will place a significant load on the system, has the experiment been designed that will measure the capacity of the system while executing this process? Have the required design modifications been made?

11. For each process that has a challenging response time requirement, has an experiment been designed that will establish the actual response time under the required load conditions? Have the required design modifications been made?

12. What risks would the project and the enterprise face if failure mode testing was skipped and a component failure and subsequent recovery took substantially longer than anticipated (hours or days)?

13. Does an environment for failure mode testing already exist? If not, is its creation part of the project plan?

14. Has a failure testing plan been established? Does the plan include at least one failure of each component, machine, and network segment?

15. Is site disaster recovery a requirement? If so, how will it be tested?

Part IX

Advanced Topics

Chapter 41

Representing a Complex Process

Before you can manage a process, you first need to define it and obtain consensus among the stakeholders that this definition is correct. This requires a representation of the process that all can share and agree upon. But many processes, particularly at the enterprise level, are complex, with many participants and many activities. An activity diagram representing the entire process in all its detail would become a large wall chart. Although such a diagram might be correct, most of its detail is of little interest to most of the stakeholders. How then do you acquaint the stakeholders with the process and get buy-in on its important aspects without burying them in detail? The answer is elision.

When presenting a complex process, you often omit some of the detail, a practice known as *elision*. When you elide detail, you are then left with a simplified representation of the process. This simplified representation is then augmented with separate representations, each showing some of the elided details. Taken together, the simplified representation and the supporting detailed representations contain all the information that would have been on the wall chart, but now organized for better comprehension.

Understanding the overall process begins with an understanding of the simplified representation. Once this simplified representation is understood, it then serves a context for understanding the process details in the supporting representations. The challenge in this game, of course, is to ensure that the simplified representation does not omit or obscure the most important aspects of the process.

So how can you elide detail in a process without creating a misleading representation of the process? While there is no one-size-fits-all answer, there are a number of techniques that you can use selectively in specific situations. Each of these techniques abstracts some portion of the process without hiding critical aspects essential to its understanding. In the end, the high-level understanding you want to preserve is the basic process flow, the breakdowns that can occur in the process, and how these breakdowns can be detected.

Eliding Communications Detail

Generally, the first thing you abstract away from a complex process representation is the detail of the communications between participants. A full UML activity diagram depiction of an interaction shows the artifact being exchanged between the participants. At an abstract level, you still want to show that there is an interaction between the participants, but you do not necessarily want to show the artifact itself. Chapter 9 showed how to do this by replacing the object flows in the diagram with control flows. Strictly speaking, this is not a "correct" utilization of the UML notation, as there is, indeed, an object flow occurring. However, by adopting the convention that a control flow that crosses a swimlane boundary is an abstracted representation of an object flow, there is no ambiguity. These control flows can be refined into object flows by adding the details of the object flow.

Eliding Participant Activity Details

The high-level representation of a process does not need to depict the detailed steps of the work being performed by each participant. What is important at the high level is the understanding that the participant performed some work as a consequence of an input and delivered some results. When a participant performs a collection of activities all belonging to the same process, you can replace this detail with a single abstracted activity in the top-level process (Figure 40–1). The details of

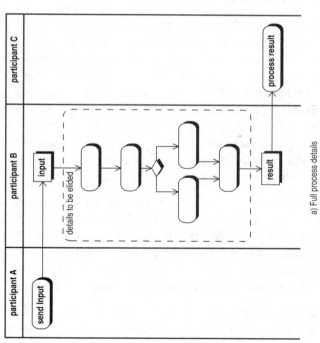

a) Full process details

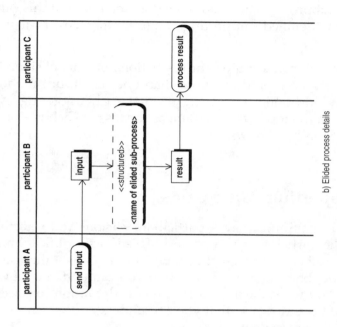

b) Elided process details

Figure 41-1: *Eliding Participant Activity Details*

this abstracted subprocess still need to be documented, but this can be done in a more detailed supporting diagram that covers just the subprocess.

There are, however, some important restrictions on this elision. This abstracted activity may produce more than one result, but it should not receive any additional triggering events. Each triggering event must be shown in the top-level diagram, as the loss of each is a potential cause of process breakdown.

Eliding Supporting Participants

Another form of simplification is participant elision: You selectively omit some of the participants in a process. This is a simplification that should be approached with a great deal of caution. One of the reasons that you are modeling the process is so that you can understand what can go wrong. You want the abstracted process definition to preserve these sources of breakdown so that you can understand which participants are in a position to detect breakdowns.

One common type of breakdown in a process is that one of the participants in the process "drops the ball." In other words, a participant that has responsibility for a task fails to execute that task. If you elide that participant from the process, you lose the understanding that this participant could ever have "the ball" to begin with. The overall process could fail as a consequence of that participant's failure to execute its responsibility, yet you would not gain that understanding from looking at the abstracted process definition. Since you want to be able to "follow the ball" of responsibility through the abstracted process representation, you cannot arbitrarily remove participants from the process.

Despite this, there are some participants that can be safely elided from the overall process. These are participants whose work is both routine and actively managed by another participant. Determining which participants fall into this category requires an understanding of both the nature of the work and the manner in which the participant's work is being managed. There are three conditions that need to be met:

1. The participant must be a performer in an interaction in which the actual work result is returned to the requestor (e.g., the invocation of the work is a request-reply interaction).

2. The task being performed must be routine (i.e., a common service) and not a task that is specific to the process.

3. The requestor managing the work must remain in the diagram and be responsible for taking action if the performer fails to return the expected result.

If these three conditions are met, the elision of the performer is generally acceptable. Since the remaining requestor is responsible for determining that the elided performer has dropped the ball, you haven't lost any understanding of how breakdowns in the process can be detected. In a sense, the omitted performer never has responsibility anyway: The real responsibility lies with the requestor, who is still represented in the model.

Note that these three conditions are not met if the work coordination involves fire-and-forget or delegation. With these coordination patterns, responsibility is truly passed from one participant to another. No other participant is in a position to detect either participant's breakdown. Therefore, eliding either participant produces an abstraction that masks breakdowns that cannot be detected by the remaining participants. Such abstractions are misleading and are to be avoided. All participants in fire-and-forget and delegation interactions should be retained in the abstracted process representation, with one exception.

This exception relates to participants who play the role of communication intermediaries. Interactions between major participants are often carried out via communications intermediaries. In fire-and-forget interactions, for example, there may be one fire-and-forget exchange between the requestor and the intermediary, and then another between the intermediary and the performer. In such cases, you can elide the swimlane representing the intermediary and replace it with an interaction arrow directly between the requestor and provider as described in Chapter 17. To indicate that elision has occurred, you label that arrow with the name of the communications service to indicate that some intermediary provided the mechanism for the interaction. Since the basic breakdown analysis asks "what happens if this participant becomes nonfunctional" for each swimlane and "what happens if this communication fails" for each communication, the breakdowns in the intermediary are still adequately represented.

This simplification can be used any time there are communications intermediaries and can be extended to cover chains of intermediary participants as was described in Chapter 18. In such cases, you create a separate activity diagram to detail the pattern of interaction between the intermediaries and give a name to this pattern. You then use that pattern name as the label on the communication arrow on the abstracted process representation.

Participant elision should be used judiciously. The abstracted representation must still convey a clear understanding of the overall process, including an understanding of breakdowns and their detection. In particular, you don't want to elide components that make decisions or perform functions that are specific to the process. Elision should be restricted to components that provide standardized supporting services.

Abstracting Subprocesses

You may find embedded within a large process a group of participants who are actually executing a subprocess. In such cases, it may be appropriate to collapse the entire subprocess (the participants and all of their activities) into a single swimlane. For such a consolidation to be appropriate, the subprocess being abstracted must adhere to the definition of process: a sequence of activities that is triggered by an event and produces countable results. The triggering event must be an interaction with a participant in the larger process, and the results must be delivered back to participants in the larger process. If these conditions are met, and the participants in the subprocess have no other interactions with the other participants that are not shown in the top-level process, then it is appropriate to abstract the subprocess into a single swimlane.

When you deal with very large scale processes (enterprise-wide processes, for example), subprocess abstraction is the primary tool you have for making the overall process not only comprehensible but manageable. But not every process can be abstracted in this manner. The requirement for subprocess abstraction is that both the activities and their performers be separable from the rest of the process. If the same participants are also involved in other activities in the larger process, then abstracting the subprocess obscures your understanding of what would happen should that participant become unavailable. There is a process management implication as well: If the participant is involved in both the subprocess and other parts of the larger process, the subprocess cannot be managed independently of the larger process. This is no longer just a technical issue of process representation—it is a process design and management issue.

Summary

Showing all the details of a complex process in a single diagram can result in an overly complicated representation that makes it difficult to understand the overall process flow and the possibilities for breakdown and breakdown detection. Simplifying the representation is important, but must be undertaken with care so as not to distort the understanding of the process.

The desired form of simplification is elision: removing selected details while preserving the structure. The details of how a communication happens can be elided as long as the fact that the interaction occurs is still represented in the remaining diagram. The details of the activities performed by a participant may be elided as long as all that participant's interactions remain in the top-level diagram. Even some participants may be elided as long as they perform routine services and the performance of those services is being managed by the remaining participants. When a collection of participants executes a subprocess, the collection can be reduced to a single swimlane in the top-level diagram and the subprocess documented separately.

Key Complex Process Representation Questions

1. If communications details have been elided from the top-level process diagram, has the diagram been annotated to indicate how the communications occurs? Have supporting diagrams been created to document the communications details?

2. Have the activity details of a participant been elided? Has that elision obscured any interactions with other participants?

3. Have supporting participants who provide routine services been elided? Do the remaining participants actively manage the work of those elided participants?

4. Have any subprocesses and their related participants been collapsed into a single swimlane? Are there any participants in common between the larger process and the elided subprocess?

Chapter 42

Process Management and Workflow

As business processes grow increasingly complex, managing them increases in complexity as well. This makes the management of the process an important target for automation. Chapter 29 introduced the basic notion of a process manager, a component whose role it is to manage the execution of a process. The requirement for this type of component arises frequently enough that a class of commercial components has arisen to address this need. These components are generally referred to as *workflow engines*. Workflow engines are process management frameworks that are configured to play the management role with respect to one or more business processes. These products have an explicit representation of the process and, in varying degrees, track or control the progress of the process.

Whether you use a commercial engine or design your own process manager, you will encounter a number of design issues in managing a process. The following sections present an overview of these issues with an eye towards understanding the interdependencies between the design of the business process and the design of the systems that support it, particularly the process manager. These interdependencies are so deep that it is virtually impossible to design the process without altering the systems. Virtually every business process design decision has system design implications, and virtually every workflow design decision has business process design implications as well.

This discussion focuses on the technical aspects of business process and system design. It makes no attempt to address the organizational and business issues that drive business process design. Such a discussion warrants a full book-length treatment of its own, such as Sharp and McDermott's *Workflow Modeling*.[1]

Process Management

So what exactly is process management? Part VI discussed how interactions between participants influence the execution of a process and, specifically, how the arrival of inputs can trigger a participant's execution of an activity. Process management is nothing more than the use of this type of interaction to explicitly manage all of the activity within a business process.

Process management is, itself, a process—a process that manages the actual work process! It determines what needs to be done, initiates the work, confirms timely completion, and determines what needs to be done next. While this sounds straightforward, there are many issues that can make process management complex.

Process Management Goals

There are many different reasons for wanting to manage a process. A few examples are:

- Ensuring that work is appropriately prioritized and scheduled to meet KPI and SLA objectives
- Ensuring that work is assigned to appropriately skilled individuals
- Ensuring appropriate responses to process breakdowns
- Ensuring that issues are appropriately escalated
- Dynamically reassigning resources to process bottlenecks

All of these, and many more, are achievable through process management. But achieving particular objectives requires design that is specific to those objectives, both at the process level and the systems level.

---

1. Sharp, Alec, and Patrick McDermott. 2001. *Workflow Modeling: Tools for Process Improvement and Application Development*. Norwood, MA: Artech House.

The mere employment of a workflow engine will not magically achieve these objectives. Beyond the design investment, achieving some objectives may require additional information and additional processes to maintain that information. For these reasons, it is prudent to determine the process management goals before embarking on the design of the business process and its supporting systems.

The possible goals for process management are pretty open-ended, limited only by the creativity and imagination of those seeking to improve the process. What you must recognize, however, is that achieving any goal is an unlikely outcome unless:

1. The goal is clearly stated in a quantifiable manner
2. The actions required to achieve the goal are clearly defined
3. Measurements are put in place to measure progress towards the goal

Clearly stating the goals is the first step in managing any process. To aid in this definition, here are a number of common process management goals for your consideration.

- Fully automate the process: Have the systems fully automate the process so that no human involvement is required in its normal execution.
- Facilitate the evolution of the process: Make it easy to alter the activity sequence or the conditions governing when activities are performed.
- Improve on-time work completion: Organize and manage the work to maximize on-time performance.
- Assign work to participants based on participant qualifications
- Manage escalation: Implement a predefined escalation chain, typically for either approvals or exception handling.
- Coordinate the execution of multiple processes: Coordinate the work of otherwise independent processes to achieve specific business goals. Batching purchase requests for common materials and consolidating the shipment of multiple orders are typical cost reduction examples.
- Dynamically define the business process results: Add a design activity in the process that defines what the process will ultimately deliver.
- Dynamically define portions of the business process: After a design activity, add an activity that defines the remainder of the process for delivering what has just been designed.

- Enable in-flight process changes: Be able to alter the definition of a process that is already executing to reflect a changing situation.

Many of these goals have design issues associated with them that will be discussed later in this chapter, but first you need to explore relationship between the work itself and the process of managing the work.

The Management Process Is Not the Work Process!

It is tempting to consider the workflow to be the actual work process, but there are some important and real distinctions between the two. To begin with, the workflow process *never* covers the complete business process. At a minimum, the workflow process does not cover the activities leading up to the start of the workflow: Activities that recognize the event and iniate the workflow are required. Secondly, most workflow engines do not actually do work—they manage work being done by other participants. Furthermore, there are usually interactions between participants that are not directly under the control of the workflow. The managed participants often interact with other participants whose activities are not being managed.

The bottom line is that the process being executed by the workflow engine is a management process that oversees a subset of the complete work process. That complete business process includes all participants and all interactions that are required to get the work done. The workflow process, on the other hand, only describes the activities of the workflow engine itself and its interactions with the participants that it directly manages. They are two distinct, though closely related, processes.

The workflow process represents the work of the workflow engine itself. This includes any activities being performed by the workflow engine itself and the direct interactions between the workflow engine and the other participants. This process is the workflow engine's view of the overall business process. It is an interesting twist of nomenclature that even though the purpose of a workflow engine is to control the flow of work (as its name implies), the engine itself is often not directly involved in either the actual performance of the work or movement of the work results. It only provides the *control* over these activities.

So now you have not one but two processes: the workflow engine's control process and the overall business process. How do you represent these two processes and the relationship between them? At the top level, the answer is that you represent the workflow process as a swimlane in the activity diagrams that represents the overall work process. When you represent the workflow engine's participation in this manner, you show the activities of the workflow engine within its swimlane as well as its interactions with the other participants. If you then extract just this swimlane and its direct interactions with other participants, what you are left with is a representation of the workflow engine's process.

Maintaining Separation between Processes and Work

When it comes to getting work done, enterprises are constantly innovating. You want to make sure that the way you are going about implementing and managing business processes facilitates rather than hinders this evolution. One key to doing this is maintaining a separation between the work and the process by which that work is accomplished.

You have already seen a couple of examples of this distinction, though you may not have recognized them as such at the time. The first example was the discussion of different processes for withdrawing cash from a bank, one involving ATMs and the other a human teller. Here there were two different processes for performing the same work. Another example was in the abstraction of milestone status from the work process. The use of milestones to communicate status (discussed in Chapters 10 and 38) serves to isolate components that require process status from changes in the underlying business process.

When you are considering the explicit management of a business process, this separation between the work and the process becomes even more important. Very often the process being managed is one of the core enterprise business processes. These are the processes that distinguish the enterprise from its competitors, and enterprises need to continually evolve these processes to remain competitive. You want to minimize the dependency of the system designs on the business process designs so that these dependencies do not impede process evolution. In fact, one of the goals of the workflow effort may be to make it easier to evolve the process. Other process management goals may require the dynamic definition or modification of business processes. These considerations lead to the following two workflow design best practices.

Explicitly Represent Milestone Status

The first design best practice is to explicitly represent the milestone status of the process. Explicitly representing the milestone status makes it easy to track the changes and capture the data required for KPI and SLA monitoring. Furthermore, the explicit status representation provides a mechanism for decoupling consumers of milestone status from the process representation and its interpretation. Even though it may be possible to derive milestone status from the process status, doing so creates a dependency on the process design that makes it more difficult to evolve the process.

Store Work-Related Data outside the Workflow Engine

The second best practice is to store all work-related information, including its milestone status, independently of the workflow engine's data representations. This work-related information is typically maintained in a database that plays the role of an operational data store (ODS) for work-related information. In keeping with the previous best practice, the current milestone status should be explicitly represented in the ODS, even if that status can be inferred from other data in the ODS. This allows the milestone status to be directly obtained without requiring any understanding of the workflow engine, its data representations, or other work-related data. In this paradigm, when the management process reaches a unit-of-work milestone, it explicitly updates the unit-of-work status in the ODS.

These best practices should be considered design guidelines, and not hard and fast rules. The guidelines are intended to minimize the design dependencies between components, and thus facilitate the evolution of the overall systems, the business processes, and the work itself. These design guidelines do, however, carry with them a performance impact. The separation of the work-related ODS from the workflow engine now requires interactions between the two whenever ODS information is needed or modified by the workflow engine. Counterbalancing this is the need for other participants (user interface components in particular) to access this same information. Maintaining the ODS separation simplifies the interactions with these other components. It is generally recommended that these best practices be followed unless a performance analysis specifically indicates that the resulting design is infeasible. In most cases, the resulting simplicity of the individual component designs and the evolutionary flexibility obtained by following these best practices will more than justify any incremental cost in machine hardware or network bandwidth.

Styles of Work Assignment

Managing a business process often requires the assignment of work. The workflow engine keeps track of what activities need to be performed, assigns the work to participants, and monitors the subsequent completion of the activities. There are four common patterns of interaction between the manager and worker that define how work queues are maintained and which party chooses the next task:

1. Individual Queues, Worker's Choice (the IW pattern): The manager assigns the work to an individual worker by placing it in a queue for that worker. The worker examines the queue and selects the next task to be performed.

2. Individual Queues, Manager's Choice (the IM pattern): The manager assigns the work to an individual worker by placing it in a queue for that worker. The manager determines which task will be performed next.

3. Group Queue, Worker's Choice (the GW pattern): All work of a particular type is placed into a common group queue. The worker examines the queue and selects the next task to be performed.

4. Group Queue, Manager's Choice (the GM pattern): All work of a particular type is placed in a common group queue. When a worker is ready for the next task, the manager determines the task that will be performed.

Work Queues and Work Assignments

When there is more than one performer for a given activity, a decision is required as to which performer will handle each work item. Implicit in this situation is the existence of at least one queue of pending work and the related issue of where work will pile up if it arrives faster than the workers can perform the work.

Individual Queues

One approach is to have an individual queue of work for each worker. With this model, the participant (usually the process manager) that places the work in the queue is pre-assigning the work to a specific worker. This approach is useful if the individual workers are not identical in their capabilities (skill level, capacity) or if the work is a continuation of earlier work that was performed by that individual.

One characteristic of this pre-assignment pattern is that queues of pending work need to be monitored and managed. Should the worker fall behind, work may have to be reassigned to ensure the timely handling of all the work involved. The current length of the queue, the individual's typical work completion rate, and the variability in effort required for each work item may all need to be considered when pre-assigning the work. These factors complicate the management of pre-assigned work queues.

Despite the pre-assignment of the work, there is still a decision to be made when the worker is ready for the next piece of work. In some cases, the queue is sorted (either statically or dynamically) to reflect the work priority. In others, the worker has the freedom to select the next piece of work based on his or her own priorities.

Group Queues

The alternative to individual queues is to maintain a single group queue for pending work of a particular type. With group queues, the work assignment does not occur until a worker is ready for the next piece of work. This greatly simplifies the management of the queue.

With group queues, the dominant decision is how to manage the work assignments: Do the workers get to select the next item, or is that choice made for them? If the workers' skills are uniform, the queue is typically sorted to reflect business priority and the first item in the queue is assigned. If the worker skills are not equivalent but still easily characterized (junior vs. senior workers) and the work characteristics are readily matched to worker skills, an algorithm may be used to select the next task.

Leaving the choice to the worker may be more appropriate in complex situations. When determining which worker has the skills to handle a given piece of work is too complex to automate, the worker can evaluate the pending work and select an appropriate work item. However, it should be pointed out that the pattern is subject to abuse: Workers may "cherry pick" easy assignments instead of choosing more urgent but difficult tasks.

Initiating Workflow

A workflow process doesn't start by itself. At some point in the larger process, some participant must explicitly take an action that triggers the start of the workflow process. You need to determine how the workflow process will actually be triggered and under what conditions this should occur. The activities and participant interactions leading up to the triggering of the workflow must be designed. This raises several key design questions with respect to initiating the workflow:

1. Under what conditions should the workflow process be started?
2. What is the mechanism for determining whether these conditions have been met?
3. Which participants are involved in this workflow initiation, and what are their responsibilities in this regard?
4. What is the mechanism by which the execution of the workflow process is triggered?
5. How will breakdowns in this triggering process be detected? What should the response to a breakdown be?

Making the Management Process Fault Tolerant

It is the nature of workflow that the execution of the management process is dependent on the proper operation of the workflow engine. If the engine fails, the management process must be properly restored or the overall work process will come to a halt. There are three common strategies that can be used to accomplish this:

1. Make the workflow engine itself fault tolerant so that it remembers exactly where it was in the management process and resumes execution after recovery.
2. Have the management process occasionally save its state (a technique known as checkpointing), and recover the process from its last checkpoint in the event of failure.
3. Invoke the entire management process using request-reply, and in the event of failure, have the requestor restart the management process from the beginning.

Of course, there is always the option of not making the management process fault tolerant at all, but if the work process warrants explicit management to begin with, it generally warrants some level of fault tolerance in the management process.

Selecting the appropriate fault tolerance strategy requires striking an appropriate balance between the time and computational cost involved in saving the management process state versus the time and computational cost involved in actually performing the work. Generally, the time is the primary consideration. Persisting the state of a management process typically takes a few milliseconds, assuming that the state is being saved on disk. In contrast, the time involved in actually performing the work can range from microseconds to months. If this time interval is large, then the additional time it takes to persist the management process state will have virtually no impact on the overall time it takes to complete the work process. On the other hand, if this time interval is only a few microseconds, then the time spent persisting the management process state will greatly increase the overall time it takes to complete the work process. Figure 42–1 shows some suggested ranges of task completion times that are suitable for the different control process fault tolerance strategies.

Task completion time is not the only consideration in selecting a fault tolerance strategy. Despite the time involved, workflow engines that save the process state after every change can provide a rich and detailed record of the process execution. This information can be used to satisfy audit requirements and provide the raw data necessary to both measure process performance and determine compliance with service-level agreements. On the other hand, while checkpointing and request-reply invocations require less management process time, recovering from failures with these strategies may result in the repetition of work tasks that were completed prior to the failure. This can

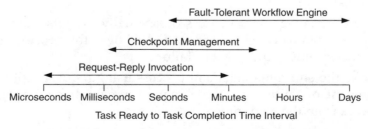

Figure 42–1: *Fault Tolerance Strategies versus Task Completion Time*

complicate the design of the management process and may make the strategy unsuitable.

Using Fault-Tolerant Workflow Engines

Fault-tolerant workflow engines save the state of the control process every time that state changes so that the exact state of the control process can be recovered after a failure. In a typical workflow engine, this state changes three times for each activity: once when the activity becomes eligible to execute, again when a participant assumes responsibility for the activity, and a third time when the activity is completed. If you assume that the state is being saved onto disk, then a reasonable working assumption is that at least three disk accesses will be required for each activity executed in the overall process.[2] This is the case whether the workflow engine employs a database as its underlying storage mechanism or writes its state directly to disk. Since there is some variation between workflow engines in this regard, the actual state-preservation strategy employed by your selected engine must be clearly understood to be able to anticipate the overhead involved in its use.

Another consideration is the manner in which the activity of starting of the management process is coordinated with the activities leading up to its creation. Bear in mind that if the workflow engine fails before the management process is successfully created, then there is no process to be recovered. For reliability, it is prudent to create the control process using a request-reply interaction that does not return the reply until the process has been successfully created and saved to disk. If the process creation should fail, then the requestor can take appropriate action. Note that a message delivery service that requires an acknowledgment of message receipt and will redeliver a message if a receipt is not returned can play the role of the requestor in this pattern. The Java Message Service (JMS) is a common example of such a message delivery service.

For true fault tolerance, the state updates must be written to disk synchronously: It is not safe (in a fault tolerance sense) for the manage-

---

2. This will vary somewhat depending upon the actual workflow engine being used. Some actually access the disk more than three times, while others may be able to do some consolidation of disk accesses. When using any workflow engine, the engine's rate of disk utilization must be clearly understood in order to determine the disk performance required to support the process.

ment process to proceed without first verifying that the state has been properly saved. Synchronous writes typically take a few milliseconds at a minimum for each save operation.[3] If the time it takes to update the disk is relatively short compared to the time that it takes to actually perform the task being managed, then these delays will not be noticeable. If, on the other hand, the activity is a small computational task that only takes a few microseconds, then the delays introduced in saving the state will be very noticeable in the overall work process. Thus, this technique for achieving control process fault tolerance tends to be used when the work tasks take a second or longer to execute. People-oriented tasks and large computational tasks fit well into this model. The time it takes to save the state can be calculated in a relatively straightforward manner, as described in Chapter 39.

You should note that disk activity is also required when a workflow process is first begun. The amount of work involved can vary tremendously from one workflow engine to another. Some workflow engines copy the entire process definition, which involves many disk accesses, while others simply reference a shared process definition and require correspondingly less activity. If workflow processes are started at a rate greater than once a minute, it is prudent to determine the practical rate at which your selected workflow engine can start processes and how that rate varies with the number of activities in the process.

There are other benefits that derive from frequently saving the process state. Fault-tolerant workflow engines typically save a wealth of information about the process execution. The times at which each task became ready to run, the work was actually begun, and the work was actually completed are typically recorded. These provide much of the raw data required to support continuous process-improvement efforts, calculate time-based key performance indicators, and determine compliance with time-based service-level agreements. Additional details, such as the identity of the individual who actually performed the task, are often recorded as well. Such data can make individual performance measurements and corresponding incentive compensation possible. It can also be used to provide an audit trail of what work was performed, when, and by whom.

---

3. There are disk subsystems available that have a shorter update time. These systems have redundant battery-backed memory-resident buffers so that a synchronous write only requires a memory update, and is therefore faster (the data is actually written to disk later). Such systems, however, tend to be expensive.

If you intend to use this additional information captured by the work-flow engine, you must not forget that the simple capture of the raw data is just the beginning. As was discussed in Chapter 38, the flow of this information into the analysis process needs to be factored into the design. This analysis process is another business process that must, itself, be driven through the design process.

Finally, you should note that the fault-tolerant recovery of the control process state may not, in and of itself, be sufficient to restore the overall work process to the correct state. If failures have occurred in other components as well, those components must also be restored to a state that is consistent with the control process state. For example, it is not unusual for a human participant to have a user interface that is populated with data related to the current task. This interface typically presents the user with a choice of possible actions, such as indicating completion of the task. If a power outage occurs, the user may need to be reminded that he or she was in the middle of a task when the outage occurred, and the user interface will need to be restored to the state that it was in at the time of failure in order to resume the work. Both the workflow engine and the user interface need to be restored to a mutually consistent state for the overall work process to proceed.

Checkpointing the Management Process State

Another approach to making the management process fault tolerant is to save its state only at selected points in the process. This approach is commonly referred to as *checkpointing*, and the saved control process state is referred to as a *checkpoint*. With this approach, the designer of the management process determines the points at which the process state will be saved. If the workflow engine should fail, then the management process is recovered from its last checkpoint and resumed from that point.

The use of checkpointing often impacts the design of the process. To begin with, you must bear in mind that if the workflow engine fails before the first checkpoint is taken, then process will not be recovered! For reliability, it is prudent to initiate the process with a request-reply exchange and not return the reply until after the first checkpoint has been reached. Then, if the process should fail prior to the reply being returned, the requestor can take the appropriate recovery action.

The process design may be further impacted by the fact that some activities are not safely repeatable. Checkpointing has the property that when a control process is recovered from a checkpoint, activities after that checkpoint that had been executed before the failure may be executed again after the recovery. But some activities cannot be safely repeated. For example, if an electronic funds transfer was completed just prior to the failure, you probably don't want to transfer the funds again. Workflow engines often have features that can be used to avoid repeating the execution of activities after a checkpoint recovery, but the use of these features must be incorporated into the actual process design. The process designer must be acutely aware of both the workflow engine's features and whether each activity can be safely repeated.

One of the features that can be used to avoid repeating an activity execution is the incorporation of the checkpoint into a database transaction. Database inserts are a common form of activity that is not repeatable. Many workflow engines with checkpointing provide the ability to include the checkpoint within the scope of a database transaction. When this is done, the checkpoint is created if and only if the database transaction successfully commits. The process designer does not have to worry about the unwanted repetition of these database operations after a checkpoint restart. If the workflow engine fails prior to the database commit, the transaction is automatically rolled back, and it is as if the database operations never occurred. If the transaction is successfully committed, the new checkpoint is created and the database operation will not be repeated after a checkpoint recovery.

Another feature that can be used to avoid repeating an activity execution is a "checkpoint recovery" flag. This flag is set to "true" when the engine is recovering a process from a checkpoint and serves as a warning that activity repetition is a possibility. This indicator can be used in the process design to initiate alternate courses of action after a checkpoint recovery. For example, if an activity after a checkpoint involves a nonrepeatable interaction with another system, the alternative course of action after recovery may be to query the other system to determine whether an interaction was successfully completed prior to the failure. The query result is then used to determine whether that particular interaction needs to be performed or can be skipped.

Taking advantage of the checkpoint recovery flag requires extra design work that may impact the design of other components in addition to the workflow engine. At a minimum, using the checkpoint recovery flag requires the design of alternate courses of action for each activity that cannot be safely repeated. Beyond this, additional interfaces on other components may be required so that the workflow engine can determine whether a particular activity has already been performed. Finally, the design of other components may need to be further altered so that sufficient data is retained to make it possible to even answer this question.

As with engines that implement fault tolerance, the use of checkpointing has performance implications that must be considered. When a checkpoint is taken, most workflow engines save the entire state of the process to disk. The volume of data and the time that it takes to write it must be accounted for in the design. In contrast with the relatively small amount of data written on an activity-by-activity basis, the volume of data written in a checkpoint can be substantially larger. In this case, the time it takes to actually transfer the data to disk may no longer be small enough to be ignored. In this case, the size of a checkpoint should be determined and the maximum rate at which checkpoints can be practically created should be computed.

Request-Reply Invocation of the Management Process

Both of the two previous approaches stressed the importance of initiating the creation of the management process using a request-reply exchange so that the requestor can respond appropriately if the process is not successfully created. But the use of request-reply makes possible a third alternative: simply doing all the work before returning the reply. This totally eliminates the need for the workflow engine to ever persist its state and sets the stage for the most efficient control process execution. When the actual work process is fully automated, the result can be a very efficient process that does not access a disk unless the actual work requires it. The request-reply pattern was discussed in Chapter 27. The most common use of this pattern is to manage a fully automated process.

Note that this use of request-reply does not alter at all the burden of fault tolerance that is placed upon the requestor! Regardless of which fault tolerance approach is selected, the requestor must still take appropriate action if the reply is not received. This means re-invoking the management process, which requires the management process to be designed so that it can be called more than once. All of the process design issues discussed in the checkpointing alternative again come into play.

Hybrid Fault Tolerance Techniques

Many business processes involve a combination of short-duration automated activities and long-duration activities. A single fault tolerance strategy may not work well for these processes. The request-reply approach may not be appropriate due to the long duration of the process. The use of a fault-tolerant workflow engine may add too much overhead to the automated activities. Checkpointing may not provide satisfactory error recovery for the manual processes. However, it is possible to combine these techniques to arrive at a satisfactory solution.

The way to combine fault tolerance techniques is to partition the process into a primary process with callable subprocesses, using one fault tolerance technique for the primary process and another for the subprocesses. One common partitioning is that the primary process contains long-running activities (usually involving people), and this process calls subprocesses that are sequences of automated activities. Here the primary process can use a fault-tolerant workflow engine, and the subprocesses can use the request-reply technique.

Another common partitioning is that the primary process is an automated one that invokes long-running processes for exception handling. Here the primary process can use checkpointing or request-reply, and the exception handling workflow can use a fault-tolerant workflow engine. The initiation of the exception handling process should be implemented with request-reply to preserve the fault tolerance of the overall process.

Human Interfaces

When people participate in workflow, they require a means of interacting with the system—a user interface. The interface makes it possible for people to understand (and possibly select) the tasks to be performed and to report back the status of tasks. Frequently, this user interface is also the means by which people perform their tasks. But the user interface is more than just a window into the system. It is a distinct component with its own specific responsibilities and system interfaces that allow it to interact with the workflow engine and other system components.

The overall role that this user interface (UI) component plays and the specific responsibilities it must fulfill are driven by both the nature of the tasks being performed by the user and the design of the process of which these tasks are a part. The UI component has specific responsibilities in coordinating the work performance with the workflow status updates. The exact nature of these responsibilities depends on the style of work assignment that is selected.

When the user interface also provides the means for actually performing the work, the UI component may play an additional role in coordinating the completion of the work with the task status in the workflow engine so that the management process state accurately reflects the true status of the work. After a system failure, the UI component must also be restored to a state that will allow work in progress to continue. The strategy chosen for failure recovery determines the responsibilities of the UI component in this regard. All of these responsibilities require both human- and system-facing interfaces. Determining the actual responsibilities of the UI component will have a significant impact on its design.

Work Assignment Responsibilities

The style of work assignment that is selected determines many of the user interface component responsibilities. If the workflow engine is actually assigning the tasks, then it is usually the responsibility of the UI component to query the workflow engine to obtain the next task assignment for the user. The performance of this query is often tied to the completion of the user's previous task in a manner that is transparent to the user. For example, the user interface may have a "Done" or "Submit" button that the user activates to indicate that a task has been completed. When the button is activated, the UI component interacts with the workflow engine to do two things: indicate the completion of the current task and obtain the next task.

If, on the other hand, the user is selecting the tasks to be performed, the UI component has a different set of responsibilities. It must query the workflow engine to obtain a list of the tasks that the user might perform and display the returned list of tasks for the user so that he or she can select one or more tasks to perform. This list often includes additional information from other sources that the UI component must also obtain. After the user selects the task(s), the UI component again interacts with the workflow engine to indicate that the user has taken responsibility for the task(s). Finally, after the work has been completed, the user interacts with the UI to indicate which tasks have been completed. The UI must, once again, interact with the workflow engine a third time to communicate the completion of the tasks.

The UI component design gets considerably more complicated when users can have more than one task in progress at the same time. This situation often arises when people are making phone calls or sending e-mail and waiting for responses. The user interface must be capable of presenting the details of these multiple tasks, either switching back and forth between tasks quickly or presenting them simultaneously. In terms of task status, this activity of switching back and forth between tasks is not necessarily of interest to the workflow engine, but many workflow processes do require the capture of statistical information, such as how long it took to perform each activity. In these cases, simply noting the start and end time of the activity will not give an accurate view. The user interface must be designed to recognize clearly which task is being performed at any given time and capture the required duration information, typically passing it on to the workflow engine.

Data Responsibilities

Many times the user interface is also the tool used to perform the task that has just been assigned. In this role, the UI component generally must obtain information from other sources and display that information so that it is available to the user. Often this involves complex navigation through information and the generation of additional queries. Performing the task generally involves the entry of information as well, whether it is the result of a simple decision or the actual entry of data. To support this, the user interface may also provide the means of entering or updating data, and may have the additional responsibility for validating the data as well.

For the overall business process to flow smoothly, the performance of the user's task, including these updates, must be accurately reflected in the task status as represented in the workflow engine. One approach is to have the user take an explicit action to indicate that the task has been completed, independent of the actual data updates. This approach has a couple of disadvantages. One is that the need to perform this extra activity can be annoying from the user's perspective. After all, the work has been actually completed and this extra activity is just bookkeeping. Another disadvantage is that it creates the opportunity for inconsistencies between the task state in the workflow engine and the actual state of the work. The user could fail to indicate that the task is complete, or could indicate that it is complete when, in fact, it is not. Either way, much of the benefit of maintaining the task status in the workflow engine has been lost.

Another approach to updating the task status is to integrate the task status update with the mainstream task performance activity in the user interface. One typical technique is to have the user edit the data into the user interface, but not apply the data to the underlying systems until a "submit" button is pressed. When the button is pressed, the user interface component both applies the data to the underlying systems and updates the task status in the workflow engine. In a variation of this, the data updates are delivered to the workflow engine which then performs the actual updates and marks the work complete. This design also affords the opportunity to invoke a data validation function as part of this operation. In service-oriented architectures, the entire activity of validating the data, updating the underlying systems, and updating the task status can be encapsulated as a service. This encapsulates all of the associated business rules and makes the same functionality available to other components as well.

User Interface Failure Recovery

The user interface generally reflects the state of the task being worked on. After a user has taken responsibility for a task, the UI component is in a state that allows the user to indicate that this task has now been completed. The UI component typically retrieves and displays task-related information so that the user can use and update this information. If the UI component should fail or be turned off by the user at this point, it must be possible to return the interface to the same state after the UI component is restarted. This becomes more complicated if the user has a number of tasks in progress, as the user may need to be reminded as to which tasks are in progress.

There are a couple of options available for restoring the user interface to the correct state. One is to have the user interface component save its state, and the other is to have it reconstruct the state based on information stored in other components. Having the interface component save its state requires that the state be saved in a fault-tolerant manner, which in turn requires that all user interfaces have high-performance access to fault-tolerant storage mechanisms. This can become increasingly complicated and expensive as the number of users increases and becomes geographically distributed. For this reason, this approach to user interface recovery is not often encountered in practice.

The other basic option for recovery is to have the user interface reconstruct its state from information persisted in other components. The list of tasks that the user was working on can be recovered from the workflow engine, and the relevant information displayed in the interface can be recovered from the original data sources. But this information may not be exactly as it was in the user interface at the time of failure. Edits that were not committed to storage prior to the failure will be lost. Thus, this recovery style operates very much like checkpointing in the workflow engine: The component will be recovered to the last saved state. While this may require some rework on the part of users, it is generally performs better, is simpler to implement, and is less demanding of system resources than having the user interface maintain its own state.

Regardless of which approach is selected for user interface recovery, it is clear that the choice will define some of the responsibilities of the UI component. If the UI component is reconstructing its state, this choice may impose responsibilities on other components as well. The workflow engine and components storing information related to the unit of work will require query interfaces that will allow the UI component to retrieve the information necessary to reconstruct its state. Thus, it is important for the recovery strategy to be well defined before these components are constructed.

Related Processes

When a workflow is dependent on other processes for triggering events, you need to document both the basic workflow and the related processes that it depends upon. Although it is theoretically possible to show all of these processes in a single UML activity diagram, the resulting diagram depicts many things going on at the same time and can be difficult to understand. Such diagrams are not particularly useful in helping people grasp how the business processes actually work. It is generally preferable to document the basic workflow on its own diagram, and then show each of the dependent processes and their interaction with the workflow process in separate diagrams.

Consider Figure 42–2, a variation on the order fulfillment process in which workflow is now being used to manage the packing and shipping of the order. The diagram depicts the events leading up to the creation of the workflow and the workflow itself, but when it comes to the interaction between the warehouse worker and the workflow needed to get the next pack-and-ship order, there is something missing. What is it?

In the non-workflow version of this process, the warehouse system printed out a stack of pick orders and associated packing slips, and the

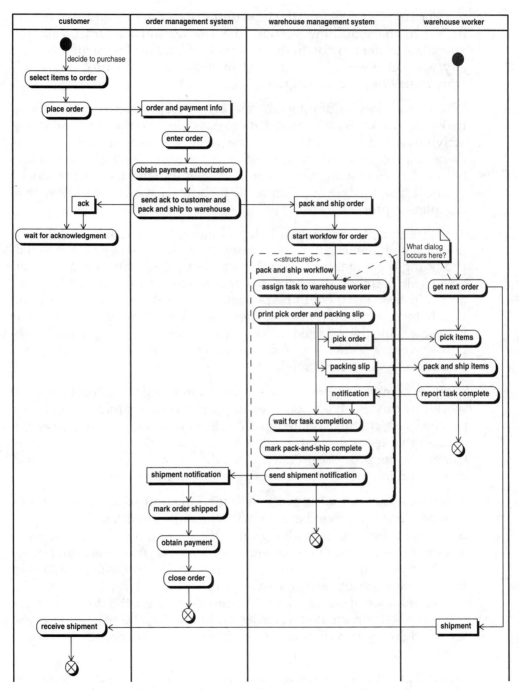

Figure 42–2: *Order Shipping Using Workflow*

worker simply picked up the next order from the pile and worked on it. But in the workflow version, the worker must interact with the workflow system to obtain the next pick order. This interaction is actually a small process—and a level of detail that you probably don't want in this high-level diagram.

When workflow is employed, one of the objectives is generally to make the worker's tasks as simple as possible, specifically eliminating activities that do not add value to the process. In keeping with this, it is commonplace to create a user interface in which a single user action both indicates that one task is complete and initiates the assignment of the next task to the user. Figure 42–3 shows a typical workflow task completion process.

This task completion process involves more than just one workflow. It interacts with the workflow containing the task that was just completed, providing the triggering event for the `wait for task completion` activity. It searches all workflows that have tasks (presumably pack-and-ship tasks) that could be performed by this worker to determine which task the warehouse worker should perform next. Finally, it interacts with the selected workflow to assign the task to the warehouse worker, providing the triggering event for the `assign to warehouse worker` activity.

The task completion process is a separate and distinct process from the workflow process. It is another example of a related process. Workflow processes *always* have related processes: At a minimum, they have the process that leads up to the creation of the workflow process instance. Generally, the processes related to workflow are triggered by external events and interact with a few steps of one or more workflows.

You will also find related processes when the unit-of-work in one process does not correspond exactly with the unit-of-work in another process. Retail store chains with regional distribution warehouses provide a common example. Different stores order stock from the warehouse, but the warehouse, in response, does not send a truck on a dedicated trip to each store. Instead, a delivery trip is planned in which one truck visits a number of stores. Here the unit-of-work for the delivery is the trip, not the individual store order. In particular, the triggering event for the delivery trip does not come from any of the orders: It is time-based instead.

Related processes always require design work. As an architect, it is your responsibility to determine the interactions between these pro-

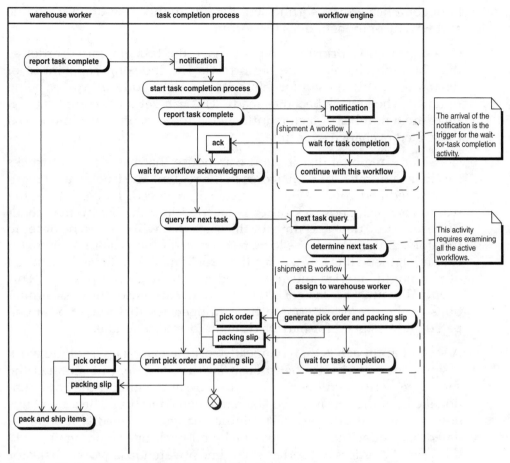

Figure 42–3: *Workflow Task Completion Process*

cesses, paying particular attention to triggering events and the potential for lost work.

Prioritized Work

Optimizing the flow of work through a process often involves prioritizing the tasks. To do this, the information required to prioritize the work must be available and readily accessible to the component prioritizing the work. Prioritization is a sorting activity and is computationally intensive. You must factor this into your design, taking into consideration how complicated the sorting will be, when and how often it occurs, and which component does the sorting.

One approach to prioritization is to save the tasks in sorted order as they become eligible to be performed. The indexing capabilities of databases are often used for this, with the task's indexed values being updated when a task becomes ready. This can get quite complicated if there are a number of factors influencing the sort, and even more so if those factors change over time.

Consider a regional distribution warehouse that has a fleet of trucks servicing a number of retail stores in the region. The trucks run a regularly scheduled route. When an order is received, its corresponding warehouse pick-and-pack order is inserted into the list by the scheduled departure date and time for the truck that will deliver the order to the store. But if a truck has to be rescheduled (due to a breakdown, for example), then all the orders for that truck must be returned to the list of pending deliveries and re-inserted into their proper position. This eventuality must be designed for, which reveals one of the basic limitations of the presorted approach: Contingencies that were not anticipated and designed for may be difficult to accommodate.

A second approach is to dynamically sort the tasks as part of the work assignment activity. This approach is very flexible, but requires the sort to be performed every time a task assignment and the computational cost of the sort must be taken into consideration. The advantage, however, is that arbitrary last-minute changes are readily accommodated. Consider the warehouse pick-and-pack operation again, only this time the orders are sorted each time a warehouse worker asks for the next order to be filled. Last-minute changes to truck schedules can now be handled automatically.

A third intermediate approach is to periodically sort the tasks. This greatly reduces the number of times that the sort is performed, but has its own limitations: Tasks that have become ready since the sort was last performed may not be appropriately placed in the list. Periodic sorts are generally used when the sorting is part of a larger scheduling activity which is, itself, performed periodically. Once again, consider the regional distribution warehouse. In this variation there is a significant variability in the volume of goods sent to any given store on a particular day. Establishing a route that has the same trucks visiting the same stores every day will result in some trucks being under-utilized while others are overloaded. Because of this, a planning exercise is performed each day that determines which trucks will service which stores, which orders will go on which trucks, and what the departure schedule will be for the trucks. One output of this process is the scheduling (prioritization) of the pick-and-pack orders for the warehouse so that the orders are filled in the same sequence as the trucks depart. Note that here, should a truck become unavailable, the planning exercise must be repeated to reallocate those orders to other trucks.

Dynamic Work Assignments

In some work situations tasks are assigned based on the nature of the individual task and the qualifications of the performer. In credit card fraud investigation, for example, fraud cases involving small losses are assigned to junior investigators, while those involving large losses are assigned to senior investigators. To make this possible, some key information concerning the work item and the performer's qualifications must be available, as must an algorithm for deciding which investigators are eligible to work on which tasks. The projected loss for each fraud case, the loss threshold distinguishing junior from senior work, and the junior/senior ranking of each investigator must be available as data items.

Dynamic work assignments have broader implications as well. The business process origins of the projected loss, the threshold, and the performer qualifications must be determined. Related business processes need to be added to the inventory and the need for additional development determined. The dynamic work assignment itself is an activity whose responsibility must be assigned to a component. Depending upon the location of the reference data, additional interactions may be required. The earlier in the design process these issues can be identified, the more easily they can be accommodated by the design.

There are other requirements that can further complicate the design of dynamic work assignment. One is the need to dynamically adjust the work assignment rules. In the credit card fraud investigation example, there may be times when there are a disproportionate number of low-loss cases and the junior investigators become overloaded. To respond to such situations, it may be desirable to temporarily lower the low-high loss threshold so that some of the low-loss cases are now assigned to senior investigators. Alternatively, it may be desirable to temporarily ask senior investigators to play the junior investigator role. Both alternatives require monitoring processes to observe the loading condition and make the appropriate adjustment. Having senior investigators play junior investigator roles additionally requires a distinction between the strict qualifications of the investigators and the role they happen to be playing at the moment. This requires a data element to reflect the current role and a process for determining what that role ought to be when a user logs in.

The business rules for assigning work can be arbitrarily complex and their implementation can have far-reaching impact on related business processes and systems. It is prudent to make sure that these business rules are well understood early in the design process. Particular attention must be paid to identifying aspects of these rules that are liable to change.

Dynamic Result and Process Definitions

For the most part, the business processes and the results they generate will be known at the time the business process and supporting systems are being designed. But sometimes the required activities and the generated results cannot be determined until the process is actually executing. This is a common occurrence when the business process itself includes some type of design activity. The results of this design activity may depend on factors that will not be known until the business process is initiated, and the activities required to implement the resulting design will likely depend on that design as well.

Consider a telecommunications company that designs and installs telephone systems in buildings. These systems can range from the simple installation of a few phone lines and handsets in a small business to the installation of wiring closets, switchboards, switches, and associated cabling in a high-rise office building. The company wants to use workflow to manage the process of designing and installing these telephone systems. Obviously, the phone system must be designed before it can be installed. Furthermore, the installation process cannot be defined until the design has been completed. Installing a few telephone lines involves different activities than wiring a high-rise office building and installing an entire telephone switching system. Business processes such as these present three major design challenges:

1. Representing a design
2. Specifying the implementation process
3. Accommodating subsequent changes

Representing a Design

The first major challenge is deciding how to represent the design coming out of the design process. In the telephone system example, the results include an inventory of the components and wiring that need to be installed and the instructions for configuring them and connecting them together. The results may also include a list of the permits required and engineering reviews that need to be conducted prior to commencing the installation.

The design representation task is somewhat simplified if the design building-blocks and the ways in which they can be assembled is standardized. In such cases, the enumeration of elements and the means for specifying their assembly can be built into the system at design time. The run-time activity then becomes a matter of selecting which elements are required, indicating how many of each are needed and how they are to be assembled. The representations of this information can be fixed and incorporated into the system along with the user interfaces necessary to capture the information.

If the design itself is open-ended, then the problem is more complex. You need to determine the manner in which the design will be represented. If the design needs to be in machine-readable form, they you must define the language that will be used to describe the design. Developing languages is a very specialized task that requires extensive modeling experience. If you, yourself, do not have these skills, engage someone who does. Much of the subsequent design will be based on this language definition. Changing it once implementation has begun will be an expensive and time-consuming process. This is one place where you should make every possible effort to do it right the first time.

Specifying an Implementation Process

The second major design challenge is deciding how to specify the process that will be required to actually execute the design. This is both a user interface challenge and a technology challenge. From a user interface perspective, it must be obvious to the user both what needs to be done (i.e., the user is expected to define the process it will take to implement the design) and how to express what needs to be done (the language used to define the implementation process).

From a technology perspective, the process being defined must be expressed in a manner that the workflow engine can then monitor and manage. The user interface is interacting with the workflow engine to either convey a new process design or modify an existing one. The challenges here are similar to those for capturing any design.

If all of the activities required to implement and assemble building-blocks are standard, then the implementation process can be assembled from these standard activities. These activities may, themselves, be standard subprocesses. The assembly approach allows the convenient use of both automated and manual activities. This approach lends itself to the management of the process as well.

A more complicated case arises when the implementation activities are not standard. Each new element in the design requires the definition of corresponding implementation activities. At this point, the user is essentially defining a business process from scratch, which potentially entails every design consideration discussed in this book! While the flexibility of this approach is attractive on the surface, the complexity of its implementation should not be underestimated.

Accommodating Subsequent Changes

The third design challenge lies in making provisions for changes in the design and in the resulting implementation process. It is a fact of life that design is often an iterative process. The result is that changes can arise virtually anywhere during the design and implementation. Such changes require both the design and the ensuing implementation process to be modified. Thus the systems supporting the design activity must allow for the modification of an existing design as well as the creation of a new one. Similarly, the systems supporting the definition and execution of the implementation process must also allow for the modification of a currently executing implementation process.

Summary

Enterprises can often benefit from the management of complex business processes. The goals for this management directly determine the manner in which the process is managed. Therefore, it is important to clearly understand the management goals before implementing any form of process management.

There is a subtle but real distinction between the management process and the work process it manages. There are always portions of the work process that precede the starting of the work processes and interactions between the participants that do not involve the management process. For the most part, the management process contains supervisory activities that interact with the real work process and its participants.

It is a good design practice to maintain a clear separation between the management process and the work it manages. Information relating to the work is best kept in an operational data store independent of the workflow engine executing the management process. It is good practice to explicitly represent milestone-level work status in this data store and have the management process update this status when milestones are reached. This facilitates the evolution of the process without impacting other business processes that utilize this status information.

Additional management processes are often required to assign work to individuals. If work is pre-assigned, it may be necessary to monitor and manage the queues of assigned work in order to ensure the timely completion of all work tasks. Alternatively, the assignment may be deferred until a worker is ready for the next task. There is variability also in which party assigns the tasks: the worker or the manager. The optimal choices depend upon the nature of the work.

There are often human interfaces associated with management processes. These interfaces allow the workers to interact with the management process, but they are typically also the vehicle for performing the work. The coordination between the actual work completion and the status update in the workflow engine needs to be carefully designed to ensure proper operation after systems and communications failures.

There are a number of design challenges often encountered in workflow design. Workflow processes generally interact with other processes, and these interactions are necessary for the proper operation of all these processes. The prioritization of work and the presence of design activities in the business process can also present challenges.

Key Process Management and Workflow Questions

1. What are the goals of the process management? Why is the process being managed, and what are the expected results of the management?

2. In the proposed design, has the state of the work process been abstracted as a series of milestones?

3. Is the milestone status obtainable in a manner that is independent of the process design and the representation of work-related data?

4. Is the milestone status stored independently of the workflow engine?

5. Is work-related data being stored independently of the workflow engine?

6. How is work assigned? Is it dynamically assigned or pre-assigned? Who made the task assignments?

7. What event leads to the initiation of the workflow, and what is the process leading up to the workflow initiation?

8. How is management process fault tolerance achieved? What fault tolerance strategy is being employed, and under what circumstances does the selected workflow engine save state? How do other components re-synchronize their state with the workflow state after recovery?

9. What are the responsibilities of the user interface component with respect to work assignment and task completion? What is the process for completing a task? What is the process for obtaining the next task?

10. How is the update of information in databases and files coordinated with the completion of the task in the workflow engine?

11. How is the user interface restored to an appropriate state after failure recovery?

12. What other processes interact with the workflow process?

13. How is the work prioritized? What information is necessary to support the prioritization, and how is this information maintained?

14. Are there dynamic work assignments? What information is necessary to decide who can work on which task? How is this information maintained? What is the algorithm for deciding?

15. Is there design activity in the business process? If so, how are the resulting design and its implementation process captured? Is the work involved in dynamic definition justified by the business benefits?

Suggested Reading

Sharp, Alec, and Patrick McDermott. 2001. *Workflow Modeling: Tools for Process Improvement and Application Development.* Norwood, MA: Artech House.

Chapter 43

The Enterprise Architecture Group

Enterprise systems are built over time, piece by piece, project by project. It is rare that an individual project team has both the time and the perspective to consider the enterprise systems as a whole. It is the enterprise architecture group's responsibility to establish this perspective and guide the day-to-day activities of individual projects.

Throughout this book there are a number of chapters that discuss specific issues requiring this type of perspective and guidance. A look at the topic areas of these chapters reveals the scope of the enterprise architecture group's responsibilities: business processes, domain modeling, communications, data, coordination, fault tolerance, high availability, load distribution, security, monitoring, architecture evaluation, and testing. In fact, the enterprise architecture responsibilities encompass the full scope of total architecture. The overall responsibility is to ensure that the people, business processes, information, and systems fit together smoothly and serve the purposes of the enterprise.

There are some challenges to be faced in this regard. Some of these are organizational in nature and are discussed in the companion work, *Succeeding with SOA*. The discussions in this book focus on the technical issues.

Half a Group Is Better than None—But Not Good Enough

Many enterprises end up with only half of an enterprise architecture group. Because of the need to share and manage infrastructure, they have created one or more organizations that address the infrastructure portions of the enterprise architecture: networks, machines, messaging, and the software platforms used for application development.

While these infrastructure groups undeniably add value to the enterprise, their contribution is not enough to ensure a robust set of solutions and services supporting flexible, efficient business processes. Without higher-level guidance, the infrastructure gets used in inconsistent and often inappropriate ways.

When this happens, the business eventually concludes that the solutions and business processes are in a state of disarray. At this point, a group is typically commissioned to examine the situation and make recommendations for moving forward. They examine the flaws in the existing systems, examine the latest trends in building business processes and systems, identify the best practices, and select the preferred hardware and software required to support these best practices. The infrastructure group retools itself to support the new tools, advertizes their availability, and goes on about its business.

The key to succeeding with this new approach lies in the appropriate use of the new infrastructure. Even the best infrastructure can be abused nearly as readily as it can be used appropriately. The best practices for its use must be established and clearly understood by all architects, particularly at the project level.

Best Practice Development

The problem with the infrastructure-only approach to enterprise architecture is that simply identifying industry best practices for business process and solution design, and then putting the infrastructure in place to support them, does not ensure that the enterprise will benefit from the infrastructure investment. Industry best practices require some interpretation in their implementation. They describe the styles in which things should be done, but these styles are only skeletons of the ideas. They must be tailored to the specific circumstances of the enterprise in order to provide their expected value.

Tailoring best practices requires making choices—choices that reflect the realities of the enterprise and its specific needs. Individual project teams, for the most part, have neither the time nor the perspective required to make these choices. Leaving these choices up to the project teams virtually guarantees inconsistency in the choices, and consistency is as important as the choices themselves in reaping the benefits from best practices.

The enterprise architecture group must assume the leadership role in introducing new technology and developing the enterprise-specific best practices for using that technology. This best practice development cannot be an ivory tower exercise. A best practice has to be effectively applied to realize its benefits, and half the challenge in its development is ensuring that it can be readily and practically applied. A major part of the challenge lies in finding the right level of formality for structuring and enforcing the best practice. Too much formality and applying the best practice becomes onerous—too little, and there isn't enough compliance to realize the benefits.

The development of workable best practices is an iterative process. It entails proposing the best practice, applying it in one or more projects, evaluating the results of that application, and then refining the best practice if the results are not satisfactory. The enterprise architecture group needs to be engaged in all four phases of this development, perhaps even modifying the best practice on the fly to ensure a good project outcome. Taking the ivory tower approach and letting the project team wrestle with an inappropriate best practice will result in both the rejection of the best practice and the loss of credibility for the enterprise architecture group that created it.

Knowledge Transfer

For best practices to be effective, project teams need to be aware of their existence and learn how to apply them. During the development of the best practice, knowledge transfer is accomplished through the direct participation of the people in the enterprise architecture group engaged in formulating the best practice. Unfortunately, direct participation doesn't scale to dozens, hundreds, or thousands of projects.

Rolling out best practices in the enterprise presents a challenging knowledge transfer problem. Solving the knowledge transfer problem requires investment in three areas: documentation, training, and mentoring.

Documentation

Documentation is the key to making knowledge transfer work. If you don't get the knowledge out of people's heads and down on paper, then the only way to transfer that knowledge is face-to-face interaction. Face time is expensive and does not scale well. Quality documentation is the key to successfully promulgating best practices.

In documenting best practices there is a tendency to just create a reference manual—a document that describes, in gory detail, the do's and don'ts of the best practice. While this type of documentation is essential, by its nature it assumes that the reader is already somewhat familiar with the best practice and its purpose, and is simply seeking clarification on the details of its application.

Best practice reference materials need to be augmented with introductory materials on two different levels. At the overview level, introductory materials are required to provide a broad overview of the architectural approach and the families of best practices needed to ensure its successful implementation. Then, on a more detailed level, additional introductory material is required in each best practice area to introduce the best practice and explain the rationale behind it. This material will give the reader an intuitive understanding of why the best practice is needed and how it satisfies the need. The intent of this introductory documentation, on both levels, is to make it practical for people to educate themselves about the architecture and the best practices for its implementation.

Training

Training is simply a structured approach to knowledge transfer. Done properly, this training should provide an introduction to the reference material along with a detailed understanding of the most important best practices. Realistically, however, there is never enough classroom time to explore all of the best practices and all of their details. Thus training, by itself, provides an incomplete and therefore unsatisfactory approach to knowledge transfer. Documentation is still the key to success.

Mentoring

Simply exposing project architects to the best practices surrounding architecture development is not sufficient to ensure that they acquire sufficient knowledge to efficiently and appropriately apply those best practices. Project architects need a place to go and seek advice when they have questions about best practices and their application. It is the responsibility of the enterprise architecture group to provide such guidance and leadership.

Governance

Another important role for the enterprise architecture group is to participate in the governance activities surrounding the development of solutions and services. As the originators of the architecture concepts and best practices, the enterprise architects comprise the only group that can meaningfully evaluate a proposed solution or service and determine whether it is both appropriate to the project challenge and consistent with the enterprise best practices.

You have to be careful, though, that governance does not become a collection of after-the-fact nay-saying activities in which the enterprise architects point out all the things that the project did wrong. Such a situation indicates a serious breakdown in knowledge transfer activities. Unless the knowledge transfer problem is remedied, governance reviews will continue to result either in significant rework to bring projects into compliance or in the project simply ignoring the review suggestions because of business pressures. The enterprise will head down the path of evolving chaos.

Designing with Evolving Requirements

Perhaps the biggest challenge faced by the enterprise architecture group is that of constantly evolving requirements. Imagine for a moment that you are architecting buildings rather than information systems. A client asks you to design a building. "What kind of building?" you ask. "A high-rise," replies the client. "Residential or commercial?" you ask. "A mixture," replies the client. Your conversation continues as you seek a better understanding of the intended utilization of the building.

Unfortunately, many of the answers in this hypothetical conversation are conjectures. For example, when you ask what kind of commercial businesses should be planned for, the client speculates about the types of business that are anticipated, but confesses that the actual commercial usage of the space will not be known until the building has been constructed and the space has actually been leased.

In this requirements-gathering conversation, you come to realize that beyond a certain level of detail, the answers to the questions have become pure guesswork. Does this mean you can't design the building? Well, that depends on what you mean by design. Do you have enough information to design the building down to the last detail? No. You do not have enough information to specify the location of every last wall, door, and closet—at least not without making many potentially invalid assumptions about how the space will be utilized. But do you need all of this information to design the building? Not necessarily.

What if you conceive of the building as a structure of relatively large interconnected but unfinished spaces accessible via common corridors, elevators, and escalators? Each space can later be customized—internally subdivided into smaller spaces—to meet the needs of a specific tenant. You can then construct the building, and later design and build the interior of each space, as it is leased. This is, in fact, a common approach for the design of commercial spaces in office buildings and shopping malls.

To execute this design strategy, you need to have an idea of the variety of tenants that may potentially occupy the space. You also need an understanding of the types of interactions that will be required between these large spaces, the common spaces in the building, and the exterior of the building. What level of human traffic will there be? What kind of vehicular traffic will there be? What material movements may be required as each space is built out? What material movements may be required daily basis in operation? How much power, water, heating, air conditioning, and sanitary drainage will be required?

Once you establish these usage boundaries, then you can go about designing the large spaces with appropriate access and the needed utilities. This overall structure and organization of the spaces, their accesses, and their utility services form the architecture of the building. Certain portions of the design, such as the external façade, the entrances, and the common spaces, can be detailed at this point so that the building can be constructed. As each space is leased, the detailed design and implementation of its interior will occur. Note that there is nothing that prevents any of these spaces from being detailed as the building is designed—the detail is just not a prerequisite for the construction of the building.

There are, of course, limitations to this approach. First and foremost you have made a fundamental assumption that there will never be a need to access one of these large spaces directly from another. All movement of people and materials between large spaces will occur via the shared common spaces (including the external environment of the building). Furthermore, in defining the accesses and utility needs of the large spaces, you are making assumptions about the utilization of these spaces that may be very difficult to alter once the building is constructed. For example, if you do not anticipate that the space might be used as a showroom for physically large items, you may not provide large-access openings. Consequently, the space may not be suitable for a tenant wishing to sell recreational vehicles or yachts. Similarly, if you do not anticipate that the space might be used for a ceramics workshop, you might not make provisions for certain things, such as adequate power or gas to operate kilns, or adequate ventilation or air conditioning to keep the space comfortable. The assumptions you make about use of the spaces will ultimately constrain the practical use of the space. After all, you are not going to be able to build a space shuttle in a shopping mall.

This methodology is a hierarchical approach to design. Rather than directly creating the complete design, you are creating a framework within which actual designs can be detailed as they are needed. The very nature of this hierarchical design approach requires placing some limitations on the utilization of the spaces in order to proceed with the design. Does this imply that the building could never be used for these other purposes? Not necessarily. It does mean that some portion of the physical structure of the building and its utility services would have to be significantly altered to accommodate these usages. This is a risk inherent in this type of design process. The extreme risk is that for some usages, the required changes to the building might not be feasible—an entirely different building design would be required. But for the most part, the risk boils down to cost—it will cost more if the building structure needs to be modified.

Hierarchical Architectures

The hierarchical approach to architecture described in this example applies equally well to the design of information systems. The "spaces" in the building correspond to the anticipated applications and business services. The accesses to those "spaces" and the provided utility services correspond to the communications facilities, physical plant facilities (heating, air conditioning, power, etc.), and infrastructure services provided to support those applications and business services. But how do you determine what kind of support will be required? What kinds of questions do you need to ask to determine the facilities and services that will be required?

These questions turn out to be the same ones you ask in any project. What are the business processes that will be supported, and what are their requirements in terms of throughput, response time, availability, security, and so forth? What interactions are required among the applications to support these processes? How will the participants interact, and how will the data be managed? What kind of coordination will be required, and how will business process breakdowns be detected? How will fault tolerance, workload distribution, security, and monitoring be addressed? How will the system be tested? Is there workflow involved? Can the proposed architecture handle the demands that will be placed upon it?

The questions remain the same, but they take on a different flavor when doing a hierarchical design because the detailed business processes are not yet known. But at the same time these business processes are not completely unknown either. Unless you are starting a new business from scratch, most of the business processes are already in place! The enterprise already has processes for taking and filling orders, hiring people, purchasing goods—the processes for performing all of the enterprise's daily activities.

The existing business processes may not be in their ultimate form yet, but you can learn a lot from them that will help you understand the hierarchical framework requirements. Remember that the activities comprising the existing business processes, and the information they produce and consume, will not, for the most part, change as the business processes evolve. What will generally change is who performs the activity (person or machine), when the activity is performed, and how the related information is managed. Process characteristics such as throughput, response time, and fault tolerance may want improvement (these are often the drivers for moving to a new architecture), but these will be improvements on the existing process requirements. Thus you can use your understanding of existing processes, coupled with an understanding of the types of improvements desired, to guide the architectural development.

For the most part, the reason you are putting the new enterprise architecture in place is to facilitate the evolution of these existing business processes. You can test your design concepts for the new architecture by taking representative examples of the existing business processes, hypothesizing the types of changes you would like to make, and then doing a high-level hypothetical design of these processes within the proposed architectural framework.

In working out the new architecture, you do not need to do a hypothetical design for every business process. Far from it! You only need to do hypothetical designs for those processes that will present challenges to the architecture—the same challenges discussed back in Chapter 7. Furthermore, you don't even need to do a design for all of these processes! Many of the processes will result in similar patterns of interaction between the participants with similar requirements in terms of throughput, response time, and so on. You only need to do one design for each pattern, scaling up its usage requirements to reflect the total volume of activity in the set of business processes that will follow the pattern.

In the end, what you seek is an understanding of the important business process patterns and the manner in which they will be implemented in the new architecture. These patterns should be documented and used as guides by project architects as they go about implementing the actual business processes. The representative business processes and their corresponding implementations in the new architecture should be documented in the same manner as an actual design. Project architects then analyze the actual business processes, identify the corresponding enterprise architecture pattern, and use the pattern to guide their actual implementation. Of course, project architects must always be on the lookout for business processes that do not have corresponding patterns in the enterprise architecture guide. These processes will require a new design pattern. The enterprise architecture group should stand ready to participate in the formulation of the new design pattern.

Geographic Deployment

One of the great variables in distributed system design is the quality of service available for communications between components. An interaction between two components that is eminently practical when they are co-located on a high-speed LAN may become completely infeasible when the components are located at opposite ends of an unreliable low-bandwidth dial-up WAN connection. While this is an obvious consideration in any design, it is an acute enterprise architecture issue as the enterprise evolves geographically. Mergers, acquisitions, and organizational realignments all impact thinking about where data centers and users may reside. Evolving technology is also changing the picture. Users who were once chained to desktop workstations now employ wireless technology in handheld devices and cell phones so that they can work wherever they happen to be.

For these reasons, you must consider the potential deployments of applications along with both business and infrastructure services in the enterprise architecture. This is not to say that the actual deployed locations for applications and services must be fixed in the architecture; rather, the variability in where they might be located must be considered. This, in turn, will impact your thinking about the choice of coordination mechanisms and the buffering of information in the design patterns. It may even impact the design of the business process itself to make it more tolerant of intermittent communications.

Organizational Alignment

Business processes rarely, if ever, take place entirely within the systems. People interact with the systems and with each other during the execution of the process, particularly when exceptions occur. As such, your patterns for business processes must include the required interactions between people as well as the interactions between systems.

In an enterprise business process, it is common to have interactions among people in different organizations. An online merchant may have one organization responsible for taking orders, another that operates the warehouse and ships the orders, and a third that operates a call center for handling customer inquiries. If the warehouse encounters a problem with an order that requires contacting the customer, it may need to interact with the call center to get the issue resolved.

Proposed business process patterns must be overlaid upon the possible organizational structures that may be encountered to determine whether the complexity of the interaction is appropriate. Typically, interactions between organizations need to be kept simple and at a fairly high level to make them manageable. This organizational overlay will also help to determine the appropriate organizational measurements and incentives required to achieve the desired level of business process optimization.

Summary

Architecture encompasses many issues with scope that exceeds the boundaries of individual projects. To achieve consistency in the overall architecture and the employment of best practices, an active enterprise architecture group is required. This group is responsible for all aspects of the enterprise's total architecture, structuring the interactions between business processes, people, information, and systems in a manner that achieves the enterprise's goals.

Many times this enterprise architecture effort focuses primarily on the infrastructure, establishing the hardware and software environment for hosting solutions and services but not directing the actual solution and service architectures themselves. The resulting unconstrained use of the infrastructure leads to chaos. The establishment and enforcement of solution and service development best practices is an essential element in attaining a flexible architecture that promotes rather than retards the evolution of business processes.

In addition to developing best practices, the enterprise architecture group has a significant knowledge transfer responsibility as well. It needs to ensure that best practice documentation can support efficient self-education, and that there are appropriate training courses in place to bring architects up to speed on the family of best practices and their application. Finally, they need to establish an effective mentoring program for project architects.

A third major responsibility for the enterprise architecture group is governance. As the originators of the enterprise architecture and related best practices, the enterprise architects are obligated to oversee and review the work of individual projects to ensure their compliance. This active involvement will further serve to stimulate the evolution of the enterprise architecture.

Developing an architecture in the face of evolving requirements is challenging. A hierarchical approach, partitioning the architecture into major interacting elements, yields a strategy that does not initially require details about the major elements. Representative business processes that illustrate typical interactions among major elements can be used both to evaluate the proposed partitioning and to document the usage patterns. These usage patterns then serve as guides for project architects as they implement the actual business processes.

Key Enterprise Architecture Group Questions

1. Is there an active enterprise architecture group?

2. Does the enterprise architecture scope encompass business processes, systems, data, and infrastructure?

3. Does the enterprise architecture group establish best practices for the use of the architecture? Are these best practices developed iteratively, factoring actual usage experience into the formulation of the best practices?

4. Is there an effective knowledge transfer program for best practices? Does it encompass documentation that supports self-education? Are there formal training courses? Is there a mentorship program in place for project architects?

5. Is the enterprise architecture group actively involved in governance with respect to project compliance with enterprise architecture standards and best practices? Does the enterprise architecture group have the requisite authority to achieve compliance?

6. Is the enterprise architecture defined hierarchically? Is its implementation illustrated through the use of representative business processes? Are these representative usages documented well enough to serve as guides for project architects?

Afterword

Focus Your Work

There are many things to consider when evolving the enterprise architecture—so many that it is not practical to consider every issue for every business process scenario. If you do, you'll end up spending the majority of your time considering issues that, in the end, don't really matter.

To maintain focus, you need to continually ask yourself three key questions about each design issue:

1. Is the design issue relevant?
2. Is satisfying the requirement important to the enterprise?
3. Is the proposed solution sufficient?

The relevance of the design issue is your first consideration. If it is not relevant, don't waste time on it. You don't need to worry about the security of information that is in the public domain, nor do you need to worry about distributing load for a lightweight transaction that only occurs once a day. Let common sense be your guide. Identify the design issues that are truly relevant and focus your attention on those.

The next consideration is the business importance of satisfying specific requirements. Many requirements are wants rather than needs, and you need to distinguish between the two before you break your back trying to satisfy the requirement. How critical is satisfying the requirement to the success of the enterprise? What level of effort is actually warranted? The enterprise will not suffer if a stringent response-time requirement for a relatively unimportant business process is relaxed a bit to simplify the design. Recognize that requirements related to less important business processes tend to be negotiable. When unimportant business processes present design challenges, your time may be better spent pushing back on the requirements and negotiating a simpler design.

The final consideration is the sufficiency of the proposed solution. You don't always need the best possible solution. If your projected demand five years in the future requires 1,000 messages per second, does it really matter whether the messaging subsystem can deliver 10,000 or 100,000 messages per second? You don't need (and probably cannot afford) the best possible solution to every design challenge. You need to know when a solution is good enough and then turn your attention to more pressing needs.

In the end, architecture is about judgment—your judgment about what is relevant, important, and sufficient. Keep focused on what is important to your enterprise.

Seek the Expertise of Others

As is evidenced by the length of this book, there are many things you need to consider as you evolve the enterprise architecture. The field is both vast and growing daily. In a practical sense, there is no way that you can become an expert in every architectural facet and fully understand every implication of every decision that you make. How then can you be successful as an architect?

The trick is to know the limits of your own knowledge and seek out the expertise of others when you reach your limits. In your dealings with others, you should never be ashamed to say, "I don't know" as long as you follow up with "… but I will find out." At the end of the day, your personal credibility is your strongest asset, and you should never do anything to compromise that.

You need a work-around for your own personal limitations. If you have concluded that a particular design issue is important, it is your obligation to see that the issue is appropriately addressed. You must either educate yourself on the topic or locate an expert in the area to assist you.

For topics that you believe will recur frequently, your best course of action is to educate yourself, although you may well choose to employ the assistance of an expert in the area as part of this educational process. That is, after all, why you take courses instead of just reading text books. At a minimum, you need to learn enough about the topic to recognize design challenges and determine when additional expertise is required. In most areas, you should find sufficient information in this book to bring you up at least to this level.

Regardless of your personal efforts, you will from time to time encounter severe design challenges for which you simply do not have the time to develop the required expertise. In such cases, you have little choice other than to engage an expert in the area. As a result and over time, you will develop relationships with experts in various areas. Treat these relationships with respect—they are as valuable to you as your own knowledge. When you approach an expert, you should have a design question formulated as concisely as you can with clearly stated scenarios and challenges. Most experts enjoy this type of challenge and will respond willingly to your requests. What they do not enjoy is answering questions you could have answered yourself. Do your homework first, and answer as many questions for yourself as you can.

Be Pragmatic, But Consider the Long View

A good enterprise architecture is an effective compromise between pragmatic needs for working solutions and the architectural ideals that enable graceful evolution. Your challenge is to guide the enterprise towards this compromise on a continuing basis as both the needs and the supporting architecture evolve.

Making these compromises requires business decisions. To be effective in your role, you need to help the enterprise understand, in business terms, the consequences of the decisions that are being made. Most of these decisions involve "pay me now or pay me later" tradeoffs that affect the viability of the enterprise in both the short term and the long term. Too much emphasis on long-range ideals may leave the enterprise ill equipped to address current market challenges. Too much emphasis on short-term pragmatics may leave the enterprise ill equipped to address future market challenges.

Your understanding of the business and your ability to help the business understand the consequences of technical decisions are critical to enterprise success. As businesses become increasingly dependent upon information technology they are becoming ever more dependent upon finding an effective architecture that meets both short-term and long-term needs. Your role is becoming increasingly important to the survival of the enterprise.

You are living and working in a world of accelerating change. Keep one eye on the present and the other on the future. Maintain a balanced view of both the business and the technology. Understand what is truly important to the enterprise. Be honest and forthright about your observations and conclusions. And above all, enjoy the ride!

Index

A

Abstraction of services, 376–377
Accept event action, 347–348
Access control
    channel enforcement, 583–585
    with a mediation service, 75–76
    policy enforcement points, 72–74
    with proxies, 74–75
Access rate, 607–608
Activity assignments, 193–198
Activity diagrams, 206–207, 358–359
Activity execution management patterns
    (AEMPS), 454–456
Activity partitions, 192–194, 577–588
Adapter(s)
    API-based, 354–355
    categories of, 353–354
    combination techniques, 356–357
    database-based, 355–356
    file-based, 357
    patterns, 358–359
    polling, 355
    protocol-based, 357–358
    standardizing, 363–364
    system of record, 386–387
    using callbacks, 355
Additive changes, 56–57
Alexander, Christopher, 33, 153
Annunciating breakdowns, 495–496,
    509–510
Annunciation, 510
API-based adapters, 354–355
Application architecture styles, 13–14
Apprenticeships, 286, 675
Architecture fundamentals
    architect's role, 29–30
    collaboration, 20–26
    enterprise architecture, 30–34
    functional organization, 15–20
    nonfunctional requirements, 27–28
    refinement, 28–29
    structural organization, 11–14
    total architecture, 26–27
Architecture in context, 96–97
Artifacts, 155–156, 165–169, 252, 284
Assertions, 580–581
Assignment strategies, 553–554
Association class, 272–273
Associations (UML), 131, 270
Asterisk, 270
Asymmetric encryption, 579–580
Asynchronous replication, 535–539,
    546–548
Asynchronous request-reply, 62–64, 527
    event driven, 463–464
    and sequencing, 374
Asynchronous status feedback, 467
ATM example
    access control, 72–73
    business process metrics, 139–140
    business process scoring, 146
    component load analysis, 603
    deployment diagram, 320
    domain model, 274–276
    goals and stakeholders, 129
    initial cut domain model, 275
    network load estimates, 611
    primary and related business
        processes, 131–134
Audit trails, 581
Authentication process, 574–576
Authorization, 576–579
Automated *versus* manual recovery,
    503–504
Availability (process constraint), 231–238
    See also High availability

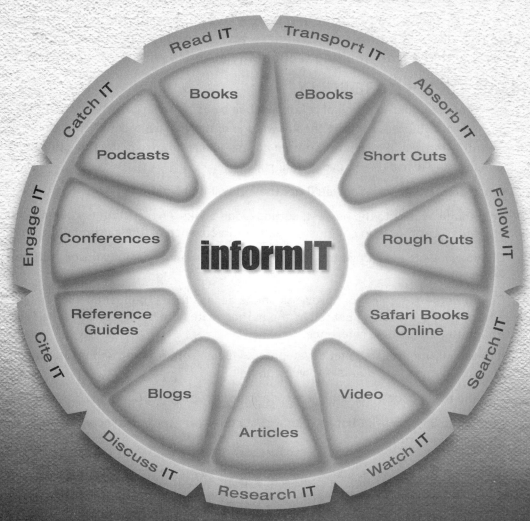

BOOKS ONLINE
ENABLED

THIS BOOK IS SAFARI ENABLED

INCLUDES FREE 45-DAY ACCESS TO THE ONLINE EDITION

The Safari® Enabled icon on the cover of your favorite technology book means the book is available through Safari Bookshelf. When you buy this book, you get free access to the online edition for 45 days.

Safari Bookshelf is an electronic reference library that lets you easily search thousands of technical books, find code samples, download chapters, and access technical information whenever and wherever you need it.

TO GAIN 45-DAY SAFARI ENABLED ACCESS TO THIS BOOK:

- Go to **informit.com/safarienabled**

- Complete the brief registration form

- Enter the coupon code found in the front of this book on the "Copyright" page

If you have difficulty registering on Safari Bookshelf or accessing the online edition, please e-mail customer-service@safaribooksonline.com.